A HISTORY *of* ITALIAN CINEMA

ALSO BY PETER BONDANELLA

Italian Cinema: From Neorealism to the Present

Machiavelli and the Art of Renaissance History

Francesco Guicciardini

Federico Fellini: Essays in Criticism (editor)

The Macmillan Dictionary of Italian Literature

The Eternal City: Roman Images in the Modern World

The Cinema of Federico Fellini

The Films of Roberto Rossellini

Cassell Dictionary of Italian Literature

Umberto Eco and the Open Text: Semiotics, Fiction, Popular Culture

The Films of Federico Fellini

The Cambridge Companion to the Italian Novel

Hollywood Italians: Dagos, Palookas, Romeos, Wise Guys, and Sopranos

New Essays on Umberto Eco (editor)

A HISTORY of ITALIAN CINEMA

Peter Bondanella

DISTINGUISHED PROFESSOR EMERITUS
OF COMPARATIVE LITERATURE, FILM STUDIES, AND ITALIAN

INDIANA UNIVERSITY

Bloomsbury Academic
An imprint of Bloomsbury Publishing Inc

B L O O M S B U R Y
NEW YORK · LONDON · OXFORD · NEW DELHI · SYDNEY

Bloomsbury Academic

An imprint of Bloomsbury Publishing Inc

1385 Broadway	50 Bedford Square
New York	London
NY 10018	WC1B 3DP
USA	UK

www.bloomsbury.com

BLOOMSBURY and the Diana logo are trademarks of Bloomsbury Publishing Plc

First published in 2009 by the Continuum International Publishing Group Ltd
Reprinted 2011, 2012 (twice)
Reprinted by Bloomsbury Academic 2013, 2014 (twice), 2016

Library of Congress Cataloging-in-Publication Data
Bondanella, Peter E., 1943–
A history of Italian cinema/Peter Bondanella
p. cm.
Includes bibliographical references and index.
ISBN 978-0-826-41785-5 (hardcover)
ISBN 978-1-441-16069-0 (paperback)

ISBN: HB: 978-0-8264-1785-5
PB: 978-1-4411-6069-0

Printed and bound in the United States of America

Contents

PART FOUR: GENERATIONAL CHANGE
IN THE CONTEMPORARY ITALIAN CINEMA

Preface

WHEN I ATTENDED DAVIDSON COLLEGE IN THE 1960S, it was virtually impossible to take a course on Italian cinema in the United States, but the rise of film studies in key places (New York, Los Angeles), along with art-film screenings in some cities and university towns, reflected a strong awareness of the contributions of Italian cinema to the development of world cinema. Yet virtually nothing in print in English could serve as a text for a university course or provide extensive analysis and real information about Italian cinematic history for the educated general reader. In my entire academic career, I was never able to take either a general course in film studies or a more specific one on Italian cinema—they simply did not exist at the otherwise outstanding institutions of higher learning where I studied. Nor were videotapes or DVDs yet available for study or for courses: 16mm prints of some Italian films could be rented from a small number of companies (Janus Films and Audio Brandon Films), but it was extremely difficult in the English-speaking world to organize a serious program of teaching or research on Italian films. It was almost impossible to see any Italian silent films or films made during the Fascist era before the advent of neorealism.

My interest in Italian cinema thus arose rather late—and quite by accident. My graduate training was actually in political science and comparative literature, with a specialization in the European Renaissance and a thesis on Machiavelli. By the time I had completed my graduate work and began teaching in an Italian program in 1970, I came to realize that Italy's cinema would be an excellent way for me to stay current with developments in contemporary Italian culture and to help attract students to the study of Italian. No usable history of Italian cinema existed in English, however, except for an excellent but already out-of-date translation of a French volume that was really not appropriate for American students. With a National Endowment for the Humanities grant, I was able to spend several months in Paris at the beginning of 1974 studying literary theory before moving on to Florence to write a study of the Renaissance political theorist Francesco Guicciardini, following up on my interest in Machiavelli. As luck would have it, at the moment of my arrival in Paris, the Cinéma d'Essai Dragon on the rue du Dragon in Paris opened a forty-five-day festival devoted entirely to Italian cinema, screening a different classic each day. I believe I saw every film they presented. (In 2004, on a nostalgic trip back to this place where I was introduced to the pleasures of Italy's greatest visual art of the twentieth century, I found myself standing, a bit horrified, before a dingy store selling and smelling of frozen fish!) The old Dragon introduced me to the best cinema school in the world: Paris and its dozens of film theaters. On one particular day, I managed by careful scheduling and the use of the Métro to see four different Pasolini films in different locations. For some reason, now mysterious to me, I never frequented the film screenings at the famous Cinémathèque Française in Paris (an oversight that I have always regretted). Thus, for the expatriate film buff I was to become, the Dragon and not the Cinémathèque always remained an inspiration and recalled my first real encounter with Italian cinema. There, the elderly women who served as ushers, with their omnipresent flashlights (yes, they still existed then), labeled me "le monsieur qui vient tous les jours," and I even tipped them by the week, so assiduous was my attendance. Without this unique experience, I could never have learned enough about Italian film to exploit my interest in it for the purpose of teaching and research. Paris at that time was an incredible place for Italian cinephiles. Most of the available literature on the Italian cinema outside publications from Italy was in French then, and the city's numerous film theaters constantly screened Italian films from all periods and genres.

Upon leaving Paris for Florence and my long-delayed book on Guicciardini, my time in that city was brightened by the hospitality of a very kind, gracious, and generous man, now departed—Count Francesco Guicciardini—who allowed me complete access to his namesake's library with its collection of fine books and manuscripts, and even encouraged me to smoke my Toscani cigars and work on the beautiful table that was given to his famous ancestor by Pope Clement VII, looking out on the busy Via Guicciardini below the library. The thought that I might well have burned down the count's library still haunts me to this day. While the prestige of Italian cinema may well have been high in Paris, it was virtually impossible in Florence to screen the great classics of Italian cinema in any real, meaningful way. Some theaters showed *prima visione* (first-run) Italian films, but nowhere could one see films from the silent era to about 1970, and of course, I had no access to commercial videotapes or DVDs, since none yet existed. At a *terza visione* neighborhood theater, the Cinema Universale in the San Frediano district—the old working-class neighborhood of real Florentines—I was, however, able to catch an important older film now and then, trudging from my apartment through the cold, dreary, rain-soaked streets to a building that served more as a hangout for older retired Italians looking for a warm place to pass the afternoon than the kind of Mecca for film buffs I had encountered in Paris at the Cinéma d'Essai Dragon. I can still recall the insect bites on my ankles while I shivered through a few Italian classics with a generally garbled sound track that was almost impossible to comprehend. As I tried to build up my knowledge of Italian cinematic history, I often rented a 35mm print and paid a union projectionist in order to see it—lonely, expensive, and time-consuming work, especially for a young, not-too-well-paid assistant professor. Yet nothing diminished my initial enthusiasm kindled by my three months in Paris, and what began as a hobby secondary to my interest in the Renaissance eventually blossomed into my major scholarly interest. My stay in Paris and Florence had, at least, prepared me to organize a university course for undergraduates that eventually expanded over the years, until it included graduate seminars and the direction of some of the first American dissertations devoted to Italian cinema.

My own research interests would eventually expand to include monographs, editions, and articles on a number of important Italian directors (Fellini and Rossellini, in particular), but my main initial focus became the production of a decent history of Italian cinema for the English-speaking world. The result was the publication in 1983 of *Italian Cinema: From Neorealism to the Present*, a book that owed its existence to a wonderful film editor at what was then the Frederick Ungar Publishing Company: Stanley Hochman. Without Stanley's enthusiasm at a time when virtually no American presses were interested in such a book, the present work would never have seen the light of day. Stanley's chance on a young writer paid off, and the book he commissioned almost against the better judgment of other editors has since its initial appearance become a standard text in the many classes that began to spring up in the 1980s and 1990s, and received a second edition in 1990 and a third in 2001. I think it is no exaggeration to state that Italian programs have embraced the cinema in a far more enthusiastic fashion than any other language department in colleges and universities in the United States, Canada, and the United Kingdom. I remain very proud that my book played a role in that curriculum change and the acceptance of cinema in Italian programs as not only an interesting but also an essential part of learning about Italian art and culture.

A few years ago, just before my retirement, in 2007, I returned to Paris in a futile Proustian attempt to recapture my film-buff past. Although the Dragon has disappeared, Paris continues to be the best place in the world to view films of all kinds, and Italian cinema remains popular there. Meanwhile, numerous scholars in the United States, Canada, Australia, and the United Kingdom had begun devoting their careers to studying Italian cinema and offering undergraduate and graduate courses and degrees in this field. American and British publications on Italian cinema now far outnumber those in France (the contrary was true in the 1970s) and have become recognized by Italian film historians as well as critics for their original contributions to the field.

The first three editions of *Italian Cinema: From Neorealism to the Present* focused upon postwar cinema (the silent film and the Fascist cinema were treated only in passing in a brief introductory chapter), with emphasis upon the art film of major auteurs. The only popular genres or "B" films (a term used here with no derogatory intent) discussed in the previous editions were film comedies and the spaghetti western, with a cursory treatment of Italian horror films; but even then I emphasized, in part out of necessity, the *commedia all'italiana* by major directors and the auteur western by Sergio Leone. With the passage of time, it became clear to me that a simple addition of a chapter or two would not suffice. A fourth edition of this work would no longer do: a new history of Italian cinema would have to be rethought, reorganized, and completely rewritten. The production of many new DVDs allowed me to examine hundreds of films that had not been available for viewing in preceding years when I first began writing on the history of Italian cinema. The present volume's first two chapters thus separately treat silent cinema and cinema in Italy from the coming of sound until 1945 (that is to say, cinema during the Fascist period, which is not the same thing as Fascist cinema). Also, it now seems clear to everyone writing on Italian film that important continuities between prewar and postwar Italian cinema exist—neorealism was not such a dramatic break as we once thought—and I hope I have argued convincingly that the prewar talkies in Italy were actually much better films than their postwar critics would admit. Since the first three editions of *Italian Cinema* slighted popular film genres, *A History of Italian Cinema* devotes entirely new, topical chapters to several popular genres: the "sword and sandal" epic or "peplum" film of the 1950s; the Italian horror film, or so-called spaghetti nightmare film (including the subcategories of horror, the Italian zombie and cannibal films), that began in the 1950s and continues through the present; the *giallo* or Italian mystery thriller; and the *poliziesco* or Italian crime film from the 1970s to the present. Although *Italian Cinema* did treat the spaghetti western and emphasized the art film aspects of Leone's work, a much longer chapter on this topic now examines in much greater detail many other directors and kinds of film. Italian film comedy was certainly analyzed in the earlier *Italian Cinema*, but *A History of Italian Cinema* not only examines Italian film comedy in a much more comprehensive manner in various chapters but also pays sufficient attention to the truly B-film comedies starring such figures as Paolo Villaggio, Franco Franchi, and Ciccio Ingrassia. Three concluding chapters treat the past several decades and the emergence of a "third wave" of new auteurs born in the 1950s, as well as an even younger group of important directors born in the 1960s who have already made their mark on the direction of the Italian cinema in the third millennium. Finally, there is a detailed bibliography on Italian cinema—modesty prohibits claiming it to be the best of its kind in any language, but it is certainly the most comprehensive one ever to be assembled in an English-language publication.

The lack of a serious discussion of Italian B films from the peplum to the present was the greatest weakness of the original three editions of *Italian Cinema*. It is also true that after teaching and writing about Italian films for almost four decades, I had managed to learn a great deal more than I knew when I first began my career. Thus, a number of my earlier ideas on various directors or on particular topics (neorealism, Fellini, the political film) and even my aesthetic judgments, have evolved over this period. I remain convinced that neorealism represents the seminal event in modern Italian film history, and that Fellini stands as the greatest figure in the past century, but I have come to be extremely impressed by many of the younger generation and some of the older figures that I overlooked in the past (Mario Bava, in particular). In the past two decades, encouraged by the existence of the Internet and abundant supplies of numerous film titles on videotape and DVD, many of Italy's popular film genres have become cult favorites, particularly after receiving praise from such American directors and writers as Quentin Tarantino, Stephen King, John Landis, and George Romero. Today, a person reading a history of the Italian cinema needs to know something about neorealism, Antonioni, Fellini, and Nanni Moretti but also requires information regarding Mario Bava, Lucio Fulci, and Fernando Di Leo. We can admire the acting talents of Massimo Girotti, Anna Magnani, Marcello Mastroianni, and Monica Vitti without disparaging those working in the popular genre B films, such as Fabio Testi, Barbara Bouchet, Edwige Fenech, and Paolo Villaggio. *A History of Italian Cinema* sets out to cover more than a century of interesting films, directors, actors, and film genres with scholarly accuracy but without academic jargon.

Acknowledgments

THE LIST OF THE PEOPLE TO WHOM I OWE A GREAT DEBT throughout my career has grown lengthy over four decades. As I look back on my relationship with the Italian cinema, good memories come flooding back: winning book awards from the Agnelli Foundation for my study of Fellini and from the American Association for Italian Studies for the first edition of *Italian Cinema*; hosting Lina Wertmüller in Bloomington, Indiana, just before she went to the Oscar ceremonies as the first woman ever nominated as Best Director; arranging for the American premiere of Pasolini's last film in Bloomington; tagging along with Francesco Rosi to a De Chirico exhibit during a break at the Venice Film Festival in 1979; receiving a book personally delivered at my Roman doorstep by Nanni Moretti riding on his soon-to-become famous Vespa before most people in America had even heard of him; driving all over the Midwest with Ettore Scola, his wife, and the Fellini scriptwriter and future director of the Fellini Foundation Gianfranco Angelucci after an Indiana University conference on European cinema (the Italians developed a certain fondness for buffalo wings!); frequently running into one of the Taviani brothers and his wife at a Roman fish market near my Roman apartment; eating in Rome at my favorite trattoria, Otello alla Concordia, where such figures as Ettore Scola, Marco Ferreri, Dario Argento, and Tonino Delli Colli would often sit at a nearby table; interviewing Bernardo Bertolucci in his home on the day that *Time* magazine photographers came to shoot his cover photo after *The Last Emperor* won numerous Oscars; having my picture taken with Liliana Cavani in Fort Worth with a daguerreotype camera (she was dressed as a Southern Belle, while I was portrayed as a slightly demented Confederate Colonel); meeting Tullio Pinelli in Rome and persuading him to persuade Fellini to give many valuable manuscripts from their years of fruitful collaboration to the Lilly Library at Indiana University; dining on several occasions in Rome with Fellini, the scriptwriter Pinelli, and Fellini's wife, the famous actress Giuilietta Masina; and visiting four different Fellini sets over two decades. I continue to maintain an active interest in Italian medieval, Renaissance, and modern classics—Dante, Boccaccio, Machiavelli, Cellini, Guicciardini, Vasari, Eco, all worth a lifetime of study—but no scholarly career could have been any more fun than spending time with such creative, intelligent, and inspiring people as those who have participated in creating Italy's greatest contemporary art form in the cinema.

Grateful acknowledgments are owed to many people. Early on, two friends of Fellini—Aldo Tassone and Françoise Pieri—became my friends as well and rented me for two years their wonderful Roman pied-à-terre, where I completed my monograph on Fellini and the second edition of *Italian Cinema*. Before the age of DVDs and videotapes, Ben Lawton of Purdue University and I drove to the Indianapolis airport each week when we both taught our first film classes, swapping prints to screen before they had to be sent back to their distributors. That began a long friendship and a professional collaboration that has not ceased over three decades. Everyone in American universities and colleges interested in this subject eventually gathered at the film conferences Ben organized at Purdue over the years. The assistance of Mario Longardi, Fellini's long-time publicity agent, was invaluable to me. The aforementioned Gianfranco Angelucci, Fellini's confidant, assistant, and eventually his scriptwriter, became one of my best and oldest friends even before he assumed the role of director of the Fellini Foundation for a number of years. At Indiana University, I would not have begun to teach Italian film without the encouragement and example of Harry Geduld, founder of Film Studies, and Carolyn Geduld. At Continuum, my wonderful relationship began with the editor Stanley Hochman and continued first with Evelyn Erlich, and then with Evander Lomke, who not only encouraged me to write a history of Italian American films but knew every line of *The Godfather* by heart! Now David Barker has brought this project skillfully into port at Continuum, and I owe him a debt of gratitude. During the course of my career, I have been guided by the scholarship and friendship of Italy's best writers on Italian film: Gian Piero Brunetta, Italy's most important film historian; the late Lino Miccichè (who generously asked me to lecture at the University of Rome in his department); the film critic Tullio Kezich (Fellini's biographer); and Vittorio Boarini, past director of the Fellini Foundation in Rimini. I cannot fail to mention my ten years of work with Amanda Ciccarelli in Indiana University's Department of West European Studies and her crucial contribution to the international conference on "European Cinemas, European Societies 1895–1995" that we organized together to celebrate the centenary of the European invention of motion pictures. Sergio Ercolessi (a film director in his own right), his wife, Patrizia, and his two children, Edoardo and Ludovica, not to mention their wonderful, generous grandparents, made my wife and me feel as if we had a surrogate family in Italy during numerous stays in Bologna, Florence, Rome, and Pesaro. And my former colleague in comparative literature, David Hertz, has always been a fertile source of suggestions and new ideas.

It has been a long journey from the Cinéma Dragon in Paris, through more than three decades of teaching about and writing on the cinema at Indiana University, to my present retirement in St. George, Utah, where I completed *A History of Italian Cinema*. I very much hope that my readers will sense the same enthusiasm and excitement that I felt when I first encountered this topic many years ago, even though now I certainly realize how little I knew about the subject when I first approached it as a young scholar. I should like to dedicate this new book to the memory of the person who first drew me to Italian cinema: Federico Fellini. As time passes since his disappearance, it is more and more clear what a towering figure he represented in twentieth-century Italian culture and what a seminal contribution he made not only to Italian film but also to cinema in general, a contribution recognized by the best directors of our day. I trust I have avoided just the kind of academic jargon and ideological claptrap he would have despised. If my writing style pleases at all, it is a testament to the editorial work of my wife, Julia, a frequent collaborator with me on other projects, who honed and polished and made of this book a much more pleasant reading experience than it might otherwise have been.

PART ONE

Early Italian Cinema

CHAPTER 1

The Silent Era

Italy's Visual Culture and the Cinema

IT COMES AS NO SURPRISE that Italy has made crucial contributions to the twentieth century's only original art form, the cinema. Italian art had virtually formed the backbone of European visual culture since the time of Giotto, who first set Western art on a trek toward representing reality with space, volume, form, light, and shadow. Much of Italy's claim to artistic hegemony on the European continent between the thirteenth and the nineteenth centuries rested not only upon a steady succession of artists of genius but also upon the resolution of certain technical problems, such as the study of human anatomy, the study of perspective, and creative uses of light and shadow. Many similar technical problems would arise as cinematic art developed, and they demanded equally ingenious artistic and technical solutions in the realm of cinematic photography.

Although the Italian artistic tradition is a long and glorious one, the particular phenomenon of large crowds in urban public spaces engaged in watching images produced by mechanical means may be traced as far back as the eighteenth century, especially in Venice and northern Italy. One of the century's greatest painters, Giovanni Domenico Tiepolo (1727–1804), created two frescos both entitled *Il Mondo nuovo* (The New World), still preserved in Venice's Ca' Rezzonico Museum and Vicenza's Villa Valmarana ai Nani, that show an excited crowd of Venetian citizens gathered around a peep show, a magic-lantern device employed to show perspective views (*vedute ottiche* or *vues d'optiques*). Bassano del Grappa, in northern Italy, in particular the press owned and operated there by the Remondini family, became one of the three major sources of these perspective views (the other two being the much larger cities of Paris and Augsburg). Such prints, perspectives taken from cities and monuments all over the world, were perforated and designed to be seen through a viewing machine, an apparatus that reflected light through the tiny holes and allowed it to pass

1

Giovanni Domenico Tiepolo, *Il Mondo Nuovo*. Excited crowds gather to view perspectives, or *vedute ottiche*. Fresco at Vicenza's Villa Valmarana ai Nani. *Credit: photo by author*

toward the peephole. The views were not always intended to be accurate depictions of distant places. In some cases, such as a view of the Teatro di Marcello in Rome, the perspective might actually misrepresent some or even many details to amuse the spectator who knew the actual site well. As the name "new world" implies, these devices astounded people in much the same way that the moving images of the late nineteenth century or the talkies of the early twentieth century enthralled their audiences. The fact that Carlo Goldoni (1707–93), Italy and Venice's most important dramatist of the eighteenth century, also employed the title *Mondo nuovo* in a play that featured such devices testifies to the thirst that people had for novelty, information about the world outside their small universe, and visual stimulation through mechanical means. A number of these precursors to cinema have been collected and displayed in Turin's important Museo Nazionale del Cinema, and at least in Italian, the term "Mondo nuovo" conjures up not only images of Columbus discovering the New World but also the "new world" of such precinematic devices.[1]

The Italian silent film follows a long tradition of visual narrative in Italy, beginning with the medieval, Renaissance, and baroque fresco cycles in churches, palaces, and public buildings and continuing through the Enlightenment with magic-lantern peep shows. It is, however, extremely difficult to see a sizable number of Italian silent films, even though the number of works produced during the silent period is astonishing. It has been estimated that between the birth of the cinema in Italy and 1930, some 9,816 films of various lengths were made. Of these, some 1,500 have survived, among them only several hundred feature films. The prints that survive usually reflect the commercial success of the works in question, not necessarily their artistic or historical value. Few titles are available for public viewing, and even fewer have been reproduced in DVD or video format. Except for special presentations at museums, film festivals, and specialized conferences, almost all these films are accessible only in major European film archives (Amsterdam, Rome, Turin, London, Bologna, Gemona del Friuli). The thousands of early films produced stand in sharp contrast to the much lower production figures in other significant periods. For instance, only about 740 feature films appeared during the sound era of the Fascist period (1930–43), and only some 1,518 films were shot in postwar Italy between 1945 and 1959—a period that produced not only neorealist cinema but some of the greatest works of such internationally renowned directors as Michelangelo Antonioni, Luchino Visconti, Roberto Rossellini, and Federico Fellini.[2] Thanks to the patient scholarship of postwar Italian film historians, we now know much more about this early period. In addition to several hundred works that have survived in at least one complete print, accurate records of the actual titles of films produced but later destroyed or lost have been compiled, plots or synopses of many of the films that disappeared are known in some detail, a sizable body of journalistic criticism and reviews testifying to the public reaction to these works remains, and much information has been unearthed on early production companies and the key individuals involved in these pioneering efforts.

"Mondo Nuovo" apparatus for *vedute ottiche* with three apertures for simultaneous viewing, now preserved in Turin's Museo Nazionale del Cinema. *Credit: Museo del Cinema (Turin)*

Filoteo Albertini and the First Years of Italian Silent Cinema

On November 11, 1895, Filoteo Albertini (1865–1937) applied for an Italian patent on an early device for the production of motion pictures, the Albertini Kinetograph. One of the first films produced for commercial use in Italy appeared the next year, *King Umberto and Margherita of Savoy Strolling in the Park* (*Umberto e Margherita di Savoia a passeggio per il parco*, 1896), directed by Vittorio Calcina (1847–1916). This brief glimpse into the daily lives of Italian royalty has the honor of being one of the first Italian films to which admission was charged. A number of such short films have survived from this period, memorable not only for the slice of life from Italy's *belle époque* that still shines through them, but also because they reveal the Italian cinema's first infantile steps toward a film language that transcends still photography: early panoramic shots of crowds, cameras placed on moving vehicles to capture the finish line of a bicycle race, and so forth. In many respects, these early documentaries were indebted to the better-known works of the Lumière brothers in France, whose films were extremely popular in the first decade of the cinema's existence in Italy. Calcina also served as the Italian representative for the Lumière brothers' company. After introducing their works to Parisian audiences in 1895 (the date generally regarded as marking the invention of the cinema), the Lumière brothers brought what they called their "cinématographe" to Italy in 1896 and screened films in Milan, Rome, and Naples. The advertising copy for the screening in Naples conjures up the atmosphere of these early years:

> This evening the reopening of Margherita Hall with a completely new program. The Lumière Cinématographe will be featured, the greatest novelty of the century. There will also be the Beneditti family, unparalleled flying acrobats expressly brought in from Berlin. The dwarf couple, the Vargas Bisaccia, recently returned from their triumphant artistic tour in Russia, Spain, and Germany. The eccentric French star Bloquette, the German singer Baroness Milford, Hermand the snake man, Belvalle the cabaret singer. In a word, a most attractive spectacle.[3]

Without doubt the cinema was first regarded as a curiosity, something akin to a country fair, where the atmosphere must have been reminiscent of the crowds depicted in the Tiepolo frescos. At the beginning of the twentieth century, the audience must have been composed primarily of relatively unsophisticated Italians, approximately half of whom were illiterate. Such films were shown virtually everywhere a space was available: in traditional opera houses or theaters (*stadia*) at fairs, and in cafes or schools. Even the short films presented during this period gave the ordinary citizen a first chance to gaze at important people, to visit foreign lands, and to take part (however marginally as passive, voyeuristic observers) in the important historical and cultural events at the dawn of a new century in the new Italian nation. Until the establishment of the first real movie theaters in the major cities after 1905, Italians often saw films screened by entrepreneurs who moved from town to town and from fair to fair, hauling their equipment in wagons, on trucks, or by train, producing what is termed in the historical literature "il cinema ambulante," or "itinerant cinema." Once fixed cinema theaters became more fashionable, these individuals often transferred their activities there. In this way, the cinema developed beyond its function as one of many diverse popular attractions at a fairground into a more sophisticated entertainment frequented not only by the poor but also by the middle class. By 1906, Turin boasted nine theaters, Milan had seven, Rome had twenty-three, and Naples had twenty-five.[4] The fact that the richer northern cities had fewer theaters than the poorer southern ones suggests that even with the emergence of stable structures, film continued to be popular, often lower-class entertainment that would develop primarily by expanding its middle-class appeal.

Albertini produced the first feature film with a complex plot in 1905: *The Taking of Rome* (*La presa di Roma*, 1905). This film is worth remembering for a number of reasons. It marked a major step forward from the brief short film designed to entertain audiences during intermissions of musical concerts or theatrical productions toward the longer, more complex feature film. The film's subject, the breaching of the Porta Pia by Italian troops in 1870, resulting in the annexation of Rome to the fledgling unified Italian state, connects the cinema to the Italian Risorgimento, the national drive to independence and the formation of a single Italian nation throughout the peninsula. (Italian cinema would continue to play a civic function in Italian society, especially during the neorealist period and afterward.) *The Taking of Rome* also set the stage for the rise of what would eventually become Italy's most successful silent film genre: the historical epic.

Film Genres in the Silent Era

Early silent cinema in Italy was never completely dominated by the historical epic or the costume drama, but films in these categories represented the industry's most profitable and popular products. Early films treated a variety of topics that ranged from the celebrated Roman epics to filmed versions of literary or operatic masterpieces; melodramas or tragedies inspired by Italian *verismo*, or regional, naturalistic narratives; adventure films in episodes or series format; comedies; and experimental art films produced by the Italian avant-garde movement futurism. All these genres contributed something to the evolution of Italian film art, but the silent historical or costume film ultimately marked the high-water mark of Italian production and its success abroad in foreign markets. Interest in literary or historical topics helped to create the need for the artistic director, in addition to the cameraman and the producer, whose task was to coordinate the necessary historical research, the construction of sets and costumes, and the increasingly central role of the often temperamental actors and actresses whose popularity would soon surpass that of the man or woman in the street of the early documentary short film. Increasingly complex plots, taken either from history or from the Italian literary classics, also required the services of another technician, the scriptwriter, even though films had yet to speak. The wealth of ancient ruins and grandiose monuments in Italy, especially in Rome, as well as the favorable climate and natural light of the peninsula, encouraged feature films shot on location. The relatively inexpensive cost of Italian labor made possible the huge crowd scenes that enliven many such historical epics, and much of the artistic value these early works possess lies in their treatment of such crowds and the spectacular sets they inhabit.

Dante and the Silent Cinema

Predictably, Dante, whose influence in Italian culture is profound, played a role in the development of cinema as a serious art form. Relying upon recognized literary or operatic classics fulfilled two functions: it provided familiar plots to Italian audiences, and it helped elevate the cinema above the fairground associations that accompanied its first decade of life. Hence, early filmmakers often pillaged authors read in Italian schools, such as Manzoni, Tasso, and Dante (not to mention popular foreign writers, such as Alexandre Dumas and Shakespeare) for their scripts. Between 1908 and 1911, eleven silent films based on Dante's life, the *Divine Comedy*, and figures inspired by Dante appeared in Italy, the most important of which was *Dante's Inferno* (*L'Inferno*, 1911), directed by Francesco Bertolini, Giuseppe de Liguoro, and Adolfo Padovan for Milano Films. It has been credited by film historians for causing a number of fundamental changes in viewing habits: it helped to establish the vogue for the multireel or feature film, it popularized the "art film" or "film of quality," it served as a forerunner to the costume epic, and it marked the most important early example of the close ties that would exist between literature and Italian cinema in the future development of this new art form.[5] One goal of the film was certainly achieved: the elevation of film above the level of popular entertainment and the attraction of the Italian intelligentsia—the audience at the Neapolitan premiere of *Dante's Inferno* included the philosopher-critic Benedetto Croce (1866–1962), Italy's most famous intellectual; the distinguished novelist Matilde Serao (1857–1927); and the playwright Roberto Bracco (1861–1943), one of whose dramas would, only three years later, become the basis for an important realist film treating Italian life.

Francesco Bertolini, Giuseppe de Liguoro, and Adolfo Padovan's *Dante's Inferno*: Lucifer devours souls in the icy pit of Hell. *Credit: DVD*

Dante's Inferno also established records for length (1,300 meters, comprising three parts and fifty-four scenes), expense (more than a hundred thousand lire at a time when only several lire translated into a dollar), special effects, and one of the first lavish publicity campaigns designed to promote a film. Its Dantesque iconography followed closely the extremely famous and familiar Gustave Doré illustrations of Dante's vision of Hell. The geography of Hell inspired the directors to create imaginative sets, monsters, and special effects, including flashbacks, superimpositions of images, and double exposures. Some of the special effects are probably indebted to the example of Georges Méliès, the French director whose imaginative work has always been contrasted to the photographic realism of the Lumière brothers in the early years of the movies.

A number of important works immediately followed the example of *Dante's Inferno*. The most successful commercially were historical costume epics, most set in classical times but some situated in other memorable periods of Italian history, such as the Middle Ages or the Renaissance. Giovanni Pastrone (1883–1959), Enrico Guazzoni (1876–1949), and Mario Caserini (1874–1920) directed a number of the most important of these films, many of which helped Italy to capture a large share of the international market before the outbreak of World War I. In *The Fall of Troy* (*La caduta di Troia*, 1910), an early work of 600 meters, Pastrone developed the aesthetic possibilities of the long shot, opening up with his camera a sense of boundless space populated by large crowds and magnificent sets that stand in sharp contrast to the operalike, one-dimensional sets of earlier historical short films. Pastrone's *Agnes Visconti* (1910)[6] reveals his mastery of creating suspense through careful editing, as parallel actions involving different characters are manipulated skillfully toward a dramatic conclusion.

The Historical Epic

Two costume films of Roman inspiration, Caserini's *The Last Days of Pompeii* (*Gli ultimi giorni di Pompeii*, 1913) and Guazzoni's *Quo Vadis?* (*Quo vadis?*, 1913), helped to popularize this kind of film among growing international audiences. Caserini adapted his film from the novel by Edward Bulwer-Lytton, while Guazzoni based his upon the novel by Henryk Sienkiewicz. Both continued the trademark aesthetic of the Italian historical epic: elaborate sets and large crowd scenes. Thanks in part to skillful distribution in the United States by George Kleine, an entrepreneur active in the industry during the silent period, Italian filmmakers could export their epic films for a brief period at virtually any price they demanded. To offer some idea of how popular such films were in America, film historians mining the Kleine Collection at the Library of Congress in Washington have calculated that *Quo Vadis?* played twenty-two weeks in New York, fourteen in Philadelphia, thirteen in Boston, eight in Chicago, and even five days in the far-off mining town of Butte, Montana![7] *Julius Caesar* (*Caio Giulio Cesare*, 1914) exploited both classical history and the universally popular Shakespearian account of Rome's most famous military leader.

Like *Julius Caesar*, the acknowledged masterpiece of this epic genre, Pastrone's *Cabiria* (1914), appeared at almost the very moment the export

Guazzoni's *Julius Caesar* dramatizes the assassination of ancient Rome's most famous leader, a typical silent film celebrating Roman glories. *Credit: AB*

In Pastrone's *Cabiria*, lavish neoclassical interiors display the wealth of the Roman Republic and the skills of Italian set designers. *Credit: DVD*

market collapsed with the outbreak of hostilities in Europe.[8] A feature film of some 4,500 meters in length, it embodied a number of artistic and technical innovations that guaranteed box-office success all over the world, and it certainly influenced the historical sets of *Intolerance* (1916) by D. W. Griffith (1875–1948). A stickler for historical accuracy and reconstruction, Pastrone spent a great deal of time at the Louvre researching the sets and costumes. The seven-month production cost 1,000,000 lire (at the time, a small fortune), including 50,000 lire paid in gold to Gabriele d'Annunzio (1863–1938), then the world's most popular novelist and a champion of self-promotion, for the use of his magic name. Publicity and rumor attributed the film to d'Annunzio, but he wrote only the intertitles. The Milan premiere featured specially commissioned symphonic music by Ildebrando Pizzetti, one of the most important composers of the era, and an orchestra of a hundred musicians performed it. Twenty thousand meters of film were shot to create a three-hour work, highlighting the important role the director now played as a film editor in producing movies.

Pastrone is credited with inventing the dolly (*carrello*), which enabled him to track smoothly in and out of his enormous sets. The technique of moving from an extremely long shot to a medium close-up or close-up was particularly successful in establishing a sense of space and grandeur. Increased attention to close-ups emphasized the facial expressions and heroic gestures of his actors, who declaimed their lines in a solemn, fustian manner indebted to the Italian theatrical style of the time. In several dream sequences, Pastrone skillfully employed superimpositions. In addition, the hand tinting of some key sequences in the film (a common but expensive process during the silent era) gave them the effect of color. Pastrone's use of artificial lighting (twelve spotlights equipped with individual reflectors) for interiors in the Turin studio—particularly for the scene in which the heroine, Cabiria ("born from fire"), is about to be sacrificed to the Carthaginian god Moloch—produced stunning effects that still seem miraculous today. Pastrone also did important location shooting in both Tunisia and Sicily, including footage of Hannibal crossing the Alps with elephants that the director had somehow transported to the mountains to satisfy his scrupulous insistence upon accuracy. Finally, his use of special effects, process shots, and scale models in two memorable scenes—the eruption of Mount Etna and the burning of the Roman fleet by Archimedes' mirrors at the siege of Syracuse—represents a most valuable and original contribution to the language of silent cinema.

No doubt inspired by d'Annunzio's neoclassicism, Pastrone's script follows very loosely the story of the epic battle between two great classical civilizations, Rome and Carthage, as it had been immortalized in Livy's history of republican Rome. In addition, to increase the film's box-office appeal, d'Annunzio and Pastrone drew on the example of the Latin epic *Africa*, composed during the early Renaissance by the virtual inventor of humanism, Francesco Petrarca (1304–74). Petrarca's epic intertwines the narrative of the Second Punic War with a love story, and *Cabiria* does the same, recounting the relationship of Cabiria, a girl whom Phoenician pirates sold into slavery to be sacrificed to the Carthaginian gods, and Fulvio Axilla, a Roman spy and patrician who, aided by his loyal slave Maciste, rescues Cabiria in the nick of time. Thus, the conflict between the virtuous Roman Republic and the evil Carthaginian Empire comes to life on the screen within a melodramatic plot that has resonance not only for the future of Italian cinema but also for works produced by Hollywood.[9]

Cabiria's popularity in Italy had other interesting causes. The film appeared around the conclusion of the Italo-Turkish War, from which Italy emerged victorious, thereby obtaining new colonies on the shores of North Africa in territory that once had been Roman. No doubt, part of the unprecedented success of the film in Italy lies in its clear analogy between past and present. Republican Rome had conquered and "civilized" the territory centuries earlier, and now history was repeating itself, as the young Italian nation that arose from the Risorgimento struggle for independence moved to reclaim its long-lost Mediterranean hegemony. Pastrone's film served not only as a model for numerous other silent Roman epics but also as a direct link to the postwar peplum or neomythological films that would eventually assume cult status. The role of Maciste, who became the ancestor of hundreds of muscle-bound heroes who would perform impossible tasks in a romanticized and fantasized cinematic past, made Bartolomeo Pagano

Pastrone's *Cabiria*: the famous set representing the Temple of Moloch in Carthage. *Credit: DVD*

(1878–1947), a dockworker from Genoa, one of the first action stars of the silent cinema. The Maciste character would survive long after the economic health of the Italian silent cinema had declined. For example, as late as 1925, Guido Brignone (1887–1959) made *Maciste in Hell* (*Maciste all'inferno*), yet another nod to Dante's *Divine Comedy* as inspiration for a silent film. In it Maciste (again played by Pagano) combats a number of devils, and the special effects and Doré-inspired sets in Hell managed to impress at least one young viewer: Federico Fellini, who lists it as the second film he remembers from his early film-viewing days, placing it between two masterpieces by Chaplin and ahead of classics by such eminent directors as Keaton, Kubrick, Hawks, Renoir, Ford, Welles, and Disney.[10]

During and immediately after the war, Italian historical epics continued to be made but were less and less likely to appeal to audiences abroad, who had grown tired of the formalized, leaden, declamatory acting style the cinema unfortunately borrowed from Italian theatrical performance. Writing in 1923 to Guido Pedrazzini, director of Cines (one of the most important Italian production companies, founded in 1906 by Albertini and closely identified with the exportation of epic films), the American distributor George Kleine bluntly stated that this kind of histrionic acting no longer attracted American audiences.[11] Some filmmakers tried to move epics in a different direction. Guazzoni's postwar films, usually featuring his favorite actor, Amleto Novelli (1885–1924), attempt to direct the historicism of Pastrone to a more fanciful and poetic treatment of the past. His *Fabiola* (1917) aims at psychological introspection in treating the martyrdoms of Saints

Agnes and Sebastian, whereas *Jerusalem Delivered* (*Gerusalemme liberata*, 1918) reflects the triumph of fantasy over archaeological accuracy, as the director places Torquato Tasso's baroque epic about the Crusaders in the Holy Land in the ancient ruins of the city of Rome. *Christ* (*Christus*, 1916) by Giulio Antamoro (1877–1945) mined an offshoot of the historical epic, the religious film, often linked to the epic in terms of style and attention to historical detail. He produced an impressive life of Christ with a simple narrative style and on-location shooting in Palestine and Egypt that stood in sharp contrast to the grandiose historical sets of period epics. Antamoro's *Brother Francis* (*Frate Francesco*, 1926) portrays the life of Saint Francis of Assisi with skill, and his visual style shows the clear influence of early Italian fresco paintings, particularly in the depiction of the saint's stigmata. Guazzoni showed that he could also skillfully produce the kind of monumental Roman potboilers that were no longer in vogue with *Messalina* (1923), a film boasting a spectacular chariot race that takes place within a set of the Circus Maximus that, for the times, was unequaled in size and historical accuracy. This scene was subsequently copied in several Hollywood versions of *Ben-Hur*.

Divismo and the Italian Star System

Immediately before the outbreak of the Great War, a phenomenon later to become known as the star system (*divismo* in Italian) arose in Italy. A number of new faces profited from the initial reluctance of established theatrical actors from the so-called legitimate theater to enter the new medium of the cinema, and as the movies grew in popularity by leaps and bounds, their role as an attraction to the public and as an economic force steadily grew. The histrionic gestures and languid style of Lyda Borelli (1884–1959) came to epitomize, in such films as Caserini's *Love Everlasting* (*Ma l'amore mio non muore*, 1913), the melodramatic genre she helped create. A number of such female "vamps"—called *dive*, literally "goddesses" in Italian, a term originally coined for star sopranos of opera—emerged to forge an image of the femme fatale in the early silent films in Italy.[12] As one film historian has put it, such a film style represents "the self-portrait, willed or not, of an era, a world as devoted to extravagance and cynicism as ours is to eroticism and violence," but that paradoxically furnished "the basis of reality in the masquerade of the upper-class drama that gives it its historical value."[13] Francesca Bertini (1888–1985) added passion to languid manner. Her life has been captured in a fascinating documentary film by Gianfranco Mingozzi (1932–) entitled *The Last Diva: Francesca Bertini* (*L'ultima diva: Francesca Bertini*, 1982). Her performance in *The Serpent* (*La serpe*, 1920) by Roberto Roberti (pseud.: Vincenzo Leone, 1879–1959), in which events marking the development of a love affair are interspersed with shots showing a snake

The Italian *diva*, or vamp: Francesca Bertini in Leone's *The Serpent. Credit: DVD*

devouring a meek and defenseless rabbit, reaches a rare level of overt sexual symbolism. Set in the midst of "Liberty" drawing rooms—the Italian term for the period style known elsewhere as art nouveau (long sold by Liberty & Co. in London)—and animated by passionate love and fatal affairs, this type of cinema, with its melodramatic mode, required an increased attention to close-up shots and a sometimes overly declamatory acting style that makes viewing such films difficult for contemporary audiences. Roberti, a.k.a. Leone, made some fifteen films with Bertini between 1917 and 1921, and he should probably also be credited with making the first Italian western: *Indian Vampire* (*Vampira indiana*, 1913). His son Sergio Leone (1929–89)—who sometimes credited himself in his early works as Bob Robertson (i.e., "Roberto's son")—would eventually become one of the Italian cinema's most innovative and original directors, reviving and transforming the Hollywood western with his famous variant of the spaghetti western.[14]

Besides Borelli and Bertini, other important *dive* include Hesperia (1885–1959), who was no great beauty but achieved renown through her unique personality; Pina Menichelli (1890–1984), who abandoned the declamatory gestures of other female leads for a wider and more contemporary range of feminine images; Maria Jacobini (1892–1944); Diana Karenne (1888–1940); and Anna Fougez (1898–1966). Few male actors in Italy, with the possible exception of Bartolomeo Pagano, became as popular as the women. The star system and its melodramatic style of acting also encouraged shooting inside studios with artificial light rather than outside on locations with natural light. The women in the silent cinema owed a great deal to preexisting literary, theatrical, or operatic traditions, including the tragic operas by Giacomo Puccini (1858–1924), such as *La bohème* (1896) or *Tosca* (1900), and the erotic and wildly popular novels by the aesthete Gabriele d'Annunzio, whose very titles, such as *The Child of Pleasure* (*Il piacere*, 1889) or *The Triumph of Death* (*Il trionfo della morte*, 1894), point to the decadence of his style, a quality that moved the critic and historian Benedetto Croce to call him a "dilettante of sensations."

One important female director from Naples deserves special notice: Elvira Notari (1875–1946), who made about sixty feature films, a hundred documentaries, and numerous short films for her own production company, Dora Film, between 1906 and 1930. What little remains of her work appears to show her films as precursors to Italian neorealism: they frequently employ real locations and nonprofessional actors, not to mention treatments of the marginalized population of the lower classes in Naples, Italy's most populous but impoverished city.[15]

Some ideologically motivated writers in the neorealist period following World War II, such as the film historian and director Carlo Lizzani (1922–), explained the collapse of the Italian silent cinema—after only a few years at the peak of its commercial appeal—by noting a number of defects in its basic structure: it was characterized by intellectual "dead ends" (historical epics such as *Cabiria*), "unreal" subject matter (a focus upon the past glories of Italy rather than its present reality), the economic burdens imposed by a star system out of control, and by the leaden weight of D'Annunzianism in film melodrama.[16] Yet the star system and the costume drama arose in Hollywood and did not lead to a similar economic collapse of the American film industry. Although critics such as Lizzani maintain that the Italian cinema would have enjoyed greater success had it focused upon "realism," it is important to recognize that the realist view of Italy in the movies has never been very popular, even during the heyday of Italian neorealism, between 1945 and 1955. Film realism may have consistently attracted the plaudits of Italian intellectuals or critics, but the truth is that the Italian public has always preferred escapism in its movies—the gestures of a Lyda Borelli, the muscle flexing of Maciste, the episodic adventure films of Emilio Ghione (1879–1930), the comic short films of Leopoldo Fregoli (1867–1936); or the fifty clown films by Polidor (Ferdinand Guillaume, 1887–1977), who was immortalized not in some surviving silent film but rather by Federico Fellini in an extraordinary sequence in a Roman nightclub for *La Dolce Vita* (*La dolce vita*, 1960). Italian audiences have always been closer to Hollywood audiences than Italian intellectuals might have preferred.

Realism in the Silent Cinema

Notwithstanding the Italian predilection for escapism, two early films deserve special mention for looking ahead to the realist current in Italian cinema that arose after the coming of sound and reached its greatest level of artistic achievement with neorealism: *Lost in the Dark* (*Sperduti nel buio*, 1914), by the director Nino Martoglio (1870–1921); and *Assunta Spina* (1915), by the director Gustavo Serena (1882–1970), with credit for direction also sometimes given to its star, Francesca Bertini. Each film was based on a preexisting Neapolitan play, written respectively by Roberto Bracco and Salvatore Di Giacomo (1860–1934).

Regrettably, *Lost in the Dark* survives solely in a few fragmentary photographs, because the Germans presumably destroyed the only extant print of the film during the last days of World War II. From what we know about the film, derived largely from accounts of important critics as well as from its recently published screenplay, *Lost in the Dark* was a forward-looking account of a lower-class girl born out of wedlock and exhibited a dramatic style of editing, juxtaposing the sunlit Neapolitan slums of the girl's world with the palatial splendor of the world of the upper-class father who abandoned her.[17] *Assunta Spina*'s plot seems melodramatic to contemporary audiences, rather than realistic: its love triangles and scuffles between suitors for Assunta's hand are now out of fashion, but its use of local Neapolitan dialect and traditional customs, its on-location shooting, and its sometimes crude, documentary photography reflect a style of cinema that points toward realist tendencies in the cinema after the advent of sound during the Fascist period and subsequently in postwar Italian neorealism.[18]

Silent Film and the Avant-garde: Italian Futurism

Italian cinema had first arisen from a popular milieu that was definitely disconnected from the high culture of Italy's ruling elites or university graduates. For some Italians, film represented a bastard art form; it was neither drama (although many films consisted of filmed theatrical works), nor literature (although many films were based upon novels), nor art (even though it employed visual images in imaginative ways). Film would have to gain respectability from Italian intellectuals if it was to attract the most talented individuals who could exploit the cinema's potential. It was only natural that the Italian futurists, then Italy's most important and influential avant-garde movement, would see in film—the only original art form of the early twentieth century—an entirely different kind of medium capable of expressing completely modern ideas and images. The futurist movement exploded upon the European scene with its iconoclastic "Futurist Manifesto," published by the movement's founder and charismatic leader,

Filippo Tommaso Marinetti (1876–1944), and a number of his associates and like-minded aesthetes on February 20, 1909, in the Parisian newspaper *Le Figaro*. The futurist penchant for modern technology, machines, and the interplay of speed, light, and space, as well as its violent opposition to tradition in the arts, recommended the cinema as the prototypical modern art form for those who claimed, as Marinetti did, to prefer the aesthetic qualities of a racing motor car to the "Winged Victory," a classical statue (*Nike of Samothrace*) in Paris's Louvre Museum.

Thus, "The Futurist Cinema," a manifesto on the movies published on September 11, 1916, represents a significant, early, and unusual appreciation of the cinema's role:

> The cinema is an autonomous art. The cinema must therefore never copy the stage. The cinema, being essentially visual, must above all fulfill the evolution of painting; detach itself from reality, from photography, from the graceful and solemn. It must become antigraceful, deforming, impressionistic, synthetic, dynamic, free-wording.[19]

While the concrete impact of the manifesto is difficult to determine, it suggested specific techniques and themes for the new art form. In futurist film, reality would be presented directly, employing cinematic analogies. For example, rather than developing various phases of the anguish of a character's suffering, it would be sufficient to show a jagged, cavernous mountain to suggest the emotion's equivalent in a single image. The manifesto also recommended filmed dramas of abstract objects, dramatized states of mind captured on film, and filmed words-in-freedom, the cinematic equivalent of futurist poetry. In the history of film theory, "The Futurist Cinema" must be considered one of the very first declarations of film's right to an autonomous existence, separate from its sister art forms.

In practice, the futurists produced few actual movies, and the most famous of these—*Futurist Life* (*Vita futurista*, 1916), by Arnaldo Ginna (1890–1982), and *The Wicked Enchantment* (*Il perfido incanto*, 1916), by Anton Giulio Bragaglia (1890–1960)—survive today only in scattered still photographs. From contemporary accounts of futurist films, it is clear that both of these films employed innovative techniques, such as hand-coloring and tinting of black-and-white film, split-screen techniques, double exposures, and the use of mirrors to distort images. *Futurist Life* consciously rejects a traditional narrative plot and employs an essentially abstract structure. Not only Ginna but also Marinetti, and the painters Giacomo Balla and Carlo Carrà planned this experimental film. Based on what has been reconstructed from descriptions from the period, the film contained eight sequences and ran for little less than an hour, but the discussions of the contents of these sequences vary, and it is difficult to say anything about the film with real precision. Bragaglia made three full-length works that ran over an hour, not only *The Wicked Enchantment* but also *Thaïs* (1916) and *My Corpse* (*Il mio cadavere*, 1916). According to most accounts of Braga-glia's works, their most interesting features were due to the truly avant-garde sets designed by the futurist artist Enrico Prampolini (1894–1956), who also worked with futurists on stage and opera productions.

It should be noted that some claims for originality in the futurist manifesto on film cannot be substantiated. Marinetti's view that film had to that time employed only outmoded literary or theatrical techniques fails to take into account, for example, the numerous aesthetic advances in film language achieved in even such a seemingly traditional work as Pastrone's *Cabiria*, based on exactly the kind of literary and historical subject that the futurists attacked as "past-loving" and out of date. Some of the ideas pro-claimed by futurists as their own might be a product of reacting to the films that were actually being made at the time. Even in the silent era, cinematic practice in Italy was often in advance of the theorists or the historians. Yet Italian futurism, the most dynamic and original avant-garde movement in Italy, had enormous influence upon other, later avant-garde movements in Europe. Its positive view of the art of the cinema certainly helped to legiti-mize this new art form among intellectuals.

Italian Intellectuals and the Silent Cinema: The Case of Luigi Pirandello

Clearly, the most prestigious Italian literary figure to boost the status of the cinema besides Gabriele d'Annunzio (who lent his name to *Cabiria* more for financial gain than for aesthetic conviction) was Luigi Pirandello (1867–1936), whose Nobel Prize for Literature in 1934 only confirmed the fact that he had long been the most innovative playwright in the first half of the twentieth century. Pirandello was fascinated by the cinema and had visited film studios in Rome as early as 1904. His novel *Shoot!* (*Si gira*, 1915) is one of the first great works of fiction about the movies.[20] Between the novel's appearance and the international success of his greatest play, *Six Characters in Search of an Author* (*Sei personaggi in cerca d'autore*, 1921), Pirandello contributed stories to various Italian studios, and a number of his short sto-ries and plays were adapted by various film directors, including Giuseppe Forti, Ugo Gracci, Augusto Genina, Augusto Camerini, Gennaro Righelli, Marcel L'Herbier, and Amleto Palermi. In 1929, the playwright visited Lon-don as Paramount's guest for a screening of *The Jazz Singer*, the Hollywood film always associated with the advent of the talkies. Shortly thereafter, Pirandello wrote the article "Will Talkies Abolish the Theatre?" ("Se il film parlante abolirà il teatro") for Milan's prestigious daily newspaper *Corriere della Sera*, and one of his short stories, entitled "Silence" ("Il silenzio"), was adapted as the screenplay for the first Italian sound film to be distributed:

The Song of Love (*La canzone dell'amore*, 1930), shot by Gennaro Righelli (1886–1949). Numerous attempts (almost fifty) were made without success to shoot *Six Characters*, despite all the energy Pirandello devoted to such a project by writing treatments for various directors and studios. His fascination with cinema resulted in a well-known Hollywood adaptation of one of his lesser plays, *Come tu mi vuoi* (1930), being filmed with the correctly translated title *As You Desire Me* (1932) by George Fitzmaurice for MGM Studios and featuring an outstanding cast that included Greta Garbo, Erich von Stroheim, and Melvyn Douglas. Since Pirandello's death, dozens of films in the postwar period have been adapted from his many theatrical and fictional works. Obviously, Pirandello's example legitimized the role of the serious literary figure as an active contributor to the creation of ideas, treatments, stories, and screenplays in Italy, leading to many such literary figures working with film directors during the subsequent history of the Italian cinema.

The Decline of the Italian Film Industry before the Coming of Sound

The Italian silent cinema never lacked directors, actors, or technicians of genius, but economic factors may explain the industry's rapid decline after its unparalleled initial success before the outbreak of World War I. A single feature of the Italian film market has remained constant from the origins of the industry to the present day: the total percentage of Italian-produced films in the Italian market has never risen above approximately one-third of the total number of films in circulation. Thus, Italian filmmakers have never dominated their home market even when both the quality and the quantity of production were extremely high; rather, American competition has been virtually hegemonic throughout its entire history. Unlike their American competition, Italian producers have proved to be comparatively poor businessmen and did not evolve, as their Hollywood counterparts did, a profitable infrastructure of movie chains and rental agencies to maximize their profits and to guarantee the distribution of their products during the silent period. The Italian state also was slow to recognize the dangers from foreign competition. Paradoxically, Italian film censorship beginning after 1913 made it possible for foreign works to enter the Italian market practically without hindrance while Italian-made films occasionally encountered censorship obstacles.

Some effort was made to meet the American challenge. In 1919, a group known as L'Unione Cinematografica Italiana (UCI) was formed, including the major Italian production companies—Cines,[21] Ambrosio-Film, Caesar-Film, and Tiber-Film. Its goal was to retain control of the Italian market, but bad planning and excessive expenditures for poorly conceived projects caused its bankruptcy in 1927. The industry's problems were further complicated by the arrival in Rome in 1923 of an American company that would produce *Ben-Hur*, a colossal costume film that challenged the Italian industry in the very film genre that had created so much of its success abroad. Although the film was finally completed in America by the director Fred Niblo, with Ramon Novarro and Francis X. Bushman in lead roles, the company's presence in Rome and its relatively inexhaustible source of funding tied up studio space and prevented progress on other domestic productions. By the time shooting had left Rome, the Italian film industry was virtually decimated. The production figures speak for themselves: from some 220 Italian films produced in 1920, the production dropped dramatically to 100 in 1921, 50 in 1922, between 20 and 30 in 1923, some 15 or 20 in 1924, around 15 in 1925–26, and fewer than a dozen in 1927–28 before the advent of the Italian talkies in 1930.[22] During this period, the more than three thousand movie theaters in Italy could procure only imported films, most from Hollywood. Oddly, this suppression occurred in a nation whose official policy after Fascism's rise to power in 1922 was national autonomy (*autarchia*). The irony of this situation was that Hollywood had taken an Italian immigrant, Rodolfo di Valentina d'Antonguolla, and made of him the quintessential silent cinema star—something the cinema of Rudolph Valentino's native Italy seemed incapable of achieving.[23]

CHAPTER 2

The Coming of Sound and the Fascist Era

Signs of Revival

GIVEN THE LAMENTABLE STATE OF THE ITALIAN FILM INDUSTRY by the end of the silent era and its inability to cope with competition from abroad, primarily from Hollywood, some form of state intervention would have probably occurred regardless of the type of government that ruled Italy. As noted in chapter 1, after the establishment in 1922 of a Fascist regime headed by Benito Mussolini (1883–1945), the official policy of the Fascist state was autonomy (*autarchia*), and Mussolini's regime eventually offered support to the industry in a number of ways until its fall in 1943, at the height of World War II, with German soldiers occupying Italy in the north and Allied troops advancing across the peninsula from the south. Mussolini is associated with his remark that "the cinema is the most powerful weapon," a statement he probably derived from the speeches of Vladimir Lenin (1870–1924), but the Fascist regime did not immediately intervene or interfere with the commercial industry upon coming to power in 1922.

Before the Fascists decided to assist Italian filmmakers, at least one partially effective private initiative took place. An entrepreneur named Stefano Pittaluga (1887–1932) began a career as a distributor of films for the some 150 movie theaters that he owned, as well as for many others that he controlled. Faced with a dearth of homegrown films and the virtual monopoly of American studios within the Italian market, Pittaluga decided to become a film producer himself. In 1926, he founded the Società Anonima Stefano Pittaluga (SASP) and bought up a number of the failing Italian companies, including Cines, Itala, and Palatina. As a result, Pittaluga became the owner of what was left of the Italian industry. After he built several sound studios, Mussolini's government, in 1927, granted Pittaluga's company the distribution of documentaries and newsreels produced by L'Unione Cinematografica

Educativa (the Educational Cinematographic Union)—known as the Istituto Luce (the acronym *LUCE* being the Italian word for light)—a move that represented the first major cooperative venture between the Fascist state and the private sector. Pittaluga offered hope for a more rationally ordered internal market with more space for Italian-made films, but his death curtailed some of the many positive steps he had envisioned for a renaissance of the Italian commercial industry. Nevertheless, Pittaluga's early support of two of Italy's best directors in the period, Alessandro Blasetti (1900–87) and Mario Camerini (1895–1981), and his salvation of Cines, the studio that produced many of the best films made between the advent of sound in Italy and the end of the Fascist regime in 1943, represent key developments in the rebirth of Italian cinema as a viable commercial enterprise. It was the Cines-Pittaluga Company, for example, that released the first Italian sound film, Righelli's *The Song of Love*, and after Pittaluga's death, Cines-Pittaluga would form the nucleus of the Ente Nazionale Industrie Cinematografiche (ENIC, or National Agency for Motion Picture Industries), a corporation the Italian government formed in 1935 to reorganize the entire industry.

Fascist Support for the Italian Cinema

After Pittaluga's death, governmental intervention in the industry increased dramatically. In 1934, the Direzione Generale per la Cinematografia (Office for Cinematography) was created with Luigi Freddi (1895–1977), a strong supporter of the Fascist regime, as its head. Until the regime's fall, Freddi would hold important administrative positions at Cines, ENIC, and Italy's major studio, Cinecittà, located on the outskirts of Rome. The Direzione Generale formed part of the Ministero per la Cultura Popolare (Ministry of Popular Culture, commonly referred to as the "Minculpop"). In 1935, a special fund for the production of Italian films was created at the Banca Nazionale del Lavoro (the "Sezione autonomo per il credito cinematografico" or the Autonomous Section for Cinema Credit).

Two years earlier, in 1933, Count Galeazzo Ciano (1903–44), first Undersecretary and then Minister for Press and Propaganda—and Mussolini's son-in-law—had encouraged the creation of "cinegufs," or Fascist cinema clubs, at the universities within the Gioventù Universitaria Fascista (Fascist University Youth, known as the GUF). These film clubs did not aim at inculcating Fascist propaganda among their members, and it was quite common for them to screen not only films from other European countries or from Hollywood but also from the hated Soviet Union. In 1934, the arts festival in Venice (the Biennale) added a category for film, and the Venice Film Festival subsequently became a showcase for the Italian film industry and the world's most important such event years before the festival at Cannes arose to supplant Venice in importance after the

Mussolini and other high-ranking fascist officials arrive in 1937 to inaugurate the grand opening of Cinecittà, the studio complex that still stands on the outskirts of Rome. *Credit: Cinecittà Archives (Rome)*

end of World War II. The government then founded the important school for training in filmmaking, the Centro Sperimentale di Cinematografia (Experimental Center for Cinematography), which opened in 1935 with Luigi Chiarini (1900–75) as its first director. Chiarini was anything but a Fascist ideologue and made a number of quite respectable films himself, and his influence at the Centro encouraged freethinking and an openness to new ideas and innovative techniques. In 1937, the Centro began the publication of a major film journal, *Bianco e nero* (Black and White), which provoked debate about film theory and practice (including film theory from Soviet Russia). After the Cines studios burned down in 1935, Freddi's leadership was instrumental in gathering government support for the creation of one of the world's great cinema complexes: Cinecittà (literally "Cinema City"). Mussolini himself inaugurated it on April 21, 1937, the choice of the date— the mythical anniversary of the founding of ancient Rome—emphasizing the importance the regime now attributed to film.

Mussolini's son Vittorio (1916–97), who was himself passionately involved with film, became editor of an important avant-garde periodical entitled *Cinema* after 1937. Using the anagrammatic pseudonym Tito Silvio Mursino, he scripted at least four films himself. Vittorio Mussolini gathered a number of "young Turks" and mavericks around him and around *Cinema*, including Michelangelo Antonioni (1912–2007), Giuseppe De Santis (1917–97), Luchino Visconti (1906–76), Carlo Lizzani (1922–), and Roberto Rossellini (1906–77). He offered them overt encouragement and implicit protection from serious political censorship. Essays and film reviews published in *Cinema* contain the seeds of postwar Italian film theory—especially the view that realism (or "neorealism") should be the preferred road for Italian postwar film to travel.[1] Most of these collaborators on *Cinema* became moderate or leftist anti-Fascists after the fall of the regime in 1943. Until that time, Italians considered them part of the left-wing Fascist intelligentsia.

Critical Reassessment of Cinema During the Fascist Period

The Italian cinema during the Fascist period was until only recently virtually ignored by mainstream film critics and historians. Thus, Carlo Lizzani once declared that the works produced during Fascist rule had not "one photogram" of the hundreds of films made that should be remembered or regretted if lost, since they constituted merely "a cold listing of commonplaces in a squalid and monotonous recipe book."[2] Italians were understandably anxious to forget the Fascist years that ended with the collapse of the regime and a bloody Resistance struggle during 1943–45 that assumed the proportions of a civil war before hostilities ended. Critics, film historians, politicians, and even veterans of the film industry, all of whom had learned their trades during the Fascist period, had every interest in emphasizing the originality and revolutionary quality of what succeeded Fascist cinema in the form of postwar neorealism, and in denigrating everything that came before it. For decades after the war until only recently, the highly charged ideological climate in Italian intellectual life simply would not allow a dispassionate analysis of the period's film production. As a result, the more than seven hundred films produced during the Fascist period were virtually ignored by scholars and critics, and this critical neglect inspired by ideological blinders has resulted in the loss of the only remaining prints of almost half these films.[3]

Numerous traditional interpretations of Italian cinema from the Fascist period have been strongly challenged by a new approach to the subject. The first and most immediate critical impression was that of surprise. Since practically no one had ever actually bothered to study the films in question, no one had ever imagined that so many were so good, or that the average quality of the industrial product of the period was so high. In the second place, virtually all the ideological commonplaces about the period were immediately abandoned. The most significant outcome of this reevaluation of an entire period's cinematic production was the assessment of the impact of political ideology on it. Virtually all recent studies of the films in question reject classifying them as a cinema of propaganda. In fact, these studies conclude that out of the seven hundred or so films made, only a small handful can reasonably be called "Fascist," although a larger number have patriotic or nationalistic themes.

Such a drastic reassessment of Fascist cinema strikes directly at one of the most deceptive myths of postwar Italian film historiography—the persistent interpretation of postwar Italian neorealism as a completely revolutionary and original phenomenon, the result of a clean and absolute break with both Italian film traditions under Fascism and those classic "rules" established by the Hollywood model. As a matter of fact, Italian film culture under Fascism was a rich, multifaceted, and highly heuristic springboard for postwar cinematic production. The most obvious contribution of the Fascist period to postwar cinema was to provide a well-trained and thoroughly professional cadre of directors, writers, and technicians no nation other than the United States could surpass. While the famous photograph of Mussolini behind a movie camera at Cinecittà with the motto "La cinematografia è l'arma più forte" ("The cinema is the most powerful weapon") seems to underscore the traditional view that the regime valued the cinema for its propaganda potential, the Italian Fascists relied almost exclusively upon the newsreels produced by the Istituto Luce to bolster their regime.[4] In these short films, screened during intermissions of commercial feature films in the thousands of movie theaters across the peninsula, such regime projects as the draining of the Pontine Marshes, the battle for grain, the regime's welfare and public works projects, and eventually the wars abroad in Spain and Africa were naturally all designed to mobilize support for the government. But Mussolini understood that controlling information was far more crucial than controlling art and entertainment. Only rarely were commercial films expected to reflect the regime's ideology, and most Fascists in the movie industry were pragmatists, not ideologues. Most preferred to produce popular entertainment, not indoctrination, and if there were a model abroad to imitate, Mussolini's would-be totalitarian regime preferred Hollywood's, not the rigidly controlled popular culture of Soviet Russia or Nazi Germany.[5]

Abundant evidence demonstrates that the Fascist regime took a genuine interest in the health of the film industry and wanted it to flourish without, however, insisting upon ideological purity in its products. Luigi Freddi, for instance, was by all accounts an able administrator interested more in promoting a profitable, commercial industry like that of Hollywood than in directing a propaganda machine. In an important article entitled "The Emancipation of the Italian Cinema" that appeared in his journal, Cinema, in 1936, Vittorio Mussolini explicitly called for a revival of Italian cinema by means of imitating the Hollywood model.[6] The dictator's son visited Hollywood in 1937 after being received by President Roosevelt in Washington, D.C. In California, he was wined and dined by such stars as Tyrone Power, Ida Lupino, Shirley Temple, and Bette Davis, and he even founded a production company with Hal Roach (1892–1992) called RAM (Roach and Mussolini), although this cooperative venture never really got off the ground.[7] The myth that the Fascist cinema was primarily one of ideological propaganda is based upon the assumption that the regime preferred a cinema designed to mobilize the masses politically. In fact, the Fascist regime preferred a successful commercial cinema complete with the star system, a collection of important auteur directors, and a genre-oriented subject matter. It was simply good business to imitate an industry, such as that in America, that made real money.

The Search for a New Film Realism

Surprisingly, the few voices calling for a realistic cinema employing documentary techniques with the goal of presenting "authentic," "believable," and specifically *Italian* landscapes or stories—the precursors for a similar vision of Italian cinema associated in the immediate postwar period of Italian neorealism with anti-Fascists and leftists—included some from within the ranks of the left-wing intellectuals associated with Vittorio Mussolini's *Cinema.* One important example of a call for film realism that advocated a move away from "escapist" cinema identified with America's Hollywood and toward filming ordinary, everyday Italian "reality" can be found in a 1933 essay called "L'occhio di vetro" ("The Glass Eye") by Leo Longanesi (1905–57). At the time the essay appeared, Longanesi was an important journalist who strongly supported the regime, and was even credited with inventing the infamous slogan "Mussolini ha sempre ragione" ("Mussolini is always right"):

> We should make films that are extremely simple and spare in staging without using artificial sets—films that are shot as much as possible from reality. In fact, realism is precisely what is lacking in our films. It is necessary to go right out into the street, to take the movie camera into the streets, the courtyards, the barracks, and the train stations. To make a natural and logical Italian film, it would be enough to go out in the street, to stop anywhere at all and observe what happens during a half hour with attentive eyes and with no preconceptions about style.[8]

A comparison of Longanesi's manifesto "The Glass Eye" to the often-cited 1952 neorealist manifesto "A Thesis on Neo-Realism" (also published as "Some Ideas on the Cinema") by Cesare Zavattini (1902–89) is extremely revealing.[9] Zavattini, the most distinguished of neorealist scriptwriters, advocates nonprofessional actors, real locations, the rejection of Hollywood conventions (sets, actors, genres), and a documentary style of photography—all elements of the conventional definition of postwar Italian neorealism. Longanesi's manifesto of almost two decades earlier sounds remarkably similar to Zavattini's, and both documents advocate a rejection of Hollywood cinematic codes.

In point of fact, it was the Fascist cinema that first began the search for a cinematic realism in Italy. This impulse later came to fruition in the immediate postwar period, when such cinematic realism was joined to a greatly increased freedom of expression after the fall of the Fascist regime. Even the use of the term "Fascist cinema" is misleading, for the films actually espousing the truly original ideology of the regime (the corporate state, the glorification of conflict, imperialism, the "Roman" heritage of Fascist Italy) as opposed to traditional values (nationalism, conservative morality, Catholicism) are few in number. It is thus more accurate to speak of "film during the Fascist period," divided into "prewar" and "wartime" (1940–43) cinema. The transition from the Fascist period to the immediate postwar period may well reflect a marked ideological change of position, but in terms of cinematic style, there is more continuity than contrast. Directors, writers, and critics in both periods often chose realism as their goal, even while disagreeing about the ideological programs such film realism might support.

Film Realism during the Sound Period: A Rediscovered Tradition

Roberto Rossellini's contribution to Italian cinema before the fall of the regime is quite revealing. Rossellini's apprenticeship in the cinema took place precisely when the interest in a new cinematic realism was being expressed by a number of ideologically diverse individuals in Italy. Moreover, he would have found numerous precedents in films made during the Fascist period for a number of the postwar techniques in his neorealist classics. In his *1860* (1934), Alessandro Blasetti masterfully employs nonprofessional actors, so striking a technique in *Open City* (*Roma città aperta*, 1945), *Paisan* (*Paisà*, 1946), or the classic neorealist films of Visconti and Vittorio De Sica (1901–74). This epic film sets the lives of simple, ordinary people against the backdrop of the invasion of Sicily by Giuseppe Garibaldi (1807–82).[10] Blasetti not only employed nonprofessionals but allowed them to speak their Sicilian dialect, a use of authentic language that was practically unnoticed by film historians until Visconti did the same thing in his celebrated neorealist treatment of Sicilian fishermen, *The Earth Trembles* (*La terra trema*, 1948). The move from constructed studio sets to authentic outside or indoor locations, another of the traditional formulae associated with Italian neorealism, was typical of some of the most important films shot during the Fascist period. Blasetti's 1860 is an excellent example of this onlocation work, but even earlier, in his silent *Sun* (*Sole*, 1929), Blasetti had celebrated Mussolini's reclamation of the Pontine Marshes in another epic production regrettably destroyed during World War II.[11] *The White Squadron* (*Lo squadrone bianco*, 1936), by Augusto Genina (1892–1957), a good example of how realistic historical themes were combined with sentimental

Non-professional actors (real peasants) wearing their own tattered garments add a touch of realism to Blasetti's *1860. Credit: AB*

love stories to ensure audience appeal, won the Mussolini Cup at the Venice Film Festival in 1936. The film's plot concerns a cavalry lieutenant deluded in a love affair. Upon having himself assigned to a native unit fighting rebels in Tripolitana (part of today's Libya), he must face a severe commander who, considering him somewhat of a spoiled playboy, doubts his devotion to duty. The lieutenant nevertheless fulfills his duty to the commander's satisfaction, and when his former lover visits the fort as a tourist, he realizes his true vocation is the life of a soldier. Genina's film is noteworthy for spectacularly beautiful shots of the desert, all done on location in North Africa. Walter Ruttmann (1887–1941) shot *Steel* (*Acciaio*, 1933) inside the giant steel mills at Terni; the film contains masterful examples of rhythmic editing within a semidocumentary style typical of many postwar neorealist films.[12] Even such an unlikely vehicle for film realism as the early comedy *What Rascals Men Are!* (*Gli uomini, che mascalzoni!*, 1932), by Mario Camerini, contains remarkable location footage of the city of Milan and its industrial fair that should not be overlooked in documenting the history of Italian film realism. *Luciano Serra, Pilot* (*Luciano Serra, pilota*, 1938), by Goffredo Alessandrini (1904–78), includes evocative North African footage that Rossellini supervised as Alessandrini's assistant director. The simple fact is that the use of nonprofessional actors, real locations, and documentary techniques reflected a growing trend toward film realism in the Fascist cinema even before the advent of neorealism, and it is doubtless in this context that Rossellini and others learned the effectiveness of such techniques.

When Italy entered World War II in June 1940, the film industry there (as in Nazi Germany, Great Britain, or America) was expected to do its bit to assist the war effort, providing not only newsreels but also popular entertainment that bolstered the regime's political and ideological goals. As a result, the most innovative aesthetic experiments in the cinema at the time involved what have become known as "fictional documentaries."[13] Essentially, such films would employ documentary footage and authentic locations (battleships, airfields, military outposts) from the war, inserting them into a fictional framework. In some cases, nonprofessional actors were employed (the actual protagonists of the events portrayed); in other instances, famous actors were mixed with ordinary sailors, soldiers, and airmen.

Augusto Genina and the Fictional Documentary Genre

Perhaps the most influential impetus to this kind of filmmaking, a model Rossellini could not have ignored, was the phenomenal success of a film of this type begun even before war broke out: Augusto Genina's *The Siege of the Alcazar* (*L'assedio dell'Alcazar*, 1940). It also led all other films at the box office during the year of its release.[14] It was awarded the Mussolini Cup at the Venice Biennale for the Best Italian Film of the year, and while its political content might cause us to question the validity of such an award, the film won fulsome praise for its innovative cinematic qualities from none other than Michelangelo Antonioni, writing in *Cinema*. He underscored its lack of rhetoric, its grounding in recent history, and his opinion that the film's value sprang from its creation of an "epic feeling" from believable acts of sacrifice and drama by single individuals. Of particular interest is Antonioni's comment that the film has a "choral" quality (one of the most typical descriptions of Rossellini's work in the Fascist period and the immediate postwar neorealist era).[15] Antonioni also notes that Genina successfully uses the group of soldiers and civilians defending the Alcázar (fortress) of Toledo for Franco's army against an overwhelming army of republican soldiers to create a microcosm (he calls it a "small city") of life that permits the intensification of emotions and drama within a tightly controlled and almost claustrophobic cinematic space. Rossellini would do something very similar in his own so-called Fascist trilogy and even more brilliantly in the torture sequences of *Open City*.

The cinematic merits of *The Siege of the Alcazar* are real, just as its clearly ideological tone cannot be ignored. A prologue tells the viewer that the heroic defense of the Alcázar represents a symbol of the ideological struggle of Franco's Fascist forces against Bolshevism in Spain; it insists, however, that the story is reported with historical accuracy, a claim that is basically true. Nevertheless, Republican soldiers are depersonalized and depicted as ugly, brutal, and treacherous, taking hostages and executing prisoners without much remorse, while the defenders of the fortress are portrayed as honorable military officers obeying the rules of civilized

In Genina's *The Siege of the Alcazar,* the strain of the long battle wears on the women who support the fighting men inside the citadel. *Credit: AB*

warfare. But there is nothing in *The Siege of the Alcazar* that should shock the viewer of the usual run-of-the-mill American combat films during the same period. Few national cinemas were able or willing to portray the enemy in a positive light. While the interior scenes were constructed at the Cinecittà studios, exterior scenes were completed on location at the site of the Alcázar amid the ruins that still remained when the footage was shot. The texture of the photography and the skillful reproduction of the interior sets, combined with on-location Spanish footage, give practically no hint that the entire film had not been done on location.

The film's unique quality arises from the distinctive rhythm that Genina produces by alternating between dramatically re-created battle scenes and more intimate moments inside the fortress, where sentimental dramas can unfold. Actual documentary footage of such historical events as the bombing of the fortress by the Republican Air Force is also skillfully edited together with the footage Genina produced. The dramatic appeal of the film derives from a highly traditional story of the conflict between love and duty, honor and sacrifice. A rich, spoiled woman named Carmen (Mireille Balin), who has taken refuge in the Alcázar, becomes transformed and learns to work for the common good by nursing the wounded, thereby attracting the attentions of the film's stalwart military hero, Captain Vela (Fosco Giachetti), who can love her only when she realizes that she must embrace the Fascist virtues of discipline and self-sacrifice.

Everyone perceived the critical problem in a film such as *The Siege of the Alcazar,* especially the Fascist officials who would have to bear the responsibility of a commercial failure if the large sums of money invested in

Genina's film did not make a profit. In a letter to the producer, Renato Bassoli, Luigi Freddi reacts to a preproduction reading of the script: defining it as a "fictional documentary" (*un documentario romanzato*), he worries about the combination of the realistic or historical part of the film with its fictional or emotional part:

> While it is certain that the part which we have defined as "documentary" (that is, the real events recreated by technical and artistic means) attains a very high emotional content (from which, however, arises a serious defect, as I will explain later), the imaginative part, that is the dramatic part in the sense of the spectacle, the part created expressly to connect the evocation of historical events with the unrelated human events, seems to me to be very weak.[16]

The completed film was certainly more successful in combining history and fiction than Freddi had predicted from a reading of its script. In fact, Alessandro Pavolini (1903–45), Fascist Minister of Education and later Freddi's successor at the Direzione Generale per la Cinematografia, wrote Genina a congratulatory letter, calling the film a "service to the country" and remarking that technically, the work is "in no way inferior" to the best films made in the world, Hollywood included, in its reconstruction of battle and crowd scenes, while it is "decidedly superior" in its "respect for historical accuracy, elegant sobriety and human emotion."[17] Moreover, the critical problem Freddi identified in Genina's film, even more clearly than Antonioni did in his own very positive review—the challenge of mixing "real" events from history with "fictional" events invented by the imagination—remains central to an understanding of Rossellini's filmmaking, from his debut with the "Fascist trilogy" in 1940–43 to the production of his "war trilogy" in 1945–47 that established his international reputation as a serious and innovative auteur.[18]

Francesco De Robertis, Vittorio Mussolini, and Film Realism

The Siege of the Alcazar was a purely commercial venture, but the other "fictional documentaries" produced before the fall of the regime in 1943 were often associated directly with various branches of the Italian armed forces. In addition to the newsreels produced by the Istituto Luce, the army, navy, and air force all had cinema departments, although the army produced very few films. In the naval ministry, at the Centro Cinematografico del Ministero della Marina (Film Center of the Naval Ministry), a man of genius, Francesco De Robertis (1902–59), took the lead in championing the marriage of fiction and documentary. Vittorio Mussolini, a captain in the air force in addition to his work in the cinema, remained a stimulating presence in its Centro Fotocinematografico del Ministero dell'Aeronautica

(Photo-Cinematic Center of the Air Force Ministry). Rossellini worked with both departments, making a film for each of them before he completed the third part of his "Fascist trilogy." The navy sponsored three films, two by De Robertis—*Men on the Bottom* (*Uomini sul fondo*, 1940) and *Alfa Tau!* (1942)—as well as Rossellini's first feature film, *The White Ship* (*La nave bianca*, 1942). These were all produced with Scalera Films, a commercial company. The Italian air force produced three more works, including Rossellini's second feature, *A Pilot Returns* (*Un pilota ritorna*, 1942) scripted by Vittorio Mussolini writing as Tito Silvio Mursino. Rossellini's third feature, *The Man with a Cross* (*L'uomo dalla croce*, 1943), was the only film of his "Fascist trilogy" produced without the assistance of the Italian armed forces.

De Robertis was instrumental in adding nonprofessional actors to the formula for the fictionalized documentary. His influential *Men on the Bottom*, the story of the undersea rescue of a sunken submarine, opens with the proud declaration: "The officers, noncommissioned officers, and the crew of one of our long-distance submarines took part in the action."[19] In this film, De Robertis employs an editing style much closer to that of Sergei Eisenstein (1898–1948) than to postwar neorealism (something Rossellini immediately thereafter imitated in *The White Ship*), skillfully focusing upon the men and their machines and creating with that editing a highly dramatic rhythm. Whereas *Men on the Bottom* is essentially a documentary pure and simple, *Alfa Tau!* (released two weeks before Rossellini's *White Ship*) completely embraces the fictionalized documentary formula. Its opening titles clearly call attention to the fact that most of its actors are nonprofessionals, but in this case, the sailor who becomes the focus of the narrative's main action (Seaman Stagi) not only plays himself but also manages to invoke a heroic gesture attributed to Enrico Toti (1882–1916), a World War I war hero for whom the submarine on which Stagi serves is named:

> In this story, all the elements respond to a *historical and environmental realism*. The humble seaman, who is its protagonist, really lived the episode that is relived in the story. In like manner, the role that every other character has in the event corresponds to the role each one of them had in the *reality of life*.[20]

Far less nationalistic propaganda presents itself in this film made for the Department of the Navy than in Genina's commercially produced film *The Siege of the Alcazar*. For example, *Alfa Tau!* openly depicts the losses suffered by the Italian navy without ignoring the poor resources at the disposal of the Italian sailors. De Robertis dramatizes the effects of the war on the home front with scenes of civilians racing to bomb shelters. The camera follows a number of sailors home on shore leave, providing proof of the war's cost: allied bombardments have even destroyed one of the sailor's homes. Humor pokes fun at the pretensions of the regime: a patriotic owner of a pensione mimics the regime's slogans, such as "Tutto al combattente!" ("Everything for the Fighting Man!"), and her name is Signora Italia! De Robertis also alternates moments of high dramatic tension with those of comic relief, a technique Rossellini would master in *Open City*. The film actually ends on a comic note: the submarine on which Seaman Stagi serves fights a duel with a British submarine, exchanging torpedoes and then surfacing to engage in a gun battle. Just when the Italians could have ended the duel with a victory, the deck gun jams, causing Stagi to become exasperated and throw his boot at the enemy in disgust! (Enrico Toti, who had lost a leg in a prewar railway accident, threw his crutch after being fatally wounded in the Sixth Battle of the Isonzo, an ultimately successful Italian offensive.) De Robertis's complex cross-cutting among four different sailors on leave and his dramatic montage editing onboard the ship, combined with the nonprofessional nature of nearly the entire cast, provide an excellent and original model for a cinematic style within the genre of the war film that any postwar neorealist director could easily adopt as a step toward a more realistic cinema.

Roberto Rossellini's "Fascist Trilogy"

Each of the films in Rossellini's "Fascist trilogy" stands in a slightly different relationship to the general formula of the "fictional documentary" genre that De Robertis adopted in part. The credits for *The White Ship* list no director, but it is clear that Rossellini and De Robertis both made contributions to the film. While Rossellini did most of the direction, De Robertis provided the script, the story idea, and assistance for his protégé. The opening credits highlight the continuity of style between Rossellini's *The White Ship* and De Robertis's earlier *Men on the Bottom*:

> As in *Men on the Bottom*, all the characters in this naval story are taken from their environment and from the reality of their lives, and they are followed through a spontaneous realism [*verismo*] in their expressions and the simple humanity of those feelings that make up the ideological world of each of them. The nurses of the Voluntary Corps, the officers, the noncommissioned offers, and the crews took part. The story was shot on the hospital ship *Arno* and on one of our battleships.[21]

De Robertis's influence is clearly visible, especially in the brilliant first half of the film, which focuses upon a naval battle in the Mediterranean. In this section, the influence of Eisenstein again is everywhere apparent, particularly in the fascinating editing patterns that juxtapose faces, equipment, and the firing of naval cannon. Eisenstein's theories of filmmaking had already been partially translated and discussed by Rome's leading intellectuals associated with the cinema, with Mussolini's journal, *Cinema*, and with the

Rossellini's *The White Ship* integrates real footage of a naval battle with a fictional narrative. *Credit: CSC*

Centro Sperimentale's journal, *Bianco e nero*. Eisenstein's major films had even been screened in Fascist Italy—if not in large public showings, at least in film clubs (the previously mentioned GUFs) paradoxically supported by a Fascist regime that claimed Russian Bolshevism as its mortal enemy. It is not surprising in the least, therefore, that the Russian director's influence can be detected in films approved by a Fascist regime. Eisenstein's impact upon Italian cinema in this period stands as yet another proof that political censorship of the Italian cinema on ideological grounds never extended to excluding the possibility of learning something important from an artist who espoused an entirely different kind of political ideology.

The "fictionalized documentary" style of *The White Ship* comes into play primarily in the second part of the film, where Rossellini used the wounding of a sailor to reveal how well the hospital ships of the regime treated Italian fighting men. The dominant image of the entire film, however, remains the dramatic picture of men trapped inside metal monsters, staring intently at dials, gauges, and instruments, while they are engaged in a dramatic struggle of life and death upon the high seas. Though the footage of the naval battle is from an actual engagement that Rossellini himself shot, it is edited so brilliantly and dramatically that certain scenes seem as if they have been lifted from an anthology of Russian cinema. It is this deft combination of documentary material with footage of daily life on Italian warships that gives much of *The White Ship* the feel of an authentic newsreel. To this documentary or pseudodocumentary section, Rossellini then added a more conventional, fictional story of a sailor and his sweetheart, who becomes a nurse; their paths cross on the hospital ship where the sailor has been brought after being wounded in combat. Thus, Rossellini joined real locations, a documentary style, and nonprofessional actors to a conventionally sentimental or melodramatic plot.

In *A Pilot Returns*, Rossellini continued the technique of the "fictionalized documentary" by weaving a personal story together with a larger, historical account of the air war over Greece and utilizing some documentary footage to show Italian air raids against the enemy. The film's sentimental plot focuses upon a glamorous, Hollywood-style protagonist played by the matinee idol Massimo Girotti (1918–2003)—a heroic pilot who escapes from English captivity, steals an airplane, and returns safely to his Italian base to fly again. Girotti's superhuman exploits stand in marked contrast to the anonymous heroes of Rossellini's *The White Ship*. In fact, the overly complex plot of *A Pilot Returns* mixes this heroic action with a love affair in captivity between the pilot and a doctor's daughter—but it does so in a very confused manner, making this particular work the weakest by far of the "Fascist trilogy." Of historical interest is that Vittorio Mussolini (as Tito Silvio Mursino) provided the story idea, and that Michelangelo Antonioni contributed to the script. The style of this second film stands apart from that of *The White Ship* in several respects. Instead of edits indebted to Eisenstein, Rossellini depended upon a very conventional assortment of wipes, fades, and transitions employing a series of newspaper headlines to advance the story. The future neorealist director Giuseppe De Santis's critical review of the film in 1942 did, however, make note of Rossellini's bold attempt to have every soldier (Italian, Greek, English) speak his native language without providing translations in the original film's subtitles.[22] This linguistic realism will play a crucial role in the best neorealist films about the war by Rossellini and other postwar directors. Exterior, realistic locations also figure importantly in the film, although many of the interiors were reconstructed at Cinecittà.

If propaganda was the intent of *A Pilot Returns*, it is hard to imagine that it had that effect. Seen today, the class divisions evident in the Italian air force between the enlisted men and the elite pilots (who live a life of luxury with service from waiters wearing white gloves, reflecting the upper-class origins of their families) speak eloquently of the inequality fostered by the regime, something Rossellini no doubt intended. Nonetheless, viewers accustomed to seeing documentaries of other armed forces during World War II cannot help but be struck by the poor quality of the equipment at the disposal of the Italian air force: men in the bombers pass notes back and forth over the din of the engines because their planes have no radios; even their oxygen masks seem to be jury-rigged contraptions that may not work. While such battle scenes will certainly persuade few viewers of the Fascist regime's technical prowess, the sequences devoted to the effects of the war— the future subject of the "war trilogy" that established Rossellini's fame after the war—are far more eloquent. Here, Rossellini's camera avoids painting a falsely optimistic picture of Italy's chances in the war and, in fact, reveals the human side of the misery it entails in a manner that is quite surprisingly honest and forthright for a man who was identified by the regime as one of its most promising directors. The film exhibits little propagandistic intent, for the director never glosses over the brutal effects of the war on civilians and soldiers alike.

The Man with a Cross continues Rossellini's progress within the "Fascist trilogy" toward a preference for fiction over documentary. In it, he uses no documentary footage at all. Rossellini re-created the battle scenes near Ladispoli outside of Rome, where he constructed an entire Russian village and staged a firefight worthy of the best Hollywood war scenes. Nevertheless, the battle scenes, unlike those in *The White Ship*, are precisely that—scenes of combat that we consider "realistic" insofar as they follow traditional Hollywood codes for war films. While the battle sequences represent brilliantly contrived examples of Hollywood "realism" rather than authentic footage of an actual battle like that in *The White Ship*, Rossellini employs some nonprofessional actors in this third work, including his girlfriend as the romantic lead and another friend as the heroic Italian chaplain who dies on the Russian front.

The titular protagonist, the man with a cross, is a figure based upon a real army chaplain, Father Reginaldo Giuliani (1887–1936), who had been killed during the Ethiopian war and was posthumously awarded various medals of honor. Rossellini's plot will remind anyone who has seen *Open City* of that later and more illustrious film, which focuses

Rossellini's *The Man with a Cross* recreates battlefield scenes from the Russian front in the Roman countryside. *Credit: CSC*

upon the anti-Fascist exploits of a partisan priest, likewise based upon an actual person who fell in the struggle against the Nazis during the German occupation of Rome. The plot of *The Man with a Cross* is deceptively simple. As the film opens, we are introduced to the various members of an Italian tank unit stationed on the Russian front during the summer of 1942, that is, before the disastrous defeats suffered by German, Italian, and Romanian troops at Stalingrad. The troops are confident in their eventual victory over the Bolsheviks, and their material and spiritual conditions are superb. We naturally see none of the infamous defective equipment or the summer uniforms issued for winter combat about which so many Italian veterans of this campaign have always complained. The film certainly contains no hint of impending military disaster. Moreover, the normally overbearing Nazi allies are completely absent from view throughout the entire film. And even more surprising to a non-Italian audience that has, no doubt, been regaled by traditional stories about Italian military incompetence in every military campaign, including that in Russia, the efficiency, professionalism, and skill of the Italian officer corps and the rank-and-file soldier are above reproach. In fact, the film concludes with a decisive Italian victory over the Russians. Still, none of this is Rossellini's main focus. Instead, he concentrates upon the selfless heroism of a military chaplain who volunteers to stay behind with a seriously wounded Italian tank man when his unit must abandon the man and move forward to the attack. The chaplain's action means certain capture by the Russians. In fact, on the following day, the chaplain and the wounded soldier are taken by Russian troops to be interrogated by a Communist officer, who orders another young Italian found with a Fascist Party card in his pocket executed on the spot for refusing to answer his questions. Too late to save the young man, the Italians attack the Russians, and the village where the priest has been interrogated is trapped between the two hostile armies in battle. The priest drags his wounded tank man inside a small farmhouse, an *izba*, where he encounters a group of Russian peasant women with their children. They are eventually joined, first, by a group of Russian partisans led by a commissar named Sergei and his girlfriend Irina, and later by some Italian tank men who abandon their burning vehicle, surprise the partisans from the rear, and take control of the *izba*. Fyodor, a terribly disfigured Russian soldier burned in a tank explosion, then arrives. Before Irina met Sergei, she had once been Fyodor's mistress. Fyodor kills Sergei in a fit of jealousy just as Sergei is attempting to overpower the Italians inside the hut. The chaplain helps to deliver a baby, baptizes it with the Christian name of Nicola, teaches the children to make the sign of the cross, and explains his religious faith to an incredulous Irina, who is grieving over the death of Sergei. Attempting to save Fyodor's life just as the victorious Italian troops retake the Russian village, the chaplain is fatally wounded.

Blasetti and Camerini: Studies in Style

Overemphasis in postwar historiography of the Italian cinema upon the question of film "realism" not only obscured the very real and original contributions of the prewar Italian cinema to the creation of this sort of style, but also distorted the place of neorealism in the overall film production of the immediate postwar period. Ultimately, a significant degree of continuity existed between the prewar and the postwar period, and the fact that film critics and historians at one time ignored this continuity led many of them to overlook other extremely noteworthy features of the Italian film industry before the advent of neorealism.

The diversity of the cinema of the Italian prewar sound era is reflected in the careers of two its most important directors: Alessandro Blasetti and Mario Camerini.

Alessandro Blasetti

Blasetti, a filmmaker both popular and prolific whose oeuvre extends into the 1960s, created dramas and comedies, documentaries and fantasies. His are some of the noteworthy works partly obscured until recently by the critical insistence on neorealism's clean break with films of the Fascist period. As was mentioned earlier, Blasetti's 1929 silent film, *Sun*, although destroyed during World War II (a few photographs survive), began the Italian cinema's march toward film realism. Treating the reclamation of the Pontine Marshes by Mussolini's regime—a grandiose project that even Julius Caesar had failed to accomplish—the film may be seen as at least outwardly favorable to the regime's policies. And yet it was no mere propaganda piece: its authentic exterior locations combined with the appeal of its contemporary social theme to produce a convincing sense of realism, according to all accounts from those who saw the completed work. Blasetti's *Palio* (1932) is a costume drama setting a romantic plot within the spectacle of the medieval festival in the city of Siena. Like *Sun*, *Palio* aimed at the creation of an authentically and uniquely Italian environment on film, rather than yet another imitation of Hollywood models. Considered by many to be Blasetti's masterpiece, his *1860* blends two tendencies typical of the director and many of his contemporaries: first, a historical theme (histories comprising the largest proportion of works produced by the Italian cinema in the period, many with literary sources); and second, an interest in regional naturalism. Against the background of Garibaldi's invasion of Sicily and his first major battle, Blasetti examines the impact of such a momentous historical event upon the lives of simple, ordinary people. Making use of nonprofessional, Sicilian-speaking characters, he shows an attention to linguistic diversity that stands in sharp contrast to the regime's efforts to standardize spoken Italian in the cinema. In addition, the complex battle scenes Blasetti designed showcase his technical skill in handling large numbers of actors, a typically Hollywood element. It was common for Italian political movements to associate Garibaldi with their ideas,[23] and Blasetti concluded the original version of *1860* with a scene linking Garibaldi's Redshirts to Mussolini's Blackshirts (*camicie nere*, also called *squadristi*)—a scene cut from postwar prints!

This same patriotic tone, concentrating upon moments of Italian history illustrative of the nation's greatness, characterizes several other films Blasetti set in the Italian Renaissance, an era when Italy achieved cultural and artistic hegemony throughout Europe: *Ettore Fieramosca* (1938), an adaptation of the historical novel of the same name by Massimo Taparelli, marchese (i.e., marquis) d'Azeglio (1798–1866), and *The Jester's Supper* (*La cena delle beffe*, 1942), derived from a Renaissance novella and a play by Sem Benelli (1877–1949). At least one of Blasetti's major films, *The Old Guard* (*Vecchia guardia*, 1935), with its clear political overtones, could be correctly labeled a Fascist film. Set in the rough-and-tumble atmosphere of 1922, when bands of Fascist *squadristi* battled with like-minded bands of leftist opponents, Blasetti's film portrays Mussolini's movement in a heroic light and concludes with a celebration of the March on Rome. Despite the work's subject matter, the director's realistic portrayal of this dramatic moment in modern Italian history employs a documentary style that found favor in the postwar period.

Blasetti's prewar works also include two outstanding films that deserve to be remembered and studied for the implications they have for the future of the industry. The most unusual of his films—and perhaps the most

The ornately stylized sets of Alessandro Blasetti's *The Iron Crown* bear testimony to the technical prowess of Cinecittà's technicians. *Credit: MOMA*

In Blasetti's *Four Steps in the Clouds*, the popular period star Gino Cervi, playing the traveling salesman who befriends a pregnant girl, buys a newspaper before boarding his train. *Credit: AB*

unusual film of the more than seven hundred made between the advent of sound in 1930 and the fall of the Fascist regime in 1943—is Blasetti's *The Iron Crown* (*La corona di ferro*, 1941). A pseudohistorical fairy tale, it may be compared to Marcel Carné's *The Devil's Envoys* (*Les Visiteurs du soir*, 1942) in its hermetic symbolism and its evocative, fanciful style. The film's theme is the journey of a sacred crown to Rome and the rise of a chosen leader who brings his people to an era of peace and prosperity. The sumptuous and very expensive sets produced for the work at Cinecittà stand in marked contrast to Blasetti's use of real locations and nonprofessional actors in previous films, and they bear witness to the technical virtuosity attained in Italy's huge studio complex only a few years after its creation. *The Iron Crown* is an ambiguous work: while its message underlines a common sentiment among Italians at the time—the desire for peace and the cessation of hostilities during World War II—the symbolic implications of the search for a charismatic leader who will restore a magic crown to its rightful place in Rome may also point to Mussolini, Il Duce of a newly revived Rome. Nonetheless, Blasetti unquestionably gave new life to the Italian treatment of heroic mythology born in the silent era with Pastrone's *Cabiria*, and *The Iron Crown* is one of several important antecedents to the postwar genre of the peplum ("sword and sandal" epic) that would become such a cult favorite among film buffs.

Four Steps in the Clouds (*Quattro passi fra le nuvole*, 1942), Blasetti's last important film before the end of the war, represents an abrupt shift away from the historical and costume epics with which Blasetti's cinema was identified and toward an infinitely simpler storyline—one that prefigures the neorealist plots of the scriptwriter Cesare Zavattini filmed by the director Vittorio De Sica. In it, a traveling salesman (Gino Cervi, 1901–74) meets a young unmarried girl who is pregnant; feeling compassion for her, he unsuccessfully poses as her husband when she visits her family; and just as the girl is about to be driven out of the house, the salesman urges the family to forgive her and to have compassion for her misfortune. (This film was remade by the Spanish director Alfonso Arau as the 1995 *A Walk in the Clouds*, starring the American actor Keanu Reeves.) Zavattini's contribution to the script must certainly have influenced Blasetti to abandon the baroque complexities of *The Iron Crown* for the discovery of the cinematographic potential inherent in the simple events of everyday life. At any rate, *Four Steps in the Clouds* provides proof that even before the fall of the regime or the experience of the Allied invasion and the Resistance, Italian cinema was already moving toward an interest in elementary but eloquent human situations and a realistic appraisal of Italian daily life.

Mario Camerini

The films of Mario Camerini, Italy's other popular director during the early sound period before the outbreak of war, are less varied in theme and style than those of Blasetti. Camerini's works are typically sentimental, romantic comedies with highly complex plots and characterization, indebted to and comparable with the best works of the French director René Clair or Hollywood directors such as Frank Capra working in the comic genre during the 1930s and 1940s. In most cases, his films provide an ironic and critical view of the polite society of middle-class Italy: the demands made upon the individual by society and the roles people are forced to play in their relationships with others constitute Camerini's favorite themes. This interest in role-playing and the interconnection of illusion and reality had already been explored in the greatest dramatic works of the Fascist era by Luigi Pirandello, and would return again in the early film comedies by Federico Fellini in the 1950s.

    Camerini's cinema launched Fascist Italy's greatest comic actor, Vittorio De Sica, who became a matinee idol, an Italian Cary Grant, long before he became identified as one of the greatest neorealist directors in the postwar period. In *What Rascals Men Are!* (1932), De Sica became a star and sang what was certainly the most popular love song of the era, "Parlami d'amore Mariù." A 1938 film review described his status and his customary role in the Italian film comedy as follows:

> With *What Rascals Men Are!* De Sica became a movie actor; but more than
> that, he become overnight the number *one* male star of our cinema. Since
> then, he has become his own character . . . a sincere, Italian character. A

sentimental young man, with simple pleasures and docile, used to hard work, and after work finding familiar and tranquil places. A really fine fellow. The shy gentleness of that young man is every bit Italian. A candor of the streets and of an unpretentious life; a liveliness one encounters by chance, genuinely, without complications.[24]

As an actor, De Sica combined acting talent, good looks, singing ability, class, and a persona that epitomized what Italians mean when they call a young man a *bravo ragazzo*. As a star, he rose above the pantheon of Italian film actors in much the same manner that Marcello Mastroianni (1924–96) would dominate the postwar Italian cinema as a sophisticated and complex comic figure. Camerini's film casts De Sica as a chauffeur/mechanic named Bruno who falls in love with the daughter of a taxi driver named Mariuccia (Lia Franca), who is a shopgirl. This sentimental romantic comedy is set within authentic locations in Milan, the city that most clearly embodied Fascist Italy's economic strength and desire for industrial modernization. As is so often the case with roles De Sica played, Bruno tries to woo Mariuccia by posing as an upper-class swell and borrows his boss's luxurious car to do so, but he damages it while taking Mariuccia to the countryside and loses his job. After a series of misadventures, Bruno and Mariuccia reconcile, and Camerini's message underscores the populist values of self-sufficiency, class solidarity, and social stability (*not* social mobility). One of the most interesting parts of the film shows the Fiera Campionaria in Milan, the trade fair that presents an attractive array of the latest commercial products available

Camerini's *What Rascals Men Are!* introduces a new matinee idol: Vittorio De Sica, here playing Bruno, a working-class protagonist flirting with three women.
Credit: AB

to the aspiring middle-class members of the audience who, like Bruno and Mariuccia, want to improve the quality of their lives.

In *I'd Give a Million* (*Darò un milione*, 1935), Camerini brings together for the first time De Sica's acting talents and Cesare Zavattini's scriptwriting expertise. In this film, De Sica plays a youthful rich man (significantly named Gold) who disguises himself in order to discover someone worthy of receiving his love and his money. He does so by changing places and clothes with a beggar (Blim) who he has saved from suicide by drowning. Before Gold disappears with the beggar's clothes, he tells Blim that he would give a million lire to meet a single person in the world who was not trying to obtain his money. The newspapers learn of Gold's offer, causing the news to spread like wildfire. Eventually, after Camerini shows a world turned upside down in which both rich and poor demonstrate their inability to think about anything but money, Gold finds a truly altruistic person in Anna (Assia Noris, 1912–98), and he eventually proposes marriage to her and carries her off on his yacht. Once again, Camerini focused upon role-playing in a stratified society such as Italy's in the 1930s, where social mobility was often viewed as a threatening possibility.

De Sica and Noris, who became one of the most popular romantic pairs in the industry, also starred in Camerini's successful adaptation of a 1918 comedy by Pirandello entitled, like the play, *It's Nothing Serious* (*Ma non è una cosa seria*, 1936). Immediately thereafter, he shot his masterpiece, *Mr. Max* (*Il signor Max*, 1937), casting De Sica as another *bravo ragazzo*—this time, a newsstand dealer named Gianni who poses as a bon vivant in the

In Camerini's *Mr. Max*, a newspaper vendor poses as a wealthy socialite to fraternize with the upper classes. *Credit: AB*

fashionable circles of Rome, the stylish Signor Max. He teaches himself to speak English and to play tennis so that he can frequent the upper-class milieu of high society, and in so doing he meets a young girl named Lauretta (Noris) who works as the nursemaid for Lady Paola, a wealthy Englishwoman. Gianni's frequent changes of name and role in society offer Camerini numerous occasions to poke fun at the pretensions of the rich and famous—without, however, suggesting that the fundamental economic relationships in the Italian society of the day ought to be changed. As one critic has aptly put it, Camerini rejects the "rags-to-riches" myth in favor of class solidarity, and Gianni and Lauretta find happiness not in upward mobility (where values are shallow and based upon pretentiousness and wealth) but in the solid values of the common people who are reliable, good-hearted, and true to their origins.[25]

Camerini's *Department Stores* (*I grandi magazzini*, 1938) again features the De Sica–Noris pair in a story that unfolds around a department store, the symbol of nascent consumer society in the advanced sectors of industrialized northern Italy. Once more De Sica plays a sympathetic working-class character, this one named Bruno again, who drives a delivery truck for the store and pretends to be injured in an accident to gain insurance compensation. Successful in his ruse, Bruno eventually meets a young salesgirl named Lauretta (Noris). Given their frequent pairing in other films by Camerini, it is obvious that, although they are meant for each other, they will be able to consummate their love by marriage only after a series of comic and near-tragic adventures. The film's final shot shows the couple outside the department store window, gazing at a display of baby dolls: they have become not only future parents but also consumers, part of the economic system represented by the symbolic department store.[26]

~

Blasetti's cinema gradually moved toward a realist interpretation of Italian life and was often based upon historical themes; Camerini's comedies stressed Italian social values, and in the more lighthearted ones he analyzed the differences between social and economic classes. Both traditions, the realistic and the comic/satiric, would continue into the immediate postwar period, and the lessons from these two masters would be retained by the next generation of neorealist directors. After all, neorealist cinema was characterized not only by the realism of Rossellini's *Paisan* or De Sica's *The Bicycle Thief* (*Ladri di biciclette*, 1948) but by the comic vision of society exemplified by De Sica's *Miracle in Milan* (*Miracolo a Milano*, 1951); Rossellini's *The Machine to Kill Bad People* (*La macchina ammazzacattivi*, 1952); or *Two Cent's Worth of Hope* (*Due soldi di speranza*, 1952); by Renato Castellani (1913–85).

Vittorio De Sica: From Matinee Idol to Director

Working with Camerini paid off immediately and may well have inspired De Sica's desire to become a film director while continuing his work as Italy's most popular matinee idol.[27] In *Maddalena, Zero for Conduct* (*Maddalena, zero in condotta*, 1940), *Doctor Beware* (*Teresa Venerdì*, 1941), and *The Children Are Watching Us* (*I bambini ci guardano*, 1943), De Sica matured rapidly and quickly showed signs of the works of genius that would explode on the international scene during the heyday of Italian neorealism between 1945 and 1955. The first film is set in a girl's school and shows a young girl named Maddalena (Carla Del Poggio) whose comic antics oppose the strict authoritarian discipline that the schoolteachers try to impose on their students. Maddalena rummages through the papers of one of the few sympathetic teachers at the school, Signorina Malgari (Vera Bergman) and discovers an imaginary letter her instructor has placed inside a book on commercial correspondence written by a man called Hartman. The young girl mails it to Hartman in Vienna, and the letter is taken to three different Hartmans: grandfather, father, and son. De Sica plays all three roles, and as the son, he decides to travel to Rome to meet the writer of the letter. Inevitably, Signorina Malgari and Hartman fall in love. Youthful refusal to obey authoritarian rules leads to a positive, romantic conclusion.

Doctor Beware replaces the school with a girls' orphanage, where a young girl named Teresa (Adriana Benetti) succeeds, by virtue of her goodness and innocence, in transforming the rakish behavior of a young doctor named Pietro Vignali (played by De Sica). The pair meets because Pietro has become the orphanage's physician, and the film predictably ends in a romantic marriage between Pietro and Teresa, who has helped change the playboy doctor into a responsible and sensitive adult. As one critic put it, De Sica's film clearly follows Camerini's formula for romantic comedies: "wealth is corrupting; businessmen are vulgar and to be ignored; happiness is with your own kind; inflated aspirations lead to difficulties."[28]

The Children Are Watching Us, however, shows a De Sica already in complete control of his own vision and not dominated by the Camerini formula for comedy. Moreover, the film takes a much darker view into the relationships between children and their parents and the nature of infantile innocence that will return in his best postwar neorealist classics. Scripted in part by Zavattini, this work has obvious links to both *Shoeshine* (*Sciuscià*, 1946) and *The Bicycle Thief* in that the director's camera adopts the perspective of a young child to criticize the callousness of society toward children. Unlike so many comedies that portray the family as a perfect harmony of love and affection, De Sica's film shows how a young boy named Pricò (Luciano De Ambrosis) becomes the victim of quarrels between his parents. The father (Emilio Cigoli) discovers that the mother (Isa Pola) has had an adulterous relationship and orders her to leave their home, but later he gives her another chance and takes the family on a beach vacation. One of the most remarkable sequences in the film is an expressionist nightmare the young boy experiences while traveling on a train, his fears projected upon the window of the carriage as if upon a movie theater screen. At the beach, his mother strikes up her love affair again when the father returns to work in the city. Pricò tries to run away out of neglect. Desperate over his failure to save his marriage, the father sends his son to a boarding school and then commits suicide. The conclusion of the film contains exactly the kind of beautiful deep-focus shot that would characterize De Sica's best neorealist films. It shows Pricò rejecting his mother's attempts to take him back under her wing after his father's death, walking in a long take toward the doorway at the end of an enormous room. Unlike the many long-suffering mothers in films of the period, Pricò's mother is a self-indulgent adulteress, and the only female figure worthy of any respect is Agnese (Giovanna Cigoli, Emilio's mother), the elderly housekeeper whose compassion for the young child clearly reflects the virtues of an older and less selfish generation of adults. De Sica's use of children to critique the lack of values in this Italian family sharply contrasts with the many films made during the Fascist period that praise the family as the most important, purest, and most benevolent institution in Italian society. If the children are truly watching their adult role models, De Sica seems to say, they will not like what they see.

Pricò's adulterous mother and her lover on the beach, shot from the young boy's subjective point of view in De Sica's *The Children Are Watching Us*. Credit: DVD

In Praise of Military Prowess: Carmine Gallone's *Scipio Africanus*

As previously noted, although the Fascist regime in theory was a totalitarian regime, in practice it was far less intrusive upon cultural matters than were the regimes in either Germany or the Soviet Union. That said, it is of course impossible to measure the degree to which Italian directors might have turned to social criticism and less oblique attacks upon Italian institutions or values had if the government been more democratic. However, a number of films, primarily those produced during the second half of the regime's twenty-one-year duration, may accurately be described as supporting the values and policies of Mussolini's government. Most of these films treated colonial wars or moments of Italian imperial glory, either under Mussolini or in a more distant Roman past. For instance, Genina's *The White Squadron* and Alessandrini's *Luciano Serra, Pilot* both celebrate the heroism of Italian soldiers in faraway Africa. Blasetti's *The Old Guard* praises the period when Fascist *squadristi* helped Mussolini seize power. Genina's *The Siege of the Alcazar* glorified the heroism (actually very real) of Franco's troops defending Toledo's Alcázar from republican forces.

Certainly the most famous of all the works that reflect the regime's praise of military prowess was a spectacular historical film on the Second Punic War by Carmine Gallone (1886–1973) entitled *Scipio Africanus: The Defeat of Hannibal* (*Scipione l'africano*, 1937). The Italian silent cinema had been noted precisely for its historical epics set in the distant Roman past,

Gallone's *Scipio Africanus* employs a huge model of the ancient Roman Forum populated by the proverbial "cast of thousands," following the epic tradition of Pastrone's *Cabiria*. Credit: AB

and Pastrone's *Cabiria*, the masterpiece of the genre, had also treated the Second Punic War. That film had appeared during a moment of Italian history involving Italian conquest in North Africa (in what would become Libya) as a result of the Italo-Turkish War. Likewise, Gallone released *Scipio Africanus* shortly after Italy emerged victorious from the invasion of Ethiopia (then called Abyssinia). When Mussolini announced the fall of Addis Ababa on May 5, 1936, and soon thereafter, on May 9 when he proclaimed Italy an empire with the conquest of Ethiopia, the regime reached the height of its popularity—although the result of his colonial adventure was to isolate Italy from the Western democracies and to squander an enormous quantity of Italy's national resources. Mussolini announced this event from his famous balcony of the Palazzo Venezia in Rome to a delirious and cheering crowd, evoking the glory of ancient Rome:

> Italy finally possesses its Empire. A Fascist Empire, because it bears the indestructible marks of the will and the power of the Roman fasces, and because this is the goal toward which for fourteen years the vital but disciplined energies of the young, vigorous Italian generations have been directed. . . . An Empire of civilization and of humanity for all the populations of Ethiopia. This is in the tradition of Rome, which, after emerging victorious, joined the defeated peoples to its own destiny. . . . [R]aise high your standards, your blades, and your hearts to salute, after fifteen centuries, the reappearance of the Empire upon the fateful hills of Rome.[29]

Thus, the regime's active support for Gallone's film about Rome's conquest of North Africa fit in perfectly with Mussolini's attempt to fashion Italians into ancient Roman imperialists abroad. Gallone received an enormous subsidy for the film—some twelve million prewar lire—and because of this assistance, it became the most expensive film ever produced in Italy to that time. Before it was released at the Venice Film Festival, where it surprised no one by being awarded the Mussolini Cup, it also became the subject of one of the most expensive advertising campaigns ever organized by the Italian industry. Furthermore, Mussolini himself visited the set in 1936 and was hailed by cries of "Duce, Duce!" from the cast of thousands of extras decked out in ancient Roman garb. Even the actors and the technical crews understood that one of the film's implicit messages was praise for the Italian Fascist empire in Africa, the reincarnation of the ancient Roman imperial spirit abroad.

Several elements in the film make clear reference to Mussolini's political movement. Scipio Africanus, victor over Hannibal and the Carthaginians, emerges from the film as a prototypical mass leader, rather than as the Roman patrician military commander he actually was. His fustian rhetoric often deadens the pace of the film and hardly represents the sober, disciplined speeches of senatorial politicians under the ancient Roman Republic (as least as those speeches are reported by Livy, the Roman historian who

Italian extras employ the fascist salute linking the glories of the vanished Roman Empire in Gallone's *Scipio Africanus* to Mussolini's imperialist adventures in Africa. *Credit: MOMA*

best described these wars). The avid response of the enthusiastic Roman crowds, however, certainly mirrored the adoring Italian crowds enthralled by Mussolini's skillful delivery of his spellbinding harangues. A more obvious link between Scipio and the modern Duce lies in the unintentionally comic frequency with which film characters give each other the "Roman" salute: they do so in the Senate, in the street, even in the privacy of their homes, and when the Roman fleet embarks for the invasion of Carthage, Gallone's frequent use of this gesture unmistakably insists on its ancient origins. If the impressive crowd and battle scenes, the thousands of extras, and the herds of elephants obey the generic rules for the Roman epic film established two decades earlier in the silent cinema, the constant references to battles in Spain and Africa in the movie were certainly not overly subtle analogies to current events: Mussolini's intervention in the Spanish Civil War and his imperialist adventures in Ethiopia.

The essence of Scipio's embodiment of a Roman way of life—discipline, the defense of the family, the belief that war was a Roman's duty and highest calling—actively supported many of the regime's most important policies, such as the campaign to raise the birthrate in Italy and to instill a warlike prowess in the Italian population. Interviews with elementary-school children in a 1939 issue of *Bianco e nero*, Italy's major film journal, reveal that the film indeed achieved its desired effect, for the children immediately grasped the implicit parallel between ancient Rome and Fascist Italy, between the earlier establishment of an empire in Africa and Il Duce's foundation of what the regime called "the fourth shore" across the Mediterranean Sea.[30]

Nationalism and Fascism in Feature Films during the Sound Era

Scipio Africanus was only one of a number of films made during the latter part of Fascism's reign that clearly supported aspects of the regime's campaign to instill nationalistic patriotism among its subjects. Guido Brignone's *Red Passport* (*Passporto rosso*, 1935), for example, highlights the love of country in Italian immigrants to South America who send their sons to die in the trenches in northern Italy during World War I. *Giovanni de' Medici: The Leader* (*Condottieri*, 1937), by the Austrian director Luis Trenker (1892–1990), presents a historical account of the Renaissance soldier of fortune Giovanni dalle Bande Nere that was extremely popular at both the box office and at the Venice Film Festival. Many critics have seen the open celebration of a charismatic leader's character as a thinly veiled reference to Benito Mussolini. Carmine Gallone's *Knock Out* (*Harlem*, 1943) takes a jaundiced look at America through the story of an Italian prizefighter named Tommaso Rossi (Massimo Girotti, 1918–2003) who comes to America to visit his older brother Amadeo (Amadeo Nazzari, 1907–79), who has made his way in the construction business. In an obvious nod to Rouben Mamoulian's *Golden Boy* (1939), the film that made William Holden a star as an Italian American violinist who discovers he can make more money boxing than playing music, Tommaso is discovered when, after being insulted, he floors a former boxing champ in a restaurant. The luster of the Italian dream of America is tarnished by the fact that Americans seek to destroy Amadeo's business and put him in jail for a crime he did not commit. Amadeo's arrest forces Tommaso to fight a black boxer in order to obtain bail money. The film concludes with a rather lame battle between Tommaso and the boxer, as crowds of black and white spectators (apparently inmates from Rome's prisons) look on. In the original film, Amadeo, who is murdered, tells Tommaso as he dies to give up boxing and return to Italy, since his own experience proves that Italy's American dream is really a nightmare. Of course, at the time the film was shot, Italy was at war with America, so a completely positive image of America would not be expected. After the war, however, the film was definitely changed and redistributed. Nazzari, one of Fascist Italy's most popular matinee idols, recalls repeating a line in the original version of the film that proclaims Americans to be corrupt and despicable; but in the postwar period this same line was dubbed to proclaim the Americans as marvelous, stupendous, and a people creating progress throughout the world![31] Yet, the picture of America even in the first version is much less violently anti-American than many Hollywood films made during World War II are anti-German or anti-Japanese.

An even-handed treatment of political ideology would not be expected in one of the few true propaganda pieces, such as *Redemption* (*Redenzione*,

Ayn Rand's anti-communist novel *We the Living* (1936) comes to the screen in Alessandrini's *We the Living* and describes an ill-fated love affair between Kira and a Russian aristocrat named Leo doomed after the Russian Revolution. The actors playing the star-crossed couple—Alida Valli and Rossano Brazzi—would later achieve fame in Hollywood in the postwar period. *Credit: MOMA*

1943), directed by Marcello Albani (1905–80), with a script by none other than the infamous leader of the Fascists from the city of Cremona, Roberto Farinacci (1892–1945), who was eventually executed by Italian partisans at the end of the war. The film's thin plot narrates the "redemption" of a Red who eventually becomes a true Fascist and dies heroically for the cause. Of much greater interest is a melodrama filmed by Alessandrini in 1942, an adaptation of Ayn Rand's novel *We the Living* (1936), which was an attack upon Soviet Communism and dictatorship in general. Ignoring Rand's intentions to criticize any dictatorship with totalitarian intentions (such as Mussolini's regime claimed to have), Alessandrini concentrated upon the anti-Soviet aspect of the original novel that had appeared in Italy in translation in 1938. The film was eventually shown in two parts: *We the Living* (*Noi vivi*) and *Goodbye, Kira* (*Addio, Kira*) and became a box-office smash after being presented at the Venice Film Festival in 1942. It featured a pair of actors who would go on after the end of the war to have a certain success in Hollywood: Alida Valli plays Kira, a middle-class woman who falls in love with a Russian aristocrat named Leo (Rossano Brazzi) after the Revolution has made such a liaison quite dangerous. In order to help Leo, whose health has deteriorated, Kira has an affair with Andrei (Fosco Giachetti), a member of the secret police. Eventually Andrei discovers Kira's subterfuge when he arrests Leo and finds her clothing in his apartment. Andrei's Communist ideals are destroyed by Kira's courageous love for Leo, and before he commits suicide, he has Leo freed and denounces his Communist comrades and the system they represent. Kira decides to leave Russia, and in the conclusion of the film, she is attempting to escape, pausing to remember the garden where she first met Leo.

Literary Adaptation and Calligraphers

Adaptations of important literary texts (European or American) would prove to be one of the most striking characteristics of postwar Italian cinema. Native literature of course was an important part of this: between 1940 and 1943, a number of directors turned to adapting nineteenth- and twentieth-century Italian novels. Since many of these individuals also worked on one another's films as assistants or scriptwriters, a certain similarity of style among their adaptations is discernable, and Italian film historians have traditionally called these directors "calligraphers"—a term underlining the filmmakers' interest in formalism, style, and, by implication, their choices of themes from past history or literature rather than from contemporary Italian culture. The implicit negative tone of this term is certainly unwarranted, since no national cinema focuses entirely on the present. Moreover, an encounter with a major writer of fiction from any modern period could not help but direct the cinema toward social problems and the complex relationships between classes.

The best known of this group of films is *A Pistol Shot* (*Un colpo di pistola*, 1942), by Renato Castellani, taken from a story by Pushkin. Luigi Chiarini, the influential director of the Centro Sperimentale di Cinematografia until 1943 and the editor of *Bianco e nero*, turned for inspiration to a story by the Neapolitan realist Matilde Serao (1856–1927) for *Five Moons Street* (*Via delle cinque lune*, 1942). Mario Soldati (1906–99) wrote and directed (and appeared in) two excellent adaptations of novels by Antonio Fogazzaro (1842–1911): *Little Old-Fashioned World* (*Piccolo mondo antico*, 1941; the novel is more often called *The Little World of the Past*) and *Malombra* (1942). (Later, Soldati was better known as a novelist influenced by American literature: he visited the United States in 1929 and 1932–33, and wrote a famous description of that country in his novel *America, First Love* [*America, primo amore*, 1935], which helped to nourish the perennial Italian dream of America.) Alberto Lattuada (1914–2005) directed *Giacomo the Idealist* (*Giacomo l'idealista*, 1943), adapting a novel by Emilio De Marchi (1851–1901). *Jealousy* (*Gelosia*, 1942) and *The Priest's Hat* (*Il cappello da prete*, 1944), both shot by Ferdinando Maria Poggioli (1897–1945), derive respectively from the naturalist masterpiece *The Marquis of Roccaverdina* (*Il marchese di Roccaverdina*, 1901), by Luigi Capuana (1839–1915), and from De Marchi's *The Priest's Hat* (*Il cappello del prete*, 1888).

A number of scriptwriters, technicians, actors, and assistant directors later associated with neorealist cinema or postwar Italian culture gained invaluable training working on these adaptations, experiences that prepared them for their more original contributions immediately after the fall of the Fascist regime. These included the scriptwriter Sergio Amidei (1904–81), the novelist Vitaliano Brancati (1907–54), the literary critic and scriptwriter Giacomo Debenedetti (1901–67), the producer Dino De Laurentiis (1919–2010), and the musician Nino Rota (1911–79).

Hollywood Withdraws from the Italian Market

Besides the institutions established by the Fascist regime that ultimately benefited the film industry (the Centro Sperimentale, Cinecittà, the Istituto Luce), other developments during the Fascist period are worthy of note. In 1938, the Italian government—faced with the fact that Hollywood films completely dominated the Italian market, generally garnering about 70 percent of box-office returns—passed the so-called Alfieri Law (Legge Alfieri), named for the then Minister of Popular Culture Dino Alfieri (1886–1966). This law, which granted state subsidies to filmmakers on a sliding scale based on box-office receipts, gave ENIC and a state institution called ENAIPE (Ente Nazionale Importazione Pellicole Estere, or National Body for Importing Foreign Films) a virtual monopoly to purchase and distribute all foreign film imports. This direct blow to Hollywood's economic hegemony within Italy's internal market resulted in the temporary withdrawal of MGM, 20th Century Fox, Paramount, and Warner Brothers from Italy. The result was a sharp rise in domestic film production. In 1937, 33 Italian films competed with 290 imports (most still from Hollywood); the next year, the proportion changed, with 45 Italian works competing with 230 imports. Italian production figures were higher throughout the war years: 77 films (1939), 86 (1940), 71 (1941), 96 (1942), 66 (1943)—and even 37 (1944) after Italy was split in half by the Allied invasion and the ensuing partisan war that lasted until 1945, when hostilities ceased on the peninsula and the war concluded. By 1942, some 470 million tickets were sold to screenings in 5,236 film theaters nationwide. Italy thus had one of the largest markets for feature films in all of Europe. Besides gaining strength from the lack of foreign competition, the industry also profited from the creation of several new production companies. Gustavo Lombardo (1885–1951) founded Titanus Films, and his son Goffredo Lombardo (1920–2005) later joined him. Although the company had little impact during the Fascist period, it acquired the Scalera Studios at this time and, in the postwar era, would become one of the most important of all Italian studios.[32] Riccardo Gualino (1879–1964) created Lux Film in 1934, and this studio made some of Italy's most original films after 1945.[33] Angelo Rizzoli (1889–1970), one of the most important postwar producers, also published a number of popular weekly magazines on the movies as well as produced a few key films in the 1930s. All of these individuals would play a vital role in the Italian film industry after 1945.

New Directions during the Twilight of the Fascist Regime

In spite of Italian Fascism's attempts to create a uniquely Italian and Fascist culture, Fascist Italy began slowly to open up to outside influences and to shed its provincial status as an European backwater. Oddly enough, some of this "subversive" cultural activity took place among artists and intellectuals who might best be described as left-wing Fascists, while other opponents of the regime silently expressed their opinions by finding value in foreign cultures diametrically opposed to the Fascist praise of war, struggle, mother-hood, and a glorious death in combat for the homeland. Under the influence of Umberto Barbaro (1902–59) and Luigi Chiarini at the Centro Sperimen-tale, translations of the theoretical works on cinema by Eisenstein, Pudovkin, Balázs, Arnheim, and others were read and discussed. The cinegufs—the Fascist-sponsored film clubs at the universities—sponsored screenings of the best films by Soviet, American, French, and German directors with relatively little opposition from the censors, since the regime's restrictions generally applied more to newsreels than to feature films seen only by an elite group of university students. After 1938, when Hollywood films ceased to come to Italy, it was the French cinema of Jean Renoir, René Clair, and Marcel Carné that had the most appeal, and a number of Italians enjoyed connections with French cinema: De Sica imitated Clair's style; Antonioni served as Carné's assistant on *The Devil's Envoys*; Luchino Visconti worked with Renoir on *A Day in the Country* (*Une Partie de campagne*, 1936) and *The Lower Depths* (*Les Bas-fonds*, 1936), as well as on *Tosca* (*La Tosca*, 1941), a film Renoir began shooting in Italy but that was completed by Carl Koch after the out-break of hostilities with France during World War II.

Visconti's *Obsession*: The Discovery of America and a New Cinema

Visconti's greatest debt to Renoir was a copy of a French translation of the American novel *The Postman Always Rings Twice* (1934), by James M. Cain (1892–1977), the basis for his masterpiece *Obsession* (*Ossessione*, 1943) a few years later. In fact the term "neorealism" was first applied not to postwar Italian films but, instead, to French films of the 1930s by Renoir and Carné, in an article written in 1943 by Umberto Barbaro.[34] Visconti's heuristic encounter with Cain's "hard-boiled" classic points to the decisive influence American fiction had upon the rise of an interest in literary and cinematic realism. English-speaking audiences familiar only with a few masterpieces of postwar Italian cinema too often overlook the fact that "neorealism" is not only an important moment in European film history: it is also a decisive trend in Italian literature between the mid-1930s and the 1950s. Many dedicated Italian Fascists admired much about American society, economy, and culture, but official governmental disapproval of all things American became the watchword as Italy moved closer and closer to being drawn into a world war with the United States as an obvious antagonist.

Italian intellectuals, both Fascist and anti-Fascist, had often viewed American literature and cinema as a countercultural phenomenon that stood in juxtaposition to the official Italian culture characterized by a strident nationalism. Still, the popularity of American fiction among the younger generation of soon-to-be-published writers had never been greater. Cesare Pavese (1908–50) defended a university thesis on Walt Whitman in 1930, translated Melville's *Moby-Dick* in 1932, and produced versions of various works by Sinclair Lewis, Edgar Lee Masters, William Faulkner, John Dos Passos, and Sherwood Anderson. His first important novel, *The Harvesters* (*Paesi tuoi*, 1941), a study of rural violence, is deeply indebted to American models in its combination of naturalism and poetic suggestiveness. Pavese's masterpiece, *The Moon and the Bonfires* (*La luna e i falò*, 1950), relates an Italian's voyage to America and his return, an event narrated against a background of partisan resistance to the Fascists. Elio Vittorini (1908–66), a self-taught worker who learned English by translating *Robinson Crusoe*, went on to translate Steinbeck and Faulkner, edited an important anthology of American literature, and exhibited the profound influence of Hemingway's literary style in his neorealist masterpiece *In Sicily* (*Conversazione in Sicilia*, 1941). Pavese, Vittorini, and Italo Calvino (1923–85) would all constitute the core of a reborn Italian literature that was resolutely "neorealist" with its quest for depicting Italian life by poetic means, and this trend was born during the Fascist period, not afterward— just as the quest for film realism was pursued, in many respects, by directors during the Fascist period. Pavese best expressed the sentiments of his generation in an essay published in 1947 by *L'Unità*, the official newspaper of the Italian Communist Party (PCI):

> Around 1930, when Fascism was beginning to be "the hope of the world," some young Italians happened to discover in their books America—an America thoughtful and barbaric, happy and truculent, dissolute, fecund, heavy with all the past of the world, and at the same time young, innocent. For several years these young people read, translated, and wrote with a joy of discovery and of revolt that infuriated the official culture; but the success was so great that it constrained the regime to tolerate it, in order to save face.[35]

The encounter with American narrative prose also moved the best and most perceptive writers and critics during the last years of the Fascist regime to reevaluate Italy's greatest naturalist novelist, Giovanni Verga.

Visconti's *Obsession* occupies a pivotal position in the history of Italian cinema precisely because it simultaneously reflects the convergence of so many of these different cultural and intellectual experiences, and establishes itself as great art rather than as an ideological manifesto. Visconti's cinematic style was first formed under the influence of Renoir, and upon returning to Italy from France, Visconti was associated with the young intellectuals and filmmakers gathered around Vittorio Mussolini and his review, *Cinema*. Visconti published two important articles in *Cinema*: a blast at the Italian commercial films of the past generation ("Cadavers," 1941), and an eloquent plea for a cinema made to human measure in which "the most humble gestures of a man, his face, his hesitations and his impulses, impart poetry and life to the things which surround him and to the setting in which they take place" ("Anthropomorphic Cinema," 1943).[36] A few years earlier, three of his colleagues on *Cinema* had written for the journal similar manifestos that called for new realist directions in Italian cinema. In 1939, Michelangelo Antonioni's "Concerning a Film about the River Po" proposed making a film about the River Po in Italy that would avoid the kinds of rhetorical and folkloric treatment so typical of Fascist newsreels about Italy and its many diverse geographical areas and provincial cultures. In another issue of *Cinema* in 1941, Giuseppe De Santis argued in "Towards an Italian Landscape" that Italian cinema should take more pains to place its protagonists into an authentic landscape, one that was specifically Italian in nature. And later that same year, De Santis and Mario Alicata (1908–66), in "Truth and Poetry: Verga and the Italian Cinema," another essay published by *Cinema*, declared that the road to film realism in Italy led through a return to an appreciation of Giovanni Verga's naturalist fiction. Later, both writers would contribute to the writing of the script for Visconte's *Obsession*. Visconti's first two films, the prewar *Obsession* and his neorealist postwar classic *The Earth Trembles*, show the lessons he learned from Renoir and French cinema of the 1930s and 1940s, from the hard-boiled American novel, and from the naturalist fiction of Verga—three diverse influences present in Italian culture during the last years of the Fascist regime.

Always a sensitive observer of trends within Italian culture, Visconti had originally intended to make a film of "Gramigna's Lover" ("L'amante di Gramigna," 1880), one of Verga's best short stories. When Minister of Popular Culture Alessandro Pavolini saw the proposed script, however, he rejected it because of its subject matter: Sicilian bandits were apparently not suitable material for Italian cinema. (A film adaptation by Carlo Lizzani finally appeared in 1969.) Then, after considering a number of literary works for adaptation, including Melville's *Billy Budd*, Visconti turned to the

French translation of Cain's *The Postman Always Rings Twice* that Renoir had given him. With a group of young friends associated with the Centro Sperimentale and *Cinema*—including De Santis, Alicata, Antonio Pietrangeli (1919–68), Gianni Puccini (1914–68), and the novelist Alberto Moravia (1907–90)—Visconti set about resetting Cain's hard-boiled American fiction in an Italian atmosphere. In the book, a crisp, hard-boiled, first-person novel narrated from the perspective of the main character as he awaits execution in prison for murder, a tramp named Frank meets Cora, the wife of Nick, a Greek American restaurant owner, has an affair with her, and is led to murder her husband. The world these characters inhabit is tawdry and absurd, a quality that explains why Cain's novel also influenced *The Stranger* (1942) by Albert Camus (1913–60). Irony abounds, for while Frank and Cora murder Nick in a fake accident and escape punishment, Frank will be executed for a murder when an authentic accident that kills Cora is considered a homicide. Cain refuses to moralize or to inject into his novel any sense of tragedy or melodrama. With rare descriptive passages, the novel consists chiefly of staccato dialogue, so sparsely written that many critics see the novel as itself a cinematic mode of fiction akin to the scenario.

As a work of art, Visconti's *Obsession* is vastly superior to either the American version of 1946 by Tay Garnett (*The Postman Always Rings Twice*) or an earlier French adaptation by Pierre Chenal (*The Last Turn* [*Le dernier tournant*], 1939), and it represents a radical transformation of the original literary source. Frank, Cora, and Nick are retained as Gino (Massimo Girotti), Giovanna (Clara Calamai), and Bragana (Juan de Landa). Cain's "grease-ball" restaurant owner becomes more complicated, if not less loathsome to his wife, Giovanna, by virtue of the fact that in Visconti's version of the story, he is a lover (as was Visconti) of Verdi's operas. Visconti totally eliminates Cain's emphasis upon the American system of justice, with such characters as Sackett, the district attorney, and Katz, Frank's lawyer. Instead, Visconti introduces into his adaptation a very ambiguous character, a homosexual nicknamed "Lo spagnolo" or "The Spaniard" (Elio Marcuzzo) who functions as an alternative to Gino's sensual obsession with Giovanna, an obsession that is Visconti's main focus in the film. The novel's first-person subjective narrative becomes in Visconti's hands a more omniscient and objective camera style where Viscount pursues his highly formal compositions as obsessively as his characters are driven by their passions.

With the example of Renoir and the manifestos of Antonioni, Alicata, and De Santis in mind, Visconti achieved in *Obsession* a magnificent linkage between his tragic protagonists and their environment—their tawdry living quarters, the provincial country inn, the streets of Ancona or Ferrara, the sandbanks of the River Po. Extremely lengthy medium shots, a typical feature of Visconti's mature camera style, allow the director to follow Gino and Giovanna, played brilliantly by Girotti and Calamai, as their destinies

The initial encounter between Gino and Giovanna leads to immediate sexual attraction and eventual tragedy in Visconti's *Obsession. Credit: DVD*

unfold while being shaped by their surroundings. Simple gestures, glances, or even the lack of any significant action at all impart to the work exactly the kind of poetic sense that Visconti recommended in his "Anthropomorphic Cinema." Cain's emphasis upon staccato dialogue disappears. In fact, the most memorable parts of the film lack any dialogue whatsoever, a technique that will be developed even further in Antonioni's early postwar films. When, for instance, Visconti shoots past Gino shaving at the inn, and his hand holding a straight razor appears in the same frame against a view in the background of Giovanna massaging her husband's corpulent body, we are prepared for the husband's eventual murder—especially since Bragana is at that precise moment discussing insurance. Even more remarkable is the famous scene that takes place after Bragana's murder: a world-weary Giovanna enters her squalid kitchen but falls asleep from exhaustion. It is a moment in which the director captures perfectly Giovanna's growing desperation and loneliness, and it is achieved by matching film time with real time. It is this characteristic of Visconti's film style that postwar critics, André Bazin in particular, came to regard as a fundamental aspect of neorealist aesthetics. By emphasizing the close interrelationship of the film's protagonists to their environment, Visconti transforms the ironic and often absurd world he found in Cain's novel into a world of genuine tragedy, a world in which the role of destiny within the plot seems inexorable and determined entirely by the logic of the situation. The fatal obsession and sensuality drive Gino and Giovanna first to murder, then to disagreement, and finally to a hopeful reconciliation just before their dreams are shattered by the automobile accident in which Giovanna and the child she is expecting by Gino are killed, sealing Gino's fate forever.

Matching film time with real time in Visconti's *Obsession* (1942): the famous scene of Giovanna eating by herself in the kitchen embodies André Bazin's concept of "duration" in Italian neorealist cinema. *Credit: DVD*

With *Obsession*, Italy produced its first real "film noir" even before this critical category had been invented by postwar French critics to describe a certain kind of hard-boiled cinema, itself derived from the American hard-boiled novel produced by such writers as Cain, Dashiell Hammett (1894–1961), and Raymond Chandler (1888–1959). Censors and government officials received the film as an act of provocation, even though Mussolini himself saw it and allowed it to be distributed. His son Vittorio, usually enthusiastic about all things American, expressed the sentiments of Italian officialdom when he stormed out of the film's first public screening, muttering that "this is not Italy!" It was certainly not the Italy that Italian audiences had been accustomed to seeing on the LUCE newsreels during the Fascist period, for Visconti had transformed the usually picturesque Italian landscape into a stage for violent passions and burning sensuality presented with a tragic intensity that had almost been forgotten on Italian movie screens. *Obsession* is thus a turning point in the history of the Italian cinema. It is a precursor to the explosion of Italian neorealism on the Italian and international scene after 1945, although it was virtually unknown outside of Italy and was actually seen by very few Italians when it was screened there. The Fascists destroyed the original negative when much of the film industry was moved north to join Mussolini's Republic of Salò between 1943 and 1945. Luckily, Visconti retained a duplicate negative. Although *Obsession* is not a film about wartime experiences, partisans, or social problems, nor one in which nonprofessional actors and a documentary-like style are employed—traits often considered to be central to any definition of Italian neorealism—it prepared Italian filmmakers, if not the Italian film spectator or the critics, for an entirely different intellectual and aesthetic climate after the end of the war.

PART TWO

Italian Neorealism

CHAPTER 3

Masters of Neorealism

ROSSELLINI, DE SICA, AND VISCONTI

Problematic Definitions of Italian Postwar Neorealism

CRITICS AND FILM HISTORIANS AGREE that the moment in Italian cinematic history known as "neorealism" was a crucial watershed in the evolution of the seventh art. Nevertheless, definitions of exactly what constitutes a neorealist film style differ widely. The term itself is problematic (meaning literally "new" realism, just as neoclassicism signifies a "new" classicism), because it limits the parameters of any critical debate to concern with the connection between the films in question and the society, culture, or time period that produced them. Indeed, one critic's list of the general characteristics associated with neorealist films shows the degree to which the traditional view of Italian neorealism, which arose during the immediate postwar period, reflects this emphasis upon social realism: social content, historical actuality, political commitment, realist treatment, and popular settings.[1] Except for the undefined "realist treatment," such a list focuses primarily on a work's content, not its aesthetic qualities. In contrast to a definition based upon content, the most original European critic of the immediate postwar period, the French writer André Bazin (1918–58), defined neorealism by its aesthetics and called it a cinema of "fact" and "reconstituted reportage" that contained a message of fundamental human solidarity fostered by the anti-Fascist Resistance taking place when the greatest Italian neorealists came of age intellectually and artistically. In Bazin's view, neorealist films often embodied a rejection of both traditional and cinematic conventions, most often employed on-location shooting rather than conventional studio sets, and made novel use of nonprofessional actors or documentary effects. Bazin defined the aesthetics of neorealism as akin to a separate and differently motivated evolution in the mise-en-scène techniques of Orson Welles or Jean Renoir with their penchant for deep-focus photography, which Bazin contrasted sharply and approvingly with the dramatic montage editing of Eisenstein and its ideologically inspired juxtaposition of images and shots. Thus, for Bazin, neorealists tended to "respect" the ontological wholeness of the reality they filmed, just as the rhythm of their narrated screen time often "respected" the actual duration of time within their narratives. Neorealist aesthetics thus opposed the manipulation of reality in the cutting room.[2]

Any comprehensive definition of Italian neorealism must come to grips with the vexing problem posed by the traditional association of neorealism with realism in both literature and film, an association that quite naturally moves critics to emphasize its often progressive or leftist ideological content, its use of nonprofessional actors, or the documentary quality of its photography. And yet, with the exception of several too frequently cited statements by Cesare Zavattini—an important scriptwriter and collaborator with De Sica, but never a major director—the remarks of the directors themselves sound quite a different note. Only Zavattini advocates the most elementary, even banal storylines Bazin prefers, and only Zavattini stresses the need to focus upon the actual "duration" of real time.[3] By contrast, while such figures as Rossellini, De Sica, or Fellini (almost as important a neorealist scriptwriter as Zavattini before he turned to direction) sympathize with Zavattini's reverence for everyday reality, what he terms an "unlimited trust in things, facts, and people," rarely if ever do they equate their artistic intentions with traditional literary or cinematic realism. Rossellini declared that realism was "simply the artistic form of the truth," linking neorealism to a moral position rather than to any preconceived set of techniques or ideological positions.[4] Fellini, who apprenticed with Rossellini as a writer and also worked with Lattuada and other lesser-known directors credited with many neorealist films, declared simply that "neorealism is a way of seeing reality without prejudice, without conventions coming between it and myself—facing it without preconceptions, looking at it in an honest way—whatever reality is, not just social reality but all that there is within a man."[5] De Sica stated that his neorealist films reflected "reality transposed into the realm of poetry."[6] Yet the best discussions of Italian neorealism during the past several decades depart from the warnings found in such fundamental discussions of the subject as those by Bazin or Roy Armes and now treat the subject as a brand of cinema quite involved with aesthetic artifice and with the establishment of its own "realistic" cinematic conventions.[7] Realism in the cinema must be created by artifice. Moreover, our concepts of what constitutes realism change. Black-and-white documentary footage seemed "real" in the postwar period when film audiences identified documentary films shown during intermissions of feature films as full of "facts." Today, however, the public watches "World War II in Color" on cable,[8] and the same documentary films about World War II once shown in black and white now seem more "real," because we can see the colors that were not developed for the weekly newscasts in the 1940s. After several decades of live news broadcasts in color, twenty-first-century audiences associate "realism" in news documentaries with color photography rather than with black-and-white images. If reporters are not speaking via satellite from the place where news events have occurred, not "embedded" with the troops in a shooting war, for example, few of us today would consider their reportage factual or "real." Italian neorealism appeared at a particular moment in the development of the cinema: it has obvious links to the events that unfolded in Italy and Europe during and immediately after World War II, but as a moment of film history, we must examine the conventions it employed to understand exactly the kind of "realism" it presented. Nor did neorealist filmmakers follow a programmatic list of ideological or aesthetic criteria. The film styles of Rossellini, De Sica, and Visconti reflect a number of similarities or "family resemblances," but they also differ in many important respects.[9]

Literary Antecedents of Italian Neorealism in Film

Early overemphasis upon the "realism" of Italian neorealist cinema might well have been avoided had film critics examined their subject matter from the broader and more general vantage point of postwar Italian culture. Certainly, they would have been forced to recognize that the major works of neorealist *literature* that appeared almost contemporaneously with the best neorealist films embodied an entirely different and more complex aesthetic than a simple interest in "realism." Novels identified with the rise of neorealist fiction include *Revolt in Aspromonte* (*Gente in Aspromonte*, 1930), by Corrado Álvaro (1895–1956); *Bread and Wine* (*Pane e vino*, 1937), by Ignazio Silone (1900–78); *In Sicily* (1941) by Vittorini; *The Harvesters* (1941) and *The Moon and the Bonfires* (1950), by Pavese; *Christ Stopped at Eboli* (*Cristo si è fermato a Eboli*, 1945), by Carlo Levi (1902–75); *The Path to the Nest of Spiders* (*Il sentiero dei nidi di ragno*, 1947), by Calvino; *A Tale of Poor Lovers* (*Cronache di poveri amanti*, 1947), by Vasco Pratolini (1913–91); *Agnese Goes to Her Death* (*L'Agnese va a morire*, 1949), by Renata Viganò (1900–76); and *The Twenty-three Days of the City of Alba* (*I ventitré giorni della città di Alba*, 1952), by Beppe Fenoglio (1922–63). The publication dates of these key novels of fictional neorealism underscore the fact that, like realism in the Italian cinema (as argued in chapter 2), neorealist fiction spans the Fascist and postwar period. Literary neorealism did not arise abruptly after 1945 but was part of a growing preference for an honest look at Italian realities (not any single "reality") that had been ignored or suppressed during the Fascist period or that, in some important cases, had been supported and encouraged by members of the regime itself.[10] Very few of these novels employ the traditional third-person, omniscient narrator

typical of the great realist novels of the nineteenth and early twentieth centuries. On the contrary, most of these narratives deal with social reality in
a symbolic or mythical fashion, and many employ unreliable and subjective
narrators, thereby embracing a clearly antinaturalistic narrative stance contrary to canons of literary realism. Calvino's retrospective preface added in
1964 to *The Path to the Nest of Spiders* makes this quite clear, for he declares
that neorealist writers "knew all too well that what counted was the music
and not the libretto . . . there were never more dogged formalists than we;
and never were lyric poets as effusive as those objective reporters we were
supposed to be," and that because of this subjective and poetic quality in
neorealist fiction, perhaps "neo-expressionism" rather than neorealism
should be the term applied to these novels.[11] Pavese strikes a similar note in
his assessment of how American fiction influenced the culture of the neorealist generation, for rather than seeking a new reality, American novelists
wanted to "readjust language to the new reality of the world, in order to
create, in effect, a *new* language, down-to-earth and symbolic, that would
justify itself solely in terms of itself."[12]

Italian novelists and directors were not concerned merely with social
realism in their works. On the contrary, they were seeking a new literary
and cinematographic language that would enable them to deal poetically
with the pressing problems of their times. As Pavese asserted, they wanted
to view their world afresh and from a new perspective, thereby creating
a "new reality" artistically. They knew, as Calvino asserts, that music was
always more significant than the lyrics, form more crucial to innovation in
language than content. Certainly, the directors we now label as neorealists
turned to the pressing problems of their day—the war, the Resistance, the
partisan struggle, unemployment, poverty, social injustice—but they never
adopted a programmatic approach to these problems, nor did they follow
any preconceived method of rendering such concerns on celluloid. Neorealism differed in significant ways from other avant-garde movements of
the twentieth century, such as Italian futurism or surrealism, for directors
known as neorealists never adhered to a governing manifesto or even felt
the need to create one. In short, neorealism was not a "movement" in the
strictest sense of the term. The controlling fiction of neorealist films, or at
least the majority of them, was that they dealt with actual problems, that
they employed contemporary stories, and that they focused on believable
characters taken most frequently from everyday Italian lives. Still, the greatest neorealist directors never forgot that the world they projected upon the
silver screen was one produced by cinematic conventions rather than an
ontological experience, and they were never so naïve as to deny that the
demands of an artistic medium such as film might be just as pressing as those
from the world around them. In many of their films, they called attention
to the relationship of illusion and reality, fact and fiction, so as to emphasize

their understanding of the role both played in their art. Any discussion of Italian neorealism must be broad enough to encompass a wide diversity of cinematic styles, themes, and attitudes. No single or specific approach was taken, and much of the discussion that arose in the next decade over the "crisis" of neorealism or its "betrayal" by various directors was, therefore, essentially groundless and founded upon ideological disagreements among various critics rather than any abrupt change on the part of the filmmakers themselves. Directors we label today as neorealists were a crucial part of a much larger general postwar cultural revolution characterized by a number of aesthetic and philosophical perspectives, all united only by the common aspiration to view Italy without preconceptions and to develop a more honest, ethical, but no less poetic cinematic language.

Neorealist Films as a Small Fraction of Italian Film Production

Other and perhaps even more pernicious myths have risen about the period running from the release and international distribution of Rossellini's *Open City* in 1945—the traditional date associated with the beginning of the neorealist era—to the mid-1950s, when it became clear that Italian cinema had shifted direction. The most surprising statistic that emerges from an analysis of the style or content of the some 822 films produced in Italy during 1945–53 is that only about 90 (11 percent) of these works could even be called "neorealist." The percentage does not change drastically if we limit our sample to the 224 films produced between 1945 and 1948. Thus, it is even misleading to identify the immediate postwar decade's film production in Italy with neorealism. The vast majority of films continued to be works associated with traditional genres (historical films, comedies, melodramas, literary adaptations). It is even more important to recognize that the vast majority of these 90 films were failures at the box office, with few exceptions (the obvious ones): *Open City* achieved first place at the box office in 1945–46; *Paisan* was in ninth place in 1949–50; *In the Name of the Law* (*Nel nome della legge,* 1949), by Pietro Germi (1914–74), reached third place in 1948–49; Vittorio De Sica's *The Bicycle Thief* managed to reach only eleventh place in 1948–49; and *Bitter Rice* (*Riso amaro,* 1949), by Giuseppe De Santis, was in fifth place in 1949–50. Most of the rest of these works were dismal box-office failures and were often even critical failures as well.[13] They were repeatedly praised more lavishly abroad than in Italy, and the small but important export market for the best films enabled the beleaguered directors to sustain their work in the face of critical opposition from Italian reviewers or even from their own government. Paradoxically, while the greatest Italian films of the era set out to project a more authentic image of Italy in as honest a cinematic language as they could create, neorealism always remained primarily an "art" cinema, never capturing the mass public it always hoped to gain in the manner of Hollywood films. Most Italians simply preferred watching movies from America or native Italian comedies and historical dramas, just as they had done during the Fascist period before the American studios withdrew from the market due to governmental controls over the sales and distribution of imported films after 1938. Italian film production rose gradually after the war, but during 1945–50 (the heyday of the neorealist period), Hollywood controlled between two-thirds and three-fourths of Italy's internal market.

Furthermore, the economic and political priorities of the Italian government, allied closely with the United States at the time, made any immediate changes in the market situation by action on the part of the Italian government unlikely. In 1951, with an accord between ANICA (Associazione Nazionale Industrie Cinematografiche ed Affine) and the U.S. MPEA (Motion Picture Export Association), the government attempted to curb the flood of American films into Italy at around 225 films per year. In principle, the accord was supposed to open up the American national market to Italian imports as well as limit American imports to Italy. Before the accord was signed, 178 Italian films had been screened in America between 1946 and 1950, whereas 1,662 Hollywood films had been shown in Italy. Yet, after the agreement, Italian exports to America rose only to a total of 220 films during 1951–55; meanwhile 1,149 Hollywood products were distributed in Italy.[14] Even the Italian Communist Party could not have invented a more disturbing illustration of American economic hegemony in postwar Italy. Directors and producers found no relief in the supposedly inexpensive production costs of neorealist films given their substantially lower rate of return at the box office and the fact that films made on location rather than in traditional studios effected only minimal savings that often disappeared with the more lengthy and costly shooting time required on location.

The contribution of Italian neorealism to the evolution of the cinema must ultimately be judged by seven films produced within a very short period in the postwar period. These seven acknowledged masterpieces are Rossellini's so-called war trilogy (set in opposition to the three films made before 1945, his "Fascist trilogy"), *Open City* (1945), *Paisan* (1946), and *Germany Year Zero* (1947); De Sica's touching portraits of postwar life in *Shoeshine* (1946), *The Bicycle Thief* (1948), and *Umberto D.* (1952); and Visconti's synthesis of the Marxist theories of Antonio Gramsci (1891–1937) and the naturalism of Giovanni Verga in *The Earth Trembles* (1948).

Rossellini's "War Trilogy"

Open City

The landmark film of neorealism and the work that announced a new direction in European cinema to the world was Rossellini's *Open City*. It so completely reflected the moral and psychological atmosphere of the moment it was created—1945, the minute the war ended, when the reconstruction of Italy had not yet begun—that it stands as a kind of symbol for the period itself.[15] The conditions of its production (relatively little shooting in a studio, film stock bought on the black market and developed without the normal viewing of daily rushes, postsynchronization of sound to avoid laboratory expenses, limited financial backing) did much to create the myths concerning neorealism. With a daring combination of styles and moods ranging from use of documentary footage to the most blatant melodrama, Rossellini captured forever the tension and the tragedy of Italian experiences during the German occupation of Rome and the beginnings of the partisan struggle against the Nazi occupiers. Its plot is an intriguing reflection of the contradictions inherent in that struggle and focuses upon a few dramatic episodes in the lives of a handful of simple characters: Don Pietro (Aldo Fabrizi), a partisan priest, joins with a Communist partisan leader named Manfredi (Marcello Pagliero) to combat the Nazis. Manfredi's former mistress Marina (Maria Michi) eventually betrays him to the diabolic Gestapo officer, Major Bergmann (Harry Feist). A working-class woman named Pina (Anna Magnani) is engaged to be married to a typesetter named Francesco (Francesco Grandjacquet), a friend of Manfredi's, and she is already expecting his child. These characters are strongly stereotyped into good and evil categories, depending upon their attitude toward the Resistance. It is not enough for Bergmann to be a monster; he is also depicted as an effeminate homosexual, while his assistant Ingrid (Giovanna Galletti) is a viperish lesbian who seduces Marina with expensive fur coats, presents, and drugs to obtain information about Manfredi. Since Rossellini cares most about how the tragedy of warfare affects common people, he concentrates the action around the impending marriage of Francesco and Pina, intertwining it skillfully with the narration of the Gestapo's brutal search for Manfredi and his comrades. As a result, Rossellini creates a narrative combining fact and fiction, reality and artistic invention. While he fuses Catholic and Communist elements of the Resistance into a coherent storyline, he never avoids the hints of tension between the two major sources of anti-Fascism, two groups who will oppose each other when the struggle against the Nazis has ended. Manfredi, for instance, expresses his mild disapproval of Pina's marriage in a church but reluctantly admits that it is better for a partisan to be married by a partisan priest than by a Fascist mayor at city hall. In spite of Don Pietro's obvious good intentions, a leftist printer tells him sharply that not everyone in Italy can hide from the Germans in monasteries. When Bergmann arrests Manfredi and Don Pietro, he tries unsuccessfully to move the priest to betray Manfredi by arguing that the Communists are the sworn enemies of the church, but Don Pietro declares that all men who fight for liberty and justice walk in the pathways of the Lord.

More than adherence to any programmatic attempt at cinematic realism, the tone of *Open City* is thus far more indebted to Rossellini's message of Christian humanism. The good characters are set sharply apart from the corrupt ones by their belief in what Francesco calls an impending "springtime" in Italy and a better tomorrow. Marina is corrupted by Ingrid not because of political convictions but because of her lack of faith in herself, which makes her incapable of loving others. Marxists and Christians alike adhere to Rossellini's credo embodied in Don Pietro's last words before he faces a firing squad at the end of the film: "Oh, it's not hard to die well. It's hard to live well."[16] Beneath the surface of the work, which often seems closer to a newsreel than to fictional narrative, a profoundly tragicomic vision of life juxtaposes melodramatic moments or instances of comic relief and dark humor with the most tragic human experiences to reconstruct the reality of a crucial moment in Italian history. When Fascist soldiers arrive at the workers' apartments near the Via Casilina to look for concealed partisans, Manfredi and the others manage to escape because the troops are preoccupied with trying to peer up the women's skirts on a staircase. A sympathetic Italian policeman looks on while Pina and other women loot a bakery, and rather than doing his duty, he only remarks sadly that it is too bad he is in uniform, because he cannot take any bread for himself. When German soldiers enter a restaurant where Manfredi is eating, we fear that he will be captured, but this moment of suspense is immediately undercut by our discovery that the Germans have only come there to butcher a live lamb and to eat it, and our fear (as well as Manfredi's) dissolves with the humorous quip made by the restaurant owner—he had forgotten that Germans were specialists in butchering!

Open City revolves around Rossellini's shifting perspective from a comic to a tragic tone, and nowhere is this more evident than in the film's most famous sequences, the search of Pina's apartment building that results in her eventual death in the street, mercilessly machine-gunned by German soldiers as she races toward Francesco, her fiancé, who has been arrested and will be taken to a German labor camp. This misfortune occurs on their wedding day. The promise of a better tomorrow, Francesco's "springtime," will never come for them, and the happy day ends in total despair. But this tragedy is preceded by a comic introduction, a sequence scripted by none other than Federico Fellini. Just before her death, Don Pietro and Marcello, Pina's son, arrive at the apartment building—supposedly to give the last

Perhaps the most famous shot in the history of the Italian cinema: Pina races toward her lover just before being gunned down by German troops in Rossellini's *Open City. Credit: CSC*

rites to Pina's father, but actually to secure and conceal weapons and bombs kept there by Romoletto ("little Romulus"), the crippled leader of a group of Roman children who have become partisans. In spite of Rossellini's often quoted assertion that dramatic editing is not required in filmmaking, here he skillfully creates a moment of suspense as he cuts back and forth between the priest's frantic search for the weapons, on the one hand, and the menacing ascent of the suspicious Fascist officer, on the other. When the Fascists enter the room, Don Pietro peacefully administers the last rites to an old man stretched out on a bed. Only after the soldiers leave and Don Pietro frantically attempts to revive the sleeper do we realize that, to keep him quiet, Don Pietro has knocked him unconscious with a frying pan and concealed the contraband weapons under the bed. But this slapstick comedy routine immediately shifts to the darkest of tragedy as Pina, in defiance of the German soldiers, runs after the truck carrying Francesco away. We hear a burst of machine-gun fire, Marcello races toward his mother screaming, and Pina lies dead in the street, her right leg bared to the garter belt, an image suggesting the obscenity of her unnecessary death. Ironically enough (and Rossellini never misses the opportunity to accentuate a sense of irony), in the next sequence partisans ambush Francesco's truck, and he escapes. Pina's death, like so many others in wartime, was pointless.

Equally unforgettable is the scene at Gestapo headquarters in the Via Tasso, and the sequences there are constructed around the juxtaposition of different moods and techniques. Here the actual structure of the set underscores the film's dramatic theme. It is also important to emphasize that, despite the myth that Italian neorealism avoided studio sets (some film

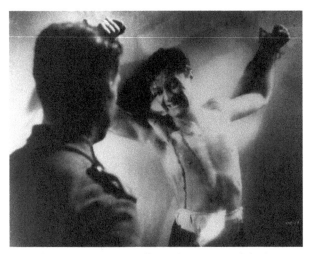

In Rossellini's *Open City*, the Nazi officer Major Bergmann calmly observes the horrible torture of Manfredi, the partisan leader. *Credit: MOMA*

historians claim that this may be explained by the fact that war damage and refugees had made Cinecittà's studios unusable), many of the most memorable parts of this film were shot in four sets that Rossellini had built in the basement of a vacant building on Via degli Avignonesi in downtown Rome. (Today a marble tablet marks the spot for tourists and film buffs.) These sets are Don Pietro's sacristy, Gestapo headquarters, the adjoining torture room, and another adjoining room where the German officers relax between rounds of interrogation. Two doors lead out from the office in which Bergmann questions first Manfredi and then Don Pietro: one opens onto the torture chamber inhabited by ghoulish soldiers whose fingers are stained with blood and who light their cigarettes from the very torch they use on Manfredi with complete indifference to his suffering; another door opens onto the parlor where Bergmann's colleagues relax with music, liquor, and female companionship, oblivious to the human suffering on the other side of the door. Bergmann moves effortlessly among these three locations, and his physical movements (viewed most often from the perspective of Don Pietro, who remains in the central room and peers through each door with difficulty, since his eyeglasses have been damaged) emphasize the emotional distance between their separate worlds.

Manfredi's torture is one of the most horrifying of many such scenes in the history of the cinema. Yet Rossellini achieves this startling impact on his audience not by showing us merely the reality of the torture with minute attention to detailed close-up shots, but rather by exploiting the power of our imaginations and focusing upon the reactions of Don Pietro, nearby. We see Don Pietro's anguished face while voice-overs convey the screams from the other room; our revulsion at this sound is further increased by masterful touches of black humor. While Don Pietro is moved to tears, a German soldier quietly sharpens his pencil and awaits Bergmann's orders without reaction. When Manfredi dies without betraying his cause, Rossellini frames this Communist partisan leader as if he were photographing the crucified Christ, employing the traditional iconography familiar to us all from numerous works of religious art. The lighting of this crucial scene also reflects that stark backlighting associated with German expressionist cinema of the 1930s.

As Manfredi is dying, a drunken Nazi officer (Major Hartmann), listening to the piano in the adjacent salon, argues against Bergmann's view that the Italian partisan will betray his cause. Bergmann believes he will talk because the Germans are a master race—otherwise, what meaning does this war have, he asks. Hartmann remembers that in World War I, French patriots refused to talk under torture as well, and in his drunken stupor, Hartmann seems to be a sympathetic German, a "good" Nazi. Yet, the next morning, when Don Pietro is led to his execution, the same Hartmann, now sober, commands the firing squad, and when the Italian soldiers forced to do the Germans' dirty work aim away from Don Pietro, obviously wanting to avoid killing a priest, it is Hartmann who arrogantly delivers the coup de grâce with his sidearm. Rossellini's concluding shots in *Open City* accentuate the religious tone of the entire film: Romoletto, Marcello, and the other children walk away from the priest's execution and are followed by the panning camera that sets them, Italy's future, against the backdrop of the dome of Saint Peter's Cathedral. Out of a moment of tragic despair, Rossellini creates a vision of hope from the first of the many symbolic images associated with children that will characterize many of the great neorealist classics.

Paisan

The melodramatic plot of *Open City* aims to manipulate its audience with different moods (now comic, now tragic) and presents obviously stereotypical protagonists (good Italians, bad Germans). In spite of the fact that this film marks the beginning of the neorealist era, Rossellini's first international success must, in retrospect, be considered a relatively traditional melodrama, both in terms of style and content, rather than an attempt to create a new film realism. To a far greater extent, Rossellini's next film, *Paisan*, reflects the conventions of newsreels documentaries, even though it too goes beyond the mere statement of facts or depictions of actual events. It is also one of the most original of neorealist works in terms of style. Its episodic organization revolves around a step-by-step narrative of the Allied invasion of Italy, beginning with the early landings in Sicily and moving successively to the occupation of Naples; to a moment six months after the

liberation of Rome; to the struggle between Fascists and partisans for control of Florence; to the visit of three American chaplains to a monastery at
Porto Tolle, in the Apennines; and finally to the capture of Italian partisans
and their American advisors in the Po River Valley. The film also exploits
many of the conventions of wartime documentaries of the 1940s (conventions that many postwar critics confused with realism): pincer movements
on a map, an authoritative narrative voice-over, and actual newsreel footage
introduce each of the six episodes, as if this were an army training film.
Made when the rubble of the destruction was still visible in Italian cities,
much of the film's photography retains the grainy quality and the immediacy of subject matter we associated with the newsreels no longer shown
in our movie theaters but that at the time were the equivalent of the evening
television news on network or cable television for us today.

Nevertheless, Rossellini's true subject is not merely a realistic view of
the Allied invasion. Instead, he aims at a more philosophical theme—the
encounter of two alien cultures, Italian and American. This encounter on
the screen had already taken place culturally during the last Fascist period,
and would continue in the first decade after 1945: Italian intellectuals had
already come to grips with American writers, and now real Italians would
meet real Americans and greet them as their liberators. The results of this
fateful juncture in history are shown in brief, individual vignettes set against
a backdrop of the Italian landscape, itself one of the main protagonists of
the film. The meeting of two different worlds involves a variety of problems subtly treated by Rossellini, such as linguistic communication or its
frequent breakdown, as well as empathy or antipathy between alien cultures
and peoples. The film's Italian title—*Paisà*, a colloquial form of the word
paesano (countryman, neighbor, kinsman, even friend)—was typically used
by Italians and American soldiers as a friendly form of address, and the
implications of its deeper meanings provide the basis for Rossellini's exploration of the Italian-American encounter.

Little indication exists that any basis of comradeship is possible between
the two groups as the film opens in Sicily. The Sicilians are suspicious and
afraid of the GIs even though one American's parents came from Gela, a
nearby town. The Americans are rightly dubious of the Italians' intentions.
After all, Italy and Germany are allied, and they have just been fighting
German and Italian troops in North Africa. The Americans call the Italians
"Eye-ties," not necessarily a friendly form of address. One of the townspeople, a young girl named Carmela (Carmela Sazio), however, volunteers to
lead the Americans through a minefield. Most of this first episode focuses
upon an incomprehensible conversation between Carmela, who speaks no
English, and Joe from Jersey (Robert Van Loon), who speaks no Italian, not
to mention Sicilian dialect. Despite the ensuing linguistic comedy of errors
("shooting star" versus *stella cadente*, "home" versus *come*), they reach an

understanding that transcends language barriers; but when Joe uses his Zippo lighter to show Carmela a photograph of his sister, its flame attracts a German's sniper's bullet, and he is mortally wounded. Carmela seizes Joe's carbine, and Rossellini sets her in a series of scenes that disorient and puzzle us, rendering perfectly the feeling of nighttime combat. Joe's friends return and find his corpse. Unaware that Carmela has attacked Joe's killers, they mistakenly blame his death on the girl ("Why, that dirty little Eye-tie!"). As Carmela is cursed by Joe's companions, the final shot of the episode shows her dead body sprawled on a rocky cliff, with German soldiers who had killed her looking down on her corpse, the result of her attempts to avenge Joe from Jersey. Rossellini's first vignette of an attempt to cross cultural boundaries in the conversation between Joe and Carmela ultimately results in the death of both characters.

Shifting to Naples in the second vignette, Rossellini portrays the disastrous effects of war upon this ancient city through the story of an African American and a young boy named Pasquale (Alphonsino Pasca) who "buys" the black soldier, Joe (Dots Johnson), while he is drunk on leave in order to steal whatever he can from him—a common occurrence in wartime Naples under the American occupation. Irony rather than realism is once again Rossellini's vehicle as he shows a member of a defeated nation literally purchasing a black man, the descendant of former slaves who has paradoxically been sent to Italy to liberate the very Neapolitans who now buy him. The irony shifts to a comic tone when Pasquale and the drunken Joe enter a puppet show featuring the traditional plot of a battle between the white Christian knights and their enemies, the black Moors, an entertainment familiar to every Italian but probably not a common sight to American soldiers. In his drunken state, mistaking this puppet show for reality, Joe leaps up on the stage and tries to assist the Moorish puppet against his white opponents. He is ejected from the theater for his foolish confusion of illusion and reality. While Joe's grotesque attempt to sort out these two vastly different realms of human experience fails, Rossellini also implicitly reminds us that the story he tells is composed of equal amounts of fact and fiction.

Not long afterward, Joe dreams of a triumphant return to America as a war hero, complete with ticker-tape parades; but as he sobers up, his joy turns into despair, since he realizes that as a black man in the America of the 1940s, he is little better off than the starving street urchins of Naples: "Goin' home! Goin' home! I don't want to go home! My house is an old shack with tin cans at the doors!" As Joe falls asleep, a moment for which Pasquale has been waiting, Pasquale steals his boots. Rossellini then fades out to a moment three days later: Joe, now driving his jeep and dressed as a military policeman, runs into Pasquale and picks him up for stealing Allied goods, and only later recognizes him as the boy who took his boots. He forces the child to go home to recover them, but he discovers that Pasquale's

In the Roman sequence of Rossellini's *Paisan*, Fred fails to recognize
Francesca, the tough prostitute he sleeps with on leave, as the young
and innocent girl he met earlier, on the day that Rome was first liberated.
Credit: CSC

home is actually a filthy cave teeming with poverty-stricken Neapolitans.
Pasquale's parents have been killed in an Allied bombing raid. The black
soldier, astonished at the level of misery and misfortune he has witnessed,
far beyond anything back in America among the poorest of his race, drops
his boots and turns away. Rossellini's subjective shots of this scene from
Joe's perspective tell the story of his empathy for his fellow sufferers more
eloquently than any spoken commentary. Joe has taken the first step, that of
understanding, toward becoming Pasquale's *paisà*.

A number of documentary clips showing the Allied liberation of the
Eternal City and the departure of German troops from Rome opens the third
part of the narrative. History quickly yields to fictional invention, however,
as Rossellini's camera dissolves to a moment six months later: a prostitute
named Francesca (Maria Michi) picks up a drunken American tank man
named Fred (Gar Moore) who knows a bit of Italian, just as she has learned
rudimentary English. When she takes him to bed, his cynical remark that
"Rome's full of girls like you" leads him to recall the more innocent days
during the liberation of Rome when everything seemed possible and when
"girls were all happy and laughing and fresh, full of color, beautiful. . . . And
now it's all different. You should've seen the one I knew—her name was
Francesca. . . ." With this remark, Rossellini dissolves to a flashback showing how Fred and Francesca actually met six months earlier, although the
drunken Fred has not recognized the girl he met on the day of liberation.
The intervening economic crisis has forced Francesca, and so many other

Roman women, onto the streets to keep from starving. The camera again dissolves back to the bedroom, and while Fred sleeps, Francesca leaves her address with the madam and hurries home to prepare for the renewal of hope in the future she feels will result from a union between them after she transforms herself from the prostitute she has become back into the innocent young girl of Fred's memory. While she waits for him in vain in the rain, Fred awakens sober, unaware that he has his ideal within his reach, and when the madam gives him Francesca's address, he throws it away, remarking bitterly that it is only the address of a whore. The entire sequence is an ironic commentary on the hope and optimism that *Open City* had expressed only a year earlier. The melodramatic plot of this particular sequence, introducing the perennial male fantasy of the whore with a heart of gold, and the uncharacteristic flashback undercutting the documentary style opening the sequence, play upon the conventions of fiction rather than documentary realism to create a moving portrait of the corruption and unhappiness that follow in the wake of military victory.

The fourth, Florentine episode stands in sharp contrast to the failure of a love story to reach its fulfillment in the Roman episode. Fred had spoken broken Italian, and his efforts to bridge the cultural gap between his culture and Italy ended disastrously; but here the American nurse Harriet (Harriet White), who had previously spent several years in Florence, speaks Italian fluently, and had also been the lover of a painter named Guido Lombardi, who has now become a partisan leader with the nom de guerre Lupo, or "Wolf." Hearing that he may be wounded, Harriet races away from her hospital and, with another partisan, crosses the Arno River through the Vasarian Corridor leading from the Palazzo Pitti to the Uffizi in search of her former lover. Nowhere else in *Paisan* does Rossellini capture so perfectly the sense of the historical present. The three earlier episodes clearly juxtapose the main storyline of their episodes to the newsreel clips preceding them, but here, with Rossellini's highly mobile camera and the grainy film stock he employs, everything seems to be filmed as if it were actually unfolding before us as historical and film time merge. After braving German bullets (part of the city on the northern side of the Arno River is still occupied by Germans and their Fascist sympathizers), Harriet learns that her former lover has died. Her pain and commitment stand in opposition to the aloofness demonstrated by two British officers who sit on a hill peering through binoculars at Giotto's Bell Tower, both oblivious to the human suffering all around them. Once again, an attempt to bridge the gap between two cultures ends in death and unhappiness.

Rossellini's fifth story, the most enigmatic of the entire film, takes place in a northern Italian monastery in the Apennines. Scripted by Federico Fellini, it represents an interlude from the war raging elsewhere: three American chaplains (one Catholic, one Protestant, and one Jew) visit a place that seems to have remained unchanged since the discovery of America. The Catholic, Captain Martin (William Tubbs), informs the monks that he has not yet converted his fellow chaplains to the Catholic faith, and his hosts begin to fast so that God may provide salvation for these two "lost souls." Martin, who speaks Italian well and must certainly have studied in Rome before the war's outbreak, reacts to their insensitivity and intolerance in a manner unlike that which we might expect. He delivers to the monks a brief speech that is incomprehensible to his two comrades and is no doubt puzzling to the average American spectator:

> I want to tell you that what you've given me is such a great gift that I feel I'll always be in your debt. I've found here that peace of mind I'd lost in the horrors and the trials of the war, a beautiful, moving lesson of humility, simplicity, and pure faith.

The puzzling intent of this speech causes us to question its significance: are the monks religiously intolerant and full of bigotry for wishing to convert the Protestant and the Jew? Or does their naive desire to save the guests they obviously like and admire represent an object lesson in Christian love of one's neighbor? In subsequent films within the next decade scripted by Fellini for Rossellini, Rossellini's cinema will explore the meaning of Christian faith in such controversial works as an episode entitled *The Miracle* (*Il miracolo*) from a two-episode film, *Ways of Love* (*L'amore*, 1948), or his *Europe '51*, a.k.a. *The Greatest Love* (1952), the story of a rich woman (Ingrid Bergman) who attempts to practice her Christian faith and is put into an insane asylum for her trouble, since her earnestness troubles her friends and relatives. Here in the monastery episode, Rossellini underlines the vast gulf that separates the two cultures represented by the Italian monks and their American guests.

The sixth and final part of *Paisan* brings together a number of elements from the other five episodes. Dale (Dale Edmonds), an American liaison officer with the partisans, is directly involved in the daily no-quarter-given struggle between the partisans and the Nazi soldiers, and his command of spoken Italian emphasizes his complete integration into this joint struggle. Rossellini employs the camera brilliantly to portray the circumscribed world of the partisans from their subjective perspective: the camera stays low just as the partisans crouch beneath the reeds along the riverbanks to avoid detection by the Germans. Thus we share, in Bazin's brilliant description of this technique, "the exact equivalent, under conditions imposed by the screen, of the inner feeling men experience who are living between the sky and the water and whose lives are at the mercy of an infinitesimal shift of angle in relation to the horizon."[17] Rarely has such a simple cinematic technique so movingly rendered a subjective human emotion. The story concludes on a note of desperation and despair rather than of hope. The

Germans capture Dale and the partisans, and while they intend to respect the Geneva Conventions with the Allied soldiers in uniform, they mercilessly execute the partisans by tying their hands behind them and pushing them into the Po River to drown. When Dale rushes forward to protest, the Germans shoot him as well. The last image we see as the film concludes is a floating partisan, and a voice-over informs us "this happened in the winter of 1944. At the beginning of spring, the war was over."

The brutality, the broken dreams, the corruption, and the compassion associated with the Italian campaign are all provided for us by Rossellini's presentation of the "facts" of the Allied invasion. But these facts do not explain the film's greatness. The confrontation of two alien cultures, that of the Old World being rescued by the New, has been marked by errors, failures of understanding, ambiguity, and, ultimately, tragedy. And yet from this pessimistic story Rossellini creates a moving testament to the human spirit. In the beginning, Joe from Jersey died on Sicilian soil by accident, unable to understand Carmela and the people for whom he sacrifices his life. At the end of the film, Dale sacrifices his life for his Italian companions and becomes one of them, a *paisà* who is a kinsman to all those who suffer to create a better world. He belongs to the same moral universe as Don Pietro of *Open City*, for he shows that the value of man's life derives from love for his fellow man, a Christian notion that transcends all the feeble intellectual attempts to comprehend or to communicate by rational means alone. Ultimately in *Paisan*, linguistic barriers, so brilliantly portrayed in the film, fall in the face of moral commitment.

Traditional definitions of Italian neorealism have always stressed its effective use of nonprofessional actors and actual, nonstudio locations. While it is clear that *Open City* does not really follow this "rule," since almost all of its protagonists were played by actors with extensive theatrical experience and the most important interior locations were actually constructed sets, in *Paisan* Rossellini remains far closer to traditional definitions of neorealism than he did in the first part of the "war trilogy." This aspect is evident first of all in the physical settings that encompass the film's action. The rubble of a bombed-out Naples in the second episode, for instance, speaks far more eloquently of the misery that followed the liberation of that city than any reconstructed movie set probably could. And the last sequence in the Po Valley, shot among the shallow inlets and canals lined with reeds and aquatic plants, represents one of the most intelligent uses of an outside location in all of neorealist cinema. In another textbook example of selecting neorealist locations, Rossellini and Fellini arranged to film bar scenes (where the American soldiers meet Italian prostitutes) from the second, Roman sequence in one of the city's best-known dives, employing some twenty actual GI's and some thirty so-called *segnorine* (the spelling comes from the Roman-dialect pronunciation), or prostitutes, who, like the female protagonist in the episode, were all forced into a life on the streets as a result of the economic destruction in the aftermath of the war. In such instances, the fact that Rossellini went to the precise physical location of his fictional story greatly enhanced the credibility of his work. Elements such as these would seem to comply with the classic neorealist dictum of taking the camera out into the streets to photograph reality. Still, other locations have been so artfully contrived that they have succeeded in deceiving critics and viewers of the film for years. One recent and comprehensive study of Rossellini's work, for example, claims that only in the monastery sequence does the director "cheat,"[18] since he filmed this segment in Maiori along the Amalfi Coast rather than in the Apennine Mountains between Florence and Bologna. The film, however, contains numerous other examples of artificially reproduced locations in the film. The Sicilian episode, for instance, is not shot near Catania in Sicily, where the events supposedly take place, but on the same coastline near Amalfi where the fifth sequence was filmed.[19] And when American tanks arrive to liberate Rome, the scene is actually shot in Livorno rather than in the capital city because only in that port city were American tanks available for use in the scene.[20] Many of the interior locations supposedly shot in Florence for the fourth part of the narrative were actually done in Rome on Via Lutezia, near the home of the aunt of Giulietta Masina (1921–94), Fellini's wife.

Rossellini's technique in choosing locations represents a mixture or medley, combining authentic locations that preserve the local color of a precise geographical spot with artfully contrived locations so similar to the real thing that they have succeeded in fooling the critics for years. This same hybrid quality, blending actual documentary footage with footage shot by Rossellini as if it were documentary footage, and authentic locations intermingled with re-created locations hardly distinguishable as such, is continued in the selection of the actors who portray the protagonists of this vast historical drama played out over the entire Italian peninsula. Few viewers of *Paisan* have failed to be impressed by the incredibly moving performances of a number of nonprofessional actors in the film. Rossellini himself has assisted in the creation of a mythology about his nonprofessional actors by describing how he would put his cameraman in the middle of a town square where he planned to shoot and would wait for the curious to gather, from whom he selected faces that interested him.[21] In the first Sicilian sequence, for example, the young Italian girl playing Carmela was discovered by Rossellini from his moving automobile as she was carrying water on her head in a small town near Naples,[22] and Robert Van Loon, her American counterpart playing Joe from Jersey, was a real GI. The Neapolitan street urchin, Pasquale, was, of course, not a professional actor, nor were the Franciscan monks, nor most of the partisans in the Florence and Po Valley narratives. In fact, in both of the partisan episodes, Rossellini questioned those who had actually lived the events he was about to film, and in the final sequence Cigolani was an authentic partisan leader who played himself in the film. Still, it is completely inaccurate to credit the film's realistic feel solely to the impact of its nonprofessional actors. On the contrary, the well-documented history of the film's production provides ample proof that Rossellini and his producer were quite eager to have American actors in the cast. Fellini has often recounted the amusing story of how the film's producer, Rod Geiger, promised Rossellini a number of major Hollywood stars, including Gregory Peck, Lana Turner, and Paul Robeson, only to disappoint them when he arrived in Naples on a transatlantic steamer with a series of unknowns in tow: Dots Johnson (the black soldier in Naples): Gar Moore (the American tank man in Rome), Harriet White (the nurse in love with the Florentine partisan), Bill Tubbs (the Catholic chaplain at the monastery), and Dale Edmonds (the liaison officer with the Po Valley partisans).[23] Even though Geiger contests Fellini's entertaining description of the arrival of this troupe of unknown actors, his own version of the story also underlines the interest Rossellini had in bringing authentic Hollywood actors to Italy to work on the film.[24]

Although these Americans were certainly not stars, they were nevertheless professionals with extensive theatrical experience in the United States. And it is instructive to note that in each episode containing large numbers of nonprofessional actors, usually in minor roles, these professionals masterfully portray the crucial parts in each chapter of the narrative. Far more important to the successful completion of the film and to its believable quality of acting was the interplay among screenwriters, director, and the actors (whether professional or not). As an assistant director, Massimo Mida, has pointed out, the script was constantly transformed and modified to suit the various personalities involved in each scene. Thus, in the Naples sequence, the script took shape only after the young street urchin (a nonprofessional) and the imported American black actor Dots Johnson met each other and developed a personal chemistry between their very different personalities.[25] Something similar must have occurred in the fifth sequence in the monastery, where three allied chaplains visit a group of secluded Franciscan monks. The Catholic chaplain is played by a professional actor (Tubbs), but the protestant chaplain was an actual army chaplain, while the rabbi was portrayed by an actual rabbi's army assistant.[26] In almost every instance where critics have traditionally been tempted to explain the film's greatness by its reliance upon "real" sets, actors, or situations, we shall discover, upon closer examination, that there is a far more complex relationship between the technical means Rossellini and his troupe employed and the "reality" they filmed. And this complexity invariably consists in Rossellini's magical combination of elements from the society around him—actual locations, real people, true stories—with the artifice of the traditional cinema: professional actors, re-created sets, invented stories.

Germany Year Zero

Shot amid the rubble of postwar Berlin, in partial imitation of some of the scenes in *Paisan*, Rossellini made *Germany Year Zero* after his first son, Romano, died in 1946, and the film is dedicated to his memory. This tragedy explains why Rossellini turns to a young protagonist, a feature more typical of De Sica's neorealist films. The film opens with an epigraph title (absent from some prints distributed in America) that announces the moralistic perspective of the film: "When an ideology strays from the eternal laws of morality and of Christian charity which form of the basis of men's lives, it must end as criminal madness. . . ." A fade-out immediately follows, moving into a long tracking shot of the bombed-out German buildings accompanied by a newsreel-like voice-over announcing that this film is

> intended to be simply an objective, true-to-life picture of this enormous, half-destroyed city. . . . It is simply a presentation of the facts. But if anyone who has seen the story of Edmund Koeler comes to realize that something must be done . . . that German children must be taught to love life again, then the efforts of those who made this film will have been amply rewarded.

Yet from the moment the director's purpose is announced, his objectivity stands in open contrast to his moralistic message.

Germany Year Zero's plot returns to a more structured, dramatic storyline like that of *Open City* and abandons the episodic collection of cinematic short stories that constituted *Paisan*'s greatest originality. Edmund (Edmund Moeschke), a young boy of fifteen, lives with his sick father; his sister Eva, (Ingetraud Hinze), who consorts with American GIs for money; and his brother, Karl-Heinz (Franz Otto Krüger), a former Nazi soldier hiding for fear of imprisonment. Edmund lacks any real friends or an authentic relationship to his family. Later we learn that he even denounced his own father to the Nazi authorities for trying to keep him out of the Hitler Youth. A former Nazi schoolteacher and an obvious pederast, Herr Enning (Erich Gühne), employs Edmund to sell souvenir records of Hitler's speeches to Allied soldiers. The unreconstructed Nazi ideology he preaches to the young boy—that the weak must die while only the strong should survive—prompts Edmund to poison his sick father in a perverted act of mercy. Lacking any sort of moral code, as the epigraph title suggests at the outset, Edmund resorts to murder and is only dimly conscious of his actions. He then commits suicide by throwing himself off the roof of a building.

In *Germany Year Zero*, Rossellini hovers between objective documentary and moralistic horror story. His camera is much more mobile than in the two earlier parts of his "war trilogy," and its characteristic movement—long, almost obsessively long tracking shots following Edmund through the rubble and debris of the desolate city landscape—portray the moral

Edmund wanders alone amidst the ruins of a bombed-out Berlin in Rossellini's *Germany Year Zero. Credit: CSC*

emptiness of his youthful protagonist by purely external means without recourse to more subjective camera techniques or rhetorical flourishes in the script. Rossellini also continues to introduce the stereotypes he created in *Open City*. With his short pants and carefully combed, straight blond hair, Edmund could be the poster child for National Socialism's Aryan race; his stiff, cadenced manner of walking and erect posture remind the viewer more of a soldier than of a young teenager. The diabolic message his teacher inculcates is linked to his sexual perversity, reminiscent of Bergmann and Ingrid in *Open City*, who were both ethical and sexual deviants.

Edmund's tragedy stems not only from the evil effects of the moral climate that produced Nazi Germany but also from his failure to find an appropriate father figure. Neither his father, nor Herr Enning, nor Hitler, nor the church has provided him with a workable moral code. Perhaps the most chilling moment in the film is created through the simple juxtaposition of sound track and photography: selling an old recording of Hitler's speeches, Edmund demonstrates his wares on a wind-up Victrola, and as Hitler's voice booms out accompanied by the delirious cheers of his followers, Rossellini shows us the rubble of the Reichskanzlei (Reich Chancellery) building, and for a brief moment, it seems that an evil spirit has returned to haunt Berlin. And the legacy of that spirit controls Edmund's mind and emotions. Rossellini's focus on a young boy in *Germany Year Zero* abandons the association he emphasized in *Open City* between the members of a new generation and his hopes for an Italian springtime, a rebirth after the disaster of the war. Clearly the director wonders if Germany will ever succeed in ridding the nation of Hitler's evil heritage.

Vittorio De Sica's "Trilogy of Solitude"

Shoeshine

When Rossellini's "war trilogy" is compared to the three major neorealist classics by De Sica, it becomes abundantly clear that there was no single aesthetic or programmatic approach to society in their films. As André Bazin perceptively wrote, "Rossellini's style is a way of seeing, while De Sica's is primarily a way of feeling."[27] Rossellini's style can be more easily described as a method that constantly explored the boundaries of fact and fiction, illusion and reality, whereas De Sica more frequently injected innovative touches into what are often rather traditional storylines typical of the films he created during the years immediately before the end of the war. Rossellini certainly began his career much closer to the film documentary, after his experiences producing his "war trilogy" and his association with De Robertis. As noted earlier, De Sica began his career as a professional actor and turned to direction in 1940 after becoming one of Fascist Italy's most popular actors and singers.

De Sica's collaboration with the scriptwriter Cesare Zavattini began in 1942 with *The Children Are Watching Us* (1944), and Zavattini scripted De Sica's greatest films after the war's conclusion. Indeed, *Shoeshine* may most accurately be seen as a continuation of some of the characteristics of this earlier work: *Shoeshine* employs the same kind of relatively elaborate screenplay (whereas Rossellini's scripts are somewhat elemental); it employs studio locations quite frequently, perhaps more frequently than Rossellini's neorealist works; and it continues the drama of childhood innocence corrupted by the adult world that De Sica presented so masterfully in *The Children Are Watching Us* and that Rossellini explored in his films as well. Two shoeshine boys—Pasquale (Franco Interlenghi) and Giuseppe (Rinaldo Smordoni)—use their hard-earned money to buy a horse, but they become involved in a black-market scheme because of Giuseppe's older brother and are sent off to a reformatory prison for juvenile offenders, where their friendship is gradually destroyed by the social injustice usually associated with the adult world and authority figures in the film. After an escape, Giuseppe's accidental death (blamed on Pasquale) concludes De Sica's exploration of the tragic impact of the adult world on youthful friendship.

Within this elaborately plotted film, De Sica's camera style incorporates a profound understanding of the aesthetic possibilities of mise-en-scène editing, a style obviously indebted to the French masters of a preceding generation, or to Orson Welles. He constantly employs camera angles or shot placements to underscore the progressive limits imposed upon the freedom of the two children. The credits of the work are superimposed over the set of the children's prison, an ominous hint of future disaster. The opening scene

In De Sica's *Shoeshine*, the faces of Giuseppe and Pasquale in prison
underscore the corruption of youthful innocence by a cruel, adult world.
Credit: MOMA

of the film, shot on an exterior location, is a view of the galloping horse that
represents the ideal of freedom in the film, a gauge against which the rest
of the film should be measured. While on horseback, the children are shot
from a low-angle perspective, one that ennobles their character and gives
them the appearance, as Bazin once noted, of an equestrian statue. When
they pursue their trade shining shoes, however, the same low-angle shot
from their perspective underscores their humble status in the world. The
sense of confinement continues to build with a number of shots through cell
windows that place the two boys in a tight, claustrophobic atmosphere and
restrict their movement. The climactic scene of the film—set outside the
prison and staged not on location (unlike the opening shot of the galloping
horse) but, instead, inside a studio—concludes the sense of confinement as
the aesthetic qualities of the photography merge perfectly with Pasquale's
tragedy. Like Renoir or Welles, De Sica frequently exploits the possibilities
of deep-focus photography to pack a great deal of visual information into
a single shot. His treatment of a prison riot is typical: three visual planes
act to delineate the human drama only implicit in the plot or the dialogue.
In the background in deep focus are the rioting children; the middle plane
contains the boy who will act as a peacemaker between the two shoeshine
boys; and in the foreground stand Pasquale and Giuseppe.

The visual complexity of De Sica's photography combines with a highly
elaborate plot. The story begins and ends with the vision of the horse, a
free spirit whose final escape symbolizes the end of a friendship. Pasquale
betrays Giuseppe in prison, revealing the details of the black-market operation, only because the prison guard fools him into believing that they are

beating Giuseppe with a leather strap. In fact, another boy pretends to scream while a guard feigns the sound of a whipping. In revenge (and not understanding that Pasquale betrayed him only by being tricked into doing so), Giuseppe arranges for the prison director to search Pasquale's cell, where the discovery of a file he has planted there leads to an actual whipping of Pasquale with the real leather belt. When Giuseppe escapes and goes to recover their horse, Pasquale follows, purposely betrays him to the guards, and beats him with yet another leather strap. Trying to avoid the blow of the belt, Giuseppe falls over a bridge to his death. Even the design of the reformatory prison contributes to the exposition of the plot: parallel rows of cells, upon which the two boys walk separately on cat walks over the cells, emphasize their similar but ultimately divergent fates.

In all his early neorealist films, De Sica is even more conscious than Rossellini that his filmed "reality" is a product of cinematic artifice, and the director takes great pleasure in revealing his art to the careful viewer. Inside the prison, an American documentary film reminiscent of the "Why We Fight" series[28] and ironically titled "News of the Free World" is screened, but it is interrupted by a freak accident as De Sica humorously but unmistakably rejects the view that cinema must necessarily reflect the outside world of social reality. Earlier, the prisoners in the courtyard are seen mimicking grand opera just before the dramatic confrontation between Giuseppe and Pasquale, warning the viewer of the melodramatic qualities of what ensues. De Sica always depicts authority figures negatively, rendering the approach of a policeman, for example, by nothing more than his disembodied and advancing legs. But even here, humor is possible. When the authoritarian warden of the prison reformatory slips up and uses the once obligatory Fascist form of address to an underling ("Voi, anzi Lei"), he reveals his true nature, just as surely as an old man does when he instinctively gives the Roman or Fascist salute to the warden while he makes his inspection tour of the premises.

De Sica creates a marvelous work of art employing nonprofessional child actors in the principal roles, a reminder that a brilliant director can combine the most complicated artifice even with inexperienced performers. De Sica stated that his method of directing nonprofessionals was "being faithful to the character," a process that involved a reversal of Hollywood techniques:

> It is not the actor who lends the character a face, which, however versatile he may be, is necessarily his own, but the character who reveals himself, sooner or later, in "that" particular face and in no other ... their ignorance is an advantage, not a handicap. The man in the street, particularly if he is directed by someone who is himself an actor, is raw material that can be molded at will. It is sufficient to explain to him those few tricks

of the trade which may be useful to him from time to time; to show him the technical and, in the best sense of the term, of course, the histrionic means of expression at his disposal. It is difficult—perhaps impossible—for a fully trained actor to forget his profession. It is far easier to teach it, to hand on just the little that is needed, just what will suffice for the purpose at hand.[29]

A consummate actor himself, De Sica was suspicious of the ease with which professionals seemed capable of leaping from one emotion to another.

The Bicycle Thief

De Sica's absolute faith in the expressive powers of ordinary people achieved perfect artistic form in his masterpiece, *The Bicycle Thief*, in which two nonprofessionals fill the leading roles of father and son. (Film historians have tended to consider as apocryphal the often-cited rumor that the Hollywood producer David O. Selznick offered to finance this film if Cary Grant were cast in the leading role as the father—an offer, if actually made, that De Sica wisely refused.) *The Bicycle Thief* continues the mise-en-scène style of *Shoeshine*, combining a number of realistic elements (nonprofessional actors, on-location shooting, social themes) with an extremely complex plot aimed at moving the sympathies of the audience. Once again, De Sica focuses upon the relationships between children and adults. Antonio Ricci (Lamberto Maggiorani), unemployed for two years, finally receives a job as a billposter, but he must have a personal bicycle to keep the job. When his bicycle is stolen, he and his son, Bruno (Enzo Staiola), search all over the city of Rome to find it but are unsuccessful, although the thief is located just after they consult a fortune-teller, called La Santona (Ida Bracci Dorati). In despair, Ricci attempts to steal another bicycle, from among dozens at a soccer match; but he fails miserably and is captured under the eyes of his terrified and humiliated son before being released by the angry crowd at the conclusion of the film.

The Bicycle Thief achieved its realistic texture not by any documentary approach to the storyline or by improvisation, a technique much more acceptable to Rossellini, but by careful, even conventional cinematic planning. The film's budget was a relatively large one, due primarily to the expensive preparations De Sica insisted upon at each stage of the work. All of the many crowd scenes in the film were carefully choreographed: forty market vendors were hired for one scene, and the Roman fire brigade drenched the set to simulate a rainstorm. De Sica selected the nonprofessionals playing Antonio and Bruno because of their particular mannerisms in their walk and facial expressions. In the classic sequence where a group of thieves steal Antonio's bicycle, De Sica employed six different cameras from a variety of angles. Thus, De Sica's direction avoided any kind of improvised work on the set; but he often injects subtle but unmistakable hints into this and other films to remind us that his neorealist films should be construed primarily as works of art—illusions of reality—and not realistic reflections of Italian society. This becomes most obvious in the scene preceding the theft of Antonio's bicycle, a scene as artistically contrived as could be imagined, where the father posts a Rita Hayworth film poster. Here the director reminds us that we are watching a film, not a sociologically correct portrait of Italy in the economic reconstruction of 1948.

It should always be remembered that De Sica defined filmmaking as transposing reality into the realm of poetry, and this approach is precisely what lies at the root of his aesthetics in all his neorealist films. While *The Bicycle Thief* certainly treats many of the pressing social problems of post-war Italy, it is not merely a film on the effects of unemployment; nor will André Bazin's often cited but basically incorrect remarks about the film— that it is "the only valid Communist film of the whole past decade," or that it represents pure cinema with no more actors, sets, or storyline—bear close scrutiny in spite of the fact that no other critic since then has ever written so passionately on De Sica's cinema.[30] The director's careful instructions to the nonprofessional actors in his cast produced a level of acting skill far surpassing the self-conscious nervousness of the nonprofessionals in the films of either Rossellini or Visconti. His scrupulous organization of the on-location shooting differs drastically from a documentary approach to his material. And the complexity of the film's plot negates Bazin's assertion that storyline has disappeared in the work. The mythic structure of *The Bicycle Thief*—a traditional quest—as well as its strange and suggestive sound track and the crucial role of chance or fortune in the film all depart from a strictly realist approach to the story and constitute the very elements of the film that make it a great work of art.

A realist reading of *The Bicycle Thief* must emphasize the film as a politically engaged film combining a presentation of contemporary social problems with an implicit denunciation of a particular socioeconomic system. Closer analysis, however, will reveal that this interpretation is only one of those possible and not even the most persuasive, for De Sica's vision also includes a pessimistic and even fatalistic view of the human condition, as well as a philosophical parable on the absurdity of life, human solitude, and the individual's loneliness in a society composed of equally alienated individuals. Antonio Ricci emerges in the film's opening shot from a crowd at the employment agency. In the deeply moving closing shot, he merges back into another crowd at the soccer match with his small son and disappears. Crowds and masses of people outside Ricci's immediate family always pose threats to him—hardly the proper iconography for a Communist film depicting class-consciousness or proletarian solidarity. When Ricci receives

Father and son face a hostile world alone in De Sica's *The Bicycle Thief* as they search in vain for a stolen bicycle. *Credit: AB*

his job, other unemployed men are more than eager to take the opportunity away from him. When he goes to his union hall to seek help in locating the stolen bicycle, vague offers of assistance are forthcoming, but he receives no actual help from a gathering that understands only collective action, not individual personal tragedy. Crowds waiting for buses threaten him, and the final destruction of his self-respect occurs before the eyes of his son, Bruno, with the hostile crowd that captures him after his attempted theft. This hostile act is in direct contrast to the complete lack of assistance Ricci receives when his own bicycle is stolen. In addition, De Sica shows us bureaucrats, policemen, and pious, churchgoing do-gooders who fail to comprehend Ricci's plight; but the fact that Ricci's fellow workers do not sympathize with him is a devastating revelation. In De Sica's universe, economic solutions are ultimately ineffective in curing what is a meaningless, absurd human condition.

De Sica's carefully contrived visual effects shed light on the hopelessness of Ricci's struggle, not merely on the economic or political aspects of Italian society that have supposedly produced his dilemma. A long, slow tilt of his camera reveals an incredible number of packages of bed linens at the pawnbroker's office when Ricci goes to sell these same materials in order to redeem his pawned bicycle—obviously the hopes of countless other Italians have already been dashed. At the police station, De Sica presents us with an equally infinite number of police dossiers—all unsolved cases like Ricci's. Even more depressing is the masterful sequence at Rome's open market where stolen items are resold to their victimized former owners: the almost endless tracking shots of countless bicycle parts, intercut with the shots of the anxious faces of Ricci or Bruno, lend their efforts a sense of futility worthy of a Kafka novel.[31] Extreme depth-of-field shots accentuate Ricci's sense of isolation. When he searches the thief's home for traces of his stolen bicycle, we see in the background most clearly a neighbor closing her window, as if to cut off all possibility of communication between Ricci and the thief's neighbors. The plot itself, as well as the evocative quality of the sound track, underscores the illogical, irrational nature of Ricci's world. Characters appear, drop out of sight, and reappear again as if by magic: the bicycle thief vanishes with Ricci's vehicle into thin air rather than actually escaping; an old man who knows where the thief lives seems to dematerialize once outside a church; Ricci mysteriously and improbably bumps into the actual thief when he leaves the fortune-teller's home; and finally the man who apprehends Ricci when he turns to stealing appears unexpectedly, almost as if the director had conjured him up by magic. While the music sometimes accentuates our sentimental response to the film, in other cases its mysterious, suggestive tunes—particularly when Ricci unsuccessfully tries to chase the thief at the marketplace—imply that events in the film result from illogical, irrational circumstances, all beyond human control.

Most of such antirealistic elements in De Sica's storyline are associated with the figure of La Santona, the fortune-teller visited at the opening of the film by Ricci's wife to pay her for having predicted that Ricci would find a job. Ricci scoffed at his wife for doing this, claiming that he found the job by himself. De Sica poses the question of Ricci's destiny squarely. Is Ricci really in command of his life, or are sinister forces at work? Time and time again before the theft of his bicycle, Ricci leaves it leaning against various buildings without a lock, and since the Italian title of the film is literally "bicycle thieves" and not just *one* bicycle thief, we should be prepared for impending disaster. Cyclical events abound in the film, perhaps not unexpected in a story about a man chasing two wheels. Ricci at first refuses to believe La Santona's predictions, but later, in despair, he returns to her for help in locating his bicycle and receives this cryptic prophecy: "Either you will find it immediately or you will never find it." This prediction, too, proves accurate, for as he steps outside her home, he runs into the thief.

Film time in *The Bicycle Thief* progresses from Friday to Sunday, a cycle of time with particular resonance in Italian or Christian culture, referring ironically not only to the death and resurrection of Christ but also to Dante's journey through Hell, Purgatory, and Paradise toward salvation. Ricci's bicycle is a brand called Fides (Latin for faith), and Ricci's failure to locate this object is intentionally ironic. The ultimately fatalistic, absurd cycle in the work concerns Ricci himself: a man loses his bicycle and becomes a bicycle thief himself, and an unsuccessful one at that. Yet this primarily pessimistic subplot is combined with another, more sentimental one. While Ricci progressively becomes a thief, his relationship to his son

Bruno gradually changes from one of the son's dependence upon his father to the father's eventual dependence upon his son.

It is no doubt true that social reform and economic development eventually transformed society in the postwar Italy of 1948. Certainly, by a decade after the end of the war, very few Italians would be on the verge of starvation if they lost a bicycle. But no amount of social engineering or even revolution, De Sica seems to imply, will alter the basic facts of life: solitude, loneliness, and alienation of the individual within the amorphous and unsympathetic body of humanity. The only remedy De Sica suggests, one typically Italian, comes from the support and love Ricci receives from his family. No amount of determinism or fatalism can destroy the special relationship between Ricci and Bruno. Psychologically, De Sica's story has only one resolution—the love between father and son. On the level of dramatic plotting, the film achieves a resolution when Ricci's tragedy links to Bruno's touching gesture of solidarity, offering his father his hand before they both disappear into the alien crowd at the film's ending. All the technical expertise De Sica can muster underscores these themes, but seldom has any film of supposedly realistic pretensions been characterized by a more problematic, ambivalent conclusion. On a positive note, Ricci puts his faith in an object, a Fides bicycle; loses it; and only then realizes that his real wealth lies in his son's love, a human emotion. The question of social change is begged at best. Viewed from a pessimistic perspective, however, Bruno's affection changes nothing. Life remains tragic and absurd in spite of it, and Ricci's frantic odyssey through Rome looking for his bicycle ends in the triumph of fate and chance without the possibility of human solidarity or economic change.

Umberto D.

Umberto D. completes De Sica's neorealist "trilogy of solitude." (*Miracle in Milan*, released before *Umberto D.*, represents a special critical problem treated in chapter 4.) It was De Sica's favorite work, produced with his own money, and its disastrous record at the box office was due in some measure to the fact that, in it, the director offered few sentimental concessions to the public's tastes. Yet André Bazin's judgment upon seeing the film when it was released—that it was a genuine masterpiece—has now been generally accepted. The film portrays a brief and traumatic period in the life of a retired pensioner, Umberto Domenico Ferrari (Carlo Battisti), as well as his complex relationship with his pet dog and the young woman in his apartment building. Once again, De Sica's choice and direction of nonprofessional actors is brilliant: he gave the title role to a professor from Florence whose facial expressions and general appearance perfectly capture the mannerisms and the moral values of an older generation. While the film deals courageously with the problem of the aged in modern society, it steadfastly refuses any sentimental resolution. De Sica pictures Umberto D. not as a lovable, jolly old man but as a cross, irritable, and grouchy type, since the director wanted him to have an untidy, unpleasant disposition and to emphasize the point that the aged can be a nuisance to others and sometimes even to themselves. Unlike Ricci, who has at least the protection of a family, Umberto lacks even this comfort, and most of his friends are already dead. There remain only his mongrel dog and Maria (Maria Pia Casilio), a pitiful unwed mother whose plight is even more desperate than Umberto's, for she will lose her position as soon as Umberto's bigoted landlady discovers her condition.

Because Umberto is part of the middle class, his life often revolves around the protection of outward appearances—a clean shirt, proper behavior, and good manners—what the Italians call a *bella figura* in public. As inflation and illness erode his meager pension, Umberto is more afraid of losing face, of appearing poor to others, than of poverty itself. De Sica thus poses a dilemma similar to that posed in *The Bicycle Thief*. Will Umberto's problems be resolved with a mere increment to his pension, or is social reform incapable of curing human solitude? Though exterior locations are important in *Umberto D.* (and De Sica exploits many of the imposing monuments in Rome to set off his protagonist's poverty against their grandeur), the bulk of the interiors were shot in the studios of Cinecittà. Thus, this film is one of the few neorealist classics to depend as much upon the resources of a professional studio as upon on-location shooting. The studio allows De Sica to express himself in a very complex camera and editing style, not typical of most neorealist films. His camera is very mobile: instead of the usual process shots simulating travel in moving vehicles, De Sica brings the camera into city trolleys and taxi cabs. He employs a wide variety of camera angles to emphasize Umberto's disorientation. He frequently shoots through keyholes and at reflections on mirrors for sophisticated visual effects. Even more remarkable are the visual effects achieved through extensive use of deep-focus photography both within studio interiors and outside on location. Umberto's insignificance in Italian society is immediately obvious in De Sica's first scene—an extremely high-angle shot down on a crowd of demonstrating pensioners. The camera's position accentuates their vulnerability, and as police cars sweep them effortlessly off the street because they have failed to request a parade permit, De Sica shows them to us as if they were insects being brushed aside, a visual hint that is reinforced later when the maid scatters a swarm of ants in her kitchen. Older people are simply expendable. In four different locations, the depth of field in his photography goes beyond the simple representation of any "real" spatial distribution of objects, producing a visual correlative of Umberto's loneliness and solitude. The long, empty hall of his apartment projects a sterile, hostile, foreboding atmosphere. The many rows of hungry men eating in

In De Sica's *Umberto D.*, the servant girl visits Umberto in the hospital, providing the director with another opportunity to use his deep focus photography to advantage. *Credit: MOMA*

a charity soup kitchen he frequents, similar to the endless rows of pawned linen in *The Bicycle Thief*, inform us that Umberto is no isolated case but only one of thousands of elderly Italians cast aside by society. The long halls of the hospital with their endless lines of elderly patients suggest the desperation people in De Sica's universe must feel. Finally, the endless rows of trees interspersed with playing children closing the film after Umberto's unsuccessful suicide attempt allow the main characters—the old man and his dog—gradually to merge into the background and out of our vision in a lyrical ending reminiscent of the disappearance of Ricci and Bruno at the end of *The Bicycle Thief*.

   Umberto D. may also be the neorealist film that most closely fits Zavattini's prescriptions for what neorealist cinema *ought* to be, a set of principles outlined most clearly in his often-cited manifesto, translated variously as "A Thesis on Neorealism" or "Some Ideas on the Cinema."[32] Zavattini advocated that neorealist films should respect real time or duration: ninety minutes in a character's life should require ninety minutes of screen time, and a film about the purchase of a pair of shoes should possess as much dramatic potential as the account of a war. Bazin's famous essays on Italian realism in *What Is Cinema?* quite rightly praise two scenes in *Umberto D.*, both of which respect duration: Umberto's retirement to bed, and the maid's awakening in the morning and her work in the kitchen. Each of these scenes, according to Bazin, show Zavattini's concept of duration, where "the real time of the narrative is not that of the drama but the concrete duration of the character . . . the film is identical with what the actor is doing and with this alone."[33] In the maid's sequence, De Sica maintains a perfect coincidence between narrative film time and that of the protagonist: refusing to give any dramatic structure to her mundane activity, respecting every intimate detail of reality equally and making no hierarchical choices among them. The sense of time's duration weighs upon the viewer just as it does upon the maid, and her simple, yet eloquent, gestures require no dialogue whatsoever to tell us all we need to know about the tragedy of her life. De Sica may well have learned something of this technique from an equally celebrated sequence in Visconti's *Obsession*, where an exhausted Giovanna sits in her kitchen (a scene analyzed in chapter 2).

In some respects, the sound track of *Umberto D.* represents a step beyond the style of *The Bicycle Thief.* Umberto's ungrateful, mean-spirited landlady, once kept alive during the war by Umberto's surplus ration coupons, now wants to evict him, and she even rents out his room by the hour to adulterers and prostitutes. Yet, she is such a hypocrite that she will doubtless fire Maria once she realizes the young woman is pregnant out of wedlock. The decor of her apartment, her lover, and her friends all show the landlady's selfishness, superficiality, and venality, and the immoral quali-ties and callous behavior she exhibits are underscored by the sound track, which always associates her with opera heard on a record. She views oper-atic music not as an expression of genuine emotions (something she would be incapable of understanding either in art or in life) but as a means of confirming and improving her social status. Opera, with its refined control of emotion and its theatrical or melodramatic qualities, stands as a coun-terpoint offered by De Sica to the genuine, elemental, and truly pathetic human suffering experienced by Umberto and the maid but completely ignored by the landlady.

The structure of *Umberto D.*'s plot may be compared to the two neo-realist films already examined: the role of Umberto's dog parallels the symbolic qualities of the horse in *Shoeshine* and the bicycle in *The Bicycle Thief.* Umberto's pitiful dog represents a burden willingly assumed by the old man, his only link to life and ultimately the only thing that prevents his suicide. No doubt De Sica was aware that the presence of such an innocent and vulnerable creature would guarantee a sentimental response to his film, just as the presence of children in other films plays upon his audience's emotions. Some critics persist in believing that playing with our emotions in the cinema must conceal some perverse ideological program, one that advocates accepting the status quo without question.[34] As in both *Shoeshine* and *The Bicycle Thief,* each of which employ parallel subplots, De Sica again delineates character in *Umberto D.* by playing the old man's tragedy against that of the maid. Throughout the film, she is his counterpart in suffering, but Umberto rarely understands how similar his or her lives actually are, just as no one else understands his plight. When Maria's negligence allows his dog to escape, Umberto scolds her for her carelessness immediately after she has told her boyfriend about her pregnancy and has been abandoned by him. In his concern for his dog, Umberto remains completely insensitive to Maria's pain, while he expects others to recognize his problems. Human loneliness fails to produce a sense of empathy in De Sica's characters, and as the film concludes, Umberto stands alone with his dog, his problems and his solitude still unresolved. Bazin cleverly remarked that "the cinema has rarely gone such a long way toward making us aware of what it is to be a man. (And also, for that matter, of what it is to be a dog)."[35] De Sica has also shown us in no uncertain terms that there is very little difference between the two conditions.

Luchino Visconti and Verga: *The Earth Trembles*

The discussion of Luchino Visconti's *Obsession* in chapter 2 reveals it as one of the precursors of Italian neorealism. After making *Obsession* Visconti became directly involved in the Resistance against the Germans, aiding escaped Allied prisoners of war behind German lines and concealing partisans in his Roman villa. Attacks on German occupiers of the Eternal City in Rome led to bloody reprisals—including the massacre of 335 Italian hostages at the Fosse Ardeatine on March 24, 1944—and a subsequent roundup of anti-Fascists included Visconti, who, though eventually sentenced to death, later escaped from prison with the assistance of his guards. In the following year, Visconti returned to work in the theater until an American psychological warfare group asked him to film the trials and executions of Pietro Koch and Pietro Caruso, the former being the very man who had interrogated him in prison. Directed by Mario Serandrei (1907–66), who collaborated with Visconti, De Santis, and Marcello Pagliero (Manfredi in *Open City*), *Days of Glory* (*Giorni di gloria*, 1945) became a collective documentary on the Resistance and Italy's liberation. But the young aristocrat had not forgotten his earlier association with the intellectuals on the journal *Cinema*, nor had he completely ignored the advice contained in the early essay by Alicata and De Santis published by *Cinema* in 1941. Entitled "Truth and Poetry: Verga and the Italian Cinema," the essay called for a return to the best realist traditions of Italian literature:

> Our argument leads us necessarily to one name: Giovanni Verga. Not only did he create a great body of poetry, but also he created a country as well, an epoch, a society. Since we believe in an art which above all creates truth, the Homeric, legendary Sicily of *I Malavoglia*, *Maestro Don Gesualdo*, *L'amante di Gramigna*, and *Jeli il pastore* offers us both the human experience and a concrete atmosphere. Miraculously stark and real, it could give inspiration to the imagination of our cinema, which looks for things in the space-time of reality to redeem itself from the easy suggestions of a moribund bourgeois state.[36]

Besides the literary example of Verga, Visconti must certainly have encountered some of the writings of the Marxist theorist Antonio Gramsci, who had focused much of his writing on the problems of Italy's impoverished southern region. Thus, with initial financial backing from the Italian Communist Party, Visconti arrived at the Sicilian fishing village of Aci Trezza, the setting for Verga's *The House by the Medlar Tree*, with the intention of filming a trilogy on a prospective revolution in the Mezzogiorno (the term used to denote the South of the peninsula) brought about by a union of fishermen, miners, and peasants, the kind of national-popular alliance Gramsci envisioned between southern agricultural workers and northern factory workers. The one film he actually completed—*The Earth Trembles* still retaining the subtitle "The Sea Episode" ("Episodio del mare")—was thus only the first part of the project he envisioned.[37]

Visconti employed absolutely no studio sets or sound stages in this film. Special lighting effects were used only during certain difficult night scenes on the sea. The characters were portrayed by the townspeople of Aci Trezza. As a result, *The Earth Trembles* fits many of the traditional definitions of neorealism perhaps better than any other well-known neorealist film besides Rossellini's *Paisan*. Visconti's method of directing the nonprofessionals involved explaining the day's shooting to the villagers, describing the events to be filmed, and soliciting their opinions as to how they would respond in similar circumstances. Their spontaneous reactions were then incorporated into the script, which thus evolved, and the film progressed. Visconti also rejected the usual Italian method of shooting without synchronized sound and dubbing the sound track afterward during editing. Instead, he insisted upon the authentic voices and sounds of the Sicilian environment, and in doing so, he also took a revolutionary cultural stance— one shunned by cinema during the Fascist period, which normally avoided using Italian dialects in favor of a standard Italian. Visconti instead used the dialect of the simple people he filmed, believing that the authenticity of the film would be achieved only if the nonprofessionals expressed themselves in their own language. Because the dialogue seemed incomprehensible to some Italians, he then chose to employ a voice-over, an objective narrative voice in Italian, to provide an often-ironic commentary to the storyline. In places, he also interjected Italian subtitles in place of subtitles in dialect. Two of his young assistants, Francesco Rosi (1922–) and Franco Zeffirelli (1923–), both became directors themselves, although only Rosi seemed to follow Visconti's interest in film realism.

Visconti modifies Verga's novel considerably, moving the focus from the father of the fishing family to his young son, Antonio, called 'Ntoni (Antonio Arcidiacono), who rejects tradition and seeks to better himself by opposing the corrupt middlemen who exploit the fishermen by paying them very little for their daily catch. Verga's novel emphasized a pessimistic fatality and did not leave room for change through social reform in what he depicted as a timeless world unchanged for centuries by history.[38] At 'Ntoni's insistence, the Valastro family mortgages the family home to purchase their own boat and so avoid working for others, but the need to meet the mortgage payments forces them to fish in bad weather, and a storm destroys the boat, resulting in foreclosure on all their real property. The family's attempts to oppose the harsh economic system fail totally, and 'Ntoni must eventually humiliate himself by begging the middlemen for a job as a day laborer on one of their boats.

Visconti's adaptation of Verga's novel is closer to Greek tragedy than to the revolutionary conclusion of the projected Marxist trilogy Visconti originally wanted to film, for that unfilmed story would have ended in the rise of a class consciousness and the growth of proletarian unity among peasants, miners, and fishermen. Visconti's aristocratic aesthetic sensibilities altered Verga's story considerably, and there was never any chance that the northern nobleman would ever produce a piece of mere propaganda for his leftist friends. In spite of his realistic attention to authentic locations, dialect, and the use of nonprofessionals, Visconti's emerging cinematic style in *The Earth Trembles* sometimes contrasts sharply with any purely ideological message.

Aci Trezza's universe is circumscribed completely by the two huge rocks in the harbor, the rocks that, according to ancient legend, Polyphemus the Cyclops hurled toward the fleeing Odysseus. The spot seems outside time or history, except for 'Ntoni's disastrously unsuccessful attempts to bring social reform to it. Visconti's plot also seems to reflect the traditional five-act structure associated with classical tragedy, with the tragic reversal and the downfall of the main protagonist occurring in the conventional place: (1) 'Ntoni first challenges traditional ways of living; (2) he then turns to direct action, first casting the fish merchants' scales into the ocean and creating a riot, leading to his imprisonment and subsequent release when the middlemen realize that they need the fishermen to survive, and this new knowledge leads 'Ntoni to persuade his family to buy the new boat, but their attempts to become entrepreneurs set them apart from the rest of the village; (3) a brief moment of happiness ensues, as the happy family salts anchovies together; (4) disaster strikes at sea, the boat is lost, and the family's last catch is sold for almost nothing, causing the family to disintegrate (one brother leaves home, a sister is dishonored, and 'Ntoni becomes a drunkard); (5) 'Ntoni encounters a young girl by his now abandoned boat, realizes his fatal error in basing his hopes on the traditional family and capitalist entrepreneurship, rather than upon a new sense of class consciousness and unity, and remains hopeful for the future, as he returns to the sea, much as the Valastros have always done, receiving his mother's blessing.

The cyclical, timeless quality of life in Aci Trezza is captured perfectly by Visconti's cinematic style. The director's signature, typically slow panning shots with a stationary camera or long, static shots of motionless objects produces a formalism that is infrequent in documentary film or feature films with realist pretensions. Characters enter into and exit from a carefully controlled frame, the pure aesthetic qualities of which once reportedly moved Orson Welles to complain that Visconti photographed fishermen as if they were *Vogue* fashion models![39] This strange objection, one that would deny beauty to poverty and restrict realism to distasteful objects, has, however, no place in Visconti's homage to the mythical dimensions of the fishermen's daily struggle to survive. In no other Italian film of the neorealist period does the photography capture the inherent nobility of its subject matter so well as in his unforgettable images of the women, black shawls wrapped about them and beating in the wind, while they wait motionlessly for their men to return from the storm at sea.

More than any other neorealist director except for Vittorio De Sica, Visconti employed extreme depth of field in both exterior and interior shots, and his careful framing of each shot embodies the same mise-en-scène techniques already examined in De Sica's best films. Visconti thus achieves a marvelous sense of open space as he shows us the Valastros' world. One brilliant shot combines the exterior world of the men with the interior female world, as the camera is placed within the dark house with the women but shoots past them through the doorway into a brightly lit exterior. Another shows us the three Valastro men washing and talking in two separate rooms, as the women carry on their activities in different locations: outside

Visconti's *The Earth Trembles* endows images of fishermen's wives waiting for their husbands after a storm at sea with all the dignity of classical sculpture. *Credit: CSC*

the depth of field Visconti captures a rooftop conversation that includes the entire neighborhood. But his use of certain techniques is never predictable: a deep-focus shot during the first part of the film may capture the family's solidarity and unity, whereas the same kind of shot toward the end of the film emphasizes something entirely different—the family's separation and alienation not only from the other villagers but from one another as well.

Visconti's personality may well be the source of some problems in an analysis of *The Earth Trembles*. The descendant of one of Italy's oldest and noblest families (the Visconti were once rulers of Milan in the late Middle Ages and early Renaissance), Visconti himself displays a progressive, if not completely Marxist, ideology in his works that often seems to clash with his obvious love for the beauty he discovers in the very society he condemns. This contradiction is true not only of *The Earth Trembles* but also of his other best-known films: *Senso*, a.k.a. *The Wanton Countess* (1954), *The Leopard* (*Il gattopardo*, 1963); and *The Innocent* (*L'innocente*, 1976), his last film. Even as 'Ntoni delivers his moving speech concerning the need for united collective action ("We have to learn to stick up for each other, to stick together. Then we can go forward."),[40] his tone of self-sacrificial martyrdom is closer to Christian than to Marxist precepts. It is no accident that when he returns to work, his sister puts the family portrait photograph back next to that of the Sacred Heart. Christian and Marxist ideas seem equally appropriate for this timeless world. 'Ntoni casts a pair of "Judas" scales into the sea to protest prices paid for fish, and behind the grinning middlemen we can dimly discern barely erased slogans from Mussolini's Fascist regime. The artist in Visconti triumphs over the party ideologue, however, for the film's storyline and its cinematic style accentuate the cyclical, archetypal quality of life in a mythical, ahistorical world much like that chronicled by the novelist Carlo Levi's *Christ Stopped at Eboli* a few years earlier. The film opens and closes with shots of fishing boats gliding over a glassy sea; they are framed between the gigantic rocks that form the symbolic boundary between Aci Trezza and the world of history and ideology (that is, the world of the North). Daily activities in the fishing village—eating, mending nets, family conversations, courtships, the mother's blessing before going to work—all become part of a timeless ritual, the character of which is emphasized by the extreme length of Visconti's shots, many of which last three to five minutes without a cut. Even the narrative voice-over serves to reinforce the sense of stoic pessimism pervading the film. Rather than a Marxist fable about the necessity of class struggle, Visconti presents an archetypal drama within the structure of the nuclear family, as old, timeless, and compelling a tale as any Homeric ballad.

CHAPTER 4

Exploring the Boundaries
of Neorealism

SUCH NEOREALIST CLASSICS AS THOSE ANALYZED in the preceding chapter captured the spirit of the times in the years immediately following the end of the war in Italy, and their reception abroad helped to establish neorealism as a vital influence upon international cinema. Although they do not reflect a coherent or programmatic style, films made by Rossellini, De Sica, and Visconti are accurately described by film historians as works by auteurs—films bearing the unmistakable signature of a single director's individual stylistic or thematic concerns. Other lesser-known films produced during the same period have a secondary role to play in the history of neorealism. Many examine some of the same problems—the Resistance, the effects of the war upon Italian society, poverty, migration from Sicily, labor unrest, the Mafia, the heavy burden of Italian history. Some drift away from a cinema of realism and may even include a mixture of styles or film genres, moving closer to a traditional kind of commercial cinema that was the very thing neorealist theoreticians such as Cesare Zavattini sought to avoid at all costs. Even when the characters in such films or their surroundings seem recognizably neorealist, they may be situated within a film genre that reminds us more of Hollywood than of Rome. Several were quite popular as well. It would be impossible to assess neorealism's place in Italian film history without reference to these works, for they bear witness to the incredible variety and richness of expression typical of Italian cinema in the decade after the fall of the Fascist regime.

Partisan Films: *Outcry* and *The Tragic Pursuit*

One interesting development grew directly from the partisan struggle and the intellectual ferment centered around *Cinema* and *Bianco e nero*, the two film journals with the greatest impact during the late Fascist period. In

1946–47, the Italian National Partisan Organization (Associazione Nazionale Partigiani d'Italia, or ANPI) produced two interesting neorealist films: *Outcry* (*Il sole sorge ancora*, 1946), by Aldo Vergano (1891–1957), and *The Tragic Pursuit* (*Caccia tragica*, 1947), by Giuseppe De Santis.[1] Even though he was well known as an anti-Fascist, Vergano had worked for many years in the industry with Blasetti and many other commercial directors as a scriptwriter, and he had also fought in the ranks of the partisans himself. *Outcry* was scripted not only by De Santis and Carlo Lizzani but also by the critic Guido Aristarco (1918–96), the future editor of the Marxist journal *Cinema nuovo* who would soon become embroiled in the debates over the "crisis of neorealism" in the mid-1950s. The film focuses upon the rise of political consciousness in a partisan named Cesare (Vittorio Duse) who flees Milan after the fall of Mussolini's regime in 1943 and returns to his hometown of Villavecchia in Lombardy. There he encounters two women symbolizing the different paths Italians would take during the period of 1943–45 when Italy was torn apart by civil war between Fascists and partisans, on the one hand, and open warfare between the German occupiers and the Allied troops moving up the peninsula. Donna Matilda (Elli Parvo) represents the kind of wealthy, middle-class Italian who, according to Marxist views of Fascism, compromised themselves with the regime and with their German allies, and the Germans occupy Villavecchia by headquartering in her villa. Cesare is attracted to Laura (Lea Padovani), who represents the kind of commitment to the anti-Fascist cause that the film's makers espouse. After the German troops execute a number of villagers, the partisans triumph: Cesare and Laura (the hope for a better future) survive, whereas Donna Matilda and Cesare's collaborationist brother Mario (Checco Rissone) are killed. Vergano's depiction of completely evil Fascists and Nazis, on the one hand, and noble partisans, on the other, recalls the stark and stereotypical dichotomy between good and evil figures in Rossellini's *Open City*, and the film's major themes—the clash between social classes in the aftermath of the war, plus hatred toward the only recently defeated Germans—are not surprising in a work commissioned by former partisans.

Credits for *The Tragic Pursuit* underscore the impact of *Cinema* upon De Santis's work, for scriptwriters include several ex-contributors to Vittorio Mussolini's review (Michelangelo Antonioni, Gianni Puccini, and De Santis himself) plus Carlo Lizzani, the neorealist novelist Corrado Álvaro, and Umberto Barbaro from the Centro Sperimentale. Once again, the development of a leftist cinema in postwar Italy owes much to the left-wing Fascist intellectuals associated with Benito Mussolini's son or institutions created by Mussolini's regime. The film's plot concerns the theft of funds raised by a peasant collective in the Po River Valley (the subject of a famous *Cinema* essay in 1939 by Antonioni, "Concerning a Film about the River Po").[2] Bandits stop a truck carrying the money along with a newly married

couple—Michele (Massimo Girotti) and Giovanna (Carla Del Poggio (1925–
2010)—and kill the driver and the accountant carrying the four million lire
destined to pay for the farmland, livestock, and farm machinery that hundreds of peasants have put together. Michele recognizes one of the bandits,
Alberto (Andrea Checchi), as a friend with whom he was interned by the
Nazis in a German labor camp (they both have tattoos on their arms with
swastikas as a result), and the bandits kidnap Giovanna to force Michele to
allow them to escape. Michele has an affair with Daniela, called Lilì Marlene
(after the famous German song that became the war's most popular ballad)
because she has been a collaborationist during the war.

The entire film focuses upon the pursuit by Michele and the peasants
of these bandits holding the money and Giovanna, and in the process De
Santis underscores the very different ideals of the two groups—those who
work for the collective good to change the world for the better and those
who are compromised with the former Fascist regime (the landowners who
have hired the bandits to ruin the farmers), or who have collaborated with
the Germans (particularly sexual collaboration, as in Daniela's case). What
is most remarkable about De Santis's film is that it presents a hybrid style
combining elements of Italian neorealism (real locations in the Po River
Valley, hundreds of minor characters played by obviously real peasants, the
themes of wartime collaboration and courage) with stylistic touches usually identified with Hollywood films. It also skillfully combines the work of
highly professional actors and actresses, playing the main characters in the
film, with very-well-managed performances by the nonprofessionals that
typify many neorealist works. The very first shot is a close-up of Michele
and Giovanna kissing on the back of the truck, but De Santis's camera
cranes up and away from the pair to reveal a larger view (one of his favorite
camera movements). He is particularly adept at using this kind of camera
movement to set off the professional actors, such as those playing the new-
lyweds, against the mass of nonprofessional peasants, and the depiction of
the crowd scenes recalls not only Soviet cinema but also such American
directors as King Vidor (1894–1982), whose *Hallelujah!* (1929) De Santis
has always cited as one of the major influences on his cinema.

The "tragic pursuit" of the bandits results in the recovery of the money
but also, somewhat surprisingly, the redemption of Alberto, who kills
Daniela, rather than allowing her to massacre the peasants who have come
to arrest them, by touching off an unexploded German minefield. At the
end of the film, popular peasant justice (and not the institutionalized justice of a new democratic regime that has too many links to its Fascist past)
spares Alberto because he did not have the advantages of a collective, such
as the group of peasants, with whom he could work. (In an act of acceptance
and inclusion, they toss earth at Alberto's feet.) Much of the power the film
possesses comes from the immediacy of its subject matter. The scenes in the

In *The Tragic Pursuit*, by De Santis, partisans administer a revolutionary brand of justice to the bandits. *Credit: CSC*

Po region are all too real: mines are still being exploded in order to cultivate the fields. The peasants rowing their shallow-bottom boats with shotguns slung across their back in pursuit of the bandits cannot help but recall the doomed partisans in the Po River Valley episode of Rossellini's *Paisan*, just as the desperate passions that motivate the guilty Daniela and Alberto remind us of the sordid and tragic love affair from Visconti's *Obsession* (to whose script De Santis contributed a great deal) that unfolds in the same geographical region. The mood of the film also recalls the actual events dominating Italian history at the time of the film's release, since it appeared only three days before the dramatic 1948 election in Italy that saw the hopes for a leftist victory dashed and the victory of the Christian Democrats, who dominated Italian politics until almost the end of the twentieth century.[3] The film's makers obviously supported the National Front of the Left in this election, and a number of important scenes in the film show various groups of veterans and peasants demonstrating their support for this political point of view.

Antonioni's Short Documentary *Sanitation Department*

Before the war, Antonioni's essays and reviews for *Cinema* had already established him as one of Italy's most important young film critics. His essay on the Po River led to his first documentary short, *The People of the Po Valley* (*La gente del Po*, 1943), but much of the film was damaged during the war and only partially salvaged for a 1947 release.[4] He also worked as a scriptwriter with a number of major directors, including Rossellini on *A Pilot Returns* and De Santis on *The Tragic Pursuit*. Between 1947 and 1950, he produced five brief documentary short films, of which *Sanitation*

Department (*N.U.* [for *Nettezza urbana*], 1948)—a brief, eleven-minute treatment of Roman *spazzini* or street sweepers—is the most original. Judging from its plot and its documentary genre, the film would seem to have its immediate origins in the neorealist interest in capturing current events and exploring the drama in the everyday lives of ordinary people. Indeed, a summary of the plot—the depiction of the banal events in the single working day of these humble city employees—sounds like just the sort of theme Zavattini's theoretical essays proposed. Yet whereas De Sica or Zavattini would uncover drama or even tragedy underneath the mundane affairs of the common people, Antonioni's style dedramatizes their lives with the abstract quality of its beautiful photography. The terse voice-over introducing the work only informs the audience that Rome's street cleaners are hardly noticed by their fellow citizens. After this comment, the film offers no further dialogue, setting quite a different mood than the often rhetorical flourishes or ideological pronouncements contained in the voice-overs of Rossellini's *Paisan* or Visconti's *The Earth Trembles*. The only other commentary provided comes from the musical sound track that juxtaposes modern jazz by Giovanni Fusco (1906–68) with classical music by Bach. The music underlines the sense of solitude captured by the camera, which dispassionately follows the *spazzini* from the time they awaken in the morning until they complete their work and return home. Antonioni resolutely refuses any development of a narrative storyline or semblance of plot from the material his camera treats. He simply records the disconnected occurrences in these humble lives without comment, creating with the rhythm of his editing and the mood of the jazz music a tone poem on loneliness, an abstract photographic vision of a world divided between two categories of people—those who pick up trash and those who throw it away. Particularly in his long shots capturing the "dead time" of his subjects, Antonioni seems indebted to Visconti's languorous film style in *Obsession*, but his dispassionate treatment of his subject matter already separates Antonioni from most neorealist films of this era and announces, in this brilliant work, the direction the evolution of his film style would take in his greatest films of the late 1950s and early 1960s, which relate characters so integrally to their landscapes.

Luigi Zampa's *To Live in Peace* and the Comedy of War

Most neorealist films approached the war and the partisan struggle with seriousness and even reverence, treating it as a tragedy. *To Live in Peace* (*Vivere in pace*, 1947), by Luigi Zampa (1905–91), does exactly the opposite, depicting the war as a comic farce. Not frequently shown today, it nevertheless won the New York Film Critics Circle Award for Best Foreign Film in 1947 and chronicles the tranquil life of a remote Italian mountain village and how the desire of its inhabitants to live in peace is disturbed

Drunken enemies celebrate what they think is the end of the war in Zampa's *To Live in Peace. Credit: MOMA*

by the appearance of two escaped prisoners of war: Ronald (Gar Moore), a journalist who eventually hopes to write a "true" account of the war, and Joe (John Kitzmiller), a black GI. Uncle Tigna (Aldo Fabrizi), a kindly peasant, helps the two American escapees, and an Italian deserter named Franco (Piero Palmarini) eventually marries his daughter, Silvia (Mirella Monti). The effects of the war seem far away and all goes well until Hans (Heinrich Bode), the single German soldier in the village—a simple peasant like Tigna—drops by the farmhouse while the group is eating, forcing the Americans and the deserter to hide. The German drinks too much wine, while Joe, downstairs in the cellar, does the same. Joe becomes violent, breaks down the cellar door, and in a magnificent scene of comic relief, confronts Hans, but instead of shooting each other, they stare, then embrace, and eventually everyone dances the "boogie-woogie" to Joe's jazz trumpet solo. Afterward, Joe and Hans stagger out arm in arm and announce to the entire village that the war has ended, shooting out streetlights and touching off a wild celebration. When everyone sobers up the next morning, they soon discover that the war continues. Hans remembers seeing escaped Allied soldiers, calls his superiors on the telephone, then has a change of heart and begs Uncle Tigna to help him desert; but as he is taking civilian clothes from Tigna's clothesline, other Germans arrive and shoot him as a deserter. As Tigna dies in his bed, surrounded by friends and relatives, Joe arrives with the advancing Allied soldiers and announces that the war really has ended in the tiny village.

Except for its wartime theme and its use of authentic locations, *To Live in Peace* stands closer in style to traditional Italian comedy than to Italian neorealism. Zampa takes the material developed tragically by Rossellini's

Open City or *Paisan* and turns it into a tragic farce. While Rossellini's Berg-mann was an evil genius and a sexual deviate, Zampa's Hans remains a stock character from traditional *commedia dell'arte*, the braggart soldier, his dignity undercut every time he appears on the screen by the musical accompaniment of the first bars of "Deutschland über alles." And although the narrative voice-over that introduces and closes the film insists that the events depicted actually occurred and were not invented, Zampa's comic style avoids any documentary realism. Uncle Tigna embodies many of the positive qualities of Rossellini's partisan priest Don Pietro from *Open City*—and is, in fact, played by the same actor. (And the same American actor who appeared as Fred in the Roman episode of *Paisan* plays Zampa's journalist, Ronald.) Perhaps most important is the fact that the message of human brotherhood André Bazin found to be characteristic of all neorealist works is present in the absurd view of warfare Zampa portrays and in his forthright stance against war's brutality and senseless killing.

From War Themes to Postwar Social and Economic Themes

Lattuada's *The Bandit* and *Without Pity*

Neorealist films focused not only on the impact of the war but on serious social problems in Italian culture (such as the Mafia) or the disastrous eco-nomic conditions that existed between the end of the war and the begin-nings of Italy's economic "miracle" in the mid-1950s. A group of important neorealist films shows this shift in focus: Alberto Lattuada's *Without Pity* (*Senza pietà*, 1948); De Santis's *Bitter Rice*; and *In the Name of the Law* and *The Path of Hope* (*Il cammino della speranza*, 1950), both by Pietro Germi.[5] These films are also important, for they show a gradual move closer to conventional and even typically American film genres or themes. Lattuada's first postwar film, *The Bandit* (*Il bandito*, 1946) deals with the role violence plays in Italian society and reminds the viewer of the conventions of the film noir or gangster film from Hollywood. Ernesto (Amedeo Nazzari), just returned from a POW camp to a Turin that still suffers damage from the bombings, learns that his mother is dead. He follows a prostitute into a brothel and is horrified to discover that it is his sister, Maria (Carla Del Poggio, Lattuada's wife), who has been forced into selling herself to survive. Ernesto kills her pimp and must flee from the police. He is attracted to the seductive Lidia (Anna Magnani), who turns out to be a gang leader herself, and she eventually turns on him and gives him over to the police.

The links between *Without Pity* and American models (film noir, the gangster film) are even more obvious. The focus on criminality in *The Bandit* continues in *Without Pity*, but the setting changes from the gritty industrial city of Turin to the port city of Livorno, which became the center for black-marketing activities associated with the American occupation of Italy and was also quite naturally a center of prostitution designed to service the Allied troops who embarked there. The cast and crew of this film bring together a number of important names in postwar Italian cinema: it was scripted by Tullio Pinelli (1908–2009) and Federico Fellini; Nino Rota, later more famous for the *Godfather* theme music and for scores for most of Fellini's films, contributed the music; and Fellini's wife, Giulietta Masina, plays a prostitute. *Without Pity* treats a daring plot for the time: an interracial love affair between a black GI named Jerry (John Kitzmiller) and an Italian prostitute named Angela (Carla Del Poggio). The film's opening information title underlines the mixture of melodrama and realism that characterizes Lattuada's hybrid form of neorealist attention to social problems and Hollywood genres:

> This is a story not of two races but of two people who met in Italy after the war. Men and women had forgotten compassion and abandoned tenderness in their desperate struggle for survival. But there was pity and devotion in the heart of one GI. This is his story.

By focusing upon a black GI, Lattuada is able to contrast American racism with Angela's affection for Jerry while, at the same time, showing that America's influence upon postwar Italy has not been all positive and is also a corrupting force. Angela first meets Jerry in a boxcar after he has been wounded in the line of duty as a military policeman. Although she obtains medical assistance for him, other American policemen take her for the gunman's accomplice, arrest her, and send her off with a truckload of prostitutes even after they learn of her innocence, merely because they do not wish to bother with the necessary paperwork to clear her name and to keep her from being branded falsely as a criminal.

Criminal activities in Livorno are controlled by a sinister character named Pier Luigi (Pierre Claudé), whose effeminate mannerisms and pure white linen suits, as well as his initials, cannot help but associate him with similar roles played by Peter Lorre in the American film noirs Lattuada admired so much. Pier Luigi exploits Jerry's love for Angela, convinces him she needs someone to protect her, and brings him into his organization; but Jerry is eventually arrested, giving Lattuada the opportunity to expose American racial bigotry in the military court system of the occupation army. Jerry is beaten mercilessly by his white guards, and, suspiciously, most of the prisoners in the army stockades are black. The composer Nino Rota's medley of black spirituals on the sound track is emblematic of the suffering not just of an oppressed race but of all oppressed people.

In *Without Pity*, Lattuada's tragic tale of interracial love in postwar Livorno, Jerry confronts the crime boss Pier Luigi. *Credit: MOMA*

Many of the film's visuals derive directly from the American gangster film: several gun battles; car chases with automobiles careening around city corners, guns blazing; a melodramatic prison break by Jerry and a black friend, who is mortally wounded but implores Jerry to go on without him; and nightclub parties featuring American jazz, presided over by the criminal mastermind and club owner Pier Luigi. In a desperate attempt to escape Luigi's clutches, Jerry and Angela rob him and try to flee, but without success: Angela steps in front of Jerry to receive a bullet meant for him and dies; Jerry vows never to abandon her, leaps into his truck to the sound of a crescendo of black spirituals, and drives off a pier into the ocean. As the military police arrive too late, we see only a spinning truck wheel with a parting shot of Angela's head and one arm clutching Jerry. At last the pair is united in death.

With its attack upon racial prejudice, *Without Pity* certainly embodies the typical neorealist message of human brotherhood. Emphasizing social conditions in the immediate aftermath of the world war in Livorno, Lattuada moves in familiar territory. His film deserves attention not for the kind of complex cinematic artifice employed by Rossellini, De Sica, or Visconti, but primarily for managing a marriage (sometimes an uneasy one) between neorealist themes and settings and the older, more familiar Hollywood generic codes of the gangster film.

Neorealist Cheesecake in De Santis's *Bitter Rice*

The main theme of De Santis's *The Tragic Pursuit*—the dichotomy between men and women who work together for the betterment of their class, on the one hand, and those outlaws from society who exploit the plights of others, on the other—finds even more satisfying expression in the director's masterpiece, *Bitter Rice*. Turning Italian neorealism toward traditional Hollywood film genres (again, the gangster film), De Santis presents a broader condemnation of both American values and the results of the cultural confrontation between Italy and America (which Rossellini had praised in *Paisan* and Lattuada had criticized in *Without Pity*). Like Lattuada, De Santis invokes melodrama, treating the disastrous effects of violent love on the relationships of two couples. Francesca (Doris Dowling) and Walter (Vittorio Gassman), fleeing from a jewel robbery, join a train carrying women (called *mondine* in Italian) to work harvesting the rice crops of the Po Valley. Francesca falls in love with an Italian soldier named Marco (Raf Vallone), while Walter jilts Francesca for a starstruck girl named Silvana (Silvana Mangano), whom he uses to help him steal the rice harvest. His crime is doubly serious, since the rice workers, in addition to meager wages, are to receive as payment for their services a significant quantity of rice—an extremely valuable commodity in a period after the war when food was scarce and the black market was still in operation in Italy. In a dramatic climax and gun battle, Francesca and Marco thwart Walter's plans, and Silvana shoots Walter when she learns that the necklace he has given her is only worthless costume jewelry; she then commits suicide out of guilt over betraying the women of her class.

De Santis's original intention was to provide a realistic study of the *mondine*, whose economic conditions force them to work under miserable conditions for only a sack of rice and 40,000 lire. He could also, in the process, condemn the corruptive influences he perceived from American popular culture upon Italian working-class values. Such a film would have satisfied De Santis's Marxist convictions; but the style of the film he actually shot represents an uneasy but brilliant compromise between ideology and his admiration for Hollywood genre films (gangster films, musicals, westerns), as well as his admiration for such American directors as King Vidor and John Ford, or the acting style of Joan Crawford. One immediate result of the huge success of the film, a success that was quite unusual for a neorealist film in Italy, was that Silvana Mangano became a box-office sensation, an international pin-up model, and one of the very first Italian "sweater girls" (in Italy called *maggiorate*).[6] Like so many other star actresses and starlets in Italy, she had entered beauty contests (yet another mark of American influence in Italy) before working in the movies and being cast in *Bitter Rice*.

With Silvana, De Santis produced a perfect symbol of the shallow fascination with movie stars, mass media, and beauty queen contests the

In De Santis's *Bitter Rice*, Silvana's betrayal of her class derives from her corruption by American values and culture. *Credit: MOMA*

director identifies with American culture in his film. But eroticism in *Bitter Rice* often undercuts social commentary: an information title prefacing the film stresses not only its theme of "hard work requiring delicate hands" but perhaps, more significantly, the "long, long nights" of the *mondine* as well. De Santis shows Silvana whenever possible in tightly fitting sweaters revealing her ample cleavage and in tight, short pants emphasizing her sensual body, and she is completely mesmerized by the facile myths of wealth and success always associated with America. In one famous scene, there is even a brief glimpse of her nude breast, a daring shot for the time. This shot was so unusual and provocative that by the time the film was being projected throughout Italy, this particular scene had been cut out by projectionists to make souvenir pin-ups. Silvana constantly chews gum, dances the "boogie-woogie" (one of De Santis's favorite musical forms), and reads pulp magazines such as *Grand Hotel*. These publications, called *fotoromanzi* (literally, photo novels or picture stories) in Italy, employed black-and-white photographs (not drawings) with comic-strip speech balloons to narrate mushy love stories. Silvana hopes to make her fortune in America, where she believes *"everything* is electric"; but Marco, the symbol of proletarian solidarity and Italian common sense, tells her pointedly that everything *is* electric in America—even the electric chair! In contrast, Marco dreams of going to *South* America, to set up a traditional family and find honest employment after he leaves the service.

Bitter Rice is a powerful film with a hybrid style. One Italian critic has called it a "neorealist colossal,"[7] and its costly production stands apart from many other low-budget neorealist pictures made with more limited financial resources. It required seventy-five days of shooting on location with a huge cast of actors, technicians, and nonprofessional extras (a total of almost twelve thousand working days). To obtain the effects of a highly mobile camera in the slippery rice fields, De Santis had constructed a wooden dolly that allowed the camera to move over the soft terrain. He also employed a crane frequently in his shooting, a type of shot rare among neorealist directors, and used this technique effectively to create a sense of epic proportion and grandeur. The famous boogie-woogie sequence danced by Silvana and Walter that leads to the first violent confrontation between Walter and Marco was choreographed down to the last detail by the director, who claimed that editing the sequence required two full months. As shot from a crane, the scenes of the *mondine* with their skirts pulled up to their thighs made conscious reference to scenes from Hollywood films showing black slaves working in antebellum cotton fields. The fact that the women were not allowed to talk among themselves while they worked also gave De Santis the chance to stage a sequence typical of American musical films: the *mondine* communicate with each other by singing in the rain. A climactic gunfight and showdown typical of gangster films and the American western, previously employed in his *Tragic Pursuit*, reappear in the splendid finale of *Bitter Rice*, when the two couples meet in a slaughterhouse, and Walter is shot repeatedly.

De Santis satirizes the mania for beauty queens and contests, yet another fad imported from Hollywood in the postwar period, and links Silvana's corruption and her betrayal of her working-class origins by having her elected as "Miss Mondina 1948." (Not only did the Italians borrow the practice of such contests but they retained the English word "Miss" as well.) Proletarian solidarity provides comfort, however. Just as his fellow peasants forgave Alberto in *The Tragic Pursuit* when they playfully pelted him with clods of their hard-earned soil, so too her *mondine* comrades pardon Silvana once the rice harvest is saved. After her suicide, she is reintegrated into their community through a highly symbolic sequence redolent of peasant folklore. As her body lies on the ground, the women file silently past, sprinkling a handful of their hard-earned rice on Silvana, while De Santis's camera shifts to a crane shot of the entire group, underlining the collective nature of the rice workers' struggle.

Bitter Rice proved that neorealism could be combined both with eroticism and with Hollywood film genres, and that films containing Marxist messages of social protest could actually make a profit. While some leftist critics attacked the director for betraying the socialist realism they prescribed as the norm, De Santis had cleverly employed the very conventions from Hollywood he was most intent upon criticizing to make a powerful statement about the disastrous effects of embracing a foreign culture rather than remaining true to the best traditions of the Italian working class. *Bitter Rice* thus rejects the more optimistic vision of the Italian-American encounter found in Rossellini's *Paisan* and extends De Santis's more critical view of America far beyond that of Lattuada's *Without Pity*. Its means for doing so make *Bitter Rice* the neorealist film most indebted to the American cinema and its rich generic traditions.

Germi's *In The Name of the Law* and *The Path of Hope*

Pietro Germi's *In the Name of the Law* and *The Path of Hope* follow Visconti's *The Earth Trembles* in their focus away from the war and the Resistance toward endemic problems in Italy's southern region. The first film is also a stylized Italian adaptation of narrative patterns Germi found in the westerns of John Ford, a Hollywood director he greatly admired. The plot concerns a young judge named Guido Schiavi (Massimo Girotti) who comes to a Sicilian village and attempts to apply northern Italian laws to a land ruled by the Mafia. The judge's *mafioso* adversary, Turi Passalacqua (Charles Vanel), stands out in the film as a charismatic leader, even though Germi obviously tries to turn Guido into the film's hero. The film's highest dramatic moment concerns a showdown (not unlike those in Ford's westerns) between Guido and the bandit chieftain over a young boy who is murdered in the town: Guido's courage moves the Mafioso to turn over the murderer to the authorities. Still, this conclusion certainly makes no contribution to an analysis of how the Mafia works in Sicily, and actually makes a hero out of a character who should really have been portrayed as a villain. The best parts of the film derive from Germi's visual style, his contrast of the black-garbed villagers with the sun-drenched white walls and homes,

Germi's *In the Name of the Law* offers a mythically heroic image of a Mafia leader who delivers a criminal to justice. *Credit: CSC*

as well as his memorable shots of the weather-worn faces of actual Sicilian peasants photographed on authentic locations in rural Sicily.

Germi's second Sicilian film, *The Path of Hope*, follows a group of exploited sulfur miners who leave Italy for employment abroad. Once again, Germi borrows a narrative pattern derived from the American western: the epic trek across a vast landscape to find a better life elsewhere. Germi's protagonists are also recognizable types from the western: Saro (Raf Vallone), a widower with three children, is the stalwart leader of the band; Barbara (Elena Varzi) is a prostitute with a heart of gold; and Vanni, Barbara's criminal lover (Franco Navarra) and Saro's antagonist. The theme of a quest for a better life combines with the motif of a developing confrontation between a noble hero and an evil villain, with Barbara's love as the reward for the victor. The customary gunfight in the western to settle such dramatic tension becomes the traditional Sicilian knife fight, a transposition of the western's code of behavior to traditional Sicilian *cavalleria rusticana*—Verga's "rustic chivalry" celebrated in one of his greatest short stories (1880), or in the opera Pietro Mascagni (1863–1945) made from it (*Cavalleria rusticana*, 1890).[8] As in the classic western, the victory of the hero is never in doubt. Germi succeeds in creating an epic tone, typical of the very best American westerns, for a rather melodramatic storyline with his brilliant photography, indebted to Visconti's example from *The Earth Trembles*. Shots of statuesque Sicilian women, dressed completely in black and waiting silently for their men to emerge from the deep-pit mines, juxtaposed strikingly against the stark, white Sicilian landscape at the opening of the film, recall sequences from Visconti's masterpiece. As the workers reach their goal and cross the

Germi's *The Path of Hope* depicts an epic trek by southern Italians to a better life on the other side of the Alps in France. *Credit: CSC*

French Alps, they are again beautifully captured in a long shot, their black garments now set off against a completely white snowscape, reversing the symbolic connotations of the opening sequence (despair) to that of hope for a brighter future.

A Change in the Political Climate in Italy and the Response of the Italian Cinema

The best neorealist films usually focused upon serious contemporary social, political, or economic problems. Most inevitably called attention to injustice and the need for social reform, if not revolution. But Italy's political climate changed between 1945 (a time when the Left felt there was a chance to remake Italian political culture) and 1948 (when the Christian Democrats gained on April 18 an absolute majority in an election marked by cold-war tensions). Strikes and political violence became common, a tense situation brought to a climax by the unsuccessful assassination attempt of July 14 1948, on Palmiro Togliatti (1893–1964), the head of the Italian Communist Party. (On January 6, 1949, Prime Minister Alcide De Gasperi would request Italy's membership in NATO; on July 13 of that year, the Vatican would excommunicate Communist voters, sympathizers, and their allies.) As a result, films with strong social statements and clear ideological positions became risky investments, as government subsidies could be withdrawn at a moment's notice from productions that were deemed dangerous. Even if such a film was made, it ran the risk of being censored or even sequestered by the government. An economic crisis in the industry thus coincided with this change in cultural climate: total film production in Italy fell from sixty-five films in 1946 and sixty-seven in 1947 to forty-nine in 1948.

De Gasperi's protégé and Undersecretary of Public Entertainment Giulio Andreotti (1919–), who decades later would himself become prime minister of Italy on several occasions, guided the industry until 1953. His open letter to Vittorio De Sica, chiding the director for exposing Italian social problems abroad with his film about the plight of aged pensioners, *Umberto D.*—and employing the popular adage that dirty laundry is best washed at home—made it clear to the industry which way the wind was blowing in Rome. Italian directors were urged to adopt a more optimistic, healthy, and constructive attitude and not to do a disservice to their nation, which, as Andreotti reminded them, boasted one of the most progressive social systems in the world. The political climate of the late 1940s and early 1950s can be gauged by the fact that a military court (not a civil court) could arrest, try, and convict distinguished journalists and critics such as Guido Aristarco or Renzo Renzi (1919–2004) in 1953 for "defaming the armed forces" by suggesting that a film on the Italian occupation of Greece be made that showed the real nature of this "harmless" occupation. Clare Booth Luce

(1903–87), American Ambassador to Italy between 1953 and 1957, could even exert pressure on the Venice Film Festival to block the presentation of an American film on the grounds that it was offensive to American prestige. Political pressure from home and abroad was thus added to economic competition as constraints upon Italian cinema, while the public's constant preference for melodrama, historical epics, or comedies provided economic incentives for moving the cinema away from touchy subjects and toward a more popular, less uncompromising social stance during the 1950s.

Melodrama, Popular Comedy, and "Rosy" Neorealism

While film historians and critics have praised the best neorealist films as the most original contributions Italian cinema made to the art of the movies, contemporary Italian audiences thronged to such popular tearjerkers as *Chains* (*Catene*, 1949), *Torment* (*Tormento*, 1950), and *Nobody's Children* (*I figli di nessuno*, 1951), by Raffaello Matarazzo (1909–66). Although despised by the critics, these three films were box-office sensations, placing respectively first, second, and third place in three successive years. Most of Matarazzo's films were never exported abroad. Other successful commercial films of the period were the comedies that were vehicles for the acting talents of Erminio Macario (1902–80), including a trilogy of works by Carlo Borghesio (1905–83): *How I Lost the War* (*Come persi la guerra*, 1947; first in box-office receipts in that year); *The Hero of the Street* (*L'eroe della strada*, 1948; eighth in popularity that year); and *How I Discovered America* (*Come scopersi l'America*, 1949). One of Italy's most popular and gifted comic actors, Totò (a stage name for Antonio De Curtis; 1898–1967), was unquestionably the most popular figure in the film industry in an era before television began to compete with the silver screen. His comic style combined elements of the classic silent comedies with the native *commedia dell'arte* and Neapolitan theatrical traditions. Totò became the darling of the less advantaged classes in the provinces and the impoverished South, and at least one of his films placed in the top ten at the box office every year from 1948 to 1957. By 1963, he had appeared in more than ninety films, often averaging six per year. Typical of his many works (most of which were never distributed abroad) is *Totò Looks for a House* (*Totò cerca casa*, 1949), directed by Mario Monicelli (1915–2010) and Stefano Vanzina (known as Steno, 1915–88), second at the box office in that year. Many of Totò's films were shot in only a few days and often reflected current events, treating some of the same social problems that were examined in the neorealist classics. Yet the farcical quest by Totò of a house in the bombed-out rubble of postwar urban Italy, and the perennial Italian penchant to laugh at rather than resolve social problems his comic mask suggested, had a far greater impact upon Italian audiences than did such films as De Sica's *Umberto D.* or even the successful *Bicycle Thief.*

Since Italian audiences preferred comedy to social criticism, and the political climate was unfavorable to harsh attacks upon Italian institutions, a comic vein in neorealism—*neorealismo rosa* or "rosy neorealism"—emerged and found favor with the public just as predictably as it was attacked by leftist critics. Renato Castellani, a "calligrapher" of the Fascist period (see chapter 2), wrote and directed a number of such films: *Under the Sun of Rome* (*Sotto il sole di Roma*, 1948); *It's Forever Springtime* (*È primavera . . .*, 1950); and his best work, *Two Cents' Worth of Hope* (1952). This last work focuses upon postwar poverty and unemployment in Naples, but its only real link to the neorealist tradition is to be found in the director's use of authentic locations and his interest in retaining the flavor of the local dialect. Based upon endless episodes employing comic gags and local color, the film offers as its hero an unemployed ex-soldier named Antonio Catalano (Vincenzo Musolino), who is finally able to marry his sweetheart, Carmela (Maria Fiore), after a series of misadventures. In a wonderful scene that parodies the departure of Saint Francis from his rich parents, before marrying Carmela, Antonio strips her of the clothes belonging to her family, tosses them at her irate father, grasps a dress from a street side peddler (on credit!), then receives donations of shoes, stockings, and a silk shirt from happy bystanders. In the concluding sequence, Antonio delivers this edifying message: "He who has created us is not poor. If He wants us to live, He must feed us. If not, what are we doing here?" Nothing could have infuriated leftist critics who were intent upon turning Italian cinema toward revolutionary goals more, and it is a measure of how different the climate had become in Italy and Europe during the height of the Cold War between 1945 and 1952 that Castellani's film was awarded the Grand Prize at Cannes.

Luigi Comencini (1916–2007) and Dino Risi (1916–2008) created an extremely popular comedy series (not usually exported abroad) that typifies "rosy" neorealism, a collection of works usually known as the *Bread and Love* series. They include Comencini's *Bread, Love and Fantasy* (*Pane, amore e fantasia*, 1953)[9]—the box-office champion in 1953–54—and *Bread, Love and Jealousy* (*Pane, amore e gelosia*, 1954); and Risi's *Bread, Love and . . .* (*Pane, amore e . . .*, 1955) as well as his *Poor But Beautiful* (*Poveri ma belli*, 1957). Comencini's two extraordinarily popular films also helped to make Gina Lollobrigida (1927–) one of Italy's best-known *maggiorate*. In both, she plays a poor but beautiful girl known as La Bersagliera, or "the girl of the rifle regiment," pursued by a marshal in the Carabinieri (state police) played by Vittorio De Sica. Lollobrigida's success in these vehicles, which did more to advertise her beauty than to analyze social conditions in the poor areas of the Italian Mezzogiorno, led to a series of international productions made in Hollywood in which she starred. The rivalry between Lollobrigida and Sophia Loren, real or invented by the film tabloids and gossip magazines such as *Dream* (*Sogno*) or *Illustrated Cinema* (*Cine illustrato*),

An original film poster from Comencini's *Bread, Love and Fantasy* illustrating the charms of Gina Lollobrigida, Italy's most popular actress in the 1950s. *Credit: AB*

became the major focus of attention in the dozens of film magazines read in Italy by avid fans of both women during the 1950s and the 1960s. Not surprisingly, with their focus upon a "poor but beautiful" female star, "rosy" neorealist films and De Santis's *Bitter Rice* implicitly encouraged the kind of uncritical spectatorship that would continue to infuriate leftist critics in Italy, who would see the politically suggestive possibilities in Italy's *commedia all'italiana* only years later (see chapter 7).

Comedies like those produced by Comencini and Risi approached poverty and social problems with a smile, not with an intention to change the status quo. Nevertheless, they were one important means of creating an international audience for Italian films, and a national interest in the *commedia all'italiana* that has always been one of the mainstays of the Italian film industry. Just as De Santis, Lattuada, and Germi had done so brilliantly with their use of Hollywood

An original film poster from Risi's *Bread, Love and . . .* shows Sophia Loren, Gina Lollobrigida's rival as the top beauty queen in the popular cinema of the 1950s, dancing with Vittorio De Sica in Risi's *Bread, Love and . . . Credit: AB*

genres (the western, the musical, the gangster film) within a somewhat altered neorealist style, so too the makers of these comic films broadened the appeal of Italian movies by treating serious problems in a comic vein. In the next generation, the *commedia all'italiana* would embrace a far more biting kind of social satire than was typical or even possible in the 1950s.

Rossellini, De Sica, and Visconti: Questioning the Power of the Movie Camera

Many critics during the 1940s and the 1950s treated any departure from social realism as either part of a "crisis" of neorealism or as a "betrayal" of neorealism. The concept of crisis is almost always something invented by critics or historians, while artists rarely think in terms of crises but, instead, of solutions to artistic problems—an entirely different matter. Moreover, it was naturally impossible to betray neorealism when there was never a neo-realist movement with a consciously agreed-upon program, manifesto, or aesthetic principle. The so-called crisis may be more accurately described as an argument between such writers or critics as Bazin, Aristarco, Zavattini, and others. Central to any belief that Italian neorealism was an important driving force behind progressive change in Italian society was a belief that film realism persuaded audiences to make certain political decisions (usually those favoring the Left). During this period, a number of important films, such as Rossellini's *The Machine to Kill Bad People* (*La macchina ammaz-zacattivi*), De Sica's *Miracle in Milan*, and Visconti's *Bellissima* (1951) all in different ways called this belief in cinema into question. By deviating from a purely realist aesthetic in order to illuminate issues crucial to any treatment of realism in the cinema, these films represent highly self-conscious treatments of the interplay between reality and appearance.

Rossellini and De Sica actually explicitly rejected a strictly realist aesthetic during this period. De Sica remarked that he had made *Miracle in Milan* to resolve problems of "form and style."[10] In 1952, when *The Machine to Kill Bad People* was finally released, Rossellini defined realism as "simply the artistic form of truth," and stated that he had made this film (completed in 1948) in order to shift his work toward the traditional Italian *commedia dell'arte*.[11] In both films, these very different directors employ a remarkable number of similar techniques, including frequent comic gags with obvious debts to silent film comedy (Chaplin and René Clair) or to the regional dialect theater of Naples (Rossellini's subject was even suggested by the Neapolitan dramatist Eduardo De Filippo [1900–84]). Rossellini's film actually opens with a traditional prologue in verse and a stage full of characters set up by the hand of a puppeteer or *capocomico* (leader of a theater company), and it closes with a rhymed epilogue and a moral. Because of this link to traditional dramatic and cinematographic conventions, both films reveal a similar approach to characterization. Neither director is particularly preoccupied with the subtle psychological nuances achieved in such masterpieces as *Germany Year Zero* or *The Bicycle Thief*. Instead, characters are almost without exception motivated by a single force—greed and self-interest, on the one hand, or pure goodness, on the other, and their actions identify them as traditional comic types. The storyline of each film is equally simple and represents what may best be described as an allegory or fable involving the relationship of the rich to the poor, the evil to the good. Rossellini's film is perhaps simpler from a technical point of view, containing fewer special photographic effects, whereas De Sica's film exploits a number of surrealist effects; but Rossellini's work is also more richly plotted, with subplots parodying both the story of Romeo and Juliet and even his own film *Paisan* (in particular, the arrival of the Americans in Italy). While the thematic content continues what may be thought of as a typical neorealist focus upon social justice and economic disparity in postwar Italy, it is precisely their attention to style that separates these works from other more conventional neorealist films of the period. Rossellini's film presents an extended meditation upon the very nature of photography itself, while De Sica calls into question the conventions associated with neorealist cinema. In so doing, each director provides the viewer with a clearer idea of the boundaries setting off neorealist aesthetics from other forms of commercial cinema.

In *The Machine to Kill Bad People*, Rossellini's plot presents a professional photographer named Celestino Esposito (Gennaro Pisano) to whom a mysterious, saintly old man (later revealed as a demon) grants the miraculous

In Rossellini's *The Machine to Kill Bad People*, a strange visitor grants the photographer Celestino frightening powers through the use of his camera. *Credit: MOMA*

power of causing evildoers to disappear from the face of the earth by means of his camera (*la macchina* of the original title). A good man consumed by moral indignation over the evil committed by others, Celestino takes his camera and turns it upon those in his village who exploit the poor and act only from self-interest. Soon, several of the town's most powerful and illustrious citizens—the town loan shark, the mayor, the policeman, the owner of a fleet of fishing boats and trucks—suffer the same fate. Once Celestino photographs a previous picture of them, they are frozen in that pose and pass to their reward. As the film progresses, Celestino becomes increasingly impatient with the town: the poor, he discovers, are no better than the rich and have exactly the same greedy motives, something that the opening prologue suggests with the line "in the end, nice or not, they resemble each other a lot." Rapidly demoralized by this discovery, Celestino embarks upon a plan to destroy everybody, since they are all imperfect, and in the process he murders the good town doctor who tries to keep him from taking a picture of the entire town. Driven by remorse, Celestino decides to punish himself with the magic camera, but only after he eliminates the demon who gave him this horrible power. Before he can succeed, however, the demon appears and is converted when Celestino makes the sign of the cross; then the demon restores Celestino's victims to life as if nothing had happened. A final moral closes the film: "Do good but don't overdo it. Avoid evil for your own sake. Don't be hasty in judging others. Think twice before punishing."

In good neorealist fashion that recalls statements made by such important figures as Cesare Zavattini, Celestino views the camera as a means of separating reality from illusion, good from evil, substance from appearance. For him, photography is a metaphor for a way of knowing, for a means of apprehending essential moral and ethical facts. It enables him, so he believes, to penetrate the surface of events to the bedrock of reality and to fulfill a godlike role in his small village, a role not unlike that of a film director on a set. Rossellini is chiefly concerned with the symbolic importance of the camera and, by extension, the nature of photography itself. Interestingly, Celestino does not directly duplicate objects from the real world with his camera. On the contrary, he must first take a photograph of another photograph to accomplish his magic. As any good Platonist knows, he is two steps removed from the world of tangible objects or sensory reality by the time he takes the second picture and engages in the essentially self-reflexive act of producing a work of art from another work of art, not from reality itself.

Rossellini thus emphasizes a fundamental characteristic of filmic art while creating an elaborate cosmic joke with Celestino's self-delusory activity. He tells us emphatically but with humor that photography (and, by extension, the cinema) is incapable of separating good from evil or of readily distinguishing reality from appearance. Celestino mistakes a demon for the patron saint of the town, and when he attacks the rich to help the poor, he learns that some of the wealthy are not entirely evil (the loan shark leaves her fortune to the three poorest people in the village), and that the poor share the selfish vices of the rich. Nowhere does any clear distinction between ethical or metaphysical positions exist. The camera, viewed as a means of acquiring knowledge of social reality by overly optimistic neo-realist directors, has been reduced to a fallible and neutral instrument that reflects not reality but human subjectivity and error.

In his 1951 film, *Miracle in Milan*, De Sica goes beyond Rossellini's suggestive treatment of the camera's relationship to reality and concentrates upon the place of the imagination itself. The film's main character, Totò (Francesco Golisano)—a figure not to be confused with the more famous comic actor Totò, discussed earlier—is as concerned with good and evil as Celestino, but he is infinitely more innocent and naive. A white dove given to him by his foster mother, Lolotta (Emma Gramatica), enables him to fulfill the wishes of every poor person living in the shantytown outside Milan. When the dove is taken away from him, he and his friends are forced to escape their wicked oppressors by flying on broomsticks over the cathedral of Milan. De Sica has clearly moved from the social reality typical of most neorealist films to a world of fantasy, fable, or fairy tale in spite of the often-cited remark by Zavattini (his scriptwriter) that the true function of the cinema is not to tell fables. *Miracle in Milan* attacks the very definition of neorealism canonized by the essays of Bazin. Although the storyline of this fable about the rich and the poor echoes the social concerns character-istic of neorealist films, De Sica's style departs from traditional definitions of neorealism even more radically than that of Rossellini's *Machine to Kill Bad People*. Chronological time is rejected, as is duration or ontological wholeness; commonsense logic is abandoned as well, and the usual cause-and-effect relationships between objects in the "real" world are replaced by absurd, surreal events (the sunlight shines in only one spot at a time; angels or magic spirits visit the shantytown; people are granted any wish they desire). The fantastic is bodied forth by a number of special effects foreign to neorealist films: people fly on broomsticks, smoke appears to reverse its course, rapid editing makes it seem that hats chase a character out of the camera's frame. The entire film is thus an extended metaphor, a hymn to the role of illusion and fantasy in art, as well as in life, but it is not merely frivo-lous entertainment. De Sica informs us that the human impulse to artistic creativity, like the broomsticks that fly over the cathedral, is capable of tran-scending social problems but not of resolving them. Film art can only offer the consolation of beauty and the hope that its images and ideas may move the spectator to social action that might change the world.

While Rossellini's film questions the cognitive potential of the camera and undermines the idea that good and evil are easily distinguished, De

In De Sica's *Miracle in Milan*, rather than organizing a revolution,
Edvige and Totò head for a better world by flying away from Milan on a
broomstick. *Credit: MOMA*

Sica's work affirms Rossellini's doubts about the moral superiority of the
poor, for the inhabitants of the shantytown all aspire only to become rich
and to act selfishly. Rossellini limits the camera's power to discover reality, but De Sica goes further: he demonstrates that the camera can uncover
new dimensions of experience through the poetry of the creative fantasy.
Although both films include a fable about the rich and the poor, they also
treat the relationship between reality and appearance. The distance traveled by Rossellini in the few years from *Paisan* to *The Machine to Kill Bad
People*, and by De Sica between *Shoeshine* and *Miracle in Milan*, marks the
outer boundaries of the Italian neorealist cinema and pushes the dialectic
between realism and illusion almost to the breaking point.

Visconti's *Bellissima* is a vehicle for displaying the melodramatic acting
talents of Anna Magnani. She plays a starstruck stage mother named Maddalena Cecconi who attempts to get her daughter, Maria (Tina Apicella), a
career as a child actor by winning one of the many contests to "discover" a
rising star that the Italian cinema sponsored in the 1950s to exploit interest in the film industry. With a nod to film history, Visconti cast the distinguished director Alessandro Blasetti as the director leading this talent
search and has him react to Maria's screen test by hilarious and demeaning
laughter. In an unbelievable reversal for a woman who has spent almost the
whole film going to extraordinary lengths to get her daughter into the movies, Maddalena, because of the humiliating trauma the director's laughter
has caused her, refuses to allow Maria to accept the contract that she is surprisingly offered. *Bellissima* shares with *The Machine to Kill Bad People* and
Miracle in Milan a metacinematic perspective on the nature of cinema itself.

Like the other two better works, it also casts doubt upon the relationship between illusion and reality in the cinema, underscoring what a venal business the industry actually is and how far removed from the real feelings of real people it seems. Thus, Visconti, Rossellini, and De Sica—the masters of neorealism—all expressed some doubts about film as a morally redemptive art form only a few years after producing their best neorealist masterpieces.

Italian Neorealism and Italian History

While some directors moved away from the recognizable historical world of postwar Italy toward metacinematic meditations upon the nature of cinema itself, other important neorealist films examined the burden of Italian history and the relation of the past to the troubled present. Two important films released in 1954 pursued this topic, Lizzani's *Tales of Poor Lovers* (*Cronache di poveri amanti*) and Visconti's *Senso*. Both films were adaptations of literary texts: the first a 1947 novel with the same title from the neorealist writer Vasco Pratolini; the second a short story entitled "A Thing Apart" ("Senso," 1883), by Camillo Boito (1836–1914). Pratolini's novel is one of the very few neorealist novels that followed the canons of traditional literary realism. In it, he examines how Fascism imposed its grip upon the simple people living in the Via del Corno in the Santa Croce district of Florence, much as the Guelphs gained power over the Ghibellines centuries earlier—by terror and violence. He thus follows Florence's medieval historian Dino Compagni (c. 1255–1324) in his use of *cronaca*, or "chronicle," and presents a historical analysis of Florence from the year 1925 with a group of more than fifty characters, revealing the complex social and personal relationships that exist among the poor people who live within the shadow of the Palazzo Vecchio. The novel's protagonist is named Corrado, but his friends call him Maciste in homage to the legendary strongman from the Italian silent cinema. His death during one of the many Fascist "punitive expeditions" against the working class results in the birth of a sense of class consciousness in a fruit vendor, who inherits Maciste's anti-Fascist sympathies and eventually becomes a member of the Communist Party. Lizzani's film is as faithful to its source as possible, and Pratolini's socialist realism finds its cinematic equivalent in an authoritative narrative voice-over in the film. Lizzani eschews any special effects or dramatic cinematic techniques, presenting all the small, seemingly insignificant details of daily life in a small street in Florence, viewing it as a microcosm of all Italy. Lizzani's film thus approaches history as chronicle, a mass of diverse facts that, taken together, explain broader historical trends. In his case, his Marxist beliefs interpret Italian history through the lens of class struggle, and he views Fascism as the means employed by the upper classes to suppress the proletariat.

Visconti's sumptuous film recounts the love affair between a Venetian noblewoman, the Countess Livia Serpieri (Alida Valli), and Lieutenant Franz Mahler (Farley Granger), a part of Austria's army of occupation in northern Italy. Unlike Lizzani, who attempts to remain faithful to his literary source, Visconti (as he had previously done in *The Earth Trembles*) transforms his source into something much closer to his own aristocratic sensibilities, aiming at a demystification of history, uncovering not only the actual events of the Italian Risorgimento but also less obvious ideological contradictions and their connections to Italy's future development. Setting the film in the nineteenth century at the height of the operatic career of Giuseppe Verdi (1813–1901) also allowed Visconti to enjoy something that was almost as dear to his heart as the cinema—producing grand opera at Milan's La Scala.

Senso opens with a re-creation of Act III of Verdi's *Il trovatore* in Venice's La Fenice opera house in the spring of 1866. As Manrico sings the famous lines "Di quella pira . . ." and the chorus joins in with a call to arms ("All'armi, all'armi . . ."), an outbreak of patriotic fervor breaks out among the Italian spectators, who direct their ire against the Austrian officers or governmental officials in the opera house. Tricolor Italian flags are displayed, the Austrians are taunted, and cries of "Viva Verdi" ring out. (Verdi's initials were employed as a shorthand way of praising the House of Savoy, the Italian ruling dynasty, by proclaiming "*Viva Vittorio Emmanuele, Re d'Italia,*" or "Hurray for Victor Emanuel, King of Italy.") In the orchestra, Roberto Ussoni (Massimo Girotti), a marquis and the leader of the demonstrators, challenges young Mahler to a duel for a disparaging remark about Italian cowardice. Meanwhile, in a box overlooking this scene, Countess Serpieri and her husband sit with high-ranking Austrians, obviously comfortable collaborating with the occupying forces of a decadent and doomed regime. (Austria will lose its grip on Venice and northern Italy as a result of its defeat by Prussia at the Battle of Sadowa that summer.) To save her cousin Ussoni from becoming embroiled in a meaningless duel, Livia speaks with Mahler and informs him that, although she loves opera, she does not care for melodrama offstage or for people who act like melodramatic heroes without considering the consequences of their actions. The duel does not take place, but the melodrama from Verdi's opera moves to Visconti's film: Livia and Franz become lovers, and Livia uses funds raised by Ussoni for an uprising against the Austrians to buy Franz's safety from military service with a forged medical certificate. But when Livia discovers that Franz has betrayed her with another woman, she reveals to the Austrian authorities the fact that his medical certificate is false, resulting in Franz's execution by firing squad—which Visconti sets against scenes depicting the Italian defeat by the Austrians at the disastrous Battle of Custoza (June 24), where Ussoni is wounded.

Visconti's *Senso* sets a melodramatic love affair doomed to betrayal and failure against the historical backdrop of Italy's struggle for national independence in the Risorgimento. *Credit: CSC*

It is clear that with *Senso*, Visconti intended to present the cinematic equivalent of a great nineteenth-century historical novel, using the private lives of individuals to analyze historical developments. Thus, the opening scene at the opera house shows one aspect of real Italian popular culture during the period, the view of Verdi and his music as a patriotic expression of Italian nationalism. True to his aristocratic background, Visconti loves the decadent world of Mahler and the countess, a way of life that he realizes is doomed to extinction, and his meticulous historical re-creations of period costumes and decor lend the film a certain sterile splendor that, as André Bazin once remarked, caused viewers to appreciate the film more with their intellect than with their emotions: we admire Visconti's art without succeeding in participating in the world it portrays.[12]

And yet, beneath the facade of sumptuous uniforms and bejeweled women, Visconti conceals a devastating critique of the Italian Risorgimento that he will continue in an even greater film, *The Leopard*. Leftist critics were quick to see *Senso* in this light, just as their more conservative opponents attacked the film for what they saw as a slanderous travesty of glorious past history. The argument obscured the film's somewhat limited merits, a fact attested to by the fact that the film did very poorly abroad, where the question of whether or not the Risorgimento was a failed revolution was simply not interesting to non-Italians. Young Vittorio Taviani (1929–)—then an organizer of film clubs in Pisa and not yet the director he was to become— grasped immediately how Visconti employed past history as a vehicle for analyzing contemporary political questions:

> More than a month after its presentation, *Senso* continues to be at the center of the cultural debate in our city. Visconti's latest film seems to

us the most coherent consequence of the premises of neorealism. If our postwar cinema was born from the Resistance—as above all a Resistance to Fascism—it was inevitable that after turning its gaze on the present, is would seek to reach the roots of political and social phenomena: that it would confront the Risorgimento as the historical moment that signals the birth of Italy as a modern nation. And it was also inevitable that with such an attentive analysis, conducted along the lines of the most illuminating results from current historiography led by Gramsci, Gobetti, and Salvatorelli, the bourgeois revolution would reveal its fundamental characteristic as an incomplete revolution.[13]

Such, indeed, was Visconti's intention when he began the film, and while the splendid sequence at the Venetian opera house captures the popular nature of Italian patriotism, the rest of the film emphasizes the ambiguities and equivocal motives behind the events of 1866. Count Serpieri (Heinz Moog) first collaborates with the Austrians, then turns to Ussoni and the revolutionaries when it is obvious that Austria will be defeated and Venice liberated, because he is basically concerned only with guarding his status, wealth, and property, not with national unification. Revolutionaries such as Ussoni are regarded as an embarrassment by troops in the regular Italian army, as were Garibaldi's Redshirts. A crucial scene in which Ussoni's offer of volunteer troops is refused by regular officers before the Battle of Custoza makes it clear that a much different result might have been expected had Italy's ascendant middle class harnessed the energies of the entire population for a true revolution; but the Risorgimento was betrayed, according to Visconti, not by passionate women such as Livia Serpieri but by others of her class who twisted the noble aspirations of patriots to ignoble, class-oriented goals. Although Visconti also intended his audience to read in his portrait of the failure of the Risorgimento a parallel to what the Left saw as a failure of the anti-Fascist Resistance, the intervention of the censors forced the elimination of a crucial sequence from the work that made this parallel much more obvious.

The structure that Visconti created in *Senso*—the marriage of spectacle, melodrama, and a critical realism based upon historical facts—would become the formula for his greatest films still to come. *Senso* represents a broadening of the horizons of Italian neorealism, a move away from the mundane facts of daily life toward more complex problems of historical development, from chronicle to history, from realism to critical realism. And yet, beneath the surface of the historical setting and the ideological issues Visconti treats in *Senso*, the pattern of passionate love leading to tragic conclusions—melodrama in the best operatic and Verdian sense of the term—shines forth.

Several facts about the film's production have some importance. *Senso* was the first major Technicolor film directed by an important Italian director. Visconti made the decision to move from black and white to color a decade before Antonioni and Fellini did so, respectively, in *Red Desert* (*Il deserto rosso*, 1964) and *Juliet of the Spirits* (*Giulietta degli spiriti*, 1965). He achieved spectacular results, particularly in the night sequences set in the tiny streets and canals of Venice and in his gorgeous re-creations of lavish interiors. He thus provided proof that Italians could match their foreign competitors in making sumptuous historical films in color. *Senso* also marks an important step toward the dependence of Italian film producers upon foreign capital. Since American financing bankrolled the film, Farley Granger was imposed upon Visconti by his backers. (Visconti had originally wanted to cast Marlon Brando and Ingrid Bergman in the main roles of Mahler and Livia.) Tennessee Williams also helped write the dialogue for the English version, but because English-speaking audiences knew little about the Risorgimento, the film did not do well in the United States. (The English version of *The Leopard* would later do badly outside Europe for the same reason.)

Zavattini and the "Film Inquiry": Neorealism as Reportage

Between the time Visconti's *Obsession* and Rossellini's *Open City* appeared to inaugurate the neorealist decade in Italy and Visconti's *Senso* moved to broaden neorealism's approach to broad historical problems, a wide diversity of cinematic styles emerged in the Italian cinema that ultimately burst the boundaries of a naive view of film realism. Despite Zavattini's insistence, at least in theory, that Italian cinema should turn toward everyday reality to avoid the "spectacular" or the "intervention of fantasy or artifice," many of the best neorealist films did exactly the opposite: they moved closer to traditional commercial Hollywood film genres and away from the intimate connection between documentary and fiction that was at least partially responsible for the appeal of the early neorealist classics by Rossellini or Visconti. Rather than concentrating upon contemporary events, directors such as Visconti began to employ the cinema as a vehicle for exploring crucial moments in Italian history (which had been one of the central goals of cinema for such directors as Blasetti, Genina, and De Robertis during the Fascist period). One particular film, *Love in the City* (*L'amore in città*, 1953) demonstrates clearly how far removed Italian cinema actually was from Zavattini's own guiding principles. Zavattini organized this anthology film to initiate a series of cinema "news magazines" in which directors would act as reporters. Impatient with scripted stories, such as his great screenplays for De Sica in which nonprofessional actors nevertheless portrayed fictional characters in fictional works, Zavattini wanted to create a new style close to *cinéma-vérité*, what he called the "film inquiry" (*film inchiesta*). He enlisted the services of six different directors for six different episodes: Dino Risi's

"Invitation to Love" ("Paradiso per tre ore"); Antonioni's "When Love Fails" ("Tentato suicidio"); Fellini's "Love Cheerfully Arranged" ("Un'agenzia matrimoniale"); Lattuada's "Italy Turns Around" ("Gli italiani si voltano"); his own "The Love of a Mother" ("La storia di Caterina"), directed with Francesco Maselli (1930–); and Carlo Lizzani's "Paid Love" ("L'amore che si paga"), censored from the original American version by the Italian government because of its shocking revelation that prostitution existed in Italy.

Zavattini's intentions in *Love in the City* were realistic in the extreme, bordering on cinematic journalism. The opening credits, for example, are listed on the turning pages of a magazine, and the narrative voice-over introducing the film informs the viewer that only the most unusual and poignant stories were selected, in consultation with the people who actually experienced the events in question. The results, however, were far removed from Zavattini's original intentions to continue the progress of Italian neorealism toward a minute examination of the daily events of ordinary Italians. Zavattini's sequence, re-creating the tragedy of an unwed Sicilian girl abandoned by her lover in Rome, is the only episode that has a recognizable neorealist style. Lattuada's sequence employs a "candid camera" technique: close-ups of thighs, breasts, and buttocks are intercut with the lecherous stares of Italian men as they leer at some twenty gorgeous women strolling down the street. Antonioni's investigation of the causes behind the suicide attempts of several women points not backward to neorealist techniques but forward to his highly abstract psychological analyses of love affairs in his masterpieces of the late 1950s and early 1960s. Fellini's sequence openly pokes fun at poor Zavattini's serious intentions by filming a story about a client who contacted a marriage bureau to find a woman willing to marry a werewolf. Apparently Fellini convinced the gullible Zavattini that this was a true story. The episode's lyricism reveals the surreal and symbolic universe in Fellini's great films of the 1950s.

Little can be learned about unwed mothers, suicides, werewolves, prostitution, or the "reality" of love in contemporary Italy from *Love in the City*. Even its use of actual locations, actual stories, and the actual people involved in the stories leads the viewer no further than the compilation of facts in a daily newspaper. Zavattini himself may have ingenuously considered the film as a new form of factual reporting and a step toward developing a new wrinkle in neorealist cinema; but it is obvious that the other directors did not accept his facile assertion that description or information would automatically lead to interpretation, understanding, and a more profound sense of the reality of Italian life. The Italian cinema, led by the makers of the two most unusual and original sequences in *Love in the City*—Antonioni and Fellini—was about to embark on an entirely different cinematic journey beyond neorealism.

CHAPTER FIVE

The Break with Neorealism

THE CINEMA OF THE RECONSTRUCTION, FELLINI'S TRILOGIES OF CHARACTER AND GRACE, AND THE RETURN OF MELODRAMA

GIVEN THE INTERNATIONAL CRITICAL SUCCESS of Italian neorealist films (even though they were not always commercially profitable), the artistic achievements of neorealism made it extremely challenging for directors with different visions to discard social realism or the semidocumentary techniques such themes seemed to demand. Yet only a few years after the appearance of the major neorealist films in the mid- to late 1940s, the direction of Italian cinema began to change, largely due to films made by individuals who had done so much to make Italian neorealism an artistic success: Rossellini, Antonioni, Fellini, Visconti, and De Sica. All five of these men had played a major role in scripting or directing neorealist classics, but for sometimes very different reasons they each felt that continued critical insistence upon social realism was artistically confining.

Rossellini and *The Ways of Love*

Because Rossellini was generally considered the father of neorealism as the creator of *Open City* and *Paisan*, the trajectory of his career in the 1950s exhibits significant artistic changes. In the same year that he completed *The Machine to Kill Bad People*, which questioned the power of the camera to capture truth, Rossellini also completed *Ways of Love* (1948), a film in two episodes that was a vehicle for showcasing the acting of Anna Magnani, the star of *Open City* and his mistress at the time.[1] In this respect, the film may be fruitfully compared to Visconti's *Bellissima*. Like many of the films Rossellini made with Ingrid Bergman, whom he married in 1950 in the wake of a widely publicized affair after he abandoned Magnani, *Ways of Love* depends upon exploiting a professional actress, and Rossellini's increasing reliance upon professionals, as opposed to his early predilection for amateurs in *Paisan* or *Germany Year Zero*, reveals his desire to explore more psychologically complex themes than the nonprofessionals in many neorealist films were capable of portraying. The first episode, *A Human Voice* (*Una voce umana*), is an adaptation of a play by Jean Cocteau (1889–1963); the second part, *The Miracle* (*Il miracolo*), was scripted by Fellini especially for Magnani, and Fellini is also the male lead. *A Human Voice* requires a virtuoso performance, for it is a monologue of a woman speaking on the telephone to a lover who has left her for another woman, a prophetic theme since Rossellini was actually about to leave Magnani for Bergman. Although Magnani's acting is always more melodramatic than is typical of American cinema, Rossellini's increasingly characteristic *plan-séquence* shooting, which organizes action normally shot in a sequence by a simple complex take, concentrates the entire force of the episode upon the actress, her facial expressions, and her solitude and suffering. No response from her lover is ever heard on the sound track.

    The Miracle is a curious companion piece. Fellini's script parodies the love between Joseph and Mary, the parents of Jesus. A demented peasant woman (Magnani) meets a man she takes to be Saint Joseph (Fellini), and she discovers afterward that she is pregnant by this mysterious stranger. When she declares her miraculous conception to her neighbors, they scoff at her and force her to run away to a deserted sanctuary to deliver her baby. Neither the mysterious Joseph nor the lover on the other end of

The scriptwriter Federico Fellini plays the enigmatic stranger who leaves a peasant woman pregnant in Rossellini's *The Miracle*, a film that resulted in a U.S. Supreme Court decision banning religious censorship of film in America. *Credit: CSC*

Brother Ginepro's humility vanquishes the wrath of the tyrant Nicolaio in
Rossellini's *The Flowers of St. Francis,* a film partially scripted by Federico Fellini.
Credit: DVD

the telephone in the first episode ever utters a word, nor does either offer
any solace to the suffering of two very different women. In *The Miracle*,
Rossellini and Fellini are interested in portraying the nature of sainthood
in a secularized and unbelieving society, for Rossellini wants to emphasize that the modern world has no understanding of religious sentiment.
The collaboration of Rossellini and Fellini on this film was not accidental: Fellini had scripted the ambiguous monastery episode of *Paisan* and
would contribute to the script for Rossellini's cinematic investigation of
the "saintly fool" in *The Flowers of St. Francis* (*Francesco, giullare di dio*,
1950), as well as uncredited work on the script for *Europe '51*. In three of
Fellini's greatest early films, which may be defined as a "trilogy of grace or
salvation"—*La Strada* (*La strada*, 1954); *The Swindle*, a.k.a. *Il Bidone* (*Il
bidone*, 1955); and *The Nights of Cabiria* (*Le notti di Cabiria*, 1957)—he
explored spiritual dimensions of human life unrelated to social, economic,
and political concerns, themes often thought unworthy of neorealist treatment. Rossellini and Fellini also managed to make American legal history
with *The Miracle*, for a clumsy attempt to ban the screening of the film in
the United States led to a landmark Supreme Court decision in *Burstyn
v. Wilson*, a judgment that reversed a 1915 ruling denying cinema protection from such restrictions and one that overturned any possible religious
censorship over works of art.[2]

Voyage in Italy: Rossellini and Ingrid Bergman— toward a Cinema of the Reconstruction

Rossellini's decision to branch off from the social realism of his early "war trilogy" toward other, more intimate psychological themes lies at the heart of a series of films he made in a relatively brief period as vehicles for Ingrid Bergman: *Stromboli* (*Stromboli, terra di dio*, 1950); *Europe '51*; *Voyage in Italy*, a.k.a. *Strangers* (*Viaggio in Italia*, 1954); *Joan of Arc at the Stake* (*Giovanna d'Arco al rogo*, 1954); and *Fear* (*La paura*, 1954). In these works, Rossellini takes the most popular international star of the day and places her into films that examine the dimensions of contemporary marriage, emotional alienation, and personal despair—exactly the opposite of the kind of film that Hollywood idols were supposed to make. They were also failures at the box office, an even more fatal flaw for any movie star, even though the young critics and intellectuals associated with the French journal *Cahiers du Cinéma* greeted them as an original and revolutionary force in film, one that transcended neorealism. In an interview with two future French directors (Eric Rohmer and François Truffaut) given to this periodical in 1954, Rossellini voices his doubts about being forever identified as the father of neorealism:

> One is drawn to new themes, interests change, and with them directions. There is no point in tarrying among the ruins of the past. We are all too often mesmerized by a particular ambience, the atmosphere of a particular time. But life changes, the war is over, what was destroyed has been rebuilt. The drama of the reconstruction had to be told.[3]

Furthermore, Rossellini declared in the same interview that the lack of "cinematic effects" noted in his latest works constituted the very essence of his newer style:

> I always try to remain impassive. What I find most surprising, extraordinary, and moving in men is precisely that great actions and great events take place in the same way and with exactly the same resonance as normal everyday occurrences. I try to transcribe both with the same humility: there is a source of dramatic interest in that.[4]

Voyage in Italy remains the most important of Rossellini's films with Bergman, and although infrequently shown today, the critics of *Cahiers du Cinéma* in 1958 considered it one of the twelve greatest films of all time. Partially indebted to James Joyce's short story "The Dead," *Voyage in Italy* relates the visit of an English couple, Alexander and Katherine Joyce (George Sanders and Bergman) to Naples, where they must dispose of property inherited from Uncle Homer. While in Italy, the couple's old-fashioned English mentalities are assaulted by the Italian gusto for both life and death, and their reactions drive them first to the brink of divorce, and then, when we least expect it, to a miraculous reconciliation at the film's ending. The Joyces have none of the close, personal connections to the past, to history, or to the forces of nature that the seemingly vulgar Italians enjoy, a fact exposed by their desire to sell Homer's villa, their only link to this past, as soon as they can. The film's loose plot centers on a number of tourist excursions they take in the surrounding area. Katherine's first trip is to the National Museum of Naples, where Rossellini reverses the typical documentary techniques of museum photography, emphasizing Katherine's shocked reactions to the nude statues in the Farnese collection rather than upon the works of art themselves. During her second visit, to the ancient site of the Cumaean Sibyl, an insinuating Italian guide embarrasses her by placing her in the same spot where the Saracens supposedly once sacrificed women (again, Mediterranean sensuality overwhelms her Anglo-Saxon reserve). As she takes a third excursion, to the nearby lava fields, Katherine is assaulted by constant images of strolling lovers and pregnant women. There, another guide demonstrates the mystery of ionization near the lava beds, where any source of fire, such as a cigarette, produces an eruption of steam from the earth. Even the very soil upon which she walks around Naples seems full of energy and life and remains in harmony with the sexual energy of the city's inhabitants. Yet when Alexander visits Capri, the site of the legendary exploits of the emperors Tiberius and Caligula, his encounter with an attractive and apparently available woman leads nowhere. Katherine later visits a church where Italians preserve the skeletons of their dear, departed relatives (Neapolitans accept death rather than attempt to ignore it). Again, observing pregnant women everywhere (six on a single street alone!), Katherine discovers that the lust for life in Italy also includes its counterpart, an acceptance of death. Finally, the Joyces make their first excursion together to the Pompeii excavations just in time to witness the discovery of the remains of a married couple, trapped in the eruption of Vesuvius and eternally locked in each other's arms. No single image could stand in greater contrast to the sterility and unhappiness of their marriage. This scene provokes not only a morbid reaction from Katherine but also her decision to obtain a divorce from Alexander. As the couple returns to the city, they are swept up by a religious procession honoring a town's patron saint, and a miraculous reconciliation takes place between them that has often offended the commonsense logic of many critics.

No doubt, the scandalous press Rossellini received in the English-speaking world during his long affair with Ingrid Bergman explains, in part, his denunciation of English morality in *Voyage in Italy*. The film never enjoyed commercial success and initially was praised only by French critics. It is also beyond argument that Rossellini's simplistic juxtaposition of Mediterranean and Anglo-Saxon culture rests upon broad stereotypes.

The controversial reconciliation of Katherine and Alexander at the conclusion of Rossellini's *Voyage in Italy. Credit: MOMA*

Rossellini's impassivity, his technique of revealing only the outer surfaces of reality, forcing the viewer to confront a seemingly inconsequential and nondramatic cinematic style without obvious clues as to how a film must be interpreted, could never gain a broad audience appeal; nor could his mise-en-scène technique, relying upon the long take, seem anything but boring to the average moviegoer accustomed to the classic Hollywood narrative with its faster pace. Nevertheless, the understated, simple images from everyday existence reveal intellectual profundity and emotional complexity. In only a few years after the appearance of *Open City*, Rossellini had succeeded in shifting the focus of Italian neorealism away from themes directly associated with the war or economic conditions and toward the analysis of emotional behavior and human psychology.

Michelangelo Antonioni's Early Films: Documentary, Film Noir, and the Psychological Film

Antonioni's films of the 1950s that are closest in tone, if not in style, constitute another important step beyond neorealism's focus upon Italian social and economic conditions. His short *Sanitation Department* had already anticipated Rossellini's evolution toward a cinema of solitude and alienation characterized by unusually long takes. Like Rossellini, Antonioni was increasingly impatient with neorealist aesthetics and themes, and he too desired to create a new type of cinema that reflected the values of the reconstruction period. As he put it:

> The neorealism of the postwar period, when reality itself was so searing and immediate, attracted attention to the relationship existing between

the character and surrounding reality. It was precisely this relationship which was important and which created an appropriate cinema. Now, however, when for better or for worse reality has been normalized once again, it seems to me more interesting to examine what remains in the characters from their past experiences. This is why it no longer seems to me important to make a film about a man who has had his bicycle stolen. . . . Now that we have eliminated the problem of the bicycle (I am speaking metaphorically), it is important to see what there is in the mind and in the heart of this man who has had his bicycle stolen, how he has adapted himself, what remains in him of his past experiences, of the war, of the period after the war, of everything that has happened to him in our country—a country which, like so many others, has emerged from an important and grave adventure.[5]

Antonioni was particularly dissatisfied with traditional narrative techniques embodied in even the best neorealist films or documentaries. As a reaction against telling a story with blocks of logically connected sequences, Antonioni employed a montage in *Sanitation Department* that tried to create an editing technique that would be "absolutely free, poetically free," and a storyline liberated from logic, lacking a clear-cut beginning and ending. Instead, he preferred to juxtapose isolated shots or sequences, rendering (rather than merely relating) the essence of his vision of the street cleaner's universe. And in his first feature film, *Story of a Love Affair* (*Cronaca di un amore*, 1950), Antonioni employed the plot of James M. Cain's *The Postman Always Rings Twice*—already the inspiration for Visconti's important *Obsession*, a work that prefigured in some important respects the birth of neorealism—to move Italian cinematic narrative toward a distinctive personal style: characteristically long shots, tracks, and pans following the actors without interruption, especially after they have delivered the lines in their written scripts. With such a dramatically new style, Antonioni aimed to capture the "intensely dramatic scene" when the actor is left "alone by himself to face the after-effects of that particular scene and its traumatic moments."[6] More than any other Italian director, Antonioni consciously aimed to produce a modernist cinema, a cinema that was tied to "the truth rather than to logic" and that responded to the rhythm of life in its daily routine, "not so much concerned with externals as it is with those forces that move us to act in a certain way and not in another."[7] This cinema would become increasingly abstract and cerebral during the course of Antonioni's evolution beyond *Story of a Love Affair* to such masterpieces as *The Eclipse* (*L'eclisse*, 1962) and *Red Desert* (both discussed in chapter 9), films that embody many of the philosophical concerns usually associated with European existentialism, the dominant trend of intellectual thought on the continent during the 1950s.

While *Story of a Love Affair* employs much of the plot from Cain's hard-boiled novel, Antonioni nevertheless uses his source to embody a personal vision. Enrico Fontana (Ferdinando Sarmi), a wealthy Milanese engineer, hires a private investigator to look into the murky past of his young wife, Paola (Lucia Bosé); the detective discovers that some years earlier Paola's girlfriend had been killed in Ferrara after a fall into an elevator shaft under mysterious circumstances. Shortly thereafter, Guido (Massimo Girotti), her fiancé (and also eventually Paola's lover) had vanished from sight. When Guido learns of this investigation, he returns to Milan to see Paola again, and their meeting initiates a chain of events leading to the rekindling of their love affair and eventually to Enrico's accidental death (a death that they have both desired and even planned). While a summary of the film's plot seems to suggest a conventional narrative based upon suspense and an affair that drives two lovers toward a crime of passion, Antonioni's techniques reject any such conventional form. He refuses to unfold the information we seek in any logical order, chance plays a greater role than cause and effect (an obvious influence of the film noir tradition), and the true drama emerges not from the plot's unfolding but from the complex emotional reactions to what are often unexplained events.

The selection of Girotti as the lead actor provides a clue that Antonioni's film should be viewed against the backdrop of both Visconti's *Obsession* and his source in Cain's novel. But Antonioni significantly shifts his focus from the tawdry provincial atmosphere of rural Italy in *Obsession* to an upper-class environment. Whereas Visconti's female protagonist, played by Clara Calamai, suggested a feminine diamond in the rough, Antonioni's Lucia Bosé came to the cinema not from the theater but rather through winning the kind of beauty contests that were imported from American culture into Italy after the war. Dressed in stunning and fashionable garments, her luxurious costumes and the elegant Milanese locations in *Story of a Love Affair* are emblematic of the director's change of perspective, for Milan was the capital of the postwar Italian "economic miracle" and the habitat of the new middle-class protagonist so central to Antonioni's greatest films in the decade to come.

Guilty passion dominates Paola and Guido just as it dominated Visconti's Giovanna and Gino. Past guilt haunts them, for they knew Guido's fiancée was walking into an empty elevator shaft but did nothing to stop her: now their guilty love leads them to consider killing Paola's husband, Enrico. Only fate spares the couple from the commission of such a crime, for Enrico apparently dies quite by accident just as he is about to drive across a bridge where Guido awaits him with a loaded pistol. Actually, it is equally likely that Enrico killed himself in despair over his wife's infidelity as it is that he suffered a fatal accident. For Antonioni, mental processes are more important than actions, and therefore the tragic results of Enrico's

Two enormous bottles of vermouth frame a powerful Maserati in Antonioni's *Story of a Love Affair*. Credit: MOMA

death affect Paola and Guido as if they had murdered Enrico, since they had already planned to do so. When the police come to Paola's home to inform her of Enrico's death, she runs from the house (obviously thinking that Guido has carried out their plan), and when she finally confronts Guido, she blames him, rather than herself, for planning what she believes to be a murder. Thus, guilt and remorse destroy their love, and Guido leaves Milan and Paola forever as the film ends.

Story of a Love Affair already reflects the masterful photography of Antonioni's mature films, his careful framing of individual shots coupled with a suggestive and rhythmic editing. Rarely has a first feature film been so attentive to formal details. One memorable shot juxtaposes two enormous bottles of vermouth placed on either side of a deserted country road where Guido (posing as a car dealer) makes love to Paola in his car while his partner demonstrates a powerful Maserati to her husband, Enrico. The incongruity of this abstract image reflects the disequilibrium found not only in the lives of these guilt-ridden adulterers but in the wealthy society they inhabit as well. Desolate landscapes (an empty soccer stadium, rain-drenched urban streets) provide poetically appropriate backdrops for the anguish of the suffering protagonists, who are always presented in carefully composed frames within such locations. Irony abounds, undercutting any logical plot development: when Paola discovers that her husband is having her investigated, she discusses this with Guido in a spot fraught with memories from their shared past—near a dark elevator shaft. The elevator that caused the accident that once separated them now provides the impulse for their resolve to commit murder. Although they commit no actual (or even legally deemed) murder, the effects of their mental resolve to do so have

Antonioni's photography in *Story of a Love Affair*, such as this scene of the guilty lovers embracing on a staircase, recalls the photography of the great classics of American film noir. *Credit: MOMA*

profoundly psychological consequences. Yet the tone of American film noir is absent, since, true to his modernist predilections, Antonioni avoids any sense of dramatic development within a crescendo of suspense.

Following *Story of a Love Affair*, Antonioni made a series of interesting films—including *The Vanquished* (*I vinti*, 1953), a three-part episodic work set in England, France, and Italy; *The Girl Friends* (*Le amiche*, 1955), an adaptation of a novel by Cesare Pavese; and one episode devoted (not surprisingly, given Antonioni's interest in the subject) to suicide, in Zavattini's *Love in the City*. He then made *The Cry* (*Il grido*, 1957), a work that embodies in a pure form for the first time in his career his mature narrative technique—what a perceptive study of his films has termed "the emotional progression and its physical counterpart, the journey."[8] This film follows the wanderings of Aldo (Steve Cochran), a worker at a sugar refinery, after he has discovered that his love affair has disintegrated. Our first image of Aldo is a high-angle shot from atop a tall tower on which Aldo is working, while his mistress, Irma (Alida Valli), hurries to the factory to deliver his lunch as well as news both good (her husband has died, permitting them to marry) and bad (after an affair lasting eight years, she loves someone else!). This shattering revelation destroys Aldo's life, and he quits his job, leaving town with Rosina (Mirna Girardi), his daughter by a previous marriage, thereby cutting himself off from both his past and his future intended. As the film's picaresque and almost plotless structure unfolds, Aldo encounters an old girlfriend, Elvia (Betsy Blair), who still loves him; he takes up with Virginia (Dorian Gray), a sensual woman operating a gas station in the provinces;

he has a brief relationship with a prostitute named Andreina (Lynn Shaw); and he sends his daughter back to Irma, his earlier mistress. None of his relationships overcomes his alienation and despair over his loss of Irma. Eventually, Aldo returns home to witness a contented Rosina and Irma changing the diapers of a new child; this happens during a strike called by his former fellow workers at the sugar refinery, with whom he no longer has any connection. He then climbs the tower that opened the film, apparently faints, and plunges to his death. The cause of his death is no clearer than that of Enrico in *Story of a Love Affair*, which may either be an accident or a suicide. We witness not his fall but Irma's terrified expression as she sees it, and the film concludes with a long shot from the tower of the couple in the courtyard, with Irma kneeling beside Aldo's lifeless body.

Completely understated methods achieve an enormous emotional impact in *The Cry*. With very little music on the sound track and sparse and elliptical dialogues, silence rather than music or words often accompanies the starkest images of alienation. A typical shot in the film involves a stroll by the muddy banks of the Po River (that region already celebrated by Visconti's *Obsession* and other neorealist films of distinction by De Santis and Antonioni). Although Aldo is accompanied by one of his lovers, the deserted riverbanks and the careful positioning of the figures in this eerie landscape always evoke a sense of solitude. The result is an existential portrait of desperation buttressed by a poetic evocation of the Po region always central to Antonioni's view of the world. Nor does Antonioni offer any resolution of Aldo's tragedy (Aldo simply gives up his efforts to live) or any injection of facile optimism. Little occurs in the film, but the spectator comes away from it with unforgettable memories of the flat, misty landscapes Antonioni photographs, where people stand out in sharp relief—solitary and sad figures whose tragedies seem inscribed in the environment. In a retrospective look at the film almost two decades after it first appeared, one critic quite correctly stated that Antonioni was less interested in Aldo than in the landscape he inhabited: "The *subject* of those sequences was in fact the desolate autumnal wastes, the oppressive horizon. These were the things that inspired Antonioni, and the plot of the film—including Aldo's state of soul—was an expression, so to speak, of the landscape, not the other way around."[9]

Fellini (and Pirandello) and the Road beyond Neorealism

Parallel to the move toward psychological introspection and new modernist narrative techniques in films made during the early 1950s by both Rossellini and Antonioni, Federico Fellini's evolution beyond his neorealist origins began with the same dissatisfaction over pressure to make films with a sociological slant. Though he never directed a film that could be termed a pure neorealist work, Fellini was intimately involved with writing the scripts of many of the most important neorealist classics: he worked with Rossellini on *Open City*, *Paisan*, *The Miracle*, and *Europe '51*; with Pietro Germi on *In the Name of the Law* and *The Path of Hope*; and with Alberto Lattuada on *Without Pity* and *The Mill on the Po* (*Il mulino del Po*, 1949). For Fellini, neorealism was always a moral position rather than a true cinematic movement, offering more a way of viewing reality without preconceptions or prejudices—but *any* reality, not just social themes. He quickly became unhappy with the insistence upon certain realistic themes or techniques that critics of the day (mostly from the leftist spectrum of Italian political culture) prescribed as crucial to the development of Italian film as an art form. As he once complained, "it sometimes seemed as if the neorealists thought they could make a film only if they put a shabby man in front of the camera."[10] Moreover, Fellini insisted upon a director's complete control of his material and emphasized the role of fantasy and imagination, as opposed to documentary and fact, drawing no real dividing line between imagination and reality. Commenting upon Rossellini's declaration that neorealism represented an act of humility toward life, Fellini set his aesthetic perspective clearly apart from those neorealist theoreticians, such as Cesare Zavattini, who insisted upon forcing cinema to reflect only "reality":

> Yes, an act of humility towards life, but not towards the camera, there I don't agree. . . . once you're in front of the camera, you ought to abandon this humility completely; on the contrary, you ought to be arrogant, tyrannical, you ought to become a sort of god, in total command not only of the actors, but also the objects and the lights. This is why, in my view, the confusion created by neorealism was a very serious matter, because if you have an attitude of humility not only towards life but towards the camera as well, carrying the idea to its logical conclusion, you wouldn't need a director at all. The camera can work by itself: all you need to do is set it up and make things happen in front of it.[11]

While not as abrupt a break with neorealism as that of either Rossellini or Antonioni, Fellini's evolution beyond film realism toward a cinema of fantasy was first apparent not in his choice of subject matter, since he never abandoned the neorealist belief in human solidarity and honesty typical of such neorealists as De Sica, nor in any particular cinematic technique in his early films. Rather, his earliest innovations lie in his conception of film character, a shift in perspective that would eventually permit his evolving film style to express a completely original and uniquely personal vision or mythology. Neorealist characters are generally defined and limited by their surroundings. Visconti's poor fishermen in *The Earth Trembles*, De Santis's exploited rice workers in *Bitter Rice*, or De Sica's pensioner in *Umberto D.*

are all "typical" figures in the sense that they reflect specific current historical conditions and may be understood, at least in part, as products of their environment. Fellini's early works, on the contrary, create completely atypical figures more amenable to the personal mythology of an auteur unrestrained by a social message.

With the wisdom of hindsight, it now seems obvious that Fellini's development of a new concept of character beyond the neorealist protagonist shaped primarily by economic and social factors parallels and even repeats an operation undertaken some years earlier in the theater by Luigi Pirandello. Like Fellini, Pirandello reacted against the conventions of realism of his day.[12] Both Pirandello and Fellini move from considering character as a function of some outside factor to a basically subjective attitude, defining character both in terms of society's influence—character as "mask"—and as the reflection of the individual's own subconscious aspirations, ideals, and instincts—character as "face." The title of Pirandello's collected plays—*Naked Masks* (*Maschere nude*)—could well serve as a title for Fellini's first three films. In both early Pirandello and early Fellini, masks worn by characters as they act out their socially defined roles are torn off to reveal something of their more intimate personality underneath the mask, that is, their "face." In plays such as *The Rules of the Game*[13] (*Il gioco delle parti*, 1918), *The Pleasure of Honesty* (*Il piacere dell'onestà*, 1917), and *Right You Are (If You Think You Are)* (*Così è [se vi pare]*, 1916), Pirandello moved from a realist focus upon a unified character in conflict with other like individuals toward the interplay and clash of mask with face. In other words, he focused upon the character's internal conflicts, the conflicts among elements of his own personality. In addition, Pirandello rejected the idea that character could even be unified or fixed or ever completely known: character was flux, an ever-changing entity beyond the grasp of human reason precisely because its foundation, the face behind the mask, was composed of raw emotions, instincts, and preconscious feelings that could be expressed outwardly only by actions that seemed irrational and incomprehensible without some knowledge of their inner motivations.

Pirandello's fundamental redefinition of the nature of dramatic character was the necessary first step in the intellectual evolution that eventually led him to question the very nature of dramatic art itself in his later "trilogy of the theater in the theater."[14] Fellini lacked Pirandello's scholarly background in European philosophy and certainly had little sympathy with his programmatic approach to literature: Fellini never produced an essay on the art of the cinema that may be compared to Pirandello's theoretical treatise *On Humor* (*L'umorismo*, 1909), an outline of the new ideas on art that Pirandello would later systematically introduce into his writings. Fellini, in fact, once declared, "I'm not a man who approves of definitions. Labels belong on luggage as far as I'm concerned; they don't mean anything in art."[15]

Fellini's "Trilogy of Character"

Variety Lights

Variety Lights (1950)—Fellini's first film, directed in collaboration with the more experienced Alberto Lattuada—turns directly to the world of the variety theater and to a world of alluring illusion beneath which the film will uncover a tawdry and mundane reality. This first step in creating what may best be described as a "trilogy of character" focuses upon Checco Dal Monte (Peppino De Filippo), an insignificant vaudeville performer whose comic illusions of grandeur are eventually unmasked to reveal a lovable but flawed personality underneath his mask. Fellini's wife, Giulietta Masina, is cast as his fiancée, Melina Amour, while Lattuada's wife, Carla Del Poggio, plays Liliana, a stagestruck amateur whose ambition and shapely figure cause Checco to betray Melina. Even though *Variety Lights* is a product of two hands, it contains the now familiar visual cues of the abandoned piazzas reflecting the inauthentic existence, loneliness, and solitude of Fellini's characters, as well as the frenzied celebrations by night followed by the inevitable moment of truth at the arrival of dawn. The variety theater (Italy's vaudeville), a collection of eccentric individuals and vagabonds, is a perfect source of figures that are not defined by social conditions as in the neorealist cinema.

This concept of character emerges clearly in the dramatic confrontation between Checco and Liliana after she abandons him for a more promising theatrical producer and a night on the town in Rome. Checco waits dejectedly for her return, and after he reminds her of what he has done for her and argues she is obliged to pay him back by sharing his bed, she demurely agrees without a moment's hesitation. Her acceptance reveals her essentially mercenary nature, shocking the basically innocent Checco, and allowing him to catch a glimpse of her true face beneath the mask of innocence she normally wears.

In this Pirandellian moment of truth, Checco allows his own pretentious mask to fall, showing that he is basically a decent man rather than the worldly actor and man-about-town he has pretended to be. Checco slaps Liliana for agreeing to sleep with him, and as he leaves her *pensione*, climbing the stairs toward his hotel, we hear what sounds like applause on the sound track. The poetic necessity of this intrusive commentary by the director would be out of place in any purely realistic treatment of the scene. We have, in effect, witnessed Checco's finest performance, an act that is both genuine and far removed from the ridiculous roles he plays in the variety theater. He throws aside the false mask he wears, revealing his true personality underneath. Reality and illusion thus fuse, as the film reveals its novel conception of character through the dramatic clash of social role (mask) and authentic personality (face). Moreover, Fellini and Lattuada have also performed a similar operation of unmasking with their portrait of the institution of the variety theater, revealing the sordid underside of this medium with its petty jealousies, irrational causes of success and failure, and the often tawdry economic motives behind the search for a pure artistic form.

It would be unfair to give Fellini the entire credit for this film, but there is also little doubt that the vision of the world it embodies lies much closer to Fellini's than to Lattuada's. The collaboration of these two very different artistic sensibilities nevertheless underlines the fact that even directors associated with Italian neorealism, such as Fellini's partner, never embraced the simplistic antithesis of illusion and reality that was so typical of critical writing on the subject. The best neorealist directors conceived of these two realms as inseparably linked together in a mutually illuminating manner by the imagination of the director's vision and the aesthetic forms of art.

The White Sheik

In spite of its complete failure at the box office, *The White Sheik* (*Lo sceicco bianco*, 1952), now recognized as the comic masterpiece it is, reveals most fully Fellini's new notion of film character, one removed from the neorealist idea of character as essentially socially constructed. Once again Fellini sets his work against the background of the entertainment world—the photo novel (*fotoromanzo*) or cartoon-romance magazine, such as the *Grand Hotel* read by Silvana in *Bitter Rice*. The *fotoromanzo*, as noted in chapter 4, carries its narrative line forward by photographs of actual people rather than cartoons (*fumetti* in Italian) but also contains the traditional speech balloons for dialogue. The title of Fellini's film also humorously evokes the cinematographic memory of Rudolph Valentino, the Italian immigrant to Hollywood, whose roles in such films as *The Sheik* (1921) and *Son of the Sheik* (1926) made him the silent cinema's first true megastar.[16]

Fellini constructs the narrative of *The White Sheik* around the visit of a newlywed couple, fresh from the provinces, to Rome for their honeymoon: he employs the fastidious Ivan Cavalli (Leopoldo Trieste) and his wife, Wanda (Brunella Bovo), as the perfect comic embodiment of the interplay between mask and face, illusion and reality. Ivan is a typically fastidious petit-bourgeois provincial, trapped within a world of mechanical forms and social conventions, the antithesis of spontaneity and emotion. Superficial piety and patriotism mark Ivan's view of life, and these elements of his personality led some early critics to see Fellini's film as a neorealist critique of Italian provincial mores. Wanda embodies a naive attempt to break out of provincial customs and her conventional marriage into a life of illusion and fantasy, symbolized for her by the world of the white sheik and the *fotoromanzi*. When she slips away from her honeymoon hotel to visit the editorial offices of *Blue Romance* (her favorite *fotoromanzo* starring this sheik), Fellini shifts back and forth between husband and wife in parallel action sequences, thereby dividing the two realms of illusion and reality in order to comment on them both. This first transition shows Fellini's attention to detail. As Wanda walks, her path is lined with film posters that refer to the illusions that dominate her character. Church bells on the sound track suggest that her illusions may well arise from the values of a very stuffy pre–Vatican II Catholic Church. At the editorial office of *Blue Romance*, Wanda agrees with Marilena Alba Velardi (Fanny Marchio), its editor, that "dreams are our true lives."[17] As she leaves the office, a strange procession of characters in the *fotoromanzo* in their Bedouinesque costumes parade down the staircase, sweeping Wanda off with them to the beach, where they will shoot the next episode of the magazine. In contrast to this magic procession, the film then cuts rapidly back to Ivan in his hotel, who has discovered Wanda's disappearance. He sets off to find her and encounters an entirely different kind of procession: a highly regimented parade of Italian soldiers that moves his patriotic impulses. The narrative continues to progress by successive movements back and forth between these two realms dominated by illusion (in Wanda's case) and by mundane reality (in Ivan's).

The sequence at the Fregene beach outside Rome, during which Wanda actually meets her sheik, and the subsequent sequence, when the *fotoromanzo* pictures are shot, allow Fellini to reproduce the process of film montage. Wanda's idol, a tawdry Lothario named Fernando Rivoli, played

In Fellini's *The White Sheik*, a comic Roman substitute for a heroic Arab sheik poses for the *fotoromanzo* photographers on the beach outside of Rome. *Credit: MOMA*

brilliantly by Alberto Sordi, presents himself; he persuades Wanda to dress like a harem girl and to play a part in the photography session, but his real aim is to seduce her. He invites Wanda to sail out onto the ocean with him, convinces her that he has been tricked into marriage by an evil woman with a magic potion, and tries to force a kiss from her, losing control of the sail boom and being struck with it several times in the process. The attentive viewer will note that Fellini actually shot the scene with a boat on the beach, not in the ocean, the first of many magic tricks that characterize his mature film style. The director's subsequent cut back to Ivan at the opera, where *Don Giovanni* is being performed, provides an ironic commentary on Wanda's bungling lover.

By the time Ivan is attending the opera with his puzzled relatives, whose queries about his new bride he is unable to answer, and Wanda is experiencing the romantic misadventure with her white sheik, Fellini's two protagonists have been frozen in their respective roles: Wanda lives a life based upon naive illusions, a position Fellini criticizes but nevertheless prefers to Ivan's conventional, humdrum existence spent conforming to society's demands. While Wanda assumes a mask she constructs for herself, Ivan wears one that is constructed by others for him. As Wanda declares before she attempts to commit suicide in a Tiber River that is far too shallow to do anything but dampen her spirits, "Dreams are our true life . . . but sometimes dreams plunge us into a fatal abyss."

Having separated the two protagonists during his narrative in order to contrast the realms of illusion and reality, Fellini now brings them back together to conclude his film with the notion that a life based either entirely upon social convention or illusion is doomed to inauthenticity. Standing before the entrance to Saint Peter's, Ivan decides to lie about the fact that he has slept with a prostitute the night before and has soiled the family honor (supposedly his primary concern), while Wanda now transfers her illusions from an absurd *fotoromanzo* figure, a fake Bedouin lover, to her husband: Ivan is now her white sheik! Social conventions and white lies triumph at the film's conclusion, and a brief shot of the statue of an angel provides an ironic benediction for the future of this couple.

I Vitelloni

I Vitelloni (1953) represents a further step in the development of Fellini's conception of film character and the dramatic clash of mask and face. Unlike *The White Sheik*, this work was a critical and commercial success and the first of his films to win foreign distribution, with which his reputation rapidly grew. Although the film seems based upon Fellini's young-adult life in his hometown of Rimini on the Adriatic coast—just as critics would later assume that his nostalgic portrait of growing up in the provinces of

Fascist Italy in *Amarcord* reflected his childhood experiences—Fellini always insisted that he was not a *vitellone* (loafer, slacker; literally, veal from an older calf) as a young man, and that most of the adventures in *Amarcord* happened to his friends, not to him. His narratives were all inventions of his fantasy, only loosely inspired by biographical events. Fellini certainly popularized the expression *vitelloni*—a local word employed to describe adult men who remain at home, being coddled by their mothers, rather than leaving the house to find a job and make their own families.

While the structure of *The White Sheik* relied upon narrative strands held together by rapid and ironic cross-cutting between them, *I Vitelloni* tells its story through a meandering, picaresque account of five different *vitelloni*: the oldest is Fausto (Franco Fabrizi), who is forced to marry Sandra Rubini (Eleonora Ruffo, who worked in genre films as Leonora), the sister of the most likable of the *vitelloni*, Moraldo (Franco Interlenghi), and the only one of the group who succeeds in leaving home at the end of the film; Alberto (Alberto Sordi) is a pathetic and effeminate wastrel who lives by sponging money off his sister, Olga, and his mother; Leopoldo (Leopoldo Trieste) is a would-be poet without talent; Riccardo's character (played by Fellini's younger brother, Riccardo) is poorly developed, but he seems to be a pleasant young man with a melodious voice. To increase the distance between his five protagonists and himself, since Fellini wanted to avoid the assumption that his stories were merely autobiographical reminiscences, Fellini employs an omniscient narrator whose voice-overs tie the rather formless plot together and provide a running commentary and an objective perspective on the action. At the close of the film, it is actually Fellini's own voice that provides the voice-over about Moraldo's decision to abandon his wastrel friends and to go to the "big city" of Rome, much as Fellini himself did two decades earlier. In contrast to this objective narrator is the highly subjective camerawork that most often reflects the more limited points of view of the *vitelloni*.

Nevertheless, the themes of *I Vitelloni* remain those of *The White Sheik*: the clash of illusion and reality and the clash of mask and face. In this, Fellini's second solo film, the director first examines each individual *vitellone*'s personal life and his pretentious social mask; then he allows these masks to be torn away, forcing his characters to confront the emptiness of their illusions. Three of the group—Fausto, Alberto, and Leopoldo—are examined in detail; Riccardo seems to have been purposely slighted; Moraldo is a bemused observer, an outsider who witnesses the crises in his friends' lives and reaches a degree of self-awareness that permits him to change his life and move away. Fellini places Fausto, Alberto, and Leopoldo in situations where the clash of mask and face, reality and illusion, arise naturally from the setting and are all connected with the world of show business: a beauty pageant, a carnival ball, a variety theater. Fausto discovers that Moraldo's sister, Sandra, is pregnant as her election as "Miss Siren of 1953" is being announced to the town. When she faints, he betrays her by flirting with another woman. Fellini's hilarious presentation of a beauty contest echoes the more serious one portrayed in *Bitter Rice* and bears witness to the influence of American popular culture here as well. Fausto is a completely unsympathetic figure whose social mask as a romantic Don Giovanni is progressively destroyed by the director. First he is forced to marry Sandra, then he is fired from a job in a religious-articles shop because of his flirtations with the owner's wife, his wife and child abandon him, and finally his father whips him with a belt in front of his family and neighbors like the spoiled brat he is and always will remain.

Alberto's moment of truth occurs in a similar situation at the annual carnival ball, where everyone comes masked and in costume—an even more obvious place to consider the interplay of mask and face. Fellini's subjective camera, with its rapid movement through a variety of positions and angles, and the suddenly increased tempo and complexity of his editing, give us an insight into Alberto's predicament. We see him lurching around the ballroom in a drunken stupor, dancing with a huge papier-mâché head or mask, and dressed in drag to underscore the effeminate qualities that set him apart from his independent and self-reliant sister, Olga, who is about to abandon life at home to run away with a married man. No other image in Fellini's works visualizes so clearly this clash of mask and face than a ballroom dance between a man in drag and an empty mask. As Alberto asks Moraldo a philosophical question—"Who are you? You're nobody, nobody!"—we realize that Alberto is really describing himself, for alcohol

Alberto's behavior at the masked ball, where he appears in drag, calls attention to his identity crisis in Fellini's *I Vitelloni. Credit: MOMA*

and Olga's departure have torn aside his social mask and revealed the miserable state of his life to him and to others. Leopoldo's moment of truth arrives when he attempts to have his wretched plays staged by an aging homosexual actor named Natali (Achille Majeroni). Horrified by the actor's attempts to seduce him, Leopoldo abandons all hopes of literary success and returns to the comforting familiarity of his home, the care of his maiden aunts, and his illusions—sadder but certainly no wiser.

Each of the *vitelloni* experiences a crisis as his illusions collide with reality, but for Fausto, Alberto, and Leopoldo, the truth that emerges from the clash of mask and face is too overwhelming. While they cling to their familiar surroundings, Fellini's alter ego, Moraldo, witnesses their failures and learns from it. With a brilliant closing shot, Fellini employs a mobile, subjective camera to let us experience Moraldo's emotions: the train pulls away from the station toward Rome, and the camera behaves as if it were on the train sharing Moraldo's thoughts, moving through each of the *vitelloni's* bedrooms, passing over each of them in their sleep with a nostalgic caress. Moraldo has begun to grow up and to experience a kind of secular conversion, an epiphany. Still, Fellini does not intend to abandon illusions entirely, even though he is certainly critical of a life entirely governed by them.

It is also interesting to note that the professional actor playing the role of Moraldo—Franco Interlenghi—began his career as the nonprofessional actor who gained fame as De Sica's orphan shoeshine boy in *Shoeshine*; Moraldo, Fellini's alter ego, has come of age. Fellini also seems to be telling his audience that the Italian cinema must do the same. Just as Fellini retained something of his neorealist heritage in *I Vitelloni* (in this case an actor), so too the Italian cinema must preserve the best of its neorealist heritage—the honesty, the belief in humanist values, the sincerity that characterized the masterpieces of neorealism regardless of ideological content or cinematic style. With this legacy of artistic integrity incorporated into his own creative vision, Fellini transcended his neorealist origins with a new perspective on the nature of film character and the dramatic possibilities of the clash between social roles and authentic feelings, between masks and faces. In so doing, he helped to lay the artistic foundations for the complicated odyssey his career was to take in the future, and his example also invited his colleagues in the film industry to do likewise.

Federico Fellini and the "Crisis of Neorealism": The "Trilogy of Grace or Salvation"

Fellini's subsequent three films—*La Strada*, *The Swindle*, and *The Nights of Cabiria*—move beyond his concern with character to a new dimension expressing a personal vision and a particular Fellinian mythology. Taken together, they form a trilogy on spiritual poverty, grace, and salvation. Such notions may erroneously be construed as indebted to Catholicism. (In fact, Marxist critics in Italy attacked these films, claiming Fellini was a Catholic apologist.) Fellini, however, generally employs Christian ideas in a purely secular context. In particular, he uses the traditional religious notion of conversion as an understandable metaphor for the personal and existential crises his lonely protagonists endure.

La Strada and International Fame

La Strada is the best known of these three works: it won Fellini an Oscar for Best Foreign Language Film; made international celebrities of his wife, Giulietta Masina, and the composer of the film's music, Nino Rota; and was a commercial and critical success all over the world. Only in Italy did it spark a polemical argument about the direction Italian cinema should take, a debate that has become an important part of what has since become known as "the crisis of neorealism." Guido Aristarco, the dean of Marxist film critics at the time, attacked *La Strada* for its lack of realism and for what he called its "poetry of the solitary man, a poetry in which each story, instead of being reflected, lived without the reality of the narrative, is, through a process of individualization, reabsorbed into itself and nullified as an historical entity only to be converted into a symbolic diagram, a legend, a myth."[18] Fellini, one of the scriptwriters who had contributed a great deal to major neorealist films by Roberto Rossellini and Alberto Lattuada, countered such ludicrous charges, charges the greatest critic of the period— André Bazin—quite rightly viewed as an attempt to impose an aesthetics of socialist realism on Italian cinema.[19] Fellini defended himself by completely rejecting the notion that neorealist cinema contained any programmatic content. He particularly rejected the idea that film characters should be "typical" in the sense that they must reflect social and economic conditions or a particular social class. In the case of the eccentric protagonists of *La Strada*—Zampanò (Anthony Quinn), the circus strongman who learns the meaning of love and human communication, and Gelsomina (Giulietta Masina), a young peasant woman who is mentally challenged but who learns from a circus acrobat and clown named Il Matto or the Fool (Richard Basehart) that her vocation in life is to love the brutish Zampanò—Fellini denied that they were particularly unusual: "There are more Zampanòs in the world than bicycle thieves, and the story of a man who discovers his neighbor is just as important and as real as the story of a strike. What separates us [Fellini and his Marxist attackers] is no doubt a materialist or spiritualist vision of the world."[20] Fellini compares his protagonists here, of course, to that of De Sica's *The Bicycle Thief*, a figure that had already become a classic instance of neorealist film character as social "type" by the time *La Strada* was released.

The "crisis of neorealism" has become no more than a subject of academic discussion, whereas *La Strada* remains one of Italy's best loved films and certainly Fellini's most popular work. The film is really more a fairy tale or a fable than a dramatic account of character development or narrative action. Its title—literally, "the road"—underlines its picaresque, antilinear plot structure, and like Antonioni, Fellini found the metaphor of the search, journey, or quest a suitable one for symbolizing the search for meaning in life that occupies most of his characters. Like Antonioni too, Fellini is most concerned with the failure of communication between human beings and the resultant spiritual poverty in life. His three protagonists are vagabonds, without any real connection to time or place, circus clowns in search of their next free meal. The film's structure follows them from one beach to another. Eventually the Fool is accidentally killed for his impudence by Zampanò after convincing Gelsomina that she has a purpose in life; Gelsomina, having witnessed the Fool's death, is gradually broken by the trauma and, abandoned by Zampanò, later dies. Their literal journey, of course, is less important to Fellini than the figurative distance the characters travel. Gelsomina moves from childish innocence toward womanhood and an acceptance of her vocation as Zampanò's companion, and her own death makes it possible for Zampanò to travel a similar road from brutish insensitivity toward a limited sort of self-knowledge. The film ends when he finally becomes capable of weeping a single tear over her death.

It is rare to discover a viewer of *La Strada* left unmoved by the film, and yet its emotional appeal cannot be explained in terms of the more complicated stylistic devices the director would employ in his future career. One perceptive critic described the work's impact better than anyone else when he noted that the most moving sequences of the film defy "confident interpretation" and are "essentially dumb"; unless the viewer is attuned to what he terms "a subliminal level, a level largely of images plus the complex associations of scarcely perceived sound," the film will remain unsatisfying.[21] Rarely has any film expressed so completely its director's sense of the wonder, fantasy, surprise, and mystery in the simple lyrical moments of life without recourse to special effects or a completely subjective camera style. As Bazin aptly put it, *La Strada* concerns "the phenomenology of the soul," which is clearly set apart from intellectual or socioeconomic concerns.[22]

Fellini achieves this sense of mystery by treating the unpredictable, the unexpected, and the extraordinary just as if it were part of everyday reality. A single celebrated sequence is illustrative of his procedure: Gelsomina runs away from Zampanò and sits by the roadside, staring at a bug with the curious, enigmatic, clownlike smile that made Masina's performance unforgettable. As she examines the insect, and without any plausible explanation whatsoever, a band of circus musicians appears as if by magic in the nearby field, forming a procession into the nearby town, and Gelsomina follows

Fellini's greatest clown figure– Gelsomina in *La Strada*–played by his wife, Giulietta Masina. *Credit: MOMA*

them. This strange event leads into another religious procession replete with traditional Catholic symbols. There, Gelsomina stands against a wall poster referring to the "Immaculate Madonna," which associates Gelsomina with the Virgin. Like the city piazza at night, in Fellini's universe of symbols the procession usually has a particular connotation, frequently preceding the ultimate Fellinian miracle, the magic moment when mental anguish or rational thought gives way to an acceptance and an embracing of life. The procession becomes, in this case, Fellini's symbol for the renewal of faith in life through grace—the mysterious quality that is bestowed by divine power without regard to the merit of the person receiving it. Fellinian grace becomes associated with existential moments where characters realize the beauty of human existence.

Fellini disliked logical, rational endings. *La Strada* is a philosophical parable with numerous possible interpretations. It is a modern fairy-tale version of the story of Beauty and the Beast; it is a version of a familiar literary motif as old as romance itself about the love of a good woman transforming a bad man. It also suggests a Christian account of a soul's redemption through sacrifice and suffering. Gelsomina reminds us of the biblical dictum that we must become like children to enter the kingdom of heaven. Gelsomina's belief in the message of the famous Parable of the Pebble that the Fool relates to her—that there must be some reason for her wretched existence just as there must be some explanation for the existence of an ordinary stone or life itself has no meaning—serves as a reminder that Fellini believes faith, a nonreligious form of faith, provides strength to humanity where reason often falls short.

The Swindle

The pattern suggesting a secular form of grace bestowed upon often undeserving protagonists established in *La Strada* is continued in *The Swindle* and *The Nights of Cabiria*. *The Swindle* represents a variation on the Christian story of the good thief: its main character is a confidence man whose characteristic swindle plays out in the disguise of a priest. With Augusto (played by Broderick Crawford, awarded an Oscar for Best Actor for his role in the 1949 film *All the King's Men*), Fellini takes a petty crook and uses him, as he had Gelsomina, as a means of exploring the implications of human anguish, solitude, grace, and existential (not religious) salvation. It is also interesting that just as he did in *La Strada* with the casting of two American actors (Quinn and Basehart), Fellini intelligently kept his eye on the American market with the use of Crawford in the lead role and with the casting of Basehart again as one of Augusto's accomplices, Picasso. Apparently he had originally considered Humphrey Bogart for the lead. In Fellini's hands, Augusto becomes an existential hero, alienated from authentic meaning in life and feeling remorse for his crimes, yet driven to commit them by some strange compulsion. After a hellish voyage of self-negation, he comes to attain a Fellinian state of grace through suffering. Once again, Fellini employs a minimum of obtrusive cinematic effects. And as in *La Strada*, his vehicle is the presentation of a poetic universe filled with symbols, and once again his plot is episodic and picaresque, following the pattern of a journey or a discovery.

One sequence depicting the discovery by his daughter Patrizia (Lorella De Luca) of Augusto's career as a confidence man may well recall a famous sequence from De Sica's *The Bicycle Thief*: the conclusion to that neorealist classic, where the young Bruno watches his father's apprehension when he fails to steal a bicycle and experiences humiliation. In Fellini's case, Augusto is spotted by one of his former victims, whose brother almost died from some fake medicine Augusto once sold him—perhaps an allusion to *The Third Man*, where the dealings of Orson Welles's character, Harry Lime, actually kill people with bad penicillin in Vienna. After Patrizia discovers that her father is the kind of man who would sell bad medicine to an ill person, his public humiliation results in a prison sentence. Yet, as usual, even though Augusto is a deeply flawed human being, Fellini feels compassion for even the most despicable of his characters. He hates the sin but loves the sinner, an attitude that sets his vision of the world apart from other ideologically oriented Italian directors and underscores his fundamental nature as a comic director.

In Augusto's case, Fellini depicts his protagonist as sinner and saint, an ambivalent assessment of his character that emerges most clearly in the conclusion of the film. Disguised as a priest, Augusto sets up his last crime: he tells a gullible peasant family that there is a fortune in stolen merchandise buried on their land, which they can have on condition that they pay 350,000 lire to say masses for the soul of the criminal who confessed his crime to Augusto. It is the kind of con game that Augusto has carried out successfully many times before, but now his conscience begins to trouble him, particularly because the peasants must sell their only ox to raise the cash, and one member of the family, a young girl, suffers from polio. Augusto, posing as a true priest, speaks to this young girl of miracles and faith in God, of learning through suffering, but his words conceal his own very troubled spirit. When Augusto drives off with his accomplices, he claims that the girl's condition has so moved him that he decided not to cheat the family out of the money. Nevertheless, after knocking him unconscious and searching his clothing, the thieves discover that Augusto really did take the money after all! No sentimental or artificial conversion occurs in *The Swindle*. Until his last gasp, Augusto remains what he is—a con artist without scruples.

And yet, at this crucial moment, Augusto achieves an apotheosis into a kind of secular saint, purified by his suffering and anguish. As he painfully crawls up an arid hill, now the victim rather than the swindler, we hear church bells on the sound track and a procession of children passes by, a familiar scene in Fellini's early works. Augusto can no longer join the process the way Gelsomina often did in *La Strada* or Cabiria will at the close of *The Nights of Cabiria*: his drama and death must take place in complete solitude. As the film ends, the camera slowly draws away from this inverted Christ figure, reminding us of a similar scene concluding *La Strada*, where Zampanò lay on the beach, weeping over the loss of Gelsomina. Here, as one critic put it, the movement of the camera is a benediction, "a short, gentle movement, one only those who have faith can truly comprehend."[23] The precedent for Augusto's miraculous redemption after a life of vice comes not from the cinema but from Christian literature, Dante's *Divine Comedy*. In the Ante-Purgatory, Dante the Pilgrim encounters Count Buonconte da Montefeltro, one of the souls who delayed their repentance until the last moment, just as Augusto seems to have done. Buonconte was saved from eternal damnation merely by uttering the name of the Virgin Mary in his dying breath. As one of the devils complained who fought over his soul with an angel and lost it, only "one poor little tear" (*Purgatory* V: 107) suffices for man's salvation, and only one measly tear is all Augusto needs as well.[24]

The Nights of Cabiria

As the Chaplinesque little prostitute Maria "Cabiria" Ceccarelli (a figure that appears earlier in a brief sequence of *The White Sheik*), Giulietta Masina delivers perhaps her finest performance, even more masterful than that of *La Strada*. In *The Nights of Cabiria*, Fellini combines many of the themes from the first two films of the "trilogy of grace or salvation" with another picaresque plot. Fellini's symbolic and poetic universe also stands out—the strange, evocative, De Chirico–like landscapes and abandoned squares inhabited by exotic figures; the wild parties with the same morning emptiness; the same quest for meaning in life. Grace or salvation still preoccupies the director (although interpreted in a secular, not overtly religious, context), and Fellini here returns to one narrative pattern employed in *I Vitelloni*. In that earlier film, he showed five different characters suffering successive soul-rending personal experiences, with only Moraldo learning from them. In *The Nights of Cabiria*, however, Fellini concentrates such events in the life of a single protagonist who undergoes five different misadventures. Like Gelsomina, Cabiria exhibits certain clownlike mannerisms and remains innocently open to unusual emotional or spiritual experiences. Yet she represents a real flesh-and-blood woman (even a prostitute) rather than a figure in a fairy tale, and her character is more well rounded, developed, and realistic.

Fellini opens his film with a sentimental, old-fashioned image: Cabiria and her boyfriend Giorgio skip through a field toward a riverbank, seemingly in love, suggesting the payoff shot of a kiss. Yet Fellini quickly deflates our romantic expectations when Giorgio steals Cabiria's purse and pushes her into the water. This trajectory of hope and illusion transformed into despair occurs repeatedly in Cabiria's experiences throughout the narrative, as the luckless but plucky prostitute struggles to survive in a hostile world. Next, she meets a famous actor—played by a famous actor, Amedeo Nazzari, a matinee idol during the Fascist period. He has just had a fight with his bimbo girlfriend and picks up Cabiria to replace her, taking her to visit an exotic nightclub where the precocious prostitute dances a frenzied mambo. Returning to his apartment, Cabiria is about to experience the romantic adventure of her lifetime when his girlfriend returns, and Cabiria is locked in the actor's bathroom while the couple makes love in the bedroom.

Cabiria's third misadventure takes place when she accompanies her prostitute friends and the crippled uncle of one of their pimps to a shrine outside Rome renowned for its healing miracles. Expecting to be cured, the uncle falls on his face after discarding his crutches. When Cabiria prays fervently for a change in her life, she receives no response at all. Grace in Fellini's universe remains a mysterious quality, bestowed most generously but only when least expected, and only after a trial by suffering. This important episode in the film foreshadows the even more radical critique of the Catholic Church in Fellini's later works and reveals how mistaken leftist critics were in their denunciation of Fellini's "trilogy of grace or salvation" for what they saw in it as an apology for conservative Catholicism. Cabiria's fourth mishap incorporates the world of show business and takes place in a variety theater, where she is hypnotized by an illusionist and forced in a trance to reveal all her hidden desires for a radical change in her life, for the normalcy of a home, a husband, and a family. When the illusionist breaks the trance,

Oscar prepares to betray the gullible Cabiria in Fellini's *The Nights of Cabiria*.
Credit: MOMA

Cabiria meets Oscar (François Périer), with whom she falls in love, but this hope for a new life, the Dantesque "new life," returns to the opening of the film, as Oscar steals her hard-earned savings and abandons her near another riverbank that recalls her bad fortune in the opening of the film.

No hope, no exit, and no redemption seem possible for Cabiria. Then the Fellinian miracle occurs: Cabiria leaves the riverbank and encounters a group of young people singing, and she is transformed by Nino Rota's music on the sound track in a manner that defies logical explanation. At the end of the film, music becomes Fellini's metaphor for salvation—a completely gratuitous, spontaneous, and unexpected experience, and his final shot is one of his most brilliant, although simple and economical. In a close-up of Cabiria's face, her gaze toward the camera crosses that of our own. As André Bazin so sensitively described the moment: "here she is now inviting us, too, with her glance to follow her on the road to which she is about to return. The invitation is chaste, discreet, and indefinite enough that we can pretend to think that she means to be looking at somebody else. At the same time, though, it is definite and direct enough, too, to remove us quite finally from our role of spectator."[25]

∾

With Zampanò, Augusto, and Cabiria, Fellini created characters that face loneliness and alienation alone, each experiencing an existential crisis. The three films comprising this "trilogy of grace or salvation" thus create three extended metaphors for the human condition and three images of the spiritual poverty of the era. A tear transforms a circus strongman's brutishness into human form when he feels love for the first time in his life as a result of Gelsomina's existence, another tear moves a swindler to repent and to thirst for salvation, and the smile on a prostitute's face signals to us that grace or salvation may befall us when we least except it. Fellini's secular version of Christian grace is ultimately one of self-revelation, a purely human experience. His female characters, such as Gelsomina or Cabiria, fare better than his male protagonists (an interesting fact in the light of the frequent feminist attacks made on his later films). Alone among the main characters in this trilogy, Cabiria joins the Fellinian procession that affirms life and continues down the symbolic path of self-discovery that all humanity must travel. Fellini's films thus celebrate the triumph of the director's lyrical and poetic vision over a material world that constantly threatens to overwhelm his embattled characters. It is a life-affirming vision almost out of place in an age characterized by a philosophy of despair and alienation expressed so eloquently in the early works of Antonioni, and one that even Fellini himself was unable to sustain consistently in his mature films.

De Sica, Visconti, and the Return of Melodrama

Vittorio De Sica's brilliant neorealist classics helped to define an entire film era in the postwar period. Yet no individual was less likely to have produced films emphasizing social realism. A prewar movie idol, singer, bon vivant gambler, and lady's man, De Sica's personality fit the template of the Hollywood movie star better than that of social activist or reformer. *Indiscretion of an American Wife* (*Stazione Termini*, 1953) represents one of the first postwar Italian attempts to make a movie with Hollywood financial backing and American stars. (Although American funding and actors were employed throughout the neorealist period, the latter were generally relative unknowns. As noted in chapter 3, the story of Hollywood backing Cary Grant to star in *The Bicycle Thief* is likely apocryphal.) Yet in *Indiscretion*, De Sica gained American support by casting the Hollywood mogul David O. Selznick's wife, the Oscar-winner Jennifer Jones, as Mary Forbes, an American tourist who comes to Rome and falls in love with an Italian named Giovanni Doria, improbably played by the American star and (then) three-time Oscar nominee Montgomery Clift. The involvement of the Italian scriptwriters Cesare Zavattini and Luigi Chiarini and the cinematographer Aldo Graziati (a.k.a. G. R. Aldo, 1902–53)—the cameraman for such neorealist classics as *The Earth Trembles* and *Umberto D.*—seemed to promise an American version of Italian neorealist cinema, as did an opening intertitle announcing that "actual settings" were employed in a story taking place exclusively in and around Rome's huge central train station. (In America at the time, a number of urban-based film noirs employed "actual settings," rather than staging city narratives on Hollywood sets, due to the

The Hollywood stars Montgomery Clift and Jennifer Jones play star-crossed lovers meeting at Rome's Stazione Termini in De Sica's *Indiscretion of an American Wife. Credit: DVD*

influence of Italian neorealism.) Nonetheless, De Sica's *Indiscretion* reverts to the very Hollywood form of melodrama that his scriptwriter Zavattini had once denounced in his influential pronouncements on neorealism.[26] Dialogue by the veteran scriptwriter Ben Hecht and novelist Truman Capote, plus beautiful costumes for Jennifer Jones by Christian Dior (justly nominated for an Oscar), mark the work as De Sica's definitive move away from a concern with social realism. The film's opening shot is a passionate and prolonged kiss by Jones and Clift in chiaroscuro lighting, and the remainder of the film stresses these close-up shots typical of a star-oriented cinema and romantic dialogue. Although far removed from the innovative style of De Sica's neorealist works, *Indiscretion* remains a fine love story in the traditional American fashion. Its most memorable sequences are paradoxically those that could have easily been used in De Sica's neorealist work: the vignettes of strange travelers hurrying through the station toward a departing train, or the concluding sequences where a police commissioner (Gino Cervi) tears up the charge of public indecency against the couple, who have tried to make love in an abandoned train compartment because Mrs. Forbes has a family back in America. Here, the humanist cinema of De Sica shines through the corny romanticism.

Visconti's *White Nights* (*Le notti bianche*, 1957) employs a melodramatic love story in an adaptation of a short story by Dostoyevsky. Mario (Marcello Mastroianni), a lonely newcomer to town, meets Natalia (Maria Schell) on four nights, and falls in love with her, but she abandons him (as Mary leaves Giovanni in *Indiscretion*) when the lover she has been waiting for over the

In Visconti's *Le Notti Bianche*, Mario looks for company in the lonely bars of the city. *Credit: AB*

course of a year returns. Visconti's narrative of loneliness seems far closer to the atmosphere of a 1950s Antonioni film than to De Sica's Italianized version of the traditional tale of the puritanical American tourist seeking love in a climate of Mediterranean permissiveness. If his earlier *Senso* embraced a sense of history within an operatic plot that often employed authentic on-location sets (such as the famous La Fenice opera house in Venice or real battlefields), *White Nights* relies heavily upon constructed studio sets that reproduce the look of the city of Livorno in the 1950s, where a small bridge divides the worlds of the two characters and the twin realms of reality (Mario's world) and illusion (Natalia's realm) in a manner that suggests familiarity with Fellini's works of the 1950s. Visconti's focus upon unrequited love moves beyond any interest in social realism to a dimension that is more typical of the great black-and-white films of the 1960s that focused upon personal psychological alienation, not overtly social problems.

By the mid-1950s, it was increasingly clear that the greatest Italian directors associated with Italian neorealism as directors and/or scriptwriters— Rossellini, Antonioni, Fellini, De Sica, and Visconti—had escaped the straitjacket of a narrowly conceived definition of Italian neorealism and were busy creating a filmic universe reflecting personal visions of their own making, rather than attempting to reflect social and economic conditions in the peninsula. In many respects, the films they made created a far more rich and complex cinema than any that might have resulted if dominated by an interest in social realism defined in a narrowly Marxist sense.

PART THREE

The Golden Age
of Italian Cinema

CHAPTER SIX

The Italian "Peplum"

THE SWORD AND SANDAL EPIC

Italian Film History, the Classical Tradition, and "Hollywood on the Tiber"

ITALIAN FILM HISTORY IN THE POSTWAR PERIOD has always been dominated by the heritage of neorealism: for better or for worse, many of Italy's greatest directors, scriptwriters, and cameramen came of age during the neorealist period (the first decade after the end of the war in 1945), and their subsequent careers were often shaped by their attitude toward the cinema of social realism. One of the most striking characteristics of Italian neorealist cinema, not counting its interest in social themes and contemporary depiction of postwar economic conditions, was a rejection of traditional film genres—highly scripted historical epics, romantic melodramas, and costume dramas that were set in a distant and often literary past. Yet toward the end of the 1950s, a version of one of Italy's most traditional film genres—the epic film set in a classical past—became redefined as the "peplum,"[1] the "neomythological film,"[2] or the "sword and sandal epic," creating a genre that gained mass audiences and often made impressive showings at the box office all over the world. These films would become the staple fare of drive-in theaters in America, a standard feature of popular entertainment everywhere—standing in clear opposition to the content of most of the "art films" associated with Italy's best neorealist directors—and would even eventually become a target of satire and parody because of their often exaggerated interpretations of classical mythology, their sometimes poorly dubbed prints intended for foreign consumption, or their often impoverished production values and camp scripts or costumes.[3]

Of course, Italy had exercised its influence abroad with the enthusiastic reception of silent epic films set in antiquity, such as Guazzoni's *Quo Vadis?* or Pastrone's masterpiece, *Cabiria*, whose protagonist Maciste resurfaced in

Bartolomeo Pagano as the bare-chested Maciste, the prototype of the classical strongman from Pastrone's silent epic *Cabiria*, became the template for all the various muscle-bound heroes of the peplum. *Credit: CSC*

the peplum era—along with Hercules, Ursus, Samson, and other renowned strongmen of steel who were favorite peplum characters. And during the Fascist period, as well as in the immediate postwar era, a number of important films set in classical times were made in Italy, including Gallone's *Scipio Africanus: The Defeat of Hannibal* and Blasetti's *Fabiola* (1949), a love story between the daughter of a Roman senator and a gladiator. Most, if not all, such films set in the classical period either aimed at a historically accurate depiction of the ancient past or attempted to inject romance and melodrama into ancient history, in the tradition of Italian grand opera and theater. Moreover, in the 1950s, the phenomenon of "Hollywood on the Tiber"—the arrival of Hollywood film studios and directors shooting in Italy to reduce production costs—revived a custom that had begun in 1923 when the original *Ben-Hur*, directed by Fred Niblo, filmed some scenes in Rome before completing shooting in America. The high point of American production in Italy was reached with a number of Hollywood films that were either partially or completely filmed in Italy. Mervyn LeRoy's *Quo Vadis?* (1951)—a remake of a tale adapted from a novel that had been shot by Guazzoni in the silent period—may be said to have launched the postwar mania for films set in the classical period and for Hollywood production in Italy. Although it lacked the wide-screen technology that would mark most of the Hollywood epics and the Italian peplums, it boasted an enormous cast and huge sets constructed at Cinecittà. Robert Wise's *Helen of Troy* (1956) was shot in Rome in wide-screen color. William Wyler's *Ben-Hur* (1959), a remake of the silent original that earned eleven Oscars, displayed a famous chariot race sequence that was, at the time, the largest film set ever constructed. (That celebrated race had been preceded by an equally complicated chariot race in Guazzoni's *Messalina* in 1923.) The international box-office appeal of Wyler's epic film provided instant advertisement for the technical and artistic prowess of Rome's Cinecittà.

The film that best characterized the "Hollywood on the Tiber" epoch and the rise to prominence of the paparazzi, the gossip-magazine photographers who preyed upon the scandalous exploits of American movie stars in Italy, was Joseph L. Mankiewicz's *Cleopatra* (1963), a film whose production moved from England to Cinecittà and whose costs spiraled out of control to become the most expensive motion picture ever made to that date. The torrid love affair between the stars Elizabeth Taylor and Richard Burton remains one of Hollywood's (and Rome's) most legendary movie love affairs. During the same year Don Chaffey's *Jason and the Argonauts* was made in Italy, featuring the justly praised special effects by Ray Harryhausen, which stand in sharp contrast to those of many Italian peplum productions of the period, whose shoddy production values could have used Harryhausen's touch to raise their filming standards. One of the last and best examples of American epic films about classical antiquity shot both at Cinecittà and in Spain was Anthony Mann's *The Fall of the Roman Empire* (1964), a film that included a scale model of the Roman Forum and an all-star cast of Sophia Loren, Stephen Boyd, Alec Guinness, James Mason, and Christopher Plummer. As so many other traditional film epics from Pastrone's *Cabiria* to the present have done, Mann's film profited from the historical expertise of one of the era's most popular historians: Will Durant.[4]

The Peplum's Defining Features

A number of important features of the Italian peplum should be noted. These films all initially appeared between the late 1950s and the mid-1960s, when the spaghetti western (see chapter 11) supplanted the peplum in popularity. Peplum films began to appear as Italian neorealism was rapidly fading in critical popularity, and whereas Italian directors associated with neorealism began to turn to more traditional concerns or to a cinema of psychological realism, peplum films rejected any concern with realism or historical reconstruction of the past. As the genre's most important historian rightly reminds us, these Italian spectacles were primarily romances, and as a genre they stand closer to opera than to history, employing a

> highly stylized pictorialism, played out in panoramic widescreen and luscious color . . . where polarized forces of good and evil vie for superiority over mortal (and immortal) souls: political and social behavior are reduced to manageable opposites—good and evil—where characters are

clearly revealed as heroes and villains, and where notions of ideal moral behavior always triumph.[5]

Even though peplum epics reject any neorealist interest in historical accuracy, or even any postrealist interest in psychological depth, peplums (at least when exported abroad) shared one thing in common with the best neorealist films: postsynchronized sound and dubbed dialogue. The clumsy and often inadequate dubbing into foreign languages typical of many peplums caused vitriolic critical attacks on their artistic merits, even though many great Italian films, including those by Fellini and Pasolini (see chapter 8), were almost always dubbed in the original version. Thus both the sound and the dialogue of the peplums are profoundly unrealistic or even unnatural when compared to their Hollywood epic cousins. American audiences familiar with the so-called art films of the most respected Italian directors generally prefer subtitles with dialogue in the original language; but Hollywood studios distributing popular genre films such as the peplum or the spaghetti western feared losing their audiences to subtitles, and so generally had these films dubbed. Unfortunately, American dubbing is generally badly done, whereas Italian dubbing of postsynchronized sound is highly professional and technically proficient, for the most part. Most audiences viewing films by Fellini, for example, are rarely aware of the fact that these films are dubbed even in the original Italian version, whereas the English dubbing done in America even of Fellini's best films (such as the first released video of his masterpiece *Amarcord*) produced almost unwatchable products.

Italian cinema in the postwar period, from the birth of neorealism to the first experiments in color photography by the greatest of the art-film directors in the mid-1960s, was characterized either by a grainy, newsreel kind of realistic photography in the case of Rossellini and De Sica, or by a painterly use of black and white in the case of Pasolini, Fellini, and Antonioni. Peplum films unabashedly adopted the latest technology, employing beautiful wide-screen color photography and an anamorphic lens. To compete with the CinemaScope technology developed by 20th Century Fox, Italian cameramen used a variety of wide-screen techniques: Totalscope, Dyaliscope, Euroscope, Super Technirama 70, Totalscope Super/100, and SuperTotalscope. The anamorphic lens employed in shooting most of these films of necessity emphasized photography not in depth but in breadth, with the result that set design followed the demands of the photography, much as it would later in the most inventive Italian color film set in classical antiquity, *Fellini Satyricon* (*Il Satyricon di Fellini*, 1969), as well as in Fellini's earlier black-and-white masterpiece, *La Dolce Vita*. Peplum colors were frequently garish, solid, and brightly lit, reminding the viewer of the colors of the classical comic strip (again, a parallel to the visual style of many of Fellini's color films).

The Mystique of the Bodybuilder

Huge sets, anamorphic camera lens, and postsynchronization of sound do not in and of themselves set the peplum apart from other typical productions of the period, either from the classic epic film treating the ancient world or other kinds of films made during the period. The single most important feature of the Italian peplum is its typical protagonist: a strong man, usually a bodybuilder, whose muscular physique dominates the screen and defines the nature of the various plots. Anglo-American bodybuilders were pre-ferred for much the same reason that subsequent genre films (the spaghetti western, the *giallo*, the spaghetti nightmare horror film), or even Italian so-called art films, liked to cast non-Italian protagonists: they believed this type of casting assisted the film in the all-important export market. The American bodybuilder who virtually defined the peplum genre was Steve Reeves (1926–2000), a native of Glasgow, Montana. Reeves earned the title Mr. America in 1947 and Mr. Universe in 1950. After Hollywood cast him in several B films, such as Ed Wood's *Jail Bait* (1954), Reeves struck gold when his physique landed him in the two blockbusters directed by Pietro Francisci (1906–77) that gave birth to the peplum genre's international popularity: *Hercules* (*Le fatiche di Ercole*, 1958) and *Hercules Unchained* (*Ercole e la regina di Lidia*, 1959).

For the next decade, Reeves starred in a number of Italian feature films, including *The Last Days of Pompeii* (*Gli ultimi giorni di Pompei*, 1959), by Mario Bonnard (1889–1965); *Goliath and the Barbarians* (*Il terrore dei barbari*, 1959), by Carlo Campogalliani (1885–1974); *Giant of Marathon* (*La battaglia di Maratona*, 1959), by Jacques Tourneur (1904–77); *The White Warrior* (*Agi Murad, il diavolo bianco*, 1959), an adaptation of a Tolstoy novel, directed by Riccardo Freda (1909–99); *Thief of Bagdad* (*Il ladro di Bagdad*, 1960), by Arthur Lubin (1898–1995); *Morgan the Pirate* (*Morgan il pirata*, 1961), by André De Toth (1912–2002); *Duel of the Titans* (*Romolo e Remo*, 1961), by Sergio Corbucci (1927–90); *The Trojan Horse* (*La guerra di Troia*, 1961), by Giorgio Ferroni (1908–81); *The Avenger* (*La leggenda di Enea*, 1962), by Giorgio Rivalta (c. 1906–84); and *Son of Spartacus*, a.k.a. *The Slave* (*Il figlio di Spartacus*, 1963), by Sergio Corbucci. His last film in Italy, a western entitled *A Long Ride from Hell* (*Vivo per la tua morte*, 1968), by Camillo Bazzoni (1934–), reminds us that the peplum and the spaghetti western are integrally related as popular genres about strong, silent heroes. Sergio Corbucci was, in fact, one of the most prolific spaghetti western directors, and Sergio Leone even considered casting Reeves in the movie that began the vogue of the Italian western, *A Fistful of Dollars* (*Un pugno di dollari*, 1964), the work that made Clint Eastwood an international star. A number of Reeves's Italian films were closer to the swashbuckler genre about pirates and bandits than they were to the peplum, but the generic boundaries of popular adventure films were highly elastic.

If Reeves was the pioneer American bodybuilder in this genre, his adversary in the Mr. Universe contests, and the eventual three-time winner of that title (after Reeves retired from competition) in 1951, 1958, and 1965, was the English muscleman Roy Park, a.k.a. Reg Park (1928–2007). His debut Italian peplum, *Hercules and the Captive Women* (*Ercole alla conquista di Atlantide*, 1961), by the director Vittorio Cottafavi (1914–98), and the subsequent *Hercules in the Haunted World* (*Ercole al centro della terra*, 1961), by Mario Bava (1914–80)—the most inventive director working in the popular Italian genre films (peplums, *gialli*, horror, science fiction, spy movies)—revealed Park as perhaps the genre's best actor. Park, who made fewer peplums than Reeves, completed some less important films such as *Hercules, Prisoner of Evil* (*Ursus, il terrore dei Kirghisi*, 1964), by Antonio Margheriti (1930–2002, directing as Anthony Dawson), who, like Bava, specialized in all sorts of popular genre films; *Samson in King Solomon's Mines* (*Maciste nelle miniere di Re Salomone*, 1964), by Piero Regnoli (1921–2001); and *Hercules the Avenger* (*La sfida dei giganti*, 1965), by Maurizio Lucidi (born 1932, directing as Maurice A. Bright). Park's filmography underscores an important feature of Italian peplum films: the interchangeability of the protagonists' names when prints were exported abroad. Hercules was always the default setting for the hero's name, but in Park's case and that of many other peplum protagonists, the popular Italian names of Ursus and Maciste were often changed to more familiar names, such as Hercules, Goliath, and Samson. Moreover, directors such as Lucidi and Margheriti often used Anglicized pseudonyms, just as many spaghetti western directors did, to improve their chances of being screened abroad. Reg Park's performances as a bodybuilder-turned-actor are notable for one other bit of cinematic trivia. Park inspired a young Austrian bodybuilder named Arnold Schwarzenegger (1947–) not only to aspire to the titles of Mr. Olympia and Mr. Universe (competitions he won on numerous occasions) but also to begin a film career in a peplum spin-off entitled *Hercules in New York* (1970, directed by Arthur Seidelman) and a contemporary peplum-fantasy, *Conan the Barbarian* (1982, directed by John Milius), the breakthrough film that launched him on his road to stardom. Schwarzenegger remains the only actor to play Hercules who has enjoyed a successful political career.

Other important peplum stars included the American actor Gordon Scott (1927–2007), who made a dozen feature films in Italy at Reeves's suggestion after starring in six Tarzan films, including *Tarzan's Greatest Adventure* (1959) and *Tarzan the Magnificent* (1960). He paired up with Reeves in *Duel of the Titans*, in which Reeves played Romulus, the founder of Rome, while Scott played his brother, Remus. One of the best actors in the peplum genre, Scott appeared in such works as *Samson and the Seven Miracles of the World* (*Maciste alla corte del Gran Khan*, 1961), by Riccardo Freda; *Goliath and the Vampires* (*Maciste contro il vampiro*, 1961), by Giacomo Gentilomo

(1909–2001); *Goliath and the Rebel Slave*, a.k.a. *The Tyrant of Lydia Against the Son of Hercules* (*Goliath e la schiava ribelle*, 1963), by Mario Caiano (1933–); *The Beast of Babylon Against the Son of Hercules*, a.k.a. *The Hero of Babylon* (*L'eroe di babilonia*, 1963), by Siro Marcellini (1921–); and three directed by Giorgio Ferroni—*The Conquest of Mycenae*, a.k.a. *Hercules against Moloch*, a.k.a. *Hercules Attacks* (*Ercole contro Moloch*, 1963); *Coriolanus: Hero without a Country* (*Coriolano: eroe senza patria*, 1963); and *Hero of Rome* (*Il colosso di Roma*, 1964).

Other non-Italian strongmen, most of them bodybuilders, worked in the peplum genre. Many of these bodybuilders had their debut in show business performing in the Mae West Muscleman Revue, a risqué show that opened in Las Vegas at the Sahara Hotel in 1954 and ran to 1957. Bodybuilders who performed on the Mae West Muscleman Revue include Mickey Hargitay (1926–2006, born in Hungary), Reg Lewis (1936–), Brad Harris (1933–), Don Vadis (1938–87), and Gordon Mitchell (1923–2003), and all of them eventually acted in peplum films. Mitchell even managed to garner an interesting role in *Fellini Satyricon* before going on to a long career in Italian popular film genres, such as the spy film, the *giallo*, and the horror film. Hargitay costarred with his wife, Jayne Mansfield, in *Hercules vs. the Hydra*, a.k.a. *The Loves of Hercules* (*Gli amori di Ercole*, 1960), by Carlo Ludovico Bragaglia (1894–1998). Subsequently, he worked in Italy on several *gialli* and horror films.

Unlike other peplum stars, such as Harris, Vadis, and Mitchell, who worked in other popular genres (especially the Italian western), Mark Forest (born Lou Degni but in Brooklyn, New York, not Italy, in 1933) quit the cinema after doing only peplum films. He employed the money he made acting in peplums to study opera in Italy before retiring to California to teach singing. His credits include *Goliath and the Dragon* (*La vendetta di Ercole*, 1960), by Vittorio Cottafavi; *Mole Men against the Son of Hercules* (*Maciste, l'uomo più forte del mondo*, 1961), by Antonio Leonviola (1913–95); *Hercules against the Mongols* (*Maciste contro i Mongoli*, 1963), by Domenico Paolella (1918–2002); *Goliath and the Sins of Babylon* (*Maciste, l'eroe più grande del mondo*, 1963), by Michele Lupo (1932–89); *The Terror of Rome against the Son of Hercules* (*Maciste, gladiatore di Sparta*, 1964), by Mario Caiano; and *Hercules against the Sons of the Sun* (*Ercole contro i figli del sole*, 1964), by Osvaldo Civirani (1917–2008).

Canadian-born Samson Burke (1930–) worked in five peplums, including one Hollywood parody of the peplum genre, *The Three Stooges Meet Hercules* (1962), directed by Edward Bernds (1905–2000). In it, the zany American comedians travel back to classical antiquity in a time machine and confront Hercules, played by Burke. This Hollywood parody was probably inspired by an earlier Italian parody entitled *Maciste against Hercules in the Vale of Woe* (*Maciste contro Ercole nella valle dei guai*, 1961), directed by Mario Mattoli (1898–1980). It featured the popular comic duo Franco Franchi (1922–92) and Ciccio Ingrassia (1922–2003), whose specialty was low-budget parodies of well-known films, and also employed the time machine device: the two comedians, brought back to ancient times, organize a match between two protagonists of many peplum films, Maciste and Hercules.

Italy, too, contributed a number of strongmen to the peplum film, although their popularity never equaled that of the imported musclemen. Kirk Morris, a former gondolier whose real name was Adriano Bellini (1937–), starred in a number of works despite his leaden acting style. (On the positive side, he did bear a resemblance to Elvis Presley.) Among his most important credits are *The Witch's Curse* (*Maciste all'inferno*, 1962), directed by Riccardo Freda (as Robert Hampton); *Maciste against the Headhunters*, a.k.a. *Colossus and the Headhunters* (*Maciste contro i cacciatori di teste*, 1962), by Guido Malatesta (1919–70); *Hercules, Samson & Ulysses* (*Ercole sfida Sansone*, 1963), by Pietro Francisci; and *Maciste, Avenger of the Mayans* (*Il vendicatore dei Mayas*, 1965), by Guido Malatesta. Alan Steel, born Sergio Ciani, who played bit roles in several Steve Reeves films, then moved to protagonist roles and starred in such films as *Hercules and the Black Pirate* (*Sansone contro il corsaro nero*, 1960), by Luigi Capuano (1904–), pitting Hercules/Samson against pirates on the Spanish Main; and *Hercules against the Moon Men* (*Ercole contro gli uomini luna*, 1964), by Giacomo Gentilomo, adding an element of science fiction to the peplum.

Peplum Classics: A Representative Sampling

Even a strict definition of the peplum—limiting it to adventures with a classical hero such as Hercules or Maciste, but eliminating biblical films or purely adventure films and swashbucklers set in different epochs—results in a total of as many as 180–200 films produced in less than a decade.[6] Given the common practices of giving the same film different titles upon re-release, and completely changing titles for foreign distribution, it is extremely unlikely that any count of these films (or spaghetti westerns) will ever be completely accurate. Nonetheless, an analysis of six important examples can capture the flavor of this highly successful film genre between 1957 (when the vogue of the sword and sandal epic was launched with the shooting of Francisci's *Hercules*) and 1964 (the year the spaghetti western craze replaced the peplum in box-office punch). The six films in question are *Hercules, Hercules Unchained, Hercules and the Captive Women, Hercules in the Haunted World, Samson and the Seven Miracles of the World*, and *The Witch's Curse*—three of the last four released in 1961, a banner year for the genre. Of these six, several became blockbusters, while others were certainly profitable. All were shot by directors who in Hollywood would have been identified as proficient and highly professional genre or B-film directors: Pietro Francisci, Mario Bava, Riccardo Freda, and Vittorio Cottafavi. These six films also feature the most important male leads in the peplum: Steve Reeves, Reg Park, Gordon Scott, and Mark Forest.

Francisci's *Hercules* and its sequel, *Hercules Unchained*, both featuring Steve Reeves, burst upon the scene in a manner not unlike Sergio Leone's westerns. Each of the films grossed almost 900 million lire in Italy alone, a huge amount of money, if one calculates that tickets cost as little as 600–1000 lire at the time, and evidence of a very large audience. More important, however, the history of the distribution of these films by the American producer Joseph E. Levine has become legendary and is probably the first example of what would subsequently become normal practice in the industry. According to one account of the American invasion of the peplum begun by *Hercules*,[7] Levine bought the rights to the film for only $120,000; spent a million dollars to promote it with lavish luncheons, four-color, full-page advertisements in major American magazines, trade papers, movie periodicals, and men's magazines, and even creating a comic-book version of the film; and opened the film in some six hundred theaters, including the popular drive-ins of the period, on the same date (July 25, 1959). The result was almost unbelievable by the standards of the day: the film grossed $18 million, with an adjusted profit of $5 million, and was seen by some 24 million people in more than 11,000 theaters! In terms of the ratio of actual profits compared to funds invested, these figures would probably put the profit margins of most contemporary blockbusters to shame.

Francisci's *Hercules* presents a classical figure from ancient mythology without undue regard for the fine points of the narratives surrounding the legendary figure of Hercules, generally associated in classical mythology with the famous Twelve Labors of Hercules, to which Francisci's Italian title refers. In myth, he was half man, half god (a son of Zeus), and his tasks included dispatching a number of monsters and performing other humanly impossible tasks. He killed the Nemean Lion, the Lernean Hydra, and the Stymphalian birds; he captured the Ceryneian deer, the Erymanthian Boar, and the Cretan Bull; he herded the cattle of the monster Geryon, tamed the man-eating horses of Diomedes, stole the belt of Hippolyte (queen of the Amazons), plucked the golden apples of Hesperides, cleaned up the filthy stables of Augeas in a single day, captured Cerberus (the multiheaded hound guarding the gates of Hades)—and still found time to help Jason and the Argonauts recapture the Golden Fleece. Considered to be more brawn than brain, he met his demise at the hand of one of his several wives before he was taken up to Mount Olympus as a god.

In the various adventures of Hercules in the peplum, following Francisci's lead, Greek or Roman mythology took second place to adventure and fantasy, and much more importance was given to his role as one of the companions of the Argonauts, since a quest plot suited the demands of the adventure film quite nicely. In Francisci's *Hercules*, the hero—played by Steve Reeves, first seen sunning himself and coincidentally showing off his physique—journeys to the city of Iolcus, invited by King Pelias (Ivo Garrani) to train his son, Iphitus (Mimmo Palmara). He is interrupted during a meal (an entire leg of beef roasting on the spit) to rescue the runaway chariot of the king's daughter, Iole (Sylva Koscina); to do so, he uproots a huge tree and stops the horse dead in its tracks. He immediately falls in love with Iole, introducing into the genre the theme of romance, always a major consideration in Hercules peplums. A flashback from Iole's point of view suggests that Iole's father and his evil partner Eurysteus (Arturo Dominici) killed the legitimate ruler of Iolcus and are responsible for the loss of the Golden Fleece, the symbol of the city. When Iphitus is killed by his presumption in accompanying Hercules to kill a lion preying on the city, Pelias obliges Hercules to kill the Cretan Bull to atone for the demise of his son.

Modifying the mythological account of this heroic figure, Francisci sends his own hero to a sybil (Lidia Alfonsi), at whose oracle Hercules asks the gods to take away his immortality and to exchange this for love, pain, and sorrow, because he wants to begin a family with Iole. Now, as the voice-over announces, "there is a woman to conquer and battles to win and the Cretan Bull awaits," Hercules overcomes the animal—but just barely, since he is now a mortal man, bloodied by the struggle—in the course of which he meets Jason (Fabrizio Mioni). On their odyssey to retrieve the Fleece, the Argonauts accompanied by Hercules encounter Queen Antea (Gianna Maria Canale), ruler of the Amazons—who intend to kill off the men after they enjoy their sexual services—and Antea naturally falls in love with Hercules. The Argonauts escape danger and stop next at Colchis, where they are attacked by ape-men. Francisci's adventure plot allows him to exploit Mediterranean locations, and he uses far fewer spectacular interior sets of the palaces, caverns, and temples that become so important a feature of other peplums. An unintentionally humorous dragon guarding the Fleece is all too easily dispatched (one of the first examples of impoverished special effects sometimes typical of the genre), and Hercules accompanies the Argonauts back to Iolcus to put Jason on the throne as the city's rightful heir. A battle ensues, in which Hercules defeats the evil tyrant's army, providing the battle scene typical of the peplum. The battle scene morphs into a Herculean imitation of the biblical exploits of Samson, as Hercules employs his chains to demolish the pillars of the tyrant's palace, burying his cavalry and winning the battle. (The destruction of a major building, sometimes even a city, from war or volcanic eruption also figures as one of the obligatory peplum scenes in future productions.) *Hercules* concludes on a domestic note: our hero departs with Iole to "find a new happiness," transforming the adventure film into a successful love story. The newly united couple is photographed against a beautiful Mediterranean sunset as the voice-over remarks: "you will have each other 'til the end of time."

On the strength of the wholly unexpected commercial success of *Hercules*, Francisci repeated the formula with variations in the sequel *Hercules Unchained*, this time employing the talented Mario Bava as his cameraman and set designer. While the original Italian title of this film refers to Omphale, Queen of Lidia (Sylvia Lopez), a sultry seductress who murders and then embalms her lovers, Levine's equally successful promotion of the film in the English-language market shifted the focus of the title to the theme of love. Hercules' chains (not referenced in the Italian title) are now not the literal chains that he broke and employed to destroy the army of Pelias in the first film but, rather, the chains of love that bind him to Iole—and, for a time, to Omphale. In promoting *Hercules Unchained*, Levine's imagination reached new levels. Not only did he run more than six thousand television spots to promote the film, but he also provided theater owners with thousands of four-pound statues of Steve Reeves, with the label: "Made from the strongest chocolate in the world, but if it breaks you can eat it!"[8] Mythology again takes second place to fantasy: one of the first adventures undertaken by Reeves's Hercules in this sequel is a confrontation with Antaeus, played by Primo Carnera (1906–67), the famous prewar World Heavyweight champion from 1933 until he lost his title to Joe Louis in 1937. Thus, the strong man from America overcomes the strong man of the Fascist era, at least in the movies. The battle between Reeves and Carnera provides one of the many humorous lines of dialogue for which the peplum is justly infamous, as Hercules/Reeves, referencing the God of the Underworld with whom he had earlier struggled, exclaims: "I don't care if he is Pluto—I'm going to knock that silly grin off his face!"

Hercules had relied primarily on exterior Mediterranean locations, relatively simple interiors, and a few uncomplicated special effects and monsters. With the contributions of accomplished set designer and cinematographer Mario Bava working for Francisci's second feature, more interesting visual effects add to the aesthetic impact of the narrative. Bava's signature use of lush, primary colors, often juxtaposed together as in traditional comic strips, create brilliant interiors. The most memorable scenes from the film are the presentation of the luxurious bedchamber of Queen Omphale, who sports 1950s-style high heels and a wig of blazing red hair, and the scene of the embalming room where her lovers are put to death. Moreover, Francisci's narrative combines the adventures of Hercules and his friend Ulysses (Gabriele Antonini)—a theme to be expected in an adventure film—with an even more pronounced emphasis upon the love theme that was treated less extensively in *Hercules*. This second film concerns itself more with the "chains of love"—Hercules's love for Iole and his ultimate ability to resist the temptations of the Circe-like temptress Omphale—than with the exploits of

In Francisci's *Hercules Unchained,* Steve Reeves as Hercules romances Queen Omphale in sets designed by Mario Bava. *Credit: CSC*

a superhero. In fact, its plot resembles a baroque or Romantic opera melo-drama: out of love for Hercules, Omphale commits suicide by jumping into her embalming fluid; this act releases him from her powers, and the film ends on Iole's remark that the gods will be kind to Hercules and her if they just love each other. The adventure plot, a confused account of a civil war between the two sons of Oedipus (Eteocles and Polynices) for control of Thebes is so convoluted and incoherent—either by the standards of clas-sical mythology or by the requirements of common sense—that it serves primarily as a means of delaying the ultimate reunion of the loving couple.

While *Hercules Unchained* stands as no masterpiece when compared to the great "art films" of the period, it still boasts the notable talents of Mario Bava and the scriptwriter Ennio De Concini (1923–2008), who had also contributed to *Hercules* and would share an Oscar in 1963 for the screenplay of that great Sicilian comedy of manners *Divorce, Italian Style* (*Divorzio all'italiana*, 1961). De Concini's remarks about the creation of a commercial phenomenon with *Hercules* and *Hercules Unchained* are worth mentioning.[9] According to his account, the desire to return to the classical hero and his adventures, for the most part abandoned by the Italian cinema since the silent era, was due to the Italian public's desire to move beyond neorealism. Ardently ideological neorealist directors such as Giuseppe De Santis hoped for a "proletarianization of the middle classes" in Italy, but what actually occurred was what De Concini calls "a middle-classicization of the proletariat," and one of its effects was the popularity of the peplum. His description of how the scripts were produced in his home shows that three or four films were written at the same time by a small group of script-writers. De Concini wandered from room to room, asking: "Where shall we put Esculapius? In this scene? No, in the other film, the one with the

Romans. But isn't Marcus Ovidius in that one? Doesn't matter, we'll move him." While Francisci was deadly serious, even ingenious, his more cynical and profit-motivated collaborators dreamed up these films between one plate of pasta and another, laughing all the way.

With the Hercules films of Cottafavi and Bava, Steve Reeves (an imposing physical presence but not much of an actor) yields the title role to Reg Park, an equally impressive muscleman but a better actor. The change in title of Cottafavi's *Hercules and the Captive Women* from its original Italian reference to the conquest of Atlantis obscures the generic contamination that takes place in the work, for Cottafavi not only changes the character of Hercules but also sets this adventure in a context that can only be called science fiction. Moreover, as is so typical of many of the Italian popular genre films, an element of comedy and parody arises in the film (one of Hercules' sidekicks in his adventures is a trickster midget). The film has in fact no "captive women" but rather the evil Antinea, Queen of Atlantis. After the Greek seer Tiresias informs the Greeks that an evil empire beyond the horizon may threaten to destroy the known world, Hercules (Reg Park), his friend Androcles of Sparta (Ettore Manni), and Hercules' son Hylas (Luciano Marin) set off to set things right. Cottafavi's Hercules is anything but energetic: for most of the voyage, he sleeps while others do the heavy lifting, and when he does perform a heroic feat, he does so reluctantly and eager to return to relaxing in the sun or the shade (thereby presenting his magnificent physique to the audience). In contrast to what the Italian critics call a "lazy" Hercules, other figures in the film serve as comic foils, outwitting rather than outslugging their opponents, and in some sequences of *Hercules and the Captive Women* the intent is parody of the peplum rather than a serious attempt to re-create the classical world in a popular adventure film.

The original poster for Cottafavi's *Hercules and the Captive Women*. Credit: AB

Hercules and the Captive Women was actually shot in 70mm (an unusual technique for Italian films at the time), and its script was written in part by Duccio Tessari (1926–94), who later became an important director of spaghetti westerns, in particular a pair of films about a character named Ringo that were quite successful.[10] Among the most interesting sequences of the film are the meeting of all the rulers of Greece to discuss the distant but very real threat to their survival (a kind of classical version of the Allies meeting to decide what to do with the Axis powers in World War II), and the depiction of the evil empire of Atlantis, whose military costumes and talk of the master race ("la nuova razza eletta") are clear references to the Germany of the Third Reich. The fact that the soldiers commanded by the evil Queen Antea are cloned and all identical certainly recalls numerous science fiction films about the role of clones in the world of the future, even though Cottafavi places this theme in the distant classical past. The conclusion of the film presents the utter destruction of a city in ways that recall the many film versions of the destruction of Pompeii, and this kind of scene, exploiting the talents of Cinecittà's special effects crews, becomes almost a commonplace in the peplum's narrative structure. Rather than the marvelous Atlantis of legend that always seems to be a kind of utopia, Cottafavi's Atlantis is a nightmare city that deserves its cruel fate.

Cottafavi's Hercules stands as the direct ancestor of Bud Spencer (né Carlo Pedersoli [1929–], an Olympic swimming champion in his youth), whose many comic films paired with the comic foil Terence Hill (né Mario Girotti [1939–]) were created by the director Enzo Barboni (1922–2002). They became incredibly successful in the eighteen films they shot together. Spencer (like Reg Park's Hercules) always plays a kind but reluctant giant ultimately forced to turn to strength to resolve problems, while his partner Hill, quite the opposite in character, was a wisecracking but likable troublemaker who uses his brain rather than his brawn. In effect, Spencer plays a modern character that continues the role played in the peplum by the various strongmen such as Hercules, Ursus, Maciste, Samson, and Goliath, all of whom seem interchangeable. Spencer's films were issued in almost every popular genre but the peplum, but unlike the peplums to which Spencer and Hill owe their cinematic personae, Spencer-Hill films were only rarely exported to English-speaking audiences. Two comic films they made that parodied the spaghetti western broke box-office records in Italy.[11]

If Cottafavi's film flirted with the generic conventions of science fiction, the most inventive peplum, Bava's *Hercules in the Haunted World*, mixes the conventions of that genre with those of the horror film. In previous work as a director, Bava, already an accomplished set designer and cameraman, had created a very popular vampire film that launched the horror-film career of the beautifully evil English actress who became known as "the scream queen": Barbara Steele (1937–).[12] In *Hercules in the Haunted World*, Bava cashed in on the phenomenal vogue of the peplum, the success of his own horror films, and the popularity of Christopher Lee's performance in the classic role of the most famous vampire of them all in *Dracula* (1958, directed by Terence Fisher). Lee is cast as the evil Lico, the uncle of Deianira (Leonora Ruffo), who is the daughter of King Eurites of Ecalia and betrothed to Hercules. Lico has placed Deianira in a trance because he has been given the possibility of eternal life if his niece's blood flows through his veins during a lunar eclipse. Hercules consults a sibyl named Medea (Gaia Germani), who informs him that in order to save his beloved, he must recover a magic stone from Hades; but before he can do this, he must steal the Golden Apple of the Hesperides (one of the original classic Labors of Hercules). In the process, Hercules defeats Procrustes (a giant made of green stone) and defeats Lico's army of zombies. He then destroys Lico just before the latter fulfills his evil designs on Deianira, and at the film's conclusion the adventure story turns into the traditional love story as Hercules is reunited with his beloved.

This outline of the film's combination of generic conventions from both the peplum and the horror film (with vampire and zombie variants) cannot do justice to the rightly praised visual qualities of what must certainly be described as the very best of the peplums. Bava's signature use of bright Technicolor exteriors contrasts brilliantly with psychedelic, dreamlike interiors. His sets (for example, the memorable throne room) combine gorgeous colors and beautifully crafted geometrical designs. Apparently Bava even employed one of the oriental masks Fellini used in *La Dolce Vita* (no doubt taken from Cinecittà's vast storeroom of props) to give his

Bava's *Hercules in the Haunted World* casts the muscleman Reg Park as Hercules and places his character in a series of stupendous, otherworldly sets. *Credit: CSC*

sibyl a mysterious, unfamiliar appearance. Like Cottafavi before him, Bava included a humorous figure to provide comic relief—Telemachus (Franco Giacobini). His sets and his monsters are a far cry from the cheap production values of many peplums. Besides a fantastic Garden of the Hesperides filled with interesting designs and a gigantic Sacred Tree containing the apple Hercules obtains with a giant slingshot, the protagonist encounters in Hades a forest of limbs and branches that scream when cut—an obvious reference to scenes from Virgil's *Aeneid* that Dante imitates in his *Inferno*. After throwing five huge boulders at Lico's zombie army (again, the casting of huge boulders has by now become one of the obligatory ways Hercules fights when he is not uprooting huge trees), the appearance of the sun's rays destroys Lico/Dracula in a manner familiar to all moviegoers who love the vampire film. Although Bava's Hercules is frequently photographed in a golden light that illuminates Reg Park's spectacular physique, absolutely nothing in the film or Bava's direction would justify the homoerotic fixation of many contemporary critics of the peplum. In fact, the film presents the triumph of heterosexual love with a kiss between Hercules and Deianira on a Mediterranean beach, as Hercules tells his beloved: "Our love will be eternal." The entire film represents a triumph of color, lighting, set design, and fantasy based on the combination of a number of film genres, all directed with a master's touch.

The final two of these peplums, Ricardo Freda's *Samson and the Seven Miracles of the World* and *The Witch's Curse*, are less interesting aesthetically than Bava's masterpiece, although they are perhaps more typical of the zany plots and puzzling historical anomalies that characterize so many of the musclemen epics. Both feature in the original Italian the muscular Maciste (familiar to Italians through Pastrone's *Cabiria*)—a character transformed into Samson in the first film by its English title. Gordon Scott, fresh from a number of Tarzan films in Hollywood, achieves a credible performance as Maciste/Samson, whereas Kirk Morris's depiction of Maciste in the second film repeats the leaden performance of his other peplum roles. The Italian title of the first film refers to the court of the Great Khan and transports the place of action from the classical world to Asia during the Mongol invasion of China in the thirteenth century. Unlike Bava's peplum/horror fantasy, the majority of the locations are exteriors shot in the light of day rather than spectacular interiors in a psychedelic Hades. Furthermore, the protagonist clearly takes on a political role, defending the downtrodden Chinese against evil tyranny. In the most famous scene, Samson escapes being buried alive and saves a number of Chinese rebels from being decapitated by a scythe-wielding chariot when the film's villain buries them up to their necks in a large amphitheater. A memorable earthquake scene (one of the classic narrative elements in the silent cinema's epic films, such as *Cabiria*) at the site of the execution is supposedly caused by Samson's heroic breakout from a

Freda's *Samson and the Seven Miracles of the World* casts Gordon Scott, most famous as a Hollywood Tarzan, as Maciste/Samson, who performs feats of strength in the China of the Great Khan. *Credit: CSC*

stone tomb beneath the royal palace. At the conclusion of the film, Freda shifts the focus of the plot away from the love interests of Hercules, central to the other peplums we have analyzed, to an overt political message about tyranny and freedom as the hero declares: "My task here is finished. Destiny brought me here. Now I must go wherever there is a fight between right and wrong."

The Witch's Curse is equally fanciful in its treatment of classical antiquity. The plot opens in Puritan Scotland at the village of Loch Laird in 1550, where a witch, Martha Gaunt (Hélène Chanel), is burned alive—but not before cursing the village and Justice Edward Parris (Andrea Bosic), whom she claims is condemning her to the stake because she refused sexual relations with him, and promising as she dies that they will meet in Hell. A cut to a century later reveals that the curse is working: women in the Scottish town are going mad as a descendant of the condemned witch, also named Martha (Vira Silenti), comes to the village to marry the local lord of the manor, Charley Law (Angelo Zanolli). The crazed villagers mob the manor, seize young Martha, and have her condemned to burn at the stake as a witch. Suddenly, Kirk Morris as Maciste turns up in a ridiculous loincloth to rescue her. First, however, he must descend into Hades through the hole in the earth revealed after he uproots an accursed tree, where his actions are observed and thwarted by the damned souls of the sixteenth-century Martha Gaunt and Edward Parris. Typical of the peplum hero, Maciste undergoes a number of adventures—he kills a lion, meets Sisyphus pushing a rock and Prometheus being devoured by a bird, and falls prey to a beautiful Circe-like woman who seduces him and informs him that he must destroy the original witch before saving her descendant. Revealed to be none other than

In Freda's *The Witch's Curse*, Kirk Morris as Maciste turns up in seventeenth-century England to save a woman accused of witchcraft—but still uprooting trees as the peplum heroes do in classical times. *Credit: AB*

the titular witch Martha Gaunt herself, this woman declares Her love for Maciste and basically commits suicide for love. After telling him that only a kiss will save the village and her descendant, she crumbles into dust at the touch of his lips. When Maciste returns to save young Martha, she is reunited with Charley, restoring peace to the village. The townspeople beg Maciste to stay with them, but Freda virtually repeats the ending of *Samson and the Seven Miracles of the World*, with Morris's Maciste echoing Scott's Samson/Maciste: "It's impossible, as my destiny leads me to help other people, people who are suffering from oppression and cruelty all over the troubled world." Although Freda continued the theme of the triumph of love so typical of other peplum classics, his films also introduced the political message that might may make right, as his musclemen protagonists also fight tyranny and oppression.

Perhaps the most interesting aspect of this film lies not in the sequences in Hell, which pale in comparison to the artistry of Bava in *Hercules in the Haunted World*. Rather, some unintentionally humorous, metacinematic moments enliven Freda's film. The original Italian title is the same as that of a famous and previously mentioned silent film starring Bartolomeo Pagano, the original Maciste: Guido Brignone's *Maciste in Hell*, a film praised by Fellini as one of the first films he remembers seeing when he was a young boy. While the modern peplum version by Freda is in no sense an imitation of the silent feature, many of Maciste's adventures in Hell certainly recall the earlier film. During the 1962 Maciste's encounters in Hell, he loses his memory and identity; he is restored to himself, however, by visions of previous adventures seen in a pool of water. In them he battles a cyclops, fights against Mongols, and tries to prevent the village mob from lynching the young Martha. But the first two scenes that help restore his memory are taken from two other Maciste films: Antonio Leonviola's *Atlas against the Cyclops* (*Maciste nella terra dei ciclopi*, 1961), where Maciste is played by Gordon Mitchell, not Kirk Morris, and Freda's own *Samson and the Seven Miracles of the World*, where Maciste is played by Gordon Scott! Apparently the audience was not expected to notice that different actors portrayed the same protagonist. Moreover, numerous sequences of the film inside the caverns of Hell were lifted from yet another Maciste film, this one actually starring Kirk Morris—*Triumph of the Son of Hercules* (*Il trionfo di Maciste*, 1961), directed by Tano Boccia, a.k.a. Antonio Anton (1912–82), with music by Carlo Franci (1927–), reappears in *Hercules against the Moon Men* by Giacomo Gentilomo.[13] This ability to use and recycle narrative sequences, sets, and music from one peplum to another speaks volumes about the production values of the genre, the budgets, and the audience's low expectations.

The Italian Film Market and the Economic and Social Place of Popular Genre Films

It is easy to denigrate the aesthetic contribution of the sword and sandal films to the history of Italian cinema because so many of the films produced during this period are almost perfect targets for parody by sophisticated film audiences. Yet we should not underestimate the impact of such films upon the imaginations of future filmmakers. Only recently, in an article on the avant-garde directors Ethan and Joel Coen, the two brothers—film buffs when being so, before videotapes and DVDs, meant watching what was on late at night—described how they watched "a lot of Hercules movies" and how they and the superstar actor George Clooney have wanted to do a Hercules picture for years![14] Of course, some of the peplum films produced during this brief, decade-long flourishing of the genre certainly merit revisiting and further study. Even more important than their aesthetic contribution, however, was their economic impact.[15] The large number of genre films made in Italy between the end of neorealism and the late 1970s—in a variety of popular genres (peplum, western, *giallo*, thriller, horror, sexy comedies, even pornography, and so forth)—provided the industry with capital, offered young technicians, writers, cameramen, and directors a chance to learn their trade, and made quite a good deal of money for their producers and distributors, since these films were particularly popular in Third World export markets as well as in the more traditional European and American markets.

The Italian film market in those days comprised three ranks or tiers of moviehouses. Major new Hollywood imports or the equivalent major Italian productions were premiered in the first-run, or *prima visione*, theaters, in the largest Italian cities (some sixteen in number). After playing in those first-run theaters, films were then cycled as they aged through the second-run (*seconda visione*) and third-run (*terza visione*) theaters in the provinces, usually in towns and small cities of fewer than fifty thousand people. Ticket prices in the second- and third-run theaters were much less expensive: a first-run film might for example cost 500 lire or more, whereas a second-run film could fall to 100–200 lire, and a third-run film to as little as 50–100 lire. (During the period, the exchange rate was approximately 600–630 lire to the dollar.) According to Giordano's figures for the peplum years, over half of the Italian industry's profits came from tickets costing 100–200 lire at precisely those theaters that, for the most part, screened the peplums and later the spaghetti westerns, *gialli*, and horror films. The vogue of any genre *filone* (literally: "thread") was generally initially consumer-driven: audiences flocked to a few specific films that gave birth to the craze for such a film. Thus when Francisci's *Hercules* and *Hercules Unchained* or Leone's *A Fistful of Dollars* made enormous and completely unexpected profits at first-run theaters—and continued to bring in revenue as they were recycled through the system—producers then sprang to imitate the trend, making dozens and even hundreds of imitations in the same genre, most of which were not masterpieces but many of which were quite respectable or even very good. During the years that peplums, westerns, and other popular genres were made in great numbers, roughly 74 percent of the box-office receipts of Italian films were derived from ticket sales in the range from below 50 to no more than 200 lire—that is, from provincial theaters. Consequently, it is obvious how important these products were to the industry. As Wagstaff explains, the Italian film market was characterized in this period by

> the production of cheap films in large quantities rather than well-financed ones in moderate quantities. The medium-level, good-quality film was poorly represented in the Italian system of production. The expansion of production had to be accomplished without an increase in creative talent.... The way to increase output without any available increase in creative resources was to have recourse to imitation and repetition. This is how the spaghetti western and its sibling formulas thrived.[16]

Moreover, it is impossible to understand the impact of genre films in Italy without some understanding of the social context of the films outside first-run theaters. Most audiences were composed of men. Films were generally shown in theaters near home, after dinner, around ten o'clock in the evening—thus not during the matinees popular in the United States, nor at drive-ins located outside the city and accessible only to those who owned an automobile. Frequently, second- and third-run theaters would change the bill daily, and spectators came and went during the projection of the films without much regard for the disturbance they made. Theaters allowed smoking, creating a huge cloud of cigarette smoke often released from the auditorium, during the obligatory intermission that interrupted every film, by a huge sliding opening in the building's ceiling. Cinema was popular entertainment, not the fare of an elite in these theaters, and it remained so until television began to overtake the cinema as a means of mass entertainment, just as the cinema had earlier gradually superseded the variety theater that was so important during the prewar and immediate postwar periods. Battle scenes in peplums or gunfights in spaghetti westerns would grab the film audience's attention for a spell, just as arias had captivated eighteenth-century opera audiences, who would subsequently turn to conversation, playing cards, and eating in the opera houses until the next aria took place. In short, viewing the adventures of Hercules, or of the Man with No Name, in an Italian movie theater was an entirely different experience than seeing the same film in a non-Italian movie theater, where smoking rules were strictly enforced, peer pressure forced spectators to remain silent during the performance, and audiences generally entered before the film began and left immediately afterward. Perhaps audiences in Italian second- and third-run theaters may usefully be compared to those in American drive-in theaters at the time. There, the attention of spectators was often directed more toward making out, or making love, in the seclusion of a large automobile with a comfortable backseat, than to the images on the outdoor screen!

CHAPTER SEVEN

Commedia all'italiana
COMEDY AND SOCIAL CRITICISM

COMEDY HAS ALWAYS BEEN the most popular film genre in Italy, and the directors who arose to prominence after the neorealist period have long constituted the economic backbone of the film industry. Although such directors as Federico Fellini are usually described as "art film directors," Fellini himself would probably have preferred to be called a comic director, and like Fellini, many of Italy's most talented directors felt most comfortable making comic or tragicomic films rather than serious dramatic films. The list of the directors making comic films is a long one: it includes Mario Monicelli, the creator of a number of box-office smashes starring the Neapolitan comic Totò (Antonio De Curtis) during the immediate postwar period; Luigi Comencini and Dino Risi, both of whom were connected with the popular comedies typical of "rosy" neorealism in the 1950s; Alberto Lattuada and Pietro Germi, two directors who made important neorealist films in a previous generation; Lina Wertmüller (1926–), the female director whose works reached the pinnacle of critical and economic success in the mid-1970s; and Ettore Scola (1931–), who first began work in the industry as a very successful scriptwriter, along with other writers of rare talent such as Agenore Incrocci (a.k.a. Age; 1919–2005), Furio Scarpelli (1919–2010), and Tullio Pinelli. In sharp contrast to neorealism, which often employed nonprofessional actors, *commedia all'italiana* depended on a large group of unusually talented comic actors and actresses—a comic star system, in effect, that included Vittorio Gassman, Marcello Mastroianni, Ugo Tognazzi (1922–90), Alberto Sordi, Nino Manfredi (1921–2004), Giancarlo Giannini (1942–), Sophia Loren, Monica Vitti (1931–), Stefania Sandrelli (1946–), Claudia Cardinale (1938–), and Mariangela Melato (1941–2013).

As these directors produced more and more comic films, they began to create a collection of comic types not unlike the figures of the traditional Italian *commedia dell'arte*, which relied heavily upon stock characters: the star-crossed lovers, the quack doctor, the shyster lawyer, the clever servant, the shrewd peasant, the braggart soldier, the pedantic professor from Bologna, and so forth. As Mario Monicelli once remarked, the Italian comic film traditionally united laughter with a sense of desperation, employing a cynical sense of humor reflecting the human drive for survival in the face of overwhelming obstacles. In its greatest moments, the *commedia all'italiana* is closer to tragicomedy than to pure comedy, often bordering on the grotesque. Unlike its more "rosy" counterpart during the Fascist period or the neorealist decade, *commedia all'italiana* almost always included an undercurrent of social malaise. Flourishing at the height of the Italian "economic miracle" after Italy's postwar recovery, it frequently underscored the painful contradictions of a culture in rapid transformation. It replaced the sometimes facile and optimistic humanitarianism typical of earlier film comedy with a darker, more ironic and pessimistic vision of Italian life. It was almost always undervalued by the progressive or leftist criticism of the era, which felt that its popular appeal deflected attention from more "serious" problems. But in retrospect, Italian film comedies may accurately be said to have treated real social, political, and economic problems quite courageously and more successfully than overtly ideological films, particularly in their portrayals of dysfunctional social institutions, reactionary laws, and outmoded customs governing the relationships between men and women.

The Comic Genius of Monicelli and Comencini

Three of Monicelli's works—*Big Deal on Madonna Street* (*I soliti ignoti*, 1958), *The Great War* (*La grande guerra*, 1959), and *The Organizer* (*I compagni*, 1963)—represent classic *commedia all'italiana* at its best. The first film portrays the futile attempts by a group of incompetent thieves to commit a robbery. A hilarious parody of the traditional Hollywood caper film, the work concludes not with the traditional gun battle or wild escape and car chase but with a bittersweet conversation among the would-be robbers over plates of pasta and beans. Monicelli's brilliant reversal of the generic expectations of the caper film establishes a pattern that became familiar in depicting the protagonists of the *commedia all'italiana*—a comic character type portrayed in its various and multifarious aspects by Mastroianni, Gassman, Sordi, Tognazzi, Manfredi, and others. This type is an inept, self-centered, shallow, yet often lovable individual, the eternal adolescent whose lack of self-awareness sometimes borders upon the grotesque, a character type immortalized a few years earlier in Fellini's *I Vitelloni*. In *Big Deal on Madonna Street*, Monicelli also reverses the audience's expectations by making unconventional casting decisions, obtaining a brilliant comic performance from a young Gassman, who was best known in Italy until this film as a Shakespearean actor in tragic roles. Monicelli also casts the

At home we say:
saucy woman makes a good mistress,

Monicelli's *Big Deal on Madonna Street*: the ultimate parody of the caper film ends over a meal of pasta and beans. *Credit: DVD*

embodiment of an earlier comic tradition, Totò, in the film, setting his older and more traditional Neapolitan comic style of acting and humor against the performances of the newer generation of comedians.

The Great War and *The Organizer* widen the thematic boundaries of the comic genre by combining the inept but sympathetic comic type of *Big Deal on Madonna Street* with controversial social issues. *The Great War* shared the Golden Lion Award at the 1959 Venice Film Festival with Rossellini's *General Della Rovere* (see chapter 8), and Monicelli's work was greeted with a wave of negative commentary from conservative elements in Italian society, especially the military, an institution that had consistently opposed any honest discussion of Italy's role in World War I. It combines the conventions of film comedy with those of the historical-colossal and the war film: it boasted a large budget, a huge cast, and the use of CinemaScope. Coming only two years after Charles Vidor's *A Farewell to Arms* (a colossal big-budget picture shot in the Italian Alps), it can also be said to represent an antiwar response to the Hollywood version of Hemingway's more romantic celebration of war as a means of testing one's manhood. Gassman and Sordi play two unwilling warriors, Busacca and Jacovacci, who spend their service time trying to avoid any dangerous combat in World War I. Through their misadventures, Monicelli creates two perfect antiheroes, bungling soldiers who recall his equally incompetent thieves. The film is full of perfect comic gags that deflate bombastic militarism: stringing telephone wires at the front, the two men cross their wires with those belonging to the enemy, creating a hilarious dialogue between the opposing sides, each of which fails to comprehend the other's language. Later, when they are finally forced to go to the front, they jeer at what they assume to be a group of motley German prisoners, only to discover that they are laughing at their own battered compatriots. The force of the comedy creates a grotesque vision of the war's absurdity and the incompetence of its commanders, portraying the so-called Great War as an idiotic and quixotic expedition in which simple working-class Italians are sacrificed to the empty ideals held by the vastly incompetent upper-class officers who lead them into battle. Italy's most disastrous military defeat before World War II, the Battle of Caporetto (also the subject of the Hollywood adaptation of Hemingway's Italian war novel) thus appears in an irreverent comic framework, something that enraged conservative Italians. Monicelli, however, rejects a comic conclusion to the film. Captured by the Germans, who accuse them of being spies because they are out of uniform, Busacca and Jacovacci are goaded out of their innate cowardice into a heroic refusal to respond to the questions of an overbearing Prussian martinet, who brags that he will soon be eating liver and onions in Venice, and they are summarily shot. The film concludes by tracing the historically successful Italian counterattack after Caporetto. As their comrades race by the undetected bodies of these reluctant heroes, they never learn of their courageous sacrifice; the two are remembered only as cowardly deserters.

The Great War is a skillful mixture of black humor, used to undermine the patriotic rhetoric unfortunately common to all cultures at war, and a superbly directed war film. The battle scenes, re-created at great expense, stand in sharp contrast to the individual but more eloquent human dramas

In Monicelli's *The Great War*, two cowardly Italian soldiers challenge their German captors and become heroes in spite of themselves. *Credit: CSC*

developing in the actions of Monicelli's two antiheroic protagonists. In *The Organizer*, Monicelli continues the successful technique of his antiwar comedy, judiciously combining black humor with an important historical issue: the rise of the socialist movement in the nineteenth century. The plot deals with the unsuccessful strike of textile workers in Turin in 1890 and examines the emergence and the weakness of class-consciousness among the workers. Marcello Mastroianni delivers a brilliant performance as an upper-class intellectual (the typical background of leftist leaders in the period) who betrays his class origins to work for the cause of socialism. Professor Giuseppe Sinigaglia, Mastroianni's character, is both a threadbare vagrant and traitor to his class. His sincerity stands in sharp contrast to his ineptitude. Sinigaglia is clearly not the classic hero of socialist realism; nor are the workers for whom he has given up wealth and social position always worthy of his gesture or cognizant of the political goals he espouses. Monicelli's proletarians are easily tricked by their employers (they claim that they, too, live on a salary!), and quicker to fight among themselves than to protect the interests of their class, dissipating their collective energies in petty squabbles.

Monicelli's film contains little of the moral indignation or the systematically defined ideology typical of the so-called political films of the early 1970s, but his denunciation of an economic system that exploited men, women, and children with a fourteen-hour working day remains moving. His genius for evoking scenes from Italian labor history in an authentic fashion in this film is as telling as his re-creation of the horrors of life in the trenches in *The Great War*. Small vignettes capture the empathy of ordinary

An impoverished union organizer, Professor Sinigaglia, stares at the luscious pastries displayed inside a chic café in Monicelli's *The Organizer*. *Credit: MOMA*

Italians for the strikers and the cruelty of their upper-class masters: troops assigned to protect the rich share their rations with hungry strikers until ordered to desist by their aristocratic officers; railroad workers, in an act of solidarity, look the other way as freezing strikers gather up stray bits of coal falling from the locomotives in the railyards. As always, Monicelli's comic cinema contrasts the simple dignity and generosity of ordinary working-class Italians with the insensitivity and incompetence of their superiors. Nowhere is Monicelli's talent for blending moments of comic relief with tragedy more striking than in a sequence in which the strikers seek to prevent imported scab laborers from taking their jobs. A carefully choreo-graphed comic brawl, reminiscent of a Hollywood western's bar fight, leads unexpectedly to disaster as one of the strike's leaders is killed by a speeding train coming from nowhere out of the fog. At the height of the crisis, Professor Sinigaglia rallies the weakening workers with a speech parodying Marc Antony's funeral oration for Julius Caesar in Shakespeare's tragedy of the same name. As is his usual practice, Monicelli provides no facile comic resolution: the strike fails, the police kill a young striker, and they arrest the professor. The only consolation offered is the hope of future success—one of the workers carries on Sinigaglia's struggle—but the last shot of the film shows the defeated men filing slowly back to work. A medium close-up focuses on the dead boy's brother, the last to enter the factory, on whom the building's gates shut as if upon a prison. Failure in Monicelli's tragicomic world does not, however, preclude the acquisition of human dignity.

Although Monicelli is universally considered one of the great comic masters, two of his works universally known and loved by virtually every-one in Italy have rarely traveled outside of the Italian-speaking world: *All My Friends* (*Amici miei*, 1975) and a sequel, *All My Friends Part 2* (*Amici miei atto II*, 1982). Set in Tuscany, a region of Italy renowned for its biting, sarcastic, and even cruel humor, *All My Friends* follows a group of Italian males who bond together by playing practical jokes on others on their *zin-garate* (what might be called "gypsy expeditions"). During their forays away from the workaday world, they invent always grotesque and often cruel practical jokes of the type that are played on the unsuspecting boobs in such famous Tuscan literary works of the Italian Renaissance as Boccaccio's *Decameron* or Machiavelli's *The Mandrake Root*. Indeed, in Tuscan tradi-tion, the witty and the intelligent are virtually required to play cruel tricks upon the foolish and the unintelligent. The group of witty pranksters com-prises Count Lello Mascetti (Ugo Tognazzi), a decadent nobleman down on his luck; Rambaldo Melandri, an architect (Gastone Moschin); Guido Nec-chi (Duilio Del Prete), the owner of a bar from which the *zingarate* expedi-tions depart; Giorgio Perozzi, a journalist and the narrative voice of the film (Philippe Noiret); and Professor Sassaroli (Adolfo Celi), a famous surgeon. All in their fifties, these men have difficulties relating not only to their

In the most famous gag of the postwar Italian film comedy, a group of Tuscan friends slaps passengers on a departing train in the face from the platform in Monicelli's *All My Friends. Credit: CSC*

wives but to their children as well, all of whom disapprove of their humor, considering their antics infantile and futile attempts to remain young by acting up. Because so many of their practical jokes depend on nonsense language to befuddle their victims, the film and its sequel are virtually impossible to explain to anyone without a rather good knowledge of Italian. Nonetheless, the most famous practical joke requires no translation: standing on a train platform, the group pretend to be waving good-bye to passengers leaning out of open windows and slap each of them in the face as the engine pulls out of the station. The film concludes with the sudden death of one friend and the cynical reaction of his comrades, who immediately decide to use their dead friend's body for one final joke negating the finality of death. *All My Friends Part 2* continues in the same vein, bringing back the dead friend by employing flashbacks to recount other *zingarate* and concluding with a famously politically incorrect sequence. After Mascetti is paralyzed by a stroke, his friends enter him as a contestant in a wheelchair race for handicapped athletes, registering him as a native of Pisa, Florence's perennial enemy, since they know he will finish last. Monicelli's Tuscan black humor, which scoffs even at death and sees male comradeship as a bulwark against old age and unhappiness, made such an impression on Italian audiences that a second sequel was virtually required. It appeared as *All My Friends Part 3* (*Amici miei atto III*, 1985), directed by Nanni Loy (1925–95). As one might expect in the *commedia all'italiana*, where comic genius consists of invention and surprise, the famous conclusion of *All My Friends* itself is now parodied. When the group of friends goes to the train station to repeat the face-slapping gag, as the train departs, the passengers slap them instead!

Luigi Comencini's *Everybody Home!* (*Tutti a casa*, 1960) represents another landmark in the *commedia all'italiana*, a perfect companion in style and content to the antiwar humor in Monicelli's *The Great War*. Comencini directs his jaundiced view of war toward Italy's disastrous role in the Second

World War, not the First. The title derives from the cheer of Italian soldiers when they learned of the armistice signed on September 8, 1943, between the Allies and Marshal Badoglio (who had been named prime minister on July 25, the day after Mussolini's arrest)—a mere flash of joy followed by the German occupation of Italy and two more years of some of the bitterest fighting in the European campaign, resulting in the almost total destruction of many parts of Italy. Alberto Sordi, the eternal goof-off comic type, portrays an Italian officer, Lieutenant Innocenzi, who is blissfully unaware of the moral consequences of his tepid support of the Fascist cause. He is an antiheroic figure whose talents on the battlefield consist of directing his troops to sing popular songs while marching. Upon hearing of the armistice, Innocenzi abandons his soldiers and heads home, and during his picaresque journey from one comic misadventure to another, tragedy always looms over him. The journey offers him three choices: a simple return home with no moral choices, fighting alongside the Germans and their Fascist allies, and joining the partisan struggles to liberate Italy. Comencini shows how this comic figure progresses from the first to the third choice, becoming something of a real hero, just as Sordi's equally ineffectual character in *The Great War* finally did.

On the road, this sunshine patriot is initially unaffected by the sight of deportees being sent to Germany in boxcars; nor does his superficial patriotism hinder his participation in the traffic of black-market food staples. After a hungry crowd runs off with the stolen flour Innocenzi has been guarding for a buxom black marketeer, one of his indignant soldiers tells him that it is precisely because of leaders such as he that Italy has lost the war. As Monicelli did in *The Great War*, Comencini uses *Everybody Home!* to mount an equally effective attack against Italy's traditional political and military leaders. And like Monicelli, Comencini employs black humor very

A deserter becomes a surprising patriot in Comencini's *Everybody Home!* Credit: CSC

effectively. When German soldiers become suspicious of a girl named Modena (they have been correctly informed that many Jewish families often bear the names of cities), a grotesque comic dialogue between the Germans and Italians on a bus ensues, as the Italians attempt to convince the anti-Semitic Germans that no such city as Modena exists in Italy! Their act of kindness does not, however, prevent the girl from being brutally executed. While hiding inside the home of one of his soldiers, the lieutenant shares a room with an escaped GI, and Innocenzi is unable to respond to the American's embarrassing question (delivered in a broken, comic Italian) as to why he has fought a war in which he did not believe.

Innocenzi's road trip throughout war-torn Italy presents Comencini's hero with numerous moral choices, each of which he fails by saving his skin and practicing the ancient Italian art of getting by (*l'arte di arrangiarsi*). Comencini shows his audience that home and family (*la casa e la famiglia*), traditionally viewed by Italian culture as ultimate values, are actually subordinate to other ethical values, some of which require self-sacrifice and a commitment to the well-being of others. Nevertheless, Comencini ends *Everybody Home!* on a more comfortable note than the ambivalent and thought-provoking conclusion of Monicelli's *The Great War*. After witnessing the death of a close friend, Innocenzi experiences a conversion, takes up a weapon, and with martial music on the sound track, joins the partisans, now content to take orders from the simple workers whom he had formerly commanded. Although the spectator may well doubt the sincerity of his new commitment, this journey from indifference to an abrupt ideological change during the last two years of the Italian campaign is not atypical of the experience of many Italians, and Comencini's film provides a trenchant critique of a way of life (getting by) sanctified by traditional Italian values.

Comedy Sicilian Style: Pietro Germi

Pietro Germi's vignettes of Sicilian social customs in *Divorce, Italian Style* and *Seduced and Abandoned* (*Sedotta e abbondanata*, 1964) dissect the senseless and unwritten codes of behavior governing relationships between the sexes in that male-dominated, insular culture. *Divorce, Italian Style* appeared before civil divorce was legalized in Italy and chronicles the comic misadventures of a decadent Sicilian nobleman, Ferdinando Cefalù (Marcello Mastroianni)—Fefé to his friends—who wants to rid himself of his wife, Rosalia (Daniela Rocca), in order to marry the young cousin he loves, Angela (Stefania Sandrelli). Since divorce is not socially or legally permitted, Fefé must find an ingenious means of driving his wife to commit adultery so that he can murder her, since Sicilian society considers murdering one's wife a necessary "crime of honor" and generally punishes such "acts of passion" with very light prison sentences. Thus, Germi's plot (and that of most Italian film comedies dealing with outmoded social customs) may be described as the reductio ad absurdum type, wherein a "social question is magnified, reducing the action to chaos and the social question to absurdity."[1] But *Divorce, Italian Style* is no simple commercial comedy poking idle fun at backward Sicilian males, for Germi's narrative employs a complex structure to develop its storyline. Germi begins his film with the conclusion of Fefé's plot—an opening scene picturing Fefé's return home after serving a brief prison sentence for murdering his wife—and then in flashback shows us Fefé's version of how he actually obtained his "divorce." Thus, while Fefé offers his own subjective and biased account, Germi's narrative voice-over provides commentary on the action, and the director inserts a number of imaginary scenes picturing fantastic murder plots into Fefé's monologue to undercut his protagonist: Rosalia is variously blasted into space, buried in quicksand, stabbed and made into soap, and shot in the town square by a Mafia assassin. The highly effective use of the sound track derives from an imaginary speech in Fefé's defense by his lawyer during the trial to be held in the future. His summation before the court is humorously juxtaposed against the more objective account of events rendered by Germi's camera that emphasizes the absurdity of Fefé's reliance upon a code of honor to justify a premeditated crime. The disparity between these various narrative perspectives forces upon the spectator a perspective highly critical of Sicilian sexual mores and gender roles.

Germi also re-creates the oppressive and repressive atmosphere of small Sicilian villages via a camera moving with masterful rapidity through endless groups of judgmental, leering men and women. Peer pressure, voyeurism, and repressed sexuality seem to constitute the basis of Germi's vision of Sicily: men aspire to seduce the married women in the town, yet ridicule their friends who are cuckolds; people incessantly watch one another through doors and windows, from balconies and opera boxes, and in the streets; fathers subject their daughters to humiliating physical examinations by midwives to certify their purity (but neglect to set the same standards for their male offspring); anonymous letters circulate with accusations of infidelity that tie up the entire post office. Women are no less guilty of following these destructive social customs: they accept sexist views of marriage, consider adulteresses whores, and seek to avenge their offended honor with violence, often more effectively than the men. In his detailed description of Sicilian mannerisms Germi utilizes a time-honored comic-film plot, what Gerald Mast defines as "riffing" or "improvised and anomalous gaggery."[2] Germi runs off endless gags revolving around the central theme, an "Italian" divorce. Typical of his technique is his description of Fefé's plot to capture his wife in flagrante with a lover. Since his wife is neither beautiful nor desirable, he must first lure his wife into falling in love with a former suitor (Leopoldo Trieste, in his greatest comic role since *I Vitelloni*). Then

Germi chronicles the meticulous details of the purchase of a tape recorder and his fumbling attempts to plant microphones in the living room, all of which fail to capture, when the machine runs out of tape, the details of the lovers' plans to elope. To allow his wife time to compromise herself, Fefé attends a screening of the hit film of the period, Fellini's *La Dolce Vita*. While Sicilian moralists condemn the film, they crowd to the theater to see it. When he confidently returns from the movie, however, Fefé discovers that he has missed his opportunity, since his wife and lover have eloped, and he then misses the train that carries them out of town. When finally he discovers their whereabouts and goes there to kill them, the wife of Rosalia's lover beats him to the location and kills her adulterous husband first. In this comedy of errors, with its convincing indictment of the retrograde Sicilian view of "divorce," Germi elicits a masterful performance from Mastroianni, whose dark sunglasses, cigarette holder, slicked-down hair, and nervous sucking of his lips set a pattern for the comic portrayal of the Sicilian or southern Italian male that was to be repeated over and over again (particularly in comedies by Lina Wertmüller, starring Giancarlo Giannini).

Although less successful than *Divorce, Italian Style*, Germi's *Seduced and Abandoned* broadened the critique of Italian divorce legislation and subjected a wider range of sexual relationships and social mores to the director's critical scrutiny. In the process, Germi examined a broader range of social types: the frustrated policeman from the North, working fruitlessly in the South, who stares at a map of Italy and sadly remarks, "That's better!" when he covers up Sicily with his hand and wonders if an atomic explosion would improve matters on the island; the poverty-stricken aristocrat (Leopold Trieste again) who receives the set of false teeth he cannot afford from his prospective father-in-law, to persuade him to marry his daughter, Matilde; the typical Sicilian father Don Vincenzo Ascalone (Saro Urzì), more concerned over his "honor" than his life or the happiness of his two daughters, Agnese (Stefania Sandrelli) and Matilde (Paola Biggio); Matilde's suitor, Peppino (Aldo Puglisi), who seduces Agnese and then refuses to marry her because she is no longer pure; and finally the courageous woman, Agnese herself, who dares to break the traditional code of *omertà* when she charges Peppino with seducing her, thus bringing down upon her and her family (but not upon Peppino) the disapproval of the entire town. Individual rebellion proves useless, however, and Agnese is eventually forced by the inflexible Sicilian moral code to marry Peppino against her will, which drives Matilde into a convent, breaks her mother's heart, and indirectly leads to her father's death.

Seduced and Abandoned is thus the darkest of grotesque comedies, combining the sharp delineation of character typical of the *commedia all'italiana* with interesting stylistic effects. Of particular interest is Germi's use of dramatic zoom-lens shots to underscore the oppressive peer pressure

Fefé records his wife's conversations with her lover in preparation for his future murder trial in Germi's *Divorce, Italian Style*. Credit: DVD

of Sicilian society upon Agnese and her family; Germi also employs a wide lens to distort the faces of the jeering citizenry. The end result is that the film audience takes part in Agnese's entrapment. A number of subjective and imaginary images from Agnese's perspective (a technique employed most successfully in *Divorce, Italian Style*), as well as a handheld camera used to capture her desperate flight from her neighbors, provide the exact stylistic counterpart for the young girl's emotions as she is hounded out of the town's main square. *Seduced and Abandoned* provides a chilling vision of how traditional social mores can destroy an individual, especially a woman with a mind of her own. Filmed long before a true Italian feminist movement had made great progress in changing Italian views on sexuality, it nevertheless provided an argument for dramatic change in the ground rules governing how men and women interrelate in modern Italian society.

Comic Views of Conformity in Society

Other directors too aimed their cameras at absurd Italian behavior. For instance, Sicilian sexual mores also preoccupy Mauro Bolognini in *Bell'Antonio* (*Il bell'Antonio*, 1960), a film based upon an important novel by Vitaliano Brancati. Once again, Mastroianni is cast as the inept Italian male (exactly the opposite of his reputation in the gossip columns or tabloids as the archetypal "Latin Lover"): Antonio, an extremely handsome man to whom most women are attracted, can function sexually only with prostitutes and is impotent with women he really loves. Brancati's novel linked *gallismo*, or the Don Giovanni complex characteristic of the southern Italian male, to a Fascist mentality. (Fellini's *Amarcord* would later make this connection between politics and sexuality even more explicit.) In fact, Antonio's father (who claims he was made the Fascist *federale*, a provincial party leader, of Catania because he once slept with nine women) dies in a brothel after he has gone there to prove to the entire town that his son's impotence has no genetic origins. Antonio's mother, however, confesses to Antonio's unhappy wife, Barbara (Claudia Cardinale), that her husband had failed to sleep with her for two years after their wedding. As in *Seduced and Abandoned*, personal feelings and emotions must always be sacrificed to public approval and family honor. The grotesque perversion of the authentic relationships between men and women concludes with a hauntingly moving final close-up of a speechless Antonio, reflected in a mirror, as his friend Edoardo, the natural father of a child Antonio must acknowledge as his own to win society's approval, congratulates him on the "normality" he will enjoy in the future.

Another Sicilian comedy of manners is Lattuada's *Mafioso* (1962), an examination of Sicilian emigration to the industrial North in an era of rapid social change. In it, Alberto Sordi portrays Antonio Badalamenti, a Sicilian transferred to Milan, where he becomes a normal part of a modern industrial community. His complacent normality is shaken during a visit home to Sicily, where he is forced by the Mafia to travel to America, to commit a murder, and then to return to his home and family in Milan as if nothing had happened. Not unlike Germi's Sicilian comedies, Lattuada's film examines the clash between modern customs and a more ancient code of conduct that resists change and survives in an era of transition. This interesting and original Mafia film may be contrasted to another and more traditional work Lattuada shot a few years later, a filmed version of the great Renaissance comic play *The Mandrake Root* (*La mandragola*, 1965), by Niccolò Machiavelli. In it, the great Neapolitan actor Totò plays the rascally and cynical priest Fra' Timoteo, but this excellent adaptation naturally lacks the trenchant contemporary social criticism typical of the best examples of *commedia all'italiana*.

The problematic nature of normality and conformity in society—experienced at great personal expense by Bolognini's and Lattuada's Sicilian Antonios—lies at the heart of several important comic films in the 1960s by Dino Risi and Lina Wertmüller. Risi's *The Easy Life* (*Il sorpasso*, 1962) may best be described as a tragicomic road picture that explores changing Italian social values during the postwar economic boom, and many critics would set it alongside Fellini's *La Dolce Vita* as a landmark film that reflects very deep social change in the peninsula. A loose, picaresque narrative structure—an automobile drive between Rome and Viareggio—provides Risi the occasion for juxtaposing two comic types: Bruno (Vittorio Gassman), the superficial extrovert obsessed with his fast sports car, the symbol of Italy's belated entry into a consumer society, and Roberto (Jean-Louis Trintignant), a pensive, introverted intellectual. Risi follows the two men in what might accurately be described as an Italian *Easy Rider*: the film ends abruptly with an automobile crash that kills Roberto. Death and disaster lurk beneath the surface

Lattuada's *Mafioso* exploits the comic possibilities of sending a Sicilian businessman to New York under Mafia orders to undertake a "hit." *Credit: AB*

of the newly found Italian prosperity represented by the automobile and the facile types who drive them.

A collection of some twenty comic sketches employing the versatile talents of Gassman and Ugo Tognazzi makes up another excellent Risi comedy, *The Monsters* (*I mostri*, 1963), the film's title providing a fitting moral judgment of a wide range of easily recognizable contemporary Italian types: the rabid soccer fan, the corrupt parliamentary deputy, the cuckolded husband glued to the television set while his wife betrays him in his own bedroom. By moving from the merely comic to the grotesque, Risi reveals himself to be a master caricaturist as he draws rogues' galleries of moral monsters that he sees running amok in Italy, driven by cynicism and self-interest and guided by no other goal than the immediate gratification of infantile desires. Here the "norm" has become perverted into abnormality.

Lina Wertmüller's Feminist Comedy

The malaise underlying the sudden prosperity of the Italian economic miracle receives satirical treatment in Wertmüller's first feature-length film, *The Lizards* (*I basilischi*, 1963). Like the *vitelloni* of Fellini's earlier dissection of Italian provincial life to which her film is deeply indebted, Wertmüller's southern males are described by analogy to the manner in which such reptiles sun themselves listlessly in the sun, but unlike Fellini's great comedy—which spawned not only Wertmüller's first film but also Martin Scorsese's *Mean Streets* (1973)—*The Lizards* offers an explicitly political and feminist interpretation of Italian provincial life. Overt class conflict among landowners, ex-Fascists, and laborers takes place, and the Fellinian juxtaposition of town and province now becomes an economic choice rather than a poetic metaphor for an individual's search for maturity. Wertmüller's vision of the Italian hinterlands is much darker than Fellini's. Whereas the latter's Moraldo eventually leaves his *vitelloni* friends and moves to Rome for a presumably richer and fuller life (like that of his creator), Wertmül-ler's provincial protagonist, Alberto, is forced to return home from Rome after an unsuccessful attempt to shake his provincial roots. Although the opening sequence depicting the entire town asleep in the afternoon, like the lizards of her title, might easily have been lifted from an anthology of Fellini's early works, Wertmüller's comedy shifts its perspective to a female, if not a feminist, point of view. The strongest characters in the film are women: we remember most vividly the outlandishly dressed woman who appears in a sports car with a movie camera and who insults the local ex-Fascist landowners (perhaps Wertmüller's self-portrait); the wealthy widow, the female physician whose parents were simple day laborers. Even the old woman who commits suicide after mourning her husband's death for five years takes on a positive light when we consider that her desperate act rejects traditional values deeply rooted in southern culture. These strongly delineated, active female figures stand in sharp contrast to the closing image of the men in the town who play cards and talk endlessly to no purpose. *The Lizards* announced the arrival of a fresh comic talent, one with a woman's point of view.

Wertmüller's international standing as a specifically feminist director took some time to attain. After a number of comic films that achieved mod-est success (two of which starred Giancarlo Giannini), and even a spaghetti western (written and directed via male pseudonyms), she burst onto the international scene with a series of incredibly successful comic master-pieces: *The Seduction of Mimì* (*Mimì metallurgico ferito nell'onore*, 1972); *Love and Anarchy* (*Film d'amore e d'anarchia, ovvero 'stamattina alle 10 in via dei Fiori nella nota casa di tolleranza . . . '*, 1973); *All Screwed Up* (*Tutto a posto e niente in ordine*, 1974); *Swept Away* (*Travolti da un insolito des-tino nell'azzurro mare d'agosto*, 1974); and her masterpiece, *Seven Beauties* (*Pasqualino Settebellezze*, 1975). *Seven Beauties* earned her the first Oscar nomination for Best Director ever bestowed upon a female director, plus three other nominations for Best Foreign Film, Best Original Screenplay, and Best Actor (Giancarlo Giannini), although none of the nominations resulted in a richly deserved award. Frequently indebted to the exuber-ant imagery of Fellini (with whom she worked on the production of *8½*), Wertmüller's cinema combines a focus on topical social and political issues (a characteristic of most of the best of the *commedia all'italiana*) with the traditional Italian taste for grotesque comedy—including its vulgarity, its stock characters, and its frontal attack upon accepted values and mores. *The Seduction of Mimì* treats both a political seduction and a seduction of the heart. After losing his job in Sicily for voting the Communist ticket against a Mafia-sponsored candidate, Mimì moves to work in Turin, where he becomes a metalworker, joins the Communist Party, and falls in love with Fiore (Mariangela Melato). Transferred back to Sicily—where his wife, Rosalia (Agostina Belli), has meanwhile become "modernized" by leaving the security of the home, finding an industrial job, and broadening her horizons—Mimì discovers that the archaic Sicilian values he thought he had abandoned still dominate his thinking where his wife is concerned. He wants sexual freedom (keeping his mistress, Fiore, and his new child, as well as Rosalia), but he cannot permit the same liberty to his wife, who has betrayed him and is now pregnant. Seeking revenge by means of the traditional Sicilian vendetta, he forces himself to sleep with an enormous Amalia (Elena Fiore), the wife of the man who has cuckolded him, and makes her pregnant in turn. When Mimì confronts Amalia's husband in the public square, his rival is shot by a Mafia gangster; but it is Mimì, instead, who is imprisoned—and who, when released, is forced to support both Rosalia and Amalia, as well as their children, by working for the very Mafia he once fled Sicily to escape. Wertmüller's view of power and authority in Italy is comically rendered by a series of characters—a Catholic bishop, a Mafia boss, a police inspector, a Communist Party official, a building contractor—all of whom sport on their faces three prominent moles captured by the director's zoom lens in close-up. Each time one of these obviously related figures appears in the film, the Italian national anthem "Fratelli d'Italia" ("Brothers of Italy") plays on the sound track, implying a common bond between the figures and the institutions they represent, both inside and outside the law.

In Wertmüller's *The Seduction of Mimì*, Mimì sets out to seduce the enormous Amalia to take revenge on her husband for seducing his own wife. *Credit: MOMA*

The outstanding comic performances of the Giannini-Melato duo made them stars. Especially memorable (and attacked by feminist critics) is the sequence, photographed with a fish-eye lens, that distorts the body of the obese Amalia when Mimì seduces her—one that certainly echoes the character of La Saraghina in Fellini's 8½.

Love and Anarchy offers a more positive male protagonist, again played by Giannini: Tunin, a southern peasant radicalized by the Fascist regime's brutal murder of an anarchist friend, comes to Rome to assassinate Mussolini, meeting there his anarchist contact, a prostitute named Salomè (Mariangela Melato), in a luxurious Roman brothel. Tunin is torn between his desire to uphold his political beliefs (anarchy) and his passion for Tripolina (Lina Polito), a prostitute friend of Salomè with whom he has fallen in love. The two women allow Tunin to oversleep rather than keep his appointment to shoot Mussolini, and when Tunin goes berserk over their actions, he is captured by the Carabinieri and eventually murdered in prison by the henchmen of Spatoletti (Eros Pagni), the macho head of the Fascist secret police who is also a frequent customer of the brothel. Wertmüller employs Spatoletti (a figure who virtually steals the film) to associate political power and macho, Fascist sexuality, while Italy metaphorically becomes a brothel in which sexual adventurers hold raw power. (The brothel scenes themselves are indebted to such scenes in *Fellini's Roma*, which appeared the year before Wertmüller's film was released.) Both Italy and the brothel are organized around authoritarian principles, whereas the more authentic human relationships between Tunin and Salomè and Tripolina embody old-fashioned romantic views of love. Indeed, Spatoletti's comic portrayal is far truer to the reigning macho ideology of Italian Fascism than the many repressed homosexuals portrayed in films by Visconti or Bernardo Bertolucci (who is discussed in chapter 8), who are meant to symbolize Mussolini's Italy. Ultimately, neither love nor anarchy leads to the end of the regime's tyranny.

All Screwed Up offers the image of a workers' commune in Milan as a possible alternative lifestyle to the dehumanizing industrial development of northern Italy. It contains some brilliant sequences: classical music accompanies a view of a slaughterhouse where beef carcasses are skinned, cut, and quartered; a virginal Sicilian girl who is being seduced uses her hands not to fend off her ravisher but rather to keep her cherished consumer object (a new television set) from falling on the floor. The film, however, never succeeds as a coherent work of art and is best seen as a series of hilarious comic sketches. With her next two films, however—*Swept Away* and *Seven Beauties*—Wertmüller's comic art combined visual exuberance and stylistic virtuosity with storylines that achieve a high level of tragicomic seriousness.

In the first film, Wertmüller employs the classic pastoral myth of a state of nature, combined with the more modern plot of a civilized European marooned on a desert island, to explore what happens when a man and a woman are suddenly cut off from the determining influences of environment, class, race, and gender. Wertmüller's two contemporary Robinson Crusoes are played by her favorite comic duo: a rich, bitchy, spoiled, married, northern Italian woman, Raffaella (Mariangela Melato), must survive on her deserted island, after her hired yacht has abandoned her, with the assistance of a Sicilian sailor named Gennarino Carunchio (Giancarlo Giannini), who is not only a sexist but a Communist who hates rich northern Italians and women who do not follow his macho southern mores. Raffaella is as prejudiced as Gennarino, believing that all southern Italians are Ethiopians or Africans. The film's plot is extremely simple. After a brief prologue presents a microcosm of Italian society, representing not only different social classes but political ideologies as well, the two main characters are cast adrift in what will become a parable about gender and class conflict. After they fall in love, the two are returned to the society they left, and its impact or its nature can be measured by their actions.

In the film's opening sequences on the yacht, Gennarino and Raffaella immediately clash. While constantly needling the southern sailor about his dirty T-shirts, his overboiled coffee, and his soggy pasta, Raffaella harangues her wealthy guests about political issues, allowing Wertmüller to sketch the perfect portrait of Italian "radical chic"—industrialists as would-be socialists or leftists pretending to a revolutionary ideology, yet loudly insisting that people of importance, even Karl Marx(!), always retained a bevy of servants. Raffaella's attitude is neatly summed up by her biting remark to Gennarino: "Anyhow, as we await the end, the revolution, let's try and make the spaghetti al dente . . . at least once."[3]

Once Raffaella and Gennarino are abandoned to their own devices on the deserted island, however, the master-slave relationship reflected in Gennarino's subordinate position to Raffaella on the yacht shifts radically. Power and command in the state of nature pass to the man because of his physical strength, not his class or gender, and the formerly insufferable *padrona* now must turn to serving Gennarino, since her lack of any real talents for survival leave her no alternative. Once the couple's social roles are reversed, Raffaella eventually rebels after she has felt what it is like to be placed in an inferior economic position. What emerges from this transformation results in a strange, almost masochistic love affair: the woman who loved to dominate Gennarino on the yacht now submits willingly to Gennarino's slaps and curses, even begging to be sodomized to show her total subjection to his affections. And subsequently Gennarino really falls in love with Raffaella, and it is he (and not Raffaella) who decides to return to civilized society when they are rescued, to determine once and for all if Raffaella really loves him. Only Raffaella realizes that this is a foolish desire, for the strength of society's class barriers will eventually destroy the love

Raffaella and Gennarino fall in love in spite of their class differences in Wertmüller's *Swept Away. Credit: MOMA*

affair that could only flourish beyond the limits of civilized society. Class always tells in Wertmüller's cinematic universe, even more than gender.

The subordination of class to gender issues in *Swept Away* explains in large measure why this film provoked such heated reactions from many feminists in the Anglo-Saxon world when it appeared at the height of the feminist movement. Many feminists felt that the image of Raffaella was degrading, particularly the sequence in which Gennarino slaps and kicks Raffaella over the sand dunes, blaming her for everything from high prices to the lack of hospital beds, and calling her all sorts of ideologically charged names ("dumb Social Democratic whore," "industrial whore")—not to mention the scene in which Raffaella begs her lover to sodomize her. Although Wertmüller has claimed that her allegory about class relationships would function equally well if the social roles the characters represent were reversed, some feminist critics of the film have preferred to see all men of whatever class as exploiters of all women.

With *Seven Beauties*, Wertmüller's cinematic art reaches its culmination in what must be called a masterpiece, and in the United States her work was championed by the most unlikely of critics, the conservative and usually caustic John Simon.[4] Once again she exploits the familiar theme of southern Italian values, but now her earlier interest in class relationships between men and women is extended to deal with questions of survival related to the Holocaust and the concentration camps of World War II. In flashbacks, the film's plot moves from wartime Nazi Germany to prewar Fascist Italy—specifically Naples—where the main character, Pasqualino Frafuso, nicknamed "Pasqualino Seven Beauties" (Giancarlo Giannini), lives by his wits, but primarily off the wages of his seven adoring but obese sisters. When one of them, Concettina (Elena Fiore), dares to disgrace the family honor by dancing in a music hall and then becoming a prostitute in a brothel, Pasqualino feels obliged to kill the man who seduced her and then became her pimp, and Pasqualino cuts up his body and mails it in pieces all over Italy. He is naturally caught, sent to prison, and then to an insane asylum, where he feigns madness, but after he rapes another female patient, he is forced to join the army and finds himself on the Eastern Front in Russia. Given that Pasqualino's only real talent is survival, when he tries to desert, he is caught by the Nazis and interned in a concentration camp. Naples has always been known as the city peopled by cunning citizens who will do anything to survive, and Pasqualino becomes the ultimate Neapolitan. He finally seduces the buxom female commandant (Shirley Stoler), who then forces him to murder another inmate to save his own life. As the film ends, we learn that Pasqualino has survived the war by engaging in every sort of degradation, but at a terrible cost.

Wertmüller avoids a linear narrative and structures her plot by jumping back and forth in tragicomic fashion between Naples (treating a single murder over an affair of honor) with German sequences (involving the wholesale slaughter of millions of people in the death camps). Hilarious Neapolitan comic scenes are juxtaposed against chilling German ones. The overriding instinct for survival that she depicts humorously in Naples, when allowed to develop unchecked by any higher moral values than survival itself, degenerates into a dehumanized obsession to live at any price in Germany. The director's sympathies are obviously with those camp inmates who rebel and are killed rather than submit to the Nazi system, particularly with the Spanish anarchist Pedro (Fernando Rey), whose political credo is

In Wertmüller's *Seven Beauties*, the director's reconstruction of a music hall number by Pasqualino's sister pays homage to Fellini's variety show scenes in various films, particularly *Fellini's Roma*. Credit: DVD

In Wertmüller's *Seven Beauties*, Pasqualino saves his life by seducing the enormous female commander of the concentration camp in which he is held prisoner. Note the Angelo Bronzino painting, *An Allegory with Venus and Cupid*, placed behind her as an ironic commentary on the lovemaking that has just taken place. *Credit: DVD*

"man in disorder," a human disorder directly opposed to the insane order of the Third Reich. Her comically vulgar tone and her rich visual style reflect the obvious influence of Fellini. The masterful music-hall sequence in which Concettina's obscene performance scandalizes Pasqualino seems lifted directly from *Fellini's Roma*, and the most memorable image of the death camp is a nightmare vision of the famous spa sequence from *8½*, now turned into a version of Dante's vision of Hell.

Pasqualino reaches rock bottom in his drive for survival with the seduction of the commandant, and as always in Wertmüller's comedies, the interrelationship of sex and politics plays a crucial role. Her screen version of the Bitch from Belsen forces Pasqualino (photographed from an angle that underscores his wormlike character) to eat a bowl of food to gain enough strength to have sex with her, and then imperiously orders him: "Now you eat, then you fuck . . . if you don't fuck, you die!"[5] Pasqualino's efforts to survive lead him finally back to Naples after the war's end, where, upon returning home, he discovers that all his desperate attempts to save his life have come to naught. Once a macho rapist, he has survived by being raped by a woman; once obsessed by his family's honor, he discovers that all of his sisters have become prostitutes who sell themselves to the American soldiers there in order to survive, echoing his own moral choice in the concentration camp. The final close-up on Pasqualino's haggard face convincingly demonstrates that some values are more important than life itself.

Comedy in an Era of Rapid Social Change: The New Monsters

During the time Italian cinema produced so many brilliant film comedies, Italian culture underwent a number of important changes, many of them signaled by the upheavals that began in 1968 with student riots. Student unrest was followed by violence and terrorism, beginning with the bombing at Piazza Fontana in Milan (December 12, 1969), continuing with terrorist bombings in Brescia (May 28, 1974) and on the Florence-Bologna express train (August 4, 1974), and culminating with the shocking kidnapping and eventual murder of Aldo Moro, former prime minister and head of the Christian Democratic Party, by the Red Brigades (March 16, 1978). Italy's economic miracle of the 1960s ended abruptly as inflation, reduced productivity, foreign competition, and the disastrous Arab oil embargo closed an era of relative prosperity. Social changes of far-ranging proportions, including the advent in 1970 of a divorce law bitterly opposed by the Vatican, took place during a time when scandals undermined public confidence in the government and led to widespread sympathy among some circles with the goals of Italian political terrorists.

Such rapid historical and cultural changes inevitably had an impact upon Italian cinema in general and film comedy in particular, which had always been characterized by a sharp, polemical edge in dealing with social issues. Moreover, the shifting patterns of popular entertainment drew people away from movie theaters and toward television (both public and private). The infrastructure of the Italian movie circuit, one of the largest in Europe and second only to that of the United States, suffered staggering losses. Many of the local theaters of the popular *seconda visione* circuit (where first-run films were repeated at lower cost) were forced to shut their doors. From 5,902 movie theaters in Italy in 1955, the number decreased rapidly to 4,619 in 1971 and 4,000 in 1975, a process that has continued until the present—although with more capital investment, the many fewer first-run *prima visione* theaters in the major cities (as in the United States) would eventually restructure themselves with wide screens and high-tech projectors and sound. Total ticket sales dropped sharply, from 513.7 million in 1975 to 276.3 million in 1979. Box-office receipts remained relatively stable (362.5 billion lire in 1975 compared to 363.6 billion lire in 1979), but this was achieved only by raising the price of admission from an average of 706 lire to 1,322 lire during the same period. The drop in total income produced a sharp decrease in film production, from a high of 294 films in 1968 to a low of 98 films in 1978, while American imports in Italy during 1968–78 remained at a high level, averaging 140 films per year. The paradoxical nature of this economic weakness in the Italian film industry came at a time when, from a critical point of view, the quality of national film production was extremely high for both the so-called art film and the more accessible genre films that appealed to a broader audience.

This social unrest did not fail to influence film comedy. The best comic directors, such as Monicelli, Risi, and Comencini, continued to make films of value. Some, such as Risi's *How Funny Can Sex Be?* (*Sessomatto*, 1973), continued the episodic tradition of collections of comic sketches established in the early 1960s. Perhaps the best of this kind of collection was *Viva Italia!* (*I nuovi mostri*, 1977), which included bittersweet sketches by Risi, Monicelli, and Scola. The title consciously refers the audience back to Risi's *The Monsters* (1963), but as the literal translation ("the new monsters") of the Italian title implies, the three directors assemble even more grotesque episodes, fourteen vignettes that are deeply pessimistic. The violence in Italian society spills over into comedy: a man sees a stabbing in the street, but is more concerned with the quality of the cheese on his pasta than in calling the police; a couple is incensed that their young actress daughter must appear naked in a pornographic film, but eventually allow her to make love to a monkey for four million lire; a rich industrialist broadcasts special radio appeals to the kidnappers of his wife to give her the medicine she needs to survive, but cuts the telephone lines to his home to prevent them from contacting him to do so; a businessman dumps his aging mother at a nursing home; a Latin-lover type seduces a beautiful airline hostess, but only to place a bomb in her plane (he turns out to be an Arab, not an Italian). In the final scene, the funeral of an Italian comic offers the hope that comedy may triumph over this dark vision of Italy.

One of the most brilliant comedies of the period that deals directly with Italian social problems is *Bread and Chocolate* (*Pane e cioccolata*, 1973), by Franco Brusati (1923–93). Largely ignored in Italy until it received rave reviews at film festivals around the world, Brusati's film depicts the conditions of Italian guest workers from southern Italy in prim, proper, and racist Switzerland. Nino Manfredi gives his greatest comic performance as Nino Garofalo, a southern Italian worker pathetically out of place in Switzerland, a country he desires to inhabit because he believes that the virtues of the Swiss people are far superior to the vices of his native land. Brusati's opening sequence juxtaposes the clean, tidy nature of Switzerland with the more exuberant but sometimes tacky Latin culture that the workers represent. While his camera pans over a Swiss family and a quartet playing Haydn in a beautifully manicured park, Garofalo appears, wearing the typically garish tie and sport shirt of the southern Italian *cafone* (boor, ill-mannered person; a word commonly employed by northern Italians to disparage southern Italian lifestyles). He immediately breaks all the rules of polite but rigid Swiss society: he litters in the park, smokes where it is forbidden, and is completely out of step with his environment. Yet death lurks in this blissful Arcadian setting. Garofalo is relaxing in the park when, nearby, a child-molesting Swiss priest

A young girl is killed not by Giovanni, the garishly dressed Italian worker living by his wits in Switzerland, but rather by a child-molesting Swiss cleric in Franco Brusati's *Bread and Chocolate*. Credit: MOMA

murders a young girl—a crime for which the obvious culprit, the Swiss assume, must certainly be the Italian foreigner.

Much of the comic force of the film derives from the competition between Garofalo and another foreigner, a Turk, for the only permanent position in a restaurant, and the misadventures Garofalo encounters as he loses his place to the Turk recall similar comic sequences in a number of Chaplin films. The most moving moments of the film show Garofalo living in a workers' barracks, where male Italian workers are squeezed into living quarters that resemble a prison or a concentration camp more than a real home. In a poignant homage to a similar scene in Renoir's great antiwar film *Grand Illusion* (*La Grand Illusion*, 1937), in which Allied prisoners in a German prison during World War I stage a variety show, Brusati depicts his homesick southern Italian men doing the same thing. When "Rosina" (a young worker in drag named Renzo), breaks into tears, unable to endure the separation from home and his loved ones any longer, Garofalo comes to understand that singing away problems, an attitude so typical of southern Italian culture, keeps Italians from changing their lives. Even more disturbing is Brusati's surrealistic vision of a group of clandestine Italian immigrants who live and work in a chicken coop. Surviving by piecework (the more chickens they kill and pluck, the more they earn), these pathetic individuals have become a grotesque parody of the very animals they kill, even speaking in henlike clucks. Outside their chicken coop home, they are treated to a vision of Germanic purity: blond young Swiss men and women bathe naked in a limpid stream to the accompaniment of Teutonic music.

We cut immediately to Garofalo, who has tinted his hair blond in a desperate attempt to assimilate into Swiss society; but even this masquerade fails when, in a crowded bar filled with German-speaking Swiss soccer fans during a match between the national teams of Italy and Switzerland, the racist remarks of the fans provoke Garofalo to scream "Viva l'Italia!" before he is tossed out of the bar. Seemingly, no room exists in Brusati's comic vision of Italy for any progress or any real social change. Italians will keep on singing and playing their mandolins to avoid dealing with the pressing issues addressing their culture.

Other comic films reflect an equally pessimistic outlook. Monicelli's *We Want the Colonels* (*Vogliamo i colonnelli*, 1973) is a thinly disguised comic version of both the dictatorship imposed by the Greek army during the period and the unsuccessful 1970 coup d'état planned in Italy by Prince Valerio Borghese with assistance from elements of Italy's armed forces and secret services. While Monicelli laughs at the ineptitude of the would-be revolutionaries, the society that produced them is decadent but comic. A more important work, *An Average Little Man* (*Un borghese piccolo piccolo*, 1977), in which Alberto Sordi gives an unforgettable performance as a minor government functionary whose son is accidentally murdered by terrorists, provides a macabre comic vision of an entire society gone berserk. When the grieving father tries to find a grave for his son, he discovers hundreds of people at the burial office waiting for endless unburied caskets. On two different occasions, a police lineup fails to identify the killer who is present, forcing the father to take the law into his own hands, capturing the killer but accidentally killing him. A similar black comedy is Risi's *Dear Papa* (*Caro papà*, 1979), the story of an ex-partisan industrialist (Vittorio Gassman) whose son studies semiotics at the university and is part of a terrorist gang planning to assassinate his own father. Only after the father is paralyzed in the assassination attempt does he discover that his son argued against the act and abandoned terrorism when his opinion was rejected. Luigi Comencini continued to make commercially successful comic films such as *Till Marriage Do Us Part* (*Mio dio, come sono caduta in basso*, 1974), a "sexy" comedy that capitalized on the widespread popularity of the scantily clad actress Laura Antonelli (1941–2009). Antonelli became the object of the sexual desire of every young Italian male in this film and in an earlier "sexy" comedy of the time, *Malicious* (*Malizia*, 1973), directed by Salvatore Samperi (1944–2009).

Comencini's darker comic films, such as *Traffic Jam* (*L'ingorgo*, 1979) and *Eugenio* (*Voltati, Eugenio*, 1980), deserve mention. The first is an episode film with numerous comic stars (Sordi, Mastroianni, Gassman) and presents a massive traffic jam that serves as a metaphor for Italy's disorganization, lack of discipline, and chaotic social conditions. As the industrialist played by Sordi remarks cynically, things are better in Moscow because there are always open traffic lanes. Every character in the film behaves badly, and the last image of the film is a long line of motionless cars going, like Italy, nowhere. *Eugenio*, on the other hand, focuses upon the private lives of a couple who have come of age in 1968 and represent a generation of protesters and would-be revolutionaries. They neglect their young son, who was conceived accidentally, treating him as a nuisance that interferes with their "liberated" lifestyle. Only the son's grandparents—representatives of an earlier era when Italian family life centered on a united family—emerge as positive figures, whereas the so-called revolutionaries emerge as nothing more than spoiled brats.

The most unusual of the Italian comic directors, Marco Ferreri (1928-97)—far more popular in France and abroad than in Italy—produced a number of outrageous but interesting works. In *La Grande Bouffe*, a.k.a. *The Big Feast* (*La grande abbuffata*, 1973), Ferreri attacks contemporary consumerism and offers an unsettling comic description of how four men (a chef, a television writer, a pilot, and a judge) go on a weekend retreat and eat themselves to death. *The Last Woman* (*L'ultima donna*, 1976) attacks the very Italian male obsession with virility. The recurrent visual image in the film is that of kitchen accidents with knives, which culminate in the nightmarish conclusion of the film when Giovanni (Gérard Depardieu) cuts off his penis with an electric knife in order to offer his wife the ultimate symbol of his manhood and, therefore, his affection.

Ettore Scola and Metacinematic Comedy

The greatest comic talent to come out of the generation after Monicelli and Comencini is Ettore Scola, whose career began first as a writer for *Marc'Aurelio*, the Roman humor magazine on which so many great Italian directors and scriptwriters (Fellini, Zavattini, and Bernardino Zapponi [1927-2000], to mention only a few) began their collaborations on filmmaking. Scola was one of Italy's most prolific scriptwriters and completed a total of more than fifty scripts before turning to direction himself in 1964. *Will Our Heroes Be Able to Find Their Friend Who Has Mysteriously Disappeared in Africa?* (*Riusciranno i nostri eroi a ritrovare l'amico misteriosamente scomparso in Africa?*, 1968), a philosophical tale indebted to the travel satires and philosophical *contes* of the Age of Reason, follows the attempts of a Roman editor (Alberto Sordi) to track a brother-in-law who has disappeared in Portuguese Angola on the eve of the end of colonialism there. Of course, like Voltaire or Montesquieu, both of whom employed exotic tales of foreign travel to comment on their own French society, Scola is actually concerned with modern upper-class Italian society rather than with Africa. When Sordi's character arrives in "exotic" Africa (actually a modern metropolis), dressed in outlandish jungle garb worthy of the white explorers in a Hollywood Tarzan film, he is obsessed with taking pictures of the "dark" continent, but an amazed African takes photos of Sordi, who has become a startlingly dated and even more exotic figure.

Scola's complicated metacinematic comedies depart, in some respects, from the traditional *commedia all'italiana* in that they also present an extremely original discourse on Italian cinema itself. *Trevico-Turin: Voyage in Fiatnam* (*Trevico-Torino: Viaggio nel Fiat-Nam*, 1973), perhaps the most obviously politically film Scola has made, creates a compelling reconstruction of the alienated existence of southern immigrants in Turin who work on the assembly lines of Italy's most important industrial complex. As such it represents a nod to Italy's neorealist heritage in cinema. Other comic films treat the very history of Italian film comedy itself, with special reference to Vittorio De Sica, Scola's cinematic model: *We All Loved Each Other So Much* (*C'eravamo tanto amati*, 1974); *Down and Dirty*, a.k.a. *Ugly, Dirty and Bad* (*Brutti, sporchi e cattivi*, 1976), winner for the prize for direction at the Cannes Film Festival (a festival on which Scola later served as jury president in 1988); *A Special Day* (*Una giornata particolare*, 1977); and *The Terrace* (*La terrazza*, 1980). Taken as a group, these films constitute the most significant and original body of comic films produced in Italy during the postwar period.

We All Loved Each Other So Much, dedicated to Vittorio De Sica (who appears in documentary footage), represents an extremely ambitious comedy, combining a consideration of the many social and political changes Italy had undergone since the fall of fascism with an equally comprehensive survey of the major developments in the history of Italian cinema. Implicit in the film's structure resides the director's belief that Italian cinema comprises the best means of understanding postwar Italy. Opening in color (the predominant tone of film when Scola shot the work), Scola presents three male friends and former Resistance fighters: Gianni (Vittorio Gassman), once the bravest anti-Fascist fighter and now a wealthy but crooked lawyer; Nicola (Stefano Satta Flores), a provincial schoolteacher and film buff who once lost his job because he defended De Sica's *The Bicycle Thief* against the conservative school administrators for whom he worked in the South of Italy; and Antonio (Nino Manfredi), a worker whose good sense and diligence serve as a corrective to the compromises and pretensions of his two comrades.

Their personal history over three postwar decades (roughly the 1950s through the 1970s) provides Scola with a microcosm of Italian history and Italian film history: the narrative recalls a number of different cinematic styles and periods. The first flashback to the Resistance, for example, shot in black in white, has a documentary style typical of many neorealist classics. Scola re-creates the tense atmosphere of social conflict during the immediate postwar period, when important films became the stuff of polemics on the Left and the Right, as Nicola defends De Sica's masterpiece against the

Nicola, Gianni, and Antonio celebrate their troubled friendship at the Half Portion Restaurant in Scola's metacinematic comedy, *We All Loved Each Other So Much*. *Credit: MOMA*

bigots of his hometown, who accuse *The Bicycle Thief* of "fomenting class warfare." Aldo Fabrizi, the actor who plays the partisan priest in Rossellini's *Open City* and represented hope for a new and better Italy after the war, now plays a disgustingly obese gangster whose daughter eventually marries Gianni, and whose wealth causes Gianni to be the first of the three friends to bargain away his belief in a new Italy. No more devastating image of the end of postwar aspirations may be seen than the actual physical degradation of Fabrizi's gangster character, whose gargantuan body bears witness to Italy's postwar excesses of self-indulgence.

Scola's references to the cinema serve a variety of purposes. The film buff Nicola playfully re-creates Eisenstein's "Odessa Steps" sequence on the Spanish Steps at the Piazza di Spagna (no doubt an oblique reference to the pro-Marxist film critics in the early postwar period), while sequences treating events in the 1950s shot in the streets and squares of Rome evoke the atmosphere of towns at night in early Fellini films. To portray the 1960s, Scola switches to color to underscore the prosperity of Italy's "economic miracle." He re-creates the single most famous sequence in Italian cinema of the time—the famous Trevi Fountain scene from *La Dolce Vita*, where Marcello Mastroianni and Anita Ekberg wade into the cold water. (Fellini plays himself shooting the scene, and in a gag typical of *commedia all'italiana* humor, an onlooker mistakes Fellini for Rossellini.) Then Scola moves from Fellini to Antonioni, parodying the mature style of Antonioni's "trilogy of alienation" (*L'avventura, La notte, L'eclisse*) in dramatizing the failure of communication (Antonioni's favorite theme) between Gianni and his wife.

The most complex linkage of fact and fiction, society and cinema, involves the figure of De Sica himself. In the 1960s Nicola had appeared on Mike Bongiorno's quiz show, *Lascia o raddopia* (literally, "quit or go for double"). This tremendously popular program from the period, when Italian television rose to challenge the hegemony of cinema in Italian popular culture, was a spin-off of similar programs in the United States, and it often received harsh criticism from Italian intellectuals for its vulgarity—most famously in Umberto Eco's essay "The Phenomenology of Mike Bongiorno" in *Misreadings*.[6] Nicola's jackpot question involves an explanation of why the boy cries in *The Bicycle Thief* at the end of the film. He provides the film-buff answer based on too much information: the boy cries because De Sica put cigarette butts in the pocket of the little boy who played the son of the man who lost his bicycle, and then the director cruelly accused him of stealing them. Nicola mistakes the "factual" answer for the "fictional" answer, but Bongiorno (played by the real Mike Bongiorno, still active on Italian television today) disqualifies Nicola and supplies the "correct" answer: the boy cries because he has witnessed his father's arrest for stealing a bicycle. Years after this crushing defeat on national television ruins his life, Nicola sees a documentary film on De Sica where the director recounts how he forced the boy to cry—just as Nicola had explained on the quiz program, but to no avail.

Each of the three friends falls in love with the same woman, Luciana (Stefania Sandrelli), but only the honest working-class stiff, Antonio, manages to win her affection. Despite Scola's intriguing mixture of historical film styles and historical moments in Italian postwar life—the metacinematic aspect of his masterpiece—the political message delivered by this leftist director is obvious. The three men represent three separate social classes (middle class, intelligentsia, proletariat), with the woman they love symbolizing Italy herself, and their evolving relationships reflect in microcosm the broader social and political interactions among Italy's major social classes.

Down and Dirty evokes De Sica by parodying the neorealist director's utopian shantytown in *Miracle in Milan*, but Scola completely overturns the happy-go-lucky image of the urban poor in that fantasy film and depicts a world without any redeeming social or moral features. Scola's protagonist, Giacinto (Nino Manfredi), is a greedy pensioner who has lost one eye in an industrial accident and now cunningly hides his insurance benefits from his huge family. He is the tragic product of a dehumanizing capitalist society that reduces the inhabitants of the slums to mindless consumers, thieves, prostitutes, and assassins. Instead of the patient, long-suffering, downtrodden poor people of De Sica's original, Scola shows us vicious, brutish, mean, and nasty individuals (albeit in a comic context). They live in a world where their desperate sexual couplings lead only to unwanted pregnancies and further squalor. In the film's ironic and metacinematic conclusion—shot

In *Down and Dirty*, Scola's parody of De Sica's *Miracle in Milan*, Giacinto's miserly character underscores the fact that the poor are not always superior to the rich. *Credit: MOMA*

from a hillside against the same dome of Saint Peter's used to symbolize hope for a new springtime in Italy in Rossellini's *Open City*—Scola offers us quite a different view of the future with a family of eighteen trapped in an inferno of ignorance and poverty. In this new period of capitalist consumerism, children—neorealism's primary symbol of optimism—become concrete embodiments of how the poor are forever doomed to repeat their deprivation.

In *A Special Day*, Scola relies upon brilliant acting performances in analyzing the emotions of his characters in a manner recalling the art of his cinematic model, De Sica, in such classics as *Umberto D.* He also casts two of Italy's most popular stars, Sophia Loren and Marcello Mastroianni, completely against type: Loren plays not the bombshell sweater girl that made her famous but Antonietta, an aging and unattractive mother of six children during the Fascist period who attempts to fulfill the regime's propaganda to raise an enormous family, while Mastroianni, in the part of Gabriele, plays a radio announcer about to be sent to confinement in Sardinia because he is a homosexual. With a casting choice consciously rejecting the commercial reputations of Loren and Mastroianni as glamour girl and Latin lover, respectively, Scola concentrates the action (as his model De Sica usually did in his films) in a short time frame—May 6, 1938, when Adolf Hitler visited Mussolini's Rome. When the crowded Fascist housing project where the two protagonists live empties, and the inhabitants of the San Giovanni district in Rome dressed in their various uniforms head for Piazza Venezia, Antonietta and Gabriele are left alone in the building, and by chance they are drawn

Scola reverses role expectations in *A Special Day,* casting gorgeous Sophia Loren as a worn-out housewife living in Rome on the day Hitler visits Mussolini there. *Credit: MOMA*

together for a few brief hours. Scola's fluid camera movements, panning up and down the apartment building and entering the two separate apartments, are juxtaposed to the jarring and omnipresent sound track of the blaring microphones announcing the triumphs of the regime. Indeed, the sound track becomes a third protagonist in the film. By showing us Antonietta's exhaustion in her kitchen, Scola borrows brilliantly from the classic scene in *Umberto D.* where the young maid prepares her breakfast, matching screen time with real time in a poignant moment of extreme psychological realism. In a change of pace from other political films of the period, it is the anti-Fascist, not the Fascist, who is a homosexual. Thrown together, the two characters make love in a desperate attempt to communicate, but Gabriele is not transformed into a heterosexual, even by the charms of Loren. "It was beautiful," he remarks, "but it changes nothing." The Fascist myth of virility has destroyed them both: it has cost Gabriele his job and his party membership (crucial for employment in the government), since such work is "only for real men"; it has destroyed Antonietta's well-being by forcing her into a life of frantic childbearing to gain government subsidies. In the evening, when the Fascist police come to take Gabriele into exile, Antonietta's Fascist husband returns home and tells her that the visit of Hitler has so inspired him that he wants to conceive a seventh child that very night.

A *Special Day* combines references to De Sica's cinematic style with amusing reversals in our expectations as spectators when Loren and Mastroianni appear on the screen. *The Terrace* narrows the metacinematic focus of other comedies that treat the relationship between Italian cinema and society. The film's characters, played by Italy's best comic actors, point to the failure of Italy's intellectuals and especially of the filmmakers to actualize the potential of the Resistance period. By employing the cream of Italy's core of comedians, Scola also implies that *commedia all'italiana* has reached an artistic impasse and no longer plays a vital role in changing the course of Italian behavior. The film's structure repeats the popular narrative structure of the episodic comedy, with different vignettes featuring various performers. Scola's camera cranes over a garden wall to reveal a Roman terrace where a reception is taking place. Thereafter, in successive episodes, the reception begins anew and follows a different figure: Mario (Vittorio Gassman), a Communist intellectual; Enrico (Jean-Louis Trintignant), a scriptwriter; Luigi (Marcello Mastroianni), a journalist; and Amadeo (Ugo Tognazzi), a film producer waiting impatiently for the script Enrico never succeeds in completing. The repetition of the episodes, all ending nowhere, emphasize the emptiness and lack of creativity typical of the evening's guests, all of whom are directly or indirectly linked to the film industry.

In effect, Scola shoots a comic film about the impossibility of making a comic film, creating a bittersweet vision of a society in which laughter can no longer serve as a corrective. Indeed, the people present even argue over the very definition of comedy. His anxiety that comic inspiration has dried up even drives Enrico to shove the finger of his writing hand into an electric pencil sharpener in a fit of frustration. The presence of most of Italy's great comic actors in a universe that is no longer funny also implies for Scola that these figures are no longer in touch with the pulse of the nation, as they were so frequently in the past in the greatest of the classic *commedia all'italiana* masterpieces. They are described by the women at the reception as has-beens, washed-out shadows of their former greatness: "It's not true that men grow old more gracefully than women," one remarks; another makes the even more damning comment, echoing the theme of *We All Loved Each Other So Much*, "if only you could have seen them during the Resistance...."

Comedies Related to *Commedia all'italiana*: Franco and Ciccio, the Fantozzi Series, the Erotic or Sexy Comedy

Several groups of comic films appeared during the height of the popularity of *commedia all'italiana* that were enormous box-office hits within Italy yet rarely received the critical attention at home or wide distribution abroad typical of other important film comedies of the period. More often than not, these films were made quickly and were what most critics would describe as B films with low production values. Normally not the work of auteur-oriented directors whose films reached wide international audiences, they had greatest appeal to *seconda visione* theaters in Italy, particularly in Rome and south of the capital. Nevertheless, they represent an often overlooked part of the Italian film industry that was extremely profitable and usually extremely amusing—if the spectator will accept the premise (one with which I strongly agree) that good comedy must allow for a certain level of blatant vulgarity if it is to be a subversive force in popular culture.[7]

Two Sicilian comics—Franco Franchi and Ciccio Ingrassia, Italy's answer to Laurel and Hardy or Abbot and Costello, but with a southern Italian accent—made over a hundred films, all low-budget works made in just a few weeks. While their comic style employed more slapstick routines, dialect, and comic devices closer to traditional *commedia dell'arte* than to the auteur-driven *commedia all'italiana*, their humor was universally loved by popular audiences and generally despised by sophisticated film critics. In retrospect, there is a postmodern quality about much of their work, as it frequently parodies important films produced by great directors, such as *Fellini Satyricon*, *The Leopard*, *The Exorcist*, *Last Tango in Paris*, or *The Good, the Bad, and the Ugly*. In the Franco and Ciccio parodies, these films become, respectively (though literal translations spoil the Italian wordplay), *Satiricosissimo* ("extremely satirical," 1970), *I figli del leopardo* ("the children of the leopard," 1965), *L'esorciccio* (*The Exorcist: Italian Style*, 1975), *Ultimo tango a Zagarol* (*Last Tango in Zagarolo* [a small town outside Rome], 1973), and *Il bello, il brutto, il cretino* (*The Handsome, the Ugly, and the Stupid*, 1967). Despite the fact that film critics considered their work trash, Franco and Ciccio achieved artistic recognition from such directors as Fellini, De Sica, Pasolini, and the Taviani brothers (see chapter 8), who cast them in at least one of their works in homage to their improvisational techniques and their unforgettable physical presence on the screen. Ingrassia is best remembered for his role as the insane and sex-starved uncle in Fellini's *Amarcord* (1973) who urinates in his pants and screams at the top of his voice, "I want a woman!" until he is taken back to his asylum by a midget nun.

A second group of extremely popular comic films focuses upon Fantozzi, a stock character invented by the actor Paolo Villaggio (1932–). Unlike many of the other stereotypical comic figures associated with Tognazzi, Gassman, or Sordi, who are usually wise guys in search of corners to cut to get ahead, Ugo Fantozzi represents the ultimate obsequious underling, an inept accountant who fawns before his superiors and cannot accomplish anything without cutting an embarrassing, pathetic figure. The first film in which Villaggio presented Fantozzi was *White Collar Blues* (*Fantozzi*, 1975), directed by Luciano Salce (1922–89), and audience reaction was so positive that the character became something of a franchise, with a new film expected every year, resulting in nine sequels by 1999. Fantozzi has an incredibly ugly daughter named Mariangela, played by a man (Plinio Fernando) to render her physical appearance more grotesque and more like a monkey—yet another example of how politically incorrect Italian film comedy generally is when it is most successful. The second Fantozzi film, *The Second Tragic Fantozzi* (*Il secondo tragico Fantozzi*, 1976), also directed by Salce, contains the most masterful sketch in the entire series. Trying to impress a superior who is a fanatic film buff addicted to repeated screenings of movie classics, Fantozzi misses a historic soccer match between the English and Italian national teams while being subjected to multiple screenings of Sergei Eisenstein's *The Battleship Potemkin* (1925), Robert Flaherty's *Man of Aran* (1934), and Carl Dreyer's *Day of Wrath* (1943)—important films but not exactly the kind of fare that the average moviegoer seeking relaxation and entertainment would screen for pleasure. Although Fantozzi's essential character is that of a lackey when confronted by orders from superiors, his love for soccer overcomes his desire for advancement, and he rebels. Risking his future, he shouts out his frustration with a remark that is cheered by the audience—and probably by some true film buffs overwhelmed by roundtable discussions, which can ruin a great film by overexplicating the obvious—"Per me, *La Corazzata Potemkin*, è una cagata pazzesca!!!" ("In my opinion, *The Battleship Potemkin* is a crazy piece of shit!") This brief moment of rebellion passes quickly, since Fantozzi's nature is that of a coward, and he and the disrespectful audience that agreed with his remark are condemned to reenact the famous "Odessa Steps" sequence of the Russian film, with Fantozzi playing the baby in the carriage that bounces down the flight of stairs. Like the film parodies of Franco and Ciccio, Villaggio's comic style frequently contains metacinematic references intended to amuse the very kind of avid film buff that Fantozzi's frustrated remark attacks. Villaggio, like Ciccio Ingrassia, received the highest possible kind of praise, not from film critics but from Italy's greatest director, as Fellini paired him with comic and fellow director Roberto Benigni (1952–) in his last movie, *The Voice of the Moon* (*La voce della luna*, 1990).

Paolo Villaggio as Fantozzi in a parody of the Odessa steps sequence of *The Battleship Potemkin*, from Salce's *The Second Tragic Fantozzi*. The anti-heroic figure of Fantozzi created by Villaggio in numerous films represents one of the most original comic inventions of the postwar cinema. *Credit: CSC*

A third group of comic films, most often described by

Italian film historians as *commedia erotica* or *commedia sexy* (erotic or sexy comedy), usually lacked the interest in social criticism typical of the best *commedia all'italiana*. While such erotic comedies generally combine traditional comic plots with soft pornography (female actresses in various states of undress), the Italian *commedia sexy* usually stopped short of the *cinema hard*, or true pornography.[8] By its very nature, *commedia sexy* focused upon naked female bodies rather than male comic figures, and the male stars of such films were often ridiculous caricatures of any imaginable Latin lover. The vogue for this kind of film probably began with Alessandro Blasetti's *Europe by Night* (*Europa di notte*, 1959), a documentary tour of risqué nightclub acts, and was certainly encouraged by the scandalous success of Fellini's *La Dolce Vita* the next year. Subsequently *Mondo Cane* (literally, "a dog's world," 1962), produced and directed (in part) by Gualtiero Jacopetti (1919–2011), and its several sequels pushed the barriers of what was permissible in the cinema insofar as sexual matters were concerned. Pietro Germi's *The Birds, the Bees, and the Italians* (*Signori & Signore*, 1965), starring Virna Lisi and Gastone Moschin, focused on the hypocritical attitudes about sexuality in the ardently Catholic provincial city of Treviso in the Veneto region of northern Italy. In the sense that the *commedia sexy* often encouraged a more honest discussion of sexuality, these films can be placed within the broader impact of *commedia all'italiana* upon important social issues in Italy—even if very few in the predominantly male audiences for these films were really interested in social reform!

A few beautiful and well-endowed actresses became famous in Italy for these pictures, particularly Barbara Bouchet (1943–), Edwige Fenech (1948–), and Carmen Russo (1959–). Some of the male actors in these films, especially Pippo Franco (1940–) and Alvaro Vitali (1950–), became stars not because they were handsome matinee idols but, on the contrary, because their grotesquely amusing facial features stood out in sharp contrast to the beautiful, breast-baring actresses with whom they starred. A number of directors—including Fernando Cicero (1931–95), Michele Massimo Tarantini (1942–2004), Mariano Laurenti (1929–), and Sergio Martino (1938–)—specialized in sexy comedies. Many of the film titles in this subgenre say a great deal about the kind of humor in the movies themselves: *Giovannona Long-Thigh* (*Giovannona coscialunga, disonorata con onore*, 1973), *La signora ha fatto il pieno* ("The lady has topped off her tank," 1977), *L'insegnante balla . . . con tutta la classe* ("The schoolteacher dances . . . with the whole class," 1978), *L'insegnante viene a casa* ("The schoolteacher makes house calls," 1978), and so forth. After the phenomenal box-office success of Pasolini's adaptation of Boccaccio's *Decameron* in 1971, no fewer than forty-eight *sexy* spin-offs with medieval or Renaissance settings but also partially nude starlets had been produced by 1975. The impact of Pasolini's "trilogy of life" adaptations of literary classics (see chapter 13) within a complicated

A medical examination in the Middle Ages provides Laurenti's cult film *Ubalda, All Naked and Warm* with the excuse to present a semi-naked Edwige Fenech to the camera. *Credit: DVD*

discourse on sexuality created an entire subgenre of the *sexy* comedy. Once again, as with the peplum epic or the spaghetti western, the Italian film industry capitalized on a popular topic by creating instant sequels. Some of the titles that Pasolini inspired are unintentionally hilarious in the original: *Master of Love*, a.k.a. *Decameron Sinners* (*Racconti proibiti . . . di niente vestiti* [translatable as "forbidden tales of bare tails"], 1972), directed by the long-time Fellini cowriter Brunello Rondi, or Joe D'Amato's *Diary of a Roman Virgin* (*Novelle licenziose di vergini vogliose* [literally, "licentious tales of willing virgins"], 1973). The working title of this last film was the most ingenious of them all: *Un mille e una notte di Boccaccio a Canterbury*—literally translated, "one thousand and one nights of Boccaccio at Canterbury," a title that managed to combine the three separate literary classics adapted by Pasolini. The cult favorite in this Decamerotic subgenre of the *commedia sexy* is most certainly Laurenti's *Ubalda, All Naked and Warm* (*Quel gran pezzo dell'Ubalda tutta nuda e tutta calda*, 1972), in which the performances of Pippo Franco and Edwige Fenech create what has become a cult classic in Italy.

Truly hard-core pornographic films eventually replaced the soft-core *commedia sexy* in special film theaters—the *luce rossa* or "red light" theater—and pornography was even shown late at night on Italian private television channels in the 1980s. Faced with this kind of hard-core competition, the relatively tame (but infinitely more amusing) erotic comedies slowly died out as frontal nudity became common even in normal Italian movies produced for family entertainment, on run-of-the-mill television advertisements, and even on weekly newsmagazine covers.

Comedy, Italian Style

Commedia all'italiana, one of the Italian film industry's staple products, reached the heights of its artistic achievements during a period of rapid social and political change in Italy, an epoch justly associated with the golden age of Italian cinema. Its cynical, sarcastic, and irreverent edge set it apart from the more traditional film comedy of the Fascist and neorealist periods (which was closer to stage comedy than to cinema), and its references to other films popular at the moment shows just how important cinema was to the popular culture of the time. In retrospect, Italian comic films at their best were far more convincing in their depictions of the defects in Italian life or character than were their more ideological counterparts in a dramatic or even tragic mode.

Like its predecessor in Italian culture, the improvised *commedia dell'arte* that dominated Italian stages for centuries before the popularity of the variety theater and the invention of the cinema, *commedia all'italiana* created a number of stock Italian types with brilliant comic actors and used them over and over again in grotesque, tragicomic, but always amusing ways. Film comedy would, of course, never disappear from the industry as a whole, and future Italian comic directors would have a legacy of great works and comic stereotypes that would be difficult to surpass in quantity and, more important, in quality.

CHAPTER EIGHT

Neorealism's Legacy to a New Generation, and the Italian Political Film

ONE OF THE REASONS WHY the period between the late 1950s/early 1960s and the mid-1970s/early 1980s may justifiably be called the golden age of Italian cinema is the successful generational change that occurred in the industry. At the same time that the great directors of the 1950s, now mature auteurs, such as Fellini, Antonioni, De Sica, and Visconti, continued to broaden and deepen their work (see chapter 9), a new group of younger men who looked back to the style and content of Italian neorealism became internationally recognized auteurs in their own right (discussed here and in chapter 13). And the foundations were laid for the enormous popularity of genre films (explored throughout the rest of Part Three). The extraordinary vitality, originality, and popularity of these various movements, most of them taking place simultaneously, were unprecedented in Italian film history, and most likely will remain so.

Roberto Rossellini's Return to His Neorealist Origins

It would be Rossellini, the director who was such a seminal force behind the birth of Italian neorealism with his "war trilogy," who would signal renewed attention to neorealism in the industry. After most of his films during the 1950s (even those made with Ingrid Bergman) had been commercial failures, *General Della Rovere* (*Il generale Della Rovere*, 1959) cost very little to make but was a huge financial success; the work won popular acclaim and a Golden Lion at the Venice Film Festival, shared with Monicelli's *The Great War*.

Bardone, the Italian con artist, gives directions to Colonel Müller, who will later have him arrested and tortured, in Rossellini's *General Della Rovere*. *Credit: CSC*

Rossellini re-creates the atmosphere of *Open City* and *Paisan* on movie sets, not the authentic bombed-out buildings that gave these neorealist classics such a documentary flavor. In fact, when Rossellini does employ actual historical footage of Allied bombing missions in *General Della Rovere*, this documentary film stands out so sharply from the footage shot on the director's sets that the contrast illuminates one of the film's major themes—the juxtaposition of reality and illusion. Set in war-torn Genoa and Milan in 1943 around the time of the Allied landings at Anzio, when the partisans were fighting the Germans and the Italian Fascists of the Republic of Salò in the north of Italy, Rossellini's film follows the adventures of a consummate con-man and gambler, Emanuele Bardone—alias Colonel Grimaldi (Vittorio De Sica)—who makes a living by helping to save Italians arrested by the Gestapo (German Secret Police), or by pretending to do so. For his troubles, he is paid with cash, jewels, and even packages of salami by the desperate relatives or friends of the prisoners. His habitual gambling and bad luck at the tables, however, leaves him constantly in need of money, and as the film opens, we discover that he has already lost the 50,000 lire he must give to a German bureaucrat named Walter at German Headquarters in Genoa in order to save the life of a client's son. By accident, Bardone meets Colonel Müller (Hannes Messemer), the commander of the German garrison, on a bridge where the German's car has a flat tire. Müller is struck by the Italian's likable personality and ingratiating manner. Later, when Bardone's confidence games go sour (he makes the amusing mistake of trying to obtain money to save a man who has already been executed), the victim's wife turns him in to the German authorities, and he once again meets Colonel Müller—under less polite circumstances. Because of Bardone's likable manner, Müller offers him the choice between being executed by the Germans or running a confidence game for him inside a prison in Milan. Müller had intended to capture an Italian general (the General Della Rovere of the film's title) after an Allied submarine landed him on the beaches near Genoa so that he could make contact with an Italian named Fabrizio, the commander of partisan forces in the Milanese area. By accident, when Müller's men tried to intercept the general, he was killed, so the colonel's plan to use Della Rovere to ferret out the Resistance leader Fabrizio has come undone. (Müller knows that Fabrizio is one of his prisoners but hasn't been able to determine which one he is.) With Bardone masquerading as General Della Rovere, Müller can pretend that the general is still alive, in the hope that Fabrizio will contact him in the prison and thereby reveal his identity. Contrary to Müller's carefully laid plans, after Bardone—alias Colonel Grimaldi, alias General Giovanni Braccioforte Della Rovere—learns the identity of the prisoner Fabrizio, he marches off with the other prisoners to his execution, refusing the colonel's offer of safe passage to Switzerland and one million lire. Rather than providing the name Müller seeks, Bardone's last act before facing the firing squad is to leave the incredulous German officer with a message for his "wife," Countess Bianca Maria Della Rovere: "My last thoughts were of you—long live Italy!"

On the level of content and genre, Rossellini moves the depiction of typical neorealist themes (the war, the Resistance) away from a strictly tragic tone to one that permits questioning, doubts, and probing questions about the nature of Italy's role in the war. Neorealist practice had transformed the Resistance into a myth; Rossellini allowed his audience to see the artifice concealed beneath the halo the saints of the Resistance wore. While the foregrounding of De Sica's histrionic acting abilities represents the most obvious and explicit emphasis upon the *artifice* in Rossellini's film, numerous other stylistic elements in the work show the attentive viewer that Rossellini's "realistic" portrait of 1943 ultimately depends entirely upon cinematic fabrication. The presence of the director is apparent in the film—one of the most surprising instances being a cameo appearance by Rossellini himself, in a crowd of Italians anxiously waiting at German headquarters in Genoa. We may expect such an in-joke from a superb commercial showman like Alfred Hitchcock, but a cameo in a "realistic" film by Rossellini has quite a different impact upon the audience.

Other more significant details of the film's style emphasize its artifice even more plainly. In this work, for the first time in his career, Rossellini employed the special, modified zoom lens known as the Pancinor, which he personally devised. This lens (known as a *carello ottico* in Italian and a *travelling optique* in French) is used sparingly but effectively in *General Della Rovere* during the important bombardment scene inside the prison, which introduces De Sica's most histrionic speech. The zoom's most obvious characteristic is its obtrusiveness: employing such a technique always foregrounds the artifice of the scene being reproduced. The results of this and other aspects of studio production stand in marked contrast to the much more believable exteriors and interiors of Rossellini's "war trilogy." So mannered are some of the sets constructed (such as the bridge on which a flat tire occasions Müller's first encounter with Bardone) that they seem taken from a German expressionist film instead of a work that supposedly pays homage to Italian neorealism. The obviously artificial lighting inside the studio settings (again, most noticeable in the bombardment sequence) increases our lack of confidence in the physical reality of what we are seeing on the screen: it is all quite clearly constructed in the dream factory of Cinecittà. Rossellini's editing style, too, foregrounds the "reality" of the filmic world portrayed as a product of cinematic illusion. For instance, he quite frequently employs the "wipe"—a transition between scenes that practically demands to be noticed. Such highlighting of the artifice behind the representation of the "reality" depicted is perhaps best achieved in the climactic conclusion of the film, when Bardone is executed against a wall. Behind the dead partisans is what purports to be the skyline of the city of Milan; but again, a closer look reveals a painted canvas backdrop so obviously contrived that it is impossible to imagine it seems so false by accident. In addition, the foregrounding of the role of the "actor" in *Generale Della Rovere*, both through the problematic treatment of "real" versus "false" identity and the use of a famed filmmaker in the lead, provides a metacinematic twist to the narrative storyline that, in one critic's words, points to Rossellini's "acceptance of cinematic artifice—role playing, the assumption of disguise—as a way toward moral truth."[1]

Rossellini's subsequent re-creation of the period of *Open City—Escape by Night*, a.k.a. *It Was Night in Rome* (*Era notte a Roma*, 1960)—is far less important a film than *General Della Rovere*, and its lack of success led Rossellini to abandon commercial filmmaking in 1963, when he turned to making a long series of historical documentary films for television. In so doing he became the first major Italian director to work exclusively for an extended period for this new medium of mass communication that would soon challenge the cinema in popular appeal. Rossellini eventually completed nine such works, but the most important by far is *The Rise of Louis XIV* (*La prise de pouvoir de Louis XIV*, 1966), in which, as in *General Della Rovere*, the puzzling interrelationships between reality and appearance, mask and face, disguise and true identity, provide a key for unlocking the protagonist's enigmatic motivations. Superficially, Rossellini returns to one element central to neorealist style: the dispassionate and documentary-like technique,

In Rossellini's *The Rise of Louis XIV*, the Sun King employs guile and deception (often signaled by his elaborate costumes) to seize and retain political power. *Credit: MOMA*

typical of *Paisan*, that collects and presents historical facts. What we learn about King Louis XIV derives from the director's understated juxtaposition of the formalized rituals at court with a number of privileged views of the young monarch's private life. Because the Sun King embraces the Machiavellian dictum that men are guided by appearances rather than by the nature of things, Louis requires extravagant robes and elegant wigs at court, forcing his noblemen to squander their fortunes (and therefore their ability to oppose his policies) by buying such ridiculous frippery. Like the con man/fake Resistance leader in *General Della Rovere*, Louis exercises power by skillfully playing a number of roles, a theme introduced at the beginning of the film when the dying Cardinal Mazarin allows the young sovereign to enter his bedchamber only after the prelate dons rouge and copious makeup: one consummate actor leaves the historical stage to make way for another. The final sequence of the film is a masterful display of Louis's true character: the king at long last slowly removes the many pieces of his elaborate costume, revealing himself to be a diminutive, rather pathetic individual without them, a man playing a role not unlike the confidence man. It is clear, however, that Rossellini has more respect for Bardone than for King Louis.

Although *General Della Rovere* and *The Rise of Louis XIV* both employ elements of Rossellini's earlier neorealist classics—the first re-creating the atmosphere and plot of the "war trilogy," the second continuing the use of nonprofessional actors and a semidocumentary style—Rossellini's cinematic style has clearly advanced beyond neorealism to something else. (His use of the Pancinor lens, introduced in *General Della Rovere*, is now more much in evidence.) By setting an example for other young and highly talented directors in his exploitation of this rich cinematic heritage, Rossellini would influence not only a new generation of filmmakers in Italy but also the New Wave directors in France.

"One Cannot Live without Rossellini"

As this quotation from Bernardo Bertolucci's *Before the Revolution* (*Prima della rivoluzione*, 1964) implies, young directors such as Bertolucci (1941–) himself, Francesco Rosi, Vittorio De Seta (1923–2011), Gillo Pontecorvo (1919–2006), Ermanno Olmi (1931–), Paolo (1931–) and Vittorio (1929–) Taviani, Pier Paolo Pasolini (1922–75), and Marco Bellocchio (1939–) all worked in the shadow of Rossellini and Italian neorealism. The members of this postneorealist generation of directors continued the interest of neorealist filmmakers in social and political problems. (If anything, they approached such issues with a stronger dose of leftist ideology; few, except for Olmi, would embrace the kind of Christian humanism typical of Rossellini or De Sica.) In many cases, their work employed a documentary or semidocumentary style with nonprofessional actors, recalling the style of some neorealist classics. Other directors, while influenced by neorealist themes or styles, were nevertheless closer in spirit to their contemporaries of the French New Wave. Intellectuals rather than artisans, they came to the cinema through a self-conscious artistic choice, often beginning their apprenticeship in film clubs; or they were inspired, like their French counterparts, by the example of Rossellini.

Vittorio De Seta and Francesco Rosi

Bandits of Orgosolo (*Banditi a Orgosolo*, 1961), by Vittorio De Seta, seems cut from the same cloth as Visconti's *The Earth Trembles*: nonprofessional Sardinian shepherds enact a drama set in their own timeless society, as De Seta contrasts their primitive codes of behavior against modern Italian culture. Like *The Earth Trembles*, *Bandits* demonstrates how economic conditions dictate social behavior, forcing honest men to embrace desperate measures to survive. The documentary style, simple plot, and stark, unsentimental narrative all recall neorealist antecedents. Wrongly implicated in the theft of some livestock by the Carabinieri (always portrayed as an occupation force sent by a distant colonial power from the mainland), an inarticulate but honest shepherd flees into the hills with his younger brother and their flock of sheep; but when all the animals perish, he must turn to banditry to survive, making a living by stealing from other men as poor as he. De Seta's powerful portrait of this elemental world moves the spectator precisely because it avoids rhetorical overstatement or patronizing attitudes toward his protagonists. His voice-over narrative intrudes infrequently, leaving his nonprofessionals to express themselves more by their stiff gestures than by their dialogue (dubbed into standard Italian from the original Sardinian dialect).

Rosi's *Salvatore Giuliano* (1962) owes little to Visconti's early neorealist style, even though Rosi had assisted Visconti on *The Earth Trembles* and sets this film in Sicily. Rosi avoids the extremely uncomplicated neorealist-like plot of De Seta, along with the use of nonprofessionals, and he prefers to present social and economic conditions in a more analytic manner. As he states, his aim was to create "not a *documentary* way of making films but a *documented* way."[2] Building upon historical facts whose veracity could not be denied even by opponents of Rosi's leftist views, the director rejects both a noncommittal, documentary presentation of "facts" and a completely fictionalized narrative. As he declares, "you cannot *invent*, in my opinion, but you can *interpret.* . . . This is the important thing for me, the *interpretation* of the facts."[3] For Rosi, politically or socially engaged cinema must provide an *inchiesta*, an inquiry into the links between past events and the reality of the present—something akin to an inquest in a trial. Rosi's film analyzes the life of Salvatore Giuliano, a Sicilian bandit who played an important role in the short-lived Sicilian independence movement immediately after World War II. Giuliano then turned to political terrorism with an attack upon a group of leftist demonstrators on May Day of 1947, killing eleven people and wounding twenty-seven at Portella della Ginestra. After the 1948 elections produced a Center-Right victory over the parties of the Left, Giuliano returned to his former criminal activities until, according to official police accounts, he was killed by the Carabinieri in 1951. Subsequently, Gaspare Pisciotta (Giuliano's lieutenant) claimed in court that he and not the police had shot Giuliano; but after Pisciotta was subsequently murdered in prison, it became clear that the official version of the bandit's death was perhaps untrue and that members of the Mafia had assisted the police in eliminating a man who had become an embarrassment to everyone. In 1960 the Mafia intermediary between the underworld and the police in the affair, Benedetto Minasola, was himself killed.

Rosi presents the "facts" within what seems to be a conventional documentary framework, but his narrative makes it clear that the facts do not explain themselves and that a darker political reality lurks beneath the surface. The figure of Giuliano himself hardly interests him: he rarely speaks, is shown primarily in distant long shots dressed in a white trench coat surrounded by men dressed in black, and he assumes an importance on the screen only in death. Indeed, the most important scene in the film is that of an overhead shot of a dead body (Giuliano's) in a courtyard which opens the movie. The death is a "fact," but Rosi claims that it is a fact that means nothing by itself. The director then moves to a number of ingenious flashbacks to interpret the historical data, completely abandoning chronological order in his treatment of the period 1945–60. The result is a legal brief against the political establishment and its underworld cronies who manipulate Giuliano and then eliminate him when he is no longer useful. The final shot of the film is that of the murdered Mafia go-between lying in exactly the same position as Giuliano at the film's opening, emphasizing

The famous opening shot from Rosi's *Salvatore Giuliano*. *Credit: DVD*

that past corruption is not merely past history but is an ever-present condition of Sicilian life.

Rosi aspires to transcend neorealism's initial postwar attempt to record or bear witness to reality and wants to move toward a critical realism with overt ideological intentions. In *Hands Over the City* (*Le mani sulla città*, 1963), Rosi uses the same style to denounce speculation in the building industry and the political corruption that encourages it. These two films were the first of many ideological attacks against Italy's ruling Center-Right government made by Italian directors with leftist sympathies, and Rosi's hybrid form of narrative, combining fiction and documentary inquiry, would later be influential in creating what many critics see as a new film genre in the period: the Italian "political" film.

Pontecorvo and Revolution in the Third World

Although Rosi's documentary investigations undoubtedly influenced Pontecorvo's *The Battle of Algiers* (*La battaglia di Algeri*, 1966), which employed one of the screenwriters from *Salvatore Giuliano*, Franco Solinas (1927–82), Pontecorvo owed an even greater debt to Rossellini. While working in Paris as a journalist, he saw *Paisan* and was so moved by the experience that he left his job, bought a camera, and began making documentaries. Pontecorvo once remarked that the ideal director should be three-quarters Rossellini and one-quarter Eisenstein,[4] and *The Battle of Algiers* combines many of the techniques he learned from these two masters, representing a major step toward an ideologically oriented cinema in Italy during the period. Shot with the encouragement of an Algerian producer, Yacef Saadi—the former military commander of the zone of Algiers for the National Liberation Front during the period treated, who played a character based on himself in the film—Pontecorvo's work presents a case history of Third World revolution in such vivid and polemical terms that it remained banned from French screens until 1971, even after it had garnered critical acclaim and an award at the 1966 Venice Film Festival. Like Rosi's *Salvatore Giuliano, The Battle of Algiers* distorts the normal chronology of the events it presents: its historically complex plot begins in 1957 as an Arab prisoner has been tortured into revealing to Colonel Mathieu and his paratroopers the location of the rebels' last leader, Ali La Pointe. Just before La Pointe's place of concealment is blown up, Pontecorvo flashes back to 1954 to trace the formation of this Arab revolutionary, the arrival of French paratroopers sent to repress native revolt, and the outbreak of a general strike that takes place between 1954 and 1957. Finally, Pontecorvo returns to 1957 as the rebel leader is killed and the rebellion is apparently destroyed. A brief coda to this central narrative flashes forward to 1960, where we witness massive anti-French demonstrations in the Casbah, after which an offscreen voice-over informs the viewer that the Algerian nation was born in 1962.

Rossellini's influence on *The Battle of Algiers* shows in many stylistic details. With the exception of the actor (Jean Martin) playing the French military commander, the whole cast is nonprofessional. Although there is not a single frame of newsreel footage in the work, Pontecorvo and his crew created an absolutely convincing reproduction of newsreel or television reportage through a variety of techniques, conveying to the viewer the actuality and insistency of history unfolding before his or her very eyes: highly mobile, handheld Arriflex cameras with fast film stock shot in diffused light;

In *The Battle of Algiers*, Pontecorvo reconstructs fictional scenes from the Algerian revolution that are indistinguishable from documentary footage of the real events. *Credit: MOMA*

the telephoto lenses common to television news reporting; and voice-overs or informational titles superimposed over an image give the visual texture and the authentic feel of the six o'clock news. By duplicating the negative of his film in the laboratory, Pontecorvo creates the same grainy, documentary tone characteristic of his favorite film, *Paisan*. And yet Pontecorvo's editing employs techniques closer to the montage of classic Russian cinema than to the neorealism of Rossellini. In most cases, the narrative advances not by linking sequences together in a traditionally Hollywood logical order but by juxtaposing images, sequences, sounds, and ideas.

Central to Pontecorvo's message—his positive view of revolutionary violence and his criticism of counterrevolutionary violence—is the contrast between the French colonel and the Arab rebel. Ali La Pointe is an illiterate, unemployed, ex–draft dodger who witnesses the execution by guillotine of a fellow Algerian and acquires a revolutionary consciousness, powerfully depicted by a dramatic zoom into Ali's eyes to capture his reaction. Colonel Mathieu, on the other hand, is a handsome, urbane, highly intelligent professional soldier whose knowledge of the dynamics of insurrections surpasses even that of his opponents. He correctly informs French journalists that if they insist upon keeping Algeria a part of France, they must also accept the logical consequences of that decision, including torture. Thus, Pontecorvo places two sets of logic in sharp contrast, both of which spawn violence and death. Much of the dramatic tension in the film derives from the conflict of two traditional film protagonists—revolutionary and military hero—and the film succeeds because Pontecorvo's ideological preferences for the side of the revolutionaries—he was an avid reader of Frantz Fanon, the major theorist of the Algerian revolution—does not cause him to picture the French as monsters.

Pontecorvo's presentation of violence has aroused criticism from both the Left and the Right. While French conservatives did not appreciate a film about a major colonial defeat, one English leftist critic complained that Pontecorvo's "dramatic irony and moral ambivalence is only a romantic humanist's sugaring of the pill for a liberal audience unwilling to stomach the hard facts of revolution."[5] The key sequence in the film for an analysis of Pontecorvo's view of violence is one that portrays the planting of three bombs by three different Arab women (dressed as Europeans and passing undetected because of their light skins) in three places where only French civilian victims will be killed: a cafeteria where a baby licks an ice cream cone; a milk bar, where teenagers are dancing to a tune ironically entitled "Until Tomorrow" (though tomorrow for them will never come); and the Air France terminal. This massive bombing attack on French civilians was a response to a similar attack on Arab civilians in the Casbah led by the French chief of police. In both cases, as the Algerians and the French extract their dead from the rubble, Pontecorvo inserts Bach's *Mass in B Minor* on

the sound track, lending both images the same tragic dignity: human suffering is always the same, and a bomb recognizes no innocent parties. Yet
Pontecorvo judges the two events differently, since the verdict of history—a
Marxist verdict in this case—condemns one side and vindicates another.
French bombs are worse than Arab bombs because a (Marxist and anti-
colonialist) theory of history demonstrates that French violence served a
lost cause, whereas Arab violence expressed a movement in the vanguard
of history.

Olmi's Postneorealist Dramas of Intimacy

Ermanno Olmi began his career as a director by making documentary
films, but his cinematic style in his early feature films shows an obvious
debt to Vittorio De Sica rather than to either Rossellini or Visconti. Unlike
so many others of this postneorealist and post-Rossellini generation of
young filmmakers, Olmi is also unusual because his ideology has obvious
links to the Christian humanism found in the neorealist works of both
Rossellini and De Sica, rather than to Marxist ideology. Although Olmi has
made relatively few films in his long career, two he shot during the first part
of the 1960s are authentic masterpieces. *The Sound of Trumpets* (*Il posto*,
1961) is a highly wrought work that examines the anguish and loneliness of
a young officeworker, Domenico (Sandro Panseri) as he seeks his first job
in Milan. In a real sense, Olmi focuses on the underside of Italy's "economic
miracle," revealing that increased prosperity does not automatically produce
happiness. Olmi employs nonprofessional actors, and his editing style, quite
impressive for a young director, emphasizes expressive deep-focus shots in
office interiors reminiscent of De Sica's *Umberto D.* and moments of psychological importance in the protagonist's life when film time coincides
with narrative time elapsed (Bazin's famous duration). Like De Sica, Olmi
has a genius for expressively employing the simple and seemingly meaningless gestures, glances, and actions gathered from the daily routine of his
rather insignificant characters. In depicting Domenico's aptitude test for the
position he is seeking (where giving the incorrect answer means nothing,
since the job requires no intelligence), his medical examination (consisting of inane questions and meaningless exercises), and his introduction to
the office where he will presumably spend the rest of his adult life, Olmi
presents a brilliant but depressing portrait of a modern office. Domenico
must first serve as an errand boy, since promotions occur only when a death
takes place.

The result of Olmi's superficially traditional narrative is a tragicomic
vision of modern labor that underlines its boring, mechanical, and tedious
nature—a vision that could well have been created by a Marxist rather than
a director with deep Catholic convictions. The film becomes increasingly

In Olmi's homage to De Sica's neorealist style, *The Sound of Trumpets* pictures work in an office as mechanical, tedious, and soul rending. *Credit: MOMA*

complex as Olmi turns from introducing us to the clerks in the office to brief vignettes concerning their personal lives: the nearsighted clerk whose eventual death opens up a position for Domenico spends his spare time in bed writing a novel, hiding his late-night use of electricity from his avaricious landlady; the clerk who does nothing but cut cigarettes in half is worried over an inheritance; a man who constantly combs his hair in the office is having an affair; another man who compulsively cleans his desk is an amateur opera singer; a woman who arrives late to work has a ne'er-do-well son who steals money from her purse. Olmi's depiction of the simple, day-to-day actions of the office staff shows that they conceal a great wealth of human interest; yet the juxtaposition of the compulsive mannerisms they exhibit at work and their more spontaneous, if often strange, behavior at home demonstrates clearly the alienating effects of the workplace.

Olmi's vision of Domenico's future becomes clear when he pictures a retired clerk who continues to come to the office because he is unable to eat lunch without the office bell that arouses his appetite, like one of Pavlov's famous dogs. Another brilliant sequence describes a New Year's Eve party. Domenico and the others without dates are given bottles of wine and silly party hats, and a series of long shots of an almost empty hall produces a depressing sense of loneliness and alienation. When the gaiety finally does begin, prompted not by spontaneous celebration but by professional revelers hired by the management, it seems clear that the frenzied dancing and party costumes conceal but do not eliminate the unhappiness of many of those present. An abrupt cut returns the viewer to the office, where an empty desk stands in mute testimony to the clerk-novelist's sudden demise.

As each employee moves furtively to occupy a desk one spot further ahead in the office pecking order, and Domenico takes his place at the end of the row, the mechanical and repetitious noise of a duplicating machine grows louder and louder on the sound track as if it were a heart beat, while Olmi's camera holds a close-up on Domenico's vulnerable face for an inordinate length of time, then fades to black.

Although Olmi's humor softens the depressing effect of the film, such an eloquent portrait of the anguish of daily labor has rarely been so successfully drawn on the screen. His next feature, *The Fiancés* (*I fidanzati*, 1963) goes beyond the simple plot structures typical of his neorealist models and moves toward a more modernist perspective, freely mixing events out of their normal chronological order in a looser plot structure, much as Rosi and Pontecorvo do. Again, Italy's "economic miracle" in the 1960s serves as the background for simple human dramas: a blue-collar worker named Giovanni (Carlo Cabrini) accepts a job in Sicily, which compels him to abandon his girlfriend, Liliana (Anna Canzi), in northern Italy. In the late 1950s and 1960s, millions of southern Italians did the same thing, and Olmi beautifully and movingly portrays the loneliness and solitude that such long work-related separations caused. *The Fiancés*, like *The Sound of Trumpets*, includes a dance-hall scene, one that opens rather than closes the film, but in both works, Olmi employs this location—a place where festivity is supposed to reign—for very precise purposes in skillfully sketching his protagonists' solitude.

The Taviani Brothers

Like Pontecorvo, Vittorio and Paolo Taviani came to the cinema through a chance encounter with Rossellini's *Paisan* one afternoon when they were playing hooky from school. Like Olmi and others, they first made short documentary films before turning to full-length features. One of these shorts, *San Miniato, July '44* (*San Miniato, luglio '44*, 1954), produced with the assistance of Cesare Zavattini, neorealism's most famous scriptwriter, chronicles the massacre of townspeople inside the cathedral of a small Tuscan town by the Germans during World War II in retaliation for the death of one of their soldiers. Shot in the realistic style typical of the 1950s, this short would later become the basis of what is perhaps their greatest work, *The Night of the Shooting Stars* (*La notte di San Lorenzo*, 1982). That postmodern masterpiece was far in the future, however, when they made their first feature film with Valentino Orsini (1927–2001), *A Man for Burning* (*Un uomo da bruciare*, 1962). Featuring the first starring role of Gian Maria Volontè (1933–94),[6] an actor who would become closely identified both with the spaghetti western and with the Italian political film a few years later, the Tavianis' film makes political ideology itself the theme of their work. Salvatore, a political activist, returns to his native Sicily after a prolonged absence from the battle waged by peasants struggling for rights to the lands they work. Salvatore imprudently confronts the local Mafia, exhorting the peasants not only to occupy the land but also to plow and plant it as well. But at a meeting of a peasants' league, the group decides that Salvatore's policy of open confrontation is too dangerous, and he is isolated. In the meanwhile, the Mafia abandons the now unprofitable agricultural sector and turns to the exploitation of day laborers in road construction work, hiring Salvatore as a foreman, thinking to compromise him with a fourteen-hour workday for his men; but Salvatore stops working after eight hours and urges his workmen to do the same. Naturally, the Mafia has him killed, and the entire town takes part in his funeral.

The Tavianis consider their first feature film an act of love toward neorealism, but this look backward toward neorealist social themes reflects ambivalence. Far removed from the ideological canons of social realism, Salvatore is an egotist, bent on exercising power and leading the peasants even if they reject him; he also is intent upon becoming a martyr, the antithesis of the simple and pure popular heroes of most neorealist films. Obviously out of touch with the working class in Sicily, Salvatore at one point addresses them in verse from an opera stage, and his gestures are comically melodramatic. Although he even has a premonition of his own assassination in a dream that represents him as a Christ figure, his actual death is brief and undramatic, set in contrast to the staged and overly literary dream sequence that reflects Salvatore's exaggerated sense of self-importance.

The Tavianis employ irony in their works, particularly insofar as their protagonists are concerned, to create a sense of detachment between the filmmakers and their characters. Irony dominates not only their presentation of Salvatore but also *The Subversives* (*I sovversivi*, 1967), a study of four Communist Party members over several days before the funeral of Palmiro Togliatti (August 1964), the party's leader throughout the Fascist period, the Resistance, and postwar reconstruction. The four people never meet in the film; their only link is Italian history and shared ideology. Rapid cross-cutting gradually reveals similar personal dramas brought on by Togliatti's death: Ermanno, a young middle-class intellectual, rejects his class origins and dedicates his life to photography; Giulia, the wife of a party official, gives in to her lesbian desires; Ludovico, a director dying of an incurable illness, seeks to complete a film on a Leonardo da Vinci turned crypto-Communist, as he abandons his art for direct communication with the masses; Ettore, a Venezuelan revolutionary in exile, breaks off a love affair to return home to continue his struggle. Far from being dangerous subversives, the four party members reveal themselves to be normal human beings with the same personal problems that afflict people who hold entirely different political beliefs.

The Early Postneorealist Work of Pier Paolo Pasolini

The most original and multitalented director to emerge in the postneorealist generation is certainly Pasolini, a poet, novelist, critic, and theorist whose first experiences in the cinema included scriptwriting for both Bolognini and Fellini. Five of his early films—*Accattone* (1961; the title means "beggar"), *Mamma Roma* (1962), *Ricotta* (*La ricotta*, his contribution to the 1963 omnibus film *RoGoPaG*), *The Gospel According to St. Matthew* (*Il Vangelo secondo Matteo*, 1964), and *Hawks and Sparrows* (*Uccellacci e uccellini*, 1966)—all build upon neorealist tradition but embody a very different style of filmmaking, one indebted far more to Marxist ideology and Pasolini's own eccentric theories about the lower classes in Italy than to the ideas contained in the neorealist classics. Pasolini was particularly influenced by the writings of Antonio Gramsci, the Marxist from Sardinia who rejected a simple, causal relationship between economic substructure and cultural superstructure. Modifying the traditional Marxist view that economic conditions determine ideas, Gramsci offered his concept of cultural hegemony: social classes exercise hegemony over other classes first through the private institutions of civil society (schools, churches, films, books, etc.) and then through political institutions, and they more often obtain such hegemony through common consent and reason than through force. Gramsci believed that the Italian Communist Party (of which he was one of the original founders) could come to power in the peninsula only after it had first established cultural hegemony within Italian culture. In a very real sense, that came very close to happening in Italy during the 1960s–1980s, and a Marxist strain within Italian film was one of the reasons why this hegemony might well have been established, had it not been for several historical events outside Italy (first, the Hungarian Revolt of 1956, then the collapse of the Soviet Union and the fall of the Berlin Wall).

For intellectuals such as Pasolini, the Taviani brothers, Pontecorvo, Rosi, and Bertolucci (to mention only a few of those influenced by Marxist culture in Italy), Gramsci's thought was attractive precisely because it gave intellectuals a privileged place in transforming society. Moreover, Gramsci was particularly interested in the peasant class in Italy—an economic class generally ignored by classical Marxist theory, and one whose members were generally dismissed even by leftists in the North as illiterate and uncultured *cafoni* (ill-mannered, uncultured people). Pasolini's fascination with the language, customs, and behavior of what he called the "subproletariat" in Italy—a term he employed to distinguish them from workers in the industrial sector and to call attention to their agrarian and preindustrial origins—owes a special debt to Gramsci. Figures from this shadowy subproletarian world of crime and poverty are prominent in two of Pasolini's early novels that are themselves part of a neorealist current in postwar Italian fiction: *The Ragazzi* (*Ragazzi di vita*, 1955) and *A Violent Life* (*Una vita violenta*, 1959).

Pasolini's writings on the cinema represent one of the most original contributions to film theory in Italy. Long before structuralism, semiotics, and deconstruction became faddish methodologies in the English-speaking world, Pasolini published a number of widely read and hotly debated essays on the semiotics of the cinema. His basic contention was that the cinema expressed reality with reality itself—an idea certainly born of neorealist cinema—and not with separate semiotic codes, symbols, allegories, or metaphors. Furthermore, Pasolini claimed that film's reproduction of physical reality was essentially a poetic and metonymic operation. The poetry of the cinema conserves not only reality's poetry but also its mysterious, sacred nature, and in its most expressive moments, film is both realistic and antinaturalistic. By communicating reality's mystery, its *sacralità*, film also projects reality's dreamlike quality, its *oniricità*.[7] The intellectual link Pasolini effected between his Marxist ideology and the semiotics of the cinema can be envisioned as early as his important collection of poetry, *The Ashes of Gramsci* (*Le ceneri di Gramsci*, 1957), in which Pasolini accepts Gramsci's praise of the working class because a specific part of this class (his beloved subproletariat) has retained a preindustrial, mythical, and religious consciousness, a sense of mystery and awe in face of physical reality that Pasolini defines as a prehistorical, pre-Christian, and prebourgeois phenomenon. The very nature of cinematic language, as Pasolini defined it, thus exhibited qualities that complemented his views on the subproletariat in Italy and the Third World.

If Marxism and semiotics provided Pasolini with his intellectual background, Italian neorealism played the decisive role in forming his cinematic culture. Pasolini preferred nonprofessional actors, natural lighting, on-location shooting, and political themes for many of the same reasons that they appealed to his neorealist predecessors. With his preference for the religious and sacred approach to reality, however, Pasolini rejected the tendency toward naturalism present in some neorealist styles. Thus his first films pay homage to neorealist style yet also assimilate it, rejecting some aspects of it in order to create a highly personal style with a very different vision of the world.

Paramount in Pasolini's early cinema is what he calls a "pastiche" construction, mixing the most disparate stylistic and thematic materials in unusual combinations. Thus in *Accattone* (and later in *The Gospel*) Pasolini juxtaposes the most sublime examples of official "high" culture with the humblest elements from "low," or popular, culture: the music of Bach or Mozart accompanies pimps and beggars; garbage dumps embody images from contemporary Italian art by Giorgio Morandi or Renato Guttuso; faces of subproletarian characters evoke scenes from early Renaissance masters, such as Giotto, Masaccio, and Piero della Francesca. This kind of dramatic juxtaposition, the essence of his idea of pastiche, points to the mythical qualities of life that modern culture has abandoned. As Pasolini frequently declared, his view of the world was always epic and religious in nature.

Accattone portrays the life and death of a thieving pimp living in Rome's poorest districts, a plot that might well have served a traditional neorealist for a critique of Italy's social conditions. Yet Pasolini portrays Accattone as an inverted, subproletarian Christ figure with citations from Dante's *Purgatory* (Canto V) opening the film, and the music of Bach's *St. Matthew's Passion* appearing on the sound track. Like Jesus, Accattone fulfills prophecy and dies in the company of two thieves; his larceny is called "divine services," and one of his prostitutes for whom he pimps is named Magdalene. A dream vision he experiences, in which Accattone attends his own funeral but is refused entrance to the cemetery, highlights the mysterious element present in subproletarian life and foretells his eventual death. With his pastiche technique, Pasolini has stylistically "contaminated" (to use his favorite term) the subproletarian world of Rome with the iconography and mythology of Christianity. Pasolini consistently searches for the aesthetic effect in each and every frame depicting this tawdry world: he treats the individual shot as an autonomous unit, the cinematic equivalent of a poetic image rather than as an integral aspect of a larger narrative design. The autonomy of his individual images is so pronounced in *Accattone* that some critics assumed this style arose from his technical incompetence (and if this was the case, Pasolini certainly made a virtue out of a necessity in this regard).

Mamma Roma continues Pasolini's interest in the urban subproletariat with Anna Magnani, a neorealist icon after the international success of Rossellini's *Open City*, playing an earthy prostitute nicknamed Mamma Roma who attempts to pull herself out of the lower classes and better her station in society. In the process, she takes her adolescent son, Ettore (Ettore Garofalo), back into her life and tries to integrate them both into the middle class formed by the economic miracle of the early 1960s in Italy. Her illiterate and shiftless son reacts negatively to her attempts to better his life, and the plot is complicated by the sudden appearance of Carmine (Franco Citti), her former pimp, who may or may not be Ettore's father and who forces her to return to the streets. Pasolini's sympathies obviously rest with the delinquent son, uninterested in the notion of "progress," rather than with his mother, who attempts to join the ranks of the bourgeoisie Pasolini despised. The director presents the back alleys and shady corners of working-class Rome in a way that endows dignity upon unsavory ambiences, the kinds privileged by Pasolini's love for the subproletariat.

Ricotta (*La ricotta*)—one episode in *RoGoPaG*, a collection of short works by *R*ossellini, Jean-Luc *G*odard, *P*asolini, and Ugo *G*regoretti (1930–)—shares *Mamma Roma*'s attack upon the consumerism of the rising middle class as well as a critique of the loss of religious values in the contemporary industrial world. Pasolini cast Orson Welles as an American director outside Rome shooting a film about the Passion of Christ. The real hero of Pasolini's film, however, is not Welles but a poor Roman named Stracci (Mario Cipriani), whose name translates as "Rags" and who works as an extra on the American director's film in order to get a badly needed lunch. Pasolini turns him into a religious figure: he dies on the cross playing the thief crucified with Jesus after having gorged himself to death with ricotta cheese. An Italian reporter on the set asks Welles's character what he thinks of the Italian people, and the response actually reflects Pasolini's opinion that they are the most illiterate people and the most ignorant middle class in Europe! *Ricotta*, perhaps the most innovative of Pasolini's three early films, combines the young director's ideology with a metacinematic discourse on the nature of film itself.

The *Gospel According to St. Matthew* operates in a direction opposite from that which Pasolini employed in *Accattone*, for now he "contaminates" the traditional biography of Jesus (something he did in small measure with *Ricotta*) with the "epical-religious" qualities he believed characterized the Italian subproletariat. Unable to locate appropriate locations in modern Israel, where Pasolini felt contemporary civilization had already erased any trace of the special archaic world he hoped to capture, Pasolini turned instead to underdeveloped regions in southern Italy (Apulia, Lucania, Calabria). Rather than reconstructing sets of the biblical world at Cinecittà in a manner typical of the peplum epics of the time or of the Hollywood biblical epics shot in Italy by American studios, Pasolini worked by analogy, finding parallels and analogues in the present. Herod's soldiers dress as if they were Fascist thugs; Roman soldiers wear costumes that resemble those worn by the Italian police; the flight of Joseph and Mary into Egypt recalls photographs of civilians fleeing over the Pyrenees after Franco's victory in the Spanish Civil War. Such modern links to what Hollywood has called "the greatest story ever told" render the emotion and drama of Christian history far more effectively than strictly archaeological reconstructions could ever have done. Pasolini continued his predilection for pastiche by juxtaposing classical religious music with Afro-American spirituals or the Congolese *Missa Luba* (a version of the Latin Mass) by setting humble elements (the faces of peasants, or impoverished locations) against sophisticated cultural references (Botticelli angels, Pier della Francesca costumes, a Georges Rouault Christ); and, in general, by presenting extremely disparate levels of style and content ranging from the vulgar to the sublime.

Nothing about *The Gospel* is more striking than its editing and sense of rhythm. A continuous process of rapid cutting and the juxtaposition of jarring images force us to experience the last days of Christ through a novel perspective. Abrupt changes of location and time—especially in the scenes evoking Jesus' Sermon on the Mount, his selection of his disciples, and a number of miracles—produce the image of a relentlessly dynamic and

The kiss of Judas recalls frescos by the medieval master Giotto in Pasolini's *The Gospel According to St. Matthew. Credit: MOMA*

almost demonic figure. Using Matthew's words, Pasolini's Jesus represents truly a man who has come to bring not peace but a sword, an appropriate Christ for an avowed Marxist who nevertheless revered the sacred qualities of Jesus' life narrative. Touches of Pasolini's Marxist ideology also influence some of the visuals. As he tempts Jesus, Satan seems to be dressed like a priest, and the Messiah indicts the rich and the poor as he drives the moneychangers from the Temple. Of course, Matthew's Gospel remains the most revolutionary of the four books in the Bible, and only Italian viewers (very indifferent readers of the Bible) felt there was any great disparity between Pasolini's "epical-religious" Jesus and Matthew's text.

Pasolini also employs a number of different camera styles, ranging from extremely brief shots in rapidly edited scenes to very long takes; a handheld camera with a subjective point of view captures the trial of Jesus (the point of view may be that of Judas or may resemble that of a modern photojournalist). Just as a backward sign of the cross shown in *Accattone* highlighted both Pasolini's indebtedness to Christian mythology and his distance from it, so too does Pasolini's version of the Deposition from the Cross reverse the traditional iconography of the event, perhaps best expressed in Jacopo Pontormo's *Deposition* (1528), for Pasolini places the camera not in front of the cross but behind it. (Many of Pasolini's images are directly inspired by the greatest of Italy's religious painters, not only Pontormo but also Giotto, Masaccio, and Pier della Francesca.) The last images of the Resurrection avoid the patently kitsch treatments typical of Hollywood versions of the Passion (at least those preceding Mel Gibson's version in 2004). Even an avowed atheist such as Pasolini made sure that the effects of this mysterious and inexplicable event would underscore the deep religious sentiment behind the belief in it, which Pasolini dramatizes by showing the disciples running joyously toward the Risen Christ in a burst of visual energy that sweeps the emotions of even the most skeptical spectator along with it.

If *Accattone* and *The Gospel* reflect in great measure Pasolini's interest in the figurative arts, *Hawks and Sparrows* marks his parting homage to the ideological and cinematic matrix of his formative years as an intellectual and a director. The film is both a comic celebration of the old-fashioned comic acting style of the great Neapolitan actor Totò and Pasolini's version of a form of *commedia all'italiana* that contains extensive social criticism. The film's structure is that of a parable within a parable. A subproletarian father and son, Innocenti Totò (Totò) and Innocenti Ninetto (Ninetto Davoli), wander about in the company of a talking crow, a Marxist intellectual who functions as Pasolini's alter ego. Within this outer plot another parabolic narrative depicts the conversion of hawks and sparrows, representing the upper and lower classes—literally, from the film's Italian title, "big birds" and "little birds"—by two followers of Saint Francis of Assisi, Brother Ciccillo and Brother Ninetto, played by the same actors who portray father and son in the outer parable. *Hawks and Sparrows* makes reference to a number of neorealist works by Rossellini that he scripted in collaboration with Fellini—*Paisan* (the convent scene), *The Flowers of St. Francis*, and *The Miracle*—as well as Fell-

ini's own trilogy of grace or salvation (especially Fellini's picaresque plot structures). Yet Pasolini emphasizes his debt to Italian neorealism to proclaim that this rich era in Italian film history has definitively ended. As the talking crow remarks, "The age of Brecht and Rossellini is finished." The crow espouses Pasolini's own ideology, declaring that the subproletarian pair of protagonists are "blessed" because they walk the streets, go into bars with workers, and kiss young girls dressed like angels from Botticelli canvases, while the crow and the bourgeois intellectual Pasolini admits he is—whose parents are

Pasolini's portrait of Brother Ciccillo unfolds within a critique of Italian neorealist cinema in *Hawks and Sparrows*. Credit: MOMA

said to be Doubt and Self-consciousness—are forever excluded from this beatific state. Since *Hawks and Sparrows* is a parable (within a parable), it has a moral, delivered through the tale of how the two Franciscans convert first the arrogant hawks who symbolize the upper classes, then the humble sparrows, who represent the less fortunate poor. Although each class of bird converts, the converted hawks then attack and murder the converted sparrows. The class struggle in the parable, as well as in life itself, will continue between men until radical change takes place in the world, as Saint Francis remarks to the two Franciscan priests—citing Pope John XXIII and not Marx, as many critics assumed.

Like the Taviani brothers in *The Subversives*, Pasolini employs documentary footage of Togliatti's funeral in the outer parable, after father and son have heard the crow's tale of the priests, but Pasolini focuses upon images of militant Communist Party members giving the clenched-fist salute of their party and then crossing themselves like good Catholics. The age of Rossellini, Brecht, and Togliatti has indeed passed. The two representatives of the subproletariat, having become exasperated with the crow's incessant chattering and ideological lecturing, devour him along the wayside, just as Pasolini believes the ideas of Marx and other intellectuals will be assimilated and eventually transcended by the working class in their march forward toward an uncertain future.

Bertolucci and Bellocchio: Young Turks Move beyond Neorealism

While Pasolini's early works both paid homage to Italian neorealism and transcended its style, Bernardo Bertolucci and Marco Bellocchio, two young talents who emerged during the same period, with ideological underpinnings as far to the Left as Pasolini's, drew much of their cinematic culture and inspiration from foreign directors (the French New Wave, in particular) and from assiduous visits to film archives, festivals, and clubs. Bertolucci was a personal friend of Pasolini, who took him on as an apprentice director in *Accattone* and who provided him with his first script, *The Grim Reaper* (*La commare secca*, 1962). Bertolucci's father was one of Italy's best poets and had introduced his son to numerous intellectuals and literary figures in Italy; Bertolucci later spent summer vacations at the Cinémathèque Française of Paris, and once declared that its director, Henri Langlois, was the greatest living professor of film history. Bellocchio's career, on the other hand, began with the formal study of cinema at the Centro Sperimentale di Cinematografia (1962) and a subsequent diploma at London's Slade School of Fine Arts. Both men brought to Italian cinema a more cosmopolitan and intellectual approach than was usual for filmmakers of the neorealist generation, given the latter's somewhat less formal entrance into the cinema.

The Grim Reaper presents a recognizably Pasolinian environment of Roman squalor, but Bertolucci's early style employs a lyrical rhythm and abrupt shifts of narrative time through dramatic editing that would be typical of his mature films. This first work is an ambitious attempt to join a commercial thriller, in which an aging prostitute is murdered and various suspects investigated, with an avant-garde treatment of time and narrative perspective. As each suspect gives an account of the "facts," the perspective on the murder changes radically. Furthermore, contrary to good neorealist practice, where some form of truth or "reality" was assumed to be objective, Bertolucci's cinephile world offers no fixed truths, only cinematic moments that cast doubt on the very nature of reality.

It was Before the Revolution, made only a few years later, that caused a number of important critics to announce the arrival of a new auteur. Based loosely upon Stendhal's The Charterhouse of Parma (1838) and replete, in good New Wave fashion, with numerous citations from literature (Wilde, Shakespeare, Pavese) and the cinema (Rossellini, Godard), Before the Revolution explores the contemporary implications of Talleyrand's statement that those who had not lived before the French Revolution could never realize how sweet life could be. Bertolucci fashions his protagonist, Fabrizio (Francesco Barilli), as a bourgeois intellectual from Parma who toys with Marxism; he has a brief affair with his Aunt Gina (Adriana Asti), and eventually marries Clelia (Cristina Pariset), preferring a safe bourgeois marriage to either Marxist revolution or an incestuous relationship. Although Bertolucci's adaptation omits Stendhal's Machiavellian Count Mosca, the novelist's most interesting character, his protagonists mirror three figures from the novel—Fabrice del Dongo; Gina, the Duchess Sanseverina; and Clélia Conti. Like Fabrice, Fabrizio has the misfortune to live in an era when his ideological aspirations conflict with his real possibilities. Rejecting his bourgeois origins, yet unable to transcend them, Fabrizio lives before the Marxist revolution that Bertolucci apparently believed was coming, and he suffers, like Bertolucci, from the "nostalgia for the present" typical of middle-class leftists. His inability to challenge society's mores by openly acknowledging his scandalous affair with his aunt parallels his failure to embrace the cause of the working class. Sexuality and politics, Freud and Marx, become uneasy bedfellows in this early film, as they will always remain in all of Bertolucci's future work.

As Pasolini perceptively noted in his essay "The Cinema of Poetry" from Heretical Empiricism (Empirismo eretico, 1972), Bertolucci's cinematic style is poetic, subjective, and elegiac. True, some awkward traces of Bertolucci's encounter with the New Wave may be traced in his Godardian citations and coded remarks, as when one pretentious intellectual declares (as previously cited), "one cannot live without Rossellini." But where the young intellectual ideologue in Bertolucci sometimes stumbles, the precocious lyric poet in him maintains a steadier hand, producing sequences of great emotional intensity. While Bertolucci the intellectual condemns his nostalgic vision of life before the revolution, declaring that there is no escape for the descendants of the bourgeoisie, Bertolucci the poet captures this way of life in lyrical images. Verdi's music and the city of Parma are never far removed from his films, and the most important sequence in this one evolves from the performance of Verdi's *Macbeth* at the Teatro Regio di Parma. As the various characters in this provincial melodrama enter the opera house, they seat themselves according to their divergent social origins. While the majestic musical tragedy unfolds on stage, Fabrizio's personal tragedy plays out in the balcony as he rejects Gina's love and enters Clelia's box after deciding to play to the bitter end his role as a disillusioned son of the decadent middle class. As his mother remarks, "Fabrizio accepts everything now."

Whereas Bertolucci examines his provincial origins and the roots of his social class with a sense of poetic nostalgia, Bellocchio's artistic perspective seems angry and provocative rather than elegiac. A native of Piacenza, Bellocchio set his first two films among the small, prosperous northern towns of the same region, which despite its reputation for supporting the Communist Party also contained a strong and very conservative middle class. Bertolucci's Fabrizio may retreat into the comforting womb of the middle-class family with his marriage, but Bellocchio attacks the very concept of

Fabrizio symbolically chooses the bourgeois world of his birth over revolution in Bertolucci's *Before the Revolution* by entering the opera box with the wealthy women of his class, suffering from what the director calls a "nostalgia for the present." *Credit: MOMA*

the family itself as well as all its traditional values and myths. In *Fists in the Pocket* (*I pugni in tasca*, 1965), Bellocchio provides a cinematic outlet for the kind of rage and anger that would burst forth from Italian universities and factories after 1968 and almost destroy Italian civil society. The family in this film, with all its physical handicaps and mental tics, stands closer to the spirit of Faulkner or Tennessee Williams than to traditional images of the family in Italian cinema. The mother (Liliana Gerace) is blind; her daughter, Giulia (Paola Pitagora), is emotionally unstable, immature, and afflicted with epilepsy; her brother Leone (Pierluigi Troglio) has mental problems; another brother, the main character, Alessandro (Lou Castel), not only has epilepsy but may also have an incestuous relationship with Giulia; only the family's eldest son, Augusto (Marino Masé), appears to be a normal, functioning part of society with a job and a future. Bellocchio's anger reaches a bitter apogee when he pictures this family around the dinner table, the traditional focus of Italian middle-class life, presenting a grotesque synthesis of the entire range of bourgeois customs and its concern with appearances, social standing, tradition, and banal ideas along with a wide range of uncontrolled emotions, illness, and madness beneath the conventional surface. Alessandro decides he must attack his family and therefore murders both his mother and Leone and attempts to suffocate Giulia when a violent epileptic attack cuts short his project of purification. Bellocchio, like Bertolucci, was fascinated with psychoanalysis, and ideas from psychoanalytic theory have informed the careers of both directors since their debut. Another link between the two directors is their love for Verdian melodrama: Alessandro's own death takes place against the moving aria from Verdi's *La traviata*, "Sempre libera degg'io, folleggiar di gioia in gioia."

Fists in the Pocket is a virtuoso first performance, one that showed Bellocchio's future career might be even brighter than Bertolucci's (something that did not turn out to be the case). Produced on a shoestring budget, with funds borrowed from the director's brother, it was shot on Bellocchio family property. Economics rather than design imposed its narrow focus upon the private life of a decadent provincial family, since the original script included a more comprehensive political dimension—a link between Alessandro and an extreme-Left student group similar to those that only a few years after the film's release gave way to terrorist cells in Italy. The link suggested by *Fists in the Pocket* between dysfunctional bourgeois families and a dysfunctional bourgeois culture in Italy becomes even clearer in Bellocchio's second film, *China Is Near* (*La Cina è vicina*, 1967), a masterful film that manages the almost impossible task of using a group of thoroughly dislikable characters to produce a brilliant political satire. During election time in an era of Center-Left coalitions, the Socialists in Imola (a town in north-central Italy) decide to nominate for city councilman Count Vittorio Gordini (Glauco Mauri), an opportunistic aristocrat and high-school teacher, thereby blocking the aspirations for this post held by an enterprising, working-class accountant and longtime party member named Carlo (Paolo Graziosi), who is subsequently named Gordini's campaign manager as a consolation prize. Elena (Elda Tattoli), the count's sexually rapacious sister, remains unmarried in order to avoid sharing her wealth with a poorer husband. Their younger brother, Camillo (Pierluigi Aprà), heads a group of Maoist students in an expensive Catholic school for the well-born, and can be found serving at Mass or playing the piano for the priest—when he is not sabotaging his brother's election campaign by means of smoke bombs at political rallies, disruptions of his speeches with attack dogs, and derisive slogans painted on the party headquarters, a location that serves more as a trysting place than as a serious center of political discussion. Set against this grotesque, aristocratic, and ideologically incoherent Italian provincial family are Carlo and his mistress, a working-class girl named Giovanna (Daniela Surina) who works in the count's home as his secretary. Joseph Losey's *The Servant* (1963) clearly influenced Bellocchio's vision of the relationships among various classes, and Bellocchio's working-class characters, like those in Losey's masterpiece, cynically insinuate themselves first into the aristocrats' beds (thanks to their proletarian sexual prowess) and then into the Gordini family itself: Elena becomes pregnant with Carlo's child, while Giovanna soon bears Vittorio's baby. Thus, Bellocchio's view of Italian politics represents a kind of "historic compromise" within the Italian family structure itself, and it also serves as an attack upon a moment in Italian political life when the Christian Democrats formed coalitions with the Socialists to exclude the Communist Party from power. Moreover, while the proletarian couple outsmarts their aristocratic lovers, in the process they are corrupted and assimilated into a class they loathe.

The Rise of the "Political" Film

The ideological issues raised by both Bertolucci and Bellocchio, as well as the extremely personal and original cinematic styles exhibited in their first works, point to a huge cultural shift in Italian life that would take place subsequent to the 1968 upheavals that began in Paris and spread throughout Europe. Both young directors, being followers of the French New Wave and cinephiles like their French counterparts, were open to new possibilities in filmmaking. They and others—the Taviani brothers, Pasolini, Pontecorvo, Rosi—were engaged in a form of radical filmmaking that called attention to social problems, undermined conventional notions about traditional values, and at times legitimized discontent, although they usually stopped short of calling for active violent revolution. The shift in focus from neorealism to the films made by this younger generation of directors who inherited neorealism's legacy would prove important in spawning another film genre in Italy in the late 1960s and 1970s: the Italian political film, sometimes called in Italian *il cinema di impegno civile*, or more simply, *il cinema civile*—perhaps best translated as a cinema of political *activism* or *engagement*. The definition of this new trend in Italian cinema must, of necessity, be broad and capable of encompassing a great many different styles and directors. Yet, many individuals not usually associated with filmmaking that arises from a political intent, such as Fellini or Antonioni, nevertheless made a number of films that fall into this category (see chapter 9). Identifying a director as an auteur, as in the case of such individuals as Fellini or Antonioni, usually separated them in critical thinking from their more ideologically minded colleagues.

Making films that reflected current political or ideological issues in Italy often made it difficult for large, commercial audiences abroad to appreciate such works. Still, some film genres during the period, such as the spaghetti western, were as politically motivated as those that were obviously so, and some directors, such as Pasolini and Bertolucci (for their mature works, see chapter 13), were obviously as "political" in their filmmaking as anyone. In addition, the division drawn here between the new generation of postneorealist directors and the political film genre serves more to indicate a certain difference in style than in content. Almost everyone of any talent in the Italian film industry learned a great deal about dealing with social "reality" from Italian neorealism, even though most directors in the 1960s–1980s were far more concerned with reaching wider commercial audiences for their works than neorealist directors ever really did within Italy, since their largest audience was always abroad. The "political film," therefore, must be understood as what Italian film historians call a *filone*: literally a "thread," here a metaphorical one that runs through many directors, many genres, and a number of decades in Italian film history, that can never really be pinned down to originating in a specific film or director, and that continues more or less uninterrupted in most of the postwar period down to the present. The following discussion isolates some of the most important examples of the "political film" *filone* during the golden age of Italian cinema.

The Political Films of Elio Petri

Perhaps the best example of the Italian political film may be found in a number of extremely popular and important works by Elio Petri (1929–82): *We Still Kill the Old Way* (*A ciascuno il suo*, 1967); *Investigation of a Citizen above Suspicion* (*Indagine su un cittadino al di sopra di ogni sospetto*, 1969); *The Working Class Goes to Heaven*, a.k.a. *Lulu the Tool* (*La classe operaia va in paradiso*, 1971); *Property Is No Longer a Theft* (*La proprietà non è più un furto*, 1973); and *Todo Modo*, a.k.a. *One Way or Another* (*Todo modo*, literally, "all means are good," 1976). The first of these films is an adaptation of a 1966 novel (published in English as *To Each His Own*) about the Sicilian Mafia by the well-known writer Leonardo Sciascia (1921–89), whose best novels lent themselves to scripts for films, since they were frequently structured around an investigation of Mafia crimes in southern Italy that could easily be turned into a more abstract discussion of the very meaning of justice. *Investigation of a Citizen above Suspicion* pairs Petri with the actor most closely identified with the Italian political film, Gian Maria Volontè (who also starred in *We Still Kill the Old Way*) and also employs a script by Ugo Pirro (1920–2008), Petri's favorite scriptwriter. Adding to the mix the brilliant music of Ennio Morricone (1928–), usually associated with the spaghetti westerns of Sergio Leone (and honored by a special Oscar Award for his film music in 2007), Petri found a winning formula. *Investigation* received not only the Grand Jury Prize at Cannes but also an Oscar for Best Foreign Language Film. Numerous other Italian directors attempted to emulate Petri's formula, most without his commercial and international success. Petri, Volontè, and Morricone teamed up again for *The Working Class Goes to Heaven* and *Todo Modo*, with Pirro cowriting the former.

Petri's success with the political film derived from his ingenious ability to blend politics and ideology with good entertainment, a lesson that other politically motivated directors such as Pasolini and Bertolucci would eventually learn. *Investigation* succeeds because it presents a specific political situation (the abuse of power by Italian institutions) within an abstract, almost philosophical framework. As Juvenal asked centuries earlier about rulers in Rome, Who will guard the guardians? A neurotic police inspector (Volontè, in perhaps his greatest performance) murders his mistress, Augusta (Florinda Bolkan), in the film's opening sequence and then defies the police to arrest him, even when he provides the investigators with ample proof of his guilt. The fact that he has transferred from homicide to the political section of the police (the DIGOS, or Division of General Investigations and Special Operations, which deals only with sensitive cases

The neurotic police inspector challenges his colleagues to find him guilty of murder in Petri's *Investigation of a Citizen Above Suspicion*. Credit: MOMA

involving terrorism, organized crime, and capital offenses) gives him virtual immunity to prosecution. For Petri, political power reduces everyone
to an infantile state. In flashback, the inspector and Augusta play ritualistic
sexual games that center around the policeman's role as father surrogate;
he interrogates her as if she were in jail, since he reminds her of her father,
and when he informs her that the police play upon the guilty feelings all
citizens share and that, confronted by the state, everyone becomes a child,
she angers him with the remark, "*You* are like a child," leading to her murder while they make love. The inspector wants to experience the cathartic
experience of confession available to others, and he commits a murder hoping to be caught. Ultimately, the highest authorities of the state confront
the inspector, but instead of arresting him, they greet him with a smile and
a scolding tug on the ear (a gesture suggesting that they are the ultimate
father figures, while he is only the son), and the murderer receives absolu-
tion as he declares: "I confess my innocence." After the inspector's superiors
leave him, we realize that the scene is a dream. Awake, the inspector adjusts
his tie as the authorities appear at his door for real, and little doubt remains
that he will actually be pardoned in reality as he was in the dream. The film
closes with a citation from Kafka: the servants of the law are above the law
and, therefore, above suspicion.

In its frontal attack upon Italy's ruling classes, *Investigation* never loses
sight of the fact that cinema is entertainment, not political theory: the
strange, jerky music of Morricone, the skillful and dramatic editing techniques, and the fast-paced rhythm of the narrative force the audience along
the director's chosen path with little time to pause for analysis or even for
a deep breath. Petri produces an exciting suspense thriller built around our
frustrated expectations that the guilty party will be eventually caught, and
then surprises us with the Kafkan ending and the ideological message about
the nature of all power. *The Working Class Goes to Heaven*, released following *Investigation*'s huge international critical and commercial success, was
a more ideologically coherent and historically accurate film but, precisely
because of this, a less entertaining political film. Volontè offers another
compelling performance as Lulù Massa, a factory worker whose life centers
around his superproductivity on the assembly line until a moment's loss of
concentration costs him the loss of a finger and drives him to consider his
condition as an alienated, exploited worker. The world of the factory in Petri
resembles that of a machine itself: its demands dehumanize the working
class. Amid a barrage of constant noise, the assembly line eventually shapes
the people toiling on it in its own image. As Massa ironically defines human
nature: "You put in a little raw material called food; various machines in
the body go to work on it; and the final product that comes out the other
end is . . . shit! Man is a perfect little shit-factory. Pity there's no market for
the stuff, we could all be capitalists!"[8] The factory reduces everything, even

sex, to the mechanical. Massa produces more than anyone else because he endows the metal products his lathe makes with his frustrated sex drive: "a piece, an ass, a piece, an ass," he mutters as he works, matching his body rhythm with that of the machine. Yet his Stakhanovist prowess on the assembly line alienates him from the other workers, who resent his productivity because the bosses use his record production as an excuse to speed up the line for others. Moreover, when a strike breaks out, Massa feels lost without the factory. Petri's ideological premises here are much clearer than in the far more entertaining *Investigation*. No need to examine the psychological results of the assembly line on a worker; it suffices merely to dramatize the brutal conditions in the factory.[9] When a company psychologist attempts to explain Massa's neurosis as a sexual dysfunction, Petri makes it clear that the factory system's cruelty to and exploitation of workers are the real culprits—the company provides him with medical treatment only to defend its production. Then, when the union finally wins its strike, Massa returns to the very place responsible for all his problems. The film closes on a chilling note, with its staccato images of the assembly line racing by on the screen in rapid, disconcerting succession, while the sound track bombards the audience with the noises and cries of the workers as Massa relates to his comrades a dream he had about breaking down a wall separating them from paradise. For Petri, workers will never enter Heaven until they destroy the wall (industrial capitalism) separating them from their dream of unalienated labor.

In *Todo Modo*, Petri adapts another Sciascia novel in a broadside attack upon the system of Christian Democratic rule that had dominated Italian political life since 1948. The film pictures a surrealistic monastery where the major leaders of an unnamed political party (obviously the Christian Democrats) retire for "spiritual exercises" established by the founder of the Jesuit order, Saint Ignatius Loyola. The film's title refers to Loyola's dictum that all measures (*todo modo*) must be employed to seek out the will of God. During this moment of spiritual inner seeking, an unknown avenger murders these men one by one until, as the film concludes, they are all killed. Sciascia's novel was a philosophical parable uncovering the guilt associated with the exercise of power—it was intended as a statement about the very nature of power itself.

Despite its closing disclaimer that any connection of the film to real events is pure coincidence, Petri's adaptation aims directly at a specific institution (and, in this sense, is far less effective as a film than the more ambiguous *Investigation*). The president of the unnamed party, played again by a brilliant Volontè, looks exactly like Aldo Moro, the two-time prime minister of Italy and president of the Christian Democratic Party who would be kidnapped and assassinated by the Red Brigades in 1978 for his role in effecting the famous *compromesso storico*, or "historic compromise," with the

Communist Party leader Enrico Berlinguer. Other characters clearly resemble other Christian Democratic party leaders (Giulio Andreotti, Amintore Fanfani). The president, like Moro, speaks of a "historic compromise" and even remarks, at one point while the murders are being investigated, that "I never distinguish between Right and Left." Thus, Petri's film attacks the political corruption of the ruling classes in Italy as well as the *trasformismo*, or "transformism" (abrupt reversals of positions; also suggested by the alternate title, *One Way or Another*), that have always constituted the root cause of political corruption in Italy, where real theoretical differences are swept under the table by deals that lump Left and Right together in compromises that avoid resolving real problems. Although *Todo Modo* is so deeply imbedded in the confusing morass of internal Italian politics that it could only with difficulty attract a commercial audience beyond the boundaries of the peninsula, it was a curiously prophetic work, coming only two years before the actual assassination of Aldo Moro.

Petri's cinema demonstrates how difficult it is to produce a genuinely political or ideological film. If the laws of cinematic spectacle are followed to guarantee a satisfied commercial audience, the polemical thrust of any political debate or historical context will most likely be obscured; but if ideology takes over the picture completely, as it seems to do in *Todo Modo* but never does in *Investigation*, only the initiated may follow the storyline.

Francesco Rosi's Postneorealist Political Cinema

Rosi's early works indebted to neorealist cinema ultimately present investigations of various scandals or political mysteries, based on documentation and the investigation of historical facts. Rosi's subsequent political films broadened his focus to include both adaptations of political novels and portraits of Italian political life similar to those identified with Petri's films. *Many Wars Ago* (*Uomini contro*, 1970) attacks the brutality and stupidity of war in an adaptation of an antiwar novel of the same title by Emilio Lussu (1890–1975), whose own participation in the bloody battles fought by Italian troops during World War I leading up to the disastrous defeat at Caporetto (1917) and the surprising Italian victories thereafter at Piave and Vittorio Veneto in 1918 were the basis for his fiction. Rosi's film recalls the futility of war satirized by Monicelli's *The Great War*, but without any of its humor. His chilling portrait of General Leone (Alain Cuny), a commander willing to slaughter his troops for no particular reason, brings to mind the inept leadership of the real General Luigi Cadorna at Caporetto. Rosi picked an easy target, but his denunciation of stupidity at the top of the army's chain of command implies that the entire Italian power structure resembles Cadorna's military debacle. *The Mattei Affair* (*Il caso Mattei*, 1972), reveals Rosi's interest in "documented" political puzzles, speculates on the reasons behind the mysterious death of Enrico Mattei (1906–62), the powerful Christian Democratic politician and director of the state-owned petroleum complex ENI (Ente Nazionale Idrocarburi), which posed a serious threat to the "Seven Sisters" (a term coined by Mattei himself), seven major oil companies that dominated the exploration, refinement, and distribution of petroleum in the mid-twentieth century, particularly in the Third World, until men such as Mattei began to negotiate more profitable contracts with underdeveloped oil-producing companies. As Italians are much given to conspiracy theories, Rosi's film clearly suggests that Americans were behind Mattei's death in a mysterious airplane crash. As Enrico Mattei, Gian Maria Volontè once again delivers a sterling performance in yet another political film. Rosi's *The Mattei Affair* and Petri's *The Working Class Goes to Heaven* represent, in a sense, the high-water mark of the Italian political film, since they jointly received the Grand Prize at the Cannes Film Festival in 1972—a tribute both to the leftist political beliefs of many of the jurors as well as the popularity of this hybrid film genre.

Another interesting "documented" political film pointing the investi-gatory finger at America is *Lucky Luciano* (1973), a probing look into the strange history of this Italo-American gangster (played by Volontè) who returned to Italy after being expelled from the United States. Rosi's film argues that Luciano's release from a New York prison reportedly came as a reward for the gangster's assistance to Allied forces during the invasion of Sicily. Released shortly after Francis Ford Coppola's international blockbuster *The Godfather* (1972), Rosi's film about the mastermind behind the Mob in America works in the same style the director had developed in *Salvatore Giuliano*. Rather than Coppola's dramatic narrative of a family dynasty, Rosi builds up a veritable legal brief against not only Luciano but also Italian and American politicians compromised by the gangster's activities.

Illustrious Corpses (*Cadaveri eccellenti*, 1976), a parable of the intricate link between political power and corruption in Italy, derives from another Leonardo Sciascia novel about Sicily—*Equal Danger* (*Il contesto*, 1971). Although the country in which the action takes place remains unnamed, the film's plot reminds us of the unstable situation in Italy at the time it was released. The investigation conducted by its protagonist, an honest and decent policeman named Inspector Rogas (Lino Ventura), begins with the assassinations of judges and magistrates but eventually turns on Rogas's belief that a right-wing plot against the government is forthcom-ing. In a meeting with the head of the Communist Party, both Rogas and the politician are shot, and the film ends with the image of anarchy about to overtake the state Rogas tried to defend. Of course, given Rosi's leftist political beliefs, it would not occur to him (nor to any of the other direc-tors of political films) to make a film about a *leftist* coup d'état. Most of the political films produced during this period share this partisan attitude, which calls attention to the ideological features of these avowedly sectarian works of art.

Two other films seemingly hark back to Italian neorealism's treatment of southern Italy. Originally made for Italian television, Rosi's adaptation of an autobiographical novel by Carlo Levi—the neorealist classic *Christ Stopped at Eboli* (*Cristo si è fermato a Eboli*, 1945), about poverty and exile in the Fascist South—appeared in 1979. In contrast to Rosi's better films, this is a slow-moving, even ponderous work that employs the same kinds of tedious film editing typical of bad American television and even includes a surprisingly bad performance (one of his last) by Volontè, as Levi. It seems strange that the film with the most direct connection to Italian neorealist literature would be among Rosi's least interesting works. A second and far more interesting treatment of the South may be found in his *Three Brothers* (*Tre fratelli*, 1981), a didactic film about the Italy of the period, still rocked by terrorism and social unrest, told through the juxtaposition of the lives of three brothers, all of whom return from the North of Italy where they work to attend their mother's funeral in the South. Their individual histories accurately reflect a decade of internal immigration from South to North: Raffaele (Philippe Noiret), a magistrate in Rome leading the fight against terrorists, is in constant danger of being assassinated; Rocco (Vittorio Mezzogiorno) retrains delinquent minors in an overcrowded correctional institution in Naples; Nicola (Michele Placido) works in a factory in Turin, rejects traditional labor unions, and has joined a workers' group that supports urban terrorism. Each of the brothers reflects upon his life, motivated by nostalgia for the peasant culture of his distant, less complicated past. In a flashback to the American invasion of Sicily in World War II, Rosi even reverses Rossellini's treatment of the meeting between American soldiers and Sicilians in *Paisan*: the soldiers Rocco encounters as a young child are Italo-Americans who jump from their tanks and kiss the soil from which their parents came. These Americans, in search of their cultural roots, stand in contrast to the rootless contemporary southern Italians, who seem to have lost their identities as a consequence of abandoning their peasant culture.

Expanding the Boundaries of Political Cinema: Montaldo, Bellocchio, and the Taviani Brothers

A fresh look at Italy's encounter with America, so crucial a theme in the neorealist period, characterizes not only Rosi's political films but also an interesting film by Giuliano Montaldo (1930–) entitled *Sacco and Vanzetti* (*Sacco e Vanzetti*, 1971), which combines Rosi's pseudodocumentary style with an attempt to re-create the authentic atmosphere of Boston's Italian community during the famous trial of the two Italian anarchists in 1927 that led to their execution. Gian Maria Volontè's outstanding performance as Bartolomeo Vanzetti, especially his moving speech during the trial, provides Montaldo with a means of effectively condemning not only American injustice in the past but also Italian injustice at the time the film was made. Disturbing parallels between the Red Scare of the 1920s in America and what Montaldo perceived as injustice in Italy were not lost on the film's Italian viewers, even though audiences outside of Italy saw the work as a historical reconstruction of a miscarriage of justice that was decades old.

The precocious talent apparent in Marco Bellocchio's first two films seems less evident in several political films aimed at a wider commercial market during the 1970s. *Slap the Monster on Page One* (*Sbatti il mostro sulla prima pagina*, 1972) examines in a rather superficial manner the way in which political factions manipulate Italian newspapers. Nonetheless, *In the Name of the Father* (*Nel nome del padre*, 1972) continues the exploration of youthful anger and generational conflict from *Fists in the Pocket* and *China Is Near*, carefully situating the action in an identifiable historical period: the academic year 1958–59, during which Pope Pius XII, the symbol for leftists in Italy of the Vatican's reactionary politics, died. It takes place in a college for the well born, clearly a metaphor for the larger social system and intended as an explanation of the causes of the social upheavals that were to sweep over Italy during this decade. The college is a microcosm of Italian society. The priests are feeble academics who try to instill in their pupils a sense of their "duties" as future rulers of Italy, but the wealthy students are a motley lot, dominated by Angelo (Yves Beneyton), who despises both the priests for their incompetence and his fellow students for their sheep-like behavior. The custodians who clean the school represent the working classes. As Bellocchio's image of a true neo-Fascist (which is what the leftist members of the post-1968 generation would call anyone to the right of the radical revolutionaries), Angelo explains that although priests have ruled for centuries through fear, secular leaders (such as he aspires to be) can do a much better job with more efficient methods. In a class play he directs that attacks all traditional values and cultural norms, a character named Faustolo (a parody of Faust) confronts God dressed in a Santa Claus suit, declaring he has no fear of losing his soul, since he has none. Bellocchio obviously believes that such puerile rebellions, like those of his middle-class protagonists in his first two works, arise more from a need to replace old authority figures than from any true revolutionary fervor. Released during the height of the student unrest in Italy, the film offers a message about the ideologically limited goals of the student population, which was not lost on those individuals who advocated a truly radical change in Italy and adopted terrorism as their means.

The political films made by the Taviani brothers during this decade were far less radical in their approach to the theme of revolution, a fact that underlines their traditional leftist views on politics, views that were not really in keeping with the sometimes mindless political radicalism of Italians who supported the Brigate Rosse (Red Brigades) and other extra-parliamentary extremist groups, such as Lotta Continua (Continuous Struggle) or Potere Operaio (Workers' Power), to name only a few such groups of the time. *Allonsanfan* (1974)—whose title derives from an Italian mispronunciation of the first phrase of the French national anthem: "Allons enfants"—recalls Bertolucci's attitude toward revolution in *Before the Revolution*. Set in post-Napoleonic Italy, *Allonsanfan* takes place during the reactionary restoration that followed the destruction of democratic changes in the peninsula. The Tavianis create a character—Fulvio Imbriani (Marcello Mastroianni)—who is an aristocratic Jacobin accused of revolutionary acts. After his release from prison, his fellow revolutionaries accuse him of betraying their cause. In spite of his desire to retire to his country home, Fulvio finds himself reluctantly drawn back into subversive schemes. For the Taviani brothers, Fulvio's reluctant attitude reflects their own view that middle-class participation in political upheavals must always be limited and constrained by a class-oriented utopianism. In fact, when the Jacobins attempt to support peasant revolt in Sicily, they are brutally murdered by the very peasants they attempt to help. Mistakenly informed that the peasants support the revolt, Fulvio dons a red Jacobin shirt and goes to meet his death. Before he is shot, however, the Tavianis show us a mass of red-shirted Jacobins and white-shirted peasants dancing a traditional Sicilian folk dance together. Although this image represents a dream experienced by one of Fulvio's friends, it remains the perfect rendition of the Tavianis' view of revolution as a utopian dream.

Padre Padrone (*Padre padrone*, 1977; literally, "father boss") launched the Taviani brothers into the international spotlight by winning the Golden Palm Award at Cannes (with a jury presided over by none other than the father of Italian neorealism, Roberto Rossellini) and the Interfilm Grand Prix at the Berlin International Film Festival in the same year. Based on Gavino Ledda's 1975 autobiographical account of how he, an illiterate Sardinian shepherd, became a professor of linguistics, it employs a number of themes typical of the political film but transcends the genre's sometimes abstract narrative structure. It is full of shifts between documentary and fiction: the real Gavino Ledda introduces himself at the film's opening and gives the actor playing him a stick, explaining that his authoritarian father (played by Omero Antonutti) once came to take him away from school brandishing a stick. From this sequence, we cut immediately to a re-creation of the traumatic moment when the father entered young Gavino's classroom and terrified everyone, including the teacher, threatening them all with the words, "Hands on the desk: today it's Gavino's turn, tomorrow it's yours!" While the stern, archaic rules of the primitive society in Sardinia

Gavino's authoritarian father removes him from school in *Padre Padrone* by the Taviani brothers. *Credit: MOMA*

provide the Tavianis with the perfect image of the primal father of psycho-analysis, this father also represents a historically accurate portrait of a real, not imagined, society. Thus *Padre Padrone* uses the theme so important in many political films, the authoritarian power of father over son and the generational conflict between older and younger generations in a time of social upheaval.

Nevertheless, the Tavianis play with, rather than follow, the conventions of film realism. Most of the film follows Gavino's slow acquisition of languages when he serves in the army and his discovery that his own language is really a dialect. Returning home, he declares his intention to attend the university, rejecting his father and the archaic, patriarchal system of repressive authority he represents. As the film ends, the real Gavino again appears, speaking directly to the camera and explaining that to employ his newly acquired education in a position of privilege would only represent his father's final victory. Yet the price of his personal evolution to literacy is quite high. As the film ends, the last image of the real Gavino (not the actor playing the young man) shows him holding his knees and rocking back and forth silently, recalling the same gesture he habitually made when he was left alone in the hills, tending his father's flocks.

The Tavianis relationship to realism in film and the tradition of Italian neorealism in film history stands out even more clearly in the film many consider to be their best work: *The Night of the Shooting Stars*, a film that received numerous prizes from the Cannes Film Festival in France, the National Society of Film Critics in the United States, and the Premio David di Donatello in Italy. It avoids even the pretense of realism and searches for a fanciful, fablelike style by reconsidering the pivotal film of Italian neorealism, Rossellini's *Paisan*. The idea for *The Night of the Shooting Stars* was born from an earlier documentary film the Tavianis had made (*San Miniato, July '44*) that recounted the massacre of the townspeople of a small Tuscan village in retaliation for the death of a German soldier during World War II. In *The Night of the Shooting Stars*, the Tavianis retell this historical event as if it were a fairy tale and reconstruct not only that moment in real history but also Rossellini's hagiographic account of the encounter of the Americans and the Italians in *Paisan*. Rossellini had narrated the encounter between these two nations by following the geographical path of the war from Sicily through Naples, Rome, Florence, and the Po River Valley.

After mining the town of San Miniato, the Nazis and their Italian Fascist allies instruct the townspeople to gather inside the cathedral there. Mistrusting the Germans, however, Galvano Galvani (Omero Antonutti) leads part of the populace toward the approaching American army. The Fascists betray those who stay behind, and many die inside the cathedral, whereas Galvano's refugees fight a deadly battle in a wheat field before reaching safety. The arrival of the Allies takes a form quite different from that in Rossellini. When "The Battle Hymn of the Republic" is heard on a record player, the group mistakes this for a sign that the liberation represents a Second Coming. Mara, a Sicilian woman (Enrica Maria Modugno) rushes forward to greet the liberators after hearing that a contingent of soldiers is composed of Sicilian-Americans, but she is shot by the Germans and, in her last moments, confuses the Nazis with her Sicilian countrymen. In her delirium, she imagines a miniature Statue of Liberty encased in a glass filled with artificial snow, and that she will be taken to visit her relatives in Brooklyn. In another encounter, two young girls meet several GIs at a crossroad, receiving the obligatory Hershey bars and inflated condoms instead of balloons. When the remaining members of the group come to greet the soldiers, they find only a half-empty package of Camel cigarettes. The shooting stars in the Tavianis' film are produced by the Perseid meteor shower, usually evident around the middle of August; they are said to be the tears of Saint Laurence, an early Christian martyr who died around 258 A.D. Attentive viewers of Rossellini's *Paisan* (as the Tavianis were) will remember that Joe from Jersey dies from a German sniper's bullet shortly after sighting a shooting star in the Sicilian episode of the film, inspiring the young Sicilian girl, Carmela, to avenge his death—an action that stands in sharp contrast to the useless, illusion-filled death of Mara. The Tavianis' film replaces Rossellini's Christian brotherhood between Americans and Italians in *Paisan* with an internecine civil war between residents of the same Tuscan town, a struggle from which the Americans are physically absent.

In *The Night of the Shooting Stars*, by the Taviani brothers, fascists and partisans momentarily suspend their hostilities to give each other water. *Credit: MOMA*

The reversal of Rossellini's major themes joins a completely different cinematic style. Rather than a documentary treatment of the narrative, *The Night of the Shooting Stars* entrusts the story to the subjective memory of the six-year-old Cecilia (one of the girls at the crossroads), filtered through her mind as an adult as she relates to her young daughter events that took place during her wartime childhood. The film's most typical editing technique is the wipe, one that highlights the film's editing and emphasizes its cinematic, not its realistic, qualities. The directors' ironic distance from their material emerges in the film's most famous sequence, the memorable battle between the black-shirted Fascists and the partisan peasants in a golden field full of ripe wheat. Interrupting this murderous battle, members of both sides pause, pass water back and forth, share it with the wounded of both sides, and then return to the killing. Equally fictitious and antirealistic in nature is a sequence where Cecilia saves herself from a bloodthirsty Fascist during the battle by reciting a magical incantation learned from her mother: this fantasy conjures up an epic scene where the partisans become Greek hoplites and impale the Fascists with dozens of spears. The Tavianis thus transform the content of Rossellini's neorealist classic into a popular legend placed within a mythological realm of poetic cinema.

Liliana Cavani's Political Cinema

Liliana Cavani (1933–) completed an education at the Centro Sperimentale in Rome and then began work with the RAI, Italy's state-owned television network. Her first film was, therefore, a documentary, and between 1962 and 1965, she produced a number of such works on Nazi Germany, Stalin, Pétain, and the role of women in the Resistance, before she produced her first feature-length film for the RAI, *Francis of Assisi* (*Francesco d'Assisi*, 1966). Her decision to cast Lou Castel, Bellocchio's angry young man from *Fists in the Pocket*, in the title role avoids the traditionally pious treatment sanctified by years of hagiography and concentrates upon a simple man who revolutionized European culture with his potentially subversive message about poverty and his distrust of the church's hierarchy and wealth. Her next film, *Galileo* (1968), again made for Italian television, provoked a hostile reaction and was never screened by the RAI, but Cavani's Galileo was not the Galileo of Brecht (a martyr of science destroyed by an ignorant church) but a Christian scientist who felt himself, a true believer, to have been betrayed by his accusers.

Cavani then moved from documentary films to feature works. Infected, as all young directors were, by the rebellious spirit sweeping over Italy and Europe in the wake of the student riots in France and Italy after 1968, Cavani first produced a political allegory, *The Cannibals* (*I cannibali*, 1970), based on a loose interpretation of *Antigone*, by Sophocles. After a military government has suppressed a revolt in an unnamed country in the present, the army decrees that the bodies of the fallen rebels must remain where they fell upon pain of death. Only a mysterious foreigner (Pierre Clémenti) shows any compassion for the rebels and breaks the law; his act of defiance moves a young Antigone (Britt Ekland) to join him in his gesture, ensuring both their deaths. As one might expect from such a mechanical scheme, plus the dreary acting style of Clémenti,[10] the film was a flop: it even included a very bad musical score by Ennio Morricone! Its failure forced Cavani to return to television for several years.

Yet with the appearance of her film *The Night Porter* (*Il portiere di notte*, 1974), Cavani became both famous and notorious. While European critics lavished praise on the film, it was bitterly attacked by New York critics for its irreverent treatment of the Holocaust.[11] A brief plot summary explains in part New York's hostility to the film: a chance encounter in Vienna in 1957 between Max (Dirk Bogarde), a former SS officer in a concentration camp, and Lucia (Charlotte Rampling), a former inmate of the camp, with whom Max carried on a sadomasochistic affair during the war, leads the couple to revert to their relationship of twelve years earlier. Max's former Nazi colleagues, all of whom are undergoing therapy to remove their guilt complexes, disapprove of Max's return to their evil past, but Max refuses to continue his therapy, locks himself in his apartment with Lucia, and they are eventually murdered by his former comrades. Cavani's plot moves in a series of flashbacks from present-day Vienna to various moments in the couple's relationship.

Many of the negative attacks upon Cavani's film hastily labeled it a "Fascist" film, but the portrayal of evil does not imply praise of it. Cavani has noted that in her earlier documentary films on the Third Reich and in conversations with survivors of the Holocaust, she was struck by a constant theme. What the victims resented most was that the Nazis had revealed to them the depths of evil of which every human being was capable, and one survivor in particular advised Cavani not to consider all victims as innocent, for like their captors they were human.[12] In her opinion, evil was not only practiced in the concentration camps; it was learned there as well. The key to the film's theme lies in a scene in which Max tells a decadent countess that "his little child" has returned to him, and when the woman replies that his affair with Lucia is "a romantic story," Max corrects her, saying instead that it is a "biblical story." This remark leads to the most shocking flashback of the film: Lucia dances in a military barracks for Max and his SS comrades. Wearing suspenders over her naked breasts and sporting an SS cap, she sings a German nightclub song in the style of Marlene Dietrich. After the number ends, when Max presents her with a gift, she opens the box and discovers the severed head of one of the prisoners who had bothered her. Her cry of mingled horror and pleasure underscores the fact that, from that moment on, she is forever linked to her lover-torturer. As Max asserts, theirs is a biblical story—in this case an imitation of the story of Salomé and John the Baptist. Lucia returns to Max in order to relive their past affair. In the clinical sense, Max is insane, but if he were ruled innocent by virtue of insanity in a court of law, how could any of the Nazis be judged guilty? Thus, when Max rejects his therapy, he asserts, paradoxically, his sanity and accepts his own guilt (at least in Cavani's eyes). And in so doing, he unburdens Lucia of her guilty conscience for having survived in the camp.

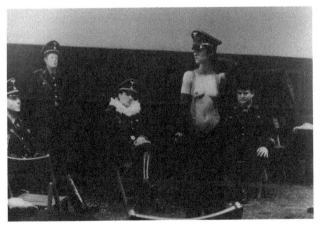

In a flashback to a "biblical" story alluding to the tale of Salomé and John the Baptist, Lucia dances for her Nazi captors before demanding the head of one of her fellow inmates in Cavani's *The Night Porter. Credit: MOMA*

This explains why Max dresses Lucia in a little girl's outfit and why he finally dons his SS uniform once again as they both walk outside to meet their deaths. What most disturbed critics about *The Night Porter* is the combination of the Holocaust and eroticism in a narrative that purports to reaffirm a traditional goal of Christianity, the consciousness of sin and guilt leading to expiation and purification through punishment. It is no wonder that Max's former comrades kill the couple as they stroll across the city bridge: their very presence undermines the men's pathetic attempts to employ psychoanalysis to sweep their criminal responsibility for the Holocaust under the rug by engaging in farcical sessions with an analyst.

Cavani's next two films examine both sexuality and the heritage of World War II. In *Beyond Good and Evil* (*Al di là del bene e del male*, 1977), Cavani moves from the Visconti-like atmosphere of *The Night Porter* to provide a highly personal interpretation of the love affair among Friedrich Nietzsche (Erland Josephson), Lou Salomé (Dominique Sanda), and Nietzsche's friend Paul Rée (Robert Powell). The liberated woman is the most uninhibited of the three, and it is she who encourages Nietzsche to share a ménage à trois. Subsequently, Cavani's adaptation of Curzio Malaparte's 1949 novel describing Naples during the American occupation in 1944, *The Skin* (*La pelle*, 1981), aims at an international market with Burt Lancaster as Mark Cork (a thinly disguised allusion to General Mark Clark), Marcello Mastroianni as the novelist/narrator, and Claudia Cardinale as Malaparte's aristocratic mistress. This moment of Italian history is a familiar one, perhaps most famously captured in Rossellini's Naples episode of *Paisan*, or in *The Four Days of Naples* (*Le quattro giornate di Napoli*, 1962), by Nanni Loy, which was nominated in 1963 for an Oscar for Best Foreign Film. Cavani pictures a much less heroic scene than Loy and a much more grotesque scene than Rossellini. Her portrayal of Naples concentrates on the relationship between Americans, seen as victors rather than liberators, and the Neapolitans, seen as victims rather than unfortunates. Implicitly her film is a protest against American cultural and political hegemony in Italy that begins with the liberation. The most effective image of this ambivalent relationship comes as General Cork finally liberates Rome: one of the Italian bystanders, who tries to grasp the symbolic Hershey bar from a soldier on a passing vehicle, is squashed under its treads.

Ermanno Olmi's Vision of Italy's Past

True to his neorealist heritage and the lessons he learned from Vittorio De Sica, Ermanno Olmi's *The Tree of the Wooden Clogs* (*L'albero degli zoccoli*, 1978)—winner of well-deserved prizes at the 1978 Cannes Film Festival as well as the 1979 New York Film Critics Circle Award, and originally made for Italian television—seems not to be a "political" film at first screening.

It focuses on peasant life on a farm near Bergamo around the end of the nineteenth century, exactly the era that a far more obviously political film, Bertolucci's *1900* (*Novecento,* 1976), depicts in a very different cinematic style. Recalling the classic conventions of neorealist cinema, Olmi employs nonprofessional actors, peasants still living in the Bergamo region, who speak their own difficult regional dialect. The film's unusual length of just over three hours aims at an elegiac re-creation of the slow rhythms of life in a culture that has almost completely disappeared in Italy but is still very much a part of the Italian collective memory.

How distant Olmi's spectators are from this world is evident from the shocking scene picturing the slaughter of the peasants' hogs. The blood and gore of the sequence makes modern audiences queasy (being all too eager to forget the origins of the meat they eat), but for the peasants, the killing of a docile animal represents a necessary part of their very existence. The film's central event, and the reason why Olmi's film can be categorized as a political film, occurs when a farmer's son breaks his wooden clogs on the way home from school. Intent upon safeguarding his son's future, his tenant-farming father (having no other wood) cuts down one of the landowner's trees to replace the clogs. This simple act results in the expulsion of the entire family from the land. With this straightforward and seemingly insignificant event, Olmi tells us more about the connection of political and economic power than most of the political films of the entire period. His patient, relentless evocation of the praiseworthy daily lives of his beloved Bergamaschi peasants contains a message that is at once revolutionary and traditional, for it contrasts the simple Christian steadfastness of these simple people to the insensitive, base cruelty of their superiors. In so doing he also reminds his viewers of the many virtues lost in the rapid transition in Italy from an agrarian, rural, peasant culture to one based upon rapid industrial development, urbanization, and class conflict.

The Heritage of the Postneorealist Generation and the Italian Political Film

The vast range of ideological positions contained within the general group of films made by young directors indebted to Italian neorealism, as well as within the subsequently popular "political film" in Italy, provides a rich commentary upon Italy's past and present, between old social problems inherited from the past and new issues that arose in an age of rapid social transition. In addition, other film genres (the *commedia all'italiana,* the spaghetti western, even the greatest "art films" of the time) quite often contained political or ideological messages at least as a subtext, if not as their primary purpose, as did these more avowedly engaged works of art. The frequent thematic emphasis on the relationships of fathers and sons quite obviously treated questions of authority or rebellion that linked to current events. In general, most of these works approached the Italian state and its institutions (schools, the police, the bureaucracy, the judiciary) with negative opinions ranging from harsh criticism to outright rejection. Regardless of their specific ideological position or their individual style, these films all remained true to the essential heritage of Italian neorealism: they cast a critical eye on the society that the films reflected, and in so doing, broadened the very idea of the cinema as "entertainment." This created a civic function for the movies in Italy, defining film as a public forum in which hotly debated social issues could be communicated through artistic means in an often uncomfortable but ultimately healthy marriage of convenience.

CHAPTER NINE

The Mature Auteurs

NEW DIMENSIONS IN FILM NARRATIVE IN VISCONTI, ANTONIONI, DE SICA, AND FELLINI

MUCH OF THE FILM INDUSTRY'S ECONOMIC SUCCESS after the neorealist era was indebted to the popular appeal of genre films. The international prestige of Italian cinema during its golden age largely derived, however, from what critics have termed "art films" directed by Italy's major auteurs, filmmakers who began work in cinema during the neorealist era but whose artistic outlooks broadened and matured as they transcended their neorealist origins. Such directors as Visconti, Antonioni, De Sica, and Fellini were frequently victorious at international film festivals and, what is more surprising, were often quite profitable at the box office, holding out the promise of a dream come true for the industry—the combination of great art with maximum profits.

Luchino Visconti: History, Literature, and the Family Romance in *Rocco and His Brothers* and *The Leopard*

In the 1960s and 1970s, Visconti made a number of important films, completing *The Innocent*, an adaptation of a novel by Gabriele d'Annunzio, just before he died. Most of his films were adaptations of literary works or treatments of important moments in European history: *Rocco and His Brothers* (*Rocco e i suoi fratelli*, 1960), *The Leopard*, *The Stranger* (*Lo straniero*, 1967), *The Damned* (*La caduta degli dei*, 1969), *Death in Venice* (*Morte a Venezia*, 1971), *Ludwig* (1973), and *Conversation Piece* (*Gruppo di famiglia in un interno*, 1974). Visconti always aimed at establishing links between his films and their historical context. He was, after all, an avowed Marxist even though he descended from the family that ruled Milan during the late Middle Ages and early Renaissance. He naturally turned to important novels reflecting

259

great historical upheavals or signaling shifts in cultural values, utilizing ready-made plots around which he erected idiosyncratic interpretations of the texts he adapted, infusing them with a distinctive Viscontian style of set design, costuming, and photography that was as indebted to grand opera as to the cinema. In fact, Visconti was one of the great postwar opera directors at Milan's La Scala and elsewhere.

Visconti always enjoyed the enthusiastic support of most Italian critics, particularly those with left-wing political views, probably because his portrayal of decadence could easily be taken as criticism of Italian institutions.[1] Visconti also privileged narratives about families—their conflicts, their disintegration, and their interrelationships. *Rocco and His Brothers,* made during the height of the Italian economic miracle, represents something of a sequel to *The Earth Trembles,* as it focuses upon the migration of southern Italians like those from the Sicilian town Acitrezza to northern industrial areas. His portrayal of the Parondi family's struggle to survive in Milan highlights the dramatic clash of different value systems—the traditional one of southern peasants, with its archaic code of honor and family loyalty, and the emerging contemporary morality linked to industrial society and the factory that loosened the ties between members of the traditional family. Rosaria (Katina Paxinou), the matriarchal ruler of the Parondi clan, arrives at the Milan train station with four sons—Simone (Renato Salvatori), a brutish but handsome lout; Rocco (Alain Delon), the kindest and gentlest of the brothers; Ciro (Max Cartier); and Luca (Rocco Vidolazzi)—to meet a fifth son, Vincenzo (Spiros Focás), who is already established in the city with steady employment and a fiancée. Each of the sons represents a different response to the immigrant experience. Vincenzo's efforts to bridge the differences between both worlds ends disastrously as his mother's interference causes him to lose his job and threatens his relationship with his fiancée, Ginetta (Claudia Cardinale). Simone becomes a boxer, a traditional route for minorities to advance even today, but his promising career collapses because of his lack of discipline, his chauvinist mentality, and his stormy love affair with Nadia (Annie Girardot), a prostitute. Rocco constantly sacrifices his interests for the interests of the clan, but he too cannot escape the burden of family. After he also falls in love with Nadia, Simone's views of traditional sexuality come into conflict with Rocco's genuine love and respect for Nadia. Under Rocco's very eyes, Simone rapes Nadia, reasserting his "property rights," and then gives Rocco a severe beating. As a result, Rocco abandons Nadia to his brother, who eventually murders her. Rocco's subservience to family comes to a melodramatic climax when, atop Milan's cathedral, he explains to Nadia that she must return to Simone because he needs her. Subsequently, Rocco becomes a successful prizefighter himself to earn enough money to cover Simone's growing debts. *Rocco and His Brothers*

Nadia dies at Simone's hand in an operatic death from Visconti's *Rocco and His Brothers*. *Credit: DVD*

omits much that a historian or sociologist would consider essential to a discussion of urban migration to the North: unions, strikes, crime, racism, and so forth. Instead, Visconti produces a melodramatic account of a love triangle among Rocco, Simone, and Nadia that is much closer in spirit to nineteenth-century opera than to a neorealist film or a naturalist novel. Nowhere is his penchant for melodrama more apparent than in the dramatic scenes cutting back and forth between Rocco's bloody fight against a superior opponent in the ring and Simone's killing of Nadia, who meets her fate as if on the stage of La Scala, with outstretched arms, embracing her former lover Simone and his knife.

Visconti's fascination with the dramatic potential of the family continues to be the director's focus in *The Leopard* and *The Damned*, which integrate family histories into broad panoramic accounts of the Italian Risorgimento, in the first case, and the rise of National Socialism in Germany, in the second. Both films display Visconti's increasing interest in re-creating lavish, carefully designed period sets and opulent costumes, props intended to evoke the spirit of eras forever vanished. Based upon the novelist Giuseppe Tomasi di Lampedusa's international bestseller of the same name, *The Leopard* opens as Garibaldi's red-shirted volunteers have invaded Sicily in an attempt to annex the island to the Kingdom of Italy. The landed aristocrats, remnants of a feudal era, must now honor their obligations to the Bourbon monarchy or come to an accommodation with the victorious middle class. Don Fabrizio, Prince of Salina and the "leopard" of the title, played brilliantly by Burt Lancaster, represents the cream of the old aristocracy: learning, culture, grace, wealth, and style. He allows his nephew Tancredi (Alain Delon), an impressive but calculating and ambitious young man, to join the revolution, a decision that eventually associates his House of Salina with the winning side and ensures their survival in the new order. A self-serving group of middle-class merchants and liberal politicians emerges to divide the spoils of the political upheaval they have engineered, and this class is personified by Don Calogero Sedara (Paolo Stoppa), a comic figure whose power derives from the ecclesiastical properties he purchased after their confiscation by the state and whose rude manners provide the aristocrats with a constant source of laughter. Yet Don Fabrizio amazes his retainers by allowing the inevitable marriage of new money to ancient titles without wealth. Tancredi marries Don Calogero's beautiful daughter, Angelica (Claudia Cardinale), thus ensuring the family a powerful future. Visconti's sordid picture of a classic example of Italian *trasformismo* concludes with a magnificent ballroom sequence in which the prince contemplates his death and his nephew's future, and overhears the sound of an execution at dawn, signaling the final destruction of any revolutionary threat to the now firmly entrenched new bourgeois regime.

The Leopard thus continues *Senso's* interpretation of the Risorgimento as a flawed, betrayed, and incomplete revolution. Still, it is more than an extremely meticulous and lavish re-creation of a great historical novel; it is also a meditation on death, historical change, and the demise of a social class to which Visconti belonged. The director identified himself with Don Fabrizio. A passionate astronomer, the Sicilian prince gazes upon the course of history swirling about him with an air of bemused detachment and slight contempt for the vulgarity of it all, just as Visconti's characteristic slow camera movements and long takes caress his subject matter in an elegiac fashion. Unlike his nephew Tancredi, Don Fabrizio takes no delight in the hypocrisy required for survival. Tancredi's credo may be summed up in a remark taken verbatim from the novel: he informs his uncle that he joins the Garibaldini because "things have to change in order to remain the same."

Visconti captures his own nostalgia for the past in the face of inevitable historical change in one of the most beautiful sequences in the film, describing the family's arrival at Donnafugata, their summer palace. As the village band serenades them with "Noi siam le zingarelle" from Verdi's *La traviata*, and the family's faithful retainer and church organist, Don Ciccio, plays "Amami Alfredo" from the same work, the family takes its traditional privileged seats at the front of the cathedral. Visconti's camera slowly tilts down from the baroque ceilings and the sumptuous statuary to the priests and the omnipresent smoke of incense, and then pans slowly and tenderly over the entire family. The actors have been made up with bluish mascara and are covered with inordinate amounts of travel dust, sitting motionless, as if they were statues. It is a stunning image of an era about to disappear, evoking thoughts of decay and death.

Don Fabrizio and his aristocratic family enter the church at Donnafugata, their summer home, in Visconti's *The Leopard*. Credit: MOMA

The prince's preoccupation with death reappears when a representative visiting him from the North, Cavalier Chevalley (Leslie French), asks him to take a role in the new constitutional monarchy. Don Fabrizio's refusal holds out no hope (his reasoning taken almost verbatim from the novel). No government has ever succeeded in changing Sicily, he maintains, because the island's physical squalor and misery reflect its obsession with death, as does the desire for voluptuous immobility, sleep, sensuality, and violence typical of the island. Sicilians do not want to change because they think they are perfect, and their vanity overcomes their misery. In the belief that no real progress can come of this new government, the prince declares that whereas the older ruling classes were leopards and lions, the era of jackals and sheep has begun. Visconti brings this theme of death and sorrow to its culmination in the spectacularly re-created ballroom scene, during which Don Fabrizio examines a painting (which the novel calls *The Death of the Just Man*) by Jean-Baptiste Greuze (1725–1805) that (anachronistically) hangs in the palace's library. The painting highlights Don Fabrizio's state of mind, leading him to imagine his own death. Yet, Visconti juxtaposes this morbid thought to the vitality of the sensual Angelica, who dances with the prince and arouses in him a sense of passion and desire that moves him to shed a single tear.

Tancredi observes that "the new administration requires order, legality and order," and the prince, hearing that deserters from the regular army to Garibaldi's short-lived attempt to effect a true revolution will be executed (after Garibaldi's defeat at the Battle of Aspromonte), walks slowly home at dawn. As the firing squad's volleys marking the end of the Risorgimento's revolutionary phase resound on the sound track, we see a yawning Don Calogero remark, "No more to worry about!" Although Visconti comes from the very class whose demise constitutes the theme of *The Leopard*, the romantic Marxist in him condemns the middle-class betrayal of Garibaldi's egalitarian Risorgimento ideals.

Visconti's "German Trilogy": *The Damned, Death in Venice,* and *Ludwig*

Visconti's interest in family narratives evolved during his career to include, in *The Damned,* a consideration of how the rise of National Socialism in Weimar Germany destroyed an aristocratic family. The other two films in this trilogy are, respectively, a reworking of Thomas Mann's 1912 novella *Death in Venice,* and an exploration of the psyche of Ludwig II of Bavaria, the "mad" king and Richard Wagner's eccentric patron. Critics speak of Visconti's "decadence" in these highly mannered films that emphasize lavish operatic sets and costumes, sensuous lighting, painstakingly slow camerawork, and a penchant for imagery reflecting subjective states or symbolic values. Responding to such complaints about his later, decadent style, Visconti makes no apology for his cinematographic signature:

> I tell these stories about the self-destruction and dissolution of families as if I were recounting a requiem. . . . I have a very high opinion of "decadence," just as, for example, Thomas Mann did. I have been imbued with this spirit: Mann was a decadent of German culture, I of Italian formation. What has always interested me is the analysis of a sick society.[2]

Both *The Damned* and *Death in Venice* were box-office successes, but in each instance, numerous critics objected to the very decadent atmosphere of these works that made them so unique.

As one perceptive reviewer put it, *The Damned* presents "the Krupp family history as Verdi might have envisaged it."[3] Visconti's film chronicles the dissolution of the von Essenbeck family (obviously patterned on the historical Krupp munitions makers) as it is caught up in the collapse of Weimar Germany and the rise of the Nazis. The family is a collection of misfits, power seekers, and perverts. The old Baron Joachim is murdered by the executive director of the steelworks, Frederick Bruckmann (Dirk Bogarde), who is the lover of the widowed Baroness Sophie von Essenbeck (Ingrid Thulin), whose son, Martin (Helmut Berger), the baron's heir, is manipulated by his mother and lover in a plot to rearm Nazi Germany with the massive steelworks the family owns. Eventually Aschenbach (Helmut Griem), a distant cousin in the SS (the *Schutzstaffel,* or "Protective Squadron"), sets Martin against both his mother and Frederick when they prove too weak for the ruthless Nazi schemes. Konstantin (Reinhard Kolldehoff), the baron's elder son, is a highly placed officer in Ernst Röhm's paramilitary SA (*Sturmabteilung* or "Storm Battalion") who opposes the power over the

Drunken revelry precedes the massacre of the SA troops during the Night of the Long Knives in Visconti's *The Damned. Credit: MOMA*

family business exerted by Hitler, the Gestapo, and the SS (which served as a kind of paramilitary Praetorian Guard for Hitler and whose militarized divisions during World War II were responsible for the most horrible atrocities). With Frederick's complicity, Konstantin dies in a bloodbath while the Gestapo and SS eliminate the SA during the so-called Night of the Long Knives—a purge that actually took place in mid-1934, before Hitler seized total power in Germany, and cost the lives of nearly a hundred people. Eventually Martin rejects the guilt caused by his various sexual perversities and completely embraces the most radical of Nazi values: he molests a young girl, rapes his mother, and forces Frederick and Sophie into a grotesque marriage and then a double suicide.

Filled with literary and historical references, *The Damned*'s plot is both baroque and confusing. The opening scene of the film, with the entire family around the dinner table, seems lifted directly from the opening chapter of Mann's *Buddenbrooks* (1901); the complicated relationships of Sophie, Martin, and Frederick show the influence of Greek tragedy, Shakespeare's *Macbeth*, and Wilhelm Reich's views on the relationship of Fascism and homosexuality. In this regard it is interesting to note that Visconti is one of the first Italian directors to bring homosexuality out of the closet with his "German trilogy." Such films as Pasolini's *Theorem* (see chapter 13), *The Damned*, and Bertolucci's *The Conformist* set a pattern, frequently repeated both in serious art films by recognized auteurs and in B films, that played on the titillating aspects of this linkage of sexual perversion and sadomasochism to National Socialism or Italian Fascism.[4] For Visconti (a homosexual himself), homosexuality becomes a metaphor embodying both negative qualities (the thirst for power in *The Damned*) and positive intellectual and cultural characteristics (a sensitivity to music, poetry, and the arts in *Death in Venice* or *Ludwig*).

The Damned should not be taken as a serious sociological discourse on the rise of Nazi Germany. The film is more accurately described as a powerful visual metaphor for the infernal nature of Nazi moral degradation, a pathological case history bordering on the Grand Guignol. The nightmarish nature of Nazi Germany jumps to our attention with the film's title credits, shot against a fiery red blast furnace. This violent and hellish color returns constantly throughout the film's visuals: in the Nazi flag and banners; in interiors lit by the menacing glow of fireplaces; in scenes of book burning; in the gory sequence, literally dripping with blood and shot in a diffused red light, depicting the execution of SA troops by the Gestapo and the SS; and finally in the red draperies serving as a backdrop for the ghoulish double suicide concluding the film. Color itself becomes a protagonist in *The Damned*, a chromatic metaphor for the family, which embodies a corrupt culture that willfully brings the world down around its ears.

Death in Venice, too often discussed solely in terms of its adaptation of Mann's novella, combines the director's characteristically lavish use of period costumes and meticulously re-created sets with a far more linear and controlled storyline than the sometimes confusing narrative of *The Damned*. Visconti transforms Mann's visitor to Venice from a writer to a composer reminiscent of Gustav Mahler. He also uses Mahler's music on the sound track, which sometimes threatens to overwhelm the visuals with its ominous, foreboding tones. Flashbacks clarify the artistic issues that intrigue Visconti and illuminate the life of Gustav von Aschenbach (Dirk Bogarde), the director's effete symbol of the *mal du siècle* decadence, whose artistic sensibilities are at war with the sensual temptations aroused by his unsettling vision of a beautiful boy, Tadzio (Björn Andrésen). Visconti's film makes the homosexuality present in Mann's novella far more explicit than in the literary original. The composer's inner thoughts—revealed to us through flashbacks—reflect an intellectual dilemma: Aschenbach's friend Alfred (Mark Burns) constantly argues for the important role of ambiguity, sensuality, and physical reality in artistic creativity, while the stuffy composer contends that beauty is a pure, cerebral quality that should function as an example of clarity. Yet *Death in Venice* succeeds most when it abandons such philosophical considerations and concentrate upon presenting a visual spectacle of *fin de siècle* society inside the luxurious Grand Hotel des Bains on the Lido of Venice. The actual hotel was the location of Mann's novella and served as Visconti's "set." In a sensuous and nostalgic farewell to an aristocratic world about to disappear in the cataclysm of World War I, much like that to the decadent world of the Salina family in *The Leopard*, Visconti slowly pans his camera around salons, dining rooms, and parlors filled with richly furnished decors, formally dressed guests, and luxurious decorations

At Venice's Hotel des Bains, Aschenbach walks by his secret object of desire, the young and beautiful Tadzio, in Visconti's *Death in Venice. Credit: MOMA*

of flowers or tables spread with exquisite foods. Aschenbach's infatuation with Tadzio becomes more than a old man's flirtation with what was then termed "Greek love"; it becomes a graphic image for the composer's confrontation with old age and intellectual sterility.

Himself a product of the decadent world he photographed, Visconti identifies himself with Aschenbach just as he did with the Prince of Salina. He retains the diabolic and symbolic figures from Mann's novella that are harbingers of death and the cholera plague that strikes Venice. Few film images of death are more haunting than that of Aschenbach on the beach, gazing upon Tadzio's resplendent, nubile body as he points toward the golden sunset. At that moment, Aschenbach's garish makeup and face powder, applied by the hotel's barber in a futile effort to disguise his age, drip down his tearful face as he dies.

The obsession in *Death in Venice* with solitude, sensuality, and mortality becomes even more pronounced in *Ludwig.* King Ludwig II of Bavaria was a romantic dreamer who constructed fantastic, fairyland castles, spent a fortune on Wagner's grandiose operatic schemes, and died a mysterious death after being deposed from the throne for mental instability. Visconti's narrative unfolds in a series of flash-forwards from the king's coronation in 1860 that move between moments in Ludwig's reign and the legal inquiry that later declared him insane. Again, the director shows his enduring penchant for the melodramatic and operatic spectacle of lavish sets and costumes. The Bavarian monarch (Helmut Berger) represents a personality type Visconti views as particularly characteristic of post-Romantic Germany that includes both utopian artists such as Aschenbach and perverted power seekers such as Martin von Essenbeck. The image of Adolf Hitler enraptured by Wagnerian melodrama while Berlin suffers Allied bombing raids suggests the historical counterpart of the kind of figure Visconti envisions in his German trilogy. Ludwig pictures himself as the embodiment of the mythical Siegfried celebrated in Wagner's opera, and while Bavaria and its Austrian allies are defeated by Bismarck's Prussia on the battlefield, Ludwig amuses himself with otherworldly things—fantastic musical projects and hours of enraptured planetarium gazing. As the monarch moves more and more into a closed and solitary existence, his physical deterioration parallels his descent into madness and homosexuality, and his drunken orgies with his male lovers are shot in almost the same manner as was the Night of the Long Knives in *The Damned*.

Visconti's German trilogy attempts no real serious historical vision or analysis of Germany's flirtation with Romantic idealism and its subsequent perversion in the Nazi era. Rather, the director allows his taste for visual spectacle, as well as his own personal preoccupation with old age, solitude, ugliness, and death, to overwhelm his narrative powers. These themes are treated in his last two works, *Conversation Piece* and *The Innocent*, two works that provide us with beautiful images of a world that has disappeared. Although he retained his matchless flair for melodramatic spectacle to the end of his life, Visconti had, by that time, abandoned more daring contributions to the art of cinematography for chilling but static visions of the passing of the culture that had produced him.

Michelangelo Antonioni and New Ways of Seeing in the "Trilogy of Alienation"

The years 1959–60 might well be remembered as miraculous ones in which everything seemed to go right for the Italian film industry, in retrospect a signal that a golden age was actually in progress. The almost simultaneous releases of *Rocco and His Brothers*, Antonioni's *L'Avventura*, and Fellini's *La Dolce Vita* provided extraordinary proof that Italian art cinema during this period had reached unprecedented commercial and critical heights. Coupled with the critical and box-office successes of such dramatic films as Rossellini's *General Della Rovere* and Vittorio De Sica's *Two Women* (*La ciociara*, 1960), or such comic films as Monicelli's *The Great War*, Italian cinema seemed poised to overtake all the rest of European national cinemas as the only true threat to Hollywood's hegemony in the important category of well-made "commercial" as opposed to "art" films (a meaningless distinction in reality, but one that was frequently made during the period). The early works by an entirely new generation of directors (Pasolini, Bertolucci, Olmi, Bellocchio, and others) promised new faces and new ideas. And the emergence of extremely profitable genre films on the horizon at this time, such as the spaghetti western or the *giallo*, all combined to make the future of Italian cinema seem not only bright but also extremely lucrative.

If it may be said that the trajectory of Visconti's career was static by the last decade before his death, Antonioni's cinema during this golden age was, with Fellini's, the most innovative of the period, winning numerous festival prizes and honors, and even making large profits in some instances. Antonioni's three great films in black and white—*L'Avventura* (*L'avventura*, 1960), *La Notte* (*La notte*, 1961), and *The Eclipse* (*L'eclisse*, 1962), which we might well term a "trilogy of alienation"—were then followed by equally innovative works in color—*Red Desert* (*Il deserto rosso*, 1964), *Blow-Up* (1966), *Zabriskie Point* (1969), and *The Passenger* (*Professione: reporter*, 1975). The last three films were shot in English, an interesting experiment with mixed results. Mention must also be made of two extremely interesting documentaries, separated by almost three decades, that harked back to *Sanitation Department*, his neorealist documentary of 1948: *China* (*Chung-Kuo Cina*, 1972) and *Michelangelo Eye to Eye* (*Lo sguardo di Michelangelo*, 2004). After less successful feature films—*The Mystery of Oberwald* (*Il mistero di Oberwald*, 1981) and *Identification of a Woman* (*Identificazione di una donna*, 1982), medical problems prevented Antonioni from pursuing the kind of active career that marked his work in the 1960s and the 1970s. Nevertheless, he filmed four short pieces, linked by a director character, as *Beyond the Clouds* (*Al di là delle nuvole*, 1995), completed with the help of the German director Wim Wenders, and attracted continued attention.

Antonioni's special genius was to stretch our understanding of the boundaries of cinematic narrative, privileging seeing and perception over storyline. Moreover, Antonioni was particularly receptive to the female sensibility, perhaps more than any other male Italian director. Nowhere is this clearer than in *L'Avventura*: Claudia (Monica Vitti); Anna, Claudia's wealthy girlfriend (Lea Massari); and Anna's lover, Sandro (Gabriele Ferzetti), take a cruise on the Mediterranean, off the coast of Sicily, during which Anna mysteriously disappears. Claudia and Sandro search for her and become lovers in the process. Outlined in this fashion, the film's plot seems rather traditional, but Antonioni's originality lies precisely in his deemphasis of the dramatic potential of film plot with its traditional problems, complications, and eventual resolutions, all developed through some notion of psychological conflict between well-defined characters. In *L'Avventura*, the crux of the story as another director might have narrated the tale—the sudden disappearance, subsequent inquest, and the mystery of what happened to Anna—is ignored, or more accurately becomes only as important as Sandro or Claudia feel they are. The storyline and the camera limit our knowledge to what these two characters know. As Antonioni put it, he felt a need to "avoid certain established and proven techniques" and was "annoyed with all this sense of order, this systematic arrangement of the material" in cinema. Breaking away from conventional narrative, here the mystery narrative first involved a destruction of convention plotting so that the story's internal rhythms, rather than logical and sequential development, would move the action: the goal of the cinema was to tie it "to the truth rather than to logic."[5]

Another aspect of Antonioni's originality is his exceptional sensitivity to the philosophical currents of the times, his ability to portray with images modern neurotic, alienated, and guilt-ridden characters whose emotional lives are sterile and who seem to be out of place in their environments. If the perfect existentialist film could be imagined, it would probably be one of the works in Antonioni's "trilogy of alienation." As the director declared in a statement distributed at the Cannes Film Festival, where *L'Avventura* was first screened, modern man lives in a world without the moral tools necessary to match his technological skills; he is incapable of authentic relationships with his environment, his fellows, or even the objects that surround him because he carries with him a fossilized value system out of step with the times.[6] As a result of this, man most often responds to this situation erotically, attempting to find in love or sex an answer to his moral dilemma, but this too proves to be a blind alley. Neither self-knowledge nor self-consciousness can make up for our outmoded values. Every emotional encounter must give rise to a new potential, a new adventure (the real meaning of Antonioni's title). Thus, his protagonists suffer from the special kind of existential boredom or *noia* Alberto Moravia described so well in his novel *La noia* (1960; the Italian title unfortunately translated as *The Empty Canvas*):

> For me, boredom is not the opposite of amusement; . . . Boredom to me consists in a kind of insufficiency, or inadequacy, or lack of reality. . . . The feeling of boredom originates for me in a sense of the absurdity of a reality which is insufficient, or anyhow unable, to convince me of its own effective existence. . . . from that very absurdity springs boredom, which when all is said and done is simply a kind of incommunicability and the incapacity to disengage oneself from it.[7]

Both Moravia and Antonioni see sexuality as a means of establishing a relationship with reality, and thus the sexual act becomes something higher, more mysterious, and more complete than love, especially if love is interpreted as the simple physicosentimental relationship between man and woman, as Moravia describes it in *Man as an End* (*L'uomo come fine*, 1964).[8] When sexuality fails as a means of communication and provides only physical relief, then, in Antonioni's words, Eros is sick.

Antonioni's genius lies not in using this theme, a commonplace in the existential literature of the postwar years, but in rendering it through starkly beautiful visual images. Ultimately, Antonioni's cinematographic

Claudia and Sandro remain without words at the conclusion to Antonioni's *L'Avventura*.
Credit: DVD

technique is his content. The visualization of subjective, often irrational states of mind by representational means—what one film historian has aptly termed "objective correlatives, visual embodiments of pervasive mood and specific psychological states"—becomes, with Antonioni, an original approach to cinematic expression.[9] A number of stylistic devices, first appearing in *L'Avventura*, characterize Antonioni's mature films. First and foremost is his absolute control of the composition of each and every shot and sequence. Every aspect of an individual shot is artfully organized for the fullest effect, just as if the director were a painter or a still photographer. Characters frequently look away from one another, or remain speechless for lengthy periods; windows, doorways, long halls, and corridors frequently frame them, as if to emphasize their separation from others and their failure to communicate. Antonioni treats both black-and-white and color films in the same manner, a painterly manner, and masses of shade or color are employed in much the same fashion as a fresco painter might use color to express weight and volume. An excellent example of the director's tight control of his shots may be found in the last few shots of *L'Avventura*. Sandro has just betrayed Claudia with Gloria Perkins (Dorothy De Poliolo), a cheap American actress whose favors he has purchased for the evening in his hotel in Taormina. Outside, Claudia and Sandro try to put their fragmented relationship back together again. First we see Claudia's hand on the back of Sandro's bench in close-up as it begins to rise and hesitates, turning into a fist; a close-up of her anguished face follows; then her hand moves to the back of Sandro's head and rests there—a white mass upon the darker mass of his hair. Antonioni then cuts to a long shot of the location—a carefully divided frame with a darker concrete wall on the right and snowy Mount Etna on the other side. As the director has declared, the shot's composition employs the couple's environment (male figure/wall/pessimism versus female protagonist/volcano/optimism) to provide a beautiful but unconventionally inconclusive ending to this problematic work. As the film ends, we know only that Sandro and Claudia have managed to communicate through a mutual sense of pity, but we are uncertain as to whether this dynamic relationship, symbolized by the frame's careful composition, will long endure.[10]

With *La Notte*, Antonioni moves from the Mediterranean island of Sicily to the northern industrial city of Milan. The characters resemble those of *L'Avventura* in their emotional poverty and upper middle-class background, and the storyline is again slim. Giovanni Pontano (Marcello Mastroianni) and his wife, Lidia (Jeanne Moreau), are no longer in love. Antonioni shows us a number of their activities during the course of a single day: they visit a dying friend in the hospital and attend a party thrown to celebrate the appearance of Giovanni's new novel; Lidia wanders by herself through Milan; later that evening they attend a nightclub and visit the estate of a rich industrialist, who offers Giovanni a job; Giovanni meets the industrialist's daughter Valentina (Monica Vitti), while Lidia is offered a ride in the rain by a man named Roberto. Both are temporarily tempted into infidelity, but neither actually commits adultery. Finally, they walk out on a golf course where Lidia reads Giovanni one of his old, passionate love letters, which he fails to recognize as his own. In a desperate effort to communicate, they make love on the grass.

After *L'Avventura*, *La Notte's* storyline seems familiar territory. Perhaps more skillfully than in the first film, the director exploits the artistic potential of duration, matching the characters' time with his film time. This matchup is most often accomplished by long tracking or panning shots

In Antonioni's *La Notte*, Giovanni and Lidia try unsuccessfully to communicate their feelings to each other. *Credit: MOMA*

following the actors after they have delivered their lines; or, in the case of Lidia's walk through Milan, an entire sequence is devoted to her random odyssey. Sound (or the lack of it) advances the analysis of character. For instance, we do not actually hear the lengthy conversation between Lidia and her would-be seducer, Roberto: the camera remains outside the car in the pouring rain and we see only the movement of lips. Antonioni's abstract and poetic use of the frame is even more pronounced than in *L'Avventura*. Characters are treated as if they are objects, captured as often by their reflection in a mirror or window as by a direct shot. They are observed in many different environments—modern homes, urban buildings, and gardens—so that it seems as if their surroundings are more important than they are. The absence of any traditional plot emphasizing dramatic conflict or character development creates an even more depressing assessment of contemporary love than does *L'Avventura*. Even as Lidia and Giovanni make love at the end of the film, this is clearly only a gesture of mutual pity (not unlike Claudia's extended hand concluding *L'Avventura*) within a marriage destroyed by the indifference of habit and an impenetrable loneliness.

In the third of these three great tone poems on alienation, *The Eclipse*, Antonioni pushes his increasingly abstract style almost to the limits of representation. Once again, plot is secondary to technique. The opening sequence, a brilliant exercise in formalism, shows the end of an affair between Vittoria (Monica Vitti) and Riccardo (Francisco Rabal); Vittoria then meets her avaricious mother (Lilla Brignone) at the Roman Stock Exchange, where she encounters a handsome stockbroker named Piero (Alain Delon) who strikes her fancy; she visits a friend who has spent time in Kenya and takes an airplane ride to Verona; she returns to the Stock Exchange, a relationship with Piero blooms, and they arrange a rendezvous they do not keep. The conclusion of the film is a cinematic tour de force, a montage of objects, people, and places at the appointed meeting site—everything except the two people supposed to meet there.

The film's opening moments present Antonioni's own view of cinema quite effectively. Vittoria is shown arranging a small abstract sculpture set on a table behind a propped-up picture frame. Antonioni then cuts to the other side of the frame, and from this new perspective the sculpture appears quite different. After this study in painterly composition that reminds us of modern abstract art, we are introduced to Vittoria and Riccardo through a skillful series of reverse-angle shots, formally framed compositions juxtaposing characters to various geometrical shapes (or to each other) as they are separated by different angles and lines. To complement this expressly modernist atmosphere, in which people and objects are interchangeable, Antonioni uses a sparse sound track on which the insistent noise of a whirling fan effectively renders the notion that their affair has died from repetitive moments of boredom. Vittoria's search for meaning—or at least some aesthetically significant arrangement—in the objects within her picture frame sets the leitmotif for the director's cinematic search for his own aesthetic organization of the starkly contemporary world his characters inhabit. The problem of human communication remains, as always for Antonioni, at the center of his work: telephones ring but remain unanswered; he photographs his characters through various barriers (doors, hallways, windows, gates, fences). On one occasion, Piero and Vittoria try unsuccessfully to kiss through a windowpane. Physical objects, most particularly various buildings, walls, or architectural components, separate characters and their gaze. One famous shot in the Stock Exchange shows Vittoria and Piero separated by a huge pillar. Not an inch of film stock is used without artistic purpose.

In *L'Avventura*, Claudia and Sandro seemed to communicate at the close of the film through a mutual sense of pity, symbolized by a touch; the end of *La Notte* showed Lidia and Giovanni attempting to rekindle a moribund passion by making love. At the close of *The Eclipse*, Antonioni is more daring. His protagonists disappear completely, and objects—other people or places and things associated with the spot in which they have previously met and at which their rendezvous was to occur—take center stage. Some of these images recall the two protagonists (for example, the water barrel into which Vittoria tossed a twig while waiting for Piero); others suggest a foreboding atmosphere (the newspapers with the headlines reading, ominously, "The Atomic Age" and "Peace Is Weak"); still others seem to symbolize an aspect of their relationship, or may be merely an intriguing composition (ants on a tree trunk, water trickling from a barrel, geometric architectural shapes, etc.). Then, in a brilliant finale, Antonioni confounds our expectations by showing us two people who look like Vittoria or Piero but who turn out to be mere look-alikes. The final shot that explains the film's title is a sudden close-up of an illuminated streetlamp with a bright halo, suggesting the eclipse of natural, physical lighting from the heavenly bodies by the artificial light of the lamp. This last shot may well be a direct quotation from a modern work of art Antonioni surely knew and admired: *The Street Light—Study of Light* (*Lampada—studio di luce*, 1909), by the futurist painter Giacomo Balla.

The enigmatic and unconventional conclusion to *The Eclipse* requires explication. This last sequence may confirm that the final meeting of Vittoria and Piero will never take place, and it may also suggest a chilling image of a completely dehumanized contemporary environment. I believe, however, that it would be a mistake to interpret Antonioni's extraordinary final sequence as a symbolic event. Piero and Vittoria are happy before their rendezvous, and there is no reason to assume that their failure to keep an appointment means anything in particular. Antonioni surely meant this sequence to remain ambiguous—a step in the direction of the poetic cinema of abstraction he often advocated. Avoiding any facile resolution of the questions the film poses, Antonioni merely invites the spectator to speculate on what the outcome of Vittoria's love affair might be.

Antonioni's Experiment in Color: *Red Desert*

Unlike Fellini, who had misgivings about moving from black-and-white to color photography, Antonioni seems to have taken immediately to the idea in *Red Desert*, perhaps his masterpiece. Its plot seems similar to those of the trilogy: Giuliana (Monica Vitti) has experienced a nervous breakdown and attempted suicide, although in the film she has left the hospital. Her husband, Ugo (Carlo Chionetti), is an electronics engineer, and she has a son, Valerio. Ugo's friend Corrado Zeller (Richard Harris) appears, and while Ugo is out of town on business, Giuliana and Corrado have a brief fling. The film ends with a view of Giuliana and Valerio taking a walk near Ugo's factory.

In *Red Desert*, Antonioni moves beyond the trilogy and now focuses on his characters' relationship to things around them, rather than on their interactions with each other. As he remarked in a conversation with Jean-Luc Godard, "it is things, objects, and materials that have weight today."[11] In the trilogy, Antonioni placed his unhappy protagonists into expressive Sicilian landscapes or modernistic Milanese and Roman buildings. Now, they move within the products of modern technology—oil refineries, radar stations, power plants—all of which possess not only recognizably contemporary geometrical shapes but specifically artificial colors and sounds as well. Yet Antonioni's point of view since his Cannes manifesto remains unchanged: modern man's technological capabilities, he feels, have far outstripped his moral values. And in contrast to the facile interpretations of *Red Desert* that would see it as Antonioni's condemnation of modern technology in the name of ecological purity and a romantic return to the past, Antonioni actually believes that Giuliana's neuroses are caused by her failure to adapt to the new world of technology, not by any dehumanizing traits of this technology. Her alienation, in short, derives from her failure to adapt to her environment:

> My intention, on the contrary . . . was to translate the beauty of this world, in which even the factories can be very beautiful. . . . The line, the curves of factories and their smokestacks, are perhaps more beautiful than a row of trees—which every eye has already seen to the point of monotony. It's a rich world—living, useful.[12]

Elsewhere, Antonioni has compared the intrinsic beauty of the computer parts in Kubrick's *2001* to the "revolting" insides of a human being: "In my films it is the men who don't function properly—not the machines."[13]

The director's surprisingly positive evaluation of modern technology finds its most complete expression in his original use of color in *Red Desert*. In fact, color emerges in the film as the protagonist, equal in importance to plot, characters, and editing. As Antonioni himself remarked to a French critic, "people often say 'write a film.' Why can't we arrive at the point of saying 'paint a film'?"[14] An obvious impression from this innovative work is its absolute modernity. Only a single scene in the film (Giuliana's fantasy of a desert island far from civilization) appears in what we have come to consider as natural color, a Kodak moment. The rest of the film presents a particularly modern form of color, the kind we associate with artificial fabrics or materials such as plastics—colors from the world of science, not the natural world, colors that only figurative artists of the past century might have had at their disposal. More important, Antonioni links his colors to character just as he linked landscape to character in *L'Avventura* or architecture to character in *The Eclipse*. In many important instances, color replaces dialogue. In what Antonioni describes as "psycho-physiology of color," the director employs color to represent Giuliana's subjective states. Subsequently, he would do something similar in *The Mystery of Oberwald*, where he used the latest videotape and laser-transfer technology, permitting him to alter colors like a painter during the very act of filming.

Several famous examples of Antonioni's "painting" stand out in *Red Desert*. When Giuliana leaves the boutique she is setting up, she sits beside a fruit vendor's cart; the fruit has been tinted a dull gray color, perhaps suggesting a monotonous sense of uncertainty on her part. Later, after making love to Corrado in his hotel room, the entire room and its objects are bathed in a pink uterine hue, expressing her physical pleasure. Not only does Antonioni change natural colors, but he also frames colored objects in a purely formalistic fashion. He invites his viewer to consider objects from the world of science primarily as art forms and only subsequently as things with utilitarian value. Close-ups of objects accomplish this goal in clever fashion. For example, before Corrado arrives at Giuliana's boutique, we see a completely filled frame that seems to be a green canvas reminiscent of many works of contemporary abstract art, but when Corrado enters the frame, we realize that this is merely a concrete wall. Perhaps the most important stylistic change in this film from the trilogy is Antonioni's rejection of great depth of focus in color photography, employing instead a diffused and often out-of-focus shot of colored objects, giving things normally possessing mundane associations the formal characteristics of objects in abstract painting. The lack of great depth of field in his backgrounds usually stands juxtaposed to the more clearly focused presence of Giuliana in the same frame, a technique present in the famous closing shot of the film. At first, we see only a hazy, diffused-focus shot dominated by a beautiful yellow color; but as the film ends, the focus sharpens to reveal a stack of yellow barrels,

In *Red Desert,* Antonioni places human figures as if they were parts of an abstract painting. *Credit: CSC*

demonstrating that even industrial debris and slag heaps have a peculiar beauty for Antonioni.

Antonioni's film represents an ecologically minded film in reverse. Giuliana's neuroses are caused by her inability to adapt to a world filled with chemicals, plastics, machines, and microwaves and not by her environment or, as Italian Marxist critics might prefer, by the capitalist economic system on display in Ravenna, the city in which the film is situated. Even her dream of a magic desert island with its clear, natural colors; wild animals; and pink sand represents a pathetic nightmare out of step with reality for Antonioni. The story Giuliana tells Valerio outside the factory at the end of the film carries the same meaning. After her son asks why industrial smoke is yellow, Giuliana explains that it is poison, and when her son remarks that it will kill the birds, Giuliana explains, "That's true, but by now the birds know this and don't fly through it any longer."[15] By this time, she has dimly comprehended that she, like the birds, must adapt herself to attain "normality."

Antonioni's English-language Films: *Blow-Up, Zabriskie Point,* and *The Passenger*

With *Blow-Up*, Antonioni turned to English-language films and new directions in cinematography. Abandoning his trademark alienated and sensitive women protagonists from his black-and-white trilogy, Antonioni now focuses upon a somewhat shallow English photographer named Thomas (David Hemmings) and sets his film in the mod London of the Beatles era rather than in Italy. He employs a new rhythm or pace in his editing, shifting from the obsessively long takes typical of the trilogy to the fast-paced editing more familiar today to audiences used to television commercials or music video. And in *Blow-Up*, his sound track assumes a greater significance than in previous works. Nevertheless, in spite of the new apparently "commercial" look of this film, it treats serious philosophical issues involving how we as an audience see and experience images.

Blow-Up makes interesting observations about the nature of the film medium itself. Thomas orders his world through his camera, controlling those around him by arranging them within his lens (not unlike Antonioni himself). In one of the film's most celebrated sequences, he practically makes love to Veruschka, a popular fashion model of the period, with his camera. But outside the glitzy and shallow world of fashion, Thomas also aspires to create realistic photographs that will expose, in typical neorealist fashion, pressing social problems and the seamy side of London's life. To conclude a book of extremely violent and disturbing images, Thomas believes he has accidentally stumbled upon a lyrical scene he describes as "very peaceful, very still"—a romantic couple in a deserted park. The irony is that Thomas has accidentally photographed a brutal murder, and his perception of the meaning of the photograph he has taken changes throughout the course of the film as the photograph is enlarged or blown-up (the source of the film's title). In *Blow-Up*, Antonioni addresses a problem as old as metaphysics itself. How do we perceive the outside world or, more specifically, in the case of modern photography (both still cameras and the movie camera), how does the camera capture what we see of reality?

Thomas discovers he has photographed the scene of a murder in Antonioni's
Blow-Up. Credit: MOMA

Antonioni is justly skeptical of the truth-value of photography:

> The camera hidden behind a keyhole is a telltale eye, which captures what it can. . . . Your task will then be to reduce, to select. . . . By making a selection, you are falsifying it [i.e., reality]. Or as some would say, you are interpreting it. . . . there is one fact that cannot be ignored, and that is that this camera, like any other, needs to be programmed.[16]

The enlargement sequence lies at the heart of Antonioni's exploration of how we see through cameras. Blowing up a photograph makes the identification of any small part of it (a gun barrel or a body) easier, but it also increases the distortion the image suffers. Thus enlargement simultaneously assists and impairs our perception of the captured object on film. During the process of blowing up his photograph, Thomas reconstructs the elements of a narrative from a moment frozen in time: we actually feel motion and energy as Antonioni's camera shifts from one enlargement to another. At first, Thomas misconstrues completely the meaning of what he has shot. Seeing only a gun barrel in the bushes but not the corpse on the ground, he thinks he has saved a man from murder; but later, as he returns to the scene of the crime—significantly enough, without his camera to back up what he thinks he has witnessed—he discovers the corpse. Even that is later removed by the murderers, who also ransack Thomas's home and steal all the evidence save one single, greatly enlarged detail of the event. Unfortunately, this detail ultimately means nothing without the context, without the other surrounding photographic information from the larger picture.

In *Blow-Up*, Antonioni moves away from the severe formalism and intellectualism of his earlier 1960s films toward a more commercial form of cinema that is both philosophically intriguing and entertaining. Whereas his earlier works avoided reliance upon plot structure, now Antonioni exploits to the hilt the suspense inherent in the classic detective thriller, replacing the detective with the inquiring photographer, Thomas. Bill, one of Thomas's friends, suggests Antonioni's move to the thriller genre when he describes his own abstract art without any obvious meaning as puzzling until the spectator finds a clue in a detail. Then, he says, "it adds up. It's like finding a clue in a detective story."[17]

Blow-Up's great impact at the box office enabled Antonioni to obtain foreign financing for two other English-language films: *Zabriskie Point* and *The Passenger*. The first of these was attacked mercilessly by reviewers and critics as a naive and simpleminded work about political unrest and revolution in America during the Vietnam era—a surprising theme for Antonioni to tackle, particularly in a country that was foreign to his experience. MGM, the major American studio that put up the cash for the production, took the rushes out of Antonioni's hands for a time and eventually forced him to edit a different film than he might have intended to make. For his protagonists,

Antonioni selected two nonprofessionals to play themselves—an anthropology student from Berkeley named Daria Halprin and a dropout named Mark Frechette. Judging from their biographies, they were perfect specimens of radical students of the period.[18] Daria works for Lee Allen (Rod Taylor), a Los Angeles real-estate developer about to begin construction on Sunnydunes, a village in the southwestern desert. Daria encounters Mark, who is on the lam from the police, accused of killing a policeman during a student riot (he is not guilty of this crime) and of stealing a plane with which he has flown into the desert. The two make love in the sand at Zabriskie Point, the lowest point in Death Valley, but Mark dies when he returns the plane to the airport. The film concludes as Daria imagines the destruction of Lee Allen's desert mansion and drives on toward Phoenix.

Antonioni exhibits a certain distaste for American consumer society, and like most leftist Italian directors of the period, his sympathies are with the revolution (whatever that might mean in Vietnam-era America), the Black Panthers, and rebellious students in general. Antonioni's Panavision shots of American streets reveal giant-sized models of human beings employed for advertising; the publicity film for Sunnydunes Enterprises uses dehumanized, plastic figures in an unnatural and artificially constructed desert, all of which is ironically juxtaposed to a sound track praising such western myths as "rugged individualism." Every visual in Antonioni's America seems out of sync and out of normal proportion: establishment figures (policemen, businessmen) are impersonal and interchangeable; the average middle-aged Americans are ugly and offensive, particularly tourists dressed in ridiculous Bermuda shorts; even Daria's visit to an old western town reveals only senile, superannuated cowboys sipping their beer and a commune of mentally disturbed children. Unfortunately, since both of Antonioni's protagonists are wooden actors, it is difficult to find much to like about them either, and the resulting commercial fiasco of *Zabriskie Point* after the huge success of *Blow-Up* can be compared only to the experience of Lina Wertmüller's fall from grace after the international success of *Seven Beauties.*

Nevertheless, two sequences in the film are remarkable, each of them presenting a vision of sexuality and violence in America. In the love scene in Death Valley, Daria's fantasies are visualized on the screen—a number of couples joyfully roll around in the dust in a hymn to the liberation of the senses, something that seems normal in a pre-AIDS world. Later, after hearing that her lover Mark has been killed by the police, Daria stares at Allen's mansion (a beautiful Frank Lloyd Wright–type building in the middle of the desert), and Antonioni provides us with a privileged view into her thoughts. Initially, she is enraged over Mark's death, and we see a spectacular series of slow-motion explosions destroying the mansion and everything in it, shot by the director with seventeen different cameras in various positions. Then Antonioni replaces these images of violence with cooler images dominated by an icy sky-blue color. Slow-motion explosions of various objects (bookshelves, television sets, refrigerators) yield to a marvelously entertaining series of free-floating objects in a sea of blue—a lobster, Wonder Bread, Special K cereal, flowers, and many other objects associated with American consumer society. Released by Daria's imagination and photographed aesthetically, they may now be perceived as aesthetic objects. As we have come to expect from Antonioni's work, the sequence involves enormously complicated technology; the cool-explosion sequence employed cameras capable of producing three thousand images per second. In its pure imagistic power, the conclusion of *Zabriskie Point* recalls the ending of *The Eclipse*, where objects take over the narration and replace characters. Antonioni's first look at America represents a flawed but interesting attempt to combine a political message—one shared by many other directors associated with the Italian political film genre and a theme atypical of Antonioni's other films—with an intense interest in expanding the technical frontiers of cinematography.

Despite the commercial fiasco surrounding *Zabriskie Point*, Antonioni managed to obtain the services of the Hollywood star Jack Nicholson in *The Passenger*, a far better work of art. Not only is this film shot in English, but it returns to *Blow-Up*'s more commercial approach to filmmaking with another suspense-story plot. Nicholson plays David Locke, a television journalist making a film about a guerilla movement in Africa, who meets a gunrunner named David Robertson (Charles Mulvehill), who sells arms to the rebels. When Robertson dies in his hotel room of a heart attack, Locke changes passports and assumes the dead man's identity. Locke's wife, Rachel (Jenny Runacre), searches for him in Africa, and she produces a television homage to his work, utilizing scraps of the documentary footage Locke has shot in Africa. Meanwhile Locke meets a girl (Maria Schneider) and uses her to dodge the investigations of his wife and producer. Unfortunately, Locke does not realize that secret agents of the government against whom the rebels are using his arms have trailed Robertson, and he is assassinated in his hotel room in Robertson's stead.

Antonioni uses *The Passenger* to inquire into the nature of documentary, and places this investigation into the context of a suspense thriller. Locke's confused identity parallels the journalist's confused attempts to reach "objective truth" in his documentary film. Of the three different kinds of documentary footage Antonioni presents in *The Passenger*, the first is an interview with an African political leader, full of lies and government propaganda; the second and most disturbing is actual footage of an execution in Africa, shown first as it actually occurs and then on a television studio monitor, juxtaposing what we first perceive as "real" with what becomes "objective" reporting; the third presents a well-spoken African witch doctor who, during Locke's interview, turns the camera around to face Locke, underlining the fact that Locke's question for information reveals more about him than about Africa.

Antonioni's customary demonstration of cinematic bravura is not missing in *The Passenger*. In a virtuoso seven-minute sequence without cuts, Antonioni's camera begins inside Locke's hotel room after his assassination, then travels outside through the barred windows, attached first to the room's ceiling, then guided by a connection to a huge crane more than one hundred feet high; the camera continues to circle about the square outside, finally peering back into the room where Locke's dead body still lies. Antonioni accomplished this beautiful ending by using a Canadian camera controlled by gyroscopes to neutralize the transition from the track inside the room to the crane shot outside. The result is a stunningly beautiful evocation of the mysterious connections between human reality and the more problematic "reality" the camera seems capable of capturing.

Antonioni's *Identification of a Woman* and Two Documentaries (on China and Michelangelo)

Antonioni never completely abandoned the interest in documentary or film realism that characterized the beginning of his career during the neorealist period. *Identification of a Woman*, which marked Antonioni's return to filming an Italian environment after many years of working abroad, continues his interest in the same crisis of values in a rapidly changing world that had been an integral feature of his masterpieces of the late 1950s and early 1960s. It traces the attempts of a film director named Niccolò (Tomas Milian) to understand his relationship with two successive mistresses: Mavi (Daniela Silverio), a rich, spoiled aristocrat; and Ida (Christine Boisson), a stage actress. Antonioni's masterful photography of environments and objects remains his characteristic signature here, but his perspective has radically changed. Now, rather than analyzing male behavior through the eyes of a female protagonist, Antonioni prefers to depict the point of view of a male director who attempts, without success, to "identify" and to understand the women in his life. For the male psyche, women present a perplexing and unfathomable mystery.

Two documentaries—one made in the 1970s, the other shortly before his death—require some attention. Antonioni made *China* after being invited by the Chinese government to make a documentary on the "new man" the regime was producing. It was intended for television and sparked a violently negative reaction from the Chinese Communist government, apparently because Antonioni's view of their "new man" was far too revealing. In *Michelangelo Eye to Eye*, made some thirty years later when a disabled

Antonioni was almost ninety years old, the director spends almost twenty minutes with Michelangelo's powerful statue of Moses in the Basilica di San Pietro in Vincoli (Saint Peter in Chains) in Rome. He visits the church digitally, since he had been more or less confined to a wheelchair since a stroke in 1985. The Oscar given to Antonioni in 1995 for a lifetime of contributions to the cinema justly honored the innovative films he had made from the 1950s through the 1970s.

Vittorio De Sica and Box-Office Success

Of the great auteurs treated in this chapter, all of whom began their careers during the neorealist era, Vittorio De Sica had the highest critical reputation prior to the 1950s. Even before the creation of the Oscar for Best Foreign Language Film, De Sica had been honored in this category by special awards for *Shoeshine* and *The Bicycle Thief*, and the latter film won several rankings as one of the best ten films made during the immediate postwar period. Nonetheless, critics lost interest in his work subsequent to the neorealist period. De Sica reached commercial success in the 1960s with two box-office hits enjoyed abroad—*Yesterday, Today and Tomorrow* (*Ieri, oggi, domani*, 1963), a tremendous success internationally that starred Sophia Loren and Marcello Mastroianni in comic roles and won the 1965 Oscar for Best Foreign Language Film, and its sequel, *Marriage Italian Style* (*Matrimonio all'italiana*, 1964), also starring Loren and Mastroianni and also nominated (unsuccessfully) by the Academy in that category. That very success translated into critical disdain among many of Italy's professional critics, despite De Sica's winning a David di Donatello Award for directing *Matrimonio*. Nonetheless, two more serious films of his from the golden age not only made money but also were recognized by Silver Ribbons from the Italian National Syndicate of Film Journalists and by the Academy Awards—*Two Women* and *The Garden of the Finzi-Continis* (*Il giardino dei Finzi Contini*, 1970). *A Brief Vacation* (*Una breve vacanza*, 1973), an unpretentious but moving work demonstrating that the old master had lost none of his touch, appeared one year before his death and earned the director another David di Donatello Award.

Two Women returns the former neorealist De Sica and his neorealist scriptwriter Cesare Zavattini to the period of World War II. It tells the story of Cesira (Sophia Loren) and her daughter, Rosetta (Eleonora Brown), who flee Rome during the Nazi occupation and take refuge in the mountains of Ciociaria between Rome and Naples. There Cesira meets a young Marxist intellectual named Michele (Jean-Paul Belmondo) who helps her to understand the political and moral issues associated with the war. An adaptation of a 1957 novel by Alberto Moravia, *Two Women* ends tragically: Michele dies at the hands of the retreating German army, and the two women are brutally gang-raped by a group of Moroccan soldiers fighting for the Allies. Cesira is generally considered Sophia Loren's greatest dramatic performance (with the possible exception of her work in Scola's *A Special Day*), and it won her the Oscar for Best Actress in a Leading Role in 1962, the second such award for an Italian star. (The first had gone to Anna Magnani in *The Rose Tattoo* in 1956, but that had been a Hollywood film, not an Italian production.)

The Garden of the Finzi-Continis, like a number of films made during the 1970s in Italy, treats the Holocaust from the Italian perspective. De Sica adapted the script based on a novel of the same title by Giorgio Bassani (1916–2000). Bassani had created a highly critical portrait of an aristocratic Jewish family from Ferrara (Bassani's hometown), whose aloofness from the more commonly born Jews in the city does not save them from destruction. De Sica's film captures perfectly the elegiac nostalgia of Bassani's portrait of the Edenic garden of the family, where the novel's middle-class Jewish narrator, Giorgio (Lino Capolicchio), would retire from the cares and threats of the everyday world. And it is in this garden, an idyllic pastoral oasis, where the narrator comes of age emotionally and sexually in his ill-fated infatuation with the enigmatically beautiful Micòl Finzi-Contini (Dominique Sanda). Unlike the grainy neorealist classics, De Sica's adaptation employs a deeply romantic diffused focus.

In *A Brief Vacation*, De Sica seems to return to his neorealist roots with a starkly simple storyline written by Zavattini that provides a memorable treatment of the Italian working class. Clara Mataro (Florinda Bolkan), a Calabrian housewife and now a Milanese factory worker, contracts

In De Sica's *The Garden of the Finzi-Continis*, Micòl (comforting an older woman) is deported to a Nazi concentration camp, never to be seen again. *Credit: MOMA*

tuberculosis and goes to recuperate in a convalescent hospital in the Italian Alps (her ironically named "brief vacation"). There, she encounters entirely new experiences, including members of the upper class, and falls in love with Luigi (Daniel Quenaud). Her married life has been miserable, but ironically her time spent in the hospital is a liberating experience. In De Sica's scenes of Milan, the romantic, soft-focus shots of *The Garden of the Finzi-Continis* shift to the gritty, industrial colors of northern Italy, reminiscent of Antonioni's *Red Desert*. Clara's brief vacation ends with her return to her boorish husband (Renato Salvatori), but now her plight seems even more miserable, since her eyes have been opened to the myriad possibilities that are closed to her. *A Brief Vacation* is a small jewel of a film, a reminder that the playboy and gambler De Sica, who had no particular political ideology (and certainly no leftist sympathies), could make films that said more about social class in Italy than all of the more politically engaged directors of his generation.

Fellini, the Director as Superstar: *La Dolce Vita*

The dominant figure of the golden age of Italian cinema is clearly Federico Fellini. His career during the 1960s and 1970s was marked by a very complicated stylistic and thematic evolution beyond neorealism that began with the international blockbuster *La Dolce Vita* and continued with his masterpiece *8½*. Inspired by psychoanalysis, Fellini's interest in incorporating dreams into his cinematic narratives influences the bulk of his later works, including *Juliet of the Spirits, Fellini Satyricon, The Clowns* (*I Clowns*, 1970), *Fellini's Roma* (*Roma*, 1972), *Amarcord*, and *Fellini's Casanova* (*Il Casanova di Federico Fellini*, 1976). His later works until his death include *Orchestra Rehearsal* (*Prova d'orchestra*, 1979); *City of Women* (*La città delle donne*, 1980); *And the Ship Sails On* (*E la nave va*, 1983); *Ginger and Fred* (*Ginger e Fred*, 1985); *Interview* (*Intervista*, 1987); and his final feature film, *The Voice of the Moon*. Fellini also made a number of brilliant television commercials—one for Campari liquor, another for Barilla pasta, and three for the Bank of Rome. In addition, he made a number of imaginary commercials in *Ginger and Fred*. Although he hated the commercial interruptions of feature films on Italian television, his commercials offer splendid examples of his cinematography and embodied his infectious sense of humor.[19] During the course of his late career, Fellini moved from autobiographical themes to political ones, and from subjective visions of the world informed by his dream life to metacinematic considerations of cinema itself. No other Italian director ever dominated the industry so completely as Fellini did during the 1960s and the 1970s; but his persistent (and often brilliant) search for a dreamlike cinema met the opposition of a new kind of popular audience, one addicted to action films, and Fellini's box-office returns thus diminished

Federico Fellini–the director as superstar–behind his beloved Mitchell camera at the height of his success during the 1960s. *Credit: MOMA*

after the international success of *Amarcord*—though his critical importance continued to grow after his premature death, in 1993.

After the international notoriety of *La Strada* and *The Nights of Cabiria*—two works from the "trilogy of grace or salvation" that won Oscars for Best Foreign Language Film, not to mention numerous other international awards—Federico Fellini's international reputation as one of Europe's most brilliant young superstar directors who could also deliver at the box office was firmly established. In the uproar and moralistic protest that greeted the first screenings of *La Dolce Vita* in Italy, however, the political or cultural affiliations of those who either attacked or defended Fellini changed entirely. Before *La Dolce Vita*, Italian Catholics and French existentialist film critics had been Fellini's champions, while Italian Marxists attacked him. With *La Dolce Vita*, Fellini became the target of outraged moralists from the Right as well as from the Catholic Church, who regarded the work as pornographic and insulting to the best Italian traditions, while the Marxist Left defended Fellini for what it regarded as a courageous dissection of bourgeois decadence and moral corruption. Furthermore, whereas the conflict over the earlier *La Strada* had largely been restricted to film buffs and critics, *La Dolce Vita* became a cause célèbre that had an enormous impact upon Italian popular culture and was a major topic in the national press for some time.

La Dolce Vita represents more than just a significant step in the evolution of Fellini's cinematic style. Like such films in America as *Gone with the Wind, Casablanca*, or *The Godfather*, *La Dolce Vita* transcended its meaning as a work of art and came to be regarded as a landmark pointing to important changes in Italian and European society. In 1960, it received the Golden Palm at the Cannes Film Festival, given unanimously by a jury that included the French mystery writer Georges Simenon and the American novelist Henry Miller. Its commercial success represented the triumph of the serious art film at the box office, and although it was a relatively expensive film to produce (600 million lire), it grossed over 2.2 billion lire in only a few years, at a time when tickets in Italy cost only 500–1,000 lire. For more than two decades, it held the European record for highest box-office grosses. Its importance can be defined as the junction of the blockbuster and the European art film, and its success helped to define a cinema of authorship that would influence even the manner in which Hollywood produced films.

Enormous social and economic changes in Italy paved the way for the film's reception. As the film was being prepared in 1958 and shot in 1959, Italy was in the midst of what would eventually be called the "economic miracle." Italy leaped from being almost an underdeveloped country into an age of rapid and unparalleled economic growth fueled by massive increases in exports of such popular products as Vespa motor scooters, Fiat automobiles, Necchi sewing machines, Olivetti typewriters, and home appliances. The rapid rise in the country's standard of living took place as vast numbers of southern Italians migrated from the impoverished areas in the Italian Mezzogiorno to the industrial zones of the North, as well as to other European countries, especially Switzerland and Germany. One of the immediate results of this new social mobility was an almost instantaneous drop of interest in religious sentiment in Italy. Thus while many conservative opponents of *La Dolce Vita* called for censorship of the film, believing it was an attack upon Italian culture in general, others even suggested that Fellini be arrested for "outrage or derision of the Catholic religion" (technically a crime listed in the Penal Code at the time). Meanwhile, supporters of the film on the Left saw the decadent lifestyle portrayed in the film (the "sweet life" of the title) as an accurate assessment of upper-middle-class and aristocratic corruption even though nothing could be further from Fellini's mind than a Marxist denunciation of class conflict.

Production on *La Dolce Vita* began on March 16, 1959. The first scene was the ascent of Sylvia (Anita Ekberg) to the top of Saint Peter's dome on a circular staircase, which was reconstructed in Cinecittà's Theater 14. Immediately following this, from April 1 to April 3, was Sylvia's famous bath in the Trevi Fountain (referenced by Scola's *We All Loved Each Other So Much*; see chapter 7); this was shot at the actual fountain, not a studio reconstruction. Thus Fellini and his brilliant set designer, Piero Gherardi, who would deservedly win an Oscar for his costume design and also be nominated (unsuccessfully) for his set design, alternated real locations (a heritage of Italian neorealism, a decisive moment in Italian film history to which Fellini had made major contributions as a scriptwriter) with stupendous studio creations. Like the staircase in Saint Peter's, the famous Via Veneto too was rebuilt, in Cinecittà's Teatro (Theater) 5—since renamed the Teatro Fellini because the director's work was so closely identified with it. The viewer may not notice, but the street in the film is completely flat, whereas Via Veneto actually runs up a relatively steep hill. Other sets that were real include the castle outside Rome where the world-weary aristocrats gather, a genuine palace in Bassano di Sutri belonging to the Odescalchi, one of Rome's oldest noble families. Shooting was wrapped on August 27, 1959, and the film premiered in Rome on February 3, 1960, opening in Milan two days later.

Guaranteeing its role as a symbol of the times, La Dolce Vita also reflected other events related to changes in mores and popular culture. Rome had come to be the focus of international cinema, even for Hollywood, after American studios set up shop in Italy (known as "Hollywood on the Tiber"; see chapter 6) to take advantage of good weather, cheap labor, and capital derived from their Italian profits, which they were prohibited from exporting back home to California. The kind of gossip column and tabloid reporting associated with the worst kind of celebrity journalist grew into a cottage industry in Rome with its center on the Via Veneto, where American and European actresses and actors came to see and to be seen. Fellini's La Dolce Vita captured the spirit of this tabloid sensationalism. Tabloid photography became one of the most popular means of chronicling this kind of Roman movie-star personality cult, and the age gave birth to the now-familiar phenomenon known as the paparazzi. The name of one of the photographers in this film, Walter Paparazzo, is actually the origin of the word. In fact, a number of the famous sequences in the film were based on actual events, published in the tabloid press of 1958 with photographs by the prototypical paparazzo Tazio Secchiaroli (of a striptease dance in a Roman restaurant) and Pierluigi Praturlon (of Ekberg's real-life wade into the Trevi Fountain in the heat of August). Thus, along with many scenes created by his own vivid imagination, or written by the gifted scriptwriters Ennio Flaiano, Tullio Pinelli, and Brunello Rondi and superbly set to music by Nino Rota, Fellini lifted these tabloid moments from the scandal magazines and immortalized them in a brilliant work of art. (In 1962, the world of Via Veneto as reported by the paparazzi and the tabloids would reach the heights of notoriety with the shockingly public love affair between Elizabeth Taylor and Richard Burton during the Roman production of Cleopatra.)

The production of La Dolce Vita was so complex and involved such an investment of resources that it must be defined as an "art film colossal." At 175 minutes in length, the film boasts over eighty different locations and a cast of hundreds. The Italian script lists four full pages of actors playing more than 120 different speaking parts, with an original screenplay divided into 104 separate scenes. La Dolce Vita avoids traditional dramatic plotting, relying instead on the power of visual images to draw the spectator's attention along a vast journey through what might well be described as a modern-day version of Dante's *Divine Comedy*, where Marcello Rubini (a journalist with serious literary ambitions, played brilliantly by Marcello Mastroianni) wanders through a Roman urban landscape and has a number of adventures. Thus, the overall structure of *La Dolce Vita*, like *La Strada*, may be said to be a picaresque adventure, where the journey has been transferred from the provincial towns and villages of Italy to the salons, cafés, and hotels of the glitterati of Italy's capital city during the height of the economic boom.

Fellini selected Anita Ekberg (Miss Sweden of 1951) for the role of Sylvia in *La Dolce Vita* not because of her acting talents, which she certainly had not displayed previously, but for her particular personification of the Nordic beauty that Italians usually identified with actresses from Hollywood, where she had spent five years in the business. Her "talent," as Fellini had her admit in the film's press conference, was her bust. She was the ultimate expression of what Italians called the *maggiorata* ("sweater girl," or buxom woman; see chapter 4) that was the rage in the cinema during the period and that produced such stars as Sophia Loren, Sylva Koscina, Gina Lollobrigida, and Silvana Mangano. As noted above, Ekberg had already waded into the Trevi Fountain and been photographed by Pierluigi Praturlon, who had sold the images for a substantial sum of money. Yet, Fellini's version of the event—shot in the icy waters of a January night, as opposed to the original hot August one—was not a simple case of art imitating life. Set within a complex series of images and visual ideas in a masterpiece, this banal, tabloid "photo opportunity" was transformed by the power of Fellini's fantasy into a symbol for feminine purity and innocence juxtaposed

Perhaps the most famous scene in postwar European cinema—Marcello and Sylvia wade into the Trevi Fountain in Fellini's *La Dolce Vita. Credit: MOMA*

against a world of corruption and decadence, which has quite rightly been called the symbolic image of postwar cinema—just what the "Odessa Steps" sequence in *The Battleship Potemkin* was to silent films. Thus Sylvia, *La Dolce Vita*'s blond bombshell and the ultimate symbol of sex appeal in the *maggiorate* style of the late 1950s, is paradoxically memorable as an image of innocence and purity—as is Paola (Valeria Ciangottini), the little Umbrian angel whose smile concludes the film.

Fellini creates his fantasy world *without* rigorous moralistic judgments. He presents his Roman metaphor for the contemporary world of image making, public relations, movie stardom, and the glamorous lifestyles of the "rich and famous" with bemused detachment, and most certainly as if the director were an accomplice, not a judge. Since Fellini is ultimately a great *comic* genius, and comedy is always an art of acceptance, even when he seems to denounce a condition or a character for some presumed moral failing, Fellini inevitably, before the "trial" ends, becomes a witness for the defense. This dual perspective informs his portrait of Marcello Rubini in *La Dolce Vita*. What redeems the sublunary, graceless world of Via Veneto in Fellini's film is poetry: vibrant images that unexpectedly are so full of life that they overwhelm any sense of futility, corruption, and despair.

After the international success of the film, Fellini was convinced that cinema should abandon traditional storylines and attempt something closer to poetry with meter and cadence. When he adopted a modernist approach to film plot with *La Dolce Vita*, Fellini himself compared it to Picasso's cubist revolution that had transformed modern art from representational to abstract artistic expression:

> So I said: let's invent episodes, let's not worry for now about the logic or the narrative. We have to make a statue, break it, and recompose the pieces. Or better yet, try decomposition in the manner of Picasso. The cinema is narrative in the nineteenth-century sense: now let's try to do something different.[20]

La Strada had moved beyond a traditional notion of the realistic representation of reality with a realistic protagonist, and image would henceforth be more important than storyline—the reversal of the traditional Hollywood reliance upon a well-made plot. *La Dolce Vita* continued Fellini's search for a new and contemporary twentieth-century means of cinematic expression, a poetic cinema on the Picassoesque model. It was a bold venture but one that made cinematic history. Rather than use conventional cinematic narrative, which aims at telling a story with a beginning, a middle, and an end, Fellini wanted to construct a film around numerous sequences, each dominated by key images, much as one might construct a poem. Such key images would provide objective correlatives, in good modernist fashion, for a number of themes, ideas, and notions that interested the director.

Fellini had reportedly considered calling the film *2000 Years after Jesus Christ*, or perhaps *Babylon 2000*. Whether these apocryphal titles were ever actually considered, they point to the fact that Fellini wished to show in *La Dolce Vita* a contemporary world cut adrift from traditional values and symbols, especially those of Christianity, and bereft of any dominant cultural center. Fellini's Rome is a world of public relations, press conferences, paparazzi, empty religious rites, meaningless intellectual debates, and unrewarding love affairs. Yet Fellini does not simply denounce the decadence and corruption he sees before him: he is actually much more interested in the potential for rebirth that such a situation offers the artist. As he once stated:

> I feel that decadence is indispensable to rebirth. . . . So I am happy to be living at a time when everything is capsizing. It's a marvelous time, for the very reason that a whole series of ideologies, concepts and conventions is being wrecked. . . . I don't see it as a sign of the death of civilization but, on the contrary, as a sign of life.[21]

The real energy in *La Dolce Vita* resides not in the jaded Marcello, nor in the beautiful but shallow Sylvia, but in the director's camera, as Fellini transforms this fresco of decadence into a vibrant portrait that intrigues viewers without necessarily drawing them into the world that passes quickly before them. He accomplishes this miracle in a number of ways. In the first place, every sequence of *La Dolce Vita* is teeming with characters. Almost every character has an unusual or interesting face, a testament to the hours that Fellini spent in the preparation of each of his films, examining folder after folder of still photographs of actors and amateurs whose physical appearance struck him for some particular reason. The Fellini cast represents a cross section of humanity that could be found in no other director's work. The director skillfully choreographs these sometimes grotesque figures, and their movements are constantly captured by masterful photography, alternating long tracking shots and traveling shots. In order to avoid distortions of the characters' background during the rapid motion of the camera in such tracking or traveling shots, Fellini instructed his director of photography, Otello Martelli, to use 75- 100- or 150mm lenses instead of the normal 50mm lens that most directors used at the time for widescreen photography. Martelli objected, but as he noted years later, Fellini's intuition was a stroke of genius, for the particular visual style it invented for *La Dolce Vita* resulted in the highlighting of figures inside a frescolike framework with only a slight distortion of their surroundings.[22] Adding to the visual appeal of each sequence were the stupendous sets designed by Piero Gherardi. As Gherardi has testified, he and Fellini would go through a ritual that was repeated throughout the production of *La Dolce Vita*. They would first attempt to find an authentic location in Rome or on its outskirts for a scene, but this search would always end in Fellini's rejection of "reality" for an artificially re-created location in the studios.[23] This rejection of specific locations occurred not only in the famous reconstruction of Via Veneto but also with the Baths of Caracalla and the aforementioned stairs of Saint Peter's. When Fellini did employ authentic locations—the Trevi Fountain, for example, or the ancient castle in Bassano di Sutri—it could be argued that these were already sufficiently "Fellinian" to need no touch of the master's fantasy.

Certainly, the world he presented in *La Dolce Vita* is a world without God. Yet Fellini's last word is not delivered by the image of the monster fish, (a traditional symbol for Christianity, once vital but now as dead as the animal itself), or the image of the jaded Marcello, (a lost soul in a Dantesque inferno of false values and spent illusions), *La Dolce Vita* ends on the close-up of Paola's beautiful smile, an image of purity and innocence that is juxtaposed (but not necessarily triumphantly) against the corruption that has preceded it. Like *La Strada*, *La Dolce Vita* ends on a poetic note of ambiguity. We leave the theater with an impression of utter hopelessness from the vast kaleidoscope of fallen humanity we have encountered during the film. Yet, the images we have seen embody such an outsized love and zest for life, with which each and every frame has been imbued by the film's creator, that we do not completely abandon all hope.

Fellini and Dreams: *8½* and *Juliet of the Spirits*

Federico Fellini's *8½* is his benchmark film, the work that confirms his status as a master and had a profound influence upon other filmmakers all over the world, including Martin Scorsese, Woody Allen, François Truffaut, Lina Wertmüller, Giuseppe Tornatore, Peter Greenaway, Terry Gilliam, Joel Schumacher, Bob Fosse, Paul Mazursky, and Spike Jonze.[24] Besides a host of awards, including an Oscar for Best Foreign Language Film in 1964, a group of thirty European intellectuals and filmmakers voted *8½* the most important European film ever made, and on the basis of this work also named Fellini as the European cinema's most important director.[25] The film occupies an important role in the director's complete works, not only because of its obvious autobiographical links to Fellini's own life but also because it focuses upon the very nature of artistic creation in the cinema.

Fellini's *8½* explores a personal fantasy world that deals self-reflexively with cinema itself. Created by one of the greatest directors of photography of the period (Gianni Di Venanzo), the black-and-white photography in *8½* is an expressionistic black and white that manages even without color to capture the essence of the irrational quality of the dream state. The protagonist, a film director named Guido Anselmi (Marcello Mastroianni), has obvious affinities to Fellini himself. The film's narrative focuses upon the extremely complex fantasy life of a film director who is in the midst of a cri-sis of inspiration and creativity, not unlike one Fellini himself experienced at the beginning of work on the film. Fellini has described the gestation of *8½* as a series of false starts, culminating in his writing of a letter to his producer to call off the entire project even while actors had been selected and crew members were constructing the sets. At that precise moment, one of the crew invited Fellini to share a bottle of champagne to celebrate the creation of what he predicted will become a "masterpiece." Embarrassed by his insecurity and the responsibility of putting all the men working in the studio out of a job, Fellini thought of himself as a ship's captain abandoning his crew. Suddenly, the inspiration for the film's subject came to him in a flash: the film would focus upon a director who no longer knows what film he is making.

Like *La Dolce Vita*, *8½* may accurately be described as an "art film colos-sal." It contains approximately forty major episodes, numerous sequences, and more than fifty-three major characters, not counting the many, many minor figures, including the entire crew shooting the film that appears in the film's celebrated ending. Shot almost entirely inside a studio on huge and imaginative set constructions, *8½* combines innumerable particular epi-sodes with a marvelously strict control of the overall narrative. Everything in the work avoids the traditional seamless storyline of the classic Hollywood film. The mass of visual images Fellini creates is held together in an almost miraculous state of grace by the use of dream and fantasy sequences. The result is one of the most convincing stream-of-consciousness narratives ever created, a storyline controlled by the subjective perspective of its director-protagonist that jumps quickly from the "real" world of a spa, where Guido has gone to take the cure for a failing inspiration, to his dreams, to waking fantasies, and to memories of his past all the way back to his childhood, an infancy characterized by a strict Catholic upbringing and a repression of sexual desire. It is most certainly not a film based upon improvisation. Only an ironclad script, as the scriptwriter Tullio Pinelli once described it, could have brought such magnificent artistic order out of such a chaotic mix of diverse materials.

The picture Guido seems unable to make is a science-fiction film about the launching of a rocket ship from Earth after a thermonuclear holocaust destroys civilization. A huge launchpad that seems to have no purpose pro-vides a concrete metaphor of Guido's creative impasse. During the many encounters at a spa resort Guido has with his producer, his potential actors, and his production staff, he also finds time for a tryst with his mistress, Carla (Sandro Milo), a marital crisis with his estranged wife (Anouk Aimée), and a number of embarrassing exchanges with a French intellectual named Daumier (Jean Rougeul)—intended as an Italian, Carini, in the shooting script—who mercilessly attacks Guido for his artistic confusion, his puerile

In Fellini's *8½*, the film director Guido summarizes the meaning of his life and of art in general in the famous circular procession where all the characters from his life and his art intermingle. *Credit: MOMA*

symbolism, his ideological incoherence, and the lack of any intellectual structure in the film Guido has proposed to make.

In *8½*, Fellini makes no pronouncements, presents no theories about art, and avoids the heavy intellectualizing about the nature of the cinema that characterizes so much academic discussion in recent years. As Fellini stated in an interview given in 1963, *8½* is "extremely simple: it puts forth nothing that needs to be understood or interpreted."[26] In light of the tremendous amount of critical exegesis on this work, Fellini's statement is extraordinary, but he means something rather straightforward. For Fellini, the cinema is primarily a visual medium whose emotive power moves through light, not words. The unforgettable circular dance that concludes *8½* is the perfect modernist image for Fellini's major preoccupation: free artistic creativity. If the audience is open to such poetic moments, no theoretical preparation is required to appreciate such a scene. Fellini wants his audience to experience an image designed to produce an emotion, not to analyze an idea designed to make an intellectual argument.

Between *La Dolce Vita* and the making of *8½*, Fellini encountered Jungian psychoanalysis and began seeing a Jungian analyst named Ernst Bernhard (1896–1965), an experience that he described as "like the sight of unknown landscapes, like the discovery of a new way of looking at life."[27] With Bernhard's encouragement, Fellini began to record his extremely active dream life, compiling large notebooks with colorful sketches made with felt-tip markers that would become the inspiration for the works shot over the rest of his life.[28] Fellini's encounter with psychoanalysis, his dream notebook, and his own predilection for a cinema of poetic inspiration all conspired together in *8½* to produce a masterpiece about artistic creativity. The domain of the dream, the irrational, is for Fellini the ultimate source of artistic inspiration and creation. In *8½*, Fellini shows (not argues) that art has its own imperatives and that it communicates a very real kind of special knowledge, aesthetically and therefore emotionally rather than logically, and that this form of knowledge has its proper and rightful place in human culture. As Fellini—who often called himself an "honest liar"—once declared, "nothing is more honest than a dream."[29] It would be an oneiric universe that concerned Fellini for the rest of his career, as *8½* bade farewell once and for all to the privileging of external reality characteristic of his neorealist origins.

Juliet of the Spirits is Fellini's first feature film in color, and this move to color also provided the director with the opportunity to test his new interest in his dream life on the silver screen. Whereas in *8½* Fellini focused on the dream visions of a creative artist like himself, in *Juliet* he cast his wife, Giulietta Masina, as a demure housewife with an unfaithful husband named Giorgio (Mario Pisu), and the film recounts her discovery of her husband's infidelities, her confused attempts to deal with her own sexuality, and her eventual emancipation and maturity. Fellini's film probably mirrors his own marriage to Masina, and it is a remarkably honest and unflattering portrait of the husband. It may well be one of the first "feminist" films shot in Italy, because it argues for women to take up what Fellini calls the woman's struggle "against certain monsters in herself, which are certain psychic components in her deformed by educational taboos, moral conventions, false idealisms. . . ."[30] *Juliet* continues *8½*'s view that childhood memories and traumatic experiences shape adult life and must be confronted to be overcome. The past is not merely a source of psychological neurosis; it is also a potential source of freedom and liberation. The healthy individual, as Guido becomes by the finale of *8½*, can be redeemed by acceptance, but *Juliet* demonstrates just how much more difficult this kind of personal liberation is for an ordinary Italian housewife in the 1960s.

Juliet's unhappy marriage appears in the very opening scene of the film. Her home resembles a doll's house, and her costume reminds us of a coolie's outfit—drab and unexciting—whereas the other female characters, particularly her sensual mother and sister, display outlandish and fashionable clothes, thus setting her apart. The picture of a desperate housewife is completed when Giorgio forgets her wedding anniversary. Juliet's life is assaulted by outside forces, her "spirits." Dreaming on the beach, Juliet experiences a surrealistic vision with obvious psychoanalytic implications: a man pulls a rope ashore and hands it to Juliet (later we learn he is the detective Juliet has hired to investigate Giorgio's philandering). As Juliet pulls the rope and brings a raft to shore, a boatload of strange savages armed with swords and horses lands on the beach just before a passing jet awakens her back to reality. Later another flashback to a dream reveals that these savages are circus characters and that her grandfather once ran off with a circus ballerina. Elsewhere in yet another flashback, we discover that Juliet suffers from a traumatic experience during a class play at Catholic school: the nuns told her that as she played the part of a Christian martyr, she would see a vision of God, but that vision was interrupted. In general, Juliet's Catholic upbringing provides the explanation for her repressed sexuality. Only after she rejects her outmoded morality does she manage to free herself from the past. The final shot of the film shows a liberated Juliet free to leave her prisonlike home, advancing in harmony toward the future without the burden of a cold husband's lack of attention or guilt. By her act of self-understanding (as Fellini understood, the goal of every psychoanalysis), Juliet now has a new future ahead of her.

Rome as Metaphor: *Fellini Satyricon* and *Fellini's Roma*

La Dolce Vita uses the Rome of public relations and the cinema to underline how much of the past Rome we have lost. *Fellini Satyricon* employs a free adaptation of the classic novel by Petronius (the very incompleteness of which forced the director to give vent to his fantasy). Since Fellini felt pre-Christian Rome was as unfamiliar to contemporary audiences as a distant planet or a dream world, he reconstructed ancient Rome in the studios of Cinecittà, just as he had done earlier with the streets and squares of the modern city. At the same time, he changed his camera style radically, seeking alienation and distance rather than identification from the characters, with the result that his characteristically mobile camera often provides extremely static shots. Indeed, the extraordinary tracking shot opening the film and following Gitone (Max Born) and Encolpio (Martin Potter) through a Roman brothel seems uniquely anomalous in this contemplative, dreamlike film. The controlling vision linking the film's many disparate episodes together is a vision of a dehumanized, chaotic, disintegrating, pagan world with important analogies to our own times.

The sequence in the comic theater of Vernacchio (Fanfulla) shows Roman literary culture to have degenerated into breaking wind onstage just as the theater of Seneca and Terence has fallen to the level of the bloodletting in the Colosseum. The poverty of Eumolpo (Salvo Randone), the unappreciated poet, emphasizes the disregard for literature and poets. Ancient myth and ancient pagan religion are equally corrupt, and Fellini's characters are clearly seeking something that is yet to come (Christianity). The episode of the Villa of the Suicides, placed roughly in the middle of the

Fellini shooting an exterior scene for *Fellini Satyricon* on the huge sound stage of Teatro 5 at Cinecittà. By the time this extraordinarily original film was made, Fellini and Cinecittà's dream factory had become synonymous. *Credit: MOMA*

film, illuminates the themes of decadence and corruption that precede and follow it. A noble republican couple, fatally out of step with the evil Roman emperor, kill themselves rather than live as slaves.

The last sequence in the film reflects the unfinished nature of Petronius' masterpiece: the young men Fellini presents as the ancient ancestors of the hippies of the day set sail for new lands and new adventures—and, presumably, new religious and moral principles that have not yet been codified and calcified into dead or degenerate forms. In no other of Fellini's films does the analogy between the corruption of the past and our own present become so manifest. The contemporary viewer can recognize himself easily in the surrealistic images, the stylized makeup, the rhetorical flourishes, and the discontinuous, fragmented narrative. Paradoxically, the frightening, nightmare universe conjured up by Fellini's fertile imagination resembles the present more closely than the Rome of the Silver Age of Latin literature.

Fellini's Roma views Rome not through the lens of past history but from Fellini's own biography. It is a completely discontinuous narrative held together only by Fellini's recollections of Rome from three different perspectives: the Rome he remembered as a young schoolboy in provincial Rimini and at the cinema, the Rome he discovered when he moved there in 1939, and the "objective" picture of the Rome of Fellini's own time when the director shoots a documentary on the Eternal City. *Fellini's Roma*, like *Fellini: A Director's Notebook* (*Block-notes di un regista*, 1969), is not really a documentary but a "mockumentary"—to employ the term used by the director Spike Jonze's *Adaptation* (2002), itself an ingenious imitation of Fellini's *8½* from the perspective of the scriptwriter rather than the film director. In *Adaptation*, one of Jonze's characters correctly credits Fellini with the invention, or at least the popularizing, of false documentaries that purport to reflect reality but that actually only mirror a subjective or autobiographical point of view.

Fellini's Rome is a city of illusions and myths; it is the center of Italian filmmaking, the headquarters of the Roman Catholic Church and the capital of the Italian state, all of which are mythmakers and manipulators of illusions. No single Rome emerges from Fellini's personal visual definition of the city; on the contrary, the many images interpenetrate and enrich the connotations of the others. The Rome of the classical world, both the virtuous republic and the decadent empire, runs together with the Rome of the popes during the Renaissance and the baroque city of the Counter-Reformation, which represents not only the Church Militant but also the darker side of the coin—the Inquisition, the Jesuits, and the "black" nobility of Rome that the church's wealth spawned. Then there is the modern Rome with its modern Caesar, the Fascist dictator Benito Mussolini, whose dream was to reestablish Rome as an imperial force. And finally, there is the Rome Fellini best understands, the Rome of Cinecittà, the prewar music halls, and the prewar brothels, where men of Fellini's generation first learned about sex. Fellini creates a number of extraordinary sequences from this aspect of the Eternal City that reflect his experiences reshaped by his fertile, active imagination: a nostalgic visit to a prewar brothel, an ecclesiastical fashion parade that shows various designer costumes for church officials and nuns, a visit to an excavation where remains of the classical past vanish into dust when confronted with the air of modern Rome, and the final concluding sequence of a group of motorcyclists roaring around the most famous monuments of the city at night that cannot help but recall barbarian invasions of this ancient metropolis.

Fellini's Roma represents the quintessential Fellinian interplay of reality and illusion, autobiography and history. Almost everything in the film—the variety theater, the outdoor scenes, even the Colosseum and the Roman autostrada—have been constructed in a studio when perfectly serviceable "real" locations could have been selected. Now the archetypal Fellinian image of parades or processions encompasses an enormous range of human experience: the theater, street traffic, the church, brothels, motorcyclists, and hippies, as all of humanity passes before the director's camera as if the world were a bizarre, grotesque circus performance. Yet, at the center of this fragmented but visually exuberant world, there is always the creative presence of the Maestro: Fellini, the character who portrays himself, continuing his role as superstar director first begun in *Fellini: A Director's Notebook* and *The Clowns*. Only the fantasy of the director makes sense out of all the confusion. And only the imagination, Fellini suggests, can lead to the creation of a new mythology for the future out of the remains of the other, older mythologies associated with this ancient city.

The Political Fellini: *Amarcord*

Throughout most of his career, Fellini was attacked by leftist critics for his lack of any social vision or political perspective. As he once declared,

> good intentions and honest feelings, and a passionate belief in one's own ideals, may make excellent politics or influential social work . . . but they do not necessarily and indisputably make good films. And there is nothing uglier or drearier—just because it is ineffectual and pointless—than a bad political film.[31]

Yet in 1973, during a period when politics and ideology had become a dominant theme in Italian cinema (see chapter 8), Fellini produced his last great box-office hit (for which he would receive his fourth Oscar for Best Foreign Language Film): *Amarcord*, a brilliant look back at the generation that produced the *vitelloni* of the 1950s, the Italians of his childhood, in a town that certainly must be based on provincial Rimini in the 1930s. Fascism ruled Italy from 1922 until 1943, when the Allies invaded Italy. Italian directors making films about Fascist Italy generally had a political ax to grind, blaming the Fascist dictatorship for various social or historical variables that usually culminated in a Marxist indictment of the middle class or a view of various personality disorders that explained Fascism by sexual perversions, ideas associated with Wilhelm Reich. Fellini believed that Fascism was caused in Italy by "a sort of blockage, an arrested development during the phase of adolescence" in people who abandoned individual responsibility for a flight toward absurd dreams, group thinking, and provincialism.[32] As *8½* and *Juliet* demonstrate, Fellini locates the focal point of creativity in the individual and his or her fantasy life. Consequently anything that deforms, represses, or distorts this creativity and the growth of an adult consciousness within the people making up society must be opposed, whether it be a Fascist regime or a consumer-oriented postmodern culture: "what I care about most," declared Fellini, "is the freedom of man, the liberation of the individual man from the network of moral and social conventions in which he believes, or rather in which he thinks he believes, and which encloses him and limits him and makes him seem narrower, smaller, sometimes even worse than he really is."[33]

Fellini's portrait of the Italian provinces during the Fascist period avoids the facile juxtaposition of good and evil (the bad Fascists versus the virtuous anti-Fascists) that characterizes most Italian films on the subject. On the contrary, rather than the jackbooted army veterans attacking the peasantry and workers during strikes, or the wealthy capitalists and industrialists who hire them, Fellini believes the causes of Italian Fascism can be explained neither by Marxist class conflict nor by neo-Freudian theories about sexual deviance (the most popular explanations of the period when *Amarcord* appeared and the two embodied in Bertolucci's *1900*, for example). His townspeople are all comic figures, clearly related to the clown figures of his earlier films. The most important group is a middle-class family headed by Aurelio (Armando Brancia), an old socialist whose wife, Miranda (Pupella Maggio), is the stereotypical Italian mother who spoils her son and her worthless brother, Lallo, a.k.a. Patacca (Nando Orfei), a gigolo who parades around in his Fascist uniform but whose main activity consists of picking up Nordic tourists. Titta (Bruno Zanin), their son, is a character often mistakenly identified with Fellini himself, even though Fellini has repeatedly denied that *Amarcord* is purely autobiographical. Titta's classmates and teachers are all caricatures indebted to Fellini's familiarity with the world of comic strips (particularly early American drawings by Frederick Burr Opper [1857–1937] and Winsor McCay [1869–1934]). Even the figures in the town directly related to the regime—the local *gerarca* (National Fascist Party leader), or the Fascist *federale* (a provincial party secretary who visits on April 21 to celebrate the anniversary of the founding of Rome)—are clowns. The cast includes Gradisca (Magali Noël), the town beauty and every male's object of desire, Titta's mad uncle Teo (Ciccio Ingrassia), and the owner of the local Cinema Fulgor (the name of the movie theater in Rimini for which Fellini drew lobby cards that were caricatures of the American and Italian actors or actresses on the screen at the time). This enormous cast of extremely funny characters interacts together on a number of occasions: the moment at the opening of the film when the town celebrates the end of winter by burning a witch in effigy on Saint Joseph's Day (March 19), the visit of the *federale* from Rome to celebrate the "Roman" character of the Fascist revolution, and the occasion on which the entire town sails out on the Adriatic to see the passage of the *Rex*, the pride of Fascist Italy's technology—an ocean liner that really existed and that, before the outbreak of World War II, held the record time for crossing the Atlantic. When the townspeople gather and resort to a kind of groupthink on these occasions, such events in Fellini's words "are always occasions of total stupidity. The pretext of being together is always a leveling process.... It is only ritual that keeps them all together. Since no character has a real sense of individual responsibility, or has only petty dreams, no one has the strength not to take part in the ritual, to remain at home outside of it."[34]

In spite of his unlimited admiration for the American films the young Fellini saw in Rimini, he believed that the repressed lives of the Amarcordians relied far too heavily upon the superficial myths they encountered at the Cinema Fulgor. Thus, before the sequence satirizing the *federale*'s visit, Fellini inserts two key sequences that explain why the townspeople react as they do to the regime's political symbols. In the first, Titta and his friends go to confession, where the priest worries only about whether they "touch themselves" or not, and his questions only arouse their sexual desire, turning Titta's thoughts to Volpina (the town nymphomaniac), the buxom math

Titta attempts unsuccessfully to seduce Gradisca in the Fulgor Cinema in Fellini's
Amarcord. Credit: MOMA

teacher, the plump peasant women at the open market with enormous rear
ends, and especially Gradisca. Within Titta's confession, the young boy
recounts how he once met Gradisca in the Cinema Fulgor alone. While
Gradisca smokes a cigarette and sits entranced by the huge close-up of Gary
Cooper in *Beau Geste*, Titta moves closer and closer to her but is eventually
rebuffed by Gradisca's question, "Looking for something?" Fellini's point
is that the mechanism attracting Gradisca to Gary Cooper works like that
which attracts the crowd to the *federale* or to the *Rex*, and the source of this
mechanism is sexual repression.

It would be untrue to see *Amarcord* as only a political film when, in
fact, it is also one of Fellini's greatest poetic creations. Like *La Dolce Vita*,
which presents countless moments of great beauty and emotional appeal
in a decadent and seemingly corrupt world, *Amarcord*'s greatest images
are not just political messages but are also metacinematic moments: Titta
approaches Gradisca in a movie theater; the Rex is a cardboard movie prop
on the back lot of Cinecittà and floats not on the real Adriatic but on an
ocean made of black plastic; the *federale* enters the town of *Amarcord* not
through the Roman arch he would have found in twentieth-century Rimini
but through the gates of Cinecittà, the Fascist architectural style of which
was right at hand for Fellini to use. Even though the argument of these three
sequences links individual and mass behavior, the subtext of them all is the
cinema. The appearance of the beautiful peacock in the snow entrances
not only the Amarcordians but also Fellini's audience, and its magic arrival
cannot but help to recall the equally magic and evocative appearance of
the musicians or the horse in *La Strada*. Fellini thus produces a political

poem with poetic images, not rhetorical speeches or ideological arguments. Whether *Amarcord* is an autobiographical film remains doubtful. As Fellini has said, "I can't distinguish what really happened from what I made up. Superimposed on my real memories are painted memories of a plastic sea, and the characters from my adolescence in Rimini are elbowed aside by actors or extras who interpreted them in my films."[35] Fellini's cinematic art has always rested upon beautiful lies (in fact, he often called himself "a liar but an honest one"), but in this regard it would be useful to recall Picasso's famous definition of art as a lie that tells the truth.

Fellini and Sexuality: *Fellini's Casanova* and *City of Women*

Coming after the international acclaim for *Amarcord*, the disappointing box-office performance of *Fellini's Casanova*—the most expensive film of Fellini's entire career—came as a great surprise and was not mitigated by Danilo Donati's well-deserved Oscar for Best Costume Design. Its commercial failure marks the beginning of Fellini's decline in audience popularity, a decline that was strangely paralleled by a dramatic (and completely justifiable) rise in publications on his films among scholars and film historians. Yet, in retrospect, *Casanova* represents one of Fellini's most original and creative films, and its theme—a complete rejection of the traditional myth of the archetypal Latin lover—presents an unusual performance by Donald Sutherland as the famous Venetian rake and adventurer. Just as he had done with his other great costume film based on a literary work, *Fellini Satyricon*, Fellini's film is an interpretive distillation. Thousands of pages from Casanova's self-serving diaries are transformed into the portrait of a mechanical man whose sexuality is reduced to the automatic movements of a machine, and whose final and most satisfying bed partner is a mechanical doll. Casanova, for Fellini, is the Enlightenment anticipation of the Fascist personality type of *Amarcord*: an eternal adolescent with no individuality whatsoever. He is, in Fellini's words, "*the* Italian." Casanova's tireless quest for ever newer sexual adventures produces no change in his character or understanding, and this insensitivity is prefigured by the opening carnival sequence, a classic example of Fellinian bravura shot not on location at Venice's Rialto Bridge but at Cinecittà, with huge, frenetic crowds of extras, lavish historical costumes, and extravagant set constructions. As Casanova makes an assignation with a nun (the lover of the French ambassador to the Venetian Republic, who likes watching his mistress make love to other men), a huge head of Venus rises momentarily from the Venetian canals, then suddenly breaks free of its cables and sinks back into the murky waters of the lagoon. This enigmatic symbol of the libido, underscoring the fact that love and women are forever inscrutable to Casanova, returns again at the stunningly beautiful conclusion of the film. In a dream, Casanova imagines himself skating upon the frozen Venetian lagoon with his mechanical doll, a chilling image of misdirected sexuality and impotence in old age. As Gerald Morin, Fellini's assistant director, remarked on the set after the sequence was shot, "So this is what Fellini thinks it all comes down to—a vacuous man dancing with a mechanical doll. Only a middle-aged man growing cynical could make such a statement. How sad. How honest."[36]

In *City of Women*, Fellini confronts the issue of feminism and his own sexual fantasies.[37] He intended the film to provide both a comic portrait of the traditional Italian male's attitude about women and a film made with the language of dreams, by now the inspiration for all his films. In fact, the story consists of a long, uninterrupted dream experienced by Snàporaz (Fellini's nickname for his star, Marcello Mastroianni, in real life), who functions in the film as Fellini's alter ego and finds himself subjected not only to attacks by outraged feminists at one of their conventions but also to Fellini's own critique of his own attitudes about women. The most memorable sequence in the entire film is a brilliant summation of Fellini's (and Snàporaz's) desire to regress to childhood, an era both unpopulated by castrating females and the source of all their fantasies. Not surprisingly, these fantasies are directly related to the cinema: Snàporaz glides down an enormous slide lit up by thousands of lights that recall those on a movie marquee. Fellini's camera moves through a series of eight scenes introduced by circles of these movie lights, each one of which introduces a different sexual fantasy from Snàporaz's past. The female figures include a singing maid from his childhood, a sensual fishwife selling eels in a provocative fashion, a Scandinavian masseuse at a spa, several sexy female motorcyclists dressed in black leather, a woman on the beach from the 1930s, and a prostitute in a brothel whose posterior is exaggerated by a wide-angle lens. Not only is each of these scenes shown through the lights of a theater marquee, but each is also depicted in a fashion that shows it represents constructions from a film set, not merely from the protagonist's imagination. Fellini thus informs us with visual images that the sexual desires of men are learned from the cinema. One particular scene, which makes this abundantly clear, pictures a huge bed on which dozens of boys are masturbating while they gaze at an enormous movie screen, where they see provocative images of women who look like Marlene Dietrich and Mae West. Disappointed by the negative reaction to both *City of Women* and *Fellini's Casanova*, Fellini would remark in a BBC documentary released a decade later that Snàporaz is a comic figure, because the mistaken notions he has about women are all generated by his own failure to appreciate women as unique individuals and his own acceptance of false images fostered by the cinema itself.

Fellini and Moviemaking: *Interview*

Fellini's last years were not happy ones. He was unable to find the financing for a number of projects that were admittedly personal, but his penultimate film, *Interview*, reveals him to be the same genius that produced *8½*. The film is a tribute to Cinecittà and to the art of filmmaking in general. In it, Fellini plays himself in his last mockumentary, and making a film is a metaphor for the creative process and becomes synonymous with life itself. This beautifully simple work actually contains four potential films, each of which is intertwined with the others during the course of the narrative. On the obvious level, *Interview* tells of a Japanese television crew's attempts to interview Fellini. The recording of the "facts" of his life leads to the more interesting personal memoirs of Fellini's first visit to Cinecittà during the 1930s where, for the first time, a young Fellini (Sergio Rubini) sees his first movie director (probably a comic version of Alessandro Blasetti) who is an awe-inspiring dictator over an imaginary celluloid universe. A third theme consists of scenes shot for a never completed film planned by Fellini that recalls the unmade science-fiction film never completed by Guido in *8½*—a Fellinian adaptation of Kafka's novel *Amerika*. Finally, as the film winds to a conclusion, we realize that we have also seen a fourth film, a film within a film, or the film *Interview*, comprising the three other films—all of which Fellini has created "live" before our very eyes with Cinecittà, his private dream world, as its main protagonist and his own artistic creativity as the film's driving force. *Interview* remains Fellini's final word about the art of filmmaking as fiction, illusion, personal self-expression, craftsmanship, and magic. His last feature film, *The Voice of the Moon*, represented

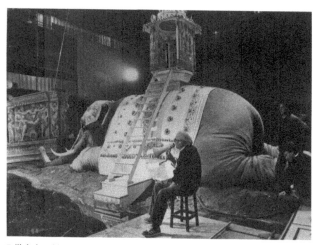

Fellini plays himself on the set of *Interview*. Credit: *MOMA*

a very negative picture of Italian culture at the end of the twentieth century. Always extremely sensitive to popular Italian culture, Fellini came to believe that the rapid social and economic changes that had taken place in the late twentieth century, particularly the rise of a homogenized form of mass media, had begun to erode the distinctive Italian virtues of creativity and authentic human communication. In *The Voice of the Moon*, only those with a form of mental illness listen to the small, still voices of the unconscious or the subconscious, for Fellini the only sources of artistic creativity. As Ivo (Roberto Benigni), the slightly addled protagonist of the film who recalls the equally intellectually challenged Gelsomina of *La Strada*, remarks, "if there were a bit more silence, if we all were a little bit quieter ... perhaps then we could understand."[38]

Auteurs and Other Lesser Mortals

Whether correctly or incorrectly, Visconti, Antonioni, De Sica (to a lesser extent), and Fellini dominated, in the eyes of critics and spectators, the Golden Age of Italian Cinema in the 1960s and the 1970s, and their artistic legacy has continued to influence international and Italian cinema to the present day. They created an image of cinematic quality and seriousness of artistic purpose that made them exemplars of what has come to be called the European Art Film. Because their works reflected the famous film theory associated with the idea of the auteur—that the body of their works reflected a personal, artistic vision rather than the product of a studio's economic projects—they were generally set apart by critical praise (or blame) from critics, reviewers, and film historians from those lesser mortals who worked in more traditional film genres, or in the so-called B films that were generally genre films. With the eclipse of the auteur theory in film history and scholarship, some of their luster wore off. Of course, as we shall discover immediately by examining the popular Italian genre films, even B films could produce auteurs of genius, and their work (often denigrated by intellectuals and pedantic critics as beneath their contempt) would eventually emerge in the postmodern future as worthy of respect and careful attention.

CHAPTER TEN

The Spaghetti Nightmare

HORROR FILMS FROM THE 1950s
TO THE PRESENT

The Background of the Spaghetti Nightmare Film and Its Different Phases of Development

IN MANY WAYS, THE TRADITIONALLY POPULAR GENRE of horror films was as much a foreign narrative form in the history of Italian cinema as was the western. While a few westerns were made in Italy before the mid-twentieth century, film historians cite a single title—*The Monster of Frankenstein* (*Il mostro di Frankenstein*, 1921), by Eugenio Testa (1892–1957)—as the only horror film produced during the silent period, and films made during the Fascist period were equally uninterested in the genre.[1] The narrative tradition standing behind the Italian horror film was thus imported from a variety of sources. Naturally, the important German expressionist films—especially Robert Wiene's *The Cabinet of Dr. Caligari* (1920) and F. W. Murnau's *Nosferatu* (1922)—were influential sources, as were the famous films produced in Hollywood by Universal Studios during the 1930s under expressionist influence, such as James Whale's *Frankenstein* (1931), starring Boris Karloff, or Tod Browning's *Dracula* (1931), featuring Bela Lugosi, or Rouben Mamoulian's *Dr. Jekyll and Mr. Hyde* (1931), with Fredric March, made at Paramount.

The first true Italian postwar horror film was Riccardo Freda's *I Vampiri*, a.k.a. *Lust of the Vampire* (*I vampiri*, 1956), a work that was completed by his cinematographer Mario Bava, who went on to become one of Italy's most inventive horror and thriller directors after setting a standard for innovative peplum epics. Following the release of Freda's film, which was not a financial success and only years later became a cult film, the revival of the horror film by Britain's Hammer Film Productions—most notably in works by the director Terence Fisher, such as *The Curse of Frankenstein* (1957), starring

Peter Cushing, or *Dracula* (1958), starring Christopher Lee—revived Italian interest in the genre. At almost the same time, American International Pictures (AIP) and Roger Corman popularized the horror genre with films based upon the tales of Edgar Allan Poe—such as *House of Usher* (1960) and *The Pit and the Pendulum* (1961), many featuring such stars as Vincent Price. This company would eventually distribute many of Italy's genre films in America. AIP had discovered the youth market: the American drive-in became the perfect venue for B films in the horror genre, and Italian genre films would eventually profit from the market they cultivated.

In contrast to the peplum film, whose production in Italy during 1957–70 reached approximately three hundred films and whose economic impact at the international box office was enormous, or to the spaghetti western, of which Italy produced almost five hundred in about a decade, and which was tremendously profitable, the Italian horror film—dubbed the "spaghetti nightmare"[2] by one of its best treatments—between 1957 and 1970 was produced in extremely small numbers and probably represented only 1 percent of total film production during that time. Yet this relatively small number of films achieved international cult status and now continues to attract viewers on DVD as well as testimonials by contemporary horror directors as to its impact on their own works.[3] Italian horror films in this discussion have been separated from another closely related popular genre, the *giallo* (see chapter 12), by the criterion of the supernatural: the *giallo* may focus upon serial killers who have all sorts of sordid psychological and sexual problems, but they are not vampires, cannibals, werewolves, zombies, or creatures with otherworldly connections. This crucial distinction between the horror film and the *giallo* in Italy is sometimes ignored by critics and film historians, primarily because the same directors—Bava, Argento, Fulci, and others—work in both popular genres, and their film styles often represent a mixture of techniques used in each kind of film narrative.

Italian horror films may conveniently be divided into several different periods. In the first or classic period (that made famous by Freda and Bava) in the 1960s, Italian horror films looked back to the traditions of German expressionism or Hollywood films of the 1930s, producing Gothic thrillers in gorgeous black and white and eventually in Technicolor. In style, they resemble the contemporary productions of the period by AIP and Hammer. Subsequently, directors who also worked in the thriller tradition, such as Dario Argento, moved the horror film away from any Romantic or Gothic atmosphere and made the genre more contemporary, inventing horror themes and narrative techniques that exploited special effects to their limit and moved away from the kinds of historic locations and stories typical of the first classic period. Finally, in the last several decades of the twentieth century, Italian directors such as Lucio Fulci, Ruggero Deodato, and Umberto Lenzi reacted to the works of George A. Romero, John Carpenter,

Wes Craven, and other highly successful Hollywood directors and moved into making extremely gory films treating zombies, cannibals, and other unusual monsters.

Freda and Bava: The Classic Italian Horror Film

It was Riccardo Freda (directing as Robert Hampton) who turned to the horror genre in *I Vampiri* on a bet that Italians could make films in this narrative tradition. At the time he was making a number of successful historical films and peplum epics (see chapter 6). A few years later, when the horror film became more popular, he shot three other important films: *Caltiki, the Undying Monster* (*Caltiki, il mostro immortale*, 1959), *The Horrible Dr. Hichcock* (*L'orribile segreto del doctor Hichcock*, 1962), and *The Ghost* (*Lo spettro*, 1963), the last two starring the British actress Barbara Steele, who became known as the cult figure "scream queen" for her work in Italian horror films. *I Vampiri* was shot in gorgeous black and white CinemaScope by the director of photography Mario Bava, who completed the film when Freda abandoned the project, and therefore much of the credit for the film belongs to Bava. It contains one important element of the *giallo*, since a Parisian journalist (not a police detective) investigates the mysterious deaths of young girls in contemporary Paris, not in some deserted castle in Transylvania. The film actually depicts no true vampire in the classic sense of the word, since a demented scientist uses the blood of young women to rejuvenate the blood of the noblewoman Giselle du Grand (Gianna Maria Canale), who is actually an older woman when the effects of this artificial

In Freda's *I Vampiri*, Giselle retains her Gothic vamp beauty by infusions of artificial blood. *Credit: DVD*

blood wear off but is a true vamp and temptress when her beauty has been refreshed by the doctor's potions. The film moves back and forth from the Paris that all tourists know to a Gothic castle that might well have come out of a 1930s Hollywood horror film, with dark staircases, cobwebs, bats, creaky stairs and doors, spiral staircases, and the like. Bava's photography captures perfectly the horror film's traditional focus upon the interplay of light and shadow. The high point of the film comes from the sequence in which Giselle ages before the camera without cutting for changes in makeup. (Bava learned this technique from the classic Hollywood horror film and achieved the editless sequence via the use of special makeup that turned color and "aged" without recourse to cuts between applications.)

Two subsequent films helped to make Barbara Steele famous. (In both of these, the credits employed Anglicized names to disguise the fact that the film was Italian—a ploy common to peplum films and spaghetti westerns as well.) *The Horrible Dr. Hichcock* shocked audiences because it treats necrophilia in gorgeous Technicolor. A wealthy English doctor invents an anesthetic that works wonders both on the operating table and in the bedroom, where his obedient wife, Margaretha (Maria Teresa Vianello), pretends to be a corpse to arouse her husband, but an overdose kills Margaretha, and twelve years later the physician marries another woman, Cynthia (Steele). Somehow, the first wife returns from the dead, and Dr. Bernard Hichcock (Robert Flemyng) must supply her with blood from his second wife in order to sustain her (somehow, she has become vampirized). The most shocking scene in the film shows Dr. Hichcock leering over Cynthia, who is tied to a bed; Hichcock's face and hands are horribly disfigured, a physical sign of the inevitable eruption of his sexual deviation. While the plot of the film leaves much to be desired, Freda's background as an artist produces a beautiful chiaroscuro color film, reminiscent of the play of light and shadow in Caravaggio.

The Ghost, set in Scotland in 1910, is not really a sequel to *The Horrible Dr. Hichcock*, even though the maid in both films is played by Harriet Medin White (an actress first seen in the Italian cinema as the American nurse in the Florence episode of Rossellini's *Paisan*). Another Dr. Hichcock (now named John, not Bernard), joins Barbara Steele, who plays the doctor's wife (now named Margaret, not Cynthia). What makes *The Ghost* interesting is that, despite the audience's assumptions that the strange occurrences in the film are caused by supernatural forces, in reality the plot derives from an elaborate crime. Cynthia and her lover, Dr. Charles Livingstone (Peter Baldwin), conspire to kill Dr. Hichcock (Elio Jotta, working as Leonard G. Elliot) with a special medicine he has devised, refusing to give him the antidote. In reality the good doctor has only pretended to be dead with the help of his diabolic maid (White), and the film ends with an Agatha Christie conclusion: everyone concerned dies by accident at the hands of another character,

The executioner places the metal mask on Asa (the shot is from the victim's point of view) in Bava's *Black Sunday*. *Credit: DVD*

and the police find only a pile of dead bodies, with no explanation of why the doctor, his wife, her lover, and the maid have all met violent ends! Once again, in these two Freda films, set design and color photography trump any search for a rigorous narrative plot.

Although Freda had initiated the vogue of the horror film, it was Mario Bava's *Black Sunday*, a.k.a. *The Mask of Satan*, a.k.a. *Revenge of the Vampire* (*La maschera del demonio*, 1960) that achieved wide, international box-office success (distributed by AIP), ensuring Barbara Steele's "scream queen" status through her striking performance. Based on Nikolai Gogol's short story "The Viy," the film presents a masterful stylistic revisitation of all the elements of the classic horror film. A prologue set in the seventeenth century opens with the execution of Princess Asa Vajda (Barbara Steele) and her brother Igor Javutich (Arturo Dominici), ordered by another brother who is the head of the local Inquisition. The film's voice-over implies that Asa is a vampire, but it is also suggested that she was probably a witch and having an incestuous relationship with Igor. Asa and Javutich die horribly by having a metal "mask of Satan" hammered onto their faces before they are burned and buried. (The huge mallet employed by the executioner looks suspiciously like the one used by the "Gongman," the famous trademark of the Rank Organisation that prefaced every film the U.K. company made or distributed.) The frightening nature of this mask becomes brilliantly clear with one of Bava's most famous shots. First Bava shoots the mask and its metal prongs from the executioner's point of view, but he then reverses the perspective in a seamless transition, moving the camera through the apertures and transferring the point of view from that of the executioner to that of the victim—just before the mask, forced by the executioner's hammer, impales the two victims' faces and forces blood to explode from the mask's apertures for eyes, nose, and mouth. Few horror films have ever opened so forcefully or so unforgettably.

Many superb Italian films by auteurs appeared around the time *Black Sunday* was released: Fellini's *La Dolce Vita*, Antonioni's *L'Avventura*, and Visconti's *Rocco and His Brothers*, all also released in 1960, spring to mind. Because Bava worked within such popular genres as peplum epics, thrillers, and horror films, his contemporary critics never considered him to be a director with auteur credentials; but on the strength of this single film alone, and judged on purely stylistic terms, Bava surely deserves to be compared favorably with the august trinity of Italy's auteurs who dominated the 1960s scene. What is most remarkable about his films is that their quality emerged from extremely low budgets and accelerated production schedules. Never once did he receive the kind of budget that even relatively capital-poor Italy bestowed on far less talented directors of many films that are long forgotten.

From the masterful prologue that introduces the witch and vampire, Bava then moves to exploit another traditional horror theme, that of the double: the witch Asa, trapped in a coffin with the mask of Satan hammered onto her face, and her descendant two hundred years later, Katia, are destined to be joined together in a common fate. Barbara Steele plays both. Asa frees herself from her coffin imprisonment when a careless professor, Dr. Thomas Kruvajan (Andrea Checchi), accidentally spills a drop of human blood on her entombed body, and Kruvajan in turns becomes a vampirized creature that serves the evil pair in Asa's quest to exchange places with Katia. The film's sets and photography are masterful. A number of sequences stand out for their eerie quality, such as a slow-motion carriage ride moving into a fog that was created simply by using a painted filter and set assistants racing

Barbara Steele, the Scream Queen of Italian horror films, plays Asa as she is about to transform herself into Katia in Bava's *Black Sunday*. Credit: DVD

around the parked carriage in the studio with cut branches to simulate a forest passing by—a trick worthy of Fellini's own studio work. Like Fellini, Bava loved creating his images and illusions inside a film studio rather than using real locations, and even the shots purporting to be external are almost always made with artificial lighting and simple effects. Bava also employed the same techniques he had used with great success in *I Vampiri* to show Asa growing old when she finally meets death in a flaming pyre. Various kinds of makeup change color under different kinds of lighting, creating this aging effect without resorting to successive shots and frequent editing.

With American International as its distributor, *Black Sunday* did extremely well in the United States. As a result of *Black Sunday's* American box-office success, Bava was even invited to work in Hollywood, but like Fellini, he refused any such offer from the American Dream Factory. Meanwhile, Steele's performance earned her a starring role in one of AIP's most important classic horror films: Roger Corman's *The Pit and the Pendulum*, in which she shared billing with the reigning star of American horror, Vincent Price. The cult status that Barbara Steele enjoyed after her first films with Freda and Bava demands some concrete explanation, and *Black Sunday* represents the film in which the reasons for this continuing fascination, through generations of horror film fanatics, may be best discerned (although the ultimate explanation is, of necessity, subjective in nature).[4]

Bava obtained Steele's brilliant performance by juxtaposing two very different roles, thus forcing a comparison between Asa (a hauntingly beautiful but diabolic witch-vampire) and an equally hauntingly beautiful but innocent and virginal Katia. In adopting his innovative version of the traditional doppelgänger horror theme, Mario Bava exploited the same facial qualities of his actress that Federico Fellini would imitate only a year later when he cast Steele as the young enchantress Gloria Morin who mesmerizes Guido's friend Mario in *8½*. In each case, Bava and Fellini captured Steele's enigmatic facial qualities with the kind of expressionistic backlighting made famous by

Bava's influence upon Fellini may be seen in Fellini's casting of Barbara Steel as Gloria Morin in *8½*. Credit: CSC the great German and American classics of horror cinema. Set in relief by stark lighting, Steele's high cheekbones suggest that there is a skull barely concealed under her beautiful face, a wonderfully suggestive quality in a horror film star and a possible visual explanation for her rise to cult status. Combining the suggestion of death behind the face of a woman embodying the traits of both virgin and temptress—and thus associating the themes of sex and death—certainly serves the many related themes found in the horror film quite well. Such visual clues explain in concrete, physical, cinematic terms why Steele attained the status of genre royalty with only eleven horror films shot during 1960–68, nine of which were completed by Italian directors. If Fellini was influenced by a screening of *Black Sunday* to cast Steele in his greatest work, he was certainly a more discerning judge of artistic talent than several generations of critics and film historians who shamefully pigeonholed Bava as "only" a B director of genre films.

All of Bava's other horror films contain delightful rewards for the discerning spectator and may be compared favorably with his best *gialli*. Unlike *Black Sunday*, these films are shot in the same kinds of innovative color that mark Bava's thriller *Blood and Black Lace* (see chapter 12). They include *The Whip and the Body* (*La frusta e il corpo*, 1963), *Black Sabbath* (*I tre volti della paura*, 1963), *Kill Baby Kill* (*Operazione paura*, 1966), *Baron Blood* (*Gli orrori del castello di Norimberga*, 1972), and *Lisa and the Devil*, a.k.a. *House of Exorcism* (*Lisa e il diavolo*, a.k.a. *La casa dell'esorcismo*, 1972). Bava's *The Whip and the Body* aroused international censors with its (at the time) shocking treatment of sadomasochistic sex between an aristocratic wastrel, Kurt Menliff (Christopher Lee), and Nevenka (Daliah Lavi), the wife of his brother, Christian (Luciano Stella working as Tony Kendall). A scene in which Kurt lashes a sensuously groveling Nevenka, who professes to hate pain but obviously derives sexual gratification from being whipped before Kurt forces himself on her was enough to cause the original film to be chopped up and distributed in a bastardized version for many years. In this film, almost everything that occurs in the film represents Nevenka's perspective. The violent murders that take place, including the death of Kurt on the night after he assaults both Nevenka and her father, all seem to be the act of Kurt's ghost. The film's final sequences, however, clarify the plot. At first we see Nevenka embracing Kurt (her demented imagination), but then we see her embracing nothing (our perspective). Clearly all the murders in the film may be attributed to Nevenka, not to any supernatural apparition, and they may be construed as the result of Nevenka's own guilt over her obvious delight in sadomasochistic sex with her villainous brother-in-law. The last shot of the film shows us Kurt's burning corpse, near which a burning whip writhes in the flames in much the same manner as Nevenka writhed under Kurt's whip.

Black Sabbath is an English title selected to bank on the much more popular *Black Sunday*: its Italian title, *I tre volti della paura* ("the three faces of fear") identifies it more clearly as one of the anthology films (*films a episodi*) that became so popular in the 1960s and 1970s. Elegantly shot in Technicolor, each of the three parts resembles a short story in a collection devoted to the supernatural or the uncanny impact of fear upon their protagonists. In it, Bava exploits the fame of Boris Karloff, who not only functions as the film's "host" in a prologue and an epilogue but also stars as a vampire in the episode entitled "The Wurdalak." Like *The Whip and the Body*, *Black Sabbath* displays Bava's treatment of color at its best as he creates beautiful sets, dominated by lights and color, in what recent critics have identified as his "baroque" camerawork and lighting. The most memorable sequence in this trilogy of brief tales is actually the epilogue, where Karloff, costumed as an Eastern European vampire, bids the audience farewell and rides off into a forest on a white horse. In a comic metacinematic moment that we may compare to the last shot of Fellini's *And the Ship Sails On* (a much later film), Bava pulls back his camera and reveals that Karloff actually rides on a mechanical horse, with only its front part constructed by Bava's technicians, many of whom race around Karloff with branches cut from trees to simulate the rider's passage through a forest; a wind machine provides further movement. Bava always worked with very tight budgets, but at least in this one case, he managed to alert his audience to the innovative source of his genius: his ability to improvise, to use tricks of the trade that go back to the origins of cinema, and his view that film was, finally, visual illusion (another obvious link to Fellini's brand of cinema).

Kill Baby Kill, *Baron Blood*, and *Lisa and the Devil* are more substantial and important films, all of which continue Bava's baroque scenography and original use of set lighting. The first film employs a Gothic atmosphere and explores the mysterious murders in a small Eastern European town associated with the appearance of the ghost of a young girl named Melissa Graps (Valeria Valeri) playing with a ball. Years ago, the daughter of the now insane Baroness Graps (Giovanna Galletti, two decades since playing Ingrid in Rossellini's *Open City*) was killed in a drunken village celebration by inebriated peasants, and now Melissa returns to claim a victim. Anyone who gazes upon her is later found dead. With beautifully staged exterior settings bathed in fog and night lighting and interior scenes that exploit spiral staircases and pursuits through endless corridors of old castles in decay shot in deep focus, the film palpably depicts the ascent into the abyss of the supernatural. As in all his color films, Bava lights up his sets (both exteriors and interiors) with primary colors in extraordinarily beautiful ways. The violence in the film—throat slashing, impalements, and the like—is also much more graphic than in earlier horror films and seems closer to the spirit of the *giallo* than of classic horror. One particularly compelling scene

The ghostly apparition in Mario Bava's *Kill Baby Kill* that influenced both Fellini's *Toby Dammit* and Stanley Kubrick's *The Shining. Credit: DVD*

features Dr. Paul Eswai (Giacomo Rossi-Stuart), a physician sent to the town to perform autopsies on the dead townspeople, racing after Melissa through the rooms of Villa Graps. Each room he enters becomes exactly the same as the next room that he enters (producing the sense of the uncanny in an original manner) until the doctor finally catches up with his target—only to encounter himself! The strange ghostly apparition with the bouncing ball most certainly influenced Fellini's creation of a young girl as the devil with a similar bouncing ball who brings about the death of the protagonist in *Toby Dammit* (one of three segments in the Poe omnibus film *Spirits of the Dead* [*Histoires extraordinaires*, 1968]), and this young female ghost may well also have influenced the two young female apparitions sporting a bouncing ball who are murder victims in Stanley Kubrick's *The Shining* (1980).

Baron Blood continues the Gothic atmosphere of *Black Sunday* and *Black Sabbath* but combines a Gothic castle setting (actually an Austrian museum) with a contemporary time frame. The titular baron, Otto von Kleist, returns from the past, invoked by an incantation read by a careless American descendant of his, to haunt the twentieth century. As Bava frequently did in his genre films, he combined American, international, and Italian cast members: Joseph Cotten as Alfred Becker (the baron's contemporary form), Elke Sommer as Eva Arnold (the beautiful girl who is the baron's target), and the onetime Italian movie idol Massimo Girotti as Dr. Karl Hummel, a professor who assists Eva and Peter Kleist (Antonio Cantafora), the baron's modern descendants in their efforts to stop the murderous fiend from returning from Hell to continue his infamous tortures and crimes. The film's plot is terribly complicated, but its key feature is an amulet that evokes the baron's past victims, who make this monster suffer "the tortures of Hell" after they, like Baron Blood, arise from the grave to take their revenge.

Lisa and the Devil, like Black Sunday, must be rated as one of Bava's finest films. It is also one of the few horror films made in Italy that reflects a sense of humor. Unfortunately, it was cut up by distributors hoping to capitalize on the success of The Exorcist and renamed House of Exorcism, even though exorcism has absolutely nothing to do with the film's plot (a cavalier attitude that was typical of how genre films from Italy were treated both at home and abroad). This film, too, exploits a link between horror in the past and the present. In the opening, Bava shows us a young woman named Lisa Reiner (Elke Sommer) who is a tourist in modern-day Toledo (Spain) and who becomes lost. She spies a strange man named Leandro (Telly Savalas), who bears a close resemblance to the figure of the devil that she sees depicted on a wall fresco outside the local cathedral. As the film progresses, the spectator is disoriented by Bava's purposely confusing plot. Wandering through the town at night, Lisa hitches a ride in an old, prewar limousine driven by a chauffeur named George (Gabriele Tinti) for a rich couple, Francis Lehar (Eduardo Fajardo) and his wife, Sophie (Sylva Koscina). When the vintage car breaks down at a villa, they are reluctantly given refuge by a blind countess (Alida Valli) and her son, Maximilian (Alessio Orano), and escorted to their rooms by the butler, who turns out to be Leandro. Telly Savalas gives a masterful performance, complete with the trademark lollipop (apparently, a means for him to avoid smoking cigarettes on the set) that he later made famous on the internationally successful television series Kojak.

Like the violence in Baron Blood, that in Lisa and the Devil contains the kind of gore quite typical of the horror films and gialli of the 1970s, and soon the bodies begin to pile up in the villa. After having sex with Sophie, George's life ends with a pair of scissors in his throat; Sophie mistakenly assumes that Francis has killed George out of jealousy and runs him over and over again with the limousine; she is then killed horribly by a mace on the head by Maximilian, who actually killed George to keep him from driving off with Lisa, whom he takes to be the reincarnation of Elena, the woman he loved years earlier. But the revelations in the film keep moving the work away from what at first appears to be a mystery thriller and toward a horror film concentrating on the supernatural, for we learn that a man who had frightened Lisa in Toledo with his rude advances was Maximilian's stepfather, Carlo (Espartaco Santoni), who, years earlier, had made love to Maximilian's mistress, Elena. (Of course, Elena and Lisa look exactly alike.) Apparently Carlo and Lisa had planned to run off together, but before that could occur, Maximilian murdered Elena and kept her skeletal corpse in a bed, so that he could be with her forever, adding the complication of necrophilia to the list of the many faults Maximilian possesses. Naturally, when

Carlo saw Lisa in the village, he assumed she was Elena, but Carlo too meets his end at his stepson's hands. Ultimately Maximilian strips Lisa naked and places her by the dead skeleton of Elena in a vain attempt to have sex with her; but when his mother objects to a marriage, her son stabs the countess to death by the coffin in which he has placed Carlo's body on display.

At each step of this complicated plot (complex but not ultimately confusing, as is sometimes the case in Italian low-budget genre films), Leandro observes the bizarre happenings in the villa and makes humorous remarks as the dead bodies pile up, all the while sucking on his lollipop. Finally confronted with a dinner table around which all the bodies are displayed (obviously Leandro's work), Maximilian recoils from the sight and falls out the window upon the spikes of a metal gate. Lisa remains the only person alive in the villa, but when she leaves and meets a group of schoolgirls playing nearby, they look at her and exclaim that she is the ghost of the villa. She returns to the city and takes a plane back to America, but on the plane she finds she is the only person in one section—and all the dead bodies are seated in another. Opening the door of the cockpit, she discovers that Leandro is the pilot. Presumably Lisa is actually the soul of the dead Elena, who magically turns into a ghostly, pale corpse that slumps to the floor of the airplane, while Leandro, the friendly embodiment of the Devil, flies the entire group off to Hell.

Although initially almost ruined by greedy distributors, today *Lisa and the Devil* appears to be Bava's most adventurous film, a modern, oneiric tale about death and the afterlife whose plot seems similar to descriptions of what *The Voyage of G. Mastorna* (*Il viaggio di G. Mastorna*)—Fellini's projected work about life after death—might have been like had he ever succeeded in shooting it. It combines all of Bava's talents: a well chosen cast; beautifully constructed sets and carefully planned lighting; skillful, even virtuoso camerawork; and a fine sense of creating a sense of the uncanny that is the key to the atmosphere of horror created in any work of art.

More Gothic Horror: Giorgio Ferroni, Antonio Margheriti, and Mario Caiano

While Freda and Bava are generally the names identified with the Gothic period of Italian horror films, a couple of other films in the same vein are worthy of note: Giorgio Ferroni's *Mill of the Stone Women* (*Il mulino delle donne di pietra*, 1960) and Mario Caiano's *Nightmare Castle*, a.k.a. *Lovers Beyond the Tomb* (*Gli amanti d'oltretomba*, 1965), which again featured Barbara Steele in dual roles. In addition, a number of horror films by Antonio Margheriti (directing as Anthony Dawson) are also interesting: *The Virgin of Nuremberg*, a.k.a. *Horror Castle* (*La vergine di Norimberga*, 1963); *Castle of Blood*, a.k.a. *La Danse macabre*, a.k.a. *Edgar Allan Poe's Castle of Blood*

(*Danza macabra*, 1964); *The Long Hair of Death* (*I lunghi capelli della morte*, 1964); *Flesh for Frankenstein*, a.k.a. *Andy Warhol's Frankenstein* (*Carne per Frankenstein*, 1973), which even had a 3-D edition; and *Blood for Dracula*, a.k.a. *Andy Warhol's Dracula* (*Dracula cerca sangue di vergine . . . e morì di sete!!!*, 1974). (The last two films were part of a contract given to the writer-director Paul Morrissey, an Andy Warhol associate, to shoot at Cinecittà in Rome; but Margheriti also earned credit for work on them, and it remains unclear exactly what contribution each individual made to both works.) A brief discussion of some of these works will underscore the continuity with themes developed by Freda and Bava but also some important stylistic and narrative differences.

Ferroni's *Mill of the Stone Women* displays none of the technical virtuosity of Bava's lighting or camera movements. Yet although it is a static, nineteenth-century costume drama, one diabolical mechanism dominates the film to such an extent that it rewards viewing. A mad Dutch art professor, Dr. Gregorius Wahl (Herbert Böhme), keeps his daughter, Elfie (Scilla Gabel), alive with the help of a criminal scientist, Dr. Loren Bohlem (Wolfgang Preiss), by extracting the blood from innocent women to rejuvenate her. The women are then turned into waxed mummies on a gigantic rotating platform of the type often found on municipal clock towers in Germany— only this one rotates by the power of a huge Dutch windmill—where they serve as a kind of horrific wax museum, masking the two men's crimes. The motif of blood transfusions between women manages to combine a number of horror themes: necrophilia (after all, the rejuvenated woman that is the object of desire is really not alive), vampirism (the emphasis on bloodletting), and mad scientists. Yet Elfie is not merely an innocent victim, because she gloats to her perspective target, Liselotte Kornheim (Dany Carrel), that

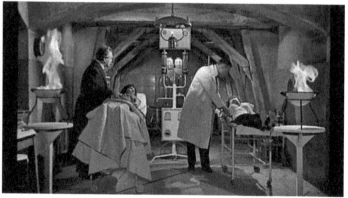

Two mad scientists prepare another innocent woman for display in Ferroni's *Mill of the Stone Women. Credit: DVD*

she will live again thanks to Liselotte's blood and will enjoy the sexual favors of her victim's fiancé, the young journalist Hans von Arnim (Pierce Brice). The Italian Gothic horror film habitually presents strong women who are also monsters, and they almost always overshadow the more traditional male monsters or mad scientists of English and American classic horror cinema.

A sampling of Margheriti's horror production in this period—*The Virgin of Nuremberg* and *Castle of Blood*—shows similar variations on typical narrative plots and techniques from the earlier works of Freda and Bava. In the first film, Margheriti clearly anticipates Bava's clever juxtaposition of past and present in *Baron Blood*. In fact, Bava was probably influenced by this film. In yet another Germanic castle with a bad historical reputation, an ex-Nazi general horribly scarred by his role in a plot to assassinate Hitler returns to his family estate and begins to take up where his sadistic ancestor, the Punisher (Mirko Valentin), left off centuries ago. His son, Max Hunter (Georges Rivière), returns to the castle with Mary, his new wife (Rossana Podestà), who is spooked by Erich (Christopher Lee), the curator of the torture museum set up in their family estate. Later we learn that Erich was General Hunter's orderly during the past war and that he and his son are trying desperately to cover up his horrible crimes. Apparently, German versions of this film cut out the links to the Nazi past altogether, but the entire plot simply makes little sense anyway. (After all, if General Hunter was a heroic opponent of the Nazis, why was he chosen to turn into a monster?) Except for the usual Gothic atmosphere and a very fine castle environment, much of the film consists of needlessly dull shots of Mary's wanderings around the castle to the tune of a jazz musical score that adds little to our suspense. Although Margheriti chose to shoot the film in color and includes all of the usual Gothic elements—a castle with a bad past, thunderstorms and lightning, candles blown out by the wind, windows blowing open, eerie screams in the dark—he exhibits none of the visual exuberance typical of either Freda or Bava.

Margheriti's *Castle of Blood*, released the following year, is a far more important film, much closer to the spirit of Bava's *Black Sunday* and, like that film, done in gorgeous black and white rather than in color. It purports to be a version of an Edgar Allan Poe tale and was apparently shot in only three weeks, employing three cameras at once—a typical technique for producing soap operas. Seeing an interview with the American writer Poe while he is visiting London, a journalist named Alan Foster (Georges Rivière) accepts a bet from a British aristocrat that he cannot last a night in his haunted castle. Foolishly accepting the wager, Foster finds himself in the midst of a perfect Gothic nightmare, a coven of vampires who, one night a year, need a victim to keep them alive for another year. Meanwhile, the vampires are doomed to repeat the events leading to their own demise and transformation into vampires before the very eyes of their yearly victim. Perhaps the key to the entire film is a statement made by Poe before Foster enters the evil castle. He claims

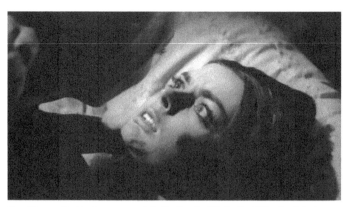

Vampirism and lesbianism are associated in Margheriti's *Castle of Blood* as Julia (a vampire) slips into bed with Elizabeth. *Credit: DVD*

that the most melancholy theme in the world is death, and that it becomes the most poetic when death is coupled with beauty; he claims the death of a beautiful woman is, therefore, the most poetic theme in all of life.

Margheriti provides us with a skillfully presented repertoire of Hollywood's entire collection of horror motifs: hansom cabs drive into thick fog; iron gates creak; black cats bar paths; bats and owls fly in the night; mist arises everywhere but especially from a graveyard; cobwebs abound; expressionistic lighting enhances the interplay of light and shadows; the sound of footsteps echo throughout the castle; sudden bursts of wind blow open windows and move curtains; and weird, discordant chords play on the sound track. The film comes alive with Barbara Steele's performance as Elisabeth Blackwood, one of the castle owner's ancestors, who is both angelically attractive to Foster and is a vampire. Foster delivers the understatement of the film to Elisabeth when he declares "your beauty is strange and very unusual." Juxtaposed to Elisabeth is another vampire, Julia (Margarete Robsahm), who has lesbian leanings and is apparently in love with Elisabeth. Reenacting all the scenes of the deaths that took place in the past establishes the theme of the film: the destructive effects of passionate love. Gradually, as the film unfolds, we learn that Elisabeth betrayed her husband with the gardener, who killed her when she refused to leave her husband. As the evening draws to a close and dawn is near, all of the vampires converge on Foster, and Elisabeth tries to save him before she turns into a skeleton. Because she loves him, she tries to repress her urge to vampirize him; but just as the journalist reaches the castle gates and closes it behind him, one of the bars impales him, turning him into one of the many lost souls trapped inside the ghoulish castle.

Caiano's *Nightmare Castle* provides yet another vehicle for Barbara Steele's talents. Once again, the setting is an aristocratic castle in the nineteenth century, and once again the film is shot in beautiful black and white. As in Bava's *Black Sunday*, Steele plays two different characters: Lady Muriel Arrowsmith (née Hampton), the lecherous wife of Dr. Stephen Arrowsmith (Paul Muller), whose adultery with David, the gardener (Rik Battaglia), costs both their lives and her husband's hands, and Jenny Arrowsmith, Muriel's stepsister, whom Stephen marries after murdering Muriel in order to gain the family inheritance that was bequeathed from Muriel to Jenny. While Steele plays Muriel with her classic long black hair, which represents the potentially evil side of femininity, she plays Jenny with a blond wig, to accentuate the two characters' quite different moral qualities.

Caiano's film contains a number of elements familiar to an audience trained in the Freda-Bava tradition. He probably imitated the mad surgeon theme from Freda's *The Horrible Dr. Hichcock* and *The Ghost*, as well as Bava's use of two wives played by the same actress, when he first employed Steele in a dual role in *Black Sunday*. The evil housekeeper Solange (Helga Liné) of *Nightmare Castle*, kept rejuvenated with the blood of other women, harks back to numerous Italian horror films: Ferroni's *Mill of the Stone Women*, for instance, or even Freda's *I Vampiri*, which began the Italian fad of horror films. Caiano's choice of Muriel's family name may also be a humorous reference to Freda, who often shot his genre films under the Anglicized name Hampton. Moreover, Caiano adds a number of sadistic twists. Stephen catches David and Muriel in flagrante, chains them up, and then murders them with a combination of acid and electric shock. Afterward he extracts both their hearts and Muriel's blood, and thrusts a dagger into the two hearts in a kind of parody of the Hampton family crest, which features two adjacent hearts. Ultimately, Jenny's psychiatrist, Dr. Derek Joyce (Laurence Clift), discovers the role Stephen and Solange have played in the death of Muriel and David. He first brings the pair back to life by pulling the dagger, buried behind the Hampton family crest, from their hearts, thereby releasing the evil pair, who murder Solange and Stephen in revenge. They almost kill Joyce and his patient, Jenny, but the young doctor throws the two hearts into the fire and escapes with Jenny from the evil castle. Although Caiano's cinematography cannot match that of either Freda or Bava, he may well have captured Barbara Steele in even more compelling shots in *Nightmare Castle* than either of them did in their own, much better, films.

The Horror Films of Dario Argento: The "Trilogy of the Three Mothers"

The Gothic period of Italian horror produced some memorable works that became cult favorites all over the world. The Italian horror film seemed to have run out of steam until Dario Argento (1940–) turned from producing films in the thriller or *giallo* tradition (characterized by graphic violence, serial murderers, and psychoanalytical plots that almost always remained in the realm of everyday reality; see chapter 12) to films that treated the supernatural or the occult—the horror genre proper. Because Argento's *gialli* were so graphic in their depiction of violence (at least for audiences at the time), discussion of them often blurred this distinction. In fact, even though Argento is known primarily as a horror film director, he has actually made more thrillers. His most important horror films include a trilogy about witches that spans three decades: *Suspiria* (1977), *Inferno* (1980), and *The Mother of Tears*, a.k.a. *The Third Mother* (*La terza madre*, 2007). Argento also became an important mentor and sometime producer to young horror directors, thus making significant contributions to the genre by producing a number of important horror films. Among these are *Demons* (*Démoni*, 1985) and *Demons 2* (*Démoni 2: L'incubo ritorna*, 1986), by Mario Bava's son Lamberto (1944–), and *The Church* (*La chiesa*, 1989) and *The Sect* (*La setta*, 1991), by Michele Soavi (1957–), who also shot an interesting documentary on his mentor, *Dario Argento's World of Horror* (*Il mondo dell'orrore di Dario Argento*, 1985). Argento also produced (and co-wrote) *The Wax Mask* (*M.D.C.: Maschera di cera*, 1997), the directorial debut of the Italian special-effects maestro Sergio Stivaletti (1957–). Argento's most ambitious and most important task as a producer was to support the making of the American horror film director George A. Romero's *Dawn of the Dead* (*Zombi*, a.k.a. *Zombies*, 1978), a seminal work that, along with Romero's *Night of the Living Dead* (1968), launched the worldwide craze for zombie-themed horror films. He and Romero also collaborated to produce *Two Evil Eyes* (*Due occhi diabolici*, 1990), a two-segment tribute to the tales of Edgar Allan Poe comprising Argento's *The Black Cat* (*Il gatto nero*) and Romero's *The Facts in the Case of M. Valdemar*.[5] Recently Argento contributed two hourlong episodes—"Jenifer" (2005) and "Pelts" (2006)—to *Masters of Horror*, an American cable TV (Showtime) series showcasing horror film directors. Argento's reputation remains quite high among such directors in Hollywood, including John Landis (who gave Argento a cameo role as a paramedic in *Innocent Blood* [1992], an amusing story of a French vampire preying on Italian American gangsters in Pittsburgh), Joe Dante, John Carpenter, Wes Craven, and Quentin Tarantino.

For many of Argento's fans, *Suspiria*, the first part of the "trilogy of the Three Mothers," represents his greatest horror film. The Three Mothers in question derive from the English Romantic writer Thomas De Quincey's *Suspiria de Profundis* (1845), where they are companions for the ancient Roman goddess of childbirth, Levana: Mater Suspiriorum (the Mother of Sighs, the subject of *Suspiria*), Mater Tenebrarum (the Mother of Darkness, the subject of *Inferno*), and Mater Lachrymarum (the Mother of Tears, the "third mother" for whom the final film is named). An examination of this literary text underscores immediately, however, that Argento's films are not in any sense literary adaptations: De Quincey's work merely provides a general framework for dealing imaginatively with the existence of witches in the world. A different mother becomes the focus of each of the three films, but since the trilogy was thirty years in the making (1977–2007), these films differ in many stylistic respects.

Suspiria establishes the basic narrative: an Italian architect named Varelli builds three buildings in Freiburg, New York, and Rome that he later discovers will house these three powerful witches and their followers. In *Suspiria*, the Mother of Sighs resides within a famous dance academy that Suzy Bannion (Jessica Harper) joins. The first twenty minutes of *Suspiria* is justly famous for setting up a masterful series of suspense-filled events where Argento's sets dominate the acting performances. Suzy arrives in a powerful thunderstorm as one of the girls, Pat (Eva Axén), escapes from the school in terror, mouthing words that are at first incomprehensible to Suzy; Pat is eventually horribly murdered with a friend by repeated stabbings (as in Argento's *gialli*, the hands doing this are his own) and thrown through a colored-glass skylight into a hallway with a noose around her neck. Later Suzy will decipher her words and discover that an iris flower on the office wall of the school's director, Madame Blanc (Joan Bennett),[6] opens up to reveal the Mother of Sighs' evil lair. Blanc is one of two rather sinister characters harbored by the school's administration; the other is a stern taskmistress named Miss Tanner (Alida Valli). The presence of Valli and Bennett—two old, distinguished actresses from prewar Italian and American films who were no longer young, sexy women—continued a practice of this kind of retro casting which had become quite popular in Hollywood horror films and thrillers. (The classic example is Bette Davis in Robert Aldrich's *Hush . . . Hush, Sweet Charlotte* [1964]. Bava's use of Isa Miranda [Gaby in *Everybody's Woman* by Max Ophüls, 1936] in *Twitch of the Death Nerve* [*Reazione a catena*, 1971], and Argento's casting of Clara Calamai [Giovanna in Visconti's *Obsession*] in *Deep Red* [*Profondo rosso*, 1975] achieved similar positive results.)

In *Suspiria*, Argento employs the same kind of "set piece" structure that he perfects in his thrillers. The most memorable include the death of one of Suzy's friends, Sara (Stefania Casini), who is trapped in a room full of barbed wire, then dispatched by a pair of hands (Argento's) with a straight razor, the weapon of choice in Argento's cinema; the death of Daniel (Flavio Bucci), a blind pianist whose seeing-eye German shepherd, through the witch's malevolent influence, turns upon him in a huge square that once hosted Hitler's most delirious speeches; maggots that infest an entire floor of the dormitory where the female dance academy students live; and Suzy's final confrontation with the Mother of Sighs, whom she dispatches with an improvised weapon—a crystal feather she desperately plucks from a glass peacock that dominates the room. (In this last scene, the film buff finds

In Argento's *Suspiria*, Suzy kills a witch with a crystal feather taken from a glass sculpture, in the process referring the spectator to the director's first big box-office hit, a *giallo* entitled *The Bird with the Crystal Plumage*. Credit: DVD

a humorous reference to Argento's first big box-office hit, one that helped invent the Italian *giallo*: *The Bird with the Crystal Plumage* [*L'uccello dalle piume di cristallo*, 1970].)

The extraordinary visual qualities of *Suspiria* make it a horror classic worthy of art film status. Films from German expressionism and images from psychoanalytical classics provided inspiration for Argento's masterpiece. The striking, sumptuous sets remain impressive and perhaps unsurpassed in any contemporary horror film. *Suspiria* predates the use of computer-generated imagery (CGI), at least in Italy, and all of the special effects are right there before the camera, produced by artisans and technicians without the use of electronic means. To show his director of photography, Luciano Tovoli (1936–), the kind of Technicolor hues he required in the film, Argento screened Walt Disney's *Snow White and the Seven Dwarfs* (1937). As it happens, new technology was just about to replace the beam-splitting, Technicolor "three-strip" camera as obsolete, but one such camera remained in Rome from the heyday of this expensive technology. Argento and Tovoli were therefore able to produce a horror film with the kinds of pure primary color typical of this process, and immediately after they locked up the film, this last machine was shipped to China. His imagery imbued with pure Technicolor tones, Argento thus managed to give the modern horror film the sense of a magic fairy tale or fable, an innovative style that enabled him to exploit the elements of the subconscious in his audience.

Although it was not possible to repeat the expensive experiment with Technicolor cameras in the second part of the trilogy, *Inferno*, Argento had as his visual effects specialist none other than Mario Bava, who served as second-unit director (and Bava's son Lamberto was credited as assistant director). Mario Bava's presence shines through in the beautiful lighting, which recalls his use of greens, reds, and blues in his own earlier horror films. In *Inferno*, the Mother of Darkness inhabits a New York apartment building constructed by Varelli. A voice-over that details Varelli's work as an architect provides a good deal of information about the Three Mothers. The architect has described his buildings and the Three Mothers who inhabit them in a book written in Latin (clearly the only language that will do for Catholic monsters!), and interest in this book touches off a series of gruesome murders: first, the beheading of Rose Elliot (Irene Miracle), who lives in the New York apartment building and bought Varelli's book from a nearby antique shop run by a strange man named Kazanian (Sacha Pitoëff); next, the beheading of Sara (Eleonora Giorgi) and Carlo (Gabriele Lavia) in Rome; then, the killing and mutilation of Kazanian in a New York park by a crew of hungry rats. Carol, the caretaker of Varelli's apartment building, played by Alida Valli, is as sinister a figure in this film as her Miss Tanner, the taskmistress, was in *Suspiria*. *Inferno* displays affinities to the *giallo* or thriller genre, since Rose's brother, Mark (Leigh McCloskey), returns from a Roman art school to investigate Rose's interest in the Three Mothers and eventually solves her murder. (The amateur detective is a key figure in the *giallo* formula as developed by both Bava and Argento.)

As did Suzy in *Suspiria*, Mark eventually confronts the second, New York witch, the Mother of Darkness, who lives in disguise as a nurse (Veronica Lazar) treating an old, wheelchair-bound invalid named Professor Arnold (Feodor Chaliapin). Mark discovers that Arnold is actually the Professor Varelli who wrote the book about the Three Mothers, who now force him to serve their evil wishes. At the close of this film, a conflagration destroys not only Varelli and the Mother of Darkness but also the building itself. Unlike *Suspiria*, a film that structures itself around a series of beautiful visual set pieces but has little coherent action (one of the reasons it may be considered an "art film"), *Inferno* moves along a narrative pattern much more typical of the Hollywood horror film and provides numerous didactic voice-overs about the myth of the Three Mothers for its audience. Nonetheless, *Inferno* lacks a convincing ending. When the nurse declares that men call the Three Mothers "Death," she turns into a figure wearing what looks like a Halloween costume—a white skeleton printed on a black jumpsuit! In fact, Argento needed something a bit flashier and more inventive to bring this otherwise fine film to a resounding conclusion.

It is unclear why it took Argento almost two decades to bring his trilogy to a conclusion, but as an examination of his entire career shows, he turned primarily to the making of *gialli* in this interval of time. *The Third Mother* reflects an entirely different kind of horror film from *Suspiria* and *Inferno*—one indebted to the stylistic and thematic developments taking place between 1980 and 2007, in particular the increase of gore and horror splatter, on the one hand, and computer-generated imagery rather than more traditional special effects employing models, rubber masks, and mechanical devices, on the other. The Third Mother, the Mother of Tears, resides in Rome. A specialist at an ancient art museum, Sara Mandy (Asia Argento, Dario's daughter), works with her friend Giselle (Coralina Cataldi-Tassoni) on an ancient urn, discovered in the Viterbo cemetery, that contains a scarlet tunic. Their examination of the urn releases the demonic power of the Mother of Tears concentrated in the tunic, and the liberation of this powerful witch in Rome leads to Giselle's horrendous death at the hands of zombielike monsters directed by an evil monkey, who feed on her entrails. It also leads to a reign of terror in the Eternal City: a mother mysteriously throws her small baby into the Tiber River, criminals gang-rape innocent passersby, and so forth. Murder and terror spread throughout the city as witches and the followers of the Three Mothers all arrive in Rome to worship this most powerful of all three wicked women. Argento's contemporary witches, who are quite amusing, sport punk costumes and exude aggressive female attitude. The Mother of Tears (Moran Atias), displays a satanic beauty quite unlike the grotesque Mother of Sighs in *Suspiria* or the comical skeleton costume in *Inferno*. She presents herself to us and to her followers in full frontal nudity, and she looks more like a stripper than a witch. Graphic gore typical of the past two decades of the international horror film fills this third film, and many of the monsters who are not witches are zombies. This fascination with zombies represents an homage to Argento's friend George Romero, but it also reflects films by the Italian horror director Lucio Fulci, especially his zombie pictures (see the next section). Like the first two films of the trilogy, *The Third Mother* ends with a cataclysm of destruction. Sara manages to throw the witch's tunic into the fire, causing an earthquake, the collapse of the building in which the Mother of Tears resides, and the desperation of her followers. Ultimately one of the ancient obelisks scattered around Rome spears the witch, and Sara escapes to safely.

Compared to the horror films made by cult directors like those discussed below, Argento's films represent an artistic achievement that rests not only on masterful suspense narrative and the skillful use of special effects but also on a cultural component that gives his films a level of sophistication and visual elegance that has yet to be matched by any of his colleagues.

The Italian Horror Film: Zombies, Monsters, and Cannibals

Italian horror films focusing upon zombies, demons, and cannibals, which owe a debt to foreign models, became extremely popular in grind-house theaters and drive-ins in the United States and Europe in the late 1970s and the 1980s. Many of these films and their directors have since become cult

figures, with numerous websites and publications devoted to them. Unsurprisingly the Italian cinema had followed the market and taken up this fad,
just as it had embraced the sword and sandal epic or the peplum, as it would
the spaghetti western, the *giallo*, and the *poliziesco*, or Euro-crime genres.
The directors usually associated with the zombie or cannibal film also
worked as scriptwriters, second-unit directors, or directors of works belonging to all of these popular genres. Among them are Lucio Fulci (1927–96),
Marino Girolami (1914–94), Ruggero Deodato (1939–), Umberto Lenzi
(1931–), Lamberto Bava, and Michele Soavi. Many of these individuals
apprenticed with other, more famous directors: Soavi with Argento, Deodato with Roberto Rossellini, Bava with both Argento and his father, Mario.
Still, because Italian cinema has always been an essentially artisanal rather
than industrial operation, these individuals all had extensive experience in
producing low-budget genre films quickly, with ingenious special effects
done by a variety of very talented Italian special-effects artists, many of
whom went on to work in Hollywood with much larger budgets and greater
production support.

    Interest in zombies and cannibals actually has something of a history
in Italian cinema.[7] One unusual peplum epic by Giuseppe Vari (1916–93)—
War of the Zombies (*Roma contro Roma*, 1964)—has Roman Legionnaires
engaged in mortal combat with undead Roman soldiers. Mario Bava's
Planet of the Vampires, a.k.a. *Terror in Space* (*Terrore nello spazio*, 1965)
features aliens who inhabit the dead, zombielike bodies of human beings.
Pier Paolo Pasolini's *Pigpen*, a.k.a. *Pigsty* (see chapter 13), employs a tale
about a sect of medieval cannibals to characterize postwar Germany as a
community founded on similar moral principles. Cannibalism even touches
the Italian Nazi sexploitation genre and again symbolizes the profoundly
immoral character of National Socialism: *The Last Orgy of the Third Reich*,
a.k.a. *The Gestapo's Last Orgy* (*L'ultima orgia del III Reich*, 1977), by Cesare
Canevari (1927–2012), completely surpasses the boundaries of decency when
it depicts a reprehensible and repugnant group of Nazis banqueting on Jewish flesh, which they describe as tasting like pork and even better than veal![8]
The mere description of this last, infamous film points to one of the aims
of horror films in this category. They are meant to shock and disgust more
than to terrify their audiences, and very little (save the production of an
actual "snuff" film) was left to the imagination of the audiences. Gore and
splatter often overcome any interest in complex narrative plotting. Descriptions of screenings of certain films that follow recount how some spectators
literally threw up in the grind houses of Times Square when these films
were first seen (that is, before they became cult objects), and similar experiences have been reported on the movie sets, where it was not uncommon
for members of the cast or crew to empty their stomachs while making the
films! An examination of several of the most important of these late horror

products—few of which ever used the tremendously expensive CGI effects that have now made such low-budget horror films impossible to make and screen in Italy—will show how the horror genre both developed and degenerated into something quite different from the far more elegant products of a Bava or an Argento.

Lucio Fulci's films during this period are most highly praised by critics and historians of these late Italian horror films. One of the most original directors of *gialli* thrillers, Fulci specialized in horror films populated by zombies, no doubt due to the impact of Romero's *Dawn of the Dead*, the 1978 sequel to the great zombie classic of 1968 that had made Romero famous, *Night of the Living Dead*. Always ready to exploit the commercial success of any American genre film, Italian producers encouraged Fulci to shoot what he called *Zombie 2* to capitalize on the Italian title of Romero's *Dawn*; originally called *Zombie Flesh Eaters* abroad, it is now known simply as *Zombie* (1979). Fulci's film ingeniously juxtaposes New York City against the Caribbean tropics, the traditional origin of zombies. The opening sequence preceding the credits shows a man shooting the corpse of a zombie in the head inside a boat, which then arrives in New York filled with zombies that attack Harbor Patrol policemen. The boat belongs to a man who has disappeared on a tropical island; his daughter Anne (Tisa Farrow) and a reporter, Peter West (Ian McCulloch), go to the island to investigate, and they discover that a strange disease causes the dead to return as flesh-eating zombies. Convinced that the rise of zombies has a scientific rather than a superstitious explanation, Dr. Menard (Richard Johnson) has begun to research this phenomenon on the island. Fulci provides a series of novel sequences: in one, an aquatic zombie combats a shark; in another, a zombie kills Menard's wife, Paola (Olga Karlatos), by pulling her through a wooden door with shutters, puncturing her eyeball with a splinter. All the gruesome detail, shown in close-up, constitutes one of Fulci's most famous special effects. Fulci's zombies are the relentless but slow variety made famous by Romero, but the novelty of his plot shows the few zombies that managed to reach New York setting off a zombie epidemic that the film somberly hints will conquer the civilized world. The final image is a crowd of zombies walking slowly over one of New York's major bridges toward Manhattan as the radio announces the invasion of its studio and a scream is heard over the sound track. Unlike Romero, whose 1978 hit at least suggested a social message (the consequences of American consumerism symbolized by the shopping mall under attack), Fulci really seems to have no "message": he is far more interested in creating believable monsters and a terrifying future.

One of Fulci's most successful films, *Zombie* soon generated many imitators in Italy, including one that appeared almost immediately: Girolami's *Zombie Holocaust*, a.k.a. *Dr. Butcher M.D.* (*Zombi Holocaust*, a.k.a. *La regina dei cannibali*, 1980). Employing some of the same actors and similar locations, and shamelessly borrowing the connection between a tropical island and New York City, Girolami also has a team of investigators from the Big Apple, a beautiful scientist named Dr. Lori Ridgeway (Alessandra Delli Colli) whose brain and body are often on display, and a policeman named Peter Chandler (Ian McCulloch). Girolami's film contains a few pretentious remarks about comparing contemporary society to one that practices cannibalism. Not surprisingly, the evil force at work on the tropical island located in the South Pacific is not therefore some strange native cult but, instead, the horrendous scientific experiments of Dr. Obrero (Donald O'Brien), who transfers the blood of live victims into dead humans, producing the zombies, who actually coexist on the island with the native cannibals. The high points of the film include Peter's dispatch of a zombie with an outboard motor's propeller, grinding its face into a bloody pulp, and Lori's emergence as the Queen of the Cannibals after being captured and stripped naked to display her ample breasts! Girolami thus packs both cannibals and zombies into this strange film.

Numerous other attempts to exploit the success of both Romero and Fulci quickly followed, and some of them favored cannibals over zombies. Deodato's *Cannibal Holocaust* (1980) has long been cited as the inspiration for *The Blair Witch Project* (1999) and as one of the most influential examples of the "shockumentary" film. The implicit juxtaposition of the West against primitive societies that practice cannibalism or harbor zombies remains a constant theme in the Italian horror films and is particularly important to *Cannibal Holocaust*. Its plot follows four filmmakers who go to the jungle to make a documentary. After they disappear, the news media sends others to recover their undeveloped film, and this footage reveals the shocking manner in which they died at the hands of the natives. These filmmakers,

In Deodato's *Cannibal Holocaust*—an influence on the Hollywood film *The Blair Witch Project*—television crews photograph killings by savage cannibals. *Credit: DVD*

however, are no innocent victims. They had intimidated natives, committed rape, and even murdered before the locals had decided to take their revenge. They are certainly less interested in the "truth" of what they photographed than in making a name for themselves and enhancing their professional reputation. Deodato's film suggests that the so-called reality in television and film documentaries is as much a product of conscious manipulation as the images from any fictional film. In *Cannibal Holocaust*, which contains graphic images of real animals being killed—one of the reasons why the film was so objectionable to many people (no doubt most of them meat eaters)—and fake images of real people being tortured and murdered by fake cannibals, the media are very much on trial. Actually, the true origins of such feigned documentary films, not to mention of "reality" television itself, more probably lie in the "Mondo" genre, born with the international hit film of 1962 *Mondo Cane*, directed by Gualtiero Jacopetti, Franco Prosperi (1926–), and Paolo Cavara (1926–82).[9] Presented as if it were a true documentary (and therefore a mirror of "reality," no matter how strange), *Mondo Cane* edits different kinds of footage together (much of it archival) to provide graphic detail of numerous cultural and sexual practices around the world that were calculated to strike the western sensibility as foreign, bizarre, ugly, frightening, or perverse.

Other films following Fulci's successful *Zombie* exhibit ingenious ways of varying the plot of his marketable venture. Lenzi uses the zombie theme in *Nightmare City* (*Incubo sulla città contaminata*, 1980) but with a twist. Like Romero's zombies, who emerge as the apparent result of exposure to some form of radiation, Lenzi's monsters arise after the spread of some form of atomic radiation that requires them to seek fresh blood to survive. Claiming inspiration from the notorious, dangerous chemical explosion and subsequent dioxin contamination in Seveso, Italy, in 1976, Lenzi created zombies that are really a radical form of vampire—they drink blood rather than actually eating flesh—but like zombies, they can be killed only with a headshot or blow to the brain. In contrast to the lumbering monsters created by Romero or Fulci, however, Lenzi's zombies are fast moving, intelligent, and capable of planning complex attacks; they also seem to be unstoppable even by military force. Lenzi's *Eaten Alive* (*Mangiati vivi!*, 1980), a film about cannibals with frequent shots of naked white women for titillation, focuses upon Reverend Jonas Melvyn (Ivan Rassimov), a Jim Jones–type cult leader who sets up shop in the middle of a cannibal-infested jungle. Banned in many countries all over the world, Lenzi's *Cannibal Ferox*, a.k.a. *Make Them Die Slowly* (1981), follows a strange team of New York drug dealers fleeing to the jungle from the Mob along with a doctoral student intent on proving that cannibalism is a myth. With that premise for her dissertation, the beautiful Gloria Davis (Lorraine De Selle) naturally discovers that cannibals exist as she watches her companions all die at the cannibals' hands. A cannibal

Cannibals execute the sexy model Pat in Lenzi's *Cannibal Ferox* by thrusting meat hooks through her prominently displayed breasts—only one example of numerous violent, gory, and extremely graphic killings in the film. *Credit: DVD*

castrates Mike, the drug pusher (Giovanni Lombardo Radice),[10] and eats his penis; another native cuts off his hand; and a third cuts off the top of his skull and eats his raw brains. Other "nonexistent" cannibals kill the sexy Pat (Zora Kerova) by hanging her by her breasts on meat hooks which a full frontal shot shows in grisly detail. *Cannibal Apocalypse* (*Apocalisse domani*, 1980), by Antonio Margheriti, depicts Vietnam veterans running amok in Atlanta, eating people after catching an infectious disease in Southeast Asia. *Anthropophagous: The Beast* (*Antropophagus*, 1980), by Joe D'Amato (a.k.a. Aristide Massaccesi, 1936–99),[11] contains a shocking scene where the cannibal Klaus (George Eastman) rips out a fetus from a pregnant Vanessa (Serena Grandi) and eats it, managing to break two taboos (abortion, cannibalism) in a single take. Ultimately this perverse cannibal meets his death by eating his own innards after being stabbed in the stomach: his desire for fresh meat overcomes even the powerful instinct for self-preservation!

Fulci's own sequel to *Zombie*, called *City of the Living Dead* (*Paura nella città dei morti viventi*, 1980), shows an aesthetic advance beyond his imitators via the creation of a mythical world closer to that of the Gothic horror film than the modern splatter film, generating a metaphysical horror ambience that he continues in *The Beyond* (*L'aldilà*, 1981) and *The House by the Cemetery* (*Quella villa accanto al cimitero*, 1981)—a group of three closely related films that some critics identify as Fulci's "zombie trilogy." Even though Fulci's horror films are justly identified with the maximum of gore and violence, they are artfully constructed around visual images rather than traditional literary plots, and thus resemble Dario Argento's horror and *giallo* cinema. Like Argento, Fulci designs horrific "set pieces" that never fully depend upon coherent storylines or cause-and-effect narratives. In discussing his work and comparing it with Argento's *Inferno*, the director declared:

My idea was to make an absolute film . . . there's no logic to it, just a succession of images. The Sea of Darkness from the final scene in *The Beyond*, for instance, is an absolute world, an immobile world where every horizon is similar. . . . Both films [i.e., *The Beyond* and *Inferno*] have no structure. We tried in Italy to make films based on pure themes, without a plot, and *The Beyond*, like *Inferno*, refuses conventions and traditional structures. . . . People who blame *The Beyond* for its lack of story have not understood that it's a film of images, which must be received without reflection.[12]

Fulci's trilogy presupposes the existence of another, parallel world of the afterlife that fundamentally embodies a nihilistic vision and a refusal of Christianity's consolation even while exploiting its mythology of Hell, Damnation, and the Rising of the Dead. Fulci's zombies in *City of the Living Dead* begin to rise after a priest commits suicide, thus opening the Gates of Hell, which must be closed again by the priest's annihilation before the risen dead take over the visible world. Thus Fulci's zombies are completely disassociated from any Caribbean connection or any link to voodoo magic; they are, rather, an atheist's spin on a Christian belief in the bodily resurrection of the dead before the Final Judgment. Like those of Argento, Fulci's horror films always have a metaphysical background and often stunning visual effects, which help to make Fulci's gory set pieces memorable. In *City of the Living Dead*, the most famous of these includes the famous "lobotomy" of Bob (played by the inevitable interpreter of Italian horror victims, Giovanni Lombardo Radice) using a mechanical drill, and a rain of worms recalling Argento's *Suspiria*.

In *The Beyond*, by general accounts Fulci's most successful work, a Louisiana hotel inherited by a New Yorker named Liza Merrill (Catriona MacColl) turns out to have been built over one of the portals of Hell. She and a doctor friend named John McCabe (David Warbeck) explore the hotel, and they enter the portal of the afterworld, from whence the dead return to walk among the living, all with blank, empty eyes that become one of the film's important images and a sign that a being has crossed over from this world to the other, the Beyond. Fulci offers a number of graphically grisly sequences, perhaps the most famous of which presents a zombie plumber grabbing a woman by the face and forcing her head against a large nail jutting out from a wall. In profile, we see the nail protrude from her eye socket with the eyeball dangling on the sharp end of the metal. Elsewhere, the camera takes a male victim's point of view as tarantulas crawl over his eyes and devour them. (The spiders literally crawl over the camera lens.) And most disturbing of all, a faithful seeing-eye dog turns on his mistress, a blind seer named Emily (Cinzia Monreale), and tears her throat apart. (Her blank stare and her expressionless eggshell-colored eyes without pupils, we

The famous lobotomy of Bob by a mechanical drill in Fulci's *The City of the Living Dead.*
Credit: DVD

discover, signify that she has come from the Beyond to this world.) As the film ends, on a desolate setting of a wasteland worthy of Dante's *Inferno*, both John and Liza stare into the camera with the same empty eyes, but the location is not Hell. It is literally nothing, a reflection of some incomprehensible evil in the universe.

The House by the Cemetery opens with a precredit sequence worthy of the best *giallo* thriller: a woman (Daniela Doria) enters the house that becomes almost the protagonist of the film. Inside, an unidentified killer thrusts a knife through the back of her head and out of her mouth, then drags her off. Someone's coming to a bad end in the house is repeated a number of times in the film. Its villain is Dr. Freudstein (Giovanni De Nava), a doctor expelled from the practice of medicine in 1897 because of his unacceptable experiments. He becomes a kind of zombie, requiring human victims to renew his cells and to stay alive, and since the action of the film takes place roughly a century later, his success is disturbingly clear. Of course, the name Freudstein evokes not only the inventor of psychoanalysis but also the archetypal movie monster of *Frankenstein*, and *The House by the Cemetery* deals not only with the unconscious (the house represents its symbolic embodiment) but also the monstrous part of humanity.

Lamberto Bava shot a number of late splatter horror films before the fad for such works ran its course and exhausted its energy, the most entertaining of which have a relationship to images from cinema and television: *Demons* and its sequel, *Demons 2* (a.k.a. *Demons 2: The Nightmare Returns*). Bava's two films are not postmodernist considerations of the horror film itself, the kind of quality that makes Wes Craven's *Scream* trilogy or the *Scary Movie* franchise begun by Keenen Ivory Wayans such a boon for film buffs. They do, however, possess their own brand of simple, uncomplicated charm and come from an era when horror films still relied upon special effects produced with gadgets, makeup, lens filters, smoke machines, and manmade prosthetics—all artisanal products that required great ingenuity and inventiveness without recourse to CGI. Obviously designed for a North American audience, the Demon films concentrate upon straight, uncomplicated gore and mayhem. In the hugely successful first one, people receive invitations to a screening at the Metropol-Theater in Berlin: the film playing presents a group of teenagers taking an ancient book written by Nostradamus and a demon mask. When one character receives a cut from the mask, the resulting infection eventually spreads and transforms the teenagers into demons. The events in the film-within-the-film suddenly begin to repeat themselves at the Metropol. After cutting herself on a prop mask in the theater lobby, a black prostitute named Rosemary (Geretta Geretta) turns into a bloodthirsty demon. Soon almost the entire audience becomes infected, with only a small group of young people escaping the disease. Most of the plot consists of various demon attacks and the survivors' unsuccessful attempts to stop the screening of the film that seems to be the source of this outbreak of demons, with the implication that the same thing is happening in movie theaters all over the world. In *Demons 2*, Bava repeats this same formula of film-causing-disaster-in-the-real-world-audience with a birthday party in an elegant high-rise apartment building replacing the cinema audience, and the infectious images emanating from a television program. Once again, demons spill out from the media world into the "real" world. In one case, a demon actually moves from a television set into an apartment. The most famous kind of demonic transformation in both films, and one of Lamberto Bava's trademarks, consists of normal teeth being transformed with a plastic mask into demon fangs. There is even a demon dog whose canines turn into demon canines before he attacks his master, the ultimate act of disloyalty. Although both films are excellent examples of the monster films that became quite popular in the 1980s, they show little of the cinematic virtuosity that characterized Mario Bava's earlier horror films—all made with even lower budgets but containing more stunning visual effects than his son's work.

Michele Soavi and the End of the Spaghetti Nightmare Era

The spaghetti nightmare film rose to prominence with the bravura of Mario Bava, continued to forge new territory with Dario Argento, and peaked in cult popularity with Lucio Fulci and a number of lesser lights in the 1980s. It died a natural death at the end of that decade, after which it was produced only in limited quantities, unlike the mass production typical of its popular heyday, when it achieved great box-office appeal in Italy and abroad. Its last and perhaps best practitioner was Michele Soavi, Argento's protégé, who worked as a bit actor or assistant director in many of the most important horror films of the time, including works by Argento, Lamberto Bava, and Fulci. He also served Terry Gilliam as second-unit director on *The Adventures of Baron Munchausen* (1988) and *The Brothers Grimm* (2005). After turning to full-time direction, he made two good horror films with religious themes that Argento wrote and produced: *The Church*, about medieval crusaders' persecution of witches and their possible return in the present age, and *The Sect*, about a satanic cult in modern Frankfurt. Next, Soavi directed a truly fine horror film: *Cemetery Man* (*Dellamorte dellamore*, 1994), which one critic has called "the most innovative and impressive horror film of the 1990s."[13] With the exception of Argento's last installment in the "Trilogy of the Three Mothers" in 2007, Soavi's film may mark the end of the long period during which the spaghetti nightmare film made international film history.

Soavi based *Cemetery Man* on a popular novel of the same name by Tiziano Sclavi (1953–), the acclaimed creator of the celebrated Italian comic series *Dylan Dog*, which Sclavi began writing in 1986. The physical appearance of his "nightmare detective," Dylan Dog, was inspired by the face of the English actor Rupert Everett, and since Everett's face was on a comic strip that sold hundreds of thousands of copies in Italy, Soavi thought him to be the perfect choice for the lead role in the film of Sclavi's novel. The Italian title of the film might be translated literally as "about death, about love," which renders most precisely the film's real subject. In a beautifully photographed return to the Gothic atmosphere of the early Italian horror films of Bava and others, Soavi places us into the bizarre, surrealistic world of the cemetery outside a small, imaginary Italian town named Buffalora. There, Francesco Dellamorte (Saint Francis of Death, as he calls himself) tends the local graveyard, painstakingly reconstructed by Soavi upon the remnants of an actual cemetery. Dellamorte's slightly retarded assistant, Gnaghi (François Hadji-Lazaro), is the spitting image of Jerome Lester Horwitz, a.k.a. Curly Howard—one of the Three Stooges. At Buffalora's graveyard, the dead generally return to life after a week in the coffin, and Dellamorte refers to them as "returners," not zombies. Dellamorte, who is a slacker, prefers to ignore the bureaucratic complications of reporting these events to the city government and simply shoots them as they arise again, and reburies them with Gnaghi's help. The wonderfully comic first sequence of the film, preceding the credits, sets the droll tone for the entire work. Wrapped in a towel and still dripping from a shower, Dellamorte speaks to a friend on the telephone. When a "returner" knocks at the door and enters the room, he shoots him without even a second thought, neither interrupting his conversation nor dropping his cigarette. Like Gnaghi, Dellamorte is a loner who is also impotent, until he meets the unnamed love of his life. We never learn her first name, but Dellamorte meets her at the funeral of her much older husband. Subsequently, her grave will eventually bear only the name "Lei," or "She." Anna Falchi, a top model whose first film was one of Fellini's last television commercials for the Banca di Roma, plays "She" as well as a grieving widow and the secretary of the local mayor. This continuous appearance of the same person as different characters in the film strongly suggests that much of the film's narrative represents either a dream experienced by the protagonist or a glimpse into his unconscious. "She" finds Dellamorte immediately attractive and delivers one of the film's best lines: "You know, you've got a real nice ossuary."[14] She becomes aroused by her visit with Dellamorte to the graveyard's collection of bones from the past, and their subsequent lovemaking not only cures Dellamorte's impotence but also provokes her dead husband's wrath, since they lie next to his fresh grave. Her husband rises from the dead, bites "She," and eventually leads Dellamorte to believe she has died as a result. When a doctor informs him the next day that the woman died while making love, it seems to eliminate Dellamorte from the list of his suspects, because the doctor knows him to be impotent. Later, in what must surely be a dream sequence, or at least a flashback in Dellamorte's mind to a past event, "She" rises up from the dead covered in a white veil, and Dellamorte shoots her in the usual way of controlling other "returners" and buries her. Later he will be overcome with guilt when he thinks that he has mistakenly thought her to be dead.

The outline of the film's plot demonstrates no objective point of view in Soavi's film, no means of determining what is true, what is false, and what is simply imagined or dreamed. Other equally bizarre events in *Cemetery Man* blur the distinction between reality and fantasy in Dellamorte's life. As Dellamorte puts it, "the living dead and the dying living are all the same, cut from the same cloth, but disposing of dead people is a public service,

Dellamorte makes love with "She" in a graveyard before her death and subsequent re-appearance as a "returner" in Soave's *Cemetery Man*. Credit: DVD

whereas you are in all sorts of trouble when you kill someone while they're still alive." Eventually, Dellamorte begins to kill the living almost on a whim. Since everyone's life ends at the cemetery, homicide only shortens the wait. Or at least it *seems* that he begins to kill the living. The film ends as it begins, with an enigmatic shot of two figures inside one of those souvenir crystal balls filled with artificial snow (perhaps a nod to *Citizen Kane*). The two figures, like Dellamorte and Gnaghi, are trapped in a world that makes no sense and from which there seems to be no escape.

By the time Soavi made this outstanding film, black humor was the only approach left unexploited to deal with the increasingly repetitive images of zombies and cannibals produced by the spaghetti nightmare tradition. Without the capital necessary to compete with the computer-generated horror films made in America, the Italian horror film factory eventually was forced to shut down. Although Italian horror films were produced in far fewer numbers than typical for other popular genre films, the best Italian horror films represent fine examples of artisanally designed special effects and original reinterpretations of traditional horror themes. In some instances, they influenced Hollywood directors producing films that had far greater appeal at the international box office. Italian horror films live on today because they enjoy widespread availability in remastered versions on DVD. They occupy numerous websites on the Internet, and they even attract real attention from academic critics. The spaghetti nightmare films have today achieved the cult status previously enjoyed by the spaghetti western and have, as it were, discovered a second life—not unlike the numerous zombies, vampires, and monsters that returned from the dead over and over again in their narratives.

CHAPTER ELEVEN

A Fistful of Pasta

SERGIO LEONE AND THE
SPAGHETTI WESTERN

The Rise of an Italian Variant on a Classic American Film Genre

AS ONE OF THE MOST POPULAR and durable of all Hollywood film genres, the western inevitably had an influence upon postwar Italian cinema, particularly during the neorealist period in certain key works by Pietro Germi and Giuseppe De Santis. A very small number of westerns were made in the silent period and during the Fascist era, such as *Indian Vampire*, made by Sergio Leone's father in 1913, or the first full-length Italian western, *Girl of the Golden West* (*Una signora dell'ovest*, 1942), shot by Carl Koch.[1] But the remarkable phenomenon we today label as the "spaghetti western"— nearly five hundred films produced in Italy between 1963 and the end of the 1970s—goes far beyond a few isolated early examples.[2] Italian westerns dominated film exports in terms of box-office profits between 1956 and 1971, a period that produced some of the most important Italian film classics in the "art film" category. Although Sergio Leone deserves most of the credit for launching this Italian genre, some twenty-five westerns had been produced in Italy before he began *A Fistful of Dollars*. And since Leone himself made only five westerns, though certainly among the very best ones, his genius does not explain the sudden production of hundreds and hundreds of films within a very brief period of time.

Economic factors played an important role in the genesis of the spaghetti western. Hollywood's annual production of westerns dropped from fifty-four in 1958 to a mere eleven in 1962–63 and would rise again to thirty-seven only in 1967 after Leone's international success gave new birth to what American producers had considered an exhausted film genre. While these were years of financial crisis in Hollywood, in Italy the huge infrastructure of the Italian film industry, second only to that of Hollywood in Europe, had just passed through the era of "Hollywood on the Tiber" (see chapter 6), a period marked by coproductions in Italy and a number of important blockbuster works. The Italian industry sought international capital for popular films, and with American money available as well as relatively inexpensive Italian or Spanish locations and extras, the western was an obvious choice. Italian directors, cameramen, set designers, and actors initially disguised their national identities by using English pseudonyms: Leone originally called himself Bob Robertson, an anglicized homage to his silent-film director father, Vincenzo, who made the first Italian western under the name Roberto Roberti; Sergio Corbucci became Stanley Corbett; Gianfranco Parolini (1930–) called himself Frank Kramer; Enzo Barboni, both cinematographer and director, worked under the name E. B. Clucher. If possible, Italian directors attempted to hire a recognizably American star or former star as well as several Hollywood character actors. Thus, not only Clint Eastwood, but also Eli Wallach, Jack Palance, Henry Silva, Robert Ryan, Telly Savalas, Lee Van Cleef, Woody Strode, Guy Madison, and a host of others came to Italy to shoot westerns. Italian actors sometimes used English screen names in these westerns. Before becoming an international star after his performances in Leone's first two westerns, Gian Maria Volontè was known as Johnny Wells; Giuliano Gemma (1938–) called himself Montgomery Wood; Mario Girotti became Terence Hill; and Carlo Pedersoli made up his stage name, Bud Spencer, in an amusing tribute to his favorite American beer and to the Hollywood actor Spencer Tracy. But Tomas Milian, a Cuban-born American actor who made his fortune in Italy, retained his Spanish first name not only for Italian westerns but also for Italian Euro-crime (*poliziesco*) films and comedies after the craze for the western passed on. Spaghetti westerns were both phenomenally successful for over a decade after the release of Sergio Leone's first *Dollars* film in 1964, and incredibly profitable: a relatively small amount of capital could produce millions in profits. As a result, before the genre exhausted itself, many ordinary Italians with money to risk invested in making a western, so certain did the prospects for gain seem.

The Classic American Western Formula and the Italian Spaghetti Western Variant

One influential study of the "classic" American western formula, John Cawelti's *The Six-Gun Mystique*, outlines it as a combination of narrative possibilities generated by three central roles: the townspeople (agents of civilization); savages or outlaws who threaten the first group; and heroes, men who share certain characteristics of the second group but who ultimately act on behalf of the representatives of civilization.[3] Elsewhere, Cawelti argues that the classic westerns of the 1940s and 1950s "depended on and reaffirmed for us the traditional American view that violence was the fault of evil and corrupt men; good men might be forced to use it in purging society of corruption, but this would lead to a regenerated social order."⁴ The fact that classic American westerns concerned the rise of a new civilization in a virgin land comes as no surprise, since this story was an integral part of American frontier history. When Italian directors appropriated the film genre in the 1960s, they inherited a large number of themes and motifs from Hollywood, but the Italian western could never become nothing more than a reflection of American history. It would become something quite different, far more violent, and a great deal more cynical about the myth of the American West.

In general, Italian films embraced a number of themes that certainly existed in American westerns, but now they were exaggerated. Christopher Frayling identifies three basic plots in the Italian western: (1) the "Servant of Two Masters" plot; (2) the "transitional plot," a variant of the "Servant of Two Masters" plot; and (3) a "Zapata-Spaghetti" plot. To these three plot types should be added a fourth: the parody of the spaghetti western genre itself.

The first type, based upon suggestions from both Carlo Goldoni's play *The Servant of Two Masters* (*Il servitore di due padroni*, 1745) and Akira Kurosawa's Samurai film masterpiece *Yojimbo* (1961),⁵ features a hero (usually a bounty hunter or an outlaw but almost always a stranger in town) who plays two rival gangs against each other. *A Fistful of Dollars* is the classic example of such a plot, with the bounty hunter played by Clint Eastwood—known variously as the Stranger or the Man with No Name—dealing with two groups: the Baxters, a family of gringo gunrunners dominated by the mother, Consuelo (Margherita Lozano); and the Rojos, a group of rum-running Mexicans led by the sadistic Ramón (Gian Maria Volontè). This plot also figures in a number of other important westerns, such as *Django* (1966), by Sergio Corbucci, where a band of murderous, racist, ex-Confederates led by a Major Jackson (Eduardo Fajardo) takes on Mexican rebels led by General Hugo Rodriguez (José Bódalo); *Django Kill* (*Se sei vivo spara*, 1967), by Giulio Questi (1924–), where a Stranger (Tomas Milian) combats a gringo gang of murderers, an entire town, and a band of Mexican homosexuals led by a psychotic character ironically named Zorro (Roberto Carmardiel); and *The Return of Ringo* (*Il ritorno di Ringo*, 1965), by Duccio Tessari, where Captain Montgomery Brown, alias Ringo, comes to town disguised as a Mexican peasant with no name. That plot offers itself to infinite permutations, as is evident by Walter Hill's remake of *A Fistful of Dollars* and *Yojimbo*, with a script that credits both Kurosawa and Leone, in *Last Man Standing* (1996), starring Bruce Willis as a Prohibition-era gunman who manipulates an Irish and an Italian mob into killing each other off.

The second plot structure combines the "Servant of Two Masters" plot with some complications, usually historical in nature. Different groups still struggle to seize control of gold or land or some form of wealth, but now other values are added by placing the action within a specific historical context, such as the Civil War or the Mexican Revolution, events that give the characters in conflict additional motives to obtain the treasure that they kill each other to possess. Leone's *The Good, the Bad, and the Ugly* (*Il buono, il brutto, il cattivo*, 1966) or *Once Upon a Time in the West* (*C'era una volta il West*, 1968) follow this pattern. Because of the historical elements in this type of film and the large budgets required to make them, such works in Leone's hands take on an epic character that is rarely matched in other lower-budget Italian westerns.

Such films as Sergei Eisenstein's unfinished *¡Que viva Mexico!* (1932) or Elia Kazan's *Viva Zapata!* (1952) were both influential antecedents of what Frayling calls the "Zapata-Spaghetti" plot (also known as the "tortilla" western). This politicized western, set in the midst of Mexican revolutions, provided a theme that many leftist Italian directors adapted as a means of making an anticapitalist or anti-American western during the ideologically charged era in which Italian westerns were extremely popular. Films in this group include *A Bullet for the General* (*Quién sabe?*, 1966), by Damiano Damiani (1922–2013); *Kill and Pray* (*Requiescant*, 1967), by Carlo Lizzani, who cast the director Pier Paolo Pasolini as a Catholic priest unsurprisingly siding with the Mexican Revolution; Corbucci's *Compañeros* (*Vamos a matar, compañeros*, 1970); and Leone's *Duck, You Sucker*, also released as *A Fistful of Dynamite* (*Giù la testa*, 1971), his fifth and last western.

The final plot type that eventually brought the craze for the Italian western to a close was the parody, the perennial treatment of popular cinematic themes in the Italian film industry that surfaces whenever a theme emerges as popular and profitable. This final plot type produced several excellent films, including *God Forgives—I Don't* (*Dio perdona . . . io no*, 1967), by Giuseppe Colizzi (1925–78), the film that first paired Terence Hill and Bud Spencer in a semiserious western; *They Call Me Trinity*, a.k.a. *My Name Is Trinity* (*Lo chiamavano Trinità*, 1970) by Enzo Barboni, a work that made Terence Hill and Bud Spencer Italy's most popular comic actors; *My Name Is Nobody* (*Il mio nome è Nessuno*, 1973), by Tonino Valerii (1934–); and the film that broke all Italian box-office records for a single film in the history of the industry, Barboni's *Trinity Is Still My Name* (*. . . continuavano a chiamarlo Trinità*, 1971).

A number of narrative themes and stylistic traits characterize spaghetti westerns. Rather than the righteous sheriff of an American western such as Fred Zinnemann's *High Noon* (1952), Italian films, following Leone's lead in *A Fistful of Dollars* and then *For a Few Dollars More* (*Per qualche dollaro in più*, 1965), preferred the bounty hunter, the relentless protagonist who kills for money rather than any higher ideal, or even an outlaw protagonist. In Leone's second *Dollars* film, there are *two* bounty hunters fighting over their target—Monco (Clint Eastwood) and Colonel Douglas Mortimer (Lee Van Cleef). The Hollywood character actor Van Cleef's performance made him a huge star in spaghetti westerns. (Unlike Eastwood, who left Italy after three films with Leone, Van Cleef remained there for years to star in a number of them.) As a corollary to the bounty hunter or outlaw hero figure, the level of graphic violence in Italian westerns was considerably higher when compared to their American counterparts. Viewed today, they seem rather tame and less graphic than is the norm even for network television programs: blood is rarely shed in the murderous gun battles that fill them, and when it shows up on the screen, it is all too often obviously fake. Moreover, the very nature of the spaghetti western protagonist increased the cynicism with which the American West was viewed, deflating the heroic aspects of a narrative about taming a wild land for civilization that typified the best products of Hollywood. Ultimately, it became very difficult to distinguish the positive western heroes from the negative ones in Italian westerns. In most cases, none of the characters possessed positive, heroic traits.

Another major theme of Italian westerns is a familiar one to theater and opera lovers, or to fans of the gangster film and the Mafia in the cinema—that of revenge, *la vendetta*, a theme that could fit into virtually any plot scheme. Of course, one of the greatest American westerns, John Ford's *The Searchers* (1956), is all about revenge. As the Italian expression puts it, "revenge is a plate best served cold," and the Italian western reflects an obsession with *la vendetta*, so essential to Italian melodrama and the Mafia films that began in the 1970s, while the western was still in vogue.

Women, so frequently a symbol of law and order and of progress toward a taming of the Wild West in American westerns, rarely play such a role in this savage world. More often than not, women in Italian westerns are prostitutes and, at the very least, women of ill repute. Like the Italian audiences themselves who flocked to see the films, the world of the spaghetti western was predominantly a masculine, or rather a macho, one. The somewhat jaundiced view of American culture typical of many Italian leftist directors also explains why race becomes so much more important in these films. In particular, westerns made in Italy frequently accentuate conflicts between the dominant white, Anglo culture of the United States and the Mexicans. That being said, if the Anglo figures sometimes seem like the essence of "white trash," the Mexicans are unabashedly caricatured as filthy "greasers" and "beaners," offering very little to prefer between the two groups.

Gunfights between opponents armed with Colt 45 pistols, so crucial to any American western, sometimes become magnified into grotesque proportions, especially in the hands of a brilliant director such as Leone. Directors modify this classic method of concluding a western film by changing the weapons of choice. In *Django*, Franco Nero, playing the title role, drags a coffin that contains a machine gun around with him, which he uses to dispatch dozens of opponents; Leone's Colonel Mortimer in *For a Few Dollars More*, and Sabata (Lee Van Cleef), a character closely modeled upon Leone's Mortimer, in *Sabata* (*Ehi amico . . . c'è Sabata, hai chiuso!*, 1969), by Gianfranco Parolini, sport unusual weapons, such as a Buntline Special pistol with a twelve-inch barrel and detachable shoulder stock that can be added to increase its range and accuracy, or derringers that shoot from the handgrip as well as the gun barrel; a mute gunfighter named Silence (Jean-Louis Trintignant) in Corbucci's *The Big Silence* (*Il grande silenzio*, 1968) uses an 1896 9mm Mauser C96 "Broomhandle" with a detachable shoulder stock that can be set on either single shot or automatic. Of course, each variation in weapon generally increases the firepower and the violence depicted on the screen. The *Trinity* films, on the other hand, also poke fun at dramatic gun battles, since Trinity's draw is so rapid he can draw and reholster his weapon before his opponent even gets his hand on his weapon, often making it unnecessary to kill him.

Given the huge number of westerns produced in Italy within a relatively brief time, including many sequels, film titles themselves often showed a sense of humor, reflected popular Italian slang expressions, or referred to previous successful films. The humor is often lost in translation with such film titles as *Sabata*, the Italian original of which literally means, "Hey buddy . . . Sabata's here, and you're through!" *Massacre Time*, by the soon-to-be-famous horror film director Lucio Fulci would have seemed much more amusing to English-speaking audiences if its Italian title had been rendered more literally (*Le Colt cantarono la morte e fu . . . tempo di massacro*, 1966; that is, "the Colts sang of death and it was . . . massacre time"). Giuliano Carnimeo (directing as Anthony Ascott) seems to have had a particular genius for inventing strange titles and unusual names for his pistoleros. Among the films he directed are these intriguing titles and protagonists: *Fistful of Lead*, a.k.a. *Sartana's Here . . . Trade Your Pistol for a Coffin* (*C'è Sartana . . . vendi la pistola e comprati la bara*, 1970); *Forewarned, Half-killed . . . the Word of the Holy Ghost* (*Uomo avvisato mezzo ammazzato . . . Parola di Spirito Santo*, 1971); *His Pistols Smoked . . . They Call Him Cemetery* (*Gli fumavano le Colt . . . lo chiamavano Camposanto*, 1971); and *Heads I Kill You, Tails You're Dead! They Call Me Hallalujah* (*Testa t'ammazzo, croce . . . sei morto . . . Mi chiamano Alleluja*, 1971); or *In the West There Was a Man Named Invincible*, a.k.a. *They Called Him the Player with the Dead* (*Lo chiamavano Tresette . . . giocava sempre col morto*, (1973), the most difficult to translate accurately, since the protagonist's name, Tresette, is a popular Italian card game unknown to most Americans (literally, "they called him Tresette . . . he always played with the dead man"). The titles themselves speak volumes about the atmosphere in which these popular films were produced, as Italian directors and scriptwriters manipulated the traditional western classic plots in an often irreverent manner. Yet, today more and more attention has been paid not only to the Leone films (always a favorite of the critics) but also to the truly B Italian genre films—not only spaghetti westerns but also the *poliziesco* (Euro-crime) movies. The driving force behind this contemporary attention to such works has been the postmodern cult director Quentin Tarantino, who cites them repeatedly—either implicitly, or explicitly in the credits—in such popular works as *Reservoir Dogs* (1992), *Pulp Fiction* (1994), *Kill Bill 1* (2003), *Kill Bill 2* (2004), and *Grindhouse: Death Proof* (2007). Moreover, he has sponsored and publicized important screenings of Italian popular genre films not only at the Venice Film Festival in 2004 but also at his own film festival in Austin, Texas.[6]

Leone's Clint Eastwood Westerns: *A Fistful of Dollars, For a Few Dollars More,* and *The Good, The Bad, and the Ugly*

Leone's *A Fistful of Dollars* plunges us into a violent and cynical world far removed from the West of John Ford or Howard Hawks. The Stranger (Eastwood), a bounty hunter, is interested only in money, a motivation he shares with the villainous Baxters and Rojos, the two opposing gangs in the town of San Miguel. Far from a microcosm of a threatened outpost of civilization (the typical nature of the town in an American western), San Miguel, is a surrealistic place where nobody works except the coffin maker, Piripero (Josef Egger), and the saloon owner, Silvanito (José Calvo), since killing has become the only means of making a living. Except for Marisol (Marianne Koch), a poor Mexican woman exploited sexually by Ramón Rojo (Volontè), women, the traditional symbol of civilization and stability in Hollywood westerns, are either absent or widows. Legal authorities are reduced to using criminals to uphold the law, and even the cavalry sells liquor and guns to the Indians rather than protecting civilization. The note of black humor always present in the most violent of Italian westerns, *gialli*, or *poliziesco* films pops up immediately even in Leone's scripts. When the Stranger confronts three Baxter men who have insulted his mule, he tells Piripero to make three coffins, but in the ensuing shootout, he miscalculates and kills four men: "My mistake—four coffins!" he remarks with a grin.

Leone's transformations in traditional Hollywood plots or even his humorous gags are only a few of the changes he initiates in the film genre he imitated. In a true stroke of genius, he employed Ennio Morricone to score his sound tracks. Morricone's music, filled with unusual sounds composed of gunfire, ricocheting bullets, cries, trumpet solos, traditional Sicilian folk instruments (the Jew's harp in particular), and whistles becomes so crucial to Leone's narratives that they shape the final outcome of both the filming and the editing process. Even more important for Leone's emerging film style is his insistence upon lengthy and extreme close-ups of the faces of

The creation of a film icon: The Stranger—chewing an Italian toscano cigar in a close-up—in Leone's *A Fistful of Dollars*. *Credit: DVD*

his actors, a stylistic trait other filmmakers imitated over and over again until it became a cliché. Leone explained his obsession with this kind of shot as part of his reaction against the formulaic codes imposed upon him by mediocre directors when he was an assistant director, codes that obliged him to follow the so-called rules of cinematic narrative rather than pursuing a personal style, that of an auteur:

> I made 58 films as an assistant—I was at the side of directors who applied all the rules: make it, for example, a close-up to show that the character is about to say something important. I reacted against all that and so close-ups in my films are always the expression of an emotion . . . so they call me a perfectionist and a formalist because I watch my framing. But I'm not doing it to make it pretty; I'm seeking, first and foremost, the relevant emotion.[7]

Leone's emphasis upon elemental and often brutal emotional impact in his works conflicted with the implicit moral message audiences expected from the classic western formula. *A Fistful of Dollars* was a revolutionary and extremely original work, a film that today would be called "postmodern" for its radical manipulation of generic rules and its playful citations of other films. It reinvigorated a dying Hollywood genre and earned more money than *any* other Italian film made until that date, at a laughable cost of some $200,000. Its success ensured that the Italian film industry would produce numerous sequels, and it made Leone's task of locating money for big budgets much easier—one of the reasons why, from a visual point of view, his later westerns appear so much richer and are so much more complicated.

In *For a Few Dollars More*, Leone creates a sequel that attempts to retain the elements that were so popular in his first film with several new narrative twists. Clint Eastwood returns as a bounty hunter, now called Monco, with his Tuscan cigars and his Mexican serape. He is joined by Colonel Mortimer (Lee Van Cleef), a retired soldier and bounty hunter motivated not by Monco's thirst for gold but by a quest for revenge against Indio (Gian Maria

Volontè, in what is certainly one of his greatest performances), the dope-crazed Mexican killer-bandit who takes a perverse pleasure in violence. Indio has a pocket watch whose chimes evoke for him memories of the moment that bound him and Mortimer together, the moment that inevitably results in the concluding showdown and settling of accounts between the two men. Like Monco, Mortimer is a professional but one who dresses like a preacher, reads the Bible constantly, and sports a series of unusual weapons. Once again, Leone provides grotesque humor in his script. When Mortimer and Monco first meet as competitors in arresting or killing outlaws who have a price on their heads, they engage in an infantile competition, scuffing each other's boots in an attempt to establish a bounty hunter's pecking order. In another justly famous sequence, Mortimer strikes a match for his ubiquitous pipe on the physically deformed back of one of Indio's men, the "Wild One" (Klaus Kinski). Elsewhere, standing on a church pulpit and preaching to his gang of murderers, Indio provides a parody of a sermon (the parable of the carpenter) as he explains that the bank they are to rob contains a safe hidden within a cabinet—a piece of secret information Indio obtained from the carpenter who built the cabinet just before Indio killed him to keep this secret location safe!

The movie inches toward the final confrontation among Monco, Mortimer, and Indio, an event whose causes Leone explains through the use of flashbacks. Not only had Indio raped Mortimer's sister and killed her husband on their wedding night, but thereafter she had killed herself with Indio's gun. Leone prefigures the end of Mortimer's thirst for revenge by giving both Indio and Mortimer one of a matched pair of pocket watches with chimes—Indio's had come from Mortimer's sister, and it is restored to its rightful family ownership after Indio's death. The final shootout is one of the best in Leone's cinema: a number of sharp close-ups captures the faces, gun hands, weapons, and minute expressions of the protagonists; the superb Morricone score based upon the watch's chimes creates an emotional climax when they cease; Indio's death at Mortimer's hands is almost an afterthought, for the settling of accounts in Leone's westerns always takes on a symbolic function, a ritual act concluding a narrative cycle and employing music in much the same way as in grand opera, where stirring arias often accompany death. With Indio's demise, the partnership between Mortimer and Monco ends. Monco piles up the bodies to collect his bounty, while Mortimer, his vendetta concluded, rides off into the distance, only to return as a different protagonist in Leone's next western, and subsequently as Santana, Sabata, and various other spaghetti western heroes in films shot by other directors.

A Fistful of Dollars and *For a Few Dollars More* were brilliantly original works that made incredible amounts of money with small budgets. In *The Good, the Bad, and the Ugly*, Leone's phenomenal success enabled him to obtain a comparatively huge budget for an Italian film, allowing the director to shift his perspective to an epic tone and to tackle a grander historical theme, the American Civil War. In his *Dollars* westerns, few values besides money or revenge motivate the characters. In Leone's depiction of the Civil War, as in his later *Once Upon a Time in the West*, with its celebration of the advent of the railroad in the West, Leone moves toward a western's more traditional concern with larger historical issues, even if these are often ambiguously treated in a manner far removed from the Hollywood model. The three protagonists of *The Good, the Bad, and the Ugly*—the bounty hunter Blondie (Eastwood), the Mexican bandit Tuco (Eli Wallach), and the murderer-for-hire Angel Eyes (Van Cleef)—all seem familiar figures motivated by gold and bounty. Yet as Leone presents them to us in separate sequences, all ending in violent murder (with a title on the screen assigning their respective moral connotations), such simplistic distinctions are immediately blurred, and it becomes extremely difficult in this ambiguous moral universe to calculate just who is good, bad, or ugly.

The film's plot centers on a complex chase by the three men for $200,000 in gold stolen from an army payroll and buried in an unmarked grave at Sad Hill Cemetery in the middle of a Civil War battlefield set in the Southwest Territory. Although most Americans know little about the Civil War in the Southwest, a Confederate force of some thirty-five hundred men led by General Henry H. Sibley left Texas to attack New Mexico in 1862; but the southern invasion ended in disaster, with numerous dead and captured after their defeat at the Battle of Glorieta Pass in the Sangre de Cristo Mountains that same year, a battle known by some historians as "the Gettysburg of the West." While Leone does not set out to create a historically accurate account of this campaign, his knowledge of it provides him with a vast historical backdrop for re-creations of contemporary warfare. Leone's complex and epic storyline culminates in a climactic gunfight among his protagonists, who struggle for the hidden gold. The injection of references to actual history into his film, however, creates a mood entirely different from his *Dollars* films. The moral ambiguity of his three protagonists, ironically labeled "good," "bad," and "ugly," is overshadowed by the even more shocking moral ambiguity of the Civil War itself. Right and wrong, good and bad, change in Leone's universe as rapidly as do uniforms. Indeed, one of the most telling comments about the two sides in this conflict comes from a comic sequence in which Tuco and Blondie, disguised as Confederates, hail what they think is a column of southern cavalry, only to be taken prisoner after the horsemen brush the gray dust off their blue uniforms! Leone bases behavior in the prison camp to which they are taken more on the Nazi *Lagers* of World War II than upon the infamous Andersonville prison (Camp Sumter). It includes a sadistic guard, Angel Eyes, now disguised as a Union soldier, who beats his "Confederate" prisoners to the tune of a prison orchestra—an obvious reference to Auschwitz. The Battle for Langstone

The greatest gunfight in the spaghetti western gets under way between Tuco, Blondy, and Angel Eyes in Leone's *The Good, the Bad, and the Ugly*. *Credit: DVD*

Bridge (which seems to be a version of the historical battle of Glorieta Pass) represents an idiotic and useless struggle for a "flyspeck on the map" at Union Army headquarters, and the bridge itself is useless to anyone except for the fact that the opposing army wants it. Employing hundreds of extras and only possible because Leone had a large, Hollywood-type budget, the visuals of the battle scene recall the senseless slaughter in the trenches during World War I. Although Leone shows automatic weapons being used in this battle—weapons that were employed only very infrequently in actual Civil War combat—his photography seems indebted to the famous battle photographs by Mathew Brady. It becomes clear that Leone prefers the smaller but infinitely less immoral universe of his three gunfighters to general warfare. At least they live and die by a code with rules and a certain sense of dignity.

In the final, triangular confrontation over the hidden gold, Leone creates the single most famous and brilliant sequence in spaghetti western history. Only Blondie knows the actual location of the grave in which the gold remains buried. He writes that name on a rock placed in the center of a ringed mudflat, the symbolic *corrida* circle of death and violence that Leone used to accentuate the symbolic character of his showdown. The three men face off against one another, and Leone devotes a full three minutes or more to the crescendo of suspense leading to the actual gunfire. Leone's manneristic style reaches an emotional peak never before achieved in a western. As Morricone's music builds the tension, the director cuts rapidly back and forth between extreme close-ups of the eyes, pupils, hands, fingers, and weapons of the three men until the inevitable shot signals the wounding and then, with a coup de grâce, the death of Angel Eye. Afterward, we discover that Blondie has tricked Tuco, removing his bullets the night before the fight to even the odds, and Leone's gallows humor returns with Blondie's callous remark: "In this world, there're two kinds of people, my friend— those with loaded guns and those who dig. You dig!"

In *The Good, the Bad, and the Ugly*, Leone's epic scope changes somewhat the completely amoral character of his gunfighters. A number of scenes underscore emotions rarely seen in the callous *pistoleros* typical of the genre. In one scene, Tuco informs his brother, a sanctimonious priest, that he was driven into a life of crime to support their parents. In another, Blondie compassionately offers a cigar and a warm coat to a dying Confederate soldier. At the conclusion of the film, although the murderous Angel Eyes must die, Blondie spares Tuco and even gives him half of the gold when he could have just as easily killed his Mexican companion. Male camaraderie, a bond central to the traditional Hollywood western formula, has crept back into Leone's interpretation of the American West, and such traditional themes become even more important with Leone's next film, his epic treatment of the arrival of the railroad and the birth of civilization in the untamed wilderness, *Once Upon a Time in the West.*

Once Upon a Time There Was a Myth: American Mythology and the Leone Western

Leone did not intend *Once Upon a Time in the West* to follow his third and last Clint Eastwood western. After his international box-office success with his first three westerns, Leone went to Hollywood to seek financial support for quite a different project, what later became his film about Jewish American gangsters in *Once Upon a Time in America* (*C'era una volta in America*, 1984). This project did not materialize at the time, but Leone returned to Italy with Paramount financing, and Henry Fonda as the star, for another western. Leone commissioned a script from Bernardo Bertolucci, who included in what he eventually showed to Leone numerous quotations from a lifetime of watching Hollywood westerns in the Paris Cinémathèque; other contributions were offered by Dario Argento. Although Bertolucci's original script was largely discarded for the final film, *Once Upon a Time in the West* remains the most deeply indebted of all Leone's works to the classic western, with references to *High Noon, Shane, My Darling Clementine, The Iron Horse, The Man Who Shot Liberty Valance,* and many other films that influenced the choice of Leone's shots, names, costumes, and even his plot. In spite of the film's obvious quality and its critical success, without Eastwood, whose contemporary popularity peaked with the release in America of Leone's third western, causing the first two to be released all over the country, Leone's most ambitious project to date, and his most elaborate effort in the spaghetti western genre he created virtually alone, never became quite as popular as the first three films. The fifth and final western he directed, *Duck, You Sucker!,* reflects the politically motivated "Zapata-Spaghetti" plot. The next time he was involved with a western it was as a producer of *My Name Is Nobody,* directed by his protégé Tonino Valerii, but based on a story in part written by Leone, which parodied the very genre he made famous.

Leone's casting of *Once Upon a Time in the West* establishes interesting links to American tradition. During the five-minute sequence opening the film with the credits, Leone presents two of the most familiar western character actors from Hollywood—Jack Elam and Woody Strode—who have been sent by Frank (Henry Fonda), the hired killer working for a railroad magnate, Mr. Morton (Gabriele Ferzetti), to a train station to murder Harmonica (Charles Bronson). The sequence is an obvious citation from *High Noon*, but Leone's style is entirely different: it is far lengthier than one might expect, given the importance of the sequence in the advancement of the plot. Leone's obsessive close-ups concentrate with extreme attention upon the mannerisms and tics of the two American actors: Elam's eye, Strode's bald head, the fly buzzing around Elam until he traps it in his revolver, the water dripping on Strode's hat. It is a brilliant segment that gives free rein to Leone's love for exploiting the emotive power of the extreme close-up. Then, as the credits come to an end, Harmonica suddenly kills off the two gunfighters, and they disappear from the story entirely. Leone tantalizes his audience with familiar iconic faces, and then removes them after they have served their purpose as citations of a familiar genre he is in the act of transforming.

An even more brilliant operation takes place in the subsequent sequence with the first appearance of Fonda. This shifts from the train station to a farmhouse in the middle of Monument Valley—John Ford country, a location Leone required to pay homage to the tradition of the Hollywood western. Leone's large budget allowed him to bypass the normal Spanish locations for the real article. At the farmhouse, the widower Brett McBain (Frank Wolff) and his family await the arrival of his new bride, Jill (Claudia

Leone recalls the Hollywood classic western *High Noon* in the opening gunfight from *Once Upon a Time in the West. Credit: MOMA*

Cardinale), from New Orleans. (Later we shall learn that she comes from the finest brothel in that city to the new town of Sweetwater to begin a new life with him.) An Irish immigrant, McBain has bought land where the railroad must necessarily build a refueling station, and it is his farsightedness that will cause his death, since Mr. Morton would rather send his gunslinger to murder McBain than pay him a handsome price for the rights to bring the railroad he is building through that property. Awaiting Jill's arrival, all the McBains except one child are viciously murdered by Frank's henchmen, who have dressed in the long dusters associated with the band of outlaws commanded by Cheyenne (Jason Robards) in order to divert suspicion away from Morton and Frank. Leone then cuts to Frank and a close-up of his cold, startlingly blue eyes; then his gun; then the lone surviving child; then Frank's shocking smile, as he brutally murders the last McBain child, the sound of his pistol blending into the shriek of an approaching train. Most theater audiences, recognizing Leone's citation and seeing that the same actor who had once played John Ford's heroic Marshal Wyatt Earp in *My Darling Clementine* had now become a despicable, cold-blooded assassin of women and children, gasped out loud at the sight. Leone's sequence juxtaposing the murdered family and the arrival of Mr. Morton's railroad introduces the film's theme, the clash of an older way of life on the lawless Western frontier with the arrival of civilization, symbolized by the railroad, but more important, the human cost of such "progress."

Unlike many classic westerns, Leone does not see the role of the frontier and the advance of civilization as completely positive. Everything connected with Morton results in violence and death, and it is all set in sharp opposition to the positive values of progress celebrated by John Ford in his own westerns, identified forever with the same Monument Valley Leone used as his location near the McBain ranch. While Jill McBain's attempts to claim her inheritance and to build her husband's refueling station show the future, Leone's sympathies are clearly with the old outlaw Cheyenne, who falls in love with Jill, and whose sense of honor reflects the traditional gunfighter's code. Cheyenne and men like him, men like the protagonists of Leone's earlier westerns, no longer have a role in the new society the railroad represents. Frank is a more complicated transitional figure. An outlaw and gunfighter like Cheyenne but with far fewer scruples, Frank seeks to make the qualitative leap from criminal to capitalist, scheming to seize Morton's fortune after his inevitable death from the paralyzing disease that eventually cuts short his dream of reaching the Pacific with his rails. When Morton asks Frank how it feels to sit behind the plush desk in his private railroad car, Frank replies: "It's almost like holding a gun, only much more powerful. . . . I'm beginning to think big too!"

Frank's desire to move from one era to another, from the code of the old gunslinger to the new age of industrial capitalism, stands doomed to failure because the sinister figure of Harmonica crosses his path. Frank's own violent past will prevent him from moving into the brave new capitalistic world. The film ultimately moves toward a climactic showdown between the two figures, with flashbacks that explain exactly who this mysterious Harmonica is and what his relationship to Frank might be. (Earlier in the film, two flashbacks shot out of focus had presented Harmonica's memory of some past event linking him to Frank which Leone leaves unexplained to tease the audience.) Each of the four main characters—Frank, Harmonica, Cheyenne, and Morton—has his own musical theme from Morricone's brilliant score, and the sound of Harmonica's mouth organ assumes an importance equal to the watch chimes of *For a Few Dollars More*, which, as noted, also used flashbacks before the final confrontation. Each time Frank asks Harmonica to reveal his identity, Harmonica's enigmatic reply is only to list the men Frank has shot dead during his career.

While Cheyenne and Harmonica work to save Jill's ranch and block Frank's plans to take it over, with Morton's men being massacred in the process, the stage is set for the final settlement of accounts, as well as the revelation of Harmonica's identity. As Frank and Harmonica face off, their conversation reveals Leone's continued juxtaposition of the Old West he loves from the movies and the new capitalist era that will eventually destroy it:

> **Frank:** Surprised to see me here?
> **Harmonica:** I knew you'd come.
> **Frank:** Morton once told me I could never be like him. Now I understand why. Wouldn't have bothered him, knowing you were around somewhere alive.
> **Harmonica:** So you found out you're not a businessman after all?
> **Frank:** Just a man.
> **Harmonica:** An ancient race.

Leone returns to the familiar circular *corrida* of his previous film, and with a crescendo of Morricone's music and a variety of camera angles and close-ups, a tight close-up of Bronson's face shifts to a final flashback that is the payoff shot of the film. It explains Harmonica's single-minded quest for revenge. A younger, perhaps even crueler Frank strides slowly forward toward the camera, stuffing a harmonica into the mouth of a young Mexican boy, on whose shoulders sits his older brother, a noose around his neck. The camera cranes back to frame this scene through a semicircular adobe structure, and through all this we catch a glimpse in the background of Monument Valley. Ford's classic geographical settings, however, never witnessed anything like Leone's ending: the older brother pushes his young brother away, preferring to die cursing Frank in a manly death rather than begging him for mercy. When Leone cuts back to the gunfight between Harmonica and Frank, we finally understand that Harmonica is the younger brother. To complete the bizarre cycle of vendetta, Harmonica thrusts the mouth organ into Frank's dying mouth as Frank finally realizes who has killed him. Leone's final shots shift from the gunfight to the arrival of the railroad at Jill McBain's refueling station. Amid the hustle and bustle of the new civilization which has symbolically replaced the archaic way of life of the gunfighter, the last images of the film are of Jill carrying water to the thirsty railroad workers. Ultimately, Leone affirms that the Old West of the solitary male gunman following an ancient code of values has been transcended by the matriarchal culture of modern civilization. Christopher Frayling concludes:

> Once upon a time, according to Leone's story, these characters lived and died in a world of simple icons, where they enacted a series of rituals in which even life and death became external, melodramatic gestures—and these gestures were codified, as the story was retold, to become a fully-fledged myth, a myth which should not be confused with a moral code, but which belongs entirely in the realms of fiction.[8]

After transfiguring this myth with his first three films, Leone's fourth work finally abandons it, but these great mythmaking films had an enormous impact upon international cinema. Leone's creative use of superb sound tracks by Ennio Morricone, his genius in employing close-ups to reveal emotions rather than information, and his brilliant dramatic editing rhythm changed the face of many different film genres, not only that of the western. Besides the hundreds of Italian imitations, it would be impossible to imagine the ethos or action of films by such Hollywood directors as Sam Peckinpah (*The Wild Bunch*, 1969; *Cross of Iron*, 1977); Don Siegel (*Coogan's Bluff*, 1968); Ted Post (*Hang 'Em High*, 1968); or Clint Eastwood himself after he turned to directing westerns such as *High Plains Drifter* (1973), *The Outlaw Josey Wales* (1976), or *Unforgiven* (1992). Even the enormously popular Dirty Harry action movies, starring Eastwood, about a violent cop out of control in San Francisco—such as Don Siegel's *Dirty Harry* (1971) and Ted Post's *Magnum Force* (1973)—have an indirect relationship to Leone's violent tales about loner gunslingers and show Leone's role as a model for action film directors.

Leone's Legacy: Django Westerns

Given the structure of the Italian film industry, it was inevitable that sequel mania would follow Leone's international success, as producers sought quick profits from this fashionable subject matter that by virtue of its links to classic Hollywood films gained easy access to markets all over the world, including America. Hundreds of Italian westerns appeared in little more than a decade, some of which were very good and most of which owed obvious debts to Leone's stunning models. One of the most interesting films was Corbucci's *Django*, appearing shortly after the Leone *Dollars* movies.

Django, one of the most imitated of spaghetti western heroes, employs a machine gun to dispatch his opponents in Corbuccio's *Django*. *Credit: DVD*

Employing the "Servant of Two Masters" plot and starring Franco Nero in the lead role as Django (a performance that made the young and inexperienced actor an international star, particularly in Europe), Corbucci's film exaggerated the violence in Leone's more elegant and stylized westerns with such touches as Django's machine gun, concealed in a coffin, or the racist Ku Klux Klan members who execute Mexican peasants for sport. Opposing the ex-Confederates are a band of Mexican outlaws led by General Rodriguez, whose men, in a scene famously contested by the censors, cut off a preacher's ear and make him eat it before they shoot him down in the town's muddy streets because of his association with the leader of the Anglo racists, Major Jackson. Tarantino cites this gruesome scene in *Reservoir Dogs*. Only at the end of the film do we discover that Django's motivation is revenge for the death of his wife many years ago after he was delayed in returning from fighting in the Civil War.

All in all, Django spawned some fifty imitations, parodies, and citations in other spaghetti westerns, and its protagonist was as imitated as Leone's Man with No Name. Interestingly enough, the one film that is most indebted to Corbucci's model in terms of its use of extremely vivid violence is Questi's *Django Kill*. But this cult western, perhaps the most violent of all spaghetti westerns, has absolutely nothing to do with Corbucci's popular film. Django was used in a completely invented English title (the literal translation of the original Italian title is "if you are alive, shoot!") to exploit the popularity of Django, a process that occurred over and over again in the sequel-oriented Italian industry. In fact, the protagonist of Questi's film, played by Tomas Milian (a role that made him famous and allowed him subsequently to pursue a career in all sorts of genre films in Italy, especially *poliziesco* works) is actually called the Stranger, one of the names for any number of solitary spaghetti gunslingers, inspired by Eastwood's role for Leone in *A Fistful of Dollars*.

Like Leone, Questi employs flashbacks to explain the Stranger's past. He is actually one of a mixed band of Anglo and Mexican bandits who massacre a trainload of Union cavalry transporting a payroll of gold; the Anglos then turn on their Mexican partners, seemingly murder them all, and bury them in a shallow grave, out of which only the Stranger emerges, surviving after being rescued by two Indians. While the Stranger heals from his wounds, the Anglo band with the gold enters a strange town that seems as if it might be the location of a horror film. When Bill Tembler (Milo Quesada), the saloonkeeper; Hagerman (Francisco Sanz), the storekeeper; and Tembler's evil fiancée, Flory (Marilù Tolo), recognize that Oaks (Piero Lulli), the leader of the band, is an outlaw wanted dead or alive, they incite the townspeople (all of whom consider themselves paragons of virtue) to murder or lynch the robbers without a trial, while Tembler and Hagerman keep the gold for themselves without revealing the motive for this bloodbath to their "virtuous" fellow citizens. The townspeople, however, are threatened by a homosexual Mexican gang leader humorously named Zorro—the name of a famous Hollywood character who always supported truth and justice. Zorro's band of homosexual "muchachos" all dress in black, embroidered costumes that appear to have come from the Versace fashion house circa 1967. Among their other escapades is the gang rape of Tembler's son, Evan (Raymond Lovelock), to force his father to give the gold to Zorro. Evan subsequently commits suicide. The Stranger, who had befriended Evan, later takes revenge by literally blowing the entire band to pieces with huge charges of dynamite.

Questi's film reaches a level of graphic violence unmatched in the genre, which cost him censorship in Italy and elsewhere. When the Stranger comes to the town and discovers that the man who almost killed him, Oaks, has a price on his head, he shoots him full of golden bullets, but leaves him alive. Subsequently, during the operation to remove the bullets and keep Oaks alive for further questioning, the townspeople discover the bullets are made of gold, and they literally rip out his stomach to obtain the gold. One of the film's most infamous scenes, perhaps an homage to the physical violence censored in Corbucci's *Django*, involves a graphic scalping. In another gruesome scene portrayed in graphic detail, the townspeople run amok and scalp one of the Indians who had saved the Stranger. Hagerman figures out that Tembler has hidden the gold in Evan's casket, buried outside the town in a desolate cemetery; he removes it and carries it home, but the Mexicans burn down his home to find it for themselves. In a scene that might have come from a horror film, the gold melts in the fire, flows down on Hagerman's face, and he dies, appearing to be a golden mummy in the flames. Ultimately, the Stranger rides out of town by the cemetery, now completely dug up by the gold-obsessed townspeople. Two children from town make strange grimaces at each other, as if to suggest that the evil and greed spawned by their parents will be visited upon their children. Questi had brought the western formula coined by Leone to a fever pitch of psychological weirdness. His single western film had few imitators but many admirers.

Leone's Legacy: Sartana, Ringo, Sabata, and Trinity

One of the links between popular genre films, such as the peplum epic and the spaghetti western, is the multitude of films that sport a protagonist with the same name. This fact is directly linked to the attempt to capitalize, in one or more alleged sequels, upon the positive public reception of a preceding work. In the peplum, there were dozens of musclemen named Hercules, Maciste, Ursus, Spartacus, Goliath, and Samson. A similar phenomenon occurs in the Italian western. Besides Leone-inspired anonymous characters called the Stranger or the Man with No Name, and Corbucci's Django, numerous Italian westerns repeated the hero's name from one film to another. Among the most popular were Sartana, Ringo, Sabata, and Trinity.

The Yugoslavian-born actor Gianni Garko (1935–) popularized Sartana, a bounty hunter dressed like a gravedigger, whose habitual comment before shooting people was, "I am your pallbearer." Several dozen of these films were produced in a brief period of time, the best of which starred Garko. Gianfranco Parolini directed the first in the series, *Sartana*, a.k.a. *If You Meet Sartana Pray for Your Death* (*Se incontri Sartana prega per la tua morte*, 1968),[9] but the rest of the official Sartana films in the short list here were shot by Giuliano Carnimeo. They include *Sartana the Gravedigger*, a.k.a. *I Am Sartana Your Angel of Death* (*Sono Sartana, il vostro becchino*, 1969); the previously mentioned *Fistful of Lead*, a.k.a. *Trade Your Pistol for a Coffin* (this time featuring George Hilton in the title role, who, dressed in the habitual black outfit, confronts his nemesis, Sabbath [Charles Southwood], dressed in white); *Have a Good Funeral, My Friend: Sartana Will Pay* (*Buon funerale, amigos!... paga Sartana*, 1970); and *Cloud of Dust... Cry of Death... Sartana Is Coming*, a.k.a. *Light the Fuse... Sartana Is Coming* (*Una nuvola di polvere... un grido di morte... arriva Sartana*, 1971). By the time the Sartana vogue died down, the character had appeared with other Italian western heroes, such as Django, Trinity, and Hallelujah, just as Hercules eventually was paired off in the peplum with Maciste, Samson, Ursus, and other popular musclemen.

As a film character, Ringo has a far more elegant pedigree. The name must certainly refer to the iconic western actor John Wayne, who played the Ringo Kid in John Ford's epic western *Stagecoach* (1939); but unlike so many other Italian gunfighters, Ringo's name was probably also suggested by a historical figure. The real gunfighter Johnny Ringo (1850–82) was associated with the Clanton gang, which took part in the famous gunfight at the O.K. Corral in Tombstone, Arizona, opposite Wyatt Earp, his brothers, and Doc Holliday in 1882. Duccio Tessari made the two best films of the Ringo series: *A Pistol for Ringo* (*Una pistola per Ringo*, 1965) and an immediate sequel, *The Return of Ringo*, both starring Giuliano Gemma (a.k.a. Montgomery Wood) in the title role. As his choice of the name for his protagonist implies, Tessari's westerns more frequently referenced the traditional Hollywood genre conventions than did Leone's.

The Return of Ringo adapts the storyline from Homer's *Odyssey* (perhaps the original revenge plot) and places it after the Civil War in a strange western town called Mimbres. After fighting for the Union, Captain Montgomery Brown (Gemma) returns to find that after gold was discovered there, two Mexicans—Esteban (Fernando Sancho) and Paco (Jorge Martin) Fuentes— have murdered his father and taken over his home. Paco plans to marry Ringo's wife, Hally (Lorella De Luca), and keeps his daughter, Elizabeth, as a hostage. Assisted by a motley crew of a drunken sheriff, a florist named Morning Glory who gives Ringo shelter, a tavern keeper, and an Apache medicine man, Ringo/Odysseus finally turns upon the evil Mexicans just as his Greek antecedent had destroyed Penelope's suitors. Tessari's most original revision of the Man with No Name formula—a rugged, bearded, serape-clad, cigar-smoking gunfighter in the *Dollars* films—imitated in costume, laconicism, and ruthlessness by directors after Leone, was Gemma's physical appearance and the way it changes as the film unfolds. When we first see him riding toward Mimbres at the opening of the film, he seems like any classic John Ford cavalryman: clean-shaven, blond, wearing the same kind

Disguised as a Mexican peasant, Ringo plots vengeance in *The Return of Ringo*.
Credit: CSC

of yellow kerchief that we have come to associate with the Seventh Cavalry. While in Mimbres, he disguises himself as a lowly Mexican peasant, sporting a stubble beard and a poncho to the extent that nobody recognizes him. When he arrives at the church to interrupt the wedding of Hally and Paco, he reappears resplendently in his cavalry uniform, surrounded by a golden light that endows him with a mythic, heroic aura through the church door.

The Return of Ringo was a box-office hit, coming in third just behind Leone's *For a Few Dollars More* and Tessari's own *A Pistol for Ringo*. Gemma became the first Italian-born actor to make a hit in spaghetti westerns, as opposed to the American import actors, such as Eastwood, Wallach, Van Cleef, and a host of others. One reason *The Return of Ringo* still deserves screening is that Quentin Tarantino's *poliziesco* idol, the director and scriptwriter Fernando Di Leo (1932–2003), coauthored the script with Tessari. Tarantino paid homage to both the historical and Italian western Ringos when he played the part of Ringo himself in the recent film *Sukiyaki Western Django* [2007] by the Japanese director Takashi Miike [1960–], a remake of Corbucci's *Django*.

Another successful Italian western gunfighter was Sabata, played in two parts of a trilogy by Lee Van Cleef after his successful roles with Leone. The first of the series, Parolini's 1969 *Sabata*, departs from his earlier *Sartana*. In the words of one film historian, Parolini "reinvigorated the Western with his own peculiar take on the 'west as carnival'. . . . If Leone's western heroes met their destiny in the arena of death, then Parolini's met theirs in a circus ring."[10] In fact, Parolini's gunfighters resemble circus performers more than bounty hunters, lawmen, or outlaws. Sabata is a sharpshooter with three gun barrels hidden in the butt of his derringer; his nemesis, Banjo (William

The bounty hunter Sabata and his Mexican sidekick wreck havoc on their enemies in Parolini's *Sabata. Credit: CSC*

Berger), sports a banjo that contains a rifle. Sabata's companions are also circus-performer types: Garrincha (Ignazio Spalla, working as Pedro San-chez) is a knife thrower, and a mute named Alley Cat (Aldo Canti, as Nick Jordan) is a gymnast acrobat. Sabata confronts an odious rancher named Stengel (Franco Ressel), whose favorite reading material is a treatise on the natural inequality of men by Thomas Dew (1802–46), president of the Col-lege of William and Mary as of 1832, and one of the South's most eloquent defenders of slavery before the outbreak of the Civil War in America. Van Cleef's character says little, but when he does speak, he often makes the kind of humorously laconic remarks that made the Terence Hill–Bud Spencer westerns so popular even before their *Trinity* series. Hence, *Sabata* became a hot ticket at the Italian box office, joining the three Hill-Spencer westerns directed by Giuseppe Colizzi, the previously mentioned *God Forgives—I Don't* (1967); *Ace High*, a.k.a. *Four Gunmen of Ave Maria* (*I quattro dell'Ave maria*, 1968); and *Boot Hill* (*La collina degli stivali*, 1969).

Parolini followed up his success in *Sabata* with a film entitled *Adiós Sabata*, a.k.a. *The Bounty Hunters* (1971), in the foreign market to exploit the popularity of the Van Cleef original: its Italian title was actually *Indio Black, sai che ti dico: sei un gran figlio di* . . . , which might best be translated as "Indio Black, you know what I say to you: you're a great son of a . . ." Because Van Cleef was temporarily unavailable, Yul Brynner played the role of Indio Black, a mercenary during the Mexican Revolution who plays clas-sical music on the piano and makes poetic pronouncements while shooting a sawed-off rifle, in the last chamber of which he keeps a cigar to smoke after he finishes off an opponent. The true sequel to *Sabata* was Parolini's *The Return of Sabata* (*É tornato Sabata . . . hai chiuso un'altra volta*, 1971), again starring Van Cleef. In this third film, the director not only continues but also exaggerates the circus or carnival motif—if anything in the popular Italian genre films and their endless sequels can ever truly be called exag-geration. The opening sequence is a bloody shootout that first plays out in a circus show, where the performers wear fake blood to simulate their deaths, but at the end of the film, the theatrical scene unfolds for real. Parolini's circus atmosphere, humor, and outlandish gadgets, coupled with the suc-cess of the Colizzi trilogy starring Hill and Spencer, set the stage for the eventual end of the traditional Italian spaghetti western and the triumph of the Italian spaghetti western parody in the early 1970s.

The "Zapata-Spaghetti" Plot: Mexican Revolution and Political Ideology in Damiani, Corbucci, and Leone

Given the heated political climate in Italy during the vogue of the western, it was inevitable that the Italian version of the genre would turn to expressions of contemporary political ideology. Of course, the classic American western

El Chuncho kills the American mercenary Bill Tate at the conclusion of Damiani's "Zapata" spaghetti western, *A Bullet for the General*. *Credit: DVD*

also contained an ideology, but rarely a Marxist one that supported Third World Revolution. Nonetheless, the traditional Hollywood film set in Mexico could easily be exploited for quite different arguments than American directors were interested in developing. The "Zapata-Spaghetti" plot generally employed two different kinds of protagonists: a Mexican peasant or bandit who is or becomes a revolutionary, and a European or American mercenary who may either oppose or assist the revolution, usually by dealing in arms. Three notable films from among the numerous works in this category are Damiani's *A Bullet for the General*; Corbucci's *Compañeros*; and Leone's *Duck, You Sucker*, also released as *A Fistful of Dynamite*, his fifth and last western as a director. Damiani's film basically set the pattern for this narrative plot. It features the familiar Gian Maria Volontè as the bandit El Chuncho; the actor apparently passed up Leone's offer for a part in *The Good, the Bad, and the Ugly* because he preferred a serious ideological statement about Mexican politics to performing in a film about the American Civil War. Klaus Kinski is El Santo, El Chuncho's brother and a priest-turned-revolutionary; and Lou Castel, an actor often appearing in political films of the period, such as those by Marco Bellocchio (see chapter 8), is the American mercenary Bill Tate, sent to Mexico by American agents to assassinate a revolutionary leader, General Elias (Jaime Fernández), whom he kills along with El Santo. When El Chuncho discovers that Tate is a hired assassin, he undergoes a kind of epiphany, embraces the Mexican Revolution, and shoots Tate before he can return to the United States with his blood money. El Chuncho gives the money Tate earned to a Mexican shoeshine boy and tells him to buy dynamite with it, not bread. Made in an era of increasing criticism of America's involvement in Vietnam and Latin America, Damiani's film has a message that is painfully obvious: Yankee go home! Much of the ideological edge of *A Bullet for the General* obviously came from the scriptwriter Franco Solinas, whose superb script for Pontecorvo's classic treatment of Third World revolution in *The Battle of Algiers* would be nominated in 1969 for an Oscar.

With its clear ideological motivations, *A Bullet for the General* became a serious dramatic film with little of the typical humor that even Sergio Leone inserted in his Italian westerns.

Quite different in tone, Corbucci's *Compañeros* is filled with wisecracks and humorous situations—an unsurprising trait, since it appeared during the heyday of the Terence Hill–Bud Spencer comic parodies of the spaghetti western. The story is almost a carbon copy of that employed by Damiani. A Swedish mercenary selling guns in Mexico (Franco Nero) encounters a peasant (Tomas Milian) named Chato but called El Vasco (the Basque) because of his Che Guevara beret. One of the most popular pieces of revolutionary garb during the period in Italy and elsewhere, it is all the more striking in the film because of the bearded and bereted Milian's resemblance to the Cuban revolutionary, considered by European leftists as a martyr to American imperialism. The Swede's actual name in the film is Yodlof Petersen, but El Vasco always refers to him as either "the Swede" or "Penguin." The epithet "Penguin" derives from the fact that when Nero's character first shows up with his trainload of weapons and explosives, he is dressed in a well-tailored black jacket and white pants. Their meeting provides one of the film's running jokes. At their first encounter, the Swede gives a silver American dollar to El Vasco, who continually asks the Swede to explain his gesture. The entire film then unfolds as a flashback to their adventures until they meet again at the same place and conclude a showdown. Ultimately, toward the end of the film, the gag is explained: the Swede says he decided that as soon as he entered the town, he was going to give the dollar to the "first turd he met"! Throughout the film, the revolution is treated in a jocular manner; even El Vasco becomes a revolutionary by accident. The plot revolves around the question of who should be allowed to buy the arms and explosives: either a fake revolutionary leader, General Mongo (José [as Francisco] Bódalo), who is interested in using the peasants only for his own gain, or idealistic students (a clear reference to the radical student groups in Italy at the time), who follow their pacifist teacher, Professor Xantos (Fernando Rey). Complicating the relationship between the Swede and El Vasco is the arrival of an American mercenary named John, played brilliantly by the veteran character actor Jack Palance. At this juncture, Corbucci injects the ideological content into his film. Xantos opposes a group of American capitalists represented by a Mr. Rosenbloom, who offer him a great deal of money and support for his revolution if their oil contracts are honored once he has attained victory with their assistance. After Xantos's refusal to play ball with American imperialists, Rosenbloom and his colleagues hire John to kill Xantos. Palance's performance in this film creates one of the most eccentric villains in the Italian western, one who has a strange relationship with a falcon. John and the Swede know each other from work in Cuba, where the Swede managed to escape capture at the hands of government

John, or Wooden Hand, smokes a joint, accompanied by his pet falcon, in Corbucci's *Compañeros*. The film's revolutionary theme music and its comical depiction of light drug use made the work a great favorite among radicals of the era. *Credit: DVD*

troops by leaving John behind, nailed to a cross. John escapes only because his pet falcon, improbably named Marsha, released him by eating off his right hand.[11] As a result, the Mexicans know John as "Wooden Hand" because he sports a wooden artificial hand within a black glove. He also constantly smokes joints throughout the film—a favorite pastime of the radical students who flocked to see Corbucci's film. Eventually El Vasco roasts the falcon, and this desecration of John's beloved pet bird provides yet another reason why he wants to kill both the Swede and El Vasco. In a stirring finale, El Vasco refuses to allow the Swede to steal a religious icon from the village after he discovers that his labors have failed to yield any financial gain, and just before they draw on each other, John appears and kills Xantos, the Swede then kills John, and neither El Vasco nor the Swede continue their quarrel. El Vasco offers the Swede a chance to continue the revolution with him, and after riding off and apparently refusing, the Swede returns, as the film's theme song (by Ennio Morricone), "Vamos a matar, compañeros," rises in a crescendo. If the normal conclusion to the "Zapata-Spaghetti" plot is the conversion of the ideologically illiterate Mexican peasant or bandit, in Corbucci's film both the peasant and the foreign mercenary yield to the revolution's siren call. Morricone's song became extremely popular among student radicals and leftist extraparliamentary groups in Italy, such as Potere Operaio and Lotta Continua. Ironically, he had based this call for political violence (its first line and refrain may be literally translated as "Let's go kill, comrades!") on a religious musical motif from a Gregorian chant.

Leone's *Duck, You Sucker* is quite clearly the most elaborate, if not the best, of all the political westerns made in Italy. The film's spectacular battle scenes, made possible in large measure by the foreign funding and thus sizable budget Leone's past box-office guaranteed, contrast greatly with the poorer effects employed in other political westerns. Although the film was never as popular at the box office or with the critics as Leone's first three westerns, it contains one of Morricone's most brilliant musical scores and must be considered one of the most interesting westerns Italy ever produced. Juan (Rod Steiger) plays a Mexican bandit who eventually becomes a true revolutionary; he is joined by John, a.k.a. Sean (James Coburn), a jaded Irish revolutionary and explosives expert who ultimately dies fighting for the Mexican Revolution. *Duck, You Sucker* had a difficult genesis, and initially Leone wanted to produce but not direct the project. Leone preferred Eli Wallach as the star and Sam Peckinpah as the American director, but United Artists, the source of Leone's distribution and much of his financing, imposed Rod Steiger on Leone as the lead actor and sent the young, precocious director Peter Bogdanovich to Rome to work on the film. By that point Bogdanovich had made only a forgettable science-fiction film for Roger Corman, *Voyage to the Planet of Prehistoric Women* (1968), and a more interesting homage to Boris Karloff in his last screen appearance, *Targets* (1968). Leone, on the other hand, had been on the cover of *Time* magazine and had revolutionized an American film genre, creating an entirely new Italian hybrid, making millions of dollars for everyone in the process. Despite Bogdanovich's future reputation as a celebrated interpreter of great film directors, such as John Ford or Orson Welles, the two men were at loggerheads almost immediately. Apparently Leone and Bogdanovich could not reach even the simplest agreement on artistic issues. When Leone described the script to Bogdanovich and would remark that here and there he would, for example, use his characteristic zoom shot, the American would reply, "I never use the zoom. I hate zooms." Eventually, Leone sent Bogdanovich packing back to Los Angeles in tourist class, calling the future wunderkind "a turd." Leone hoped to delegate the task of directing to a younger colleague, Giancarlo Santi. He told Steiger, who had agreed to do the project only with the understanding that it would be Leone directing him on the set, that since he would supervise everything Santi did, it would be the same as if Leone were actually directing. Steiger replied that he would send his cousin to the set, and that it would be the same as if Steiger were actually acting! So Leone relented and did the film.[12]

The film's opening title card—a quotation from Chairman Mao to the effect that revolution is not elegant or pretty but an act of violence—seems quite out of place in a Leone western, but it shows that the director wanted to keep up with the growing popularity of political westerns in Italy. The initial sequence that follows is a masterpiece of cinema. A filthy and badly dressed Juan, clearly out of his social element, joins a wagonload of wealthy travelers, including not only Mexican landowners and a priest but also an American who compares peasants like Juan to pigs. The close-ups of them eating and speaking show Leone's continual debt to Eisenstein in technique. In this film, flashbacks, so important in *For a Few Dollars More* and *Once Upon a Time in the West*, reveal Leone's doubts about the morality of social upheavals, perhaps an unusual idea in a political western. From

Because he is a dirty, illiterate peasant, wealthy Mexican aristocrats insult Juan before he robs their train in Leone's *Duck, You Sucker*. *Credit: DVD*

the flashbacks we learn that Sean's best friend had betrayed him during an Irish uprising, and that Sean had been forced to kill this friend in a gun battle, resulting in his escape from the British authorities and his career as a professional foreign mercenary working for other revolutions abroad. History then repeats itself in the film as one of the Mexican Revolution's leaders, Dr. Villega (Romolo Valli), betrays Juan under torture. Sean, because of his past experience, has compassion for Villega when he discovers what the doctor has done (something he failed to show toward his best friend), and he grants Villega the chance to die as a hero of the revolution by ramming a locomotive into a troop train. Sean tells him: "When I started using dynamite, I believed in many things. Finally, I believed only in dynamite. I don't judge you, Villega. I did that only once in my life." Later, as he lies mortally wounded in the fight around the derailed troop train, Sean bids farewell to Juan, experiences one last flashback, in which he, his best friend, and his friend's fiancée are all reunited in an Irish meadow, photographed in a romantic and elegiac manner; he then blows himself to bits with the dynamite that has become his signature.

The devastating comparison of rich and poor à la Eisenstein that opens Leone's film certainly demonstrates that he stands for the exploited against the exploiters. Still, *Duck, You Sucker* actually questions the value of revolutionary violence rather than celebrates it, as occurs in *A Bullet for the General or Compañeros*. At the height of the ideological upheavals going on in Italian society in the late 1960s and early 1970s, Leone clearly understood that the simplistic political slogans of the time, the Italian leftist version of "radical chic" that seemed so superficially clever, were really incapable of capturing life's complexities—let alone the complexities of the western as an art form. Sean's transformation from the embittered killer of the best friend who betrayed him to a man who learns to forgive another traitor reflects a far more nuanced treatment of the complicated role of politics and revolution in history than that of most Italian political westerns.

The distance that stands between Leone's film employing the "Zapata-Spaghetti" plot and other political westerns may be seen in Jean-Luc Godard's *Wind from the East* (*Le Vent d'Est*, 1970), originally conceived with a script by the German revolutionary Daniel Cohn-Bendit and with Gian Maria Volontè cast as an Indian-torturing American cavalry officer, emphasizing the supposed parallel between the conquest of the American West in the nineteenth century and American "imperialism" in the Third World during the Vietnam War era. That the ruling deity of political correctness (not a term used at the time) in French cinema and the darling of the French New Wave directors among leftist intellectuals would treat the western in *any* form testifies to the popular appeal of the Italian variant of the Hollywood genre. Although set on a Caribbean island, Gillo Pontecorvo's *Burn!* (*Quiemada*, 1969), cowritten by Franco Solinas, also reflects the influence of the political spaghetti western. It stars Marlon Brando as Sir William Walker, a British agent and soldier of fortune who first foments a native revolution against the Portuguese and then helps to organize middle-class settlers to exploit the peasants, keeping the island open to British trade. When the man Walker has trained to overthrow Portuguese rule leads another uprising against the landowners, Walker returns to the island, destroys the rebellion, and hangs his friend. Just as Walker approaches a ship in the harbor to leave the island, a dockworker and revolutionary assassinates him. Popular revolutions seem impossible to control, Pontecorvo seems to imply, echoing the theme of *The Battle of Algiers*. While not technically a western, *Burn!* certainly employs the "Zapata-Spaghetti" plot typical of the films about the Mexican Revolution, but places its action slightly outside the normal geographical location of the spaghetti western.

Don't Touch the White Woman (*Non toccare la donna bianca*, 1974), by the comedy director Marco Ferreri, represents an even more unusual political western, with the surrealistic touch usually associated with Ferreri and the political ideology of Paris's Rive Gauche. In it, Ferreri parodies the famous Errol Flynn role in Raoul Walsh's *They Died with Their Boots On* (1941), setting a ludicrous combination of characters—General Custer (Marcello Mastroianni); Buffalo Bill (Michel Piccoli); Sitting Bull (Alain Cuny); Custer's favorite Indian scout, Mitch (Ugo Tognazzi); and a CIA agent (Paolo Villaggio), as well as the Battle of the Little Big Horn—in the excavations made during the construction of a shopping mall on the site of the old Les Halles market in Paris. Ferreri's sense of the ridiculous manages to save the film from its Godardian pretensions and propagandistic content. The sight of Sitting Bull riding into contemporary Paris with his braves in the midst of rush-hour traffic to meet Custer, who is seated with the men of the Seventh Cavalry at a sidewalk café, in some respects alleviates the heavy-handed parallel of the Indian Wars in America in the nineteenth century with what Ferreri views as President Nixon's genocide in Vietnam. *Don't Touch the White Woman*, however, reveals just how flexible the formula of the spaghetti western could be and how easily it could accommodate a wide range of themes, characters, and plots.

The Apex and Decline of the Spaghetti Western: Western Comedies and Genre Parodies in *They Call Me Trinity, Trinity Is Still My Name,* and *My Name Is Nobody*

As was the case with many Italian genre films, B-film parodies appeared almost as quickly as a successful film was released. The comic duo of Franco Franchi and Ciccio Ingrassia (see chapter 7) were shameless in their cheaply made but hilarious send-ups of box-office hits. A list of some of their titles shows how they employed funny variants of the original films' titles to alert their audiences to the target of their satirical barbs: *The Two Sons of Ringo* (*I due figli di Ringo*, 1966), directed by Giorgio Simonelli; *The Handsome, the Ugly, and the Stupid* (*Il bello, il brutto, il cretino*, 1967), by Giovanni Grimaldi (1917–2001); *Two R-R-Ringos from Texas* (*Due rrringos nel Texas*, 1967), by Marino Girolami, the father of the *poliziesco* director Enzo C. Castellari (see chapter 14); *Ciccio Forgives . . . I Don't!* (*Ciccio perdona . . . Io no!*, 1968), by Marcello Ciorciolini; and *Two Sons of Trinity* (*I due figli di Trinità*, 1972), by Osvaldo Civirani. The kind of parody involved in their comedies did little damage to the reputation of the western itself, since the slapstick quality of the parody never called the myth of the western into question.

The attack on the myth of the western came, however, when Terence Hill and Bud Spencer teamed up with the director Enzo Barboni to make *They Call Me Trinity*. The duo had already done extremely well at the box office with such serious westerns such as *God Forgives—I Don't*, which, like Leone's classic model, always contained a good deal of wry humor. Although Barboni's films had far higher production values and featured true box-office stars, his humor was much closer to the Franco and Ciccio variety. Both Leone and Corbucci have claimed that Barboni's *Trinity* films gave the coup de grâce to the genre. Leone believed reducing the western to farce, however, demystified the more than three hundred films that had been made after *A Fistful of Dollars*, whereas Corbucci felt that once the western hero had been reduced to ridicule, it would be very difficult to conceive of a *pistolero* who would shoot a gun seriously in a dramatic role.[13] Barbone, who had worked as the director of photography on Corbucci's *Django*, felt, on the contrary, that the genre had run its course and that the stereotypical solitary gunfighter dressed in a serape and smoking a cigar had become boring. His hero, Trinity, "the right hand of the devil," is dirty, shiftless, and carefree, entering and exiting the film sleeping on an Indian travois, being dragged along by his horse because he is too lazy to ride. His outlaw half-brother, Bambino (Bud Spencer), "the left hand of the devil," criticizes Trinity's lack of ambition:

> **Bambino:** Ain't you got no ambition in life? Do somethin', rustle cattle, hold up a stagecoach or play cards or somethin' . . . once you were a good cardshark . . . but do somethin'!
> **Trinity:** Who's got the time? I'm already busy doin' nothin'![14]

They Call Me Trinity contains all the familiar elements from Leone's films or those of his imitators: bounty hunters; innocent Mormon settlers who refuse to defend themselves from a band of idiotic Mexican bandits; the bandits' leader, Mezcal (Remo Capitani), an exaggerated parody of the many other Mexican bandits or generals in other spaghetti westerns; and an equally idiotic group of yahoos led by the jaded southern aristocrat Major Harriman (Farley Granger), the comic epitome of all aristocratic southerners in other westerns. None of the gunfights involve epic showdowns typical of the classic spaghetti western. For example, when Major Harriman sends for two hired killers (appropriately dressed in black) to take care of Trinity and Bambino, they are introduced by a long trumpet solo that clearly recalls Morricone's music before a Leone showdown. Still, the possibility of high drama disappears instantly as Trinity manhandles both gunfighters in the General Store, ordering them to drop their pants, and off they run (alive) in their long johns. Trinity shoots several opponents backward, without even looking in their direction (an obvious impossibility), even castrating one that he hits in the crotch; but most of the normal spaghetti violence dissolves into epic barroom brawls that surely employed most of the stuntmen on the European continent. Political themes are conspicuously absent; the religion of the Mormons (like the religion of everyone else) becomes a target for sarcastic humor of the following type:

> **Brother Tobias [the Mormon leader]:** It's the Lord that sent you!
> **Bambino:** We wuz just passin' by!
> **Brother Tobias:** Have you seen what faith can do?
> **Bambino:** It'll work, if you put it in a rifle barrel!

The conclusion of the film involves a plot to persuade both the Mexicans and Harriman's cowboys to discard their weapons and fight the Mormons "like men" with their fists, and the entire film is given over to an epic fistfight that makes up the longest sequence of the film. Leone's black humor vanishes entirely, as slapstick and comic gags recalling early silent film take over completely. A typical scene is the one in which Trinity hits a man's head on a cash register that obligingly registers "Thank You." While *Trinity Is My Name* completely deflates the idea of a serious western, both the classic Hollywood variety and the Leone-Corbucci-Questi-Parolini hybrid, such a film probably tells us more about the Italian audience and film industry at the time than about the generic formula that went into the spaghetti western. The film aims at pure matinee entertainment for the entire family, and its violence, like that in a Sicilian puppet show, was never considered "real," unlike the scenes in such works as Questi's *Django Kill,* which were frightfully graphic for the period and received the opprobrium of the censors. Clearly, Barboni's film managed to exploit the daydreams of a rather unsophisticated audience of young Italian males, who projected themselves onto Trinity's cool style, his aversion to serious work, and his macho prowess. Barboni's exaggerated style went even further into the realm of slapstick in the sequel, *Trinity Is Still My Name:* Trinity's bad table manners become even more elaborate when he eats at a chic restaurant rather than in a saloon, the slaps in brawls become even more mannered as the duo, disguised as monks, slap an entire company of authentic monks, or when Trinity slaps the face of a gunfighter at a card table even before he can draw his pistol, and so forth. These Trinity films and their imitations may seem childish and silly today, but *Trinity Is My Name* became the twenty-second most successful Italian film of all time, just behind Leone's *The Good, The Bad, and The Ugly.* Topping that, *Trinity Is Still My Name* made a phenomenal amount of money, becoming the fifth-largest grossing film in Italian industry history, outperforming even Leone's most successful work, *For a Few Dollars More.*[15]

Perhaps it was appropriate that the last word on the western in Italy would be delivered by Sergio Leone's production of *My Name Is Nobody,* directed by the Leone protégé Tonino Valerii. Leone saw the western as a collection of myths, not merely a target for parody, and his idea for an answer to the *Trinity* series that demystified the western was to create a sort of comic counterpart to his *Once Upon a Time in the West* by treating the passing of the era of gunfighters and cowboy heroes in an elegiac form. Henry Fonda, the iconic western hero of such Hollywood classics as William Wellman's *The Ox-Box Incident* (1943) and two classics by John Ford, *My Darling Clementine* and *Fort Apache* (1948), plays Jack Beauregard, an aging gunfighter whose only goal is to leave the West and to retire to Europe (where, of course, the western had migrated). He is plagued by a young aspiring gunfighter, Nobody (Terence Hill), who has idolized Beauregard's reputation as the fastest gun in the West since childhood. Nobody aspires to be "Somebody" by replacing Beauregard in the history books, once he ensures the latter's fame in a successful shootout with "150 pure-bred sons-of-bitches on horseback," a grotesque enlargement of the gang of washed-up gunfighters made immortal by Sam Peckinpah's *The Wild Bunch.* This Hollywood western treated the myth of the West in a manner that must have impressed Leone, who could rightly consider Peckinpah a like-minded director. Thus, Leone cast two actors in diametrically opposing roles: one, the Hollywood embodiment of the classic western; the other, the personification of the Italian spaghetti western and its comic version as well, the star of the *Trinity* series that had just broken box-office records in Italy.

The basic gag of the film revolves around Nobody's name, which can be traced back to Homer's *Odyssey*, where Odysseus cleverly tells the cyclops Polyphemus his name is No Man, so that the other monsters on the island will think Polyphemus has been drinking when he claims "No Man" has blinded him. This comic reference to classical mythology comes right at the opening of *My Name Is Nobody*, when Beauregard shoots three men out to murder him outside a barbershop so quickly that the sounds of the three bullets he uses blend into the sound of one shot. When the barber's astonished son asks his father how the gunfighter did it, the following conversation takes place:

> **Son:** How'd he do it, Pa? I only heard one shot.
> **Barber:** It's a question of speed, son.
> **Son:** Ain't nobody faster on the draw than him?
> **Barber:** Faster than him? Nobody.[16]

My Name Is Nobody contains numerous citations from the classic American western, Leone's own hybrids, and Barboni's *Trinity* series, as well as its Morricone music. In the segments in which Nobody dominates the narrative, comic gags abound. When a number of cowboys throw custard pies at some hapless blacks for amusement, Nobody replaces the custard

Inspired by Sergio Leone's vision of the mythical dimensions of the Hollywood western, *My Name Is Nobody*, directed by the Leone associate Valerii, casts the Italian actor Terence Hill, famous for his roles in the *Trinity* series of parodies of spaghetti westerns, in his most interesting role as a comic gunfighter. *Credit: MOMA*

pie with one made of concrete and hits a white man with it. When he confronts a dwarf on stilts, he whittles the stilts down with shots from his Colt Navy revolver—the same pistol Beauregard uses, as well as some of Leone's protagonists—until the dwarf is his size. Elsewhere Nobody displays his lightning-fast speed by engaging in a face-slapping contest with an arrogant gunfighter, who is so much slower on the draw than Nobody that he cannot even reach his revolver before his face is smacked over and over again.

The event by which Nobody intends for Beauregard to attain mythic status, a gun battle alone against 150 men whose saddlebags have been stuffed with dynamite by Nobody to ensure an explosive finale, clearly parodies Peckinpah's slow-motion photography of violence in *The Wild Bunch* (for whom Valerii's *mucchio selvaggio* is named). But unlike the archetypal gunfighters in Peckinpah's western, who all die in a shootout with Mexicans, Beauregard in *My Name Is Nobody* triumphs, with Morricone's usual music of trumpets, gunfire, Jew's harp, and whistles replaced by Wagner's *Ride of the Valkyries.* (Among the many unaccredited riders and stuntmen in the "Wild Bunch" destroyed by Beauregard was the future Hollywood director John Landis, creator of such hits as *Animal House* [1978] and *The Blues Brothers* [1980], who had dropped out of high school and gone to Yugoslavia and then Spain to work on spaghetti westerns and war films.)[17] Of course, before Beauregard can fade out into history, myth, and legend, Nobody, in order to replace him, must kill him in a final gun battle; but the outcome is rigged so that Nobody's hero escapes unharmed and boards a ship in New Orleans bound for Europe. As he is about to depart, Beauregard writes Nobody a letter, declaring that his era, in which men still believed a pistol shot could resolve everything, had now been transcended. In like manner, the new western has transcended not only the classic Hollywood model but also that of Sergio Leone, replaced by the *Trinity* parodies—just as Nobody replaces Jack Beauregard. The new era is quantitatively and qualitatively different from the era that practiced the code of behavior by which Beauregard and men like him lived. Earlier in the film Nobody had told Beauregard a parable about a little bird, a cow, and a coyote: the bird became trapped in cow manure, and the only one willing to help the bird out of the mire turned out to be a hungry coyote, who ate it. Now Nobody explains his parable's meaning: "Folks that throw dirt on you aren't always trying to hurt you. And folks that pull you out of a jam aren't always trying to help you. But the main point is: when you're up to your nose in shit—keep your mouth shut!" As Christopher Frayling notes, such a moral could never have summed up a classic Hollywood western.[18]

⸾

The history of the spaghetti western represents a remarkable chronicle of film history, a moment when the Italian film industry changed the course of world cinema, dominated throughout the twentieth century by its Holly-wood competition, by changing the face of what almost anyone would agree is the archetypal American film genre. Even the greatest Italian auteur and art film director, Federico Fellini, was tempted to try his hand at the western during the height of its commercial and artistic success. Fellini had collaborated with the French directors Roger Vadim and Louis Malle on the 1968 *Histoires extraordinares*, an adaptation of various short stories by Edgar Allan Poe. Fellini's episode, *Toby Dammit*, followed the adventures of a British Shakespearean actor (Terence Stamp), usually high on drugs and alcohol, who has come to Italy to shoot the first Catholic western, financed by the Vatican. As a cardinal informs Dammit after meeting him at the Rome airport, "the first Catholic Western, do you understand? The return of Christ in a desolate frontier land. If it reflects the crisis, the upheavals of our society, the explanation for the decadence of our system, which is so capitalistic, even an Italian-style western can be a work of the most seri-ous engagement."[19] Fellini shot over a quarter of an hour of actual western sequences, all three of which were eventually cut from *Toby Dammit* even though they had cost 50 million lire to make. They had required the con-struction of a western set at Cinecittà, herds of horses, and dozens of extras. Apparently Fellini, sensing the audience's mood at the time, also wanted to shoot a true western of his own, something that would have been extraordi-nary if it had actually been made. Fellini's scriptwriter, Bernardino Zapponi, eventually advised him to cut the three scenes from *Toby Dammit* because they were not really necessary to Fellini's adaptation of Poe. Unbeknownst to Fellini, however, Zapponi himself was at the same time secretly composing spaghetti western scripts for three other obscure directors: Demofilo Fidani (1914–94), Giovanni Fago (1933–), and Giulio Petroni (1920–2010). That Italy's greatest art film director and one of its most original scriptwriters would both consider working in the western genre represents perhaps the most striking proof of just how completely the spaghetti western craze had overtaken Italian cinematic culture for more than a decade. Unlike the first popular genre fad to dominate the Italian film industry in the 1950s—the peplum epic—Italy's contribution to the evolution of the western, a proto-typically Hollywood genre, was both profound and lasting.

CHAPTER TWELVE

Mystery, Gore, and Mayhem

THE ITALIAN GIALLO

The Term *Giallo*

JUST AS THE ITALIAN WESTERN was being launched on an international
scale with the phenomenal success of Sergio Leone's first spaghetti westerns, another popular film genre came into fashion that would prove to be
not only profitable and popular but also durable. Like the western, which
produced its auteurs (a term normally used to refer to art film directors),
the *giallo*'s success also earned auteur or cult status for several Italians who
worked in this particular genre on an international level. The term *giallo*
(the Italian word for the color yellow) derives from the extremely popular
series of mystery novels introduced in 1929 by Mondadori, the gigantic
Milanese publishing house, since the books were promoted with a very
bright, even garish yellow cover. The series continues to be popular today
and still sports the characteristic cover in its paperback editions. Virtually
all of the books published in the series were Italian translations of English
whodunits, not Italian mystery novels, and they included not only the classics from Edgar Allan Poe, Sir Arthur Conan Doyle, and Agatha Christie,
but eventually the American "hard-boiled" novel written before and after
World War II by such figures as James M. Cain, Dashiell Hammett, and
Raymond Chandler.

One of the characteristics of modern Italian fiction in the nineteenth
and twentieth centuries is its relative dearth of books written in such
popular literary genres as science fiction, thrillers, or mysteries, genres that
in Italy were almost always, until recently, associated with Anglo-Saxon
and, to a lesser extent, French literature. Lacking a flourishing tradition
of indigenous mystery and crime fiction was obviously an impediment to
the creation of a similar tradition in the cinema, and this partially explains
why Italian cinema was so late in embracing themes related to mystery
and detection. The same kind of high-culture denigration of such popular

literary forms carried over into a contempt for popular cinematic genres in Italy, and each successive wave of new film genres (peplum, western, *giallo*, Euro-crime *poliziesco*, horror, and so on) became the object of scorn among intellectuals or highbrow critics who decried each new genre's "vulgarization" of taste while the public embraced that genre as entertainment. One early Italian critic (Alberto Savinio) declared that mysteries were unnatural and foreign to Italian culture, and that they had no place in the presumably law-abiding Italian urban areas and countrysides. Such an attitude would today puzzle many very popular non-Italian mystery writers—Donna Leon, Thomas Harris, Magdalen Nabb, Michael Dibdin, and David Hewson come immediately to mind—who have chosen to situate their own mysteries in Italian cities and provinces, and who now join a completely new group of Italian novelists who all practice the art of the mystery or detective novel.

Only in the postwar period has Italian literature shown a remarkably successful reversal of this traditional contempt for popular literary genres. Important practitioners in this genre, such as the Kiev-born Giorgio Scerbanenco (1911–69), Andrea Camilleri (1925–), Carlo Lucarelli (1960–), Massimo Carlotto (1956–), Gianrico Carofiglio (1961–), and Niccolò Ammaniti (1966–) are not only widely read in Italy but are also increasingly translated abroad. The single most successful twentieth-century Italian novel, *The Name of the Rose* (*Il nome della rosa*, 1980) by Umberto Eco (1932–), sold tens of millions of copies worldwide and is a postmodern version of a traditional mystery novel that looks back to the Anglo-Saxon mystery tradition from Poe to the present. Other innovative postwar writers whose novels rely upon the detective fiction tradition include Carlo Emilio Gadda (1893–1973) and Leonardo Sciascia (see chapter 8), to name only the most important writers that traditional criticism identifies with "serious" literature as opposed to pulp fiction. Early examples of Italian mystery films, usually cited by critics searching desperately for historical antecedents, are Visconti's *Obsession* and Antonioni's *Story of a Love Affair*. Both of these films are essentially loose adaptations of the hard-boiled novelist James M. Cain's *The Postman Always Rings Twice*—another confirmation, if any were required, of the essentially foreign origins of this kind of literature and film in Italian cinematic culture.

The *Giallo* as *Filone*

Italian *gialli* may be identified with a number of mystery, detective, or thriller films—several hundred, depending upon how we may define the term—that flourished between the mid-1960s and mid-1970s. Although the peplum and the spaghetti western crazes have come to a more or less definitive end in Italy, Italian directors still produce *gialli*, although in far fewer numbers, to the present day. Chronologically, the *giallo* led to subsequent popular genres—the Euro-crime, *poliziesco* films during the 1970s (see chapter 14), as well as horror films in the same period (see chapter 10). It is extremely difficult to pin down any rigid definition of the *giallo*, since these films cross the generic boundaries of crime films, horror films, and thrillers in general, and film historians often place them quite as easily in the horror genre as in the mystery or thriller camp. Italian film historians and scholars are more likely to call a collection of films, such as the spaghetti western or the *giallo*, a *filone*—literally meaning a large thread, but used by Italians to indicate a collection of similar themes or styles, a genre or subgenre, perhaps also a formula or pattern. As our discussion of *gialli* will demonstrate, there is no fixed group of traits that can be found in every *giallo*. A number of traits or family resemblances are, however, typical of this particular *filone*, and in order for a film to be defined as a *giallo*, at least a number of these traits should be present.[1] Directors associated with the *giallo*'s best films are Dario Argento, Mario Bava, Giuliano Carnimeo, Lucio Fulci, Aldo Lado (1934–), Sergio Martino, Luciano Ercoli, Umberto Lenzi, and Pupi Avati (1938–). It comes as no surprise that many, if not all, of these figures had learned to practice their trade on productions associated with other genre films, such as the peplum, the *commedia all'italiana*, or the spaghetti western.

Perhaps the most obvious characteristic of the Italian *giallo* is graphic violence, but the entire concept of "gratuitous violence" is essentially foreign to the *giallo*. The graphic, cinematic nature in which ingenious methods of killing are devised explains why these films are often placed in the horror genre. The *giallo* stands close to the horror film, but in this chapter most *gialli* that contain supernatural explanations of the actions they describe shall be excluded: in other words, no witches, werewolves, vampires, or monsters. Plenty of "monsters" in the Italian sense of the word populate these films, for in Italy serial killers are frequently called *il mostro* in the newspapers when journalists do not actually use the English term "serial killer." Besides this element of graphic violence (tame compared to today's standards), the appeal of the *giallo* abroad was its sexual content. A number of *giallo* protagonists are characterized by sexual vices (at least those considered to be vices during the period), and one of the most frequent scenes in a *giallo* displays a seminude woman, often the victim of a killer. Again, the *gialli* seem relatively tame today, but when they first appeared they seemed quite sexy and audacious, and they were often censored in Italy and abroad for their violence, just as were some of the more daring spaghetti westerns.

Gialli are usually the opposite of police procedurals, particularly in the earliest films of the genre by Bava and Argento. That is to say, the investigation that takes place in the *giallo* frequently features someone *not* professionally involved with police work: it may be a foreign tourist in Italy, an Italian living abroad, or simply a curious individual who stumbles across something fishy or criminal in nature. In this sense, the *giallo* may follow the lead of Alfred Hitchcock, whose thrillers often feature everyday characters that fall into similar situations, forcing them to seek the identity of a murderer or to search for the truth. That the police are often inadequate or even incompetent has a long tradition in the mystery novel, going back to both Poe and Conan Doyle, and when the Euro-crime film became popular, this trait of the professional police and police detectives was drastically exaggerated because the political obstacles to solving crimes force them, on occasion, to take the law into their own hands.

Basically, the world of the *giallo* is one of cynicism, greed, sexual depravity, and violence: everyone, not just the murderer, probably has something to hide. Virtually every *giallo* contains ample evidence that human behavior rests upon irrational and frightening foundations.[2] Unlike the classic mysteries featuring Sherlock Holmes, where the solution of a crime involves an affirmation of the Victorian moral order, no such reaffirmation of traditional values takes place in the Italian *giallo*—on the contrary, the violent, sexual, immoral nature of the crimes and the actions of their perpetrators can lead us only to doubt that any order actually exists to be reestablished at all. Since *gialli* pay close attention to eyewitnesses of crimes (the Italian term is *testimone oculare*), ways of seeing or of not seeing become one of the genre's basic themes. A corollary to this obsession with sight is the frequently employed zoom shot. Moreover, another popular technique allows us to share the perspective of the killer (that is, the "killer cam") or even of the victim. Early on in the *giallo*'s development, again thanks to Bava and Argento, the killer sports a distinctive disguise that involves a trench coat, slouch hat, stocking mask, and gloves, all usually black. Most murders take place because the murderer has experienced a trauma in the past, and the murders are photographed and edited in a spectacular manner, usually as what one critic has called a "set piece" that guarantees the audience's attention by stressing suspense, sex, violence, and then murder.[3] In this regard, *gialli* function much like all other popular forms of entertainment with a formulaic structure: in the peplum, the confrontation of the strong man with the tyrant represents the set piece; in the western, the attention-getting set piece is usually the gunfight; in the opera or musical, the aria or solo always trumps the chorus; and of course in the pornographic film, the set piece is generally the orgasm.

Many critics have traditionally viewed *gialli* negatively because of a perceived lack of interest in tight narrative plotting. In fact, some *gialli* make very little rational sense at all (a common trait of low-budget B films of any kind made by any national cinema). If the *giallo* sometimes fails to live up to the high standards of art film narrative in its plotting and the characterization of its protagonists, it privileges, on the other hand, dramatic visuals and music—in set design, color photography, special effects, sound tracks, and editing. The Italian *giallo* film represents a profoundly cinematic product, one primarily designed to entertain a popular audience by manipulating it with stunning visual effects built around the set-piece extravaganza. One other characteristic also marks many of these films: the "red herrings" liberally sprinkled throughout the narrative. The *giallo* frequently provides its audience with false trails, information that turns out to be false or misleading, as a means of building suspense and frustrating the audience's normal desire to figure out "whodunit."

The Birth of the *Giallo*: Mario Bava

Film historians generally agree that, along with Dario Argento's first films in the early 1970s, several of Mario Bava's films made in the preceding decade launched the *giallo* as a film genre: *The Girl Who Knew Too Much* (*La ragazza che sapeva troppo*, 1963); *Blood and Black Lace* (*Sei donne per l'assassino*, 1964); and *Twitch of the Death Nerve*, a.k.a. *A Bay of Blood*, a.k.a. *Chain Reaction*. Unlike the majority of the *gialli* that follow, Bava shot his first *giallo* in a distinctive black-and-white that stands comparison with the best art films of the period, just before the move to color in the works of such auteurs as Antonioni or Fellini. Bava's skill as both a lighting designer and a cameraman stand out in his *gialli*, as they do in the peplums or horror films he made. In fact, he has clearly become a cult figure today with a huge following on Internet sites and with a relatively large number of his works available in DVD format.

Bava's title, a clear reference to Hitchcock's *The Man Who Knew Too Much* (1956), traces the visit of a young American girl, Nora Davis (Letícia Román), to Rome to visit her aunt, who dies almost as soon as she reaches the city. As the plane reaches Rome, we see Nora reading a *giallo* ominously entitled *The Knife*, and a voice-over informs us that Nora reads this kind of literature fanatically. A man named Pacini sitting next to her offers her a Kent cigarette and gives her the entire pack. Later at the airport as she stands in line for customs clearance, the police arrest Pacini and discover his entire suitcase is filled with packets of Kent cigarettes laced with marijuana. (At the film's conclusion, the same voice-over raises the question: Did what Nora experience in the interim really happen, or was it merely the effect of a joint smoked by accident?) Shortly after her aunt's death near the Spanish Steps in the very heart of the Eternal City, Nora witnesses a woman die with a knife in her back and a bearded man who drags her body away through the rain. Like many of Hitchcock's figures, however, Nora is not believed by anyone to whom she reports this, except perhaps by Dr. Marcello Bassi (played by John Saxon, an Italian American actor). Because Nora is an avid reader of mystery novels, she decides to prove that what she saw actually happened.

The birth of the *giallo* in Bava's *The Girl Who Knew Too Much*: while Nora reads a thriller (a *giallo*) on her flight to Rome, as the plane lands a friendly passenger offers her what turns out to be a drug-laced cigarette. *Credit: DVD*

At her aunt's graveyard burial, Nora meets Laura Craven-Torrani (Valentina Cortese), the wife of a Dr. Torrani, whose sister was the third woman killed ten years earlier by the infamous Alphabet Murderer, who chose his victims by the first letter of their last name (A, B, C)—a nod to Agatha Christie's *ABC Murders* (1936), one of her classic thrillers featuring the detective Hercule Poirot. Laura invites Nora to use her apartment midway up the Spanish Steps while she is in Switzerland with her absent husband, and the film narrates Nora's attempts to solve the murder, as well as her growing infatuation with Marcello. A typical red herring throughout much of the film is provided by a strange man who shadows Nora for some time, until we eventually learn that he is Andrea Landini (Dante DiPaolo, another American actor—and, much later, Rosemary Clooney's husband), a journalist whose obsession with the Alphabet Murderer resulted in the loss of his job. Even when Nora joins forces with Landini, the murderer seems to have outsmarted everyone, finally killing Landini and staging his death as a suicide with a note stating that he, Landini, was actually the culprit.

Just when the mystery seems to be solved, Laura returns from Switzerland. That night, Nora finally meets her husband—with a knife in his back, courtesy of the now obviously demented Laura, whose crimes he has feverishly tried to conceal. Thus when Nora had seen the first murder victim's body dragged away by the man she now recognizes as Dr. Torrani, she had misinterpreted what she saw, failing to understand that it was Laura who had killed her, not the man she saw pulling the knife out of her back. (This error of sight is a kind of misapprehension typical in the Italian *giallo*.) Just as Laura is about to shoot Nora, Dr. Torrani, as his last act before dying, shoots his wife through the door of the large armoire where his wife has now concealed him. While the film concludes with the forthcoming marriage of Nora and Marcello, Bava cannot help but insert a comic ending. Nora offers her husband-to-be a cigarette, realizes it is from the pack of marijuana-laced Kents she still has in her purse, and throws the entire package down to the street, where a priest picks them up and will certainly have a mystic experience when he smokes them!

Bava's first *giallo* displays many of the future traits of the genre: the amateur investigator, the demented murderer, and the red herrings to send us off in the wrong direction. With his first scene of Nora's arrival in Rome, Bava even provides the new genre's name by prominently displaying Nora's mystery novel, or *giallo*, and having the police warn Nora that mysteries are dangerous reading. But the style of the film remains resolutely linked to the traditional Hollywood film noir, with the kind of expressionist, chiaroscuro, black-and-white lighting that we have come to identify with such works. With *Blood and Black Lace* in the following year, however, Bava employed Technicolor film stock to produce a true work of original genius, a film that was to be much more influential on subsequent directors of *gialli*, such as Dario Argento. The Italian title literally means "six women for the murderer," and it is therefore one of the first thrillers with a title that points to a body count, a frequent element in the slasher films and their sequels made in Hollywood after the phenomenal success of Sean Cunningham's *Friday the 13th* (1980), a Hollywood film indebted to Bava's other body-count classic, *Twitch of the Death Nerve*.

Blood and Black Lace takes place in and around a fashion house, Cristina's Haute Couture, where Contessa Cristina Como (Eva Bartok) and her manager, Max Marian (Cameron Mitchell), manage a number of beautiful models inside a beautiful villa populated by a group of beautiful people whose appearance conceals all kinds of vice—drug dealing, blackmail, murder, and so forth. The stunning visual beauty of the low-budget production emerged from a lack of resources that would have astounded a Hollywood director. The exquisite tracking shots at night in the fashion salon filled with surrealistic, De Chirico–like mannequins were produced by placing the camera on a child's simple toy wagon rather than the more expensive dollies that are usually required. As the film progresses, models are murdered one by one through the use of various graphically depicted methods by a murderer photographed with a black fedora, a black jumpsuit, and the obligatory pair of black leather gloves, the outfit that would become de rigeur in future *gialli*. The murderer kills his second victim, Nicole (Ariana Gorini), by pommeling her with the macelike gauntlet of a suit of armor in an antique store; the third victim, Peggy (Mary Arden, an actual famous American model of the period), dies after the murderer presses her face against a red-hot pot-bellied stove. All of the crimes are set in motion by the first murder, of Isabella (Franceca Ungaro), who has kept a diary with incriminating information on a number of the people at the fashion house and who, we discover, has also been blackmailing Contessa Cristina for murdering her husband to obtain his money and to live with Max after they secretly marry.

Focusing upon an haute couture studio and beautiful, sexy models shot in lush Technicolor, Bava's film calls attention to the ugliness behind the facade of glamour. The official policeman in charge of solving the crimes, Inspector Silvestri (Thomas Reiner), incorrectly sees them as the result of a sex maniac—not an implausible theory given the body count of beautiful female models. Yet, this theory is the ultimate red herring in the plot, revealed to be spurious at the conclusion of the film when we learn that not one black-clad murderer but two exist. Both Max and Cristina join in their first murder, that of Cristina's husband, before the action of the film begins; they are forced thereafter to murder Isabella, who has blackmailed them both for their first crime. One killing leads to another by a kind of implacable logic that forces the evil pair to act out the crimes of a serial killer, who really does not exist, in order to recover Isabella's diary, which could lead the police to the real culprits. The sixth person to die is actually Cristina, who falls from a loose drainpipe and mortally wounds herself after killing Tao-Li (Claude Dantes), the fifth model to die, in a bathtub. Returning to her studio, she discovers Max stealing her jewels and shoots him before expiring herself. Max had loosened the drainpipe to kill her, knowing she would be using it, because they had planned that devious means of reentry into the home to avoid police detection.

With *The Girl Who Knew Too Much* and *Blood and Black Lace*, Bava provided a number of the features that would come to define of a new genre, even pointing to its nomenclature through Nora Davis's fascination with *gialli* novels. As in all formulaic forms of art, subsequent directors would embellish, exaggerate, and extend the generic boundaries that Bava had originally provided. One completely camp *giallo*, *Bloody Pit of Horror*, a.k.a. *Crimson Executioner* (*Il boia scarlatto*, 1965), by Massimo Pupillo (1929–), deserves some mention here for its explicit announcement of a genre change similar to Bava's depiction of the reading of *gialli* at the opening of *The Girl Who Knew Too Much*.[4] It stars Mickey Hargitay as Travis Anderson, a former muscleman who had acted in peplum films and now lives as a recluse in a Gothic castle, obsessed with the legend of the Crimson Executioner, who had been executed in 1648 for the horrendous crimes he had committed. Travis dresses like the Executioner, and when a carload of cover girls for *gialli* arrive at his castle for a photo shoot of various kinds of killing, Travis obliges them by killing them in earnest with a variety of medieval mechanisms, including an iron maiden and an ingenious and enormous spiderweb with a venomous mechanical insect that devours its victims, designed by a very young Carlo Rambaldi (1925–2012), the future Oscar winner for special effects on *King Kong* (1976), *Alien* (1979), 5 and *E.T.* (1982). Hargitay was, of course, in Italy to make several peplum films with his then wife Jayne Mansfield (*Hercules vs. the Hydra*, a.k.a. *The Loves of Hercules*; see chapter 6), and *Bloody Pit of Horror* reminds us in a camp fashion that the male bodybuilder image celebrated in the peplum, in which both Travis and Hargitay worked, now yields pride of place to the equally fetishized female body in the *giallo*, such as the murdered models in Pupillo's fictional photo shoot or in Bava's *Blood and Black Lace*.

Twitch of the Death Nerve, less visually complex than *Blood and Black Lace*, had an enormous influence upon the Hollywood slasher film that became very popular in the 1980s. Made with a low budget like most of Bava's works, it nevertheless featured a cast of important Italian actors, as well as special effects by Carlo Rambaldi. Isa Miranda, one of the most important stars of the Italian cinema during the Fascist period, plays Contessa Federica Donati, the owner of extremely valuable property on a bay that has remained unspoiled by commercial development. Leopoldo Trieste, famous for starring roles in films by Fellini and Germi as well as an important role in Coppola's *The Godfather II*, plays Paolo Fossati, an eccentric collector of insects at the bay who is married to Anna, a woman addicted to Tarot card fortune-telling, played by one of Pasolini's favorite actresses, Laura Betti (1927–2004). Bava's film stands as the forerunner of numerous body-count slasher films made in Hollywood, such as the *Halloween* franchise begun by John Carpenter in 1978, the *Friday the 13th* franchise by Sean Cunningham in 1980, or the *A Nightmare on Elm Street* franchise by Wes Craven in 1984. In those and many other similar series of films, deranged or deformed serial killers (respectively, Michael Myers, Jason Voorhees, and Freddy Krueger in the three franchises mentioned here) murder a succession of people, frequently young people having sex, generally leaving one character alive at the end of each film (if a woman, critics often call her the Final Girl) to prepare for the next sequel. *Twitch of the Death Nerve*, however, contains a total of thirteen victims dispatched by various means—hanging, decapitation, stabbing, impalement, choking, gunshot, while featuring a group of people all of whom are capable of murder and a plot that revolves around control of the seaside real estate owned by the countess, who is the first to die. Bava's most brilliant stroke in this film lies in his ingenious invention of murderers who in turn are murdered. Greed ultimately explains the motives behind all but the last two murders. Bava's graphic depiction of such violent acts continues from *Blood and Black Lace*, and his style continues the sometimes all-too-frequent zoom shots on the corpses. A grotesque sense of humor pervades the film, as bloody killings often segue into sentimental piano sonatas on the sound track or beautifully romantic shots of idyllic sunsets over the bay. Ultimately the film concludes as Renata (Claudine Auger), the contessa's daughter, and her husband, Albert (Luigi Pistilli), manage to dispatch all the characters not eliminated either by the greedy real estate developer Frank (Chris Avram) or by the contessa's illegitimate son, Simon (Claudio Camaso). Just as Renata and Frank are now poised to be the only legitimate inheritors of the bay, Bava ends the film with an even more astounding conclusion than he employed in *Blood and Black Lace* when we discover that not one but two killers dressed in black are at work in the film. As if to underline Bava's belief that murder resides in all of us, Renata and Frank are killed by a shotgun blast from their young son and daughter, who think they are using a toy gun. The last line of dialogue from the children sums up Bava's black humor: "Gee, they're good at playing dead, aren't they?"

Dario Argento and the *Giallo*

Bava's early *gialli* had a formative influence on the genre and an enormous impact upon Hollywood films, but his low-budget B films never enjoyed a comparable success at the Italian box office. Until recently he was never really given the credit his talent deserved as a true auteur who made fundamental contributions to a number of film genres. It would be the early *gialli* of Dario Argento, greatly indebted to Bava's work, which established these films as a box office phenomenon and launched the craze for making *gialli* by other directors. In rapid succession, Argento made *The Bird with the Crystal Plumage*, *The Cat o' Nine Tails* (*Il gatto a nove code*, 1971), *Four Flies on Grey Velvet* (*4 mosche di velluto grigio*, 1971), and a few years later *Deep Red*, perhaps his masterpiece. Each of these four films employs the amateur-detective motif borrowed from Bava's *The Girl Who Knew Too Much*. In his first film, shot with the brilliant support of Vittorio Storaro (1940–) as director of photography and Ennio Morricone's splendid music, Argento adopted and popularized the favorite *giallo* killer's costume from Bava's *Blood and Black Lace*: the black slouch hat, trench coat, and gloves, worn in Argento's films by the director himself rather than his actors, perhaps as a nod to Hitchcock's cameo appearances in so many of his films. By continuing Bava's intelligent system of mixing British or Hollywood actors with Italians, Argento aimed at the export market in which his films were highly successful. In *The Bird with the Crystal Plumage*, Tony Musante plays an American writer Sam Dalmas, in Rome, who witnesses what he thinks is the attempted murder of Monica Ranieri (Eva Renzi) by a black-clad serial killer in the art gallery she and her husband Alberto (Umberto Raho) operate. Even though Mrs. Ranieri survives, something strange about the scene he witnessed haunts him, and Sam decides to play detective when Inspector Morosini (Enrico Maria Salerno) seems to make no progress. As his investigations go forward, he discovers that the serial killer's first victim was a lesbian who sold a strange painting just before her death—a naive and macabre work depicting a murder. Argento then quickly cuts to the actual painting with the dark figure of the murderer staring at it. After giving a television interview about the killings, the killer himself calls Morosini, taunting him and declaring that there will soon be a fifth victim. Sam, too, is attacked several times (once by a professional hit man fittingly dressed in a yellow jacket), but manages to escape. Recording one of the killer's calls to Sam and detecting a strange clicking sound on it, the police then receive a call themselves. A comparison of the two tapes reveals the two voices to be different. This apparent breakthrough raises the question about the number of the killers. Are there perhaps two, as was the case in Bava's *Blood and Black Lace*? Argento's narrative technique, one that becomes standard procedure in most of the *gialli* that copy his success in the next decade, revolves around a mysterious killer who somehow manages to stay just one step ahead of his pursuers, even when his or her success defies logic. In the midst of this cat-and-mouse game between amateur detective and killer, any number of red herrings are thrown across the trail of the hunter and the audience's screen that raise all sorts of possibilities, hopes then dashed. The strange clicking noise on the phone calls turns out to be produced by an extremely rare bird that exists only in one specimen at the Rome zoo, and its cage stands near the Ranieri apartment. Assuming that the killer is a man, the police arrive to see a replay of the same scene Sam saw at the art gallery (two people struggling), and they draw the same mistaken conclusion from this sight that Sam had reached—that the male figure (in this case clearly identified as the husband) is trying once again to kill his wife before plunging to his death off the balcony. Ultimately, this conclusion proves to be incorrect, yet another red herring. The strange painting of a murder turns out to be an account of a traumatic attack against Monica ten years previously. When she saw the painting in the antique shop, that event triggered a psychotic spree of killings wherein she reverted to her past but identified with the killer rather than with the victim (herself). The scene Sam witnessed at the opening of the film of a black-clad man trying to kill Monica was actually Monica trying to murder her husband, who nevertheless covered up her crime spree out of love.

The Argento brand of suspense continuously opens up questions, and then answers them in ways that the spectator least expects. Focusing on Sam's inability to see properly (a theme that can be traced through all of Argento's work), such a *giallo* keeps the audience on the edge until the very last minute, dashing expectations until the final frame of the film unfolds. With its use of flashbacks to Sam's memory, zooms on the actual graphically depicted violent killings, and the now-standard killer cam to provide the assassin's perspective, Argento's first and extremely successful film, an elegant, well-made work, launched the craze for Italian-style thrillers during the next decade.

His next two films—sometimes referred to with his first *giallo* as the "animal trilogy" because of their titles—continue the amateur-detective narrative framework. In the case of *The Cat o' Nine Tails*, Argento's detectives are a blind writer of crossword puzzles named Franco Arnò (Karl Malden) and a nosy journalist named Carlo Giordani (James Franciscus). Again with an eye to the export market, Argento selected well-known American actors to join the lesser-known Italians. At the opening of the narrative, Franco overhears a conversation about blackmail and discovers the next day that a murder occurred in the medical institute outside of which he had overheard the information. As the film progresses, we learn that the institute not only works on important drugs that could easily be the target of industrial spies, but that they are also doing research on the link between the double-Y chromosome and criminality (a link currently rejected by scientific studies but popular when Argento's second film was shot). Throughout numerous sequences in the film, Argento's camera takes on the perspective of the killer. Victims begin to pile up at the institute: Dr. Calabresi (Carlo Alighiero), the man Frank earlier overheard, whose head is cut off at the train station when the killer pushes him onto the tracks of an oncoming engine; Righetto (Vittorio Congia), the photographer whose picture of Calabresi's death contains a clue to the killer's identity, whose throat is slashed by the ever-present straight razor before he is strangled; and Bianca Merusi (Rada Rassimov), who worked with Calabresi in seducing researchers at the institute to gain information for the purposes of blackmail, and whom the murderer eventually strangles. The mysterious killer also tries to murder both Franco and Carlo (echoing the attacks on Sam in *The Bird with the Crystal Plumage*). Ultimately the young genius researcher Dr. Casoni (Aldo Reggiani) turns out to be the killer with the double-Y chromosome who kills anyone who discovers his genetic makeup. Even though blind, Franco eventually pushes Casoni down an elevator shaft when he corners him and the killer falsely claims to have killed a little girl named Laurie, who is Franco's niece.

The Cat o' Nine Tails works wonderfully well as a suspense-filled thriller, although more reflection reveals that it is virtually impossible to explain how Casoni manages to arrive on the spot before the two amateur detectives each time they find a clue. The title of the film itself represents a kind of red herring, which derives from Franco's remark that the nine leads they have to follow are like a cat with nine tails, and that to solve the mystery of the killer's identity, they must grasp on to at least one of the tails. Seeing or the inability to see properly becomes Argento's visual focus and the frequent shots of the killer's eye mark each crime, as if to push us to take on the killer's point of view. Before the killer is unmasked at the conclusion of the film, Carlo makes a remark about Casoni, saying that there is something fishy about him, since he was fired from his last position in spite of his brilliance as a scientist. Franco's reply, one that could well serve as the motto for the entirety of Italian *giallo*, sums up Argento's cinematic universe: "Isn't there something fishy about all our lives?"

The third of the "animal" trilogy, *Four Flies on Grey Velvet*, appeared in the same year that the second film was released, but with far less success. Like *The Cat o' Nine Tails*, this film rests on the false claim of forensic science folklore that the police are capable of testing with a laser the eyeball of a murdered victim, since the retina supposedly will retain the killer's image (an idea inspired by untested hypotheses of nineteenth-century studies of the eye). For an interesting twist the murderer turns out to be the amateur detective's wife, and the four flies on gray velvet are actually a piece of jewelry comprising a fly in clear plastic that swings back and forth around the wife's neck—the last thing the murder victims saw before expiring.

This analysis of Argento's first three thrillers shows that the *giallo* shares with both the peplum and the spaghetti western the genre film's fascination with establishing generic "rules" and styles and then bending them to frustrate the audience's expectations, trained as they are to expect a genre film to follow the formula and obey the so-called rules. Undoubtedly Argento's best *giallo* during his initial work on thrillers, one that helped to launch the craze for the genre, is *Deep Red*.[6] Like every great genre picture, it not only follows many of the generic "rules of the game" but also adds subtle (and not-so-subtle) new wrinkles to the ever-evolving understanding of just precisely what these rules might entail. Argento's most interesting decision was to select a different kind of music for *Deep Red*. Rather than employing Ennio Morricone as he had for his first three *gialli*, he commissioned a contemporary rock group named Goblin (all conservatory graduates), and their music was a great success, particularly with its use of different keyboard instruments (synthesizer, organ, piano) and scary percussion instruments. The group continued to work with Argento on a number of horror or thriller films as well as on the Italian version (1978) of George Romero's *Dawn of the Dead*, and Argento has declared that the music on *Deep Red* had an important influence on the sound track of John Carpenter's *Halloween*. Worthy of note is his choice of the coscriptwriter Bernardino Zapponi, whose interest in the supernatural and the grotesque also found resonance in such important Fellini films as *Toby Dammit, Fellini Satyricon, Casanova,* and *Roma*.

Deep Red's plot of the amateur detective repeats that of *The Bird with the Crystal Plumage* or Bava's *The Girl Who Knew Too Much*. (Behind all of the films made with this sort of plot we may see Alfred Hitchcock's many films about out-of-place individuals who become entangled in dangerous espionage adventures abroad.) In this case, the British pianist Marcus Daly (David Hemmings) witnesses the murder of a German performing psychic named Helga (Macha Méril), who has sensed the presence of a murderer among her audience and later dies for her prescience. Eventually, Marcus gains the assistance of the journalist Gianna Brezzi (Daria Nicolodi, who subsequently became Argento's companion), and some advice from his jazz pianist buddy, Carlo (Gabriele Lavia). The casting for Carlo's strange mother, Martha, recalls Bava's use of Isa Miranda in *Twitch of the Death Nerve*. Argento cast Clara Calamai, forever identified with the birth of Italian neorealism and as the vamp in Visconti's *Obsession*. (Both Bava and Argento seem to be echoing Hollywood's frequent use in horror films, noted in chapter 10, of aging actresses who were once femmes fatales.) Of course, following the genre's rules, the discovery that Martha is the killer comes as the film concludes; but the black-gloved hands we see throughout the film as the murderer's are Argento's own. These gloves, like the *giallo* disguise in *The Girl Who Knew Too Much* and *Blood and Black Lace*, conceal the fact that the culprit is actually a woman. Argento almost always stands in for the serial killer in his *gialli*, using his own hands to enact the murders and even his own voice dubbed as the murderer's.

Once again, a traumatic experience from the past eventually explains the killer's motives. Years earlier in a beautiful Roman art nouveau villa, Carlo witnessed his deranged mother stab his father just before he was forced to have her committed. The film actually opens with a flashback to this moment as the credits begin, and Argento's sound track always associates this earlier crime with a strange lullaby and future killings. Architecture also plays a major role in the film, along with Argento's extremely creative use of vivid colors and unusual camera angles and point-of-view shots. For example, in the center of Rome and between Piazza Navona and the Pantheon, Argento constructed a set that copies Edward Hopper's famous painting *Nighthawks*, at the Art Institute of Chicago: this is the Blue Bar, where Carlo plays when he is not covering up for his mother's murders. The most striking set is a stunningly beautiful art nouveau villa known in the film as the House of the Screaming Child; its florid and sensuous lines,

In Argento's *Deep Red*, the director transforms a sidewalk near Rome's Piazza Navona into the café of Edward Hopper's famous painting, *Nighthawks*. Credit: DVD

Marcus discovers the key to the mystery behind the killings in Argento's *Deep Red*. Credit: AB

even when abandoned, suggest something out of place and threatening. At this somewhat sinister site, Marcus uncovers the original traumatic killing of Carlo's father which explains everything in the film. The set-piece murders are longer than in Argento's other thrillers and much more skillfully handled. Martha dies at the end of the film as her necklace, caught in an elevator that Marcus sets in motion to save his skin, decapitates her in a symphony of blood gushing around the gold chain. Argento also deals with the theme of homosexuality in *Deep Red*, as Marcus discovers Carlo's sexual preference even before he realizes that Carlo has been covering up for his mother's crimes, identifying with her rather than with his dead father.

Deep Red shares a connection with Antonioni's *Blow-Up*: the directors' choice of actor, David Hemmings, for their protagonist, who struggles to decode a visual clue that leads to discovering a crime. Marcus's search to find the killer involves deciphering something strange he saw when he ran to find the German psychic murdered in an apartment near his own. His experience resembles that of Sam Dalmas in Argento's first *giallo*, who sees a couple struggle but confuses the victim with the killer. The troubling thing Marcus cannot remember is actually the image of Martha, reflected from behind him onto the front of a grotesque painting that he only subliminally remembers at the first crime scene. In almost every respect—plot, dialogue, camerawork, music—*Deep Red* is a huge leap forward from Argento's first three *gialli*, particularly in its use of color, which stands comparison with the brilliant work by Bava on *Blood and Black Lace*.

Post-Argento *Gialli*: Luciano Ercoli, Paolo Cavara, and Lucio Fulci

Within only two or three years after the international success of Argento's first *giallo*, Italian genre directors jumped on the box-office bandwagon and began to roll out similar films, many of which remain worth screening. Argento himself moved from *Deep Red* to the horror genre for a brief time (see chapter 10), and by the time he returned in *Tenebrae* (*Tenebre*, 1982) to the classic *giallo* formula, one not "contaminated" by horror-film elements (such as witches and other supernatural phenomena), the Italian film industry had produced more than a hundred thrillers following the generic "rules of the game" established by Bava and Argento's seminal films. A number of actors became associated with the *giallo*, just as some had with the spaghetti western: the Uruguayan leading man George Hilton (1934–); the Spanish beauty Nieves Navarro, a.k.a. Susan Scott (1938–); the Brazilian actress Florinda Bolkan; the French leading man Jean Sorel (1934–); the Swedish actress Anita Strindberg (1944–); the Italo-Croatian Ivan Rassimov, who also was closely associated with the Euro-crime films of the 1970s; the American Eugene Walter (1921–98), famous for his portrayals of characters with ambiguous sexual identifications;[7] the Czech-born but California-educated Barbara Bouchet, who moved to Italy from Hollywood in 1970 and immediately became a star in *sexy* comedies, *gialli*, and crime films; and the Algerian-born Edwige Fenech, whose career resembles Bouchet's in its trajectory of film genres. The cosmopolitan backgrounds typical of the actors and actresses who worked extensively in the *giallo* call attention to the fundamentally contemporary and cosmopolitan nature of the genre itself, which is clearly displayed in the typically contemporary and cosmopolitan locations, architecture, interior furnishings, fashion, automobiles, and a variety of non-Italian names. Relatively few Italian *gialli* portray Italy as a land of ancient monuments unless they are juxtaposed against the resolutely modern. Films are often shot abroad, and they often have the feel of generic locations that become almost interchangeable: London, Berlin, Paris, Turin, Milan, and the business-suburban EUR (Esposizione Universale Roma) district of Rome. Important exceptions exist, of course, but in general the varied national origins of many of the popular actors that turn up repeatedly in the *giallo* cast aim at a mass foreign audience that does not immediately recognize the ambience of a *giallo* as being too foreign. Critics have remarked incredulously at the frequent appearance of a bottle of J&B scotch in an Italian *giallo*, but the 1970s coincide with an era that viewed scotch (not white wine, cold vodka, or the martini) as chic and international in Italy—exactly the kind of audience appeal the *giallo* sought.

Luciano Ercoli

One of the first directors to jump on the thriller bandwagon was Luciano Ercoli, who made three films in three years: *The Forbidden Photos of a Lady above Suspicion* (*Le foto proibite di una signora per bene*, 1970), *Death Walks on High Heels* (*La morte cammina con i tacchi alti*, 1971), and *Death Walks at Midnight* (*La morte accarezza a mezzanotte*, 1972). Susan Scott, who is featured in all three films, married the director shortly before he inherited a fortune and retired from the film industry in the late 1970s. Although few stylistic traits set Ercoli's films apart from those that follow, they are relatively restrained in their depiction of violence, elegantly photographed, and a bit more interested in the erotic potential of filming beautiful women in various stages of undress than in pushing the limits of the permissible. In the first film, for example, Minou (Dagmar Lassander), the wife of a businessman, who may be a killer, according to a violent blackmailer (Simón Andreu), who assaults and rapes her. Her best friend, Dominique (Susan Scott), practices promiscuous sex and loves pornography from Denmark. Flashbacks reveal Minou's thoughts while she was being raped (she enjoyed it and now feels guilty). When she finally confesses all this to the police and her husband, Peter (Pier Paolo Capponi), no one believes her. Like all of Ercoli's plots, the conclusion of the film must be regarded as both surprising and far-fetched. Peter's apparently unexpected return home, where he finds his wife and the blackmailer, who is trying to kill Minou, is actually a carefully planned event, since Peter has hired the blackmailer to drive his wife crazy, then murder her. Upon his arrival, he shoots the blackmailer and then makes a phone call to an accomplice, revealing that he was behind the entire plot to kill Minou, who was only temporarily unconscious. Anyone in the audience must assume that Peter has called Dominique, but when the police commissioner arrives and shoots Peter before he can finish the blackmailer's task, we discover that it was in fact Dominique who had alerted the police, since she recognized the blackmailer from her Danish pornography and had also learned, by sleeping with Peter's partner, George (Salvador Huguet), that Peter had recently taken out an enormous insurance policy on Minou. We learn that Peter's real business was pornography plus "personal demonstrations" of his products. As this outline makes clear, Ercoli's convoluted plots are often confusing, and the resolution of the thriller requires great leaps of imagination.

The sophisticated atmosphere Ercoli created in his first *giallo* continues in his third, *Death Walks at Midnight*. This time, Susan Scott plays an aspiring fashion model named Valentina convinced to take part in a hallucinatory drug experience by an ambitious journalist named Gio Baldi (Simón Andreu). One of the elements of contemporary life that *gialli* introduced into Italian cinema was the widespread use of illegal drugs, and *Death*

Walks at Midnight unfolds as a thriller whose resolution rests upon the drug trade in Milan. One of the unusual aspects of the film is the weapon employed by the film's serial killer—a spiked metal glove or gauntlet typical of those used by soldiers wearing medieval or Renaissance body armor also employed in *Blood and Black Lace*. Ercoli continues his skill at capturing the wealthy, contemporary atmosphere of upper-middle-class Europe: his films feature fashionable bars where patrons consume enormous quantities of J&B scotch and listen to the latest rock music, luxurious interiors with the last word in Milanese designer furniture, and the like. Once again, it seems that the impact of Antonioni's *Blow-Up* upon the *giallo*'s development is evident. The film's entire plot revolves around a scene Valentina saw across the internal courtyard of her high-rise apartment building—the violent murder of a woman by a man with a spiked glove.

Ercoli's style combines an elegant patina of urban life photographed beautifully within a violent storyline of murder and mayhem, all of which he wraps up in a conclusion that is virtually impossible to imagine from the few clues provided to the spectator. Once again, we have the obligatory policeman who refuses to believe Valentina's story (a generic trait of the Italian thriller that begins with Bava's *The Girl Who Knew Too Much*); but instead of the leather-clad murderer with black gloves, the single spiked glove takes center stage in this thriller. The film's conclusion is complicated almost beyond verisimilitude. Valentina's boyfriend, Stefano (Pietro Martellanza), turns out to be the drug lord behind a bewildering series of deaths; he apparently was interested in sleeping with Valentina only because her apartment gave him a direct view of the apartment across the courtyard, where his competitor in the drug trade was located—and where the murder Valentina saw in a drugged state took place. Yet all of Ercoli's *gialli* display very high production values, and *Death Walks at Midnight* has an excellent and clever script (to which Sergio Corbucci and Ernesto Gastaldi [1934–] contributed), a fine musical sound track, a good group of well-cast actors, elegant photography, and skillful editing that intensifies the narrative suspense.

Paolo Cavara

Another interesting *giallo* appeared immediately after Argento's success: *The Black Belly of the Tarantula* (*La tarantola dal ventre nero*, 1971), by Paolo Cavara (1926–82), a film that sports contributions to the script by Tonino Guerra, the talents of Ennio Morricone's musical score, and three Bond Girls (Claudine Auger from *Thunderball* [1965], Barbara Bouchet from the spoof *Casino Royale* [1967], and Barbara Bach, who would be in *The Spy Who Loved Me* [1977]), plus the Italian stars Giancarlo Giannini and Stefania Sandrelli. Cavara's plot represents the classic *giallo* storyline: a deranged killer injects a series of beautiful women with the venom of a black wasp that preys on tarantulas, paralyzing them so that, while he rips open their stomachs with a sharp blade, they can witness their own deaths. Inspector Tellini (Giannini)—one of the brighter detectives in a genre that generally shows the police to be incompetent, rather than the amateur detectives popularized by Bava and Argento's early *gialli*—focuses his investigation upon an exclusive, ultramodern, and terribly expensive spa. Given this focus upon fashion and beauty, Cavara's film also lingers as long as possible on the beautiful female bodies in the film. In fact, the fascination with murdering beautiful women Bava exploited in *Blood and Black Lace* becomes one of the most important traits of these Italian thrillers, along with the by-now classic technique of focusing upon the killer's gloved hands (in this case, a yellowish rubber glove, rather than the black leather variety accompanying a black trench coat).

The killer dispatches the first victim, Maria (played by Barbara Bouchet in one of her earliest Italian roles, before she became a star), as an adulterer. After a second victim, the owner of a dress shop, dies in the same fashion, the inspector discovers a large quantity of cocaine on her premises. No connection can be found between the two women except the method of death: the paralyzing venom and the stomach wounds. This fact leads Tellini to an entomologist for information about the special wasp that kills tarantulas. In the midst of his discussion with the scientist, Tellini discovers that this researcher actually traffics in cocaine, bringing it into the country by passing it off as white sand inside insect cages! By this time, the audience must certainly be aware of the premise of the film: everyone has dirty little secrets. Cavara drives home his point even more strongly when he shows one of the murder suspects taking pictures of Tellini and his wife, Anna (Stefania Sandrelli), making love in their bedroom; the entire homicide squad screens the footage in a moment humiliating for the detective, who considers quitting his job. More murders follow, now reaching into the ranks of spa employees. After the killer eliminates Jenny (Barbara Bach) and stuffs her body in a garbage bag, Tellini believes the owner of the spa, Laura (Claudine Auger), is the key to the mystery, along with her blind masseur (Ezio Marano). In fact, Laura offers to reveal the entire truth to Tellini if he meets her at the spa at night, but Tellini finds only Laura's bloody body and a pair of contact lenses on the floor. Realizing that the blind masseur has been faking his blindness, and that the photographs of him and Anna making love mean that his wife may be the next victim, Tellini rushes home in a crescendo of suspense as the director cuts between the masseur's progress in slowly slicing off Anna's clothes to prepare her for the paralyzing venom and Tellini's frenzied drive home to save her. He makes it in time, and later at the hospital, a motive for the masseur's crime spree comes to light. He had killed his wife five years earlier and became obsessed with torturing and murdering other beautiful women who surrounded him; he feigned blindness as a means of remaining invisible to the women who revealed all their secrets to him, because they thought he could not identify them. Once again, a *giallo* underscores the theme of sight and the inability to see clearly.

Lucio Fulci

Fulci's *A Lizard in a Woman's Skin* (*La lucertola con la pelle di donna*, 1971) and *Don't Torture a Duckling* (*Non si sevizia un paperino*, 1972) move quickly beyond the most obvious and most easily imitated characteristics of the *giallo* genre as practiced by Bava and Argento, such as the simple crescendo of suspense, the traumatic past experience that explains a present crime, or the stereotypical black-gloved assassin. Like Argento, Fulci vacillated between genres, making violent thrillers as well as even more violent horror films, and he had learned his trade by previously working as the director of one of the most violent of the spaghetti westerns, the 1966 *Massacre Time*, a film scripted by the screenwriter Fernando Di Leo, who was also the best-known director associated with the equally violent Euro-crime films of the 1970s and 1980s.

A Lizard in a Woman's Skin exhibits the same cosmopolitan, upper-class atmosphere typical of Ercoli's films shot abroad. The world Fulci dissects mercilessly for its corruption is aristocratic England, the wealthy residential area of Belgravia in London and the opulent country homes of the dynastically wealthy, a dysfunctional, fashionable world that rests upon a substratum of drugs, blackmail, self-indulgence, and homosexuality. Carol Hammond (Florinda Bolkan), the rich daughter of an important lawyer and politician, Edmund Brighton (Leo Genn), is married to Frank (Jean Sorel), who works for her father and is carrying on an affair with his own secretary, Deborah (Silvia Monti). Brighton receives an anonymous telephone call, warning him that someone in his family is engaged in scandalous activity that could damage his political career. What Brighton fails to realize is that the call comes from Julia Durer (Anita Strindberg), the beautiful but promiscuous lesbian who lives in Carol's building, and that the scandalous behavior referred to in the call is Julia's affair with Carol. Fulci opens the film with a highly imaginative dream sequence reminiscent of those in Fellini's *8½* in their surrealistic visual qualities, but in Fulci's case, this sequence of lesbian love is quite explicit (both women are nearly naked, with only a fur coat covering Carol's body). In another of Carol's dream experiences, Fulci clearly employs the visual images derived from Francis Bacon's paintings (artwork that also influenced Bertolucci's *Last Tango in Paris* several years later). In this second scene, Carol stabs Julia with a letter opener as a pair of stoned hippies watch them from the balcony.

Carol dutifully reports the dreams to her psychoanalyst, who believes that the murder of Julia represents a dream of liberation for Carol, freeing her from things she does not wish to accept (her temptation to have a lesbian affair). Immediately afterward, however, we discover that Julia actually has been murdered, and the police find her apartment full of all sorts of drugs employed in her regular orgies. When the police find that virtually everything in the apartment seems as if it was taken from Carol's dreams and that her fur coat from the opening dream sequence is even in Julia's apartment, she is arrested for murder. Fulci complicates his narrative of the events tremendously, since the film basically reflects Carol's point of view, which is totally unreliable. Actually, Carol had killed Julia and used the account of her dreams related to her analyst and recorded in a falsified dream diary as a red herring to complicate the forensic evidence of the case. Her aim was to avoid a charge of premeditated murder and to be diagnosed with a split personality. (The original American release title of the film was *Schizoid*.) Ultimately, her machinations lead to her father's suicide, after he falsely confesses to murdering Julia because he realizes his daughter is the culprit. The explanation for the film's strange title comes from the police testimony of the hippie couple, Hubert (Mike Kennedy) and Jenny (Penny Brown), the two stoned onlookers who saw Carol stab Julia. Although Carol manufactured the entire dream fantasy out of whole cloth, because she thought they had seen her commit the murder, they had, in fact, experienced an LSD hallucination of a "lizard in a woman's skin"—referring to her naked body inside the fur coat she was wearing. In this instance, the psychoanalyst misses the point entirely, and the policeman from Scotland Yard, Inspector Corvin (Stanley Baker), figures it all out. Of course, English policeman have the example of Sherlock Holmes to follow, something that Italian policeman in *gialli* set in Italy cannot match.

Fulci's film represents a brilliant use of surrealistic dream sequences and an extremely complicated but intriguing plot that plays with the unreliable point of view of the murderer, a woman who fools (at least for a brief time) not only her doctor, her family, and the police but also the audience. *Don't Torture a Duckling* in the following year shows Fulci as the equally original creator of an entirely different kind of mood and setting for an even more disturbing take on a serial murderer, set in a southern Italian village called Accendura. (The actual location was Monte Sant'Angelo in Puglia, the easternmost region of Italy). Everything about the location stands in contrast to the wealthy, cosmopolitan, sophisticated world of his first film. Fulci creates a town that stands apart from the modern world, even though the autostrada sweeps through the nearby countryside and links the two. Only Patrizia (Barbara Bouchet), a young woman from Milan whose father was born in the town but who has gone north to make his fortune, connects us to the ambience of Fulci's first *giallo*, and her contemporary mountain villa stands in sharp contrast to the whitewashed traditional structures typical of Puglia. The townspeople consider Patrizia a slut. The real powers

In Fulci's *Don't Torture a Duckling*, a naked Patrizia (played by Barbara Bouchet, one of the stars of Italy's "sexy" comic films) tempts Andrea, a Roman journalist. Besides the almost obligatory *giallo* killer wearing gloves and sporting a sharp blade and a trench coat or a slouch hat, the Italian thriller film also delighted in photographing beautiful naked women whenever possible. *Credit: DVD*

in the town are those with links to magic and superstition: a gypsy witch named La Magiara (Florinda Bolkan), and Francesco (Georges Wilson), a kind of magician. As a kind of premodern peasant world best described in Carlo Levi's classic neorealist novel *Christ Stopped in Eboli*, Fulci presents it visually in a fundamentally neorealist style. One after another, male children are being murdered in the town without being sexually molested. A Roman journalist, Andrea Martelli (Tomas Milian), arrives to investigate the crimes and pairs up with Patrizia, since only outsiders seem to be interested in uncovering the truth. Townspeople are frightened of something, and the police resign themselves to the belief that, in the Mezzogiorno, they will receive no assistance from the population.

Fulci employs a number of red herrings—suspects that prove to be innocent—to heighten the suspense, but it comes as a shock to any viewer of the film to discover that the young village priest, Don Alberto (Marc Porel), is the serial killer. His crimes come to light because of his retarded six-year-old sister, who compulsively tears the heads off her dolls. Patrizia buys her a Donald Duck doll and later finds the duck's head near the scene of one of the murders. Patrizia and Andrea confront the priest as he attempts to throw his sister off a steep cliff, and in the process he himself falls like Lucifer from Heaven, his face horribly disfigured and graphically portrayed by Fulci's camera as he dies. The priest's motives had been "pure": he strangled the young boys not because he was a sexual pervert but because of his perverted religious fears about sex. Convinced that they would become sinners after meeting girls like Patrizia, he preferred to send them off to paradise with immaculately innocent souls! In Italy, priests have traditionally been held in high esteem—except, of course, in the comic literature, which portrayed them as gluttons and fornicators but rarely child murderers or molesters. Hence, Fulci's choice of a murderer priest for essentially religious reasons did not please the Italian censors.

Earlier, in *A Lizard in a woman's skin*, Fulci inserted a shocking scene in one of Carol's dreams—cut from most subsequent versions of the film—depicting a laboratory filled with horribly dissected but live dogs employed for medical experiments, their bodies cut open and their organs still palpitating. These mechanical special effects had been created for Fulci by the famous Carlo Rambaldi, who was obliged to testify in court that no real animals had been harmed during the making of the film and to produce his realistic handiwork to win the case. Fulci's future work in both the *giallo* and the horror genres would rely increasingly on such special effects, as would Dario Argento's post–*Deep Red* work.

Post-Argento *Gialli*, Continued: Sergio Martino, Giuliano Carnimeo, Emilio Miraglia, and Aldo Lado

Sergio Martino

After rounding up the usual suspects (George Hilton, Susan Scott, Anita Strindberg, Edwige Fenech, and Ivan Rassimov, among others), Sergio Martino turned out several well-received works in only three years: *The Strange Vice of Mrs. Wardh* (*Lo strano vizio della Signora Wardh*, 1971); *The Case of the Scorpion's Tail* (*La coda dello scorpione*, 1971); *All the Colors of the Dark* (*Tutti i colori del buio*, 1972); *Your Vice Is a Locked Room and Only I Have the Key* (*Tuo vizio è una stanza chiusa e solo io ne ho la chiave*, 1972); and, the most controversial, *Torso* (*I corpi presentano tracce di violenza carnale*, 1973).

After an opening citation from Sigmund Freud to the effect that murder is in humanity's blood, Martino's first *giallo* opens with a streetwalker killed with a straight razor by a man who picks her up outside of an Austrian airport. This provokes a flashback in which Julie Wardh (Edwige Fenech) relives what appears to be a rape that she enjoys and then treats the audience to one of Fenech's obligatory shows of nudity in the shower. Mrs. Wardh's "strange vice" of the title turns out to be the enjoyment of sadomasochistic sex with a sinister character from her past named Jean (Ivan Rassimov), who, in a flashback to a dream, pours liquor over her, breaks a bottle over her body, and uses the pieces to scratch her body bloody. In the middle of this dream, Julie wakes up in bed next to her inattentive husband, Neil (Alberto de Mendoza). Subsequently, in a shower scene that cites Hitchcock's *Psycho*, the classic black-gloved *giallo* murderer slits the throat of a girl Julie has met at her friend Carol's party. Julie becomes romantically involved with Carol's cousin George (George Hilton), but the strange Jean continues to pursue and haunt her, sending her flowers with an inscription so amusing that it will become the title of Martino's fourth *giallo* ("Your vice is a closed room . . ."). The narrative contains a bewildering number of corpses and murders, numerous red herrings, and a startling ending. Jean places Julie's body in the kitchen and turns on the gas; George and Julie's doctor arrive apparently too late. Subsequently, George meets Jean in a deserted spot, but instead of paying Jean off for killing Julie, George shoots him. George then drives back to meet Julie's husband, Neil—they joke about throwing away the obligatory killer's black gloves. Finally the motive behind the bizarre series of events in the confusing narrative becomes apparent: Neil needed the payoff from his insurance policy on Julie.

In a coup de théâtre that completes the film in a completely unexpected manner, Neil and George suddenly see Julie alive on the road, and they drive off the road, over a cliff, and die as the police arrive to arrest them. Against all odds, the doctor managed to revive Julie, and justice triumphs in one of the most surprising plot twists in any *giallo* ever made. (Quentin Tarantino uses the "Dies Irae" musical theme composed for Martino's film by Nora Orlandi [1933–] and associates it with the character Budd, a.k.a. Sidewinder, played by Michael Madsen in *Kill Bill 2* [2004]—only one of many such references to Italian genre cinema in his works.)

All the Colors of the Dark, inspired in part by the success of Roman Polanski's *Rosemary's Baby* (1968), continues the use of non-Italian locations (this time London) typical of many *gialli* and adds the narrative complication of a satanic cult to give a dimension of horror to the story. It opens with a dream sequence involving a pregnant woman, one of the most nightmarish of such sequences in any Italian thriller, following the success of both the opening in Fulci's *A Lizard in a Woman's Skin* and the dream sequence in Martino's first *giallo*. In this powerful film, Martino stresses how strong premonitions may actually be fulfilled by real events, as well as the inability of his protagonists to distinguish reality and fantasy. Jane Harrison (Fenech) and the man she calls her husband, Richard (George Hilton), are recovering from Jane's recent miscarriage and car accident, actually caused by an abortion (events dimly seen through the opening dream sequence of the pregnant woman). Terrorized also by dreams about the murder of her mother when she was a child and a knife-wielding killer, Jane takes the advice of various people to cure her psychological problems. George, a pharmaceutical salesman, thinks vitamins will cure her, and scoffs at Freudian solutions; her sister, Barbara (Susan Scott), sends her to a psychoanalyst, Dr. Burton (George Rigaud); her strange neighbor, Mary (Marina Malfatti), suggests a Black Mass. Then Jane receives a strange call from a lawyer, Franciscus Clay (Luciano Pigozzi), requesting an appointment; she puts it off and decides to attend the Black Mass, where she drinks the blood of a slaughtered animal and participates in a group orgy, photographed by Martino from her subjective point of view as the group caresses and kisses her. A sudden cut to Jane and George making love seems to suggest that the satanic cult ritual solved her psychological problems.

Continuing to frequent the cult rituals, Jane becomes involved in Mary's death, receiving a cult tattoo as a symbol of her membership in the group, a group she learns can be abandoned only by death. When she attempts to escape from the cult, a number of people associated with her die mysterious deaths. Meanwhile, George discovers the strange reasons behind the killings. Before Jane, her and Barbara's mother had been in the cult and died trying to leave it. Barbara, a major player in the cult, received information from the lawyer, Clay, that the murderer of their mother repented in New Zealand and left the sisters £300,000. Barbara has decided to use the cult to rid herself of her sister and to pocket the inheritance. When she offers herself to Jane's husband and then tries to shoot him, Richard shoots her instead! All seems well at last, but Martino adds yet one more sudden twist, as if the story to this point were not sufficiently confusing, to conclude the film. Suddenly, McBrian (Julián Ugarte), the surviving cult leader who escaped the police, appears and tries one more time to kill Richard and Jane. In this instance, Jane's dreams provide her with a sense of premonition, and she manages to warn Richard in time. In a struggle, McBrian is thrown over a tall balcony (an extremely popular means of dispatching characters in the *giallo*, because it allows the director to film the body bouncing down a number of flights of stairs in intricate architectural spaces with great visual impact), and finally Jane's monsters are exorcised. Martino seems to have learned from Argento's practice of employing extremely interesting buildings to create extremely satisfying aesthetic effects. In this case he uses a beautiful art deco apartment building featuring an old-fashioned elevator in the middle of its stairway.

Martino's *Torso* has been discussed in terms of its important links to what later becomes the slasher film.[8] It focuses upon a group of mostly promiscuous American students studying art history in Rome—and anyone who spent time as a student in Italy during the 1970s living hand to mouth in wretched but expensive apartments will be amused by the luxurious quarters these lucky young people seem to have found for themselves. Everyone in their group attends the art-historical lectures of Franz (John Richardson), an academic obviously attracted to the oldest American of the group, Jane (Suzy Kendall). Jane's friends, however, are more interested in sex and drugs than in frescoes: Carol (Conchita Airoldi), Flo (Patrizia Adiutori), Katia (Angela Covello), and Ursula (Carla Brait) are also eventually revealed to be lesbians, or at least bisexual. Even before the film's credits run, an opening sequence shows two women making love slightly out of focus and being photographed by an unknown cameraman. Ultimately, the serial killer, who uses a scarlet scarf to strangle his victims, turns out to be the photographer, the victim of blackmail at the hands of the girls in his pictures.

After two girls (Flo and Carol, the two we later learn were being photographed) are murdered in Rome, Jane, Daniela (Tina Aumont), Katia, and Ursula go off into the countryside to a villa situated high above a small village, where the killer pursues them and dispatches Jane's friends. In a powerfully suspense-filled segment lasting more than twenty minutes, the murderer plays cat and mouse with Jane until she is rescued at the last moment by Roberto (Luc Merenda), a medical doctor who had earlier treated her twisted ankle. Finally, the audience learns the identity of the photographer–serial killer: he is her enamored art professor Franz, whose perverted, murderous acts stem from one of the more unbelievable traumatic past events that thriller directors and their scriptwriters have invented in the *giallo* tradition: As a child, Franz had seen his brother fall to his death trying to rescue the doll of a girl who had promised to lift her skirt for Franz's brother if he would retrieve her doll. Thereafter, Franz considers women as sluttish dolls; he feels compelled to destroy them, driven further astray by Jane's lesbian friends. He murders the two lesbians blackmailing him and soon finds occasion to murder two other lesbians in the group of art history students.

Martino's original Italian title focuses our attention upon the bodies in the film: they are beautifully and frequently shot naked in lesbian embraces, and when murdered, they literally "bear traces of carnal violence" as the title suggests, with far more realistically bloody wounds than typical of *gialli*, where the blood-covered bodies appear to be doused with ketchup or commercial makeup rather than real *sangue*.

Giuliano Carnimeo and Emilio Miraglia

Italian directors freely migrated from one popular genre to another. Once it was clear that well-made thrillers had an international market, it made sense to move to *gialli*—particularly from the then expiring western, as did the director Guiliano Carnimeo (still working as Anthony Ascott). His *The Case of the Bloody Iris*, a.k.a. *What Are Those Strange Drops of Blood Doing on Jennifer's Body?* (*Perché quelle strane gocce di sangue sul corpo di Jennifer?*, 1972), opens and closes with a telephone call from one woman to another from a pay phone—both lesbian assignations, as we later discover. Carnimeo thus exploits the Italian male audience's repulsion and attraction to female homosexuality that was so successful an element of the narrative in Fulci's *A Lizard in a Woman's Skin*. When the caller enters an apartment building, an ultramodern structure in Rome's EUR district, a killer dressed in a black overcoat and wearing rubber gloves slits her throat with a scalpel. Later Andrea (Hilton), the designer of the building in which the woman was murdered, meets Jennifer (Fenech), who is participating, nearly naked, in a fashion shoot. We discover later that her ex-husband, Adam (Ben Carrà), had married her in a flower-child ceremony that introduced her to a cult marriage and group sex: "a single body made up of many members as this flower has many petals" in the words of the ceremony, a line that explains the film's English title. After adding cult sex to lesbianism, the film moves to a third and even more intriguing scene. A black girl named Mizar (Carla Brait), who just happened to find the first woman's body in the building's elevator, performs a strip act in a private club to which Andrea belongs, a dance devoted to the enslavement of blacks by white men. Mizar challenges the audience (all men) to wrestle with her and make her their slave, openly insulting their Italian manhood. She wins the bouts easily, ending in a triumph of muscular nudity under the club's spotlight; but just as predictably, she becomes the killer's next victim, knocked out with a judo chop by the killer in the classic black stocking mask, rubber gloves, black coat, and black slouch hat, and dies in her bath. Luckily for Jennifer and for her model friend, Marilyn (Paola Quattrini), this frees up Mizar's apartment for them; but when Andrea shows it to them, he becomes deathly ill at the sight of a pinprick of blood, an important element for the conclusion of the film.

The enormously long shots of flights of stairs through triangular or oblong or circular stairways offer Carnimeo a perfect visual metaphor for the killer's twisted psyche, but numerous red herrings obstruct his or her identification. Jennifer and Marilyn meet Sheila (Annabella Incontrera), a gorgeous woman with obvious lesbian leanings who lives with her retired father, a university professor of music (George Rigaud). Sheila must have been the woman to whom the first telephone call that opened the film was made, as bodies now begin to pile up: Adam is stabbed; Marilyn is stabbed and dies in Andrea's arms outside her apartment, the sight of her blood making Andrea almost faint. The police are virtually nonexistent and, as usual, ineffectual, leaving the solution of the crimes to Jennifer and to Andrea, who may perhaps be the actual murderer, as the plot constantly suggests.

David, the strangely disfigured son of an old woman who lives next to Jennifer's apartment, thinks of beautiful women as whores and sluts, suggesting that he may be the killer; but he turns out to be just another red herring provided by the director. Sheila dons a black leather coat, hinting that perhaps *she* is the mysterious figure. Both are murdered. Ultimately Jennifer discovers that Sheila's father, who accidentally killed his daughter with a blast of hot steam in the furnace room, mistaking her for Jennifer, is the assassin. His fascinating motive is not surprising: he blames all beautiful women for corrupting Sheila with lesbianism! Just as the mad professor is about to throw Jennifer over the ubiquitous balcony, Andrea shows up, almost faints from the sight of blood, but recovers in time to toss the professor over instead. A flashback explains Andrea's reaction as the result of a car accident many years before, in which his dying father's blood dripped on the horrified young boy trapped beneath the car.

Carnimeo's black humor concludes the film. Another woman from the same pay phone that opened the film calls up to yet another lesbian lover, who answers: "Come on up, I'm alone!" Lesbian love trumps the happy heterosexual ending of Andrea and Jennifer. Carnimeo's skillful combination of point-of-view shots, beautifully photographed interiors, flashbacks, and red herrings conducive to creating confusion among his spectators make for a powerful and entertaining story.

Emilio Miraglia, who had directed in a number of genres, filmed a noteworthy *giallo* released in 1972, *The Red Queen Kills 7 Times* (*La dama rossa uccide sette volte*), which combines the completely contemporary environment of a large German city, the couture of a German fashion house called Springe, and the Gothic atmosphere of a mysterious castle filled with a legendary ghost, the Red Queen. Kitty Wildenbrück (Barbara Bouchet) believes she had accidentally killed her sister Evelyn in an argument, an incident covered up with the help of her other sister, Franziska (Marina Malfatti). Evelyn's body apparently lies hidden in the family castle crypt while Kitty pursues a career with the fashion house: Evelyn, people are informed, has gone to America. Now, as people around Kitty begin to be murdered by a woman wearing a red cloak and cackling fiendishly after she commits her crimes, it seems that the family curse, illustrated by a painting in the castle, has struck. As their grandfather had told them when they were children, every hundred years the Red Queen kills seven people—the seventh of whom is the Black Queen, her sister.

Miraglia's film offers no original cinematic effects but marries the world of haute couture with Gothic horror. The film's most typical shot is from the killer cam, showing the subjective perspective of the killer as she attacks each successive victim. The film might also be called an homage to the fashion designs of the then tremendously influential Italian-born designer Mila Schön (1916–2008), whose creations are featured throughout the film, returning us to the high-fashion world of Bava's *Blood and Black Lace*. Bodies pile up as the Red Queen approaches victim number seven, which according to the legend would be Kitty: the first victim is the grandfather (frightened to death by an apparition); then Hans (Bruno Bertocci), the director of Springe Fashions (stabbed); Lenore, one of the workers at the fashion house (stabbed); Elizabeth, wife to Martin Hoffman (Ugo Pagliai), successor to Hans (impaled on an iron fence); Peter, a drug addict blackmailing Kitty (head bashed against the curb while dragged by a Volkswagen driven by the Red Queen); and Lulu (Sybil Danning), a promiscuous associate of Springe who jumps from Hans's bed to Martin's (shot). Finally the still plotting Franziska dispatches Rosemary (Pia Giancaro), whom she has known to be the *real* Evelyn: the grandfather, it seems, had switched the infant Evelyn with a peasant girl in an attempt to obviate the family curse! Thus the sister Kitty believes she has killed was actually really a peasant girl, whom Franziska had then found in the castle moat, semiconscious but still alive, and finished off herself. Later, Franziska found the *real* Evelyn (that is,

Rosemary), kept her drugged (courtesy of the addict, Peter), and gotten her to kill the other victims. As usual, the motive was greed: the family inheritance. While Miraglia's film begins as a Gothic thriller and piles up serial killer victims, as is expected in a *giallo*, the film ends happily with Martin and Kitty headed for marriage—in short, the classic conclusion of a comedy.

Aldo Lado

Aldo Lado came to direction after working as assistant director on a spaghetti western (the normal progression for thriller directors) and then on one of the great ideologically engaged "art films" of the period, Bertolucci's *The Conformist*. Thus, it is no accident that the three films he directed in rapid succession, establishing him as one of the major *gialli* directors in the wake of the genre's invention, convey an implicitly ideological message. These include *The Short Night of Glass Dolls* (*La corta notte delle bambole di vetro*, 1971), *Who Saw Her Die?* (*Chi l'ha vista morire?*, 1972), and *Night Train Murders* (*L'ultimo treno della notte*, 1975). Shot in Prague, Lado clearly intended the first work to reflect in some measure the frightening portrait of power found in the fiction of that city's greatest writer, Franz Kafka. Its journalist protagonist, Gregory Moore (Jean Sorel), stumbles upon a worldwide chain of private clubs called Club 99 that houses a satanic cult of old men and women who exert power through using and discarding the young and beautiful people that they kidnap and kill. Lado's original take on the thriller genre derives from his decision to tell the story from the perspective of the journalist, who lies paralyzed in the city morgue, waiting for an autopsy that will kill him. Thus, Gregory speaks frequently through a voiceover, and the story that explains how he ended up on the autopsy table unfolds in flashback: the amateur detective of the genre as prime victim. His girlfriend, Mira (Barbara Bach), disappears after being chosen to be one of those used and discarded by the cultists. Everyone Gregory meets in Prague who has some official standing in the government or in civil society belongs to this cult. Perhaps the most memorable sequence in the film, depicting the satanic rituals taking place at Club 99, represents an orgy of old, fat, and ugly people—for Lado, the ideal visualization of those who hold power in society—while the power holders take the lives of the young and the beautiful, those we might normally expect to see depicted in an orgy scene.

Who Saw Her Die?, set in Lado's native Venice and beautifully shot during the unique, foggy, and suggestive winter weather there, rests upon similar assumptions about how political, social, and economic power may be exerted by a small but coordinated group of secretive people. This film features not just an ex–Bond villain, Adolfo Celi (Emilio Largo, Spectre No. 2, from *Thunderball*), but an ex–James Bond (George Lazenby, from *On Her Majesty's Secret Service* [1969]), who plays a sculptor named Franco

Serpieri working for Celi's character, a shady art dealer named Serafian. The film opens with the abduction and killing of a small girl in the French Alps in 1968. What appears to be a woman's skirt appears on the screen, the only visible part of the kidnapper and killer, who grabs the child and crushes her head with a stone to the accompaniment of a perfect Morricone musical score, with a choir of children singing in unison. Lado then cuts to Venice in 1972 with Franco at the airport greeting his redheaded young daughter, Roberta (Nicoletta Elmi), who has come from London, where she lives with her mother. On their way home, they meet a jovial young priest, Father James (Alessandro Haber), who greets them kindly. As Franco buys Roberta some ice cream to celebrate her arrival, a killer cam shot (more accurately, a "killer lace-cam shot") focuses on Roberta through a woman's veil of black lace. Lado repeats this particular modification of the traditional killer cam shot several times until the inevitable occurs: the apparently female killer murders Roberta.

Franco and his wife, Elisabetta (Anita Strindberg), become the amateur detectives virtually demanded by the *giallo* rules of the game, receiving practically no assistance from the ineffectual police of the city. (A journalist friend of Franco's tells the police inspector, "I don't think you can catch pneumonia!") They discover the existence of an entirely unsuspected serial killer, and a conversation with the grieving father of one victim reveals that he had been mysteriously assisted by one of the city's top lawyers, also a colleague of Franco's agent, Serafian. Moving from one red herring to another, Franco learns of the existence of a network of pedophiles and sexual perverts whose targets all apparently have red hair, like Roberta and the young French girl killed in 1968. Ultimately, the murderer of young children turns out *not* to be a woman, despite the shots of the skirt, black lace gloves, and veil, but the cross-dressing priest, Father James, whose identity comes out only at the film's conclusion! For an Italian audience, this revelation must have been as disturbing as the knowledge that the serial killer in *Don't Torture a Duckling* was a village priest. For Lado (unlike Fulci), this information points to a structure of corrupt power in society, not merely a psychological perversion, even though the film also informs us that the killer attacked redheads because his mother was a redhead, and by killing them he would prevent the little girls from becoming whores like his mother. Like Fulci, Lado provides much more detailed information about his characters than is typical of the usual cursory *giallo* treatment, which is generally heavy on astonishing plot twists but much lighter on personality development.

Lado's most disturbing film, *Night Train Murders*, stretches the boundaries of the *giallo* almost to the breaking point, presenting a rape-and-revenge narrative that owes its ultimate narrative plot not only to Ingmar Bergman's Oscar-winning *Virgin Spring* (1960) but also to its Hollywood imitation by Wes Craven, *The Last House on the Left* (1972). The story of how two beautiful and innocent young women are brutalized, raped, and murdered on a train ride from Munich to Verona on their way home for Christmas is one of the most disturbing films ever made in Italy—disturbing not because of the kinds of gore and violence it shows, which we have come to expect as the artistic conventions of a film genre, but because it visualizes a dehumanization of people that seems all too true to life. Lado intended exactly this effect upon his audience. Furthermore, by the way in which he differentiates the killers from their accomplices and their victims, Lado also makes a political statement about how retribution differs by class rather than by guilt.

Two lower-class thugs, Blackie (Flavio Bucci) and Curly (Gianfranco De Grassi), hopping a train to escape a police chase after a petty robbery in Munich, encounter Lisa Stadi (Laura D'Angelo), an Italian returning home to visit her wealthy parents, accompanied by her German girlfriend, Margaret Hoffenbach (Irene Miracle). In their compartment is also "una signora per bene"—a "respectable lady" with no name, played with incredible duplicity by Macha Méril, who represents for Lado all the hypocrisy and corruption that the Italian Left of the 1970s saw personified in the European bourgeoisie. This Respectable Lady, who initially rattles on about immorality, allows Blackie to have sex with her in the train's toilet, returns with him to the compartment where the two young girls are riding, and eggs both thugs on. They first rape both girls, then kill one with a knife in a drug-crazed attempt to deflower her and drive the other to jump off the moving train. By setting all this within a train compartment that can hold only eight people, Lado creates a stifling atmosphere of claustrophobia, an effect enhanced by the blue light that suffuses the entire location. Very few people are on the train, since everyone is already at home for the holidays. The exception is a middle-class man described as the Perverted Passenger (Franco Fabrizi), who, upon the Respectable Lady's invitation, first has sex with a catatonic Margaret as Curly, Blackie, the Respectable Lady, and Lisa observe (the first three amused, the latter horrified) and then, after leaving the train, tips off the police about the location and identity of the murderous trio.

The Respectable Lady and the two killers detrain without any problem. As fictional coincidence would have it (and as *Virgin Spring*'s plot demands), they fall into the company of Lisa's father, Professor Giulio Stradi (Enrico Maria Salerno). He courteously invites them to his home to dress a cut the Respectable Lady actually received from Blackie on the train, and feeds the trio before taking them back to town for another train. Radio announcements, along with Curly's stupidity in wearing a tie Stradi's wife knows to be a Christmas present for Lisa's father, reveal the truth about the Stradis' guests. The normally law-abiding doctor goes justifiably berserk and kills both thugs, but he runs out of adrenalin to complete the job by killing the Respectable Lady, while police sirens blare on the sound track. As the film ends, the Respectable Lady lowers the black veil on her hat: it is obvious that the entire blame for the girls' murders will fall on the two usual suspects, the working-class thugs, and that their "respectable" accomplice, in line with Lado's perspective on social class, will escape any punishment or retribution.

Night Train Murders represents an extremely troubling film about the nature of violence. It deserves classification as a *giallo* largely because Lisa's father assumes the role of amateur detective and "solves" the crimes without any assistance from the established authorities.

Other Thrillers by Andrea Bianchi, Luigi Cozzi, Pupi Avati, Antonio Bido, Lamberto Bava, and Lucio Fulci

The formulaic nature of a genre film does not generally detract from its enjoyment as entertainment if the "rules of the game" are applied intelligently and an appropriate visual style carries the storyline forward. In genre films, however, some touch of originality and intelligence is required to make any film following a general formula worth screening. These were apparently lacking for *French Sex Murders* (*Casa d'appuntamento*, 1972), by Ferdinando Merighi (1924–). Even with a plot involving a series of killings connected to a Paris brothel and a cast featuring Anita Ekberg and Barbara Bouchet, the photography, editing, and script are so poorly done that this incoherent film apparently ended Merighi's career as a first-unit director.

Andrea Bianchi

A first-rate film like *Strip Nude for Your Killer* (*Nude per l'assassino*, 1975), by Andrea Bianchi (1925–), which follows the *giallo* formula almost to the letter, demonstrates that by the time Bianchi shot the film, the *giallo* conventions established by Bava and Argento and elaborated upon by a number of directors in the early 1970s had become well codified. *Strip Nude for Your Killer* makes the often implicit connection between the thriller and the "sexy" film very explicit and deals with a number of themes (abortion, lesbian sex, frontal nudity) that were treated much less openly than in other earlier thrillers of the period.

The film opens with a frightening presentation of a fashion model named Evelyn, who has an abortion that results in her death. Subsequently, an assassin kills one after another of the people connected with the Albatross Modeling Agency, while dressed in a *giallo* disguise slightly modified from the classical norm. Rather than a black overcoat, leather gloves, and slouch hat, this villain wears a black motorcycle helmet and a black motorcycle outfit even when driving a normal car—a disguise punctuated by heavy breathing through the helmet worthy of a Darth Vader. The film concludes with a perfect reversal of expectations: Patrizia (Solvi Stubing, a real top model, identified by everyone in Italy with an extremely successful series of ads for Peroni beer that was made at the time) turns out to be the murderer, rather than the male killer her costume causes us to expect, and she killed because Evelyn was not only her sister but apparently also her lover! Carlo (Nino Castelnuovo), an oversexed fashion photographer, and his assistant, Magda (Edwige Fenech), form another duo of amateur sleuths who solve the crime and unmask the killer.

Besides a certain sense of humor in the script that is often missing in the *giallo*, Bianchi's film really raises the bar on female nudity and almost matches the same daring advances in presenting his male leads as all but naked. Although the English title (falsely) suggests that characters are ordered to strip nude by the killer, in fact they are all too willing to strip naked in the film without orders from anyone!

Luigi Cozzi

The Killer Must Kill Again (*L'assassino è costretto ad uccidere ancora*, 1975), made by the Dario Argento assistant Luigi Cozzi (1947–), demonstrates how the rules of genre films can be broken if they are broken intelligently. In this case, unlike the classic *giallo* plot in which we learn the identity of the assassin only at the dramatic conclusion of the story, Cozzi reveals this identity within the first two minutes of the film's opening. Observing a serial killer (Antoine Saint-John) disposing of the body of one of his victims, an adulterous husband, Giorgio Mainardi (George Hilton), blackmails him into adding his wealthy wife, Nora (Teresa Velázquez), to the body count. The film also features a stupendously bright yellow interior in the Mainardi apartment that certainly signals a high-water mark for unusual (yet literally *giallo*) contemporary set design in the genre. In a stroke of originality, Cozzi replaces the search for the identity of the killer in the opening moments of the film with the search for the location of the body. While the killer cleans up after his crime once he has placed Nora's body in the trunk of his Mercedes, and Giorgio attends a cocktail party to establish his alibi, a carefree, second-rate Bonnie and Clyde—Luca (Alessio Orano) and Laura (Cristina Galbó)—steal his car (with the body) and head for the beach, forcing the killer to steal another car to recover the dead woman. The suspense normally generated by the search for a killer now comes from the back-and-forth editing in this film between the killer's search for the wife's body and the husband's behavior back in the city, including his relationship with the police, who think they have discovered a kidnapping. Clearly Cozzi had learned a great deal from his work with Argento, for the film's suspense derives from a convoluted storyline that brings Giorgio back to the scene of the serial killer's original crime to repeat what Giorgio saw (the killer pushing a car into a canal with a dead body inside); only this time, a suspicious police inspector brings the guilty husband to justice.

Pupi Avati

One of the more successful and original *gialli* was shot by Giuseppe, or "Pupi," Avati, as he is known, an eclectic but highly skilled director who has worked in many different film genres and in television; he has also served on juries at film festivals in Cannes and Venice and as the president of the Federico Fellini Foundation. Like most of his films, he sets *The House with Laughing Windows* (*La casa dalle finestre che ridono*, 1976) in his native Emilia-Romagna. Shot on an extremely low budget but made extremely well, the film concerns a young art historian named Stefano (Lino Capolicchio), who comes to a tiny town in the region to restore some frescoes describing the martyrdom of Saint Sebastian by a twentieth-century painter named Legnani, who was famous for painting people after their death. Spectators should know something very wrong is taking place in the town in terms of sexual identification when we see Legnani's first painting: a woman with Legnani's ugly features (the lame explanation being that he could not find a model).[9] Legnani supposedly committed suicide back in 1931 as a young man, leaving two sisters who apparently disappeared.

The entire town resembles that of *Don't Torture a Duckling*: the townspeople all seem to resent outsiders and share secrets. Unlike many *gialli* that resemble their predecessors, the spaghetti western in relying heavily upon music on the sound track, Avati's *The House with Laughing Windows* emphasizes natural sounds—creaking doors, strange birdcalls in the night, unusual noises in attics or basements—to create suspense without the kinds of dramatic musical intervention typical of a director such as Dario Argento.

As Stefano works on the fresco, he begins to understand the secret hidden by the inhabitants of the village and takes on the familiar role of the amateur sleuth. As occasionally happens in the *giallo*, the amateur sleuth dies because of what he or she has discovered. Stefano stumbles onto the fact that the two insane sisters are still alive and still provide corpses for the dead Legnani to paint, while preserving their brother's body in formaldehyde. Stabbed by one of the two, Stefano manages to make it to the church where he has worked on the fresco, only to discover that the second sister is actually the priest. (The camera provides a close-up of her breast to establish the character's true gender.) Our amateur detective expires as the police arrive too late to learn what he has learned.

Since the *giallo* treats both murder and sexuality in sometimes shocking ways, this cross-dressing murderous priest—a figure encountered a few years earlier in *Who Saw Her Die?*—was no doubt even more disturbing to

Italian audiences than was the priest-murderer of *Don't Torture a Duckling*. On this occasion the priest is a woman.

Antonio Bido

Another priest-murderer appears in *The Blood Stained Shadow* (*Solamente nero*, 1978), by Antonio Bido (1949–). Bido's debt to Argento's thrillers can be seen not only in his use of the group Goblin to arrange and perform the music composed by Stelvio Cipriani for the sound track, but also in his cameo appearance in his own film (Argento's omnipresent black-gloved hands appear in his) as a man at a cemetery. He also imitates other directors by injecting not one murderer but two into the plot to make it even more complicated. And like Lado, Bido's preferred setting is Venice. Although most of the sequences were shot in the neighboring island of Murano, his creation of a spooky, mysterious atmosphere during the Venetian winter, with its foggy waterways, silent *calli* (streets), and deserted squares stands in sharp contrast to the sunlit city typically visited by tourists in spring and summer.

Even before the opening credits roll across the screen, the first sequence shows a young girl being strangled by a man dressed in black. A young boy has witnessed this event, as we later learn through flashbacks experienced by the film's protagonist. Years later, this same boy—now the art historian Stefano D'Archangelo (Lino Capolicchio)—comes to visit his brother, a priest named Don Paolo (Craig Hill), who is outraged over the behavior of three of his parishioners, who attend séances held by a medium. These are a decadent Venetian aristocrat named Count Pedrazzi (Massimo Serato), who is guilty of pedophilia; Signora Nardi (Juliette Mayniel), a midwife who performs abortions and who has a son with mental problems; and a doctor named Aliosi (Sergio Mioni), whose wife's death years ago under suspicious circumstances was ruled an accident. The art historian naturally becomes the amateur detective in this film, and it is probably no accident that this character bears the same first name as the protagonist of Avati's *The House with Laughing Windows*, exercises the same profession, and is played by the same actor. (*Gialli* frequently associate sex and violent crime with beauty and art in all forms and places, from fashion houses and modeling agencies to church frescoes and art galleries.) After Paolo witnesses the medium's murder outside the window of his bedroom, a killer stalks and kills each of the three characters who attended the séances.

Stefano's traumatic experience of seeing the murder of the young girl years ago slowly begins to make more sense to him under the shock of the serial killer's onslaught. Ultimately he remembers that it was his own brother, the priest Don Paolo, who had killed the girl. Still, the murders in the present cannot all be blamed on Stephano's brother. It is Signora Nardi's deranged son who attacks the medium and later Paolo, whereas Paolo himself kills the others before committing suicide. Yet Don Paolo remains somewhat unique in the list of serial killers presented by Italian *gialli*, because he has successfully fought the temptations of the flesh to which he succumbed years ago and has become an outstanding moral leader of his community. He kills again now only to cover up his first crime, after discovering that one of the trio attending the séances has found the breviary, with his name inscribed in it, from which the girl he had killed years ago had ripped out three pages—enough to pinpoint him as her killer.

Lamberto Bava

As the son of the legendary Mario, the inventor of the *giallo* tradition, Lamberto came to the cinema by working for both his father and for Dario Argento before making his second *giallo*, *A Blade in the Dark* (*La casa con la scala nel buio*, 1983), a low-budget thriller shot quickly in several weeks and almost entirely in a single location: the beautiful villa owned by his producer. Bruno (Andrea Occhipinti), a composer who has rented the villa from Tony Rendina (the Argento assistant Michele Soavi, a horror film director in his own right; see chapter 10), must compose music for the sound track of a horror film shot by Sandra (Anna Papa). This kind of plot would have been the perfect excuse to shoot the kind of postmodern, self-referential send-up of the *giallo* genre that the Hollywood director Wes Craven accomplished in the smash-hit horror classic *Scream* (1996).

Bava's killer is the cross-dressing Tony, who once experienced the trauma of being dared to venture into a dark stairway to retrieve a tossed tennis ball or to be called a girl by his young male friends. Later he becomes Linda, a cackling serial murderer who uses a box cutter (a much more frightening weapon after the events of 9/11 than it was when Bava shot the film) to dispatch a number of women who cross his path. Bava's relatively low budget has an impact upon this film's production values, but the director's camera movements are quite skillful, creating a claustrophobic atmosphere within the villa where almost all the events in the film take place. Since the film is about a film music composer, it is natural that his main musical motif becomes a haunting reminder of the murderer's presence each time he strikes, accompanied by his cackling, his remarks whispered to himself, and the subjective point of view through the classic killer cam. After Tony as Linda kills five different victims, he himself dies in a struggle with the film's amateur sleuth/musical composer. His dying words—"I am not a female child"—underscore the event years ago that scarred his psyche and turned him into a demented assassin. As we have seen, such confused gender roles often play a part in creating the killers of the Italian *giallo* genre.

Lucio Fulci

By the time Fulci made *The New York Ripper* (*Lo squartatore di New York*, 1982), the craze for the Italian *giallo* had run its course, even though Dario Argento, as its most accomplished and famous practitioner, continues to work in the genre in these early years of the new millennium. Like other directors (even Argento) who worked on thrillers, Fulci took advantage of the increased interest in horror films (with their zombie and cannibal variants) to make films that seemed to embody characteristics of both the traditional Italian thriller and the newly popularized horror film. Fulci's killer, the deranged murderer of beautiful but promiscuous women, speaks like Donald Duck. In this film without a real amateur detective, the jaded New York detective Lieutenant Fred Williams (Jack Hedley) eventually solves the series of killings by taking on as his advisor a brilliant psychotherapy professor from Columbia University, Dr. Paul Davis (Paolo Malco), who accurately profiles the killer as a man of very high intelligence. Fulci himself appears as New York's Chief of Police. Throughout most of the film, attention focuses on a sinister Greek immigrant named Scellenda (Howard Ross), who has two fingers missing from his right hand, but this character is merely an elaborate red herring, since Scellenda only serves as the procurer of victims for the Duck Murderer. The bodies begin to pile up: first a prostitute named Ann-Lynne; then a young woman named Rosie, riding her bicycle on the Staten Island Ferry; then a female sex-show performer named Eva. The killer slips up, however, only wounding Fay (Almanta Keller), the girlfriend of a physicist named Peter Bunch (Andrea Occhipinti). A rich woman in an open marriage, Jane Lodge (Alessandra Delli Colli), carries on sadomasochistic but anonymous affairs. She crosses paths with Scellenda at the sex show where Eva performs right before she is murdered. Later Scellenda has Jane tied up in a hotel room while calling to somebody (presumably the real Ripper), informing him that Jane is just the kind of woman he likes. Eventually, when Jane escapes from the hotel room, she is brutally murdered in the hallway. And finally, Fay is attacked in Peter's home but again escapes death when Peter returns and drives the Ripper away.

Ultimately, the Duck Murderer challenges Lieutenant Williams and brutally murders Kitty (Daniela Doria), a prostitute he sees on a regular basis. When Scellenda's body turns up, apparently killed four days before the attack on Kitty, Williams realizes that Davis's profile of a superintelligent killer with a girlfriend must lead directly to Peter and Fay. After Fay discovers that Peter has a young daughter, Suzy, dying in the hospital of an incurable disease (she has already had her limbs amputated), she overhears Peter's conversation on the phone, during which he speaks to the girl like a duck. (Fay also spies a Donald Duck toy in the child's hospital bedroom.) Thus alerted, she manages to stab Peter when he attacks her, just before

Williams arrives to arrest him and literally blows his head apart with one well-placed shot from his service revolver. Professor Davis explains that Suzy is Peter's motive. He saw the Duck as the avenger of his daughter's problems, and killed beautiful women, because his child would never enjoy the kinds of sensual pleasure once enjoyed by the women he killed.

Once again, the motive for the serial killer in this *giallo* seems a bit far-fetched, but Fulci's cinematic style in this film is highly polished: the editing is exceptional, the plot full of suspense, and even the dubbing of New Yorker accents is outstanding. In short, this film has high production values, good dialogue, and skillful camerawork. What bothered some critics about it was its incredibly realistic violence: the razor blades or knives slicing through the women's throats, stomachs, or other body parts (a nipple, for instance) seem absolutely true to life—no ketchup for blood, real arteries pumping what seems like real blood, numerous close-ups of the physical damage to the beautiful female bodies in question. The charge of misogyny is often aimed at films with violence against women in them, and Fulci certainly received his share of criticism for his graphic violence, which far surpasses that of the early *giallo*. Lesser films are perhaps no less misogynistic, but Fulci's far more skillful rendering of the physical details of his killer's hatred of women has a more forceful impact upon his audience.

Argento's Later *Gialli*: *Tenebrae, Opera, The Stendhal Syndrome, Sleepless*, and *The Card Player*

After *Deep Red*, Argento turned for a while to making horror films, films with supernatural agents rather than the classic serial killer of the Italian *giallo* thriller, in the process stretching the generic boundaries between these two popular art forms and making important contributions to this related genre. His later thrillers employ many of his familiar themes, but the production values of his work are substantially higher, commensurate with the larger budgets his reputation allowed. *Tenebrae* represents his first major film after his flirtation with horror in *Suspiria* and *Inferno*, two parts of a horror trilogy he completed in 2007 (see chapter 10). It stars the American Anthony Franciosa as Peter Neal, a writer of thrillers who comes to Rome to promote his new novel, also called *Tenebrae* (literally, "shadows"). John Saxon (Dr. Bassi from Bava's first *giallo*) is Bullmer, Neal's literary agent in Rome. Veronica Lario (who in 1990 would become Mrs. Silvio Berlusconi) plays Jane McKerrow, Neal's former lover, while Giuliano Gemma portrays Detective Inspector Germani. The famous Italian transgender actor Eva Robins portrays a woman who appears only in flashback and helps to explain the serial killer's motives. And Daria Nicolodi is Ann, Neal's love interest in Italy.

In Argento's *Tenebrae*, the killing of Jane (played by Veronica Lario, then wife of Italian Prime Minister Silvio Berlusconi) sprays blood around the walls as if she were painting one of her abstract canvases. *Credit: DVD*

In *Tenebrae*, the police are more resourceful than is usually the case in the *giallo*, and not one but two killers are at work in the plot. The real serial killer, called the Razor Killer, in the film is Christiano Berti (John Steiner), a television journalist and critic who admires Neal's writing; the second killer turns out to be Neal himself, who first dispatches Berti and then continues killing to murder both Jane and Bullmer, since the two are having an affair. Argento handles the direction with much more confidence than he exhibited in his early thrillers. Neal's answer to a lesbian journalist, Tilde (Mirella D'Angelo), who attacks his novels for treating women in a misogynistic manner, echoes one of the common attacks upon Argento's own work, in which women are murdered by male serial killers on a regular basis. Argento's opinion of this critique produces one of the most brilliant sequences of the film. His camera moves along one side of Tilde's apartment building, peering into the windows, then over the roof and to the other side of the house, and down past other windows, before breaking into the apartment along with the Razor Killer, who kills not only Tilde but also her lesbian lover, Marion, all in one brilliant shot.

No amateur sleuth really exists in *Tenebrae*, since Neal only pretends to try to discover the killer's identity, but as a writer of murder mysteries, he declares at the end of the film he had figured out immediately that Berti was the Razor Killer even when the police were baffled. In *Tenebrae*, the police are not exactly incompetent, but Neal manages to kill both Inspector Germani and his overly ambitious female assistant, Detective Altieri (Carola Stagnaro), when he is finally uncovered as one of the murderers (after a body count of nine victims, between him and Berti). In one of the most brilliant coups de théâtre in the *giallo* genre, Neal cuts his throat with a straight razor just before Germani takes a frightened Ann out to his car—Neal had murdered Germani's partner, mistaking her for Ann. When

Germani returns, Neal dispatches him with an ax. The straight razor he had employed to feign suicide was actually a cinematic prop razor that squirted blood yet had no cutting edge. Then Ann accidentally kills Neal in the house by impaling him with a metal sculpture that she inadvertently knocks over on Neal when she realizes he is still alive!

Opera (1987) is an even more brilliant thriller and exploits the splendid natural set of Parma's Teatro Regio, where an English director of horror films, Marco (Ian Charleson), is presenting his unusual staging of Verdi's *Macbeth*, setting the drama during the time of World War I. Betty (Cristina Marsillach), the understudy of a major soprano, sings the starring role when the diva has an automobile accident. Once again, as in *Tenebrae*, autobiographical elements have a role in this film. Argento has himself been tempted to direct operatic productions, following a tradition that has been long practiced in Italy by such directors as Visconti, Zeffirelli, Rosi, Cavani, and many others. By inserting various "high culture" attacks on Marco's production and his understanding of both Verdi and Shakespeare, Argento also implicitly defends his own "low culture" genre of the *giallo*.

This film features a number of absolutely virtuoso sequences. In one, after Betty makes love to Stefano (William McNamara), the young stage manager of the production, the classic black-gloved and masked *giallo* serial killer, who is obsessed with her brilliant performance on her opening night, ties her up and inserts a series of sewing needles under her eyes, forcing her to keep them widely open or cut her eyelids. Then he butchers Stefano in front of her, with a huge Renaissance dagger visible inside his mouth after being jammed through his throat. In yet another brilliant sequence, Betty's agent, Mira (Daria Nicolodi), is shot in the eye as she peeks through a keyhole at the killer on the other side. We first see the bullet leave the barrel of the pistol, then smack into Mira's eye and exit the back of her skull, striking the telephone Betty is trying to use to notify the police. Finally, by removing the enormous chandelier from the Parma opera house and

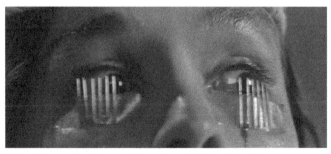

The sadistic murderer in Argento's *Opera* forces Betty to witness his gruesome killing of her boyfriend, Stefano, by inserting sewing needles under her eyes to hold them wide open. *Credit: DVD*

substituting it with a circular mechanism that moves a remotely controlled camera around in a circle, lowering and raising it at will, Argento shows us a seemingly literal bird's-eye view of a flock of ravens that are employed in Marco's avant-garde production. The ravens have had an early encounter with the serial killer, who murdered one of their flock, and Marco, knowing that the killer cannot help but attend Betty's performances, decides to let the birds fly freely in the production, knowing that they will attack the killer in return. As a result, the serial killer loses his eye to one of the black birds and is revealed to be none other than Inspector Alan Santini (Urbano Barberini), who then seemingly dies in a fire in a room of the opera house. As in *Tenebrae*, however, the logical ending is not Argento's finale. When Marco and Betty go to Switzerland to rest and recuperate from her ordeal, Santini suddenly reappears (the body in the fire had actually been a stage mannequin), murders Marco, but fails to kill Betty, who manages to turn him over to the pursuing policemen. At this point we discover another almost unbelievable coincidence, so typical of the *giallo* genre: Santini had earlier played sadomasochistic games with Betty's own mother, killing women for her amusement until he strangled her as well. The film then *really* concludes with Betty shouting to Santini that she is nothing like her mother.

Argento's fixation with eyes in *Opera* continues the most important theme of the *giallo* and of his first film: vision and seeing (or the failure to do so). When Santini believes he can replace Betty's mother with her daughter, he keeps her eyes open while he commits his gruesome crimes; but when he has finally decided to kill her, he blindfolds her for the first time.

In *Opera*, Argento used only traditional mechanical effects—no digital tricks or electronic tinkering. In *The Stendhal Syndrome* (*La sindrome di Stendhal*, 1996), he employs a number of electronic special effects and casts his own daughter, Asia, in the lead role as a police detective, Anna Manni, who suffers from the titular Stendhal syndrome, a psychosomatic illness some people experience when overwhelmed by too many works of art in a museum or church. (The French novelist Stendhal first described this puzzling syndrome, reporting in his diary that he was overcome by the artworks he observed during a visit to Florence's Basilica di Santa Croce in 1817.) When Anna goes to Florence to follow up on clues to the identity of a rapist, she faints in Florence's Uffizi Museum while she looks at Bruegel's *The Fall of Icarus*. By means of electronic special effects, she seems to enter the picture and, like Icarus, to swim in the ocean. The rapist-murderer she is seeking—Alfredo Grossi (Thomas Kretschmann)—intercepts her, rapes her as well, and then forces her to watch while he rapes another woman, shoots this other woman through the jaw, and finally peers through the hole in her head that his bullet caused. As one might imagine, these traumatic events cause a series of changes in Anna's personality that culminate in her own murderous rampage. After she exacts her vengeance upon the murderer, she kills not only her doctor but also her boyfriend. In effect, Anna Manni becomes a female version of Alfredo. Argento's film attempts a level of psychological complexity that rarely occurs in a *giallo*, and it also ignores some of the genre's conventions: we learn the identity of the killer almost immediately, no amateur sleuth takes part, and the police in this case are actually quite competent, despite the fact that it is a policewoman who becomes a killer herself through her traumatic encounter with a serial rapist. Critical opinion of the film was, at best, mixed.

Argento's next two *gialli*—*Sleepless* (*Non ho sonno*, 2001) and *The Card Player* (*Il cartaio*, 2004)—were not only more favorably received, but they also had successful box-office runs. *Sleepless* features the veteran actor Max von Sydow as Inspector Moretti, now retired, who seventeen years ago in 1983 had been in charge of the investigation in Turin of a serial killer called the Dwarf, identified as Vincenzo De Fabritiis, a writer of *gialli* whose pen name was John MacKenzie. The corpses the Dwarf left behind were always discovered with a piece of paper shaped like an animal. Now, even though De Fabritiis has been dead for many years, it seems that the serial killer has returned. Years ago, Moretti had promised Giacomo (Stefano Dionisi), the son of one of the victims, that he would find his mother's killer. Now in retirement and out of step with the police department's "new" methods, he and Giacomo form a team—the *giallo*'s usual amateur sleuths—to hunt this new criminal, who is either a copycat of the Dwarf or the real Dwarf who somehow escaped Moretti's clutches almost two decades earlier. In *Sleepless*, Argento combines the usual almost unbelievable plot with a skillful stylistic cinematic style. Ultimately, Giacomo discovers what Inspector Moretti understood just before he dies of a heart attack: it was not the mystery-writing dwarf Vincenzo who had been the serial killer but a mutual friend of Vincenzo and Giacomo, a certain Lorenzo, who had memorized a violent nursery rhyme as a child and taken it literally. Initiating a life of serial killings in Turin, he had continued in New York, where he was also a university student, but was never caught—which explains the apparent hiatus between the original murders and those that began again in the present upon his return to Turin.

The Card Player marks a shift in Argento's cinematic style for the *giallo* genre. Normally, his films focus on scenes with enormous amounts of non-natural light, which allow his various directors of photography to carry out his plans to use color as part of his narrative, creating a mood with a particular hue just as he does with various kinds of music on the sound track. This film, however, employs natural light in the daylight sequences and a few streetlights for scenes shot at night (since Rome is notoriously poorly lit during the evenings). As a result, *The Card Player*'s visual surface seems much more realistic than most of his other thrillers, with very little blood (bucketsful being a trademark of the usual Argento *giallo*) but a great deal of understated violence. Its plot is also much more contemporary than most of his *gialli*, which seem to have grown out of the traditional detective tale. The killer, called the Card Player, is what an American FBI profiler would call a "risk-taking hedonist" who captures women and then challenges the police to play electronic poker on the Internet with him to decide the woman's fate. Winning three of five hands will save the woman, but each time the police lose, some part of the woman will be excised with a box cutter. Argento's hero, Inspector Anna Mari (Stefania Rocca), a policewoman whose father committed suicide because of his gambling obsession, is the one the Card Player contacts. The killer's first victim is a British tourist, resulting in the arrival of the Scotland Yard detective John Brennen (Liam Cunningham) to Rome to assist in her investigation, and the two detectives eventually fall in love. Their liaison turns out to be a fatal mistake, since the culprit is actually a corrupt policeman, Carlo Sturmi (Claudio Santamaria), whose constant advances Anna always rejected. *The Card Player* stands apart from other Argento *gialli* in its essentially cool presentation of the facts of the case. It is relatively easy to guess the identity of the killer during the course of the narrative's unfolding, since there are far fewer red herrings than normal for the genre, and the usual gallons of fake blood the viewer has come to expect from other Argento suspense thrillers are missing. Nevertheless, the director manages to concoct an extremely entertaining ending. Carlo locks himself and Anna to the middle of a railroad track, puts the key to the handcuffs in front of his portable computer, and challenges Anna to play him one last round of poker, with the key and survival as the reward. Anna manages to win and rolls off the track just before the train crushes the Card Player—an homage to one of the silent cinema's first popular serials, *The Perils of Pauline* (1914), one episode of which took place on a railroad track, with Pauline saved at the last minute from an oncoming train.

The *Giallo*: An Assessment

Italian suspense thrillers developed an entertaining set of conventions: a black-gloved killer, amateur detectives, international characters and casts, contemporary settings with luxurious furnishings and striking architecture, red herrings to heighten audience confusion, violent set pieces that featured gruesome gore, and a loose narrative framework that concluded with psychological explanations about a killer's (or killers') motives that often strained credibility. The highly polished scripts of such Hollywood suspense thrillers as, for example, Brian De Palma's *Dressed to Kill* (1980) were not really the goal of these films. On the contrary, Italian thriller directors would frequently leave all sorts of loose ends in their plots, aiming for audience reaction from their set pieces of murder and mayhem rather than sophisticated character development. Nevertheless, the *giallo* was an important force in Italian cinema during the 1970s, even if only Dario Argento, the genre's acknowledged master, has consistently made thrillers since 1970, when his first *giallo* helped launch the craze.

The *giallo* certainly did emphasize a certain kind of sexuality and corruption in modern society, themes that would thereafter become easier to exploit in both cinema and television as a result of the *giallo*'s sometimes daring brushes with the censors. The several hundred Italian genre thrillers provided a great deal of income for the industry both domestically and internationally. Like that of the spaghetti western, their popular appeal demonstrated that Italian films could make inroads into international markets hitherto dominated by Hollywood products, and that Italians too could produce popular and profitable commercial films for the general public, not just art films for an elite audience. The *giallo*'s emphasis upon graphic violence would be matched both by the Italian horror film and by the Eurocrime film, two genres that also attracted a loyal and even fanatic following among international audiences in the 1970s and the 1980s.

CHAPTER THIRTEEN

Myth, Marx, and Freud in Pier Paolo Pasolini and Bernardo Bertolucci

PASOLINI AND BERTOLUCCI stand out in the postneorealist generation of directors for their impact upon Italian and international film culture. Both directors developed entirely different but highly personal cinematic styles that owe a great deal to an interest in myth, Marxist ideology, and Freudian psychoanalysis. Even though some of their early films were clearly noncommercial or experimental in nature, both directors eventually managed to transcend the limited appeal of such films to engage large commercial audiences all over the world. Pasolini's career, cut short by his violent murder in 1975, seems the more complex, since his work in the cinema links directly to his important theoretical essays on the semiotics of film, as well as to several important novels and a great deal of good poetry. After *Hawks and Sparrows*, Pasolini began to shoot his films in color as he moved further and further away from his neorealist heritage and toward a concern with myth, politics, and psychoanalysis.

Pasolini's Exploration of Mythological Consciousness Viewed through the Prism of Marx and Freud

In *Oedipus Rex* (*Edipo re*, 1967); *Theorem* (*Teorema*, 1968); *Medea* (1969); and *Pigpen*, a.k.a. *Pigsty* (*Porcile*, 1969), Pasolini alternated highly personal adaptations of classical tragedies by Sophocles and Euripides with narratives of his own invention to explore various aspects of mythical consciousness. Each of these films owes a debt to both Freud and Marx, but they were also imbued with his own unique interpretations of these systems of thought, which often had very little to do with orthodox Marxism and Freudianism.

In *Oedipus Rex*, Pasolini takes great liberties with the Sophoclean text, re-creating the protagonist to suit his own personal sensibilities. He sees Oedipus less as a tragic figure destroyed by a mysterious fate than as an individual whose ruin derives from a consciously willed refusal to examine himself rationally. Rather than a tortured intellectual, Pasolini's protagonist responds to intellectual problems with violence and rage. The classic Freudian interpretation of the Greek play appears in a brief autobiographical prologue taking place in Bologna around 1930, during the Fascist era. In it we see a middle-class family much like Pasolini's: a tiny baby provokes resentment in his soldier father since the child (obviously the young Pasolini) competes for attention from the wife and mother (Silvana Mangano, who wore a dress in the scene that once belonged to the director's own mother). When the father cruelly squeezes the young baby's foot, the film shifts to the more traditional version of Oedipus ("swollen foot," the meaning of his name in Greek), where Pasolini uses locations in Morocco rather than in Greece, continuing his characteristic construction by analogy that had been so successful in *The Gospel*.

The most important changes to the classical text occur precisely in the traditional section of the narrative. Oedipus (Franco Citti) blunders into his tragic destiny, murdering his father and escort in an incident that has no apparent relationship to any mysterious or predetermined fate that might explain his actions. Unlike the Oedipus of Sophocles, who solves a difficult riddle in a contest with the Sphinx (thereby establishing himself as an intellectual), Pasolini's character attacks the Sphinx and kills it. The blind, brutal nature of his character overshadows either the theme of parricide or that of incest Pasolini found in Sophocles, and Oedipus' blindness derives from his rigid refusal to understand his destiny. Pasolini's interpretation of the Greek myth concludes with an epilogue that returns to the modern era: a blinded Oedipus absurdly wanders among factories and buildings in northern Italy, returning finally to the place of his birth. Thus, Pasolini juxtaposes the classic Freudian prologue and epilogue, suggesting that the Oedipal myth of parricide and incest serves as the mythical structure underlying all modern human relationships centered on the institution of the family, with his own take on the classical myth, utilizing the metaphor of blindness to underscore modern man's refusal to come to grips with his consciousness and to chart his own destiny.

If Sophocles served Pasolini as a springboard to comment on human destiny completely unconnected to a religious notion of fate, Euripides' *Medea* offers Pasolini a convenient vehicle for the personal mythology he had developed in *The Gospel* and his early films on the subproletariat. His plot is outwardly traditional. Medea, played brilliantly by the opera diva Maria Callas in her first cinematic role, is a sorceress and daughter of Aeëtes, King of Aea in Colchis. With her help, Jason and his Argonauts steal the Golden Fleece, which Jason needs to regain his kingdom, and during the theft Medea kills her own brother, Apsyrtus. After she returns with Jason to Corinth, she is abandoned by Jason, who marries Glauce, daughter of King Creon. When Medea regains her magic powers, she destroys Glauce and Creon, and then vengefully murders the two children she has borne Jason. Influenced not only by Pasolini's attachment to preindustrial peasant cultures but also by readings in the anthropologists Mircea Eliade and James George Frazer, Pasolini transforms Euripides' classical drama into a clash between two cultures with diametrically opposed views of reality, a struggle having more relevance to philosophical and religious problems than to traditional Marxist theories of class struggle. Medea represents for Pasolini the archaic, clerical, and hierarchical universe of human prehistory, a stage of civilization typical of the peasant cultures Pasolini still finds in the Third World. Working by analogy, Pasolini sets the ancient mythical kingdom of Colchis in remote portions of Syria and Turkey. Jason (Giuseppe Gentile), on the other hand, embodies the rational, antimythical, and pragmatic universe of the technician. Pasolini's *Medea* thus serves as a long, extended metaphor for the disastrous encounter of a Third World culture with a rationalistic, materialistic Western civilization, while Jason's inability to understand such a preindustrial civilization marks him as part of the modern, bourgeois world we now inhabit. The Piazza del Duomo, the famous courtyard of Pisa's cathedral, serves Pasolini as his location for Corinth, and he chooses it because for him it symbolizes the triumph of reason over myth that occurred during the Italian Renaissance when middle-class merchants established their hegemony over Western culture.[1]

The most impressive sequences in *Medea* present dramatic imagery reflecting the clash of two worlds, the "barbarian" world that Pasolini loves and the "civilized world," aspects of which he hates. Jason's blindness to the power of ancient myth becomes clear from the opening sequence of the film, where he receives instruction from his tutor, the Centaur, the half-man, half-beast who explains to the young child that "all is holy, wherever you look, there is a god; when nature seems natural, that is the end; everything is holy." In successive cuts, Jason grows to maturity, and the Centaur (Laurent Terzieff) becomes a mere man, symbolizing the drastic diminution of Jason's mythic consciousness. Later, after Jason steals the Golden Fleece, two centaurs appear—the mythical centaur remains silent, since its message can no longer be understood by the rational Jason, and the now completely human Centaur must explain its sentiments. Yet Pasolini believes that a prehistorical mythical consciousness cannot ever be entirely destroyed, and the heritage of modern man's origins in preindustrial mythical culture remains under the surface in the human psyche, as the mute presence of the original centaur implies.

The sequences devoted to the Centaur lead to Pasolini's brilliant cinematic evocation of mythical culture on Colchis depicting peasants who gather for a human sacrifice that is part of a fertility cult, which uses the victim's blood to fertilize the wheat fields. After this beautiful dramatization of an ancient ritual, Pasolini shifts the narrative to the class struggle between the rational Greek invaders and the relatively defenseless peasants. Jason and the Argonauts overwhelm Medea's countrymen just as the Spanish Conquistadores destroyed Indian civilizations in South America. When Medea betrays her origins and runs off with Jason, she discovers that outside the mythical realm of Colchis, she no longer has roots or identity. Thus, Pasolini's Medea finds herself in the same position that Pasolini posits for contemporary humanity, in a world where she is alienated, without the sense of identity provided by ancient myths and separated from the beneficial power of illusion.

Nonetheless, when Medea resumes her magical powers, they ultimately triumph over the facile rationalism of Jason and Corinth. Pasolini dramatizes this revenge by providing us with two different versions of the fiery deaths of Glauce (Margareth Clémenti) and Creon (Massimo Girotti): the first embodies a subjective insight into a dream Medea experiences, while the second scene constitutes the actual event. True to his personal interpretation of Gramsci's Marxist writings, Pasolini believes that both capitalism and orthodox Marxism aim at the destruction of the preindustrial cultures he so admired both in southern Italy and in the Third World. Alienation derives not just from working in a factory where an exploitative capitalist class controls one's work product (as Marx suggested), but also may be caused by the loss of a sense of mythical identity, a sense of harmony with nature destroyed by industrial civilization. Medea's revenge provides Western audiences with a profoundly prophetic vision of the anger alien cultures feel when their values are underestimated and undermined. Pasolini's encounter with classical mythology, Freud, Jung, and cultural anthropology plus Marxism produces in *Medea*

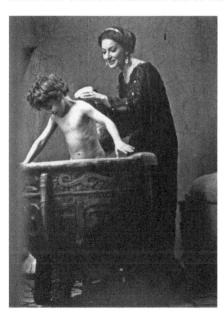

Medea prepares one of Jason's children for execution in Pasolini's *Medea*. Credit: *MOMA*

an engagingly original synthesis of the director's understanding of these texts as well as a highly successful cinematic spectacle.

Pasolini places us in totally unfamiliar territory with *Theorem* and *Pigsty*, relying upon a mythology entirely of his own invention rather than well-known literary texts he reinterprets. Yet, these two films reveal more about Pasolini's cinematic techniques and his personal ideology than any of his more accessible films. The entire film *Theorem* consists of a hypothesis (a theorem) and a demonstration of an abstract idea resembling a parable or an allegory. What if, Pasolini asks his audience, a god or some form of divine being appeared before a middle-class family, formed relationships with each of its members, and then departed? His unequivocal response to his own implied question is that the bourgeois family would achieve a sense of self-consciousness that would cause it to self-destruct. He adds an important corollary that any element of the subproletariat (specifically the peasantry) would manage to survive. Such self-awareness on the part of the members of the bourgeois class derives from various kinds of sexual encounters.

A prologue shot in color and utilizing documentary techniques reveals a factory owner, Paolo (Massimo Girotti), turning over his plant to his workers, followed by an abrupt cut to the arid, smoking slopes of a volcano. Pasolini then shifts to a soundless, black-and-white introduction to the family: Paolo; his son, Pietro (Andrés José Cruz); his daughter, Odetta (Anne Wiazemsky); his wife, Lucia (Silvana Mangano); and the maid, Emilia (Laura Betti). A sudden cut moves us back to color and a cocktail party during which a divine messenger, significantly named Angelino (Ninetto Davoli), delivers a telegram to announce the imminent appearance of a "visitor." This person (Terence Stamp) suddenly appears and makes love successively with the servant, the son, the mother, the daughter, and the father. This action contains several abrupt cuts to the volcanic wasteland. Another message announces the visitor's departure and leads to the second half of the film, in which the visitor speaks to each member of the family. He has revealed the son's true nature, uncovered the mother's false values and shown her to be a promiscuous slut, caused the daughter to see her life as an illness, and destroyed the father's smug complacency. Only the servant fails to speak to the visitor, but she returns to her peasant origins (her name, Emilia, also refers to Pasolini's native region), where she fasts, cures the sick, levitates, and becomes transformed into a saint before she goes to a construction site and cries "tears of renewal." Juxtaposed to the epiphany made possible by her class origins is the disintegration of the family. The daughter falls into a catatonic state; the son urinates upon his abstract paintings but continues his ill-chosen profession without skill or sincerity; the mother cruises around town, picking up strangers at street corners; and the father strips himself naked in the Milan train station as the camera follows his bare feet directly from the train station to the volcanic slopes to which the film has repeatedly referred. The volcano provides a graphic image for the emptiness of the values held by Pasolini's hated middle class.

As Pasolini puts it bluntly, "the point of the film is roughly this: a member of the bourgeoisie, whatever he does, is always wrong."[2] This bitter hatred of a class that has, according to Pasolini, destroyed his beloved subproletariat by assimilating its values into those of petit-bourgeois consumer society, involves not a small amount of self-hatred: "I, too, like Moravia and Bertolucci, am a bourgeois, in fact, a petit-bourgeois, a turd, convinced that my stench is not only scented perfume, but is in fact the only perfume in the world."[3] *Theorem* makes extraordinary demands on its audience. Pasolini insults his middle-class audience (the odds that working-class people would sit through a film of this nature are almost zero) and their values, providing them anything but entertainment; he presents them with a religious parable but one that includes scandalous transgressions of sexual taboos, both heterosexual and homosexual in nature. For Pasolini, the real scandal is that middle-class society has destroyed any sense of the sacred.

Pigsty offers an even more complicated personal allegory. It employs the same abrupt editing techniques used in *Theorem* but sets two very different narrative storylines in completely different eras. In one, we witness the origin and spread of a society of cannibals during the fifteenth century on the slopes of Mount Etna, the volcanic wasteland used in *The Gospel* and in *Theorem*. A strange individual (Pierre Clémenti) feeds first upon insects, then snakes, and finally upon human flesh, hurling the decapitated heads of his victims into the volcano's mouth, an action that eventually becomes part of a community ritual, a perverted form of religion. The local representatives of church and state naturally capture the cannibals as heretics, and all but their leader repent: he merely declares that "I killed my father, I have eaten human flesh, and I tremble with joy" before he and his followers are staked down and devoured by wild animals. A second storyline takes place in postwar, neocapitalist West Germany and follows the adventures of a reconstructed Nazi industrialist named Klotz, played by Alberto Lionello, who bears an uncanny resemblance to Adolf Hitler and who plays the "Horst Wessel Song" on the harp; and a rival ex-Nazi industrialist named Herdhitze (Ugo Tognazzi), a former Nazi who once collected the skulls of Jewish Bolshevik commissars (a kind of Nazi trifecta). Klotz's son, Julian (Jean-Pierre Léaud), is a superficially revolutionary student capable of responding sexually only to swine. These themes—the transgression of society's taboos, cannibalism, and gargantuan consumption—represent two separate but related stories with important philosophical parallels.

Theorem is a humorless film; *Pigsty* contains a great deal of humor, albeit much of it in questionable taste. Herdhitze and Klotz oppose each other as business rivals but then decide to forget the past and effect a merger, which, as they put it, "is as natural as the return of spring." Klotz exclaims in a burst of joy: "Germany—what a capacity to consume and defecate!" Their understanding comes at a high price, because Klotz trades his silence about Herdhitze's Nazi past for Herdhitze's silence about Julian's erotic affairs with the pigs. Thus, as they consummate their partnership with laughter, they obscenely swap a story about pigs for a story about Jews! The poor pigs of the film are employed by Pasolini as a metaphor to symbolize the gigantic German neocapitalistic machine of consumption that has arisen from the ashes of the Holocaust. Both the leader of the cannibalistic cult and Julian are "perverts" as society defines the term, but the cannibal is a classic heretic destroyed by the church, whereas Julian is a "modern" deviate and a greater threat to the ruling classes of modern Germany, because his secret, in Pasolini's view, reveals the true essence of the ruling industrial class—its Nazi past. Unlike the fate of heretics, removed from society by the Inquisition, Julian is treated in the "modern" way—by secret understandings, agreements, and compromises—in order to cover up the real scandal of the past. The pigs eventually eat Julian, removing the embarrassment of his sexual preferences. In the last shot of the film, Herdhitze speaks directly to the camera, warning the audience to remain silent about what they have discovered.

Pigsty was completed in 1968, the pivotal year of student unrest in Europe that seemed to promise radical change throughout the continent. And yet, Pasolini's depiction of student radicals in *Pigsty*—Julian and his girlfriend, Ida (Anne Wiazemsky)—is a totally negative one. Ida eventually becomes part of the system she claims to detest; Julian is a self-absorbed intellectual who remains totally unaware of his father's past and withdraws into his perversity until it destroys him. Although an avowed Marxist, Pasolini nevertheless attacked radical Italian students during the 1968 demonstrations as anticultural, antihistorical, self-indulgent, and ignorant sons of the middle class, while he defended the embattled policemen sent to restore order as the impoverished sons of the southern peasantry—one of his most controversial opinions, and one that still makes perfect sense in retrospect. In his contempt for Julian resides the genesis of the shifts in Pasolini's personal ideology that will shape in important ways his bleak vision of the world in his final film.

Pasolini's "Trilogy of Life"

By the time Pasolini turned to three medieval masterpieces in what he would call his celebration of the revolutionary power of sexuality, he had become Italy's most controversial intellectual, and except for art theaters in Paris where *Theorem* and *Pigsty* were considered profound ideological statements, his films were decidedly noncommercial. With *The Decam-eron* (*Il Decameron*, 1971), *The Canterbury Tales* (*I racconti di Canterbury*, 1972), and *Arabian Nights* (*Il fiore delle mille e una notte*, 1974), Pasolini abandoned the gloom and doom of his previous ideological films and celebrated the liberating force of sex, a force he identified with the non-bourgeois subproletariat, another strange intellectual choice given that the sexual revolution of the period during the political upheavals was largely the product of middle-class protagonists. Even more important was the fact that he abandoned his small, elite, *rive gauche* audience and its intellectual pretensions (mostly borrowed from the French cinema of the period) and broadened his appeal to tell, as he put it, stories for the simple pleasure of telling them, still maintaining an implicit ideological message about human sexuality. His highly personal interpretation of Boccaccio's great prose mas-terpiece was a deliberate choice. For Pasolini, *The Decameron* reflected the historical optimism of an era that would eventually witness the triumph of the newly formed merchant class.[4] Boccaccio's collection of one hundred *novelle* (short stories) was set within a frame of ten days of storytelling by ten different narrators (three men and seven women). Of the 338 characters it contained, 140 came from the middle classes but 68 from lower-class, proletarian origins. In this first masterpiece of Italian prose, as Erich Auer-bach's *Mimesis* (one of Pasolini's favorite books) described it, "the literature of society acquired what it had not previously possessed: a world of reality and of the present."[5] In the magnificent fictional universe Boccaccio created from his portrait of the dawn of the Italian Renaissance, the author outlined a noble human goal—earthly glory attained through praiseworthy deeds, a goal implicitly rejecting the otherworldly goals of his great contemporary, Dante, in *The Divine Comedy*.

Pasolini's *Decameron* modifies the humanistic message embodied in his literary source, not because Pasolini rejects Boccaccio's anthropocentric view of the world but, rather, because he considered Boccaccio's perspective a class-based one. Therefore, Pasolini omits the celebrated frame describ-ing the plague of 1348 and its ten storytellers, thereby eliminating the per-spective of the merchant class to which these young storytellers belong.[6] In its place, we see only a single narrator—a popular Neapolitan storyteller whose obscene gesture and remark that one of Boccaccio's tales should be sold "in the Neapolitan way" emphasizes Pasolini's geographical, ideologi-cal, and linguistic departure from his original. The aristocratic locations or Florentine middle-class settings of Boccaccio's stories are replaced by those of the Italian Mezzogiorno (Naples), the middle class in Boccaccio yields to the historical ancestors of Pasolini's beloved subproletariat, and Boccaccio's elegant literary language of an elite leisure class (Florentine) becomes contaminated by the speech of the ordinary people of southern Italy. Pasolini tantalizes the viewer familiar with Boccaccio's original by

making references to the careful symmetry of *The Decameron*: he takes ten
episodes from Boccaccio and adds to them ten of his own invention. The
film is framed by two characters—the first from *The Decameron* (I: 1), Ser
Ciappelletto (Franco Citti), and the second of his own invention, Giotto's
best pupil, a role played by Pasolini himself—in a story based upon Boccaccio's novella about Giotto (VI: 5). Pasolini's ten episodes are scattered
asymmetrically through the two parts of the film (three in Part 1 and seven
in Part 2), a conscious reference to the number of storytellers in the original. He also transforms his adaptation into a film that is both self-reflexive
or metacinematic and ideologically quite sophisticated, but not so boring
or intellectually pretentious that it precluded a vast commercial audience.
For example, Pasolini exploits for his own ends two of the most famous
stories in Boccaccio—the tale of Riccardo and Caterina, who "listen to the
nightingale," or enjoy sex (V: 4), on the one hand, and that of Lorenzo,
Isabetta, and the famous pot of basil (IV: 5), on the other. His adaptations
reflect his clever insights into the conversations that Boccaccio's tales often
carry on among themselves, connections many modern critics have overlooked. Two pairs of lovers brave the objections of their families to enjoy
each other carnally, but class determines the radically different outcomes
of each story. Because Riccardo comes from a wealthy family, when he and
Caterina are discovered naked on a balcony with the famous "nightingale"
in Caterina's hand, her father resolves the moral dilemma with a merchant's
quick wit, forcing the well-born Riccardo to marry Caterina on the spot. To
set up a contrast to this triumph of "business logic," Pasolini then relates
the tragic end of Lorenzo, who has been transformed from the Pisan in
Boccaccio to a Sicilian servant and a member of a despised, exploited lower
class, who is murdered by Isabetta's brothers because his origins provide no
economic advantage to their family. With only a few subtle changes, Pasolini manages to attack a specific class (the bourgeoisie) and an institution
(the family) that is its typical expression, completely reversing Boccaccio's
admiration for the practical sense his merchant heroes display, guilelessly
reconciling economic interests and sexual drives. Elsewhere in his film, the
hilarious tale of Ser Ciappelletto's sanctification despite the fact that he is
the worst man in the world (I: 1) becomes a metaphor for the predatory
practices of both the church and the middle class, Father Gianni's magic
transformation of an ignorant peasant woman into a mare by having sex
with her from behind (IX: 10) attacks the clergy's exploitation of the working classes, and the tale of Meuccio and Tingoccio (VII: 20) concludes with
the ultimate message of Pasolini's film—that human sexuality is no longer
a sin. Pasolini's expressed intention in *The Decameron* was to celebrate in
his "trilogy of life" what he called "the ontology of reality, whose naked
symbol is sex," and it was the sexual explicitness of his film (by the period's
somewhat strict standards) that gained him one of the largest box-office

Pasolini casts himself as Giotto's best pupil in *The Decameron*. Credit: MOMA

grosses in the postwar era of the Italian cinema.

By casting himself as Giotto's best pupil, Pasolini makes important comparisons between writing Boccaccio's masterpiece and making a film. In the Neapolitan marketplace, we see Pasolini/ Giotto's best pupil framing various characters with his fingers, much as a director does with a camera lens. His re-creation of the painting of a fresco in Santa Chiara Church reminds us of the collective effort required in producing cinema. Finally, at the end of the film, the director/artist dreams a vision, that of Giotto's *Last Judgment*—the masterpiece of the fresco cycle at the Arena Chapel in Padua, completed around 1306. In Pasolini's version, however, a benevolent figure of the Madonna portrayed by Silvana Mangano (Pasolini's mother in *Oedipus Rex*) replaces Giotto's figure of Christ the Judge. Such a substitution is quite appropriate, since the lower classes of Italy have always embraced the Madonna more than Christ or even God in their brand of Catholicism. The director/artist poses an enigmatic question to the audience in the final frames of the film: "Why realize a work of art when it is so nice simply to dream it?" As Pasolini later explained, the making of his "trilogy of life" represented an examination of

> the most mysterious workings of artistic creation. . . . I find it the most beautiful idea I have ever had, this wish to tell, to recount, for the sheer joy of telling and recounting, for the creation of narrative myths, away from ideology, precisely because I have understood that to make an ideological film is finally easier than making a film outwardly lacking ideology.[7]

The astounding box-office success of *The Decameron* not only made Pasolini, the avowed Marxist, a very rich man, but it also provoked a polemical reaction from some of Italy's intellectuals. Writing on the six-hundredth anniversary of Boccaccio's death in 1975 in the prestigious *terza pagina* (its "third page," or literary section) of Milan's *Corriere della sera*, the late Vittore Branca, the dean of Boccaccio scholars, fulminated against works like Pasolini's, without even mentioning his name, describing such contemporary readings of Boccaccio as examples of a kitsch approach to Boccaccio's "higher" culture.[8] In Branca's defense, this erudite scholar was doubtless provoked less by Pasolini than by a group of blatantly semipornographic sequels to Pasolini's masterpiece that were rapidly produced as sequels (see chapter 7), a frequent phenomenon in the Italian cinema (see chapters 7, 10–12, 14 on Italy's *commedia all'italiana* and other genre films).

Pasolini continued his experiments in cinematic narrative that were devoted both to self-reflexive film and to the celebration of human sexuality as a means of undermining middle-class values in *The Canterbury Tales* and *Arabian Nights*. In the first film, Pasolini himself plays Chaucer: the tales he adapts include the Merchant's Tale, the Friar's Tale, the Cook's Tale, the Miller's Tale (never so graphically portrayed), the Wife of Bath's Prologue, the Reeve's Tale, and the Summoner's Tale. Although Pasolini seems less at home with the English text, many of the themes from *The Decameron* continue in this work. The hypocrisy of the church emerges in his account of the Summoner, who spies through keyholes in pursuit of homosexuals, bribing wealthy gays and condemning poor ones to be burned alive while the public looks on, eating griddle cakes sold at the executions. Perkyn in the Cook's Tale (Ninetto Davoli) assumes the dress and mannerisms of Charlie Chaplin, and the entire sequence becomes an homage to the gags and comic sketches of the American silent cinema. Still, unlike his evocation of early Renaissance Italy, Pasolini's picture of Chaucerian England seems to reflect a gradual loss of confidence in the liberating powers of human sexuality. The director's preoccupation with bodily functions of all sorts, evoked throughout the film by images of anality, voyeurism, and grotesque exploitation, culminates in the bizarre vision of Satan's anus at the conclusion of the film, inspired not only by the Summoner's Tale but also by the art of Bosch. These infernal visions of human sexuality running amok and ending in the very bowels of Hell stand in dark contrast to the Edenic vision of a pure, earthly paradise that opens the film in the Merchant's Tale sequence. As a perceptive critic put it, "the powers of creation—tale-telling—have thus reduced themselves punningly to powers of excretion and exhaustion—tail-telling."[9] Only the redemptive power of art, embodied in the enigmatic smile of Chaucer/Pasolini that closes the film, seems to offer a positive note.

With *Arabian Nights*, Pasolini searches for idyllic sexuality in the Third World, shooting on various exotic locations in Nepal, Yemen, Iran, and Ethiopia. The director hoped to discover there a joyous sexuality freed from the exploitive conditions he felt existed in Western industrialized culture. As in *The Decameron*, his narrative aims at pure storytelling, and true to its literary original, this film has a structure that is the most intricate of the "trilogy of life." In the original text, the stories evolved from a series of tales told each night by a woman, Scheherazade, to her husband, the king, in order to avoid execution. Pasolini's *Arabian Nights* plays once again with a narrative-framing device that he had already found in both Boccaccio and Chaucer. In this film, he frames his stories within the "Tale of Nur ed Din and Zumurrud," a single episode in the original (where the young man's name was Ali Shar). By inserting a number of stories within this opening episode, Pasolini creates a narrative that resembles a Chinese box: stories set within stories set within stories. The most remarkable feature of the film is its use of breathtakingly beautiful, exotic, and unfamiliar Oriental land-scapes and locations, on the one hand, and Pasolini's unique interpretation of Oriental sexuality on the other. Zumurrud (Ines Pellegrini), an extremely clever slave girl, is separated from Nur ed Din (Franco Merli), a rather dim-witted young man, and the account of their eventual reunion becomes Pasolini's account of the triumph of feminine sexuality and intelligence over male dominance and presumption. When Zumurrud reaches the magic city of Sair, she becomes heir to the throne, because she is the first to arrive after the previous ruler's death. Her disguise fools everyone, including Nur ed Din, who is brought to the king's bedroom. Expecting a homosexual rape, a fate he fears worse than death, he is amazed to discover his smiling mistress is the kingdom's ruler. The ironic conclusion to *Arabian Nights*—the tri-umph of female heterosexuality—comes as a surprise from a director who was an avowed homosexual and who consistently viewed homosexuality as a weapon for undermining middle-class values. The joyous expression of unfettered sexuality in the film, both heterosexual and homosexual, stands as Pasolini's final elegiac tribute to a force of nature he then considered, along with the redeeming power of art, to be a vital civilizing presence in the modern world.

Pasolini's "trilogy of life" juxtaposed the carefree sexuality of the past in three very different cultures to his own era's manipulative, exploitive sexual-ity and deceptive sexual freedom. But the director's darkening mood and his increasing sense of alienation from the world around him caused him to reject not only the trilogy itself but also most of the key ideas embodied in his major films that praise the subproletariat. In one of his last important essays, "Disavowal of the 'Trilogy of Life,'" published as a preface to the scripts of the three films, Pasolini outlines why in his next and final film he had revised his earlier views on the mythical potential of sex and on the subproletariat's view of sexuality. In an era of sexual freedom, he believed, all forms of sexuality have been assimilated into the cultural system Pasolini despised: consumer capitalism. Even Pasolini's trilogy had been co-opted into the system of values he rejected, since many viewers went to see the three films as a form of soft pornography. Now, Pasolini declared, it was clear that the lower-class characters he had formerly praised and admired and had seemed to discover in a purer form in the Third World than in Italy were always potentially petit-bourgeois figures, anticultural members of an ignorant lumpenproletariat whose only remaining function in life was that of consumer. Of course, Pasolini's admiration for the lower classes had always been something of a romantic illusion, a view that could have been held by only a leftist intellectual. Why should he have been surprised that people who had endured poverty for centuries would want to have the same access to education, consumer goods, and well-being that he himself enjoyed? At any rate, his conclusion in this essay is bleak: "I am adapting myself to the degradation and I am accepting the unacceptable. . . . Here before me—slowly materializing without alternative—is the present. I am readapting my own commitment to a greater legibility [Salò?]."[10]

Pasolini and the Marquis de Sade: An Unhappy Ending to a Director's Career

Salò, or The 120 Days of Sodom (Salò o le 120 giornate di Sodoma, 1975) presents one of the darkest visions of life imaginable but one that was ironically appropriate to the violent manner in which Pasolini met his death, shortly after the film's release.[11] It combines a storyline Pasolini took from the Marquis de Sade's novel 120 Days of Sodom, describing four powerful individuals who retire to a secluded villa to satisfy all their lustful, cruel, and powerful desires. On this frame, Pasolini then imposes a structure taken from Dante's Inferno—concentric narrative circles descending into the depths of Hell. Pasolini locates this pastiche of Dante and de Sade in Salò, the capital of Mussolini's Social Republic during the last days of the Fascist regime before the end of World War II. In Pasolini's version, the four individuals are all Fascists, each of them representing an arm of society's power: a magistrate, a banker, a duke, and a bishop. Following de Sade's mania for symmetry, Pasolini includes in his cast four female narrators (ex-bawds), four of the men's daughters (who are married off among them), four soldiers, four collaborators, eight male and eight female victims, and five servants.

The film depicts the progressive unfolding of sadistic power wielded by contemporary consumer society (a bit of an antihistorical leap, since Italy never experienced anything like a consumer society until after the "economic miracle" of the 1960s). The film moves from the "Ante-Inferno," in which a town is destroyed by the Fascists and the quartet's victims are assembled, through three Dantesque "circles": the "Circle of the Manias," which portrays the lust for power; the "Circle of Excrement," which represents consumption and defecation (two sides of the same coin for Pasolini); and finally the "Circle of Blood," which concludes with the gruesome destruction of the victims. In contrast to the exuberance and vitality of his "trilogy of life" set in distant epochs, Salò presents a somber visual style that emphasizes highly stylized modernist period sets (art deco, Italian

The young victims in Pasolini's *Salò* are first reduced to the status of animals by their fascist guards before they are executed for the amusement of the four powerful figures that dominate the villa. *Credit: Donald Krim Jr. and United Artists (New York)*

Bauhaus), intricate but static formal compositions, and relatively long takes and few camera movements, all of which intensify the effects of the increasingly closed and repressive nature of the activities taking place in the villa. Storytelling, a creative, liberating activity in the "trilogy of life," now becomes a prelude to torture and violence with no redemptive end in sight. The female narrators (all bawds) appear in formal dress and relate scabrous events from their lives to the carefully posed torturers, guards, and victims, which result in sexual arousal. The earlier redemptive sexual desire now represents only one stage in a sadistic ritual. Pasolini employs sadistic parodies to attack a number of institutions—the family, marriage, religion—and human sexuality in general. The most shocking moment in the film, one clearly designed to reflect Pasolini's fixation with contemporary consumerism, presents a meal in which human excrement is consumed. The ending of the film presents a ritualistic slaughter of the remaining victims, observed from a distance through binoculars with no sound of the victims' screams on the sound track, thus transforming the static tableaux and the suffering human beings they contain into abstract objects for aesthetic contemplation. To continue the dominant metaphor of the film, *Salò* represents a film that Pasolini designed to be difficult to swallow. It is difficult to see why he chose to represent his own sexual choice (homosexuality) as the epitome of sexual repression rather than as a countercultural phenomenon capable of undermining conservative social mores, as he had in his earlier works and writings, or why he chose to associate homosexuality so directly with Fascism. Because he was murdered shortly after the film reached the public, he had no time to move beyond this bleak vision of a totally unredeemed humanity, and thus his life ended on this artistic note of despair. His passing removed one of the Italian cinema's most original and controversial figures from the scene and denied us many more films that he might have produced, to the end of the century and beyond.

Bertolucci's Intellectual Background and the Trajectory of His Career

Bernardo Bertolucci began his cinematic career as Pasolini's assistant, and both directors shared many of the same ideological interests. Bertolucci's works embody a more orthodox understanding of both Freudian psychoanalysis and Marxist political theory, and Bertolucci himself underwent analysis for a number of years. Like Pasolini, Bertolucci moved from making films for a small, elite intellectual audience, the kind of audience that he found in Paris among like-minded film buffs and where he learned about the history of the cinema by attending numerous screenings at the city's famous Cinémathèque. Eventually he broke out of the art film circuit into large-budget commercial distribution, using American capital, English-language versions, and carefully chosen American actors whose renown might guarantee box-office success, and finally earning a number of Oscars and other film prizes from institutions all over the world. His abilities seemed to have been liberated by his move away from the hermetic, self-absorbed world of the Parisian cinephiles where his career began.

Partner (1968) appeared at the height of the 1968 upheavals, when Bertolucci was still under thirty—the age past which, according to popular belief among the young, one could not be trusted. It is a very free adaptation of Dostoyevsky's *The Double*: Jacob (Pierre Clémenti) is a young drama teacher in love with his professor's daughter, Clara (Stefania Sandrelli), and is rescued from committing suicide by his alter ego, Jacob II (also Clémenti), who engages him in a number of philosophical conversations about the nature of theatrical spectacle that reflect the theories of Judith Malina and Julian Beck's Living Theatre, then very popular in Italy. Jacob I suggests that the stage should become the entire world, with revolution as its text. When the two Jacobs are deserted by the students who betray their planned revolutionary spectacle, Jacob II informs Jacob I that the spectacle must go on without them. Before joining his double on a balcony to commit a double suicide, Jacob II turns directly to the camera in a Godardian moment and announces abruptly that the major enemy in the world is American imperialism. *Partner* thus bears the heavy imprint of the 1968 era and is humorlessly didactic, but a number of lighter moments surface from the Godardian maze of political messages. A baby carriage rolls down a series of steps with a bomb in it (a clear reference to the "Odessa Steps" sequence of Eisenstein's *The Battleship Potemkin*). A detergent saleswoman visits Jacob II and, in a parody of advertising based upon sex appeal, offers herself to him. She is eventually murdered by him in a washing machine overflooding with suds.

Much of *Partner* relates intimately to Bertolucci's obsessive personal concerns, problems he confronted under analysis. Yet the seemingly Freudian theme—a man who meets his alter ego or his double—seems less indebted to Freud than to Marx, since their encounter allows Bertolucci to construct a dialectical argument between Jacob I and the more politically engaged half of his split personality. *Partner's* style combines elements from both noncommercial art films and popular, commercial cinema. Since Bertolucci then believed that a frequent use of cuts in editing implied a conservative ideology, he consistently searched for the extreme long shot, avoiding dramatic cuts and transitions at places we would expect them in a studio-produced work. Still, relatively sophisticated special effects such as matte shots are employed, and the film is in Techniscope. As Jacob remarks, such a process suits a film with broad ideas, but even in a film that today seems almost unwatchable, Bertolucci's eventual move toward a very different kind of cinema can be detected. The upper-class students who betray the revolution remind us of Fabrizio in *Before the Revolution* (a much more traditional work). The schizophrenia inherent in the split personality of the would-be revolutionaries may well serve as Bertolucci's admission that revolutions are carried out by the masses and not by middle-class directors with movie cameras, such as he or his one-time mentor Godard. Years later, in *The Dreamers* (*I sognatori*, 2003), Bertolucci returns to the Paris of the student upheavals and shows us quite a different picture of Paris in 1968.

A Quantum Leap of Quality: Bertolucci's Films on Fascism

The striking natural talent displayed in *Before the Revolution* emerged almost immediately after *Partner* in a minor masterpiece made for larger mass audiences on Italian television, *The Spider's Stratagem* (*La strategia del ragno*, 1970), and again that year in an adaptation of Alberto Moravia's novel *The Conformist*, perhaps Bertolucci's most brilliant work. The first of these films, based on the extremely short story by Argentina's Jorge Luis Borges entitled "Theme of the Traitor and the Hero," marks the rejection of the Godardian tone of *Partner* and a return to the lyrical evocation of Bertolucci's provincial origins in *Before the Revolution*. Bertolucci transposes Borges's setting from revolutionary Ireland to the tiny Renaissance ideal city of Sabbioneta (in Lombardy), called Tara in the film after the plantation in *Gone with the Wind*. The film moves back and forth between the present of postwar Italy and events that took place in Tara in 1936 during the height of the Fascist regime's greatest popularity. Athos Magnani Jr. (Giulio Brogi) returns home to Tara thirty years after the assassination of his father, an anti-Fascist hero, and meets his father's former mistress, Draifa (Alida Valli), so named because of her leftist father's support for Captain Alfred Dreyfus (1859–1935) during the infamous Dreyfus Affair in France during the 1890s and 1900s. Athos Jr. tries to discover the truth behind his father's death by speaking with his father's old anti-Fascist friends. During the film, Freud eclipses Marx as Bertolucci chronicles the oppressive hold of father over son. We see this theme vividly represented on the screen from the beginning, when Athos Jr. upon his arrival encounters a statue erected to his father's memory in the town square: its blank, unchiseled eyes accentuate the persistent motif of blindness and its Oedipal connotations that will also mark Bertolucci's imagery in *The Conformist*. Gliding past the statue, Bertolucci's camera uses the statue to obliterate our view of the son, prefiguring his eventual entrapment in the father's web at the film's conclusion.

A series of repetitions dramatizes how the present repeats and explains the past. Numerous flashbacks to 1936 employ exactly the same actors and locations as in the present with no change of costume, and the flashbacks are so abrupt and continuous that they obscure chronological distinctions.

In Bertolucci's *The Spider's Stratagem*, Athos Jr. confronts the statue of his father Athos Sr. and solves the mystery of his death during the fascist period.
Credit: MOMA

When Athos Jr. accompanies his father's friends to the shack where they had met years ago to plan the assassination of Mussolini, before his father betrayed the plot and was killed, past and present merge. Athos Jr. becomes terrified of these old men, runs away, and Bertolucci cuts back and forth between the present (Athos Jr.) and the past (Athos Sr., also Brogi). Moreover, he employs a technique he had used to great effect in *Before the Revolution*. His fluid camera captures a running figure of father blended with son, the figure's identity obscured by its constant motion, and his swiftly moving camera provides a brilliant visual evocation of the protagonist's inability to escape not only from his father's shadow but also from Bertolucci's obsessive camera as well.

The notion of political spectacle introduced in *Partner* now finds its perfect aesthetic expression. Athos Jr. learns that the traitor in the group of plotters was actually his own father, who had collaborated with his comrades out of guilt in order to produce an operatic anti-Fascist myth that results in the Fascists being falsely blamed for his murder and not his friends, the actual perpetrators of the crime. Athos Sr. dies in a drama marked by numerous citations from Verdian melodrama and Shakespearean tragedy for which the town of Sabbioneta becomes a theatrical backdrop. As Gaibazzi (Pippo Campanini) tells Athos Jr., it is not truth but the consequences of the truth that matter. Sabbioneta/Tara becomes a mythical location of the mind, and the son learns the truth about his father's guilt at the precise spot (the opera house) and the precise moment (during the famous *Rigoletto* aria "Maledizione") as when, years ago, his father met his death during the same opera performance. Learning the unpleasant truth that his father was a traitor and that the anti-Fascist myth built upon his death has false foundations does not, however, set Athos Jr. free. On the contrary, the truth literally imprisons him in a mythical web his father, not unlike a predatory spider, has spun. When Athos Jr. attempts to leave Tara by train (one that never arrives), he sees that the tracks have been completely overgrown by weeds, as if the train on which he came to town never existed. The father and the past triumph over the son and the present: Athos Sr. remains an enigma to his imprisoned son. Whether he betrayed his comrades because of cowardice, or whether he embraced his martyrdom consciously, engineering his melodramatic assassination in the opera house to create hatred in his native city for Fascism, can never be completely clear.

Italian critics actually ignored Bertolucci's precocious insight that much of postwar anti-Fascism rested upon a resistance that was as much myth as historical truth, construing Bertolucci's unusual take on the Italian Resistance as an uncomplicated anti-Fascist film. They somehow missed the fact that *The Spider's Stratagem* already prefigures the manipulation of the Resistance by Italian postwar politicians on the Left. With Bertolucci's adaptation of Moravia's novel *The Conformist*, the director produced what many critics consider his most visually satisfying work, although the cinematic brilliance of his narrative also conceals some ideological incoherence. Working with a fairly conventional chronological narrative told by an omniscient narrator—Moravia's tale of a child's psychic development begins with a view of his parents making love, leads to a traumatic homosexual encounter with the chauffeur, and results in his compulsive search for normality or conformity by joining the Fascist Party—Bertolucci produced a completely different kind of film narrative shaped by his own experiences under analysis. He rejects a linear chronological narration and juxtaposes time sequences in a manner even more complicated than that in *The Spider's Stratagem*, thanks to the brilliant editing of Franco "Kim" Arcalli (1929–78) and the outstanding camera work of Vittorio Storaro, who would go on to win three Oscars, for Coppola's *Apocalypse Now* (1979), Warren Beatty's *Reds* (1981), and Bertolucci's own *The Last Emperor* (*L'ultimo imperatore*, 1987).

The *Conformist* also marks Bertolucci's deliberate break with Godard's brand of noncommercial cinema. Made with American capital from Paramount, the film caused a rupture between Bertolucci and his former mentor, a biographical fact that Bertolucci inserts into the script of the film. Although *The Conformist* owes a huge debt to the cinema, it is not to that of the French New Wave: its lighting reflects that of a 1930s Hollywood studio film in its expressive and poetic qualities, and Bertolucci himself has mentioned his debt to Von Sternberg, Max Ophüls, and Welles.[12] Thanks to Arcalli's suggestions on editing, Bertolucci's storyline is constantly interrupted in its chronology, as the many flashbacks and even flashbacks within flashbacks disrupt any sense of linear development. As Bertolucci's most perceptive critic has noted, Bertolucci's editing techniques present what must be called a dreamlike, oneiric narrative where such techniques as condensation, displacement, projection, and doubling are at work—all techniques that Freud identified with the latent dream work.[13]

Marcello Clerici (Jean-Louis Trintignant) uses a honeymoon trip from Rome to Paris with his new wife, Giulia (Stefania Sandrelli), to cover up a political mission he undertakes for the Fascist Party: he must eliminate a bothersome anti-Fascist Italian refugee, Professor Quadri (Enzo Tarascio), his former philosophy professor at the university. Along the way, Special Agent Manganiello (Gastone Moschin) escorts Clerici, who encounters the professor's wife, Anna Quadri (Dominique Sanda), a bisexual who allows herself to be manipulated by Marcello so that she may seduce Giulia. Bertolucci begins the story through a complex series of flashbacks that begin at the moment Marcello and Manganiello pursue Quadri into a dark forest outside of Paris to kill him. The action shifts back from that moment in time (October 15, 1938) to follow Marcello's search for conformity within Fascism; his marriage; his homosexual encounter as a young child with Lino (Pierre Clémenti), his family's chauffeur, on March 25, 1917; and back to his eventual meeting with Professor and Anna Quadri in Paris. The film culminates with the assassination of the professor and his wife in the forest, and ends with a coda set in 1943 as the Fascist regime crumbles in Rome with the Italian invasion of Sicily by the Allies.

With this ingenious confusion of different time periods, Bertolucci brilliantly renders the deep sense of entrapment in the past felt by Marcello. Central to Bertolucci's reconstruction of Moravia's novel is Marcello's constant search for surrogate fathers, authority figures he seeks both to appease and, in typically Oedipal fashion, to destroy. In flashback at the film's beginning, we encounter the first of these figures, his blind friend, Italo Montanari (José Quaglio), a Fascist ideologue who broadcasts a radio program somewhat deliriously proclaiming the "Prussian aspect" of Mussolini and the "Latin aspect" of Adolf Hitler! Later, when the regime disintegrates and Marcello seeks to distance himself from it, and from his involvement in it—purchased at the price of Quadri's death—Marcello denounces Italo to an angry crowd of anti-Fascist rioters. A flashback within a flashback moves from Italo's radio broadcast to a government ministry richly decorated in period art-deco style, where Marcello visits another father surrogate, a highly placed Fascist minister. This interview takes place in a building actually constructed during the Fascist period, where the visuals underline Marcello's position behind barred windows and doors, a motif of entrapment continued throughout the film. Moreover, he catches a glimpse of the minister's sexy mistress, a woman who reappears twice more in the film, once as a prostitute in a brothel on the Franco-Italian border that serves as a front for Fascist secret police headquarters, and again in the person of Anna Quadri (all three characters played by Sanda). Thus, when Marcello finally encounters Anna, he has an uncanny sense of déjà vu that disconcerts him during his entire stay in Paris. Special Agent Manganiello provides yet another father surrogate, since he is charged with Marcello's "education" as an assassin. And Professor Quadri himself, the father-teacher par excellence, eventually replaces Manganiello. To highlight the repetition of this intimate relationship between father and son in Marcello's life (and in Freudian psychoanalytic thought), Bertolucci confronts Marcello with his real father, who has been placed in an insane asylum that visually resembles a De Chirico surrealistic painting, where Marcello's father rejects him. Thus, Marcello's entire existence revolves around a desire to please successive father figures. A chance homosexual encounter in his youth has brought on a sense of inadequacy that motivates his search for "normality" in the present by embracing a totalitarian philosophy and murdering one of several surrogate fathers in his life.

Marcello's assignment to eliminate Professor Quadri reflects not only the protagonist's Oedipal conflicts but those of Bertolucci as well. Quadri's address and telephone number (17 rue Jacques; MED-15-37) belonged in

1971 to Jean-Luc Godard, once Bertolucci's good friend and mentor. As Bertolucci declared:

> *The Conformist* is a story about me and Godard. When I gave the professor Godard's phone number and address, I did it for a joke, but afterwards I said to myself, "Well, maybe all that has some significance. . . . I'm Marcello and I make Fascist movies and I want to kill Godard who's a revolutionary, who makes revolutionary movies and who was my teacher."[14]

Thus, Bertolucci's private neuroses are transposed to those of his screen protagonist, Marcello, and once again, as in *The Spider's Stratagem*, the framework of Freudian psychoanalysis provides the inspiration for a unique work of art. Of course, Bertolucci was no more a Fascist filmmaker than Godard was a true political revolutionary, but such exaggerated statements were typical of the highly charged times.

Even though some knowledge of Freudian ideas is required for an understanding of *The Conformist*, this stunningly beautiful film cannot be exhausted by a psychoanalytical interpretation. As a coherent explanation of the birth of Italian Fascism, *The Conformist* fails just as certainly as did the theories of Wilhelm Reich in *The Mass Psychology of Fascism* (1933), or Erich Fromm in *Escape from Freedom* (1941), books that obviously influenced Bertolucci's understanding of Moravia's novel. By placing the ultimate origin of Marcello's search for conformity in the realm of Marcello's unconscious and the lingering memory of a homosexual encounter during his childhood, Bertolucci undermines any Marxist explanation of the rise of Italian Fascism based on the theory of the class struggle or the view that Italian Fascism protected the middle and upper classes in Italy. In fact, the only milieu represented in *The Conformist* is that of a decadent bourgeoisie on both sides of the political struggle: Marcello and Quadri come from the same social class, and the film ignores the working class almost entirely. Anna Quadri's bisexuality, as well as her husband's obvious voyeuristic pleasure in observing her sexual escapades with members of her own sex, mark the anti-Fascist exiles in Paris as members of the same decadent class of which Marcello is the expression. Thus, far from providing a coherent explanation of Italian Fascism, *The Conformist* presents only an indictment of it, and the verdict had already been delivered before the film was made.

Of course, the cinema does not rest on a rational political theory, and no viewer of the film can ignore its strikingly beautiful visual texture. Careful composition of individual shots and intricate attention to the effects of light and shadow emphasize the film's dominant motifs of Marcello's entrapment and the metaphor of blindness. Light and shadow in the film often say more than the dialogue. For example, in Bertolucci's version of Plato's Allegory of the Cave, transferred to Quadri's office, the interplay of

In *The Conformist*, Anna and Giulia dance a sensuous tango in one of the most celebrated and brilliantly shot sequences in Bertolucci's entire cinema. *Credit: DVD*

shadow and silhouette underscores the ambivalent relationship in the film between illusion and reality, sight and blindness. Marcello faces ambiguous ideological guides: not only is his Fascist friend Italo sightless, but so is the little Parisian flower girl who sells him violets from Parma, Bertolucci's hometown, and sings the Socialist "Internationale." Consciously or unconsciously, Bertolucci suggests with these two blind figures that ideologies on both the Right and the Left are a dead end, just as in *The Spider's Stratagem* he casts doubts upon the most sacrosanct mythology of the postwar Italian Left: the anti-Fascist Resistance.[15] The images of bars and prisons, suggested first by the horizontal and vertical windows of the Fascist ministry, are constantly repeated in the film. Light and shadows pick up this motif at Giulia's home, where Marcello's impending marriage to her represents another form of bourgeois entrapment and conformity, symbolized by her zebra-patterned dress. Marcello finds himself constantly trapped in tight spaces, such as church confessionals, and in Manganiello's automobile, en route to Quadri's assassination. The eerie and surrealistic asylum where Marcello's father lives also resembles a prison, and he is even locked inside a straitjacket. A recurrent pattern in the cinematography is a shot of Marcello through a pane of glass that picks up the reflections of others outside his imprisoned psyche—at the radio station, in the train heading for Paris, in the sequence in which Anna and Giulia perform a sensual and celebrated tango, and inside Manganiello's car. Bertolucci's mature grasp of his craft leaps to the fore in the famous tango scene, with its rapidly shifting camera angles, positions, graceful motions, and superlative editing. Ultimately, his poetic talents and his unerring understanding of the technology of the art of film triumph over the sometimes fuzzy ideological structure that purports to explain the rise of a Fascist in the storyline.

Last Tango in Paris: Bertolucci's International Success

The Conformist may well be Bertolucci's most brilliant work, but *Last Tango in Paris* (*Ultimo tango a Parigi*, 1972) was an international box-office draw and a critical triumph that won Bertolucci a front-page photograph on *Time* magazine. As Bertolucci intended, it was also a shock to any Puritanical spectators still interested in the movies. New York's most influential critic, Pauline Kael, declared somewhat deliriously that it was "the most powerfully erotic movie ever made, and it may turn out to be the most liberating movie ever made," while the novelist Norman Mailer asserted about the famous scene in which Paul (Marlon Brando) couples with his young French girlfriend, Jeanne (Maria Schneider), that "the cry of the fabric is the most thrilling sound to be heard in World Culture since the four opening notes of Beethoven's Fifth."[16] In this film, Bertolucci's narrative rests almost entirely upon Freudian concepts of sexuality, but the almost explicit sex in the story has a tremendous impact upon the spectator's emotional response to the film. True to his cinephile origins, Bertolucci rightly noted that the film is a tragic version of Vincente Minnelli's *An American in Paris* (1951), but certainly Gene Kelly's amorous attentions to Leslie Caron in that picture differed entirely from those depicted in Bertolucci's updated version of that story.[17] For Bertolucci, *Last Tango in Paris* was also "a form of a dream" in which the entire story represents an Oedipal projection on the part of Jeanne (age nineteen) and the older Brando (age forty-eight), who is a surrogate father for the girl as well as her lover, whom she eventually kills.[18]

The dominant image of the film is a starkly empty room in which Paul and Jeanne accidentally meet while both look for an apartment. After their first passionate lovemaking, in which no words or names are exchanged, each is drawn back to this location for a number of different and increasingly kinky liaisons, the most famous of which involves the use of butter as a lubricant for sodomy, during which a whole range of society's sexual taboos are broken. In their trysts, Paul sets the rules, forbidding the use of names or any discussion of the world outside their little room. As Bertolucci remarked, sex in *Last Tango in Paris* is "simply a new kind of language that these two characters try to invent in order to communicate. They use the sexual language because the sexual language means liberation from the subconscious, means an opening up."[19] This perspective is most apparent in their third act of love, where their words degenerate into animal grunts. Yet their futile attempts to maintain a purely sexual relationship stand doomed to failure, because "every sexual relationship is condemned," as Bertolucci has put it, and the psychological and sentimental backgrounds of the two characters interfere with this sexual experiment and ultimately destroy them both.[20]

Paul and Jeanne meet just after Paul has lost his wife, Rosa, to suicide and clearly seeks a sexual experience without emotional ties: Rosa and

Jeanne are linked by Jeanne's dress when she appears at the vacant apartment clad in wedding attire that resembles the clothes worn by Rosa in her coffin. Jeanne obviously had an incestuous affection for her dead father, a colonel in the French Army, and Paul reminds her of him; but when Paul follows her home at the end of the film and playfully dons her father's kepi (the traditional French army cap), Jeanne kills him with her father's revolver. These psychoanalytical overtones are enriched by references in *Last Tango in Paris* to cinema itself, through Brando's own previous film roles. One of the film's characters describes Paul in this manner:

> Nervous type, your boss. You know he was a boxer? . . . That didn't work . . . so he became an actor, then a racketeer on the waterfront in New York. . . . It didn't last long . . . played the bongo drums . . . revolutionary in South America . . . journalist in Japan. . . . One day he lands in Tahiti, hangs around, learns French . . . comes to Paris and then meets a young woman with money.[21]

Bertolucci employs Marlon Brando in *Last Tango in Paris* as a living icon of the American cinema, much as Sergio Leone was in *Once Upon a Time in the West* and Tonino Valerii did in *My Name Is Nobody* with Henry Fonda. Thus, this description of Paul also fits Brando's résumé as an actor—his early, defining role as a boxer in Elia Kazan's *On the Waterfront* (1954) and his famous performances in Kazan's *Viva Zapata!* (1952), Joshua Logan's *Sayonara* (1957), and Lewis Milestone's *Mutiny on the Bounty* (1962). One perceptive critic noted that Brando was the "last romantic cinematic idol," much of whose appeal was based upon his "rebel" image, a connection that was born from his famous performance in László Benedek's *The Wild One* (1953), his breakthrough starring role as the iconic, motorcycling rebel Johnny.[22] In *Last Tango in Paris*, Bertolucci has the actor mount a quite different saddle than that in his earlier film, transforming Brando's character Paul into a sexual rebel. Yet when Paul succumbs to his romantic attachment to Jeanne and wants to deepen his relationship beyond a purely sexual level, his romanticism leads to his death.

Bertolucci also juxtaposes the myth of the romantic "leading man" associated with Paul to the ludicrous figure of Tom (Jean-Pierre Léaud), Jeanne's cinephile fiancé, whose silly attempts to produce a film about their engagement parody aspects of both Truffaut (who casts Léaud frequently in his films) and Godard. Tom reduces the sexually charged emotion of Paul to game-playing with a movie camera and silly discussions about naming their children after famous revolutionaries. As portrayed by Brando, Paul expresses a level of stoic suffering beneath which there exists a layer of genuine feeling, set in relief by the superficiality of Tom's shallow sentiments. The two figures represent two historic cinematic styles, the older of which (Brando's Hollywood image) Bertolucci obviously likes, even though

In Bernardo Bertolucci's *Last Tango in Paris*, Paul's comic tango with Jeanne in a Paris music hall will soon be revealed to have been a dance of death for him. *Credit: MOMA*

the director must have realized that this style embodies an attitude doomed to failure in a world composed of shallow people such as Jeanne and Tom.

Bertolucci prefaces the dance-hall scene in which Jeanne and Paul stage a ridiculous parody of the tango with a number of Paul's imitations of American cinema (James Cagney plus a number of film tough guys). Moreover, when this tough-guy facade disappears, Paul becomes transformed for Jeanne from a mythic embodiment of her father into an aging American with no future. Cinematic conventions fail to function in the pop-culture ambience in which Jeanne lives. The film ends with a bleak portrait of broken illusions taken from both cinema and from life. "Trapped in the conventions and fantasies of their culture," as two reviewers put it neatly, "Tom is ridiculous, Paul is dead, and Jeanne is a killer."[23] Paul's failure to establish a new sexual language and his subsequent death ultimately argue not for more eroticism in the movies but, paradoxically, for more old-fashioned love and romance of the kind contained in the classic American cinema Bertolucci knew and loved as a child, and to which he now nostalgically refers us.

One important feature of *Last Tango in Paris* is the role played by Brando in the film's production. No Italian director, regardless of his or her knowledge of American culture, could have created dialogue with such authentic and complex cultural and cinematic references. Brando's advice and improvisation on the set were instrumental in creating Paul's character. Storaro's role as director of photography constituted a major contribution in the film's brilliant use of light and shadow. Lighting in the empty apartment reflects what Bertolucci calls a "uterine" or "prenatal" state, and the dominant imagery of the film is heavily influenced by the disturbing paintings of the English artist Francis Bacon, whose canvases are displayed under the film's opening credits. When *Last Tango in Paris* was being shot in Paris, Bertolucci, Storaro, and Brando all went to study the artist's works at a Bacon show at the Grand Palais, assimilating the "devastated plasticity" of these works into the film's visuals.[24]

Bertolucci's Marxist Epic: *1900*

Fresh from the astounding box-office triumph of *Last Tango in Paris*, Bertolucci obtained American capital to finance *1900*, a Marxist extravaganza, and employed well-known American actors to guarantee the film's reception at the box office. When *1900* was finally completed, it was the most expensive film ever to have been produced in Italy until that date. The original Italian version was over five and a half hours long and was reduced by about one third for the version eventually sent abroad. Even with cuts, this version, like the Italian version, had to be shown in two separate parts: *1900 Act I* and *1900 Act II*.

In this film, Bertolucci's obsession with sublimating personal problems into art takes second place. The director concerns himself with offering a grandiose and ambitious Marxist vision of modern Italian history from the rise of socialism in the late nineteenth century through World War I, the rise and fall of Italian Fascism, the anti-Fascist Resistance, and the liberation of Italy ending World War II. It is a work that sets out to rival the epic sweep of a historical novel like Tomasi di Lampedusa's *The Leopard* and its cinematic adaptation by Luchino Visconti. With *1900* Bertolucci hoped to produce the Italian equivalent of *Gone with the Wind* but with a leftist flavor, a film that combined the demands of commercial spectacle with the concerns of a Marxist intellectual. Like *The Leopard*, Bertolucci's *1900* analyzes Italian history through a focus upon family history by telescoping the events of the twentieth century into the juxtaposed chronicles of two different clans. On the first day of the dawn of the twentieth century, two sons are born: one, Alfredo (Robert De Niro), the grandson of the wealthy landowner Alfredo Berlinghieri (Burt Lancaster, the star of Visconti's earlier epic); the other, Olmo Dalcò (Gérard Depardieu), the grandson of the peasant Leo Dalcò (Sterling Hayden). Bertolucci follows the two children, whose twin destinies are closely intertwined from the day of their birth through their old age, touching upon all the major historical themes of the century. As he did in *The Conformist*, Bertolucci's narrative avoids any linear storytelling: it opens with the liberation of Italy on April 25, 1945, then cuts back to the birth scene in 1900 and ends act I with the apparent victory of the Fascists under the violent leadership of Attila Mellanchini (Donald Sutherland) and the apparent destruction of agrarian socialism in northern Italy. Act II follows the demise of Mussolini's regime, shows the end of the *padrone*, or boss, in northern Italian agrarian farming, and ends with a comic picture of Olmo and Alfredo as old men in 1975, still struggling with each other. Along the way, Alfredo marries Ada, a liberated young woman who takes cocaine and declaims futurist poetry (Dominique Sanda), whereas Olmo weds a young Socialist teacher named Anita (Stefania Sandrelli). Juxtaposed to these two couples are the evil Attila and his perverse wife, Regina (Laura Betti), Alfredo's cousin.

Bertolucci's romanticized version of modern Italian history may easily be attacked as either too idealized a portrait of his beloved peasants or too softhearted a depiction of Alfredo, a weak-willed bourgeois whose friendship for Olmo does not prevent him from being used by Attila and his Fascist bullyboys, who terrorize the peasants and murder a number of them. Set against the decadence of the Berlinghieri family—especially Alfredo's Uncle Ottavio, who dallies with Alfredo in casinos and Mediterranean resorts, snorting cocaine and taking photographs of nude and seminude peasant boys dressed in classical garb—the humanity of peasant culture and the generosity of the lower classes provide an element of sanity in a world that seems terribly out of joint. Alfredo's ambivalent character reflects that of Bertolucci himself, who was born only a few miles from the enormous nineteenth-century farm in northern Italy where he shot *1900*. Indeed, there is much in the film that reflects more of the director's biography than authentic social history.

Partisan justice: fascist Attila dies on the grave of some of his peasant victims in Bertolucci's *1900*. Credit: MOMA

Even though some critics have attacked Bertolucci for his film's ahistorical character, Bertolucci intended the film to represent a utopian dream— the end of the boss, or *padrone*, with the liberation in 1945. As an astute observer of the Italian scene, Bertolucci knew full well that the *padrone* did not disappear at the end of the war and that the system that the *padrone* represents in the film regrouped its forces in the postwar Reconstruction. As a result, the liberation failed to generate a true social or socialist revolution, and the opening sequences of *1900* show us a liberation manqué, just as those in Visconti's *The Leopard*.

The most memorable sequences of *1900* show Bertolucci at his best and most lyrical. Many of the evocative scenes of peasant life come from an intimate knowledge of the canvases of the Italian *Macchiaioli*, a school of nineteenth-century Florentine painters influenced by French impressionism that concentrated upon rural life of the period. The ideology of *1900* repeats the substance of that in *Before the Revolution*. As a middle-class intellectual like Fabrizio in that earlier film or like Alfredo in this one, Bertolucci believes he or characters like him can never become an integral part of the class he admires for its progressive role in Italian history. For this reason, *1900* is a utopian view of a revolution that has yet to occur made by a director who is doomed (or so he professes to believe) to make films *before* the revolution. Although very different filmmakers, Bertolucci and the Taviani brothers share this view of the revolution as a utopian dream. Bertolucci's ideological compromises stem from this perspective: to make a film in a capitalist system, he must follow the unwritten rules of cinematic spectacle and bow to some of the dictates of his financial backers (none of whom were Marxists). The finished product therefore reflects the director's ambivalent personal position and makes of it a far more honest work than many of its severest critics admitted.

Luna and *The Tragedy of a Ridiculous Man*: A Return to Freud

While *1900* recounts a story that rests upon a Marxist foundation, Bertolucci's view of the landed gentry in the film remains both biblical and Freudian—the sins of the fathers are visited upon their sons. With *Luna* (*La luna*, 1979), Bertolucci turns from his preoccupation with the father to the image of the mother. After years of being obsessed in analysis with his father, Bertolucci began to speak of his mother, and his first memory of her recalls an evening when she was pedaling her bicycle down a country road with the infant Bernardo in a basket facing her; he remembers confusing the face of the moon with that of his mother. This childhood recollection becomes the inspiration for *Luna*.[25] This film was financed entirely by American capital,

stars Americans, and was shot in English, another conscious attempt on
the director's part to ensure a wide international audience and to have an
excuse finally to make a film, at least in part, in the land of Hollywood and
Marilyn Monroe. Its plot is not so far from Italian culture, however, since
the protagonist is Catherine Silvers (Jill Clayburgh), an opera singer who
takes her teenage son, Joe (Mathew Barry), with her to Rome when she is
scheduled to sing at the Baths of Caracalla. Along the way, she discovers
that her own neglect and the absence of Joe's father have turned Joe into
a drug addict, and in an attempt to save him, she not only provides him
with the drugs he needs but even offers herself to him sexually. *Luna* thus
analyzes an incestuous relationship between mother and son, breaking one
of the few cinematic taboos left untouched by *Last Tango in Paris*.

    Luna resembles *The Spider's Stratagem* in the way it combines Freud-
ian plot with Verdian melodrama. Two prologues preface the New York
sequence and the death of Joe's legal father before the film moves to Rome.
The first shows a baby choking on the thick honey his mother has fed Joe
with her finger (a reference to Joe's later dependence on heroin plus his
attraction to his mother). A shadowy figure, as yet unidentified, dances the
twist with Catherine while the baby Joe drags a ball of unwinding twine
toward his grandmother, playing the piano (an image meant to suggest the
umbilical cord linking mother and child). Only at the conclusion of the
film do we learn that the unidentified figure was his real father, an Italian
named Giuseppe (Tomas Milian). A second, stunningly beautiful sequence
follows, capturing Bertolucci's own personal memory of the moment when
he confused his mother with the face of the moon. As the film shifts to
Rome, Joe takes a young Italian girl to the movies to see Marilyn Monroe in
Henry Hathaway's *Niagara* (1953). While Joe tries to make love to her in the
darkened movie theater, a sliding roof opens (a typical feature of big-city
Italian cinemas before air-conditioning) to reveal a full moon. This causes
Joe to abandon the girl and to seek out his mother at the opera, where she is
starring in Verdi's *Il trovatore*.

    Later, at Joe's fifteenth-birthday party, Catherine discovers her son
shooting up with a girl and is horrified, whereas her earlier thought that
they were only making love raised no more than a mischievous smile. When
Joe expresses his total lack of interest in life, in an effort to communicate
with him she caresses his genitals and he suckles her breasts. These sexual
overtures, however, fail to bridge the gap between them, and a trip to Verdi's
birthplace in Busseto (also one of Bertolucci's hallowed spots) provokes
only bored indifference in Joe. Although Catherine has a surrogate father
in Verdi, Joe has lost his legal father, who died in New York before they left
for Italy, and he does not even know his true father. Catherine finally relents
and tells Joe where his true father, a schoolteacher, lives. As Joe goes there
to meet him, we recognize the location of the film's opening sequence, but

his father throws him out of the house. Rejected, Joe goes to the Baths of Caracalla, where Catherine is rehearsing Verdi's *Un ballo in maschera* and where life begins to copy art (or opera) as the scene onstage begins to reflect what is happening in the audience. Joe watches his mother walk through her role, Giuseppe suddenly appears, slapping him, then making up as Catherine sings the line "lasciatelo" ("leave him alone"). The stage immediately darkens as Bertolucci's camera moves in to focus upon Catherine singing, and a full moon (with all its psychological associations for Joe) appears over the stage at the Baths. Joe finally encounters his real father, and although Giuseppe and Catherine will not be united—Joe's father cannot tear himself away from his own mother—Catherine's last lyrics ("ei muore"; "he is dying") reinforce the fact that Joe has finally become an adult, and the child within him has died. What this growth implies for Joe's relationship with his mother, Bertolucci leaves unanswered.

In *The Tragedy of a Ridiculous Man* (*La tragedia di un uomo ridicolo*, 1981), Bertolucci comes to grips with contemporary Italy's pressing social problems—drug addiction and terrorism—themes that became increasingly common in the Italian cinema between the 1970s and the present. In this milieu, Bertolucci returns to investigate his interest in the relationship between fathers and sons: an industrialist (Ugo Tognazzi) learns that his son has been kidnapped, and when the boy is killed, his father exploits the situation in order to divert the ransom money to rebuild his shaky business.

Triumph at the Oscars: *The Last Emperor*

If *Luna* and *The Tragedy* were not the kind of critical and box-office successes to which Bertolucci had become accustomed with *The Conformist*, *Last Tango in Paris*, and *1900*, Bertolucci's epic account of the bizarre life of China's last dynastic ruler in *The Last Emperor* not only enjoyed an enormous budget (for an Italian film), expensive on-location shooting abroad, an international cast, and an epic scope similar to that attempted in *1900*, but also earned an unprecedented nine Oscars, an unheard-of achievement for an Italian film, a record for any foreign director, and third place (then) in the history of the Academy Awards.[26] Initially rejected both by Italian producers and by the major Hollywood studios, Bertolucci obtained support for the project from an independent producer (the type of source that had become increasingly essential in Hollywood by the time he shot the film). Even more important, he obtained the crucial permission to shoot on location in Beijing's Forbidden City at a time when the entire world was fascinated with events in China, a condition that guaranteed him an enormous audience all over the world.

As Bertolucci remarked, the theme of *The Last Emperor* is change: "Can a man change? The story of Pu Yi is a story of metamorphosis. From emperor to citizen . . . from caterpillar to butterfly."[27] As described in the memoirs of Sir Reginald Johnston, the emperor's English tutor during 1919–22, or in Pu Yi's own autobiography, written with the approval of the Maoist government after the emperor's "reeducation," the life of Pu Yi (1906–67) spans all the tumultuous events of modern Chinese history. Named emperor at the age of three by the empress dowager on her deathbed in 1908, Pu Yi (John Lone) was shortly thereafter deposed by republican nationalists in 1911 and remained confined inside the Forbidden City in the center of Beijing until 1924. When he was finally evicted by a Chinese warlord, he took refuge in the Japanese legation at Tianjin. After passing a few years as a Western-style playboy, Pu Yi finally agreed to serve the Japanese puppet state of Manchuria (the birthplace of his ancestors) as a collaborationist emperor until he was arrested by Soviet troops in 1945. The Soviets turned him over to the victorious Communist regime established by Mao in 1949. After ten years of relatively gentle "reeducation," he was released as a simple citizen, finding employment as a gardener in the botanical gardens of the imperial city he had once ruled. After publishing his autobiography in 1964, Pu Yi died during the upheavals of the Chinese Cultural Revolution.

Bertolucci's interpretation of the last emperor's life employs a narrative structure similar not only to two of his best films (*The Spider's Stratagem* and *The Conformist*) but also to Sergio Leone's epic film about Jewish American gangsters, *Once Upon a Time in America*, a work that appeared only three years before *The Last Emperor* and an equally ambitious film with an epic scope set not in Italy but abroad. A series of twelve major symmetrically balanced flashbacks and flash-forwards, beginning with Pu Yi's reeducation in Fushun Prison, weave an intricate web of details from which the spectator must reconstruct the protagonist's chronology. Unlike Leone's quite different shifts back and forth in time that tend to negate the difference between past and present, Bertolucci's narrative relentlessly returns over and over again to the prison scene, where Pu Yi's motives are constantly called into question by the prison's governor, Jin Yuan (played by Ying Ruocheng, then China's vice minister of culture). Accordingly, the jumps in narrative continuity in *The Last Emperor* analyze and explain the protagonist's motives and actions. This jumping from the prison to the past and back again abruptly ceases during the film's last three sequences, the only parts of the film arranged in accurate chronological order. Significantly enough, these three sequences represent the final stages of Pu Yi's metamorphosis: his release from prison in 1959, his witnessing of the Cultural Revolution and the public humiliation of his former prison interrogator in 1967, and his final visit as a simple tourist to the throne room of his former palace in the Forbidden City.

Bertolucci's film reflects both his encounter with Freudian psychoanalysis and his utopian search for a Marxist revolution with a human face. Pu Yi's sheltered existence within the Forbidden City is shot with what the director of photography Vittorio Storaro has called " 'forbidden' colors, the warmest colors, because it [the Forbidden City] was both a protective womb for him and a kind of prison . . . the more we go into his story, the more we discover new colors, new chromatics."[28] The collaboration between Bertolucci and Storaro in utilizing the lighting of the film to advance its narrative content, an achievement already brilliantly realized by the two men in *The Spider's Stratagem, The Conformist, Last Tango in Paris,* and *1900,* constitutes one of the film's most original features. Light and shade are juxtaposed to suggest a psychological struggle between Pu Yi's conscious and unconscious. For Bertolucci, the young emperor trapped inside the Forbidden City represents the kind of flight from painful self-awareness common to all human beings. Bertolucci depicts Pu Yi's eventual exile from his womblike residence as the departure of a blind man, his dark glasses testifying not only to a lack of self-knowledge but also to the effects of an Oedipal complex growing out of the emperor's unusual family history and the lack of a strong paternal presence. As Pu Yi matures and reaches a greater understanding of his life's meaning, the lights and shadows of the film's photography move into greater balance.

Nowhere is Bertolucci's belief that the child is father to the man clearer than in the brilliant and complicated sequence narrating the young boy's coronation. The three-year-old scampers through the ranks of his courtiers on the Upper Terrace outside the Hall of Supreme Harmony, lured not by a thirst for adulation from his assembled retainers (a group of some two thousand extras supplied by the Chinese People's Liberation Army, producing the proverbial Hollywood "cast of thousands"), but rather by the child's attraction to the chirp of a cricket. The director's highly mobile and fluid camera movements follow the young boy (Richard Vuu) with a difficult Steadicam shot as he races along through the throng; the young Pu Yi eventually encounters the cricket's owner, who shows the child the insect inside a small cage that the mature Pu Yi will eventually rediscover in 1967 when he returns to his former throne room at the end of his life. Bertolucci's use of this simple incident to provide narrative closure for the story underlines Pu Yi's intellectual and psychological growth.

The Last Emperor provoked criticism in some quarters as an "official" view of Pu Yi's past and as pro-Maoist propaganda, and the Chinese government always referred to Bertolucci as "a member of the Italian Communist Party." Clearly, Bertolucci's ideological views assisted him in obtaining the support of the Chinese regime. Yet to construe the film as mere propaganda would be a mistake. In fact, Bertolucci shows how Pu Yi suffered from ideological manipulation not only by the Japanese but also by the Maoist regime. The last Chinese emperor's conversion from ruler to common citizen may well, by Western standards, represent only a transition from one form of authoritarianism to another, but in the concluding scene of the film, the now wiser ex-emperor dimly perceives that like the cricket, he, too, had been trapped throughout his life by ideological myths. Pu Yi's release of the insect testifies not only to the emperor's final acceptance of his new personality but also to Bertolucci's deep faith in the possibility of changing human nature.

Bertolucci's "International" Films: *The Sheltering Sky, Little Buddha, Stealing Beauty, Besieged,* and *The Dreamers*

Although it would be impossible to equal the success of *The Last Emperor*, Bertolucci's production after this unqualified triumph may be said to follow the same pattern of shooting films that seem more like the product of Hollywood than of Cinecittà. Most often, he shoots such "international" films with English rather than Italian as their "original" language, and non-Italian scriptwriters rather than Italian writers may generate the scripts that underpin the stories. Such films may have independent producers, who assemble enough international capital to complete the film, and they may reflect foreign cultures rather than Italian ones (although this is not a requirement); but preproduction, casting, shooting, and editing are all basically under the Italian director's control. The Hollywood connection comes into play when the completed film enters the distribution phrase, especially in the United States.[29] Bertolucci's last five films employ foreign locations (Africa, Seattle, Tibet) or track the adventures of expatriate foreigners in Rome, Tuscany, or Paris. They have not been as successful as *The Last Emperor* and are essentially less ambitious works in which beautiful photography often replaces strong narrative plots with engaging characters.

The Sheltering Sky (*Il tè nel deserto*, 1990) offers an adaptation of Paul Bowles's 1949 cult novel lavishly photographed by Vittorio Storaro in the Sahara. Bowles himself appears as a narrator who comments on the film's events while relaxing in a café. Despite the valiant efforts of John Malkovich and Debra Winger, who play out a love affair between Port and Kit Moresby, the film's appeal rests more upon the beautiful photography of the African desert than upon its psychological insight into the protagonists. When Kit goes native and takes up with a Tuareg caravan, becoming the mistress of a desert nomad, little in the film explains her existential angst. *Little Buddha* (*Piccolo Buddha*, 1993) and *Besieged* (*L'assedio*, 1998) provide glimpses into cultures quite different from that in Italy and contain some extraordinarily beautiful sequences. In the first film, Bertolucci employs two different but interrelated stories: the life of the Buddha in Nepal five centuries before Christ (Siddhartha is played by Keanu Reeves), and the story of a nine-year-old Seattle youngster named Jesse, who may possibly be the latest incarnation of the Buddha in the twentieth century. In the second film, a foreign pianist living near the Spanish Steps in Rome falls in love with an African woman studying medicine who cleans and washes in the apartment building in return for her board and some pocket money. Knowing no other means of showing her his love, he sells everything he owns, including his art collection, tapestries, furniture, and his beloved piano, in order to pay to free her husband from an African jail and to bring him back to her. Moved by this demonstration of selflessness, she grants him a single night of love just before she reunites with her spouse. Whereas *Little Buddha* boasts spectacular scenes set in the majestic mountains of the Himalayas and near Seattle's Mount Rainier, *Besieged* is, by Bertolucci's standards, a low-budget film. Neither film has the kind of narrative power or compelling intellectual structure typical of Bertolucci's best films. Even the influence of psychoanalysis, so seminal a force in the plots of his most famous works, seems unimportant.

Stealing Beauty (*Io ballo da sola*, 1996) and *The Dreamers*, on the other hand, exhibit many of Bertolucci's unique talents as a director. The first film is Bertolucci's foray into "Chianti-Shire"—the Tuscan countryside beloved by so many English and American expatriates. In it, Bertolucci combines the extraordinary beauty of his photography of the landscapes justly celebrated by all visitors to the region with a firmer psychological grounding for his characters. Bertolucci explains his interest in this story as follows:

> I felt the need to rediscover my country through the eyes of a foreigner. Whence the story of Lucy, this young American girl who comes to spend her vacation in a Tuscan villa. Her pretext for being there is to have her portrait done by an artist friend of her parents, but her secret goal is to discover the identity of her real father. Like me, the people who make up this cosmopolitan community she enters had been very politically engaged twenty or thirty years previously; but, out of despair, they decided to abandon their political dreams at a certain moment and seek refuge from the vulgar crowd, at the top of a hill, overlooking a unique landscape whose incredible beauty inspired the Tuscan painters of the fourteenth and the fifteenth centuries.[30]

The stormy relationships between parents and children depicted in *Stealing Beauty* are obviously related to the psychoanalytic themes in some of Bertolucci's greatest films. Bertolucci shifts, however, from his habitual masculine protagonist with whom he identified in earlier films to a young woman named Lucy Harmon, played by a precociously talented Liv Tyler, who would eventually reach superstar status in Peter Jackson's *Lord of the Rings* trilogy. Lucy's arrival in Tuscany makes her the center of attention of a group of bohemian expatriates who marvel at the fact that she has remained a virgin until the age of nineteen. In a beautiful villa decorated by the real sculptures of the English artist Matthew Spender, Lucy befriends a terminally ill artist (Jeremy Irons) while she has her very first love affair. Bertolucci's film succeeds because its structure resides upon a double mystery: Lucy's quest to discover her true father's identity, and her decision of whether or not to surrender her virginity to one of the many willing males who hover around her at the villa like animals in heat.

At the conclusion of this simple but beautifully photographed work, Lucy discovers that her mother's artist friend is her true father (explaining why his sculpture portrait of her is so movingly wrought); she also surrenders herself to a romantic liaison with a poor Italian boy she had known years earlier who had written her passionate love letters and wants to follow her to America. Her choice for a first lover thus rejects all the jaded Italian aristocrats and expatriate houseguests with whom she might well have been partnered. In a sense, Bertolucci supplies a Hollywood happy ending to his story (something he would never have done in his earlier, more ideologically leftist career), but it seems appropriate here and is rendered in a lyrical camera style that equals that of some of his best work.

With *The Dreamers*, Bertolucci sends a love letter to the cinema and to his cinephile experiences in Paris. By placing his film in the Paris of 1968, Bertolucci restages the student demonstrations against the firing of Henri Langlois (1914–77) at the French Cinémathèque in February 1968, and those following in May of that same year that, for a brief time, seriously threatened the stability of President Charles De Gaulle's government. Matthew (Michael Pitt) is a young student and film buff, not unlike Bertolucci, who comes to learn French in Paris and meets a pair of twins, Isabelle (Eva Green) and Theo (Louis Garrel) at Langlois's Musée du Cinéma, then at the Palais de Chaillot (from which the French Cinémathèque has since been transferred to a Frank Gehry–designed postmodern structure in the twelfth *arrondissement* of the city). Isabelle and Theo are two decadent European intellectuals, incestuously linked to each other, who apparently need to be part of a ménage à trois to go beyond temptation to action. Once they invite Matthew to stay in their apartment while their parents are out of town, spectators familiar with *Last Tango in Paris* may feel they have returned to the claustrophobic apartment of that film, with similar kinky sex.

Yet *The Dreamers* also looks back on the sexual transgressions of 1968 as somewhat childish. Matthew understands something the twins will never learn: they will never grow and mature unless they abandon their childish, regressive lifestyle. When Theo seems to spout the kind of foolish political jargon so typical of the period among intellectuals, comparing Mao's Cultural Revolution to a huge epic movie, Matthew's common sense causes him to object, saying that the only problem with this epic film is that all the people are only extras, not actors, since Mao controls their thought, their actions, and most certainly the films they see.

What strikes the viewer who is not nostalgic about sixties radicals in this film is its visual beauty: Bertolucci continues to be one of the most skillful directors in the Italian industry in creating breathtaking camera movements. At one moment, his camera follows Matthew into an old-fashioned European elevator mounted on the interior of a staircase and follows the twins up all the way to their apartment and then even inside in a single take; elsewhere, Bertolucci moves from a crane shot to a Steadicam shot without missing a beat. Even though it is not a large-budget film, *The Dreamers* might well be taken as a demonstration of virtuoso filmmaking. Moreover, it also pays homage to the history of the cinema, particularly the French New Wave. Throughout the film, the three friends constantly refer to other films, and film clips are often interspersed with the action. The films Bertolucci cites either visually or musically (a favorite practice of the French New Wave, which was the dominant cinema school during the time of the film's action) comprise the kind of film-buff history lesson that Bertolucci would have enjoyed when he, like Matthew, "studied" the history of cinema at the feet of Langlois. They include Charles Chaplin's *City Lights* (1931); Josef von Sternberg's *Blonde Venus* (1932), with Marlene Dietrich; Howard Hawks's *Scarface* (1932); Tod Browning's *Freaks* (1932); Rouben Mamoulian's *Queen Christina* (1933), with Greta Garbo; Mark Sandrich's *Top Hat* (1935), with Fred Astaire and Ginger Rogers; François Truffaut's *The 400 Blows* (1959); Jean-Luc Godard's *Breathless* (1960) and *Band of Outsiders* (1964); Sam Fuller's *Shock Corridor* (1963); and Robert Bresson's *Mouchette* (1967). Perhaps the most remarkable thing about this list is the absence of citations from the history of the Italian cinema (no Rossellini, no Antonioni, no Fellini). For Bertolucci, the great lesson that the history of the cinema teaches comes primarily from old Hollywood films or from the French New Wave. Although loosely based upon a novel, *The Dreamers* seems to be more a remake of Godard's *Band of Outsiders*, a film also admired by the postmodern director Quentin Tarantino. That film too featured a trio of friends who were film buffs, and Bertolucci even imitates their race through the Louvre Museum as Matthew, Theo, and Isabelle beat the record of Odile, Franz, and Arthur (Godard's characters) by just a few seconds.

≈

As a survey of their works shows, both Pasolini and Bertolucci were responsible for a broadening of Italian film culture through their interest in Marxism and psychoanalysis, as well as their penchant for the French cinema of the New Wave, their cinematic model, for incorporating ideology into film. Pasolini's career was cut short in the mid-1970s, just when

Bertolucci's career was taking off toward the kinds of high-visibility commercial films that made him internationally famous and extremely successful. In spite of the unfulfilled promises associated with Pasolini's untimely demise, the kind of ideologically challenging cinema Pasolini always espoused was taken up, developed, and expanded by Bertolucci, once his assistant and disciple.

CHAPTER FOURTEEN

The Poliziesco

ITALIAN CRIME FILMS
FROM THE 1970S TO THE PRESENT

The Origin and Historical Matrix
of the Italian Crime Film

IN THE LATE 1960s AND 1970s, during the same period that the spaghetti western flourished and the *giallo* rose to prominence, the Italian cinema developed another popular genre, the crime film—referred to as *il cinema poliziesco*, or as *il cinema poliziottesco* by negative critics. Over a hundred of these popular films were shot in a decade, and they bore a close relationship to the far more popular western film. Actors, directors, scriptwriters, and others working in the cinema moved from one genre to the other quite effortlessly, since the two kinds of films were in such high demand that producers could not obtain enough of them during the period of their success at the box office. The Italian *giallo* film is a genre in which the police are always present because the horrendous crimes committed by their villains inevitably require police investigation; this element, therefore, is a direct link between the *giallo* and the *poliziesco*. Yet one of the most important features of most, if not all, *gialli* is that amateur detectives, nonprofessionals, who sometimes show up the professionals as inept bunglers, following the tradition established by Conan Doyle's classic Sherlock Holmes mysteries, usually solve the crimes. Furthermore, the crimes committed almost always revolve around psychological traumas suffered by the criminal, and their concrete expression is most often sexual in nature. So in many respects, even though violent crime takes place in both the *giallo* and the *poliziesco*, the Italian crime film stands closer to the kind of violence we associate with the spaghetti western as well as to the social concerns typical of the Italian political film—the so-called *cinema di impegno civile* (see chapter 8)—than to the *giallo* thriller.

453

The Italian police film represents a completely *contemporary* popular genre in the sense that, not unlike the content of the American *Law & Order* television series, many of its plots and its most popular themes could easily have been lifted from the pages of the *cronaca nera* (crime news) of any urban newspaper from the 1960s to the early 1980s, a period of great social, economic, and political unrest in Italy. The first great postwar Mafia bloodbath in Palermo (or First Mafia War) was touched off by the Ciaculli massacre in 1963, where a number of policemen were killed trying to defuse a bomb meant for a rival clan boss. This war reflected the penetration by organized crime of both political and civil institutions associated with the building trade, which became known as the "Sack of Palermo," when Mafia-controlled construction businesses destroyed much of the charming urban setting of Palermo and replaced it with ugly concrete buildings. An even more violent Second Mafia War broke out in the early 1980s between various families based in Palermo, on the one hand, and, on the other, several crime families associated with the nearby town of Corleone (the home of Mario Puzo's fictional godfather). Eventually, the Corleone faction virtually eliminated its competition and, in the process, killed a great number of important Italian judges, labor leaders, politicians, and magistrates (the *cadaveri eccellenti* ["excellent cadavers"] Francesco Rosi employed as the title of one of his films), including General Carlo Alberto Dalla Chiesa (1920–82), who had been successful in his campaign against the Red Brigades of Turin, but whose attack on the Mafia of the Second Mafia War provoked the wrath of the victorious Corleonesi gang. The fugitive leader of the Corleonesi, Salvatore "Totò" Riina, a far more deadly opponent than any of Dalla Chiesa's terrorist adversaries, gave the order to kill him and, later, his successors, the Anti-Mafia Commission magistrates Giovanni Falcone (1939–92) and Paolo Borsellino (1939–92).

Besides the widely publicized and explosive Mafia violence in the South of Italy, a number of other developments heightened the social tension in the peninsula. There were widespread strikes and labor unrest. Important national referenda on divorce (1974) and abortion (1975) showed that ordinary Italians were no longer content to allow the Catholic Church to dictate rules about family life. (Of course, the rise in the use of birth control had already signaled these profound shifts in public opinion.) The spread of the use of narcotics not only enriched organized crime but also caused an explosion of petty burglaries, shoplifting, purse snatchings, and minor violence—occurrences virtually unheard of in the traditionally safe Italian urban areas outside the Italian Mezzogiorno. In this period, terrorist attacks from both the Left and the Right ranged from simple kidnapping to knee-capping and to brutal assassinations and terrorist bombings.

Among the most famous of these terrorist events are the Piazza Fontana bombing in Milan in 1969, the kidnapping and murder of Aldo Moro in

1978, and the planting of a bomb at the Bologna train station in 1980. Dozens of less notorious but equally brutal events occurred. Eight major bomb attacks killed or wounded nearly a thousand people between the Piazza Fontana bomb of 1969 and the explosive device hidden on a Florence-bound train in 1984. In the case of the 1984 attack, the Italian government claimed that right-wing terrorists had cooperated with members of organized crime to carry it out. In the case of the more famous Piazza Fontana bombing, the perpetrators were originally presumed to be anarchists, and two of them—Giuseppe Pinelli and Pietro Valpreda—were arrested immediately. Shortly after his arrest, Pinelli allegedly committed suicide by jumping from the fourth floor of the Milanese police station after interrogation by a policeman with a reputation for toughness, Commissioner Luigi Calabresi (1937–72). Absolved of any guilt by a subsequent investigation but vilified by leftist newspapers and politicians, Calabresi was assassinated outside his home in 1972. Years later, in 1988, the police arrested Adriano Sofri, a former leader of the extraparliamentary group Lotta Continua (Continuous Struggle). His conviction for ordering Calabresi's death earned Sofri a prison sentence. Evidence of his guilt came from the detailed testimony of one of the members of Lotta Continua who, like so many ex-Mafiosi, became what Italians popularly call a *pentito*—a collaborator (literally, "penitent")—an ex-criminal or terrorist who cooperates with what Italians call "the forces of order" (*le forze dell'ordine*). Based on the Pinelli "suicide," or "assisted suicide," depending on your political point of view, the leftist playwright Dario Fo (winner of the Nobel Prize for Literature in 1997) dedicated one of his most popular plays, *The Accidental Death of an Anarchist* (*Morte accidentale di un anarchico*, 1970), to Pinelli. For Italy's leftist intellectual culture, Pinelli and Sofri have become political martyrs (Sofri is now free and engaged in writing for major Italian newspapers), whereas Calabresi's murder receives scant attention. Thus, during this period in Italy, the numerous interconnections among organized and disorganized crime, terrorists, government agencies, the secret police, policemen, and judicial magistrates (both incorruptible and corrupted) created an environment of tension and fear. The Italian cinema in various ways reflected these current events—not only the political cinema praised by the critics and intellectuals of the day (see chapter 8) but also the crime films discussed in this chapter, generally disparaged at the time as B films and ignored by most critics and scholars, with their predictable leftist views on current events.

In addition to terrorists and organized southern Italian criminals, a number of violent robber gangs—groups of criminals not associated with the traditional southern Italian Mafia, Neapolitan Camorra, or Calabrian 'Ndrangheta—operated in central and northern Italy, usually attacking banks and credit unions with automatic weapons and fleeing via fast automobiles. Among them, a group in Turin led by Pietro Cavallero committed dozens of robberies that led to a famous shootout in 1967 after the gang had robbed the Bank of Naples in Milan and left four dead and twenty-two wounded. The events surrounding this robbery became the material for Carlo Lizzani's *The Violent Four* (*Banditi a Milano*, 1968). Renato Vallanzasca (1950–), whose exploits were popularized with the nickname "Bel René" bestowed upon him by the tabloid press, led another infamous gang of bandits. Arrested in 1972, he made a clamorous escape from jail in 1976, thereafter completing more than twenty robberies and kidnappings before he was caught again in 1977 and sentenced to four consecutive life sentences plus an additional almost three centuries in prison. In Rome, the so-called Banda della Magliana (Magliana Gang), known by the neighborhood from which some of their members originated, engaged in kidnappings, robberies, and drug dealing between the mid-1970s and the early 1990s, maintaining connections with both right-wing terrorist organizations and the Italian Secret Service. Finally, in and around Bologna during 1987–94, the Uno Bianca Gang used stolen white Fiat Unos, the most common car on the streets at the time, to commit more than a hundred robberies in which both civilians and policemen were killed. When they were finally apprehended, most of the gang's members had ties with the police! This gang inspired one of the best crime films ever made for television in Italy, Michele Soavi's two-part miniseries *Uno Bianca* (*Uno bianca*, 2001).

Cinematic and Literary Antecedents for the Italian Crime Film, Domestic and Foreign

The raw materials for interesting crime films based on Italy's dazzlingly confusing conglomeration of various kinds of shady, subversive, and illegal activities were therefore more than any social historian, let alone a film director, could ever completely digest. Even skilled Italian writers of contemporary crime fiction, such as Giorgio Scerbanenco, Andrea Camilleri, or Carlo Lucarelli, to cite only a few examples, can scarcely make the many mysterious events in postwar Italy all fit into a neat pattern.[1] This Byzantine collection of facts, lies, plots, and judicial processes that have dragged on for years and even decades would challenge any writer or filmmaker to make sense of it all without simplification and radical editing. Even the gruesome murder of Pier Paolo Pasolini in 1975 took place under the same murky and puzzling circumstances that have typified almost every major political, social, and economic event in postwar Italy. Real events of the period inspired many Italian crime films, and the *cronaca nera* of most metropolitan newspapers furnished plenty of raw materials. Many of the protagonists of the spaghetti western phenomenon—not only actors and directors but all of the other technicians required to shoot a film—easily moved from producing films about gunfighters on horseback to urban gunslingers working for the police or criminal gangs. In each case, the gunfire and violence were similar. Fernando di Leo (1932–2003) contributed to the scripts of Sergio Leone's two *Dollars* westerns (see chapter 11) before establishing his reputation as a director of action crime films; *The Last Round* (*Il conto é chiuso*, 1976), by Stelvio Massi (1929–2004), is clearly an updated remake of *A Fistful of Dollars*. The ideological content of the Italian political films by such figures as Petri and Rosi suited the cynical view that most Italian crime films expressed about the corruption and ineffectiveness of many Italian civil and political institutions, although very few directors of B crime films had any other goal but to entertain the audiences that had previously filled movie theaters to see Italian westerns.

Like the Italian western, crime films did not have a long pedigree in the domestic industry's prewar past, largely because urban violence was deemed unsuitable to the kinds of films the Italian Fascist government wished to see presented. The Fascist regime preferred to envision Italy as a land without crime. In the aftermath of World War II, however, a number of crime films emerged during the neorealist period, in particular those by Pietro Germi, including *Lost Youth* (*Gioventù perduta*, 1947), *In the Name of the Law*, *Four Ways Out* (*La città si difende*, 1951), and *The Bandit of Tacca del Lupo* (*Il brigante di Tacca del Lupo*, 1952), to all but the first of which Federico Fellini contributed as scriptwriter. Other important neorealist films dealing with crime included Lattuada's *Without Pity*, De Santis's *Bitter Rice*, and two works by Luigi Comencini: *Behind Closed Shutters* (*Persiane chiuse*, 1950), also scripted in part by Fellini, and *The White Slave Trade*, a.k.a. *Girls Marked Danger* (*La tratta delle bianche*, 1952). They were all closely related to the immediate postwar economic crisis, in which the black market, prostitution, and banditry were common phenomena. While most of these films tended to focus upon the plight of unfortunate and impoverished people driven into a life of delinquency, subsequent crime films by directors associated with the Italian political film, such as Carlo Lizzani, Elio Petri, and Francesco Rosi used the existence of criminal behavior as a springboard to far more radical critiques of Italian society.

Eventually, as always occurs in the history of a popular cinematic theme in Italy, serious early treatments of crime in the immediate postwar neorealist cinema turned to comic parodies, as in the classic spoof of a caper film, Mario Monicelli's *Big Deal on Madonna Street*. The same shift from violence to slapstick comedy came in crime films as it had in the spaghetti western (with the tremendously popular Hill–Spencer *Trinity* series; see chapter 11). In the early 1970s, Bud Spencer made the transition from comic western to comic *poliziesco*, almost at the moment the genre gained steam, with a series of extremely popular films directed by Stefano Vanzina, a.k.a. Steno (1915–88), in which Spencer plays Inspector "Flatfoot" Rizzo, a.k.a. Piedone: *Flatfoot* (*Piedone lo sbirro*, 1973), *Flatfoot in Hong Kong* (*Piedone a Hong*

Kong, 1975), *Flatfoot in Africa* (*Piedone l'africano*, 1978), and *Flatfoot on the Nile* (*Piedone d'Egitto*, 1979). Just as predictably, Franco Franchi turned his talents for parody and inventive comic titles to sending up the *poliziesco* genre, just as he and Ciccio Ingrassia had done with the spaghetti western, in films such as *Il giustiziere di mezzogiorno* (1975; directed by Mario Amendola), a play on words of the Italian title of Charles Bronson's vigilante film *Death Wish* (*Il giustiziere di mezzanotte*). And since the erotic comedy was one of the other staples of Italian genre films during this period, Edwige Fenech jumped easily from sexy roles in the Italian *giallo* to sexy roles as a policewoman in a trilogy by Michele Massimo Tarantini: *Confessions of a Lady Cop* (*La poliziotta fa carriera*, 1975), *A Policewoman on the Porno Squad* (*La poliziotta della squadra del buon costume*, 1979), and *A Policewoman in New York* (*La poliziotta a New York*, 1981). Tarantini played both sides of the field, as it were: not only did he parody two separate genres (the *poliziesco* and the sexy comedy) in these three films, but he also shot two perfectly conventional *poliziesco* action films at virtually the same time: *Crimebusters* (*Poliziotti violenti*, 1976) and *A Man Called Magnum* (*Napoli si ribella*, 1977). The appearance of parodies of popular film genres tends to announce their demise. As with the spaghetti western, the rise and fall of the Italian police film within virtually a single decade confirmed this rule.

Italian crime film directors certainly had in mind the elegant models of the French and American film noirs when they worked in this genre; but with respect to film style, the classic noir model had a greater impact upon the neorealist crime films, since both were shot in black and white and relied on the kinds of chiaroscuro lighting effects long associated with this quintessential American or French genre. By the late 1960s through the 1980s, when the *cinema poliziesco* gained popularity, almost every film genre had permanently shifted to Technicolor or other forms of color photography, and Italian directors were more likely to look for models in the Italian *giallo* film or, even more important, in the contemporary Hollywood police procedural and Mafia film, works that emphasized graphic and often gratuitous violence with cynical and even corrupt policemen. One early *poliziesco*, *Red Hot Shot* (*Colpo rovente*, 1969), by Piero Zuffi (1919–2006), a designer turned director who shot only a single film, underscores the crime film's direct link to the *giallo*. The film opens with the familiar black-gloved assassin, preparing a Styrofoam box to hold a pistol to be used in the assassination of a high-placed pharmaceutical company executive who is in reality a drug dealer. Barbara Bouchet, the sexy protagonist of so many Italian *gialli*, plays the victim's daughter, who ends up drugged in a brothel, sent there to die by her father's evil associates. Similar to the *giallo*'s surprise ending, the conclusion of this film reveals the murderer of the drug kingpin to be the investigating New York City detective. Like so many *giallo* casts, *Red Hot Shot* also includes American actors, starlets in various stages of undress, and even faded stars from both American and Italian film history. In this case, Isa Miranda, star of the Fascist era cinema, plays the madam of the brothel, while Edward (Eduardo) Ciannelli portrays an aging crime boss, a role he had performed in 1937 in Lloyd Bacon's *Marked Woman*, where his character, Johnny Vanning, was a thinly disguised Lucky Luciano.

The universal popularity of Francis Ford Coppola's *The Godfather* (1972) and *The Godfather: Part II* (1974) had an impact, particularly upon Sergio Leone's 1984 venture into the crime genre with *Once Upon a Time in America*. Both Coppola and Leone aimed at a certain kind of epic grandeur and historical sweep, but this kind of film required a huge budget, something not typical of the *poliziesco* genre. Hollywood films had a profound influence upon Italian crime films of the period, but most influential were less the "art film" versions by Coppola and Leone than the more commercial "action" films that leftist critics on both sides of the Atlantic would brand as "fascist" in their choice of protagonists—the tough, no-nonsense cops who bent the law in numerous ways, shot to kill, and were politically incorrect. These cop heroes and their underworld opponents appear in a number of tremendously popular Hollywood films that were released in time to influence Italian cop films. The first was Peter Yates's *Bullitt* (1968), starring Steve McQueen as the hard-boiled San Francisco cop who provides the cinema with one of the best car chases ever filmed in that city. William Friedkin's *The French Connection* (1971) and John Frankenheimer's *French Connection II* (1975), both starring Gene Hackman as the tough cop Jimmy "Popeye" Doyle, provided more stirring car chases as well as international drug connections and political corruption. Clint Eastwood, the ultimate spaghetti western hero, traded his Colt pistol for a Smith & Wesson .44 Magnum revolver on the mean streets of San Francisco in Don Siegel's *Dirty Harry* and Ted Post's *Magnum Force*. Eastwood's performance as Inspector "Dirty" Harry Callahan made him a superstar and provided the Italian cinema yet another role model for cops who pursue criminals even if it requires breaking the law. Finally, Michael Winner's *Death Wish* (1974) began a popular series of films (the original spawned four sequels) based on the private war waged against criminals by Paul Kersey, an architect whose wife is murdered by street punks, turning him into a vigilante. Played by Charles Bronson, an actor already famous from his role in Leone's *Once Upon a Time in the West*, this very influential (and much criticized work) popularized the theme of vigilante revenge, a motif that becomes central to the Italian police film.

King of the B's: Fernando Di Leo

Italian *poliziesco* films moved from cult status to international exposure only recently with Quentin Tarantino as their champion and a series of retrospectives of Italian B films at the Venice Film Festival, beginning in 2004.

After years of focusing on either Italian and European auteurs or Hollywood stars, the oldest film festival in the world (began in 1938) finally turned to the commercial genre film with a series called "The Secret History of the Italian Cinema."[2] Its first retrospective, sponsored by the Prada Foundation, the institution funded by Miuccia Prada's fashion house in Milan, boasted as cocurator Tarantino himself, whose own works contain numerous citations from Italian B films, not only the spaghetti western (the object of another Prada-sponsored retrospective at the Venice Film Festival, in 2007) but also the *poliziesco* film. Besides the screening of major films by Di Leo, a man whose death in Italy in 2003 passed virtually unnoticed, Prada also supported the reissue of newly mastered DVDs of his works, complete with new English subtitles. Whether or not there is universal agreement with Tarantino about Di Leo's importance as a director, little doubt remains that his crime films, along with those of such B directors as Stelvio Massi, Massimo Dallamano (1917–76), Umberto Lenzi, Enzo G. Castellari, Damiano Damiani, Sergio Martino, Mario Caiano, and Sergio Sollima (1921–), offer a template for this highly successful genre. His works, which span the entire period of the genre's commercial success, include the following as his most important films: *Naked Violence*, a.k.a. *Sex in the Classroom* (*I ragazzi del massacro*, 1969); *Caliber 9* (*Milano calibro 9*, 1972); *The Italian Connection* (*La mala ordina*, 1972); *The Boss*, a.k.a. *Wipeout!* (*Il boss*, 1973); *The Cop Is Crooked*, a.k.a. *Shoot First, Die Later* (*Il poliziotto è marcio*, 1974); *Kidnap Syndicate* (*La città sconvolta: caccia spietata ai rapitori*, 1975); *Rulers of the City*, a.k.a. *Mr. Scarface* (*I padroni della città*, 1976); *Madness* (*Vacanze per un massacro*, 1980); and *Killer vs. Killers*, a.k.a. *Death Commando* (*Killer contro Killers*, 1985).

Naked Violence is a low-budget shocker that opens with the brutal gang rape and murder of a female teacher during an evening course for troubled teenaged students. The graphic close-ups of this event take place before the credits are run: the violent precredit prologue is one of Di Leo's trademarks. Much of the rest of the film takes place in the interrogation room of Detective Lieutenant Marco Lamberti (Pier Paolo Capponi), whose queries turn up drugs, prostitution, homosexuality, and transvestites before he discovers that a police informant who is also a cross-dresser has such a hold over the young boys who murder and rape their teacher that he bears the ultimate responsibility for her death. Di Leo offers few moral lessons: the one innocent student in the group commits suicide because he is gay, Lamberti complains that the murderer will be released from prison in only a brief time, and justice is certainly not achieved.

Di Leo's next three films, often described inaccurately as a trilogy, are far more interesting and showcase his talents. *Caliber 9* opens with a brilliant prologue that begins with a package of money being transferred from one courier to another, until the criminals making the switches discover that the real cash has been replaced with paper. Subsequently, the film moves backward through various violent scenes as the masterminds of the money transfer torture each of the couriers in turn and then blow the three of them up in a cave with dynamite before the credits appear. In this film, Di Leo has selected his protagonists perfectly. As will be the custom in *poliziesco* films, at least one American actor appears: here, the veteran character actor Lionel Stander, also employed by Sergio Leone and others in spaghetti westerns, plays "the American," the Italian crime boss. Gastone Moschin is Ugo Piazza, the hard-luck antihero who has been sent to prison for four years on a minor charge and whom the American suspects of stealing the money that disappeared in the film's opening sequences. As the Mob boss's second in command, Rocco Musco, Mario Adorf's fine performance anticipates Tommy DeVito, the psychotic personality played by Joe Pesci in Scorsese's *Goodfellas* (1990). Milan at the height of Italy's boom years is the setting for the film, but Di Leo shows us the underside of the "economic miracle"—strip clubs, gangland executions, graphic physical violence, and most particularly Italian institutional inefficiency and corruption. Two policemen of ideologically opposed opinions—Right and Left—supply caustic commentary about the causes of crime in the city. The leftist from the North believes the true criminals are the rich Italian industrialists who export currency abroad to Swiss banks (the particular destination for the packet of cash that is stolen at the film's opening) rather than the petty gangster Ugo Piazza, whereas the right-wing cop from the South just wants to jail anyone breaking the law.

Ugo Piazza continues to deny he heisted the stolen currency, but in point of fact he is the culprit, and he hopes to go away with his girlfriend Nelly Bordon (Barbara Bouchet). Nelly does a stupendous striptease dance in a nightclub where she works—and where the bartender, unbeknownst to Ugo, has replaced him in her affections. Ugo cannot rest easy and retrieve the money as long as the American suspects him of hiding it. Nonetheless, since the gang's modus operandi is laundering cash abroad, another package of cash, transferred among a number of couriers, in an almost exact replica of what occurred at the beginning of the film, disappears as well! With the assistance of an old-time Mafia hit man, Ugo manages to eliminate the American; he retrieves the stolen cash and, in the first twist of the film, dies at the hands of Nelly's secret boyfriend, who shoots Ugo when he brings her the recovered currency. In the shootout, Nelly too is killed, but by Rocco, who has followed Ugo to the apartment and who bludgeons the boyfriend to death, screaming "that man deserves our honor" while the police come in to arrest him as the only survivor. Di Leo's last, sad shot is a close-up of Ugo's still burning cigarette in a solitary ashtray, an apt metaphor for his lonely antiheroic existence.

Caliber 9 shows any heroic potential in organized crime of the type Coppola explored in *The Godfather* has long since passed away in the squalid underworld of petty thieves and psychotic gangsters of modern Milan. *The Italian Connection* continues to explore that city's underworld culture. Now Mario Adorf is cast as a small-time loser named Luca Canali who has been demoted from criminal member of an active gang to pimp. The New York Mob boss Corso (Cyril Cusack) sends two American hit men, played by two iconic Hollywood gangster figures—Henry Silva as Dave Catania and Woody Strode as Frank Webster—to Italy to kill the man who hijacked a shipment of their heroin, the blame for which has been placed on Luca by the Milanese Mob boss Don Vito Tressoldi, played by the Bond veteran Adolfo Celi. In spite of the fact that Luca seems to be a loser, he also is quite clever and manages to survive repeated attempts on his life. Typical of the kind of dialogue and violence in the film is the sequence following Luca's escape from two of Don Vito's men. The New York "professional" Dave Catania tells Don Vito "only a shit surrounds himself with shit" and shoots both men in the legs. Don Vito's response is to up the ante by killing both of his own men, exclaiming, "Now you know I mean more business than you do!"

When Luca's wife and daughter are killed in an attempt to put pressure on him to deliver the heroin he does not have, this act finally pushes Luca over the edge. First he kills the assassin who ran over his family, and then he surprises Don Vito in his office. Before Luca kills him, Don Vito grudgingly admits that Luca is no small-time crook but a real man of respect, and asks that he shoot him with one bullet "and look me in the eyes if you are the

In Di Leo's *The Italian Connection*, the small-time hood Luca Canali dispatches one of two American hitmen sent to Italy to kill him with a huge metal hook used to crush cars in a junkyard. *Credit: DVD*

man I think you are." Finally, in an epic battle in a junkyard, Luca eliminates both American hit men, crushing Dave Catania with a huge metal claw used to pick up crushed junk cars. Di Leo's last shot in the film reminds us of the nihilistic single cigarette at the end of *Caliber 9*. After killing everyone in the film, Luca Canali simply shrugs. It is an ending that lacks heroic dimensions; it offers no hope.

In *The Boss*, Di Leo continues the revenge motif exploited in *The Italian Connection* as well as the discourse about the contrast between the old "men of honor" from the past who, with their professional standards, adhered to a rigid code of gangster ethics (such as not slaying a victim's family, unlike what happened to Luca's wife and daughter) and the new punk gangsters who understand only killing. Set in Palermo, capital of the historic Mafia, this film opens with a sequence depicting a Mafia killer named Nick Lanzetta (Henry Silva) who destroys an entire movie theater with a grenade launcher to kill a number of old Mafia bosses associated with the Attardi family (a total of ten people) as they watch a porn film together. In *The Boss*, Di Leo's critique of Italian institutions becomes quite apparent: one of the police inspectors, Commissioner Torri (Gianni Garko), is actually in the pay of Don Corrasco (Richard Conte), the secret overboss of Palermo's Mafia. Vittorio Caprioli skillfully plays the *questore* of Palermo (the provincial chief of the state-run police), whose cynical remarks about the city, delivered with a southern accent, are worth the admission price of the movie. At one point, the *questore* tells the corrupt cop that Italy is being Vietnamized by Mob violence, while Torri informs him that the rule of law and the rule of the Mafia are similar to the extent that they both bring stability and order.

In Palermo, the ever-present His Excellency—always an unnamed Italian politician—gives orders even to Don Corrasco, while a crooked lawyer, Avvocato Rizzo (Corrado Gaipa), works as a go-between for the criminal and political bosses. Di Leo's portrait of the link between gangsters and politicians is so believable that a well-known political leader of the Christian Democratic Party in Sicily initially sued him for libel before realizing that bringing such a suit would be an obvious sign that he was completely corrupt, since Di Leo had never even thought of linking him to the character of His Excellency in his film. He wisely dropped the suit before anyone looked into his bank accounts! The level of the corruption in the city is highlighted by the fact that no one other than the *questore* realizes that Don Corrasco is the Mob's highest boss. The anti-Mafia commission from Rome remains unaware of his very existence, thanks to the good offices of the corrupt policemen in his pay, such as Torri. Even the Catholic Church seems involved with Don Corrasco's schemes in return for charitable contributions; the Mob boss and Torri actually meet in a courtyard of the cathedral.

Di Leo's portrait of organized crime with its connections to Italian political figures in Palermo is an intricate puzzle. As one boss kills another and takes his place, the real power always remains lodged in the hands of the politicians who, for unknown and ambiguous reasons, protect the gangsters. In collaboration with a friend named Pignataro (Marino Masé), the cold and efficient Lanzetta ultimately organizes the massacre of everyone above him, including the last of the Attardi family and even Don Corrasco himself. On the orders of Rizzo the lawyer, Pignataro tries to eliminate Lanzetta, but the latter is too wary to be tricked so easily and kills Pignataro first. Di Leo ends the film on an inconclusive note. He replaces the traditional "Fine," or "The End," with "Continue," or "To Be Continued," over the screen as the lawyer go-between Rizzo answers the telephone. Is it Lanzetta threatening him, or might it be another order from Rome? The director provides no answer, but the tag "To Be Continued" leaves no doubt that the link between Mob and government will endure forever in Sicily. *The Boss* displays a dazzling array of methods to kill one's opponent, with rapid editing, car chases, gunfights, and everything one could desire from a gangster movie. Unlike the world of Coppola's *The Godfather*, however, the environment of this film has nothing of the heroic. Its protagonists are brutal murderers who can never be trusted and who have no respect for the "rules" followed by a true "man of honor." Di Leo's use of two iconic American actors—Silva and Conte—gives this essentially low-budget film a touch of class.

Kidnap Syndicate continues Di Leo's clever use of foreign actors, with James Mason playing an engineer named Filippini whose son, Antonio, (Francesco Impeciati) is kidnapped along with the son of a much poorer mechanic and former motocross racer, Fabrizio (Marco Liofredi). The instigators of these kidnappings function like a business enterprise: they even hold board meetings in a fancy office with the name Istituto Finanziario Internazionale La Falange. These criminals meet in a corporate boardroom and dress like business executives, not the mobsters they are. When the rich engineer decides to dicker over the amount he is willing to pay for his son's ransom, the kidnappers murder Fabrizio to show they are serious, driving that boy's father, Mario (Luc Merenda), to take his revenge. Cleverly, Mario convinces them he wants to use the ransom he has stolen from the kidnappers to buy into the kidnap syndicate. Once at the meeting, he dispatches the entire crew with a machine gun just as the police arrive to clean up the mess. Merenda, a French actor, would become one of the most popular male leads in the genre, but it is Vittorio Caprioli, as the talkative Police Commissioner Magrini, who steals the show with his cynical, witty remarks (as when he played the questore from *The Boss*) about the difference between rich and poor in Italy.

Rulers of the City combines the revenge motif with an opening sequence that recalls some of the explanatory flashbacks in Sergio Leone's westerns, such as *For a Few Dollars More* or *Once Upon a Time in the West*. In it, a gangster played by the American Jack Palance kills his partner over the loot from a robbery in an old, abandoned slaughterhouse and receives a scar on his face as the man's son throws something at him. Later, we learn that the gangster has become Mr. Scarface, while the boy, Tony (Harry Baer), has become a collector for Scarface's gambling and loan-sharking operations. In reality, however, he is seeking revenge for his father's death years earlier. The entire film builds up to a reckoning of accounts in the same slaughterhouse, where Tony, his friend Rick (Al Cliver), and an over-the-hill mobster named Vincenzo Napoli (Vittorio Caprioli) take part in an enormous shootout. The three friends kill carloads of their opponents in a conclusion that contains some fine comic elements, thanks to the presence of the always-amusing Caprioli. The fact that such graphic and senseless violence can be joined to moments of comic relief raises moral questions about the world that Di Leo creates, but it is a world that several decades later morphs into the comic violence typical of Tarantino's *Pulp Fiction* (1994). The amoral and nonjudgmental quality of his fictional universe must certainly be one of the elements of Di Leo's cinema that appeals to the American director.

Di Leo's *Madness* is something of an anomaly, since it is as clearly an imitation of Wes Craven's *The Last House on the Left* as is Aldo Lado's thriller *Night Train Murders* (see chapter 12). Far more interesting is Di Leo's last film, *Killer vs. Killers*, a loose remake of John Huston's classic film noir *The Asphalt Jungle* (1950). Two members of a team hired to steal the formula for a synthetic fuel that is potentially priceless even bear the names of two of the actors in the Huston original: Sterling (Henry Silva) and Jaffe (Fernando Cerulli). The film belongs to the caper subgenre of the crime film and easily divides into two parts. In the first, a small team of specialists in various criminal activities is formed under the orders of His Excellency, the mastermind from Monte Carlo who arranges for the theft. In the second, when the group pulls off the impossible and grabs the formula, His Excellency then sets out to eliminate them all. After three of the group are killed, Sterling and Ferrari (Albert Janni), the driver whose comical personality stands in unexpected contrast to the professional seriousness of Sterling, manage to take on carloads of assassins sent from His Excellency's office, Petroleum, Inc. (Sterling employs a bazooka to eliminate his enemies.) As one might expect from a film that embodies Di Leo's nihilism, the concluding gunfight results in Sterling's death and Ferrari's paradoxical survival. Throughout the film, the only moral code of values exhibited by the protagonists is that of the professional crime figure. Sterling constantly complains about a contemporary lack of professionalism in the criminals around him, particularly apparent in the frivolous attitude toward his work typical of Ferrari. Di Leo's film ends on this note, as Sterling says to Ferrari, "Now you're a professional!" and then dies. The film offers no more uplifting message than this one. Di Leo's protagonists in this and his other films clearly must have caught the attention of Quentin Tarantino for their nihilism and their complete rejection of any idealistic notions of justice. Nonetheless, they certainly lack the tongue-in-cheek postmodern humor and metacinematic citations that lift Tarantino's films from the mundane to an entirely higher intellectual level.

Umberto Lenzi

With many film titles that include the names of specific geographical locations, Italian crime films clearly aimed to endow criminal activities taking place in specific Italian cities with an enhanced realism and immediacy. Localizing the setting heightened suspense in the *poliziesco* by emphasizing crimes happening right outside the doorsteps of the spectators, who screened the movies in their local neighborhood theaters (many of which still existed in the early 1970s). Examples of such localization include Michele Massimo Tarantini's *Napoli si ribella* (literally, "Naples Rebels"); *Milano violenta* (1976; literally, "Violent Milan"), by Mario Caiano; and *Torino violenta* (1977; literally, "Violent Turin"), by Carlo Ausino (1938–). Their respective English-language titles are *A Man Called Magnum*; *Bloody Payroll*, a.k.a. *Commando Terror*; and *Double Game*, but those do not fully express the uniquely time-and-place-bound character of the Italian *poliziesco* film. This quality remains less apparent in the more ideological, metaphor-driven political films of the *cinema di impegno civile* (see chapter 8), practiced by directors such as Petri or Rosi, considered closer to art film auteurs. Location may be seen in the Italian titles of some of Lenzi's *polizieschi—Gang War in Milan* (*Milano rovente*, 1973); *Almost Human* (*Milano odia: la polizia non può sparare*, 1974); *Death Dealers*, a.k.a. *Violent Naples* (*Napoli violenta*, 1976); *Assault with a Deadly Weapon* (*Roma a mano armata*, 1976). Still others do not name a location—*Free Hand for a Tough Cop*, a.k.a. *Tough Cop* (*Il trucido e lo sbirro*, 1976); *The Cynic, the Rat, and the Fist* (*Il cinico, l'infame, il violento*, 1977); and *Brothers Till We Die* (*La banda del gobbo*, 1978). *Almost Human* and *Free Hand for a Tough Cop* star the spaghetti western actor Tomas Milian and the American crime film icon Henry Silva. *The Cynic, the Rat, and the Fist* employs another male lead popular in this genre—Maurizio Merli (1940–89), reprising a role he played in *Assault with a Deadly Weapon*—along with the veteran expatriate American actor John Saxon, known for his role in one of the films that initiated the craze for the Italian thriller genre, Bava's *The Girl Who Knew Too Much*.

The mixed quality of Lenzi's films, typical of virtually every genre director's works, marks three of his best-known works: *Almost Human, Death Dealers*, and *Free Hand for a Tough Cop*. The first film contains what Tomas Milian has always considered his best performance in any film genre—that of a totally despicable, violent, sadistic, and cowardly killer named Giulio Sacchi, who organizes the kidnapping of a rich man's daughter and leaves a trail of bodies behind him before he is stopped by Inspector Walter Grandi (Henry Silva in an unusual role as a policeman rather than a murderer). Lenzi himself describes *Almost Human* as indebted to the French *série noire* crime films of the period, particularly such films by the director Jacques Becker (1906–60), who made such classics as *Grisbi* (*Touchez pas au grisbi*, 1954) and *The Night Watch* (*Le Trou*, 1960). Whatever Lenzi's inspiration, *Almost Human's* convincing portrait of a low-life criminal represents one of the most complex villains in the entire repertoire, and Milian's performance belies the roles he often played in films unworthy of his considerable talents. The film relies less on the elements that made some of his other roles popular (special effects, dazzling car chases) and develops the character of this villain far more effectively than those in most Italian crime films. In this regard, the character of Giulio Sacchi stands closer to the psychotic killers of the Italian *giallo* than to the traditionally drawn urban criminals from the North of Italy or the classic Italian Mafiosi of the South. The musical composer Ennio Morricone contributed a memorable and pounding sound track, while the screenwriter Ernesto Gastaldi demonstrated why his scripts for crime films were always regarded as among the best Italy produced in this period. Partly because Sacchi's psyche is so well developed in the film, the film's graphic violence makes more sense than the habitually gratuitous kind so typical of the B film in a variety of genres.

Ultimately, without a gun in his hand and as a helpless victim, Sacchi is a coward; his violent impulses also have a sexual component. After kidnapping his target, he and his two accomplices take refuge in an upper-class home and sequester its inhabitants, first forcing them to engage in oral sex with each of the gang and then stringing them up to a chandelier before murdering them all. Even a man in the house is forced to fellate Sacchi himself, who ghoulishly grins and announces that "I am in favor of sexual equality" while the other two women are forced to service his accomplices in the same fashion. Sacchi's psychotic character leads him to believe that killing all witnesses to his crimes makes it virtually impossible for Inspector Grandi to arrest him. Because very few Italian *polizieschi* from the 1970s pay any attention to fingerprints or forensic evidence from scientific tests (DNA analysis would come later), and police investigators almost always depend upon eyewitness testimony—which gangsters can easily destroy by threatening ordinary people—it is understandable that Inspector Grandi cannot obtain enough evidence to arrest Sacchi, and even runs into opposition from his superiors. Driven by his thirst for justice, Grandi feels he has only one choice: he personally condemns Sacchi to death and shoots him mercilessly on the top of a garbage dump in the suburbs, an appropriate metaphor for Sacchi's criminal's nature. Part of the rubbish of contemporary Italy, Sacchi can be swept into the dustbin only by an indignant representative of the law, who must break it in order to preserve social order.

Lenzi's *Free Hand for a Tough Cop* introduces one of Milian's most popular characters, a kind-hearted thief with a penchant for witty sayings in Roman dialect. He is called "Er Monnezza," whose name may best be translated as "Garbage," or "Trash," a reference to his unkempt and generally disreputable appearance. Lenzi's opening sequence during the film's credits seems at first a mistake—a shot of John Ford country, a stunningly beautiful sequence shot at Monument Valley, from a Western film. The audience learns immediately that it comes from a film being watched by Er Monnezza and others in a Roman jail. This sequence seems to be Lenzi's metacinematic salute to the link between the spaghetti western and the *poliziesco*. At his wit's end over a kidnapped child who will die if not given her medicine, Inspector Antonio Sarti (Claudio Cassinelli) decides to employ criminals to combat the kidnappers led by a murderous villain named Brescianelli (Henry Silva in a role much more typical for him). Er Monnezza and Sarti eventually triumph, saving the young girl and killing all her kidnappers, but the film's almost nonexistent narrative plot and even a lack of exciting special effects or action scenes make *Free Hand for a Tough Cop* hard to screen, except for the occasional relief of Er Monnezza's one-liners. Nevertheless, this film repeats the habitual argument that emerges as characteristic of the Italian crime film. Since governmental institutions are ineffective or even corrupt and cannot protect the citizen, police must break the law in order to obtain justice.

Eventually, Milian portrays not only Er Monnezza but his twin brother crime boss, "Il Gobbo," or "the Hunchback," in *Brothers till We Die*, an unusual double role. Exploiting his success at comic roles in the crime genre, Milian then shot no fewer than eleven comic police films, all completely forgettable and all directed by Bruno Corbucci (1931–96), brother of the spaghetti western director Sergio Corbucci. Like the popular Piedone/Flatfoot comic crime series created to exploit the box-office appeal of Bud Spencer and transfer it from the comic spaghetti western to the comic police film, Corbucci's highly profitable but truly B films devoted to Inspector Nico Giraldi were extremely popular among the diminishing Italian male audiences of the period, before the franchise died the usual natural death of overexposure. A representative sample of some of these titles would include *The Cop in Blue Jeans* (*Squadra antiscippo*, 1976), *A Crime in a Chinese Restaurant* (*Delitto al ristorante cinese*, 1981), and *Cop in Drag* (*Delitto al Blue Gay*, 1984).

If *Almost Human* was closer to a study in psychotic behavior than an action thriller, and *Free Hand for a Tough Cop* depended so heavily upon wisecracks in dialect that it was virtually impossible to export it profitably, Lenzi's *Death Dealers* contains all the best elements of the most successful *polizieschi* dramas and shows Lenzi to be a highly competent director of action films. It displays an almost endless series of well-paced action sequences, superb car chases, and respectable production values in special effects, even with miserably minimal budgets compared to those for even mediocre Hollywood crime films. It also boasts a superb sound track composed by Franco Micalizzi (1939–), who first became known for a track composed for the original Trinity western and then contributed music to a number of Italian films in this genre. Lenzi provides the obligatory Hollywood actors in decline: Barry Sullivan as the General, a criminal mastermind in Naples, and John Saxon as Francesco Capuano, a financier of the Mob who betrays the General. After the two gangsters touch off a gang war, the tough cop Commissioner Betti, played by Maurizio Merli, exploits the conflict. Hollywood action films such as Paul Greengrass's *The Bourne Ultimatum* (2007) have demonstrated conclusively by winning three Oscars that action films with virtually no real story or script can nevertheless win over audiences by substituting dramatic editing and sound for anything even resembling an interesting story. In *Death Dealers*, Lenzi shows that he can achieve almost the same results with a small percentage of Hollywood's expense.

Death Dealers does not allow its audience to relax for a moment, moving rapidly from one action sequence to another without pause. The key to Lenzi's success in this film is his skillful use of the city of Naples itself as a backdrop for stunning motorcycle- and car chases through the crowded streets and marketplaces of the old city. One of Betti's targets is a vicious bank robber named Casagrande (Elio Zamuto), who is out of prison on parole and must sign a register in Betti's police station each day at precisely the same time. Casagrande concocts a clever scheme to rob a bank a few minutes before his obligatory appointment and then hop on a swift motorcycle, whose skilled driver (played by an actual Italian champion racer) will deliver him to the police station so soon after the robbery that his very presence at the station will constitute his alibi. Betti figures out Casagrande's scheme and sets out by car on a parallel course to intercept him on the motorcycle, thereby providing the proof of Casagrande's guilt that Betti's superiors continuously deny and the criminal's lawyers habitually refute. Merli performed his own stunt driving, and Lenzi mounted a camera on the motorcycle passenger's thigh so that the rapid trip through Naples would be captured "live." Thus, Lenzi cuts back and forth between Betti in a fast car and Casagrande on a motorcycle, weaving around in breathtaking defiance of gravity and any regard for safety. They literally crash into each other, touching off another equally gripping chase through real Neapolitan outdoor markets peopled by nonactors startled by the sudden appearance of this frantic chase, shot by the director from a number of cameras placed on balconies or hidden in the crowd. By accident, a traditional Neapolitan funeral carriage showed up during the shooting and is incorporated skillfully into the sequence. Then, as if this were not enough, a final sequence shows Betti chasing Casagrande inside one of the celebrated inclined railways in Naples, the *funicolare*: Casagrande takes a female hostage and pushes her face against the *funicolare* carriage in descent, all the while shooting his machine gun at Betti, perched on the top of the car, before the policeman shoots him. Once again, Merli shot the sequence without a stuntman, lying only fifty centimeters from the electrically charged wires that operate the *funicolare* car. The series of sequences that begin with the parallel car-motorcycle chase, moves through the marketplace, and concludes with Casagrande's death on the *funicolare* is as memorable as any Hollywood chase ever was.

Known for his use of graphic violence in all his genre films, Lenzi provides some memorable images in *Death Dealers*: one criminal impales himself upon a fencepost while trying to escape Betti's clutches; the General smashes the skull of an undercover cop by tying him down in a bowling alley and rolling a perfect strike to his head. And the film's conclusion continues the now classic solution to the policeman's investigation. Betti arranges a meeting of Capuano and the General, shoots the General, and places the pistol in Capuano's hands to frame him. Once again, only by taking the law in one's own hands can one achieve justice.

Damiano Damiani

Damiani certainly established his credentials as a politically engaged director with his 1966 western *A Bullet for the General*. His *The Day of the Owl*, a.k.a. *Mafia* (*Il giorno della civetta*, 1968), based on a 1961 Leonardo Sciascia Mafia novel and scripted by the veteran political-cinema scriptwriter Ugo Pirro, might be seen as an early example not only of the political film but also the *poliziesco* genre. Three of his films rank among the best examples of explicitly political spin on the *poliziesco*: *Confessions of a Police Captain* (*Confessione di un commissario di polizia al procuratore della repubblica*, 1971), *L'istruttoria è chiusa: dimentichi* (1971; literally, "The Investigation Is Closed: Forget It"), *How to Kill a Judge* (*Perché si uccide un magistrato*, 1974), and *The Sicilian Connection* (*Pizza Connection*, 1985). In 1984, Damiani directed a television miniseries entitled *La Piovra* (literally, "The Octopus," a slang term for organized crime, the tentacles of which reach everywhere), starring Michele Placido. Although never imported into the United States, his miniseries and the numerous sequels that it inspired over the next decade were exported widely, and in its impact upon Italian audiences, *La Piovra* might well be compared to that of David Chase's *The Sopranos* in America.

Confessions of a Police Captain and *How to Kill a Judge* demonstrate both the strengths and weaknesses of Damiani's particular approach to the crime film. *A Bullet for the General* was an engaging western first, and only secondly a political tract on the methods employed by America in dealing with Mexico and the Third World; Damiani's approach to the crime film

In Damiani's *Confessions of a Police Captain,* the victims of the mob (including this naked young lady who was a dangerous witness) end up in the concrete pillars of the construction industry, a mobbed-up business. *Credit: DVD*

is somewhat heavier handed and almost pedagogical in nature. In the first film, the jaded policeman Commissioner Bonavia (Martin Balsam) seeks to put away the crime boss Ferdinand, not only for his present crimes but also, and even more important, for his brutal murder of a union organizer named Rizzo years earlier, in his ascent to power. Using the kinds of flashbacks employed by Francesco Rosi in *Salvatore Giuliano,* Damiani dramatizes this early crime, cutting back and forth between the event in the past and the present explanation of Di Brosio's crimes to a young, idealistic magistrate (district attorney) from the North named Traini (Franco Nero). The high point in the flashback sequences depicts a contest of wills between the organizer and the future crime boss. Shot in a public square, Rizzo lies bleeding on the ground in front of Di Brosio, but he continues to stare the criminal in the eye with an unfaltering gaze until finally Di Brosio leaves the square, vanquished. Ultimately, as so many other honest Italian policemen in the film conclude, the justice system is not only inefficient but corrupt and in the service of the criminals. After Bonavia confronts Di Brosio in a restaurant with his henchmen and shoots him dead, he turns himself in, only to be murdered in prison. His death, however, convinces Traini that Bonavia had been right, and the film closes with the district attorney staring down a high-placed magistrate on a staircase at the Palace of Justice in the same way Rizzo had earlier done with Di Brosio.

On the surface, *How to Kill a Judge* concerns the Mafia's ability to murder even the highest and most honest judges in Sicily. Damiani's protagonist, a journalist and film director named Giacomo Solaris (Franco Nero), is shooting a movie about a corrupt judge that apparently refers to Judge Traini

(Marco Guglielmi), who is later brutally murdered. While everyone in the city assumes the Mafia is responsible for the murder, and even Giacomo believes it at first, the director discovers that the judge was actually murdered by his wife, Antonia (Françoise Fabian), and her lover, Dr. Valgardeni (Giorgio Cerioni). Paradoxically, this revelation makes nobody happy. Giacomo angers his journalist colleagues, who had planned a sensational Mafia scoop; he upsets his friends in the police because they had followed the wrong clues and failed to solve the case, leaving it to an amateur; and worst of all, the Mafiosi and their political and judicial cronies originally accused of the murder can now breathe easier for a bit and continue their corruption and influence peddling in Palermo. They even smile at Solaris at the end of the film, leaving Damiani's audience to consider whether or not the truth in this case was more important than slapping a number of influential criminals with jail terms.

A Constellation of Crime Film Directors: Sollima, Dallamano, Massi, Castellari, Tarantini, and Ausino

By the early 1970s, the generic boundaries of the Italian *poliziesco* were reasonably well defined, and such seminal directors as Di Leo, Lenzi, and Damiani had in large measure fixed the rules of this game. Numerous other directors turned out Italian crime films of varying quality over a decade or more until the genre gradually disappeared as a recognizable fad in the early 1980s. Films that still merit attention in this large and uneven collection of films include the following: *Revolver*, a.k.a. *Blood in the Streets* (*Revolver*, 1973), by Sergio Sollima; *What Have They Done to Your Daughters?* a.k.a. *The Police Want Help* (*La polizia chiede aiuto*, 1974) and *Colt 38 Special Squad* (*Quelli della calibro 38*, 1976), by Massimo Dallamano; *Emergency Squad* (*Squadra volante*, 1974), *The Last Round*, and *Convoy Busters* (*Un poliziotto scomodo*, 1978), by Stelvio Massi; *High Crime* (*La polizia incrimina, la legge assolve*, 1973), *Street Law*, a.k.a. *The Citizen Rebels* (*Il cittadino si ribella*, 1974), *The Big Racket* (*Il grande racket*, 1976), and *The Heroin Busters* (*La via della droga*, 1977), by Enzo G. Castellari; *Bloody Payroll*, by Mario Caiano; *A Man Called Magnum*, by Massimo Tarantini; *Double Game*, by Carlo Ausino; *Gambling City* (*La città gioca d'azzardo*, 1975), by Sergio Martino; and *Contraband* (*Luca il contrabbandiere*, 1980), by Lucio Fulci. A rapid consideration of a representative sampling of these films will show how the *poliziesco* genre developed during this brief decade before more complicated works involving crime after the 1980s eventually transformed the fad of such B films.

Sollima's *Revolver* aims at a delineation of character infrequently found in this genre. A veteran of writing numerous scripts for the sword and sandal epics, as well as the direction of spaghetti westerns and of espionage films imitating the success of the James Bond series, Sollima had the original notion of juxtaposing a lawman and a criminal. When gangsters kidnap Anna (Agostina Belli), the wife of Vito Cipriani (Oliver Reed), the director of an Italian prison, they demand the release of one of the prisoners, Milo Ruiz (Fabio Testi), to return her safely. With an excellent musical score by Ennio Morricone and impressive stunts done by Testi himself (who had worked eight years as a stuntman while studying at the university), Sollima's direction emphasizes elegant violence with long tracking shots, carefully choreographed fight scenes similar to martial arts encounters, and intelligent dialogue. Although neither Cipriani nor Ruiz understands it, the criminals want to kill Ruiz because he is the only person alive who knows where the body of his friend and partner in crime is buried. As long as this body remains undiscovered, the French police will continue to believe that it was he was who committed a political assassination in France and will investigate no further. Thus, Ruiz must be silenced in order to protect the high-placed instigators of that assassination. Despite the fact that Cipriani and Ruiz stand on opposite sides of the law, the policeman and the bandit become friends, and in effect *Revolver* turns into a buddy movie. Nevertheless the hidden and high-placed political forces behind the assassination decide that Cipriani has only one choice: he must eliminate Ruiz or his wife will be killed, and his complicity in Ruiz's death will guarantee his future silence. Cipriani's reluctant compliance leads to the final scene of the film, in which he reports a completely fabricated version of events to the authorities while his horrified wife (who knows the truth), wordlessly, by her facial expression, registers her disgust with his abandonment of his moral values. What began as a typical plot of the *poliziesco* genre—a cop seeking revenge—develops into something far more disturbing.

One interesting point may be made about the film's title. Very few Italian policemen or criminals employ revolvers. Beretta automatic pistols are their weapons of choice, and Cipriani is no exception in this film, when he kills Ruiz with a clip-loaded automatic forced upon him. The title of Dallamano's excellent *Colt 38 Special Squad* calls attention to the unexpected use of the revolving cylinder handgun among Italian cops and robbers. At the very time many American law enforcement officials and the armed forces were adopting the very popular Beretta 7.65mm automatic because of its firepower and the additional supply of ammunition in its large clip, a special group of policemen in Dallamano's film are equipped with old-fashioned revolvers, possibly another homage to the link between the spaghetti western and the Italian *poliziesco*.

Like Sollima, Massimo Dallamano had worked in other popular genre films before making crime films. He had been a cinematographer for Sergio Leone on the two *Dollars* films, and the plot of his crime film *What Have They Done to Your Daughters?* owes a great deal to his earlier

giallo, What Have They Done to Solange? (*Cosa avete fatto a Solange?*,
1972), since both treat the touchy subject of sex crimes linked to adolescent girls in a private school. In the *giallo*, a teacher suspected of committing a series of gruesome murders decides to uncover the real culprit (the
classic *giallo* plot), an individual who turns out to be motivated by the
expected psychological defects of most thriller assassins. But Dallamano's
What Have They Done to Your Daughters? departs from the *giallo* skepti-
cism of the police and is one of the very few films made during the 1970s
that might well be identified as a form of the police procedural, a plot
structure extremely popular in Hollywood films and British or American
television, including an uncharacteristic interest in scientific forensic
investigation. What initially appears to be an adolescent suicide turns out
to be the first of several young girls killed by a group attempting to cover
up their having taken part in an adolescent prostitution ring. One of the
policemen in the investigation, Inspector Valentini (Mario Adorf), discovers that even his own daughter has participated! Eventually a number
of adults, including a psychiatrist who treated the young girls and even
a government minister, are implicated in the ring; but the heroic Inspector Silvestri (Claudio Cassinelli) and Assistant District Attorney Vittoria
Stori (Giovanna Ralli) are ultimately blocked, by political interference at
the highest levels in Rome, from arresting the big shots behind it. Unlike
so many of the lesser films in the crime genre, Dallamano's work is well
paced, skillfully shot, and characterized by a fine script with good dialogue, all packaged in a suspense-filled narrative. The police procedural
aspect of the film provides the kind of shocking information concerning
the murders that would have been censored in an American film of the
same period: the first poor girl to be found dead (killed, not a victim of
suicide) is reported to be filled with sperm in all her bodily orifices and
stomach and to be pregnant at the age of fifteen. Dallamano, however,
boldly rejects the view that such children are totally innocent even though
they all come from "good" families. During an interrogation, another
underage girl arrogantly and defiantly responds to Silvestri's questions
with the dismissive comment, "What a lot of talk about four screwings!"
Disturbing physical evidence continues to pop up throughout the story,
always presented in a matter-of-fact manner. Unlike most violence in
crime films of the period, Dallamano usually leaves it off camera, but one
private detective is decapitated, and later his body appears on an autopsy
table, having been sliced up into different parts by the assassin employed
by the prostitute ring's operators. This unknown individual carries a
butcher's hatchet and dresses in dark, black motorcycle leathers with his
head covered by a full-face helmet—details obviously connecting Dallamano's crime film to his earlier interest in the conventions of the *giallo*.
As in *Revolver*, powerful and evil forces in *What Have They Done to Your*

Daughters? control the reins of government. These forces, whom one of the criminals identifies as "saints in paradise," protect the real malefactors and stymie the honest investigators.

At times, such policemen refuse to be stopped by political interference. In Stelvio Massi's *Emergency Squad*, Inspector Tommaso Ravelli (Tomas Milian) of Interpol stays on the job, after his wife was killed accidentally in a robbery, only in order to find the killer and seek revenge. In this film, the impact of *Dirty Harry* upon Ravelli's character is very evident, but Massi actually anticipates the ending of *The French Connection II* (1975), where "Popeye" Doyle executes the French criminal mastermind the Frog at the dock of the port of Marseilles. The villain of this film, like those in the two *French Connection* blockbusters, also hails from Marseilles and is called Il Marsigliese (the Man from Marseilles; masterfully played by Gastone Moschin). Among other interesting features of the film are slow-motion sequences of violence indebted to Sam Peckinpah—two such scenes juxtapose the accidental death of Ravelli's wife with Ravelli's assassination of the Man from Marseilles at the dock just as he is about to escape by boat to Tunisia. Ravelli himself recalls Sergio Leone's taciturn spaghetti western hero (Clint Eastwood) with the unlit Toscano cigar hanging from his lips, dominating the last shot of the film even after he has executed Moschin's character, thrown away his badge, and surrendered. In fact, in an interview included on the DVD of this film, Milian asserts that transferring the spaghetti western antihero from his horse to a squad car and exchanging a modern automatic pistol such as the Italian Beretta for the Colt 45 created the Italian *poliziesco* genre. In both genres, revenge serves as one of the most important plot devices throughout their short-lived development.

Not only policemen but also private citizens in the *poliziesco* world sometimes lose control when faced with rampant, unpunished criminal activities. Films such as Enzo G. Castellari's *Street Law* investigate this phenomenon, owing an obvious debt to the impact of *Death Wish* and Charles Bronson's performance in what became a five-film franchise. Perhaps its alternate title, *The Citizen Rebels* (which literally translates the Italian), is more apt, since the film depicts an upper-class professional named Carlo Antonelli (Franco Nero) who does an extremely poor job of taking the law into his own hands. Castellari's direction features all of the expected car chases, and like Maurizio Merli and Fabio Testi, the athletic Nero does virtually all his own stunts. (Indeed, one of the most attractive elements of the *poliziesco* genre lies in the well-paced stunts performed by its principal actors. Hence Castellari and many other crime film directors always preferred large interior spaces, such as abandoned warehouses or slaughterhouses, in which to bring their films to an exciting and violent climax.) Although some critics attacked Castellari, as they did the director of *Death Wish*, as a right-wing cryptofascist for showing a vigilante in action, the two films found resonance both in Italy

In Castellari's *Street Law,* criminals driving an improbable Ford Mustang chase Carlo.
Credit: CSC

and America during a period of exploding and visible crime. In Italy, *Street Law* was the box-office champion for a number of months. Castellari's directorial style featured numerous zoom shots, handheld cameras for action sequences, slow-motion violence, and frequent car chases (including the memorable one of Franco Nero attempting to run away from a Ford Mustang, an apparent homage to Steve McQueen's famous car in *Bullitt*). What no doubt irritated left-wing critics who attacked *Street Law* was the fact that the single thing moving Carlo Antonelli to act as a vigilante is a framed poster from the partisan war against the Nazis, a legacy from his partisan father. Its capital letters ITALIANI RIBELLATEVI! urge his countrymen to rebel against their oppressors in 1944, and the sight of this poster in his living room shames Antonelli to do the same in 1974.

Castellari's subsequent *Heroin Busters* profits from good acting by Fabio Testi and David Hemmings as a pair of cops attempting to halt a flourishing drug traffic ring operating with the approval of a high-placed official at Leonardo da Vinci–Fiumicino Airport in Rome. Although the film's fast-paced action begins on a didactic note, with endless and boring scenes of the international scope of drug trafficking throughout the entire world, Castellari finally offers his audience dramatic car chases and even an airplane chase designed to satisfy the most demanding of action-film audiences.

A Man Called Magnum by Tarantini highlights the acting talents of Luc Merenda, the Frenchman who joined Fabio Testi, Franco Nero, and Maurizio Merli as the principal actors in the *poliziesco* genre. The English title is inexplicable, since the Italian title, which translates as "Naples Rebels," describes the film more aptly; moreover, Merenda's character, Inspector Dario Mauri, bears no resemblance to the main character of the popular American television show *Magnum P.I.* starring Tom Selleck, shown on the Italian small screen. (Like the confusion between revolvers and automatic pistols, English titles for Italian genre films sometimes raise puzzling questions.) One of this film's most interesting features juxtaposes the character and mannerisms of a tough cop from northern Italy (Mauri) with a wise-cracking local policeman, Sergeant Nicola Capece, played by the veteran Neapolitan comic actor Enzo Cannavale (1928–2011). Tarantini's camera style, which also displays a number of interesting close-ups of criminal faces with distinctive southern Italian features, may owe a debt to Sergio Leone's similar stylistic preoccupation with faces in his westerns. While the film's plot seems confusing during its opening, eventually it becomes clear that the story involves a drug war between a gang boss named Domenico Laurenzi (Claudio Gora) and various of his underbosses who are trying to betray him. One original element of Tarantini's plot involves a child's drawings and furtive telephone calls directed to Inspector Mauri which warn of forthcoming gangster activities linked to Laurenzi, tips that we discover are provided by Laurenzi's adopted daughter. Tarantini's visual style privileges low-angle shots (often positioned upward near the gear shift during dramatic car chases, something Tarantini obviously liked to present); he also places his cameras at tire level or on car fenders to make the scenes more dramatic. In one memorable sequence, Mauri, in a squad car, follows the commuter train around Naples, the famous "Circonvallazione Vesuviana" service running around the major tourist attractions, eventually stopping the train by driving onto the tracks. The chase then continues through a Neapolitan market and features numerous handheld cameras as well as stationary cameras mounted at various locations (particularly on balconies overlooking the market). It offers a memorable journey through many of the most characteristic sights in this remarkable city. In a dramatic ending to the film, Laurenzi dies at the hand of one of his underlings, Bonino (Ferdinando Murolo), who kidnaps Luisa, the little girl who has tipped off Mauri on numerous previous occasions. After a final showdown with Bonino, resulting in the gangster's death at Mauri's capable hands, Luisa is rescued. While *A Man Called Magnum* certainly shows us a world of organized crime protected by higher political figures, Tarantini's focus remains solidly upon the figure of the heroic and incorruptible policeman, rather than upon the corruptive interplay of organized crime and political bosses.

Released a year after *A Man Called Magnum*, *Convoy Busters*, by Stelvio Massi, actually contains no convoys (any more than there is a character named Magnum in Tarantini's film). Its Italian title, literally meaning "an inconvenient cop," is a far better description of Massi's film that stars

Maurizio Merli as Commissioner Olmi, a cousin of Dirty Harry in his tough character and ruthless but sometimes illegal methods. The first half of the film is set in crime-infested Rome, where Olmi's tactics eventually result in his accidental killing of a civilian after his fanatic attempts to arrest a diamond smuggler named Degan (Massimo Serato) at the Rome airport. Olmi's sometimes violent approach to lawbreakers nevertheless derives from the political coverage such criminals enjoy from corrupt judges and politicians. After Degan's son confesses to the smuggling to protect his father, a car carrying him to jail is ambushed and the Carabinieri guards are murdered; but Olmi pursues the criminals with a helicopter and single-handedly kills two crooks and then Degan's son from the air, in a sequence that can only remind the audience of Hitchcock's famous crop-dusting plane chase sequence in *North by Northwest*. After Degan escapes to Zurich through a judge's warning, Olmi gives up the fight against urban crime and transfers to a small village by the sea, Civitanova Marche, where he intends to stay out of trouble and falls in love with Anna (Olga Karlatos), a schoolteacher with whom he hopes to spend the rest of his more tranquil life. When drug smugglers take Anna and her students hostage, Olmi dusts off the pistol he had hoped never to use in this quiet town and dispatches four of them before throwing his badge away at the conclusion of the film. In Rome, he was unappreciated as a tough, honest cop, and in the provinces he proves unable to escape the ubiquitous presence of organized crime and violence.

Carlo Ausino's *Double Game* appears toward the end of the genre's popularity, and it reflects the loss of energy that eventually overtakes a dying film genre. George Hilton, the star of many Italian *gialli*, plays Inspector Ugo Moretti, a tough cop in Turin's most violent decade. He is also the Avenger, a vigilante who kills criminals in cold blood. Moretti's equally frustrated colleague, Inspector Danieli (Emanuel Cannarsa), stands for the other kind of justice—not vigilante revenge but due process of law. The film fizzles out in a totally confusing plot, an incomprehensible script, and an unmotivated shootout between Moretti and Danieli that the totally inept Danieli surprisingly wins. This conclusion is hardly a stirring argument that honest cops with the support of judges and politicians may pursue justice. Lucio Fulci's *Contraband*, one of the last of the *polizieschi*, already announces in its gory scenes of physical violence a transition to the horror films that would make Fulci a cult figure in the 1980s–90s (see chapter 10).

The End of the Classic *Poliziesco* and the Rise of a More Complex Italian Crime Film

In spite of the praise heaped upon the Italian *poliziesco* by such figures as Quentin Tarantino, its heyday was shorter than that of the more popular spaghetti western, and its impact upon international cinema was less profound. Still, the more than one hundred police films made reflected the very troubled decade in Italian society from which they emerged, one characterized (and occasionally overcharacterized) by drug dealing, terrorism, and a sharp rise in violent street crime. The classic *poliziesco* of the 1970s embodies an almost universal suspicion of the very social institutions charged with protecting Italian society from criminal violence. (Only a few decades later, in the 1990s, this contempt for the "forces of order," to use the Italians' term for law enforcement, would be replaced in large measure, even in the regions plagued by endemic organized crime, by increased respect for martyred judges and policemen who had died battling either the Mafia in Sicily or other similar miscreants in Naples or Calabria.) Italian police films, with few exceptions, replaced the gunslinging loner of the spaghetti western with an equally aggressive urban policeman fighting crime with what were often illegal means and even vigilante violence. Popular Hollywood police films of the period certainly provided an excuse for such plots, but the kind of institutional suspicion common in Italy during the 1970s found a direct expression in such *polizieschi*. Later Italian crime films would present a far more nuanced treatment of organized crime in the peninsula.

The rise and fall of the classic genre in the 1970s coincides with dramatic changes in the very fabric of the Italian film industry. Between 1974 and 1976, court decisions resulted in the deregulation of Italian public television, the end of the RAI's monopoly, and the sudden rise of numerous local private television stations. Between 1968 and 1981, local TV stations grew in number from 68 to 808. Eventually Mediaset, a corporation founded and owned by Silvio Berlusconi, came to rival the structure of Italian public media with its three large television channels, ownership of Italian newspapers and periodicals, and investment in movie production. Berlusconi, who in 1990 married the actress Veronica Lario (mentioned in chapter 12), would go on to become Italian prime minister several times as founder of Forza Italia, and leader of the Center-Right political coalition in Italy. The impact of this sudden rise of nonmonopoly private television led to a disastrous drop in cinema revenues, from 455 to 374 million lire in 1976–77, and another drop to 276 million lire in revenue in 1979. Even more serious was the virtual destruction of the chain of film theaters in Italy, from eleven thousand moviehouses in the peninsula in 1975 to a little more than five thousand in 1984. Since censorship was virtually nonexistent and hard-core films often constituted the mainstay of private television fare during the very late hour evening and the early morning, many theaters were also turned into pornographic film venues. These *luci rosse* or "red-light" theaters certainly attracted an entirely different kind of clientele from the first-run moviehouses of previous decades, and they prevented any investment in new technology that might upgrade the moviegoing experience inside Italy's very outmoded film theaters.

Nonetheless, detective fiction in Italy was developing a sophistication in the latter part of the twentieth century that surely had an influence upon the cinema. Films about cops and robbers would eventually number among the most interesting works from the 1980s to the present, and the door to this far more serious approach to the genre was opened by the greatest of Italian western directors, Sergio Leone, in his *Once Upon a Time in America*. Damiano Damiani's internationally acclaimed 1984 television series *La Piovra* launched a television franchise whose subsequent miniseries (ten in all) ran until 2001. Italy's best young directors, all brought up on a diet of traditional American and French detective novels plus an infusion of newly discovered indigenous Italian detective fiction, began to turn to crime narratives to recount more than car chases and showdowns between evil criminals and tough cops. These films include Giuseppe Tornatore's first work, *The Professor* (*Il cammorista*, 1986), starring the American Ben Gazzara as a character loosely based upon the career of the Neapolitan Camorra boss Raffaele Cutolo (1941–), who today remains in prison after reinvigorating the older Camorra by transforming it into the Nuova Camorra Organizzata. *La Scorta* (*La scorta*, 1993), by Ricky Tognazzi (1955–), son of the actor Ugo, is an action-packed film about the dangerous lives of police bodyguards for Italian judges targeted by terrorists or organized criminals. The rising-star female director Roberta Torre (1962–) actually made a prizewinning film musical about the Mafia, *To Die for Tano* (*Tano da morire*, 1997). The pervasive power of the Mafia is the subject of *The Hundred Steps* (*I cento passi*, 2000), by Marco Tullio Giordana (1950–), as well as *Placido Rizzotto* (2000), by Pasquale Scimeca (1956–), both of which are biopics celebrating two Sicilians who fought against the Mafia and paid with their lives. The made-for-TV *Uno Bianca* by the horror film actor-director (and Dario Argento disciple) Michele Soavi provides a fascinating account of a band of criminals who terrorized northern Italy in the late 1980s and early 1990s. Other important contemporary films dealing with crime in often unusual ways include *Lo zio di Brooklyn* (literally, "the uncle from Brooklyn"; 1995) and *Totò che visse due volte* (literally, "Totò who lived twice"; 1997), by a pair of Sicilian directors—Daniele Ciprì (1962–), who also served as cinematographer on *To Die for Tano*, and Franco Maresco (1958–)—who broke into the media with their work for local television; *The Embalmer* (*L'imbalsamatore*, 2002) and *Gomorrah* (*Gomorra*, 2008), by Matteo Garrone (1968–); *I'm Not Scared* (*Io non ho paura*, 2003) and *Quo Vadis, Baby?* (2005), by Gabriele Salvatores (1950–), winner of the Oscar for Best Foreign Language Film for his earlier *Mediterraneo* (1991); *The Consequences of Love* (*Le conseguenze dell'amore*, 2004) and *The Family Friend* (*L'amico di famiglia*, 2006), by Paolo Sorrentino (1970–); and *Crime Novel* (*Romanzo criminale*, 2005), by Michele Placido (already famous as the actor playing Commissioner Corrado Cattani throughout the TV series *La Piovra*), an account of the Magliana Gang that dominated Roman crime in the 1970s. Many of these titles have won numerous festival awards, and although they are fewer in number than the dozens and dozens of *polizieschi* that were shot in the classic period of the 1970s, they represent an important development in contemporary Italian film narrative.

Leone's *Once Upon a Time in America*

Once Upon a Time in America is an ambitious film that may be compared favorably to Francis Ford Coppola's landmark Mafia movie *The Godfather*. Always obsessed with the cinema as a repository of cultural myths, Sergio Leone moved from his radical and original interpretation of the American western to a highly personalized interpretation of the Hollywood gangster film, with expensive on-location shooting abroad, a large Hollywood-style budget, an international cast, and an epic scope audiences have tended to identify with American products rather than Italian films. Leone no doubt chose to portray Jewish—not Italian—American gangsters in an attempt to avoid the sometimes stereotypical presentation of American organized crime as the product of only one ethnic group, when in fact virtually every immigrant group that came to America played a part in the rise of American mobs. Leone's film earned critical acclaim in Europe and America as well as a special premiere at the Cannes Film Festival, but its length (218 minutes) caused its American distributor to mutilate the film in a shamefully abbreviated version (139 minutes) that weakened its aesthetic impact and distorted its meaning. (The copy currently available on DVD contains his original version.)

Leone based his film on a novel entitled *The Hoods* (1952), by Harry Grey (pseudonym for Harry Goldberg), and although there was clearly some polemical intent in shifting his attention from Italian American to Jewish American gangsters, it is nevertheless true that Jewish gangsters played an important role during the Prohibition and Depression eras in America.[3] Bearing in mind the epic scope and historical foundation of Coppola's classic *Godfather* series (the first two parts of which Leone surely screened before making his own film), Leone focused upon Jewish gangsters in the Lower East Side of New York City, tracing the careers of two close friends— David "Noodles" Aaronson (Robert De Niro) and Maximilian "Max" Bercovicz (James Woods)—from their childhood in 1922 through 1933 (the Prohibition era), then concluding with their final encounter decades later in 1968. Even though Leone spent thirteen years preparing to shoot this work and almost a year actually working on location in America, his perfectionism and meticulous attention to historical detail in his sets, costumes, and dialogues owe little to realism. The key to this film, like those Leone made in the genre of the western, is to be found in his title: "Once upon a time . . ." is the traditional opening line in fairy tales in both Italy and America. As Leone noted, "My America is a land magically suspended between cinema and epic, between politics and literature."[4] In Leone's America of the imagination, the passage of time dominates the actions of the film's protagonists. *Once Upon a Time in America*'s narrative hinges upon a complicated series of flash-forwards and flashbacks among the three crucial years in the film—1922, 1933, and 1968—and the film opens and concludes in the 1930s. In one of the initial sequences and at the end of the work, Noodles rests in a Chinese opium den that features a shadow-puppet theater, a subtle reminder that what is to unfold before the spectator's eyes is a cinematic work based on fantasy, not merely a historical reconstruction of Depression-era America.

Barely escaping from gangsters who are trying to kill him, Noodles flees the opium den and leaves New York City from a bus station dominated by a wall painting in the period style advertising the amusements at Coney Island. When we then jump forward in time to 1968 to observe Noodles's return to New York, the station's original advertisement has been replaced by an enormous Big Apple (a popular symbol for the city in 1968) as "Yesterday," by the Beatles, plays on the sound track. The intricate narrative of the film gradually reveals the explanation for Noodle's flight. For years, he and Max had argued over the direction their criminal enterprises should take. While Noodles wanted to remain small and in control of his bit of gangster turf, Max aimed at an alignment with larger criminal syndicates, those run by other ethnic groups, including, naturally, the Italian Americans. Max also backed the organizing efforts of a young union figure,

Noodles begins his journey through time from the Coney Island Amusement Park in the 1930s to the "Big Apple" of the 1960s in Leone's *Once Upon a Time in America*. Credit: Sergio Leone

Jimmy O'Donnell (Treat Williams), who reminds us of the historical figure of Jimmy Hoffa. When Max appears to have lost his senses and launches an impossible attack upon a Federal Reserve bank, Noodles informs the police to save his friends and Max from almost certain death, but something goes horribly wrong: Max and his other Jewish gang members are all killed (or at least that is what Noodles is led to believe). Noodles flees from the Syndicate's sure revenge to Buffalo in 1933 and remains there in hiding until 1968, when he receives a mysterious summons to return. For thirty-five years, he has lived with the remorse he felt over his tip to the police.

What Noodles discovers is that his own betrayal pales before that of his friend Max. The elimination of the old Jewish gang associated with Max and Noodles was part of a plot organized by the Syndicate, and Max actually survived and has assumed the character of a powerful but mysterious figure—Secretary Bailey—who now stands accused, finally, of ties to the criminal underworld. Not only did Max betray Noodles and ruin his life, but he also stole his childhood sweetheart, Deborah (Elizabeth McGovern), in the process. In partial atonement, Max offers Noodles a fortune if his former friend agrees to kill him, since Max realizes that the Mob will kill him eventually in order to cover up his years of collaboration with them as the influential politician he became. Noodles refuses this offer and walks out of Max's Long Island mansion, but soon thereafter Max dies in a surrealistic garbage truck that mysteriously appears outside his home and apparently mangles his body beyond recognition. Leone ends his film with a close-up of Noodles's smiling face in the opium den of the opening sequences as the credit titles run across this final enigmatic shot.

In the process of creating his mythical view of American gangsters, Sergio Leone destroys our comfortable notions of narrative time and character development. His mobsters are trapped in their immutable past. While the episodes of 1922 and 1933 represent flashbacks from 1968, the episodes of 1968 are flash-forwards from the past: as the director declares, "there is only the past seen from the future and the future seen from the past, memory is confused with fantasy, without reference points."[5] Given that Leone opens and concludes the narrative in an opium den where the narrator (Noodles) is certainly in a drugged state of consciousness, the intervening narrative, with its complicated jumps back and forth between past and future, suggests that the entire story actually projects Noodles's guilt-ridden fantasy, dreamed in a narcotic stupor, in an attempt to relieve himself of the guilt for the death of his childhood friends and fellow gang members. Far from detracting from the dramatic impact of the work, as its American distributors believed, the unusual length of the film is essential for the unfolding of Leone's treatment of time. The spectator observes all the protagonists of the film passing from adolescence through maturity into old age, and as they all embody one of Hollywood archetypal cinematic myths—that of the gangster—their gradual deterioration before our eyes demythologizes this cinematic tradition in much the same manner that Leone's laconic gunfighters and bounty hunters altered the conventions of the American western in the 1960s.

Cops and Robbers in Contemporary Italy: The Birth of a New Crime Cinema

Without question, the classic Italian *poliziesco* of the 1970s, with its hard-boiled, freewheeling inspectors and commissioners, made tangible the fears and concerns of the Italian movie audience. Whatever the quality of these films (and some were frankly quite inferior products in terms of production values), they were utterly contemporary: they highlighted authentically modern city environments with all their old and new problems, and they also underscored a widespread lack of confidence in Italian political, economic, and social institutions, which characterized an Italy torn apart by political terrorism, organized criminal activity, and violent street crime. Sergio Leone's Jewish gangster masterpiece stands apart from this focus on current events in Italy, and while it seems closer in spirit to the long line of classic Hollywood mobster figures, from *Scarface* to *The Godfather*, and obviously deals not at all with contemporary Italian society, Leone's film nevertheless encouraged young directors to consider the crime genre as a vehicle for other nontraditional narrative themes.

Italian crime films after Leone revert in some measure to an interest in depicting contemporary social problems, sometimes realistically but often quite fantastically (as in the aforementioned Mafia musical). Ricky Tognazzi's *La Scorta* belongs in the realistic tradition of crime films. A relatively low-budget venture that turned out to be a commercial and critical success, its appeal derives from shifting its focus from the hard-boiled inspectors and commissioners of the classic *polizieschi* to the simple policemen who serve as undertrained, underpaid, and undersupported bodyguards for judges and politicians targeted by the Sicilian Mafia during the 1990s, an era that culminated in the infamous assassinations of Giovanni Falcone, Paolo Borsellino, and General Carlo Alberto Dalla Chiesa. In large measure, it is based upon a true account of bodyguards assigned to protect a real judge in the resort town of Trapani, Sicily. Shot on location in fewer than eight weeks, Tognazzi employed a Steadicam to reproduce the rapidly moving camera typical of many Hollywood action films. A splendid Ennio Morricone musical score heightens the dramatic tension building up in the film as Judge Michele De Francesco (Carlo Cecchi) transfers from the North to uncover the facts surrounding the intersection of political and criminal power that controls the water supply of the city. His bodyguards—Angelo (Claudio Amendola), Andrea (Enrico Lo Verso), Fabio (Ricky Memphis), and Raffaele (Tony Sperandeo)—become completely isolated from the rest of the police force, trusting nobody but themselves and their judge, who quickly becomes more like a father figure than a magistrate to them. The same corrupt politicians and bureaucrats in the court system plague De Francesco's investigation, and one of the escorts (Raffaele) dies in an assassination attempt against the judge's daughter. The film concentrates, however, more upon the simple bravery of these unheralded policemen than upon a sophisticated analysis of the Sicilian underworld, and it is this psychologically sophisticated account of how four simple but honest policemen learned the difference between good and evil by protecting a surrogate-father magistrate that produces a compelling narrative.

Giordana's *The Hundred Steps* avoids the epic approach to gangsters typical of Hollywood epics: his Mafia reaches down to the very core of everyday life for the Impastato family, who live only one hundred paces from the home of the local drug boss Gaetano, or "Tano," Badalamenti (Tony Sperandeo) in the Sicilian village of Cinisi. Luigi Impastato (Luigi Maria Burruano) works for Badalamenti, but his son, Peppino (Luigi Lo Cascio), becomes an impassioned critic of his father's boss and livelihood and symbolically refuses to walk the "hundred steps" to bow to the Mafia chieftain's power. Giordana filmed this work in the real town of Cinisi, and the major characters in the film were all real people, not fictional characters. Badalamenti (1923–2004) was the boss of the Sicilian Mafia Commission (the so-called Cupola) during the 1970s and the mastermind behind the infamous "Pizza Connection" drug-smuggling ring in the United States that sold drugs throughout the American Midwest in pizza parlors controlled by the Mafia. Eventually sentenced to an American prison term of forty-five years in 1987 for this conspiracy, Badalamenti subsequently died in an American jail. The real Peppino (1948–78) was murdered by Badalamenti's henchmen on the very day that Aldo Moro's body was discovered in Rome, the victim of Red Brigade terrorists. He spent his brief life fighting the Mafia by mocking them with humor on a private radio program with accounts of Mafiopoli (he called the town of Cinisi "Mafia City") and caricatured Badalamenti as Tano Seduto—literally "Sitting Tano," a parody of the Italian translation of Sitting Bull, Toro Seduto. (Shortly before Badalamenti's death, he was also sentenced for his complicity in Peppino's killing.)

Giordana's biopic reverses the hagiography of the Mafia that begins with the epic tone of Coppola's *Godfather* trilogy and attacks the entire notion of "family" that Coppola's depiction of organized crime families celebrates, the same concept examined in such successful series as David Chase's *The Sopranos*. In this Italian film, Tano is a close friend of the Impastato family. Peppino's father earns a living by being associated with the Badalamenti clan, but the Mafia forces Luigi to drive his son, Peppino, out of his home. Giordana opens the film with a scene taken directly from

Coppola's *The Godfather*—all the associates of Don Cesare Manzella (Pippo Montalbano) gather at his country villa. Tano, Luigi, and even a young Peppino attend a huge dinner party, but later it is Don Cesare who is blown up in his car to make room for Tano, who becomes the new power behind the local Mafia. Even the family portrait from Coppola is repeated in the opening sequence, but for the last time one "family" supports without question the other "family." Peppino refuses to "honor his father," as the biblical commandment requires, but this refusal extends not only to his biological father, Luigi, but also his other "father," the head of the Mafia who controls the entire region.

In *The Hundred Steps*, Giordana shows Peppino fighting the Mafia alone, with little institutional or local support, until his death galvanizes the Sicilian populace, a multitude of whom turn out for his funeral, even after Don Tano warns Peppino's mother to stay away from the service. The upbeat, positive ending of the film represents not the situation in Sicily in 1978 when Peppino died but, rather, the glimmer of hope in Sicily after the fall of Italy's First Republic in the 1990s removed much of the Mafia's political support among politicians in Rome. It affirms that the Mafia can be fought and even defeated if only the Sicilian populace demands it, but one of the themes of the film remains that the Mafia exists not because Sicilians are afraid but because deep down they identify with it and love it, no matter at what cost to their lives and institutions.

After Giordana reenacts Peppino's funeral, he concludes the film with photographs from Peppino's actual life, linking the style of his film to the long tradition of Italian film realism—a connection that is brought up during the film when Peppino himself screens Francesco Rosi's *Hands Over the City*, one of the first Italian films to denounce the Mafia and its corruption of the Italian construction industry, which was one of the real sources of organized crime's wealth in Cinisi. Of course, the citation of Rosi's film poses the question of whether anything will ever change in Sicily.

Soavi's *Uno Bianca* blends the search for film realism typical of *The Hundred Steps* with the police procedural subgenre, an approach to making crime films typical of Hollywood products (particularly films shot for TV series) but rarely employed by the Italian cinema during the 1970s in the *poliziesco*. An "Uno bianca" is a white Fiat sedan called the Uno, the most popular car sold in Italy between 1987 and 1994, when a criminal band terrorized northern Italy and was able to use a different, stolen, white Fiat Uno in each of their robberies to escape detection, because these cars were present on the streets by the thousands.[6] Besides its police procedural type of plot, the most important innovation in this film is that the cops were the robbers! Two small-town policemen from Rimini, Valerio (Kim Rossi Stuart) and Rocco (Dino Abbrescia)—obstructed by arrogant superiors in Bologna, who continuously attempt to pin the robberies on immigrants or Albanians or terrorists—persevere, and by a meticulous sifting through the evidence ignored by their big-city colleagues in a special task force set up from Rome, manage to conclude that the criminals are policemen who have access to police communications through their mastermind, Michele (Pietro Bontempo). Unlike the protagonists played by Franco Nero, Luc Merenda, or Tomas Milian in the earlier *polizieschi*, the policemen in *Uno Bianca* are not gunslinging cowboys, out of control, but shy and even introverted men doing a boring but necessary job with courage and dignity. The realistic photographic and editing styles are rather unanticipated from a director who apprenticed in *gialli* thrillers and spaghetti horror genre films with Dario Argento. Whereas the film's focus on forensics places the work closer to commercial Hollywood products, the cultural elements at work in the narrative (the search to pin the crimes on foreigners or terrorists, the obstructions typical of Italian bureaucracy) link it with the earlier *polizieschi* of the 1970s. Unlike many of the crime films in this tradition, however, *Uno Bianca* offers highly professional acting, a fine script, and a carefully crafted series of dramatic events that masterfully build suspense and engage the viewer's interest.

The other recent film that continues the tradition of realism within the crime film genre is Placido's *Crime Novel*, an engaging account of how a group of low-life delinquents from the Roman *borgate* (slums), whose social and cultural background recalls that of Pier Paolo Pasolini's characters in *Accattone* or *Mamma Roma*, graduate from small-time thievery to the control of Rome's gambling, prostitution, and drug rackets with the eventual support not only of the Sicilian Mafia but also of the Italian Secret Service. Placido's direction attempts to provide a realistic account of the dramatic rise to power of the Magliana Gang and its inevitable end in death and bloodshed, but from an innovative point of view—that of the criminals, who display the same sense of camaraderie and devotion to one's colleagues in the face of danger that characterized the policemen of *La Scorta* or *Uno Bianca*. Placido emphasizes with flashbacks how three young boys, known primarily by their criminal nicknames—Il Freddo ("Ice"; Kim Rossi Stuart), Libano ("the Lebanese"; Pierfrancesco Favino), and Il Dandi ("Dandy"; Claudio Santamaria)—begin their gangster career as the closest of friends but eventually are destroyed one by one by the environment in which they have chosen to live. Thus, *Crime Novel* may be compared to the treatment of friendship among thieves in *Once Upon a Time in America*. Although Placido's film lacks the epic quality of Leone's gangster classic, its attempt to trace a trajectory of criminal activity from the gangster perspective, including the subplot of friendship and betrayal at the film's center, makes it a true Italian portrayal of historically real people. Whereas in Leone's film the lighting, musical score, and editing make the finished product closer to the epic scope of Coppola's *Godfather* series, Placido's lighting, music, and editing show a clear link to the gangster films of Martin Scorsese, particularly *Goodfellas*, especially in his choice of music contemporary with the action on the screen and performed by a mixture of Italian and American pop singers and rock groups. Now, however, the traditional problems of political interference and corruption that we normally view from the perspective of the police are displayed from a criminal point of view. The Magliana Gang apparently had links to right-wing elements of the Italian Secret Service, who the film implicates in the infamous bombing of the Bologna train station in 1980. Likewise, the mysterious sniper who kills Ice, the last surviving member of the original gang, is also obviously under the control of a branch of Italian state security. *Crime Novel* represents a compromise between film realism—in its careful reconstruction of the rise of the Magliana Gang—and entertainment—the invention of sexual relationships carried on by a high-class prostitute named Patrizia (Anna Mouglalis) with both Dandy and Police Commissioner Nicola Scialoja (Stefano Accorsi), who is charged with investigating Dandy's gang. Unlike the early *polizieschi*, where good acting was less common than violent action, films like *La Scorta*, *Uno Bianca*, and *Crime Novel* enjoy outstanding scripts that suit the admirable acting talents of a new generation of young Italian stars.

Crime stories in contemporary Italian literature deal with more than realistic accounts of the activities of gangsters. As great detective fiction writers and directors discovered in America during the heyday of the hard-boiled fiction of Hammett, Chandler, and Cain, or in the important film noir variant of the traditional detective story, criminal narratives could easily be adapted to a wide range of important literary or cinematic themes that allow the exploration of quite different problems. Just as recent Italian fiction has rediscovered this aspect of the crime story, so too have a number of Italy's best directors—Garrone, Sorrentino, Salvatores—explored the existential dimensions of similar narratives in film. Matteo Garrone's *The Embalmer* provides a disturbing and grotesque account of Peppino (Ernesto Mahieux), a Neapolitan taxidermist whose growth has been stunted almost to dwarf-hood. When he is not crafting beautifully stuffed animals, he works with the local Camorra to conceal drugs inside dead bodies and unstitches them when they reach their destination. Nevertheless, the plotline of the Neapolitan Mob provides the gruesome background to what is actually an obsessive love story, since Peppino's sexual interests focus upon Valerio (Valerio Foglia Manzillo), his handsome young assistant who, in turn, is in love with Deborah (Elisabetta Rocchetti). Peppino's tragedy is that he has a sparkling personality trapped in an ugly and unattractive body, resulting in his need for love without the ability to find it. Shot in direct sound (recall that most Italian films feature dubbed sound tracks), Garrone's film style employs the kind of somber yellow and blue filters that set it apart from the usual picture of "sunny Naples" in bright and happy colors, so often our only image of this mysterious and unhappy city. Kinky group sex in the film functions not to tit-illate our imaginations but to underscore the lengths to which poor Peppino will go to be near Valerio's beautiful body. The desolate landscapes and life-less suburban neighborhoods Garrone photographs provide a perfect visual image of Peppino's unhappiness. The taxidermist's oppressive obsession with Valerio finally drives the young man and Deborah to kill Peppino and dump his body in a river. Even though they had eventually become genuinely fond of him, his death offers the only means of escaping his clutches.

The skillful ability Garrone demonstrated in this film to pair protagonists with an appropriate physical environment and unusual visuals—something Michelangelo Antonioni made so crucial an element in his great films on alienation in the 1960s—reappears in *Gomorrah*, winner of the Grand Prix at the Cannes Film Festival of 2008. An adaptation of Roberto Saviano's 2006 international nonfiction report on the impact of Camorra corruption on the construction, fashion, and waste-management industries in Naples and its attendant political corruption and social violence, *Gomorrah* (like its liter-ary source) presents Naples not as a sun-bathed metropolis full of folkloric and entertaining vignettes but as a descent into a contemporary vision of Dante's *Inferno*. Garrone concentrates upon five different seemingly uncon-nected stories taken from Saviano's book, but eventually links these sepa-rate narratives by the pervasive and morally corrosive force of organized crime. Although the atmosphere created by this hellish but original vision of Naples stands far removed from the traditional "political" cinema of such directors as Rosi or Petri, Garrone's use of real locations and local dialects (with subtitles for non-Neapolitan audiences, even in the Italian prints), as well as his skillful mixture of professional actors with nonprofessional citizens of Naples' underworld, remind us of Italy's neorealist heritage. Of particular note is Toni Servillo's performance as Franco. After only a few years of acting in a variety of works by young film directors, he has become the most exciting dramatic actor in the contemporary Italian cinema.

The Neapolitan Camorra controls the waste disposal industry, and in Garrone's *Gomorrah*, gangsters sometimes use their garbage trucks to dispose of their victims, such as this young aspiring criminal who ran afoul of their activities. *Credit: DVD*

The popular director Gabriele Salvatores has recently shot two quite different films that may be rightfully placed within the crime film category. In the critically acclaimed *I'm Not Scared*, based on a 2001 novel by Niccolò Ammaniti, Salvatores returns to another neorealist strength: directing outstanding performances by nonprofessional child actors. In this case, Michele (Giuseppe Cristiano) is a boy of ten who lives in a desperately poor village in Basilicata, where the entire population (only three or four households) has apparently engaged in kidnapping wealthy northern children for money, a cruel form of crime practiced by both Calabrians and Sardinians during the 1970s and 1980s (the film is set in 1978). The entire narrative is shot from the perspective of Michele, who discovers that his own father and mother (albeit reluctantly, in her case) are involved after he finds the kidnapping victim, Filippo (Mattia Di Pierro), chained in an underground cave like a wild animal. His place of captivity has rendered him completely white, almost blinded by sunlight, and nearly insane, but Michele brings him food and water and even walks him in the beautiful wheat fields near his horrible prison. Because Michele cannot comprehend the evil nature of any human being who would inflict such pain upon a child his own age, he at first interprets what he sees in terms of the fables, comic strips, and fairy tales that all young boys know. Thus, *I'm Not Scared* represents more than a believable account of a kidnapping and becomes a coming-of-age tale where both adults and children have secrets (many of them dark and horrible), and where the discovery of truth usually involves a destruction of childhood fantasies and innocence.

While Salvatores's *I'm Not Scared* harks back to many neorealist and postneorealist films dealing with childhood, his *Quo Vadis, Baby?* constitutes a true detective film, another genre very rare in Italian film history, with a female protagonist that qualifies the work as an authentic film noir *all'italiana*. Salvatores derives his title from a line delivered by Marlon Brando, the protagonist of Bertolucci's *Last Tango in Paris*, to his young mistress Jeanne, a relationship that eventually ends in his death at her hands (see chapter 13). Set in a beautifully photographed Bologna, with its porticos, foggy nights, and shadows, Salvatores's narrative follows the peregrinations of Giorgia Cantini (Angela Baraldi), a private detective working for her father's agency. Receiving videotapes shot by her sister, Ada, who had killed herself almost two decades earlier, Giorgia begins a troubling quest for the truth. In her search, she meets a film professor at the university named Andrea Berti (Gigio Alberti), with whom she has a sexual fling and who, she discovers, was Ada's lover years earlier. After they make love, she discovers a copy of a book he has written: *Jumping-Back Flash: Temporal Paradoxes in the American Cinema*, a key to the film's plot. Her authoritarian father—called by everyone, including his children, "the Captain"—warns Giorgia to "be careful, you can't play with the past, especially if it's not yours."

Eventually, Giorgia learns from Berti that he had left Ada alone, returned to find that she had hanged herself, and cleaned up the drugs and his fingerprints before leaving her body there. Yet this is not the whole truth either, for after Giorgia leaves her apartment for a date with a cop friend, with a tape of Fritz Lang's *M* still running, the end of the tape—which includes footage showing Ada in a confrontation with the Captain, who throws Berti out of the apartment—informs the audience that Ada tells her father she saw him kill their mother, the traumatic event in the past that has governed her personality and her family relationships for the rest of her life. Ada said nothing to her sister about all this. At the film's conclusion, we see a clip from yet another home movie showing Giorgia's mother going over the side of a balcony with Ada on a bike and Giorgia behind her. Presumably the Captain killed his wife at this point, although it is equally possible that she fell by accident and the entire narrative about a murder was a child's interpretation of that momentous event. Giorgia does not see this clip—the director shares it only with his spectators. Thus, the existential detective narrative yields no conclusive truth, while even our partial vision of what might be the truth remains fuzzy and confused.

Paolo Sorrentino's two crime films—*The Consequences of Love* and *The Family Friend*—explore the implications of human loneliness through fascinating portraits of two grotesque male criminals: respectively, a Mafia banker, Titta di Girolamo (Toni Servillo), exiled to ten years of solitude in a dreary Swiss commercial hotel for losing a fortune through bad investments for his gangster friends, and a repulsive loan shark, Geremia de' Geremei (Giacomo Rizzo), living alone with his mother, squeezing every penny he extorts from his victims, some of whom are killed if they fail to pay up. Both lead actors deliver brilliant performances in demanding and difficult roles. Banished for his bad financial judgment, Titta delivers a suitcase filled with Mob money to a local bank once a week. His entire life rests upon absolute control, impassivity, routine, and eternal boredom until he suddenly becomes attracted to a young hotel-bar waitress named Sofia (Olivia Magnani, granddaughter of the famed actress Anna), for whom he suddenly departs from his sterile emotional life and takes $100,000 to buy Sofia a BMW convertible. The consequences of his act (the key to the meaning of the film's title) unleash a series of surprising events that begin with Mafia hit men betraying Titta's boss by stealing his weekly consignment of cash and concludes with Titta killing them, retrieving the suitcase, yet refusing to return it to the Mafia even though he realizes that this means his death. All this information emerges to our view, however, only through flashbacks at the end of the film. Sorrentino's talents in *The Consequences of Love* are evident in his dark humor (a Mafia hit man wearing glasses held together with Scotch tape), his skillful use of Toni Servillo's extraordinary acting talents, and his ingenious use of screen and off-screen space, with beautiful cinematography from fluid camera movements through sterile hotel hallways, corridors, bedrooms, and bars. One memorable sequence opens with an extremely long Steadicam journey through hotel corridors lined with Mafiosi soldiers to meet the assembled elderly *capi* (bosses) to whom Titta must answer for the missing suitcase of money. They are all gathered together in an auditorium, the kind that convention hotels employ for large meetings, and a banner at the front of the room announces that what is being held is an introductory course to cures for the prostate—certainly the most laughable cover for a criminal meet ever devised on the screen! The final scene shows Titta returned to the earlier imperturbable persona that he had abandoned only long enough to steal the funds from his bosses: he is slowly lowered into wet cement by an enormous crane, showing no hint of emotion, fear, or regret. Titta dies alone, an enigmatic figure who finds consolation only in the fact that he gave the suitcase full of money to an elderly couple living in the hotel who are not his friends in what might be called an *acte gratuit* worthy of Gide or Camus, and in the belief that a man whom he has not seen in over twenty years may, from time to time, think fondly of him, "his best friend."

Sorrentino's *The Family Friend* features another lonely man, a small-time crook who, like Titta, goes completely out of control when he falls in love with a woman: Rosalba (Laura Chiatti), a winner of the Miss Agro Pontino beauty contest. Sorrentino thus sets his film in one of the towns Mussolini built in the marshy regions south of Rome when he drained the Pontine Marshes (*Agro pontino*), and its extreme, rationalist architectural style typical of Fascist town planning sets the tone for the almost surrealistic environment in which Geremia plies his trade of usury, all the while claiming that he has a heart of gold and only wants to help people—until they fail to meet their payments. Giacomo Rizzo's performance as Geremia is as splendid in this film as Toni Servillo's is in *Consequences*. A physically repulsive individual, he shuffles along or trots through the streets like a rat, carrying his possessions in a cheap plastic grocery bag. He employs a fanatic fan of American country music, Gino (Fabrizio Bentivoglio), to research his prospective loan customers/victims. Geremia is another control freak (the kind of male figure Sorrentino privileges in his films), but in a surprising turn of events, Geremia's henchman Gino connives with his two enforcers, Rosalba, and even his father (also a loan shark, one who abandoned his wife and son years earlier to eke out a living in Rome), to plan an elaborate sting that relieves Geremia of his entire fortune of more than one million euros. As the film ends, Geremia survives alone, stitching in his tailor shop late into the night. Both Titta and Geremia are humanized by their directors: they are criminals and disgusting individuals, but their personalities contain a spark of goodness and a modicum of humanity that the films call to the fore in an entertaining manner.

Toni Servillo delivers another memorable performance in Sorrentino's biopic of the Italian politician Giulio Andreotti, *Il Divo* (*Il Divo: la straordinaria vita di Giulio Andreotti*, 2008), the recipient of the Jury Prize at the 2008 Cannes Film Festival. Sorrentino avoids the normal treatment of political figures reserved for the traditional political film and presents Andreotti in a grotesque and almost surrealistic manner. In fact, he may well have been influenced by a brilliant but little-known portrait of the Italian political leader by Giorgio De Chirico that focuses not just on the man's face but also upon peculiar features and mannerisms associated with Andreotti's hands, displayed throughout Sorrentino's film. Servillo becomes the perfect physical and emotional embodiment of this powerful Italian politician who famously embraced Salvatore "Totò" Riina—longtime boss of the Sicilian Mafia—years before he was captured and sent to prison. Although a strange and enigmatic figure who has never been accused of corruption for financial gain but only for obtaining and exercising power, Italians refer to him as "Il Gobbo" ("the Hunchback"). (His unattractive physical features should not obscure the fact that Italians also superstitiously believe that good luck derives from touching a hunchback's hump!) Cynical Italians also admire Andreotti's witty quips—the most famous of which is that "power wears out those who do not have it"—a particularly cynical Italian twist on the famous and often quoted dictum of Lord Acton that "power corrupts and absolute power corrupts absolutely." Coppola recreated Andreotti's persona and his famous declaration about the nature of political power in the violent conclusion to *The Godfather: Part III*, in which the Andreotti figure, Don Licio Lucchesi (Enzo Robutti), dies on the orders of Michael Corleone (Al Pacino) at the hands of Michael's former Sicilian bodyguard, Calo (Franco Citti), just after Calo whispers Andreotti's famous remark into his ear. Andreotti has always been considered by his political enemies to be the mastermind behind the complex system of

Toni Servillo's performance as Italian politician Giulio Andreotti in Sorrentino's *Il Divo* confirms his rise to stardom as Italy's top dramatic actor in the twentieth-first century Italian cinema. *Credit: DVD*

corruption that for years linked Italian organized crime with Italian political parties, before these links were publicly revealed and weakened in the wake of the "Mani pulite" ("Clean Hands") scandals of the 1990s that completely changed Italy's political landscape.

The many critical awards and impressive box-office results garnered by the crime films of the past decade and a half—not to mention the recent twin successes at Cannes of *Gomorrah* and *Il Divo*—demonstrate a healthy, ongoing Italian interest in the crime genre, one that transcends the quickie exploitation-film production values of many (but certainly not all) of the hundred or so *polizieschi* generated when the genre first became popular in the 1970s. Given the prestige of the directors working now in this genre (most of whom would have been art film directors in the postneorealist generation) and the high production values in their films (including the acting, musical scores, and editing), works such as those from *La Scorta* to *Gomorrah* continue to show us an undiscovered Italy and chart new directions for the crime film—a genre that the Italian film industry had traditionally left for Hollywood to exploit.

PART FOUR

Generational Change in the Contemporary Italian Cinema

CHAPTER FIFTEEN

The Old Guard Never Surrenders
ITALY'S PREWAR AUTEURS IN THE 1980s AND 1990s

Generational Change in the Italian Auteur Film

WHILE ITALIAN FILMS OF QUALITY continued to earn festival awards, Oscar nominations, and critical acclaim between the 1980s and the end of the twentieth century, the industry as a whole experienced a prolonged economic crisis. By the end of the 1970s, De Sica, Visconti, Rossellini, Germi, and Pasolini had all died, depriving younger generations of models to follow. Nevertheless, the Italian film industry was still dominated by directors born before the outbreak of World War II. Fellini and Antonioni, of course, were the preeminent names of this prewar generation, but even such renowned figures as these two masters—each of whom finally received an Oscar honoring his entire career from the Academy of Motion Picture Arts and Sciences, Fellini in the year of his death—faced increasing difficulty in financing their projects after the end of the 1970s. The major names associated with Italy's "art cinema," as opposed to the directors of genre films, still included directors born before the beginning of World War II, who had come of age during the neorealist period: the Taviani brothers, Francesco Rosi, Pupi Avati, Franco Zeffirelli, Ermanno Olmi, Ettore Scola, Mario Monicelli, Liliana Cavani, Nanni Loy, Marco Bellocchio, to list the most important ones. Two successive generations—directors born after 1945 (see chapter 16), and directors born near or around the important cultural date of 1968 (see chapter 17)—often seemed to float adrift upon a cinematic ocean buffeted by an indifferent public, a neglectful national government, and an increasing sense that Italian cinema had become irrelevant to younger generations who had lost touch with Italy's cinematic traditions and political or cultural concerns.

Not surprisingly, during the last two decades of the twentieth and the first decade of the twentieth-first century, Hollywood continued to dominate the internal Italian market. More important than the number of American films screened in Italy was the fact that the most popular ones among them were often produced with technical or economic means (expensive special effects, distribution patterns that blanketed the entire country with numerous copies, huge advertising budgets, and so forth) with which Italian producers could not possibly compete. In Italy in 1998, 2,600 film theaters were available for screening motion pictures; this dropped to 2,400 in 2000. After a remarkable period of decay and neglect in which many elegant old moviehouses in urban centers were allowed to fall apart or lie abandoned, some additional capital finally began to flow into the industry, allowing for the creation of multiplex facilities familiar to American audiences, theaters that could accommodate the screening of more than one picture at a time. Yet if the number of Italian theaters in 1998 is compared to those in either France (4,465) or Germany (3,814) during the same year, the rather grim condition of Italian cinema becomes clearer, particularly since there had been 4,885 theaters in Italy in 1985.

A proper context can put ticket sales figures in perspective. During the 1990s, ticket sales actually increased a bit from a low point of 91 million in 1995 to 104 million in 1997 and 125 million in 1998. But compared with figures from the enormous Italian market of the past—661 million in 1950, 744 million in 1960, 525 million in 1970, and 240 million even in 1980—such small increases were inconsequential. Moreover, total tickets sold represent revenues generated for *all* films, Hollywood movies included, not just Italian productions or Italian coproductions. In the first six seasons of the 1970s, a period of great artistic and commercial strength for the native Italian cinema, Italian films earned an average of 61.1 percent of total revenues; but this figure declined sharply in 1976–79 to 47.4 percent, then to an average of 39.8 percent between 1980 and 1985, before sinking to the abysmal figure of 13 percent in 1993. During the 1990s, between 140 and 180 American films circulated in Italy, whereas Italian productions or coproductions averaged about 100 per year; and yet non-Italian films earned almost 75 percent of total revenues.[1] In short, the Italian cinema earned a smaller and smaller slice of a rapidly shrinking pie in a market dominated almost completely by American movies. In spite of this depressing situation, works of great quality continued to be produced in Italy by many of Italy's older generation of art film directors, whose contributions are the subject of this chapter.

Carrying on the Traditions of *Commedia all'italiana*: Scola, Monicelli, Loy, and Wertmüller

Ettore Scola

Few directors during the 1980s were as effective as Ettore Scola in combining box-office appeal with critical praise. Making use of traditional

Italian film comedy's ability to combine laughter with serious topics (see chapter 7), Scola created some films with historical themes that relied upon traditional dramatic structures requiring strong acting performances. In these works, he also continued to entertain the kinds of metacinematic themes that distinguished his best comedies of the 1970s. *La Nuit de Varennes* (*Il mondo nuovo*, 1982) analyzes French society on the eve of the Revolution and presents a cross section of the ancien régime who come together in a carriage ride: Thomas Paine (Harvey Keitel), an aging Casanova (Marcello Mastroianni), the French intellectual Restif de la Bretonne (Jean-Louis Barrault), and the Countess de la Borde (Hanna Schygulla). When they reach the town of Varennes, they arrive just in time to witness the French king's unsuccessful attempt to flee Paris and his capture on June 22, 1791.

The film's Italian title, which translates as "The New World," refers not only to the tremendous social and political upheavals that promptly give rise to a new world after the fall of the French monarchy but also, by allusion, to the sort of magic lantern that showed reproductions of perspective views, the period's precursor to the cinema projector (see chapter 1). To capture this special moment in French history, Scola uses a perspective similar to the one that was so successful in *A Special Day*: private points of view reveal how the most earthshaking historical revolutions may ultimately depend upon small, seemingly banal personal decisions. The events leading up to Varennes appear as a flashback from an opening prologue, where a group of Venetian actors operate the magic-lantern peep show through which they invite the audience to observe the spectacle that follows.

Reprising this metacinematic approach to the history of the distant past, Scola sets *Le Bal* (*Ballando ballando*, 1983) entirely inside a Parisian dance hall and films it as if it were a silent film. *Le Bal* examines changes in French morals and attitudes over five decades of the twentieth century. After an opening prologue set in the present (1983), flashbacks focus upon crucial periods in contemporary French history: the Popular Front of 1936; the early days of World War II and French collaboration with the Nazis during the Vichy regime; the liberation in 1945 with the arrival of the Americans, the black market, and jazz music; the colonial war in Algeria in 1956; student riots in 1968; and finally a return to 1983. During the course of the film, 24 actors portray some 140 characters. They provide caricatures of basic human emotions buffeted by the changing tides of historical events, the kind of characters Scola had drawn (beginning in high school) for the humor magazine *Marc'Aurelio*, the same periodical on which both Federico Fellini and Cesare Zavattini had also worked, both in the Fascist period and after the war. Hence, *Le Bal* encompasses a panorama of fifty years of French history, using only the possibilities of mime, choreography, and the traditional gestures and facial expressions from Italy's *commedia dell'arte*.

Its view of recent French society should be compared to Scola's treatment of postwar Italian society and cinema in his much more famous *We All Loved Each Other So Much.*

Less daring but no less interesting projects—*Macaroni* (*Maccheroni,* 1985) and *The Family* (*La famiglia,* 1987)—focus Scola's comic eye upon the sentiments typical of basic human relationships. In the first film, Scola cast Jack Lemmon as an American businessman named Robert Traven who meets an archivist named Antonio Jasiello (Marcello Mastroianni) in Naples during the war. Years later, while visiting Naples for three days, Traven comes to the realization that his frenetic life, devoted almost entirely to business, lacks meaning without friendship, and he reestablishes his link to his old friend, learning how to savor life's fleeting moments of happiness by following Jasiello's dictum, "How beautiful wasting time is!" At the film's premiere, Scola announced that he had hoped to contrast two very different ways of life through a metaphoric juxtaposition of two different cuisines: American fast food, consumed hurriedly, often while standing up and alone, and Neapolitan macaroni, an even simpler fare that nevertheless requires more attention to detail and is best eaten with friends and relatives.[2] American critics treated *Macaroni* as no more than a vehicle for showcasing the talents of two famous actors, but *The Family* received international critical recognition. It combines the superb acting talents of major stars and telescopes a considerable range of historical change into the microcosmic lives of a few individuals, a technique Scola had used to perfection in earlier films. *The Family* recounts the bittersweet adventures of an upper-middle-class Italian family from 1906 to 1986, narrated in the first person by Carlo (Vittorio Gassman), whose transformation through the course of the film takes him from childhood to grandfatherhood. Scola employs dissolves to mark shifts from one decade to the next and to heighten the concentration of dramatic tension achieved by employing the family apartment in the posh Prati district of Rome as the film's sole setting. In his portrait of the patriarchal family, traditionally represented by Italian cinema as the focal point of Italian life, Scola dramatizes its metamorphosis into an entirely different kind of institution over the course of several tumultuous decades. Most of the film's drama takes place at the family dinner table, and Scola, with his insight into the role of individuals in large social movements, demonstrates just how adept he is at using subtle innuendos and undercurrents in domestic life to portray an entire society in transition. *The Family* justly attained enormous critical and commercial success.

Scola's next films, which gained less critical attention and earned less at the box office, decreased in number—even though, paradoxically, his stature grew, based upon the growing recognition that his comic vision was the achievement of an authentic auteur. (This realization was confirmed by Scola's nomination to preside over a Cannes Film Festival jury.) *Splendor* (1989)—a

The dinner table becomes tense as Carlo, seated by his wife, entertains his former sweetheart with her fiancé, toward whom his barely concealed jealousy is transformed into open hostility in Scola's *The Family. Credit: Ettore Scola and Mass Films (Rome)*

work that bears comparison to the far more commercially successful *Cinema Paradiso* (*Nuovo cinema Paradiso*, 1988), which made Giuseppe Tornatore internationally famous—pays homage to a bygone era when moviehouses were the focal point of Italian popular culture. To highlight the acting talents of Massimo Troisi, who had played the projectionist opposite Marcello Mastroianni's theater owner in *Splendor*, and later earned international recognition in Michael Radford's *Il postino* in 1994 just before his tragic and untimely death, Scola cast him in a comic adventure film in costume, *The Voyage of Captain Fracassa* (*Il viaggio di Capitan Fracassa*, 1990). *The Dinner* (*La cena*, 1998) employs the microcosm of a family restaurant to study the small details of everyday life, attempting with some success to capture the energy of the kind of convivial meals and the friendships dramatized in *We All Loved Each Other So Much*. And *Unfair Competition* (*Concorrenza sleale*, 2001) returns to the Fascist era of 1938 and the atmosphere of *A Special Day* to examine the relationships between two shop owners, one Catholic and one Jewish, in the Roman Ghetto. It is a portrait of anti-Semitism in Italy that deserves more attention than it has received.[3]

Mario Monicelli, Nanni Loy, and Lina Wertmüller

Let's Hope It's a Girl (*Speriamo che sia femmina*, 1986) ranks as one of the greatest film comedies of Italy's proud comic tradition. Appearing a decade after the heyday of the *commedia all'italiana*, it was created by the director Monicelli and several of Italy's greatest scriptwriters. Its artistic energy puts to shame many of the frivolous comic films produced during the last two decades of the twentieth century, and it was a box-office success. Boasting a magnificent female cast, the film provides an engaging approach to feminist debates in Italy. The setting is a Tuscan farm, where Elena (Liv Ullmann) lives, separated from her ineffectual husband, Leonardo (Philippe Noiret), who is more concerned with his mistress, Lolli (Stefania Sandrelli), than with his wife or his two daughters, Franca (Giuliana de Sio) and Malvina (Lucrezia Lante della Rovere). Completing this collection of sharply drawn, strong, and spirited female characters are Elena's sister, Claudia (Catherine Deneuve), and her housekeeper, Fosca (Athina Cenci). The only male in the house, the senile old uncle (Bernard Blier), spends most of his time knitting, typically a female task. A series of crises shakes up this female community, causing many of them to leave the farmhouse, but when the women learn that Franca is pregnant, they all return to support her (including even Leonardo's mistress!) and to await the birth of her child, hoping it will be another girl. Although critics sometimes denounce a certain kind of Italian film comedy as sexist, Monicelli makes the persuasive and humorous argument that men are rather superfluous in the lives of these independent women. The history of the cinema is filled with stories about male bonding, but *Let's Hope It's a Girl* demonstrates the possibility of a similar kind of close relationship between women who live, by choice, in a world without men.

The veteran director Nanni Loy, best known for his stirring account of the popular uprising against the Nazi occupiers of Naples in *The Four Days of Naples*, and several successful comic films, such as *Café Express* (1980) and *All My Friends Part 3*, made a masterpiece with *Where's Picone?* (*Mi manda Picone*, 1983). This chilling comic portrait of crime-ridden Naples revolves around Giancarlo Giannini's memorable performance as a small-time con artist named Salvatore who assumes the identity of Pasquale Picone, after this apparently unemployed steelworker sets himself on fire in protest during a government hearing about unemployment in the South. With the assistance of Picone's wife, Luciella (Lina Sastri), Salvatore soon discovers that Picone had never been employed (and therefore never unemployed), that he has disappeared, and that his true occupation was that of a collector and runner for the local Mob. In fact, Picone has faked his own death by using an asbestos suit to shield himself from the flames. Why Picone simulated such a dramatic demise never becomes clear, increasing the mystery for both Salvatore and the spectator. Salvatore follows Picone's traces through the underworld in a picaresque journey that owes more to the novels of Franz Kafka than to the sunlit world of the tourist's Naples. When he prepares to attend Picone's funeral, the same kind of mysteriously appearing ambulance that had taken Picone away carries Salvatore off in the same way, and the film leaves the spectator to wonder about the possibility of ever comprehending the morass of corruption and criminality that characterizes this ancient and beleaguered city.

Although nothing Wertmüller directed after *Seven Beauties* could possibly match the critical and commercial success of that important and original work or her other political comedies of the 1970s, she went on to make good comic films in the *commedia all'italiana* tradition of mixing comedy and politics or social criticism. Perhaps her critical downfall arose from her decision to sign a contract to make English-language films, since her meteoric rise to international fame came to an abrupt halt with the failure of *A Night Full of Rain* (*La fine del mondo nel nostro solito letto in una notte piena di pioggia*, 1978), which received in the United States the same kind of brutal critical reaction that Antonioni had experienced a decade earlier with *Zabriskie Point*. Nonetheless, subsequent Italian-language films—including *Blood Feud* (*Fatto di sangue fra due uomini per causa di una vedova—si sospettano moventi politici*, 1978); *A Joke of Destiny* (*Scherzo del destino in agguato dietro l'angolo come un brigante da strada*, 1983); *Ciao, Professore!* (*Io speriamo che me la cavo*, 1992); *The Worker and the Hairdresser in a Whirlwind of Sex and Politics* (*Metalmeccanico e parrucchiera in un turbine di sesso e di politica*, 1996); *Ferdinando and Carolina* (*Ferdinando e Carolina*, 1999), a historical account of Naples in the nineteenth century; and *Too Much Romance . . . It's Time for Stuffed Peppers* (*Peperoni ripieni e pesci in faccia*, 2004)—demonstrate her unique mastery of combining feminist issues with Italian political matters. These films tackled complex contemporary problems, such as sexual roles in a changing Italian society, the ecological crisis, and the Neapolitan underworld, all rendered with her characteristically exuberant camera style. Besides work in the cinema, Wertmüller has also directed operas and made films for Italian television. In 1988, she joined the administration of the Centro Sperimentale di Cinematografia, the state film school in Rome.

Films of Quality by the Taviani Brothers

After the international acclaim for *The Night of the Shooting Stars*, a film characterized by its "magic realism" and its metacinematic homage to the neorealist era, the Tavianis' films, frequently underwritten by the RAI, Italy's national television network, often took their point of departure from literary works. *Kaos* (*Kàos*, 1984) and *You Laugh* (*Tu ridi*, 1998) draw inspiration from Luigi Pirandello's short fiction, *Elective Affinities* (*Le affinità elettive*, 1996) adapts one of Goethe's best-known works of the same title, and *The Lark Farm* (*La masseria delle allodole*, 2007) has its origins in a novel about the Armenian genocide in Turkey during the early twentieth century. *Good Morning, Babylon* (*Good Morning Babilonia*, 1987) considers the possible relationships between silent cinema in Italy and America during the birth of the motion pictures (another metacinematic work). Finally, *Fiorile*, a.k.a. *Wild Flower* (*Fiorile*, 1993), marks an apparent return to the elegiac magic realism of *The Night of the Shooting Stars*. A brief examination of three of these films—*Good Morning, Babylon*; *Kaos*; and *Fiorile*—offers insight into the range and depth of the Tavianis' cinematic vision.

With its celebration of the artisanal origins of Italian cinema, *Good Morning, Babylon* follows two Italian brothers, Nicola (Vincent Spano) and Andrea (Joaquim de Almeida) Bonanno, who have followed their father (Omero Antonutti) in his ancient trade as a cathedral builder in Tuscany. After the family business fails, the two sons immigrate to America and eventually find work in the studio of D. W. Griffith (Charles Dance) as carpenters. During the filming of *Intolerance*, the brothers produce exactly the kind of elephant Griffith desires for his lavish sets, copying an animal they had observed while repairing the facade of Pisa's cathedral. This work launches them as set designers in Hollywood, but the Great War intervenes, with the brothers united again on the Italian front to shoot a film for the Italian army.

Numerous details of *Good Morning, Babylon* call attention to the Taviani brothers' views on cinematic art. The fact that the two protagonists are brothers working together in the film industry is clearly autobiographical. It is a historical fact (depicted in the film) that Pastrone's *Cabiria*—particularly its lavish sets—influenced Griffith when the American director shot *Intolerance*. The Tavianis' comparison of Master Bonanno, the old cathedral builder, and the great American silent film director, the creator of the new "cathedral" made out of celluloid, seems explicit in Griffith's declaration: "I do not know whether our work, that of your sons and mine, is as fine as that of those who built the Romanesque cathedrals. I do know that those works were born as these are born today—of the same collective dream. . . . This is why I love movie-making, and I respect it."[4] Even though the ideological and aesthetic underpinnings of the cinema of the Taviani brothers and Federico Fellini seem miles apart, *Good Morning, Babylon* and Fellini's *Interview* celebrate a certain kind of filmmaking that the three men believe to be most typical of Italy's cinematic heritage. It is an artisan's cinema, a poet's cinema, a kind of cinema close in conception to the honest labor and personal expression of a simple craftsman and far removed from either the ideologically engaged cinema aimed at a minuscule audience of like-minded intellectuals or the commercial brand of industrialized filmmaking for vast international audiences we associate with the Hollywood system.

Kaos adapts five short stories from Pirandello's voluminous collection *Short Stories for a Year*, published in a two-volume edition in 1937 shortly after his death. Most of the best stories in the collection, particularly those the Tavianis selected for adaptation to film, treat Sicilian folklore and customs, but the film represents a serious cinematic statement about the role of the creative imagination. In his fiction, Pirandello (see chapter 5), an extremely cerebral writer, a rationalist playwright, dramatized the sudden and sometimes tragic eruptions of the irrational into daily life. The opening epigraph title of *Kaos* cites Pirandello's remarks about his birthplace in Sicily, a spot near the modern city of Agrigento (then called Girgenti) that has ancient Greek origins: "I am a son of Chaos; and not allegorically, but in true reality, because I was born in our countryside, located in an entangled wood, named *Cavusu* by the inhabitants of Girgenti: a dialectal corruption of the genuine and antique Greek word *kàos*." Employing the name of Pirandello's birthplace for their title, the Tavianis remind us that Pirandello himself struggled during his entire career to produce literature that bridged the gap over the nothingness that the word "chaos" suggested to him.

The film employs versions of four different short stories—"The Other Son," "Moonsickness," "The Jar," and "Requiem," and an epilogue, "Dialogue with the Mother"—set within a frame inspired by a fifth story, "The Crow of Mízzaro." The Tavianis' Sicily exhibits nothing of the picturesque that even remotely resembles the renowned tourist attractions of Greek temples and sandy white beaches. Although agonizingly beautiful, it is a violent and tragic land, beset by murderous Sicilian bandits who, in a flashback, behead a woman's husband in the first episode, "The Other Son." The Tavianis remind us (as Coppola had in the *Godfather* trilogy) that the antiquated social system of the ancient island produced not only violence but also strange folk beliefs (the werewolf of "Moonsickness"), forced immigration to America because of the grinding poverty most Sicilians experienced before the postwar period ("The Other Son"), and greedy landlords whose wealth and attachment to material goods outweighed their concern for their impoverished workers ("The Jar").

On the set of "The Jar" episode of *Kaos*: Franco Franchi, Paolo and Vittorio Taviani, and Ciccio Ingrassia, from left to right. *Credit: Paolo and Vittorio Taviani*

An intriguing and unusual episode, "The Jar" includes in its cast two Sicilian comics who have made repeated appearances in this history (see, for example, chapter 7): Franco Franchi and Ciccio Ingrassia. The Taviani brothers cast them in *Kaos* precisely for Sicilian qualities that the teams' critics disliked. Their unforgettable physical presence on the screen had earlier inspired Federico Fellini to cast Ingrassia as the insane, sex-starved uncle in *Amarcord* who screams, "I want a woman!" at the top of his voice until he is taken back to his asylum by a midget nun. The fact that the Tavianis and Fellini skillfully employed such iconic popular figures rather than more traditional comic actors proves once again that film directors are often cleverer than critics.

The film's epilogue sets all of these Pirandello stories in the proper aesthetic prospective. In it, the playwright's mother admonishes Pirandello (Omero Antonutti): "Learn to look at things with the eyes of those who can't see them anymore. It will be painful of course, but that pain will make them more sacred and more beautiful." The beautiful stories adapted by the Taviani brothers all represent examples of the author's adherence to his mother's teachings. Like Pirandello's short fiction, their *Kaos* views the past from the eyes of those who are no longer with us, creating a fabulous, musical, and poetic world, filled with violence and pity, comedy and tragedy, to which Pirandello's posthumous collection gave timeless literary form. With this original adaptation of stories by Italy's most Sicilian of writers, Vittorio and Paolo Taviani have produced a minor cinematic masterpiece, a film worthy of comparison with their best work.

With simplicity and elegance, *Fiorile* presents a visually rich account of how a family curse has dominated the lives of a Tuscan family from the French Revolution to the present day. By allowing their narrative to rest upon folklore and legend, the Taviani brothers evoke the hidden and mythical meanings behind the dry details of academic history. The film opens in the present, as Luigi Benedetti (Lino Capolicchio) and his French wife, Juliette (Constanze Engelbrecht), are taking their two children to Tuscany to visit Massimo Benedetti, the grandfather (Renato Carpentieri) they have never met, since Luigi had been sent away from Italy as a young boy to live abroad. As the story unfolds in successive flashbacks to the eighteenth, nineteenth, and mid-twentieth centuries, the reason for his exile becomes clear. Luigi tells his family about the curse of the Benedetti family and why they became known in the Tuscan countryside as the "Maledettis" (that is, the "cursed," rather than the "blessed," the latter being the literal translation of their family name).

The family curse dates back to the Napoleonic invasion of Italy in 1797–99. A handsome, young French lieutenant named Jean (Michael Vartan) falls in love with Elisabetta Benedetti (Galatea Ranzi), a poor peasant girl. Jean makes love to her rather than guarding the strongbox full of gold coins he is entrusted to protect, and as a result he is shot by a firing squad. In a letter written to Elisabetta before his execution, Jean calls Elisabetta "Fiorile," the Italian translation of Floréal (literally "blossom"), the month of springtime in the French Revolutionary calendar that corresponds roughly to the period between 20–1 April and 20–1 May in the traditional Gregorian calendar. Unbeknownst to Elisabetta/Fiorile, it was her brother, Corrado (Claudio Bigagli), who took the gold, which established the financial basis for their wealthy and powerful family dynasty, along with a family curse for taking the money that cost Jean his life. When Elisabetta finds herself pregnant with Jean's child, she vows revenge for Jean's death, not knowing that the curse will fall upon her own descendants.

A century passes and the Benedettis become powerful enough to send the ambitious Alessandro Benedetti (Claudio Bigagli again) to the Chamber of Deputies in Rome. Nevertheless, the stolen coins, the family curse, and Fiorile's thirst for revenge resurface. Fiorile's descendant Alessandro prevents Elisa Benedetti (Galatea Ranzi again) from marrying a young peasant boy who has made her pregnant. In this new generation, however, Elisa embraces Fiorile's desire for vendetta and kills her two brothers with poisoned mushrooms when they are traveling to Rome. Another jump in time moves from the late nineteenth century to the last months of World War II. Elisa Benedetti's grandson, Massimo (Michael Vartan again), who is obsessed with the family curse, even writes his university thesis on the French army in the countryside between 1797 and 1799 and keeps a mannequin of his French ancestor Jean in his home. His fascination with the revolutionary ideals for which Jean fought—liberty, fraternity, and equality—convinces him to participate in the anti-Fascist Resistance even though most of the partisans belong to an entirely different economic class, the Tuscan peasantry, the class of his ancestors before they were corrupted by the wealth from the stolen gold coins. Captured by the Fascists, Massimo's life is spared because of his social prominence. A Fascist militiaman recognizes him and pulls him out of the group of condemned partisans because he recognizes the value of having a rich friend after the Fascists lose the war. The family curse and the guilt he feels for having been singled out and saved because of his wealth color the rest of Massimo's life. His desire to spare his son, Luigi, from the negative results of the family curse explains why he has sent him to France, and why Luigi and his family have never before visited Massimo in his old age on his Tuscan property.

In telling this charming story that is a combination of Tuscan folklore and history, the Taviani brothers return to many of their favorite themes. The French Revolution has always represented a utopian notion of revolution for these two Marxist directors and inspired their *Allonsanfan* of 1974. *Fiorile*'s portrait of the anti-Fascist Resistance in the Tuscan countryside recalls *The Night of the Shooting Stars*. *Fiorile* embodies the directors' habitual use of a kind of cinematic magic realism, where the simple folktales and customs of the peasantry in Tuscany are imbued with a beauty and charm that even the passage of two centuries of history cannot erase. The skillful use of Claudio Bigagli, Galatea Ranzi, and Michael Vartan to play characters from different historical periods helps to ensure the continuity of tradition in the narrative. It would not be inaccurate to call *Fiorile* a kind of Marxist fairytale, where money, "filthy lucre," functions as the driving force of the narrative and as the root of all evil. Yet the film's political message, always understated and subordinated to the aesthetic demands of storytelling, remains overshadowed by the beauty of the film's photography and the magic unfolding of how the past resurfaces in the present in the most surprising ways imaginable.

Music and Other Themes in Zeffirelli, Rosi, Cavani, and Olmi

In the 1940s and 1950s, operatic films flourished, often casting film actors in the leading roles with dubbed singing on the sound track. In the most famous of these films, Sophia Loren, criticized by many musical purists for her inability to lip-synch to the music and to Renata Tebaldi's lyrics, played the title role in the film version of Verdi's *Aida* (1953), directed by Clemente Fracassi (1917–93).

Franco Zeffirelli

True to his early apprenticeship with Luchino Visconti, who became both a famous film director and an opera producer, Franco Zeffirelli made a number of opera films, including productions of three Verdi operas: *La Traviata* (*La traviata*, 1983), *Otello* (1986), and *Don Carlo* (1992). Zeffirelli's Verdi films were directed at an audience of music lovers rather than film buffs, but their sumptuous settings and rich detail certainly owe something to Visconti's film and operatic style. In addition, Zeffirelli also directed biographical films about musical personalities: *Young Toscanini* (*Il giovane Toscanini*, 1988) and *Callas Forever* (2002). Both pay particular attention to their protagonists at a critical moment in their lives. The biopic of the internationally famous conductor (portrayed by C. Thomas Howell) focuses upon his debut with Verdi's *Aida* in Rio de Janeiro at the age of eighteen and his love affair with an imposing opera diva named Nadina Bulicioff (Elizabeth Taylor). Zeffirelli's tribute to one of his closest friends, Maria Callas (Fanny Ardant), provides a fictionalized account of the diva's last days, when the music promoter Larry Kelly (Jeremy Irons) offers her an opportunity in 1977 to star in filmed versions of operas with her earlier recordings dubbed on the sound tracks. In the process of completing a version of Bizet's *Carmen*, an opera she had previously never performed but only recorded in the studio, Callas experiences a moment of artistic creation of the kind that had made her such a celebrated singer.

In Zeffirelli's mature career, opera productions and opera films overshadowed his direction of fiction films. He based *Tea with Mussolini* (*Un té con Mussolini*, 1999), however, on events from his own extraordinary autobiography.[5] Much more admired abroad than in Italy, this film gives insight into an outsider's appreciation for a very different foreign culture by focusing upon Luca (Charlie Lucas as a child, Baird Wallace as a young man), the illegitimate son of an Italian businessman befriended by members of the Anglo-American expatriate community in Florence during the years before the outbreak of World War II. Drawing bravura performances from five famous women—Cher, Lily Tomlin, Judi Dench, Maggie Smith, and Joan Plowright—Zeffirelli juxtaposes the older English Grand Dames to the young American upstarts to propose an extremely subtle metacinematic discourse about the contrasting acting styles associated with the London stage, on the one hand, and the Hollywood screen, on the other. Set in the Florence of the 1930s and 1940s, Zeffirelli's film provides sympathetic portraits of these expatriate women, called the "scorpions" by the Florentines, who promenade daily up Via Tornabuoni for tea at Doney's Bar, while scolding the locals for not measuring up to their Anglo-Saxon standards of morality, cleanliness, and decorum. Naturally, the women fail to understand anything of importance about the Italy of these times, and they are united only by their affection for Luca. Their naïveté becomes quite apparent when the widow of an English ambassador, played by Maggie Smith, uses her political connections to arrange a meeting with Mussolini himself, at which he serves them tea and reassures them with unblinking hypocrisy that he hopes to avoid war with their two countries. After the outbreak of war, the English and America women are interned by the Fascist government, and the story becomes one of endurance and courage as they all, largely through Luca's influence, come to appreciate one another and work together to survive to see the war's conclusion.

Francesco Rosi and Liliana Cavani

Like Zeffirelli, Francesco Rosi began work in the cinema as Visconti's assistant on *The Earth Trembles*, one of the classics of Italian postwar neorealism. Rosi showed an interest in opera films, creating realistic sets for Georges Bizet's *Carmen* (1984)—as Luigi Comencini, who shared this interest, would later do for Giacomo Puccini's *La Bohème* (*La bohème*, 1988). Rosi's most important work in this period is his historical reconstruction of the Holocaust in *The Truce* (*La tregua*, 1997), an adaptation of *The Reawakening* (1963), the memoir by Primo Levi (1919–87) that narrates Levi's odyssey following his release from the concentration camp in Auschwitz to his arrival in his hometown of Turin. With a large budget and huge cast of extras, *The Truce* was shot in English and featured John Turturro, the Italian American actor, as Primo Levi, but the film was unsuccessful at the box office. Its attitude toward the Russian liberators of Levi's concentration camp points to the director's nostalgia for an era when Italian intellectuals looked to the now defunct Soviet Union for an alternative to American economic and intellectual hegemony in Italian postwar life.[6]

Liliana Cavani, in her film *The Berlin Affair* (*Interno berlinese*, 1985), provides a portrait of sexual mores in prewar Nazi Germany (Berlin in 1938), recalling both Visconti's German trilogy and her own controversial work *The Night Porter*. In its depiction of a ménage à trois among a German official in the Foreign Office (Kevin McNally); his wife, Louise (Gudrun Landgrebe); and Mitsuko (Mio Takaki), the daughter of the Japanese ambassador to the Third Reich, *The Berlin Affair* approaches this kind of kinky relationship from a female perspective rather than the male point of view typical of most sexually explicit films. Morally and sexually, Mitsuko completely dominates the German couple, and her actions reflect a complete disregard for considerations of sexual gender, an attitude obviously designed to shock Cavani's audiences. Like her male counterparts, Liliana Cavani also worked on opera films during this period, producing versions of Verdi's *La Traviata* (1992), Pietro Mascagni's *Cavalleria Rusticana* (1996), and Puccini's *Manon Lescaut* (1998) for Italian television. Her fictional films included a revisitation of her 1966 film *Francesco d'Assisi*, entitled *Francesco* (1989), with an improbable Mickey Rourke as Saint Francis, and *Ripley's Game* (*Il gioco di Ripley*, 2002), an adaptation of the second of Patricia Highsmith's Ripley novels—with John Malkovich playing an older Tom Ripley. (Highsmith's intriguing murderer and con man had previously been adapted for the cinema by Wim Wenders in *The American Friend* [1977] and then again by Anthony Minghella in *The Talented Mr. Ripley* [1999].)

Ermanno Olmi

Ermanno Olmi carried on his commitment to making straightforward but subtle films influenced by his neorealist heritage. Recalling in many ways the protagonists Olmi presented in his masterpiece *The Tree of the Wooden Clogs*, the religious narrative in *Keep Walking* (*Cammina, cammina*, 1982) retells the Journey of the Magi with nonprofessional actors. Most critics see Olmi's critique of contemporary intellectuals in the Wise Men's failure to intervene to stop King Herod's Slaughter of the Innocents. In *Long Live the Lady!* (*Lunga vita alla signora!*, 1987), he provides an amusing allegory of authority in a treatment of the adventures of six adolescents, the best students of a school for hotel workers, who have been summoned to serve an important banquet given for a mysterious but powerful woman. With little dialogue and fine attention to detail and facial expressions, Olmi draws masterful performances from his nonprofessional actors that recall those of the protagonists in *The Sound of Trumpets.* Olmi's Christian perspective provides little ideological denunciation of society's power elite, but the film concludes with the message that love could change the powerful woman's loneliness and might transform her sterile power into a force for good.

Olmi's penchant for nonprofessional actors and simple, original scripts did not prevent him from trying his hand at literary adaptations in which he cast professionals. *The Legend of the Holy Drinker* (*La leggenda del santo bevitore*, 1988) brings to the screen a novella by Joseph Roth starring Rutger Hauer and Anthony Quayle; and *The Secret of the Old Woods* (*Il segreto del bosco vecchio*, 1993) presents an ecological fairy tale, an adaptation of a 1935 novel by the Italian surrealist writer Dino Buzzati (1906–72), replete with talking animals, starring Paolo Villaggio. Even more surprising, however, was his direction for the stage of Verdi's opera *Un ballo in maschera* (directed for television by Don Kent), with unusual sets and costumes provided by the Italian sculptor Arnoldo Pomodoro (who, in addition to his famous spherical sculptures, also designed Fellini's funeral monument in Rimini). Subsequently, Olmi turned to two historical films. *The Profession of Arms* (*Il mestiere delle armi*, 2001) represents a splendidly meticulous recreation of the last days of the famous sixteenth-century Medici *condottiere*, Giovanni dalle Bande Nere (1498–1526), the father of the first grand duke of Tuscany, Cosimo. In it, Olmi employs stupendous Renaissance costumes, real locations from famous Renaissance buildings, and dialogue taken from period documents (especially the letters of the Venetian writer Pietro Aretino [1492–1556], one of Giovanni's closest friends). For Olmi, Giovanni incarnates the prototypical Renaissance warrior before the triumph of guns, but he uses the *condottiero*'s death from a wound caused by small cannon fire from a falconet as emblematic of a technological and ethical shift in European culture connected with the eclipse of traditional personal weapons (the sword, the lance, or the mace) by gunpowder and deadly firearms that took place in the early sixteenth century. Particularly interesting are his beautifully surrealistic scenes of knights in full armor riding through the misty regions close to the Po River in wintertime, his carefully re-created casting of primitive cannon in Ferrara, and the etiquette surrounding the medical operations and ritualistic death of important figures connected with Italian Renaissance courts. In his following film, Olmi turned to an almost completely Oriental cast (with the exception of Bud Spencer playing a Portuguese sea captain) to make *Singing behind Screens* (*Cantando dietro i paraventi*, 2003), an epic treatment of eighteenth-century Chinese pirates commanded by a woman, which used digital technology to re-create the Chinese Imperial Fleet on the high seas. *With One Hundred Nails*

(*Centochiodi*, 2007), a complex film about the relationship between the intellectual life and the spiritual vocation, Olmi announced his intention to renounce fictional filmmaking, opting to devote the remainder of his career to his first love, documentaries. *One Hundred Nails* opens with a man we later discover to be a philosophy professor at the University of Bologna (Raz Degan) who nails one hundred manuscripts (incunabula, actually) to the floor of a library with the kinds of huge spikes usually associated with Christ's Crucifixion. Feigning suicide, he then abandons his post at the university and discards his BMW by the shores of the Po River in favor of a simple life in the countryside, where the locals begin to treat him as the incarnation of an impoverished saint much like Saint Francis. Although this film has high aesthetic qualities, Olmi's ultimate image, captured by the ex-professor's remark that a single cup of coffee with a friend is more valuable than all the books in the world, unfortunately panders to the rampant anti-intellectualism prevalent not only in Italy but in the rest of the world of moviegoers. Not surprisingly, this film aroused a heated critical discussion in Italy, and though it received a number of festival prize nominations, it was not overly successful at the box office.

The Versatile Lightness of Pupi Avati

Less well known abroad than within Italy, Pupi Avati has become one of Italy's best and most successful commercial directors while gradually attaining the status of auteur or art film director (which for some Italian critics, apparently, represents the only category that counts in the history of the cinema). Like his predecessors Mario Bava and other directors associated with the genre or B film, Avati tried his hand quite successfully at a number of different genres, with original forays into both the universe of the *giallo*, or thriller, with *The House with Laughing Windows* in 1976 (see chapter 12), and the world of the spaghetti nightmare zombie film with *Revenge of the Dead* (*Zeder*, 1983). His passion for American jazz led him to shoot *Bix* (1991), a fascinating biopic of the American musical legend Leon "Bix" Beiderbecke (1903–31), which he filmed partially on location in Davenport, Iowa, Beiderbecke's hometown. Avati's American sojourn no doubt influenced him to use Davenport and another of the Quad Cities (Rock Island, Illinois) as the setting for a recent *giallo*: *The Hideout* (*Il nascondiglio*, 2007) is about an Italian woman (Laura Morante) who moves there to set up an Italian restaurant in a house where, fifty years earlier, while it was an orphanage, some brutal murders had taken place.

American music also inspired what is perhaps Avati's best film, *Help Me Dream* (*Aiutami a sognare*, 1981). It combines a film genre most unusual in Italian cinema—the musical—with an original discourse on Italy's postwar love affair with America and American culture that blossomed during the

Francesca and the village children listen to the radio and wait for the arrival of the American army in Pupi Avati's *Help Me Dream. Credit: MOMA*

last several years of World War II and the decade dominated by neorealist film culture (1945–55). Opening with a prologue showing the train on which the songwriter "Fats" Waller (1904–43) died (leaving a legacy of such classics as "Honeysuckle Rose" and "Ain't Misbehavin'"), the film then cuts to a farmhouse in Emilia-Romagna in 1943, where groups of upper-class Italians are awaiting the arrival of the American army and liberation. Francesca (Mariangela Melato) is a starstruck movie fan whose cinematic education was based upon her memories of American musicals and the popular entertainment fare permitted for importation by the Fascist regime. Albeit tinged by a highly romantic and superficial view of it, her love of American culture is emblematic of the hope an entire Italian generation felt. The group sits around the fireplace, playing old American records and breaking into full-blown production numbers worthy of American musicals. It is doubly humorous to hear them sing such classics as "Pennies from Heaven," "Jeepers Creepers," and "Some of These Days" with a pronounced Italian accent. One day the American observation plane that flies over every day has engine trouble and is forced into an emergency landing on the farm. Out jumps an Italo-American airman named Ray (Anthony Franciosa), who has relatives in Castellammare and who, like Francesca, is a passionate jazz pianist. His plane is named *Help Me Dream*, and he claims (probably falsely) to be on intimate terms with Bing Crosby, Glenn Miller, and other famous jazz artists in the States such as Fats Waller.

Of course, the obvious happens, since this film is a musical. Ray and Francesca fall in love, but eventually Ray repairs his aircraft and returns to the war, never to be seen again, while Francesca and the children in her hometown wait in vain for years for his return. Besides a film belonging to the musical genre, *Help Me Dream* also represents a final good-bye to the optimistic postwar myth of America that had been so important to Italian popular culture. Attracted by the enigmatic innocence and enthusiasm embodied in American music and in soldiers like Ray, Francesca and her friends are ultimately betrayed not by America itself but by their own naive perception of American culture that was ultimately as much a projection of their own desires and illusions as of any real America. If Rossellini's *Paisan* opened this cross-cultural dialogue on a romantic note, films like Avati's *Help Me Dream* bring the dream down to earth.

Since most of Avati's films are set in his native Emilia-Romagna, they possess as sure a sense of place as the Taviani brothers' settings in Tuscany. Apart from his comic irony and light touch, which have led critics to compare him to both Truffaut and Ernst Lubitsch, what makes Avati such an appealing auteur is that he boldly explores a number of film genres: musicals, horror films, sentimental comedies, thrillers, fables, sports films (*The Last Minute* [*Ultimo minuto*, 1987]), and historical costume dramas, such as *We Three* (*Noi tre*, 1984), a touching portrait of the young Mozart who comes to Bologna in 1770 at the age of fourteen to prepare for an examination on musical composition. The drama of this little jewel of a film—released only a few months after Milos Forman's *Amadeus* broke international box-office records with another Mozart biopic—Avati's work focuses upon the marked conflict between Mozart's genius and future greatness, on the one hand, and his adolescent temptation to abandon his destiny for a more emotionally rewarding life that allows room for simple pleasures and human passion.

Avati's nostalgic look at Mozart's youth shares the mood of other films made during this creative period in the 1980s: *School Trip* (*Una gita scolastica*, 1983), *Graduation Party* (*Festa di laurea*, 1985), *Christmas Present* (*Regalo di Natale*, 1986), *Impiegati* (literally, "employees," 1984), and *The Story of Boys & Girls* (*Storia di ragazzi e di ragazze*, 1989). Three of these films profit from the acting talents of Carlo Delle Piane, whose characters project an ingenuousness and basic goodness that more than compensate for their extremely homely features. (In all, Avati has directed Delle Piane in twelve films and two TV miniseries.) *School Trip* recounts the bittersweet events of a high-school excursion in 1914 from Bologna to Florence, narrated from the viewpoint of the last surviving member of the class, an aging spinster named Laura (Lidia Broccolino). On this trip, the bashful literature professor Carlo Balla (Carlo Delle Piane) experiences his first taste of passion in a relationship with Serena Stanziani (Tiziana Pini), the drawing instructor who later betrays her husband with a student and loses her job. The last sequence of the film shows each of the children on the school trip crossing over a river and into a thick fog bank, a metaphor for their deaths. Love fails to conquer death, but the director's nostalgia saves their personal dramas from oblivion. In *Graduation Party*, Avati treats the conflict between innocence and experience. Vanni Porelli (Delle Piane) is a pastry maker and former factotum of the rich Germani family whose life was forever changed when the beautiful daughter of the house, Gaia (Aurore Clément), kissed him in her excitement over Mussolini's declaration of war on June 10, 1940. Exactly ten years later, Gaia asks Vanni to remodel her country villa and to handle all the details for the graduation party of her daughter, Sandra (Lidia Broccolino), consciously exploiting Vanni's obvious crush on her to obtain these services without paying for them. Vanni loses his illusions about Gaia and her entire family: Sandra has lied about graduating; Gaia, her family, and her friends are all superficial egotists. He realizes that the woman of his dreams was only a creation of his own imagination and refuses payment for his ruinous expenses from these wealthy but morally bankrupt remnants of his past. In *Christmas Present*, Avati reverses Delle Piane's previous role as an innocent, transforming him into a calculating card shark named Antonio Santelia, a performance that earned him a Golden Lion for Best Actor at the 1986 Venice Film Festival. Santelia is introduced into what is usually a friendly card game among four close friends by one of the men; the latter, willing to betray his friends for money, has agreed to split his earnings with Santelia. During this all-night Christmas Eve card party, it becomes clear that the close relationships of these four individuals have much less firm foundations than they had imagined, and card cheating becomes emblematic of a wider range of inauthentic emotional relationships.

Demonstrating a mastery of the light, poetic touch, Avati's later works also show an obvious affection for the countryside and customs of his native province. His best work is almost always set in the near-distant past, frequently in the prewar Fascist period. *The Story of Boys & Girls*, perhaps the most successful of his films, provides a wonderfully entertaining portrait of a wedding feast that takes place in the countryside of Emilia-Romagna during the Fascist period, before the war that would destroy this idyllic rural and romantic life. Comparable in certain respects to Scola's *The Family*, it provides a slice of everyday life from a past that must be drawn from Avati's own recollections of his youth. The film is memorable not only for its skillful handling of a large group of active and energetic actors, but also for the incredible depiction of the almost endless array of wonderful Italian dishes served to the guests. Avati sets his romantic comedy *Incantato*, a.k.a. *The Heart Is Elsewhere* (*Il cuore altrove*, 2003), in his favorite city of Bologna during the Fascist period. Nello (Neri Marcorè), a scholarly bachelor nearing middle age, teaches Greek and Latin. Nello's father, Cesare (Giancarlo Giannini), who runs a tailor shop in Rome for ecclesiastics and provides sartorial garb for cardinals and popes, sends him to Bologna, not only to teach but also to lose his virginity and to find a wife, relying on that city's reputation for pliant women and famous brothels to change his son's shyness toward the opposite sex. Nello meets a rich, spoiled, and beautiful girl named Angela (Vanessa Incontrada), who has become temporarily blind, and falls in love with her; she uses Nello shamelessly, parading him around as her fiancé in order to arouse the jealousy of her former real fiancé, Guido (Pietro Ragusa), who dumped her after learning of her blindness. Once Angela regains her sight, she, in turn, dumps Nello and marries her surgeon. Eventually Nello and Angela meet at the Vatican at the time of a papal audience. Nello, who has abandoned his teaching career in Bologna and gone to work for his father, has been assigned to stitch up a damaged garment. Once there, he discovers that the person who needs his assistance is none other than Angela. Since she had never seen him because of her temporary blindness, she does not recognize him until, after he has stitched up her dress, Nello cites a Latin verse. *Incantato* offers a beautiful but simple exploration of the dimensions of selfish and unselfish love, and confirms Avati's ability to depict, deftly and with great insight, complex human passions on the screen.

Marco Bellocchio

Marco Bellocchio's debut on the international scene coincided with that of Bernardo Bertolucci in the early 1960s (see chapter 8). Characterized as the enfants terribles of that period, both directors had a serious interest in psychoanalysis, and both made politically themed films typical of leftist Italian cinematic culture. Although Bellocchio never achieved the international commercial success of Bertolucci, he continued to make films that were well received in Italy and Europe (less so in the United States). Like so many other directors of this generation and in the 1980s and 1990s, Bellocchio adapted several literary works to the screen, including *Henry IV* (*Enrico IV*, 1984), an intriguing version of Luigi Pirandello's 1922 play about an existential madman in which Marcello Mastroianni contributed one of the best dramatic performances of his career; and *The Prince of Homburg* (*Il principe di Homburg*, 1997), a less successful filmic version of Heinrich von Kleist's play of that name (1811). Bellocchio's literary adaptations proved more successful when they included an exploration of psychological problems, such as *The Nanny* (*La balia*, 1999)—a film set in early twentieth-century Rome and based on a short story by Pirandello. Professor Mori (Fabrizio Bentivoglio), a wealthy psychiatrist, hires a wet nurse for his infant child when his wife, Vittoria (Valeria Bruni Tedeschi), finds herself unable to nurse the baby. The woman he hires, Annetta (Maya Sansa), is an illiterate peasant with a leftist lover in jail for subversion and a child of her own for whom she must care. Bellocchio sets his psychological study of motherhood, which contrasts the neurotic behavior of the doctor's wife to the healthy maternal instincts of the peasant girl, in an atmosphere of "subversive" political upheavals in Rome, and the clear implication is that the rich exploit the poor even in depriving them of mothers' milk. The film provides a telling portrait of the strict social separation of rich and poor in Umbertine Italy.

Bellocchio's later works—*The Religion Hour*, a.k.a. *My Mother's Smile* (*L'ora di religione* [*il sorriso di mia madre*], 2002); *Good Morning, Night* (*Buongiorno, notte*, 2003); and *The Wedding Director* (*Il regista di matrimoni*, 2006)—treat a wide variety of subjects: the canonization of an intellectual's mother, the killing of Aldo Moro, and a metacinematic consideration of a film director, respectively. In *The Wedding Director*, Bellocchio provides an uncharacteristic comic touch to the portrait of a film director named Franco Elica (Sergio Castellitto), who is engaged in filming Alessandro Manzoni's nineteenth-century novel *The Betrothed*, a great literary work that, like Dante's *Inferno*, has bored generations of Italian schoolchildren largely because of the sanctimonious manner in which it has been taught. When the project runs into trouble because of the director's sexual peccadilloes, he takes refuge in Sicily and encounters a sinister figure, the Prince of Palagonia (Sami Frey) who wants Franco to film the wedding of his daughter (Donatella Finocchiaro), with whom Franco immediately falls in love. In the process, Bellocchio provides a witty but cynical description of the state of affairs in an economically exasperating Italy and the deplorable condition of his own art form, the cinema.

My Mother's Smile and *Good Morning, Night* explore more familiar Bellocchio themes: social hypocrisy, religious cynicism, and political unrest in Italy. The first film tackles the question of religious faith, imagining that the Catholic Church considers the beatification of a mother murdered by one of her sons, now locked up in an insane asylum. Another of her sons, an atheist artist named Ernesto (Sergio Castellitto), opposes treating his mother as a saint, believing that her enigmatic smile of the film's title was actually one of indifference, and that she actually drove his brother to kill her. Interestingly, the family bands together to support this beatification as "insurance"—Aunt Maria (Piera Degli Esposti) spells out their self-interest when she advises Ernesto to go along with the family, avoid causing trouble, leave his wife, get himself a mistress, and stop being a moralist! A saint in the family will work wonders for everyone, she insists, and Ernesto will profit from the canonization as much as the rest of the family.

Freely adapted from a book (*Il prigioniero*, 1988) by Anna Laura Braghetti (1953–), one of the terrorists involved in the Moro assassination, *Good Morning, Night* presents a sympathetic look into the psychology of terrorism, but the director's position suggests that by killing the Christian Democratic leader Aldo Moro, the terrorists dehumanized him as a political abstraction and, therefore, committed inhuman acts in the name of humanity. In fact, Moro's idea of a "historic compromise" between Christian Democracy and Italian Communism helped change the face of Italy's political parties. The same kinds of thinking characterized the worst periods of leftist, totalitarian rule in the Soviet Union, Cambodia, and China. From his leftist perspective, however, Bellocchio also reserves a good deal of criticism for the Italian political system, which in his ideologically tinged view, is almost equally guilty of the politician's death for refusing to negotiate with terrorists.

Just before Moro is taken off to his death, the character in the film named Chiara (Maya Sansa), in whose apartment Moro has been held (as he had been in Braghetti's), and whose doubts about killing the politician are followed throughout the narrative, dreams that Moro is walking out of apartment and into freedom while the terrorists sleep. And yet Bellocchio's attempts to "understand" the terrorists who killed Aldo Moro cannot change the historical judgment on the uselessness of their cruel act. Since most of the surviving Italian Red Brigade terrorists associated with Moro's murder and other violent assassinations are currently out of jail, on parole, on work release, or actually done with their relatively light sentences, it remains difficult for a fair-thinking person without ideological blinders to work up much sympathy for the perpetrators of such crimes, which accomplished nothing and tore Italy apart for many years.

Always willing to provoke his audiences with social and political issues, Bellocchio's latest film *Vincere* (literally, "to conquer"—the title derives from a popular Fascist slogan, 2009) explores the little-known story of the Italian dictator Benito Mussolini's secret and illegitimate son. It is likely to prove as controversial as his work about the assassination of one of Italy's most important political leaders.

~

It is essential to understand the significant contributions to the Italian film industry of this older generation of major directors. After the giants of the postwar period (Rossellini, Visconti, De Sica, Antonioni, Fellini) finally passed from the scene into film history—along with many of their less illustrious but often immensely talented comrades (De Santis, Comencini, Bava, Germi, Lattuada, Pasolini, Petri, Risi, Pontecorvo, Ferreri, Leone, Fulci)—figures such as Scola, Avati, Bellocchio, the Taviani brothers, and others, all born before the outbreak of World War II, continued to form the backbone of the industry and to create original, exciting films.

A generation of young filmmakers born in the 1950s, and who came of age around the time of the social, political, and cultural upheavals associated with the date of 1968, would strike off in very different directions. It is they who are the subject of chapter 16.

CHAPTER SIXTEEN

The Third Wave

A NEW GENERATION OF AUTEURS

ITALY NEVER EXPERIENCED the generational conflict that occurred in France during the New Wave period, when such young directors as Truffaut, Godard, and others rebelled, before and immediately after the end of World War II, against what they considered an outmoded kind of filmmaking practiced by directors from the prewar generation. Because of the social and aesthetic importance of Italian neorealism in the immediate postwar period, the generation that included such Young Turks as Bernardo Bertolucci, Pier Paolo Pasolini, Francesco Rosi, and others had, if anything, an attachment to the neorealist past. Yet it was inevitable that an even younger generation, those born after the war and who had come of age during the upheavals of the 1960s, would eventually search for aesthetic and economic solutions to the almost perpetual crisis in the Italian film industry after the 1970s, when the rise of private (as opposed to government controlled) television seemed to be destroying this original form of cultural expression. Thus, a new group of talented directors emerged, one that would not only take account of Italy's cinematic traditions but would also attempt to explore a new cinematic language, all the while coming to grips with entirely different problems of production and distribution: the threat of television; new technologies, such as video and DVDs; the lack of Italian capital to produce quality films; the increasing hegemony of Hollywood; and the decline of international interest in Italian films. Taken together, and in spite of the ink spilled during this period on the supposed "decline" or even the "death" of the Italian cinema, these new faces constitute a highly creative and successful group of filmmakers: Andrea (1944–2006) and Antonio Frazzi (1944–), Gianni Amelio (1945–), Maurizio Nichetti (1948–), Marco Risi (1951–), Roberto Benigni, Nanni Moretti (1953–), Sergio Castellitto, Massimo Troisi, Giuseppe Piccioni (1953–), Marco Tullio Giordana, Cristina Comencini (1956–), Giuseppe Tornatore, Davide Ferrario (1956–), Silvio Soldini (1958–), Mario Martone (1959–), and Ferzan Ozpetek (1959–).

Nanni Moretti

The closest thing to a rebellion against the Italian cinema of the past occurs in the films of Nanni Moretti. Called narcissistic because his work reflects not only his personal autobiographical views on life but also because he acts in so many of them, Moretti frequently combines typically cynical and intellectual perspectives on political events in Italy, and has had perhaps more impact upon that part of Italian life than any other director of his generation. From humble and impoverished beginnings with Super-8 filmmaking, Moretti moved to commercial films in 35mm and eventually founded his own production company (Sacher, named after his favorite desert, the Sachertorte), his own movie theater in Rome's Trastevere district (called the Nuovo Sacher), and a short film festival (again, the Sacher Festival). Always scripted by Moretti himself, with only occasional contributions by others, his films are among the most popular and highly regarded in Italy and Europe, even though none of them has yet to achieve blockbuster status in the United States. They include his early *I Am Self-sufficient* (*Io sono un autarchico*, 1976), shot in Super 8 and then reprinted in 16mm, which enjoyed a highly favorable reception in film clubs; *Ecce Bombo* (*Ecce bombo*, 1978), shot in 16mm with direct sound, and received at the Cannes Film Festival with great enthusiasm; *Sweet Dreams* (*Sogni d'oro*, 1981), his first 35mm film, awarded the Grand Jury prize at the Venice Film Festival; *Bianca* (1984); *The Mass Is Ended* (*La messa è finita*, 1985), awarded the Silver Bear at the Berlin Film Festival; *Red Lob* (*Palombella rossa*, 1989); *Dear Diary* (*Caro diario*, 1993), for which Moretti received the Best Director award at Cannes; *April* (*Aprile*, 1998); *The Son's Room* (*La stanza del figlio*, 2001), for which Moretti won the Golden Palm Award at Cannes and the three David di Donatello film prizes (the Italian equivalent of Oscars) in Italy; and *The Caiman*, a.k.a. *The Crocodile* (*Il caimano*, 2006).

Moretti's films constitute a coherent body of work that treats a number of recurrent themes: metacinematic considerations of the state of cinema, particularly in Italy; a focus upon Moretti's own personal problems and intellectual or artistic concerns, sharpened by the fact that he always acts in his own films and has created an alter ego named Michele Apicella, who is the protagonist of *I Am Self-sufficient, Ecce Bombo, Sweet Dreams, Bianca,* and *Red Lob*; a critique of useless rhetoric and political jargon in which the precise use of language (even in a visual medium like cinema) becomes extremely important; and political concerns that culminate in his support for a true leftist government in Italy, a stance that has provoked a visceral dislike for the Italian media mogul and politician Silvio Berlusconi in his works. His unabashed self-referentiality, his caustic wit and sense of humor, and his passionate political views have made Moretti Italy's most thoughtful, original, and influential director of the post-Fellini era; but it is often lost on critics of Moretti that he, perhaps better than any other living director in Italy, has understood that Fellini's special talent lay in a single-minded pursuit of autobiographical themes. Moreover, Moretti may well be regarded as the inheritor of the civic mission of filmmaking we associate in another generation with Pier Paolo Pasolini, whose idiosyncratic ideas about the cinema find resonance in Moretti's works. Perhaps most of all, Moretti hates the clichés, banalities, and homogenized kitsch taste spread by the mass media, and he presents all of these interrelated ideas with a remarkably keen sense of humor and self-parody, never taking himself too seriously.

The Michele Apicella films all concern the construction of a personal identity. The first, *I Am Self-sufficient*, pokes fun at experimental theater that drives away any potential public it might enjoy, mixing this aesthetic discourse with caustic comments about Lina Wertmüller's comic films. When Michele hears that she has been offered a professorship at the University of California at Berkeley, he foams at the mouth! *Ecce Bombo*[1] famously attacks the actor Nino Manfredi for making commercials and the film comedies of Alberto Sordi for lacking any kind of ideological content. As Michele puts it to a man in a bar who is spouting clichéd ideas, "You deserve Sordi!" *Ecce Bombo* also casts a jaundiced eye on Moretti's own post-1968 leftist generation, viewing his contemporaries as silly role-players who are far closer to their parents, whom they pretend to hate, than they realize. In fact, unlike many of the directors of *commedia all'italiana* (a genre Moretti despises), who made fun of social groups lower or different from themselves, Moretti believes in ironic and caustic critiques directed not only at his own generation and social class but also at himself.[2] *Sweet Dreams* is a full-blown metacinematic work about a young director (Michele again) who is frustrated by the vulgarity and lack of comprehension of his work. His film, "Freud's Mamma," is never completed, and Michele is even humiliated on a vulgar television show in competition with his hated rival, a director who is making a ridiculous musical on the Vietnam War. In *Bianca*, Moretti's alter ego, Michele, is a math teacher. Moretti's sarcastic opinion of the disastrous leveling effects of the cultural upheavals in Italy after 1968 finds perfect expression in the humorous description of Michele's high school. Named after Marilyn Monroe, it boasts a headmaster who tells Michele his task is to "inform" rather than to "form" his students, a psychoanalyst for the faculty (not the students), and various forms of games (toy trains, pinball machines) that attract the students more than their education. As in the other Apicella roles Moretti plays, Michele is litigious, intolerant of the ideas of others, and compulsive. The film became famous for a single scene—Michele eating compulsively from an enormous jar of Nutella, the habit-forming Italian chocolate–hazelnut spread. In this film, however, Michele's neuroses hide the fact that his mental state has driven him to begin killing his friends and neighbors because they have disappointed him in his search for order and meaning in life. Finally, in his last Michele Apicella role, in *Red Lob*, Moretti's alter ego becomes a Communist Deputy in the Italian Parliament who loses his memory. The film takes place during a water polo match (another one of Moretti's obsessions, like Nutella and Sachertorte), and as it unfolds, we eventually learn what Michele has forgotten—that he had taken a highly public stand against the traditional politics of his own party in a legislative debate. Thus, Michele's loss of memory and identity parallels the ideological confusion of the Italian Communist Party (PCI) in this era that would eventually change the PCI into the Democratic Party of the Left (PDS) after the fall of the Berlin Wall and the crumbling of the old cold-war divisions between Right and Left all over Europe.

In *April*, Moretti plays himself rather than his Michele Apicella persona, but this overtly political film may be seen as the logical sequel to *Red Lob* and an anticipation of *The Caiman*. It opens with the announcement on Berlusconi's private-television Channel 4, a pro-Right station in the manner of America's Fox News, that Berlusconi has defeated Moretti's beloved leftists in the political elections of 1994. Although Moretti decides to shoot a documentary on Berlusconi, he puts the project aside in order to make a musical, and then returns to the original project in 1996. Meanwhile, his son is born (in April, the reason for the film's title), and ultimately neither the documentary nor the musical is made. *April* became famous in Italy for a single line, an impassioned outburst Moretti aimed at the head of the Italian Communists, Massimo D'Alema: "D'Alema, react, say something, react, say something, answer, say something left-wing, say something even not left-wing, something civilized!"[3] Moretti's cinematic dissatisfaction with left-wing politics in the movies would later be repeated in a life-copies-art moment in February 2002, when at the end of a major political rally in Rome, Moretti took the microphone and accused the leaders of the Left seated on the podium behind him of being bureaucrats who had failed to understand the power and appeal of Berlusconi and his Forza Italia party. A great many people in Italy agreed with him, as subsequent newspaper polls and articles discovered.

Moretti's obsession with Silvio Berlusconi culminated in *The Caiman*, a fictional film about Berlusconi that was released in 2006 just before Berlusconi lost the general elections. (Subsequently, Berlusconi returned to power as prime minister of a Center-Right coalition by winning the elections of 2008.) Once again, Moretti mixes politics with a discussion of the state of the cinema and the media in general. A film director named Bruno Bonomo (Silvio Orlando) receives a script after his project of a film on Christopher Columbus comes to nothing, and Bruno realizes that the script is about Berlusconi. He decides to make the film, and as usual in a Moretti film, this question becomes intermingled with all sorts of personal problems (love affairs, divorce, lack of finances). Nevertheless, one completed scene shows Berlusconi (played by Moretti himself) at one of his trials in which he is convicted. After the verdict, Berlusconi leaves the courtroom to a cheering crowd, underscoring Moretti's belief that the Left has never understood Berlusconi's ability to sway the electorate.

Films such as *Red Lob*, *April*, and *The Caiman* will never reach a large non-Italian audience due to their close relationship to current political events in Italy, even though Moretti's humor translates into any language quite well (not unlike that of Woody Allen, to whom Moretti is often compared). Moretti's reputation, however, would rest on more than solid foundations if one were only to consider three of his works whose aesthetic and narrative appeal are not so specifically tied to Italian political events: *The Mass Is Ended*, *Dear Diary*, and *The Son's Room*. In each of these films, Moretti's acting contributes in large measure to their success. *The Mass Is Ended* and *The Son's Room* cast Moretti in roles that suit his actual personality and that of his alter ego, Michele Apicella. In *Dear Diary* (as its title implies), Moretti plays Moretti. His first international success at the Berlin Film Festival, *The Mass Is Ended* examines the life of Don Giulio (Moretti), a young priest whose personality has obvious affinities with the Apicella characters: he is impatient with empty rhetoric and cannot abide imperfection and frequently finds faults in his parishioners and family. Nonetheless, *The Mass Is Ended* is never a predictable film about a priest's loss of faith or even sexual temptation; Don Giulio has a genuine vocation for his job and believes his mission in life is to help those in need. Yet, at every turn he is thwarted in his efforts to attend to his neighbor: his father abandons his mother for a younger woman; his sister becomes pregnant and insists on an abortion; his former friends from earlier, more revolutionary days are either ex-terrorists, slightly mad intellectuals, or selfish egotists. The common denominator of all those who surround him is their complete and absolute indifference to his desire to exercise his vocation as a priest. Don Giulio finally decides to abandon his Roman parish and to work in a

The director Nanni Moretti plays an unorthodox priest in *The Mass Is Ended*. Credit: *Nanni Moretti and SACIS*

tiny church in South America, where the parishioners truly need and seek out priestly assistance. *The Mass Is Ended* paints a powerful portrait of the drastic changes in traditional Italian religious and family values during the postwar period without, however, being replaced by any new system of values that can sustain and strengthen social bonds.

With *Dear Diary* and its numerous awards, Moretti achieved not only Italian popularity but also worldwide renown. In this film, Moretti's love-hate relationship with modern Italy is clearer than in any of his other works. As he has remarked, Italy is a country characterized by "false appearances, vulgar words, media culture, and loss of taste, ideological and moral renunciation, and pseudo-modernity."[4] It would be most accurate to describe Moretti's film as a form of cinematographic essay. As he has remarked: "I am not a director. I am one who makes films when he has something to say."[5] Rather than searching for specifically cinematic effects, Moretti in this film concentrates upon making his audience think about the moral and social problems of contemporary Italy by focusing upon the single protagonist (Moretti as Moretti, not an alter ego) of the three episodes that make up this film journal: "On My Vespa," "Islands," and "The Doctors." Each of these episodes reflects Moretti's famous contempt for claptrap, conformity, politically correct thinking, and the use of platitudes as a means of false communication. It is the first episode that captures perfectly the persona Moretti has projected in all his films. In it, we see him riding through Rome during the summer on his Vespa scooter, when most of the city is at the beach or planning to go there. A voice-over provides commentary on what we see, with Moretti the director analyzing what Moretti the actor does on the screen. In Italy, unlike America, where summer is one of the most important seasons for the opening of major films, the cinema goes into hibernation, with everyone heading to the beach. Consequently, during Moretti's peregrinations through his favorite sections of the city (usually quarters others despise), he begins to discuss the status of Italian cinema as he is forced to watch films he would not normally have selected. He runs into the star of *Flashdance*, Jennifer Beals, who is walking with her boyfriend in Rome, and he explains how he has always wanted to dance. He sits practically alone in a movie theater, suffering through one of the boring pseudointellectual films of the past decade (one he invents, not an actual film), in which all the characters of his generation speak constantly of how their lives have failed and how as a group they have wasted their potential. In the audience, Moretti begins to argue with the people on the screen, reacting in disgust to their vapid remarks, rejecting their argument that "we" have failed: "*You* shouted awful, violent slogans. *You've* gotten ugly. *I* shouted the right slogans, and *I'm* a splendid forty-year-old!"[6] After reading a laudatory review of John McNaughton's *Henry: Portrait of a Serial Killer* (1986)—apparently the prototypical vulgar Hollywood film that Moretti detests—he confronts the critic who wrote the silly review and reads him examples of his writing while the critic hopelessly tries to sleep, until the hapless intellectual begs for mercy.

Much of the charm of *Dear Diary* derives from these amusing episodes and from the sarcastic voice-over of the director as he drives through the deserted city. The most moving sequences of the film occur when he drives to the outskirts of the city to visit the spot where the director Pier Paolo Pasolini met his death in 1975 at the hands of his gay lover.[7] The degradation of the physical site itself, when contrasted to the importance of the life wasted there, forces us to consider the state of Italy's cinema today. This episode also encapsulates Moretti's debt to both Fellini and Pasolini. Although his films are an integral part of a debate on civic issues in Italy (the heritage of Pasolini), they stem initially not from a preconceived ideological position so typical of many "political" directors in Italy but from Moretti's private life, his preoccupations, and even his egocentric fantasies (the heritage of Fellini).

"Islands," the second episode, chronicles the disastrous and comic attempt by Moretti and a friend to visit the Aeolian Islands (Lipari, Stromboli, and others) in a fruitless search for a tranquil spot where one can be alone to think and to write. His friend, who claims never to have watched television in his entire life and to have devoted the past decade to a close reading of James Joyce's *Ulysses*, makes the mistake of watching a soap opera and becomes a fanatical follower of *The Bold and the Beautiful*, the American television program that enjoyed an enormous Italian audience when Moretti shot this film. Moretti is eventually forced to interrogate American tourists on the edge of the volcano at Stromboli (a spot made famous by Roberto Rossellini's famous film of the same name, starring Ingrid Bergman) in order to give his friend plot summaries of future episodes of the program, which have already run in the United States! "The Doctors," the final episode of the film, is the most personal and the most moving. In it Moretti explains how an endless succession of doctors and clinics failed to diagnose a case of cancer (Hodgkin's lymphoma) from which he was suffering. After trying everything, including acupuncture, he consults a single-volume encyclopedia on medicine, a self-help guide that can be purchased at any bookstore: this act saves his life. This absurd situation captures perfectly Moretti's wry sense of humor, which informs the entire film.

Paradoxically, this most private of cinematic diaries managed to capture the attention of audiences all over the globe, who obviously saw in Moretti's film persona (and in his actual life) something that spoke intimately about their own lives. The artistic and commercial success of *Dear Diary* also provided a model for other Italian film directors. From it, they had hard and convincing evidence that interesting ideas and a good script can produce an outstanding work of art without investing millions of dollars in computerized special effects, action-film car chases, and violent explosions to compete with Hollywood forms of storytelling.

The Son's Room picks up the serious themes of life and death evoked in *Dear Diary*. Moretti's least political, least humorous, and most personal film, it is a deeply moving treatment of a psychoanalyst named Giovanni (Moretti) who loses his son, Andrea (Giuseppe Sanfelice), in a tragic accident, a death that has an enormous impact upon him; his wife, Paola (Laura Morante); and his daughter, Irene (Jasmine Trinca). Before the son's death, Giovanni's family had seemed to be the perfect, harmonious contemporary Italian family, unlike the comic stereotype celebrated in dozens of Italian films about family life. As modern parents, both Giovanni and Paola have an extremely close relationship with their children, and meals together are a picture of domestic bliss, serenity, and affection rather than the neurotic, temper-tantrum-filled moments found in other classics of Italian cinema (Fellini's *Amarcord* may be the classic case from film comedies). On the day his son died, Giovanni had promised to go jogging with him but was called away to attend to a suicidal patient. His failure to prevent his son's death fills him with a sense of guilt that begins to poison his and his family's life together. Yet the film ends on a note of hope: it is also his family that saves him from sinking into the kinds of mental aberrations or obsessions that had characterized so many of his other film characters. In so many other films, Moretti had criticized the defects of the traditional Italian nuclear family, the patriarchal model that had endured for centuries. Now, himself a father (his son is prominently displayed in *April*), both Moretti and Giovanni seem to have come to the conclusion that although a healthy family is no panacea for all the world's ills, it remains the bastion of human happiness. In an era when young Italians marry much later (if at all), practice divorce, and are suffering from a negative birthrate, the film's message is one of the most personal and yet the most relevant of all his films.

Maurizio Nichetti

Whereas Moretti's vision of the world would be more accurately described as tragicomic rather than purely comic, Nichetti's films owe more to his early work with cartoons and to silent cinema (the Marx Brothers, Chaplin, Buster Keaton) than to traditional *commedia all'italiana*. Unlike Moretti, Nichetti has a strong interest in the technological aspect of making films. His first film—*Ratataplan* (1979; the title is the Italian onomatopoeic equivalent for a drum roll)—stole the show at the Venice Film Festival that year from older directors such as Bertolucci, Pontecorvo, and the Taviani brothers, as well as a host of foreign directors. Made in 16mm at very little cost (another parallel to Moretti's early career), its skillful use of pantomime in its treatment of a waiter's misadventures in Milan made it commercially successful and launched this director's career. Like Moretti, Nichetti most often stars in his own works. His second feature, *Splash!* (*Ho fatto splash!*, 1980), continued his exploration of pantomime as it presented a satirical view of modern advertising.

Perhaps the best and most original comedy of the 1980s, Nichetti's *The Icicle Thief* (*Ladri di saponette*, 1989) has attracted the most serious critical attention of all his works. Setting forth a postmodern revisitation of De Sica's neorealist classic *The Bicycle Thief*, it is an ingenious amalgamation of a number of neorealist clichés, drawn not only from De Sica but also from Rossellini, Fellini, and others. Nichetti himself stars as a film director named Nichetti being interviewed by a film critic (Claudio G. Fava, one of Italy's best-known television film critics) in a television studio just before the transmission of De Sica's moving film. A strange family consisting of a pregnant woman, a man reading his newspaper, and their children personifies the television audience. Nichetti narrates his story on three levels: the film the director has made, interrupted by the kinds of obnoxious television commercials that Fellini attacked in *Ginger and Fred*; shots of the director at the television studio and then within his own film; and scenes showing the family watching the television program, often surfing the channels with the remote control and interrupting it as occurs so often in normal life. The plot of the director's film consists of a parody of neorealist social realism. An unemployed worker named Antonio Piermattei (also played by Nichetti) steals a chandelier (not a bicycle) during his first day at work in a light-fixture factory. The original script called for Antonio to be paralyzed after being struck on his bicycle by a truck while taking his stolen chandelier home. The accident was supposed to have forced his son Bruno (Federico Rizzo) to make the bicycle into a wheelchair to help his paralyzed father, to have sent Bruno and his brother to an orphanage, and to have driven his wife, Maria, into a life of prostitution. In short, the script as laid out by the director would have produced a perfect work of leftist social criticism.

After an electrical failure causes a studio blackout, however, the director's film, which is being broadcast by the television studio, begins mysteriously to intersect with the world of television just as Antonio cycles past a riverbank on his way home with the chandelier. During a commercial break that precedes the power failure, a blond bombshell named Heidi dives into the blue waters of a swimming pool, only to emerge in color after the power returns but in the black-and-white water of Antonio's river. He saves her, though drying her off changes her from color to black-and-white, and she changes places with his wife, Maria, who, in turn, enters the world of colorized commercials. The most original aspect of Nichetti's parody of De Sica is that rather than using actual footage from *The Bicycle Thief*, he creates his own version of the neorealist classic that is constantly interrupted by commercials and contaminated by references to other famous films. From Rossellini's *Open City*, for example, Nichetti borrows a priest that resembles Don Fabrizio. Although the director Nichetti is concerned with making a film about social problems, his characters harbor entirely different aspirations. Maria wants to become a dancer, and Bruno becomes the perfect consumer, fascinated by the Big-Big candy bars he has learned from television ads to eat. Ultimately, Nichetti transforms the classic neorealist family of De Sica into the kinds of consumers (not spectators) assumed by television advertisers, rolling into their home enormous quantities of goods in huge shopping carts. Nichetti deftly fashions this exceptional film by using bits and pieces of neorealist cinema in the same manner as his television spectators channel-surf constantly, creating, in effect, their own film. Nichetti's Italian title (literally, "thieves of soap bars" in English) not only points back to Italy's great postwar cinematic tradition in metacinematic terms, but also provides the kind of critique of television that both Fellini and Moretti would applaud. Nichetti's subsequent films—including *To Want to Fly* (*Volere volare*, 1991), *Stefano Quantestorie* (literally, "Steven Manystories," 1993), *Luna e l'altra* (literally, "The Moon and the Other," 1996), and *Honolulu Baby* (2000)—could only with difficulty match the masterful comedy of *The Icicle Thief*, but they all continue to combine reality and fantasy. *To Want to Fly* represents the most innovative of Nichetti's use of new technology, featuring a character who turns into a cartoon figure that interacts with real actors. This technique was made famous by Robert Zemeckis in *Who Framed Roger Rabbit?* (1988), but Nichetti has insisted (possibly correctly) that although he actually conceived the idea first, the production of his work was delayed until after Zemeckis's work appeared and scooped the idea.

Massimo Troisi

As in the cases of Moretti and Nichetti, Troisi's brief but important career as actor and director reminds us that the comic films of this new generation of auteurs often combine the tasks of direction and acting. His acting skills reflect more of the venerable *commedia all'italiana* tradition, which Moretti avoids like the plague, or that of Neapolitan popular dialect theater; but Troisi's works, like those of his colleague Roberto Benigni, enjoyed far greater appeal with Italian audiences. His first feature film, *I'm Starting from Three* (*Ricomincio da tre*, 1981), cost only $450,000 to make but broke box-office records in Italy and earned David di Donatello awards for Best Film and Best Actor. In it, Troisi plays a Neapolitan named Gaetano who moves to Florence, where he encounters the usual diffidence that Florentines and northern Italians often show toward Italians from the Mezzogiorno. Troisi's comic persona reverses the usual Neapolitan stereotypes perennially associated with characters from that inimitable city. Rather than being vivacious, likable, and outgoing, he is the essence of insecurity, timidity, and clumsiness. When Troisi teamed up with Benigni, with both men writing, codirecting, and acting, their film *Nothing Left to Do but Cry* (*Non ci resta che piangere*, 1984) enjoyed enormous success at the Italian box office. The film's storyline recalls some of the most outrageous comic plots conceived by the team of Franco and Ciccio: Saverio (Benigni), a schoolteacher, and Mario (Troisi), a school janitor, after stopping at an inn when their car breaks down, wake up the next morning only to discover that they have been transported back to the year 1492 in an invented town called Frittole. While in the past they meet Leonardo da Vinci, to whom they impart a good deal of modern knowledge—supposedly the origins of his later status as a genius inventor—including modern capitalism, the railroad train, the Oedipus complex, thermometers, and even stoplights. At the film's conclusion, they encounter Leonardo again, but in the present he is oddly enough the engineer of a locomotive. Another version of the film's ending (now available on the Italian DVD) has Saverio trying to prevent the departure of Columbus to forestall his discovery of America because, in the present, his sister is engaged to an American soldier in Italy with NATO, and if Columbus fails to discover America, this American could never ruin his sister's life!

Troisi's greatest performance was in *The Postman* (*Il postino*, 1994), a film directed by the British director Michael Radford, who adapted a Chilean novel by Antonio Skármeta: *Ardiente Paciencia* (1985), originally translated into English as *Burning Patience* but republished in English as *The Postman* to complement the release of Radford's film in the United States.[8] Troisi's brilliant performance was followed by his premature death only a day after filming ended (he required a heart transplant). The astounding commercial and artistic success of the film all over the globe made Troisi the sentimental favorite for Best Actor at the 1996 Oscar ceremonies, even though he did not win. *The Postman* also marked the vigorous entrance into the field of foreign film distribution in America by the powerful Miramax Company, which later distributed such popular works as *The English Patient* (1996) and Benigni's *Life Is Beautiful* (*La vita è bella*, 1997).

Skármeta's novel had depicted a friendship between Pablo Neruda, the Chilean Marxist poet (and winner of the Nobel Prize for Literature in 1971), and a young man whose job is to deliver his fan mail. To accommodate the story to Troisi, Radford changed the setting from Salvador Allende's Chile in the late 1960s through Allende's overthrow in 1973 to the Italy of 1952. In that year, Neruda, who was living in exile, had passed some time on the famous Italian island of Capri. Thus Radford, although English by birth, intended to make a completely Italian film with a predominantly Italian cast led by Troisi, an original sound track in Italian, and an Italian crew. In Radford's adaptation, Neruda (Philippe Noiret) introduces Mario

In Michael Radford's *The Postman*, Mario delivers the mail to the exiled poet Pablo Neruda and learns to love poetry in the process. *Credit: DVD*

Ruloppolo (Troisi) to the lyrical world of poetry and its erotic metaphors, and Mario begins to write poetry to win the hand of his beautiful island muse, Beatrice (Maria Grazia Cucinotta). In the process, his association with Neruda politicizes Mario, who becomes a Communist, and Neruda serves as Mario's best man when he eventually marries Beatrice. Years after Neruda leaves the island, he sends a very impersonal letter to Mario, asking him to forward his belongings. Believing that his friendship with the poet was an empty illusion, Mario is inspired to take his tape recorder and to record all the poetic sounds and images (the sea, the cries of birds in flight, his unborn child's heartbeat) that he experiences every day on his island to remind the forgetful poet in Chile that, at least on his island, poetry exists in its pristine purity. About to read a poem entitled "A Song for Pablo Neruda" at a rally of Communist workers in Naples, Mario is killed when a riot breaks out. Years later, after winning the Nobel Prize, Neruda returns to Mario's island and listens to the tapes Mario made for him but never sent. Neruda understands that Mario has left behind a poetic legacy worthy of his own best work.

The international success of *The Postman* offered still more proof that a simple, uncomplicated, and inexpensive *Italian* film, shot even without an English sound track, could communicate effectively to American audiences and might break into the lucrative market dominated at home by Hollywood. It is ironic that an English director managed to produce a work dealing with Italian culture that could span the linguistic and cultural divide between Hollywood and Italian filmmaking. Bridging these gaps would become the goal of many directors of Troisi's generation, in particular Tornatore and Salvatores, whose films have also been successful in doing so.

Gabriele Salvatores

Salvatores began his career in the theater before making his first feature film, *Marrakech Express* (1989), which was followed by *Turné* (1990); the surprise Best Foreign Film of 1991, *Mediterraneo*; *Puerto Escondido* (1992); *Sud* (literally, "South"—that is, the Mezzogiorno; 1993); and a science fiction film (a rare excursion into that genre by an Italian director) entitled *Nirvana* (1990). Of late, his most important works have been two crime or detective films—*I'm Not Afraid* and *Quo Vadis, Baby?* (see chapter 14). One of Salvatores's contributions to the Italian cinema has been his skillful use of several actors, such as Diego Abatantuono and Fabrizio Bentivoglio, who have since become two of the Italian cinema's central figures. His early films have been labeled "road" films, since one of Salvatores's major themes is the idea of escaping from a reality that is overpowering and unacceptable. *Mediterraneo* provides a key to understanding this director. Its opening epigram announces "escape in these times is the only means of surviving and continuing to dream" (a citation from Henri Laborit, a French physiologist). Withdrawing from society in one way or another thus becomes, in many of his films, the only means of maintaining one's identity. *Mediterraneo* chronicles the mishaps of a company of Italian soldiers sent by Mussolini's regime in 1941 to occupy a small Greek island. This group includes the misfits typical of many film treatments of this subject and certainly represents a cliché that does an injustice to the many Italian soldiers and civilians who died bravely defending an indefensible cause during Italy's imperialistic adventures. Indeed, the soldiers resemble contemporary slackers more than Italian soldiers of the 1940s; this bunch even anachronistically smokes hashish provided by a friendly Turk who then steals everything they own while they are sleeping off their high. Providing the basis for what many Italian critics have said about the film, this episode suggests that Salvatores's picture of the war on a small Greek island really represents the generation to which Salvatores belongs, which has abandoned dreams of revolution without seeking and finding some other ideal in which to believe and for which to struggle.

Other film comedies about Italians at war—Monicelli's *The Great War*, Luigi Comencini's *Everybody Home!* or Wertmüller's *Seven Beauties*—raise far more perplexing questions, either about Italy's role in World War I or about Italy's complicity with Nazi Germany in the often brutal treatment of native populations under their occupation or in shipping people to concentration camps. *Mediterraneo* glosses over an idea that Italians might have been anything but benefactors to those they invaded with a phrase uttered numerous times in the film: "stessa faccia, stessa razza," or "the same face, the same race." This groups all Mediterranean peoples together as if they had always been peaceful brothers, when in fact the history of the Mediterranean has been, in large measure, the conflict among them. During the three years the soldiers remain on the island, living a pastoral existence far from the fighting, they mingle with the Greek population. No Greek men remain on the island—presumably they are away fighting the Germans and not the Italians, whom Salvatores transforms from invaders into happy tourists. They amuse themselves with regular visits to the town prostitute, interrupted by discussions about whether or not they want to return to Italy to build the future.

Ultimately the English arrive, announce that Italy now fights with the Allies, and take them away, with only one Italian deserting to remain with the prostitute and to open a restaurant. Instead of ending the film on this happy note, more in keeping with the traditional *commedia all'italiana*, Salvatores concludes with a flash-forward to our times, where two of the men, Lieutenant Montini (Claudio Bigagli) and Sergeant Lorusso (Diego Abatantuono), return in old age to die on the island. After building a new democratic nation in Italy, they have concluded that it was not worth the trouble, and that it is better to be a slacker on a beautiful island than to construct a democratic nation out of the ruins of a dictatorship and create an economy that pulls Italy out of centuries of poverty as an agricultural country to the ranks of the major industrial powers. Salvatores seems to share this conclusion, and as a result, *Mediterraneo* represents light entertainment with a message that, resembling an easy pastoral ideal, seems somehow wrongheaded.

Without a doubt, both *I'm Not Afraid* and *Quo Vadis, Baby?* represent far more substantial films, in terms of both an unsentimental approach to their subject matter and Salvatores's development as a director of genre films. Likewise, *Nirvana* demonstrates his ability to branch out into new directions, including science fiction and cyberpunk. Cyberpunk films usually feature a dystopian future dominated by technology. Computers become a central part of society, and computer hackers are often the protagonists of such works. Salvatores obviously owes a debt to Ridley Scott's *Blade Runner* (1982) in the film's pessimistic view of a cyberpunk future, its unusual costumes, and its sets, which were located and shot in an abandoned Alfa Romeo car factory in Milan. *Nirvana*'s protagonist, Jimi Dini (Christopher Lambert)—like that of *The Matrix* (1999), by the Wachowski brothers, released two years later—works as a computer programmer who designs video games. Somehow Jimi's creation, the protagonist of his video game, named Solo (Diego Abatantuono), has become sentient and realizes that, since the game is a first-person shooter, he is trapped in an endless series of episodes in which he will be killed over and over again. Solo's name means "alone" in Italian as well as in English, and it is quite apt for the film's theme, which represents the interchange between human beings and their computerized avatars—the advance of technology makes machines more human and human beings more like machines. After Solo makes contact with his creator, he begs him to erase him from the memory bank of the mainframe of the computer corporation for which Jimi works, and Jimi's quest to do so constitutes the film's plot. On the strength of his Oscar-winning *Mediterraneo*, Salvatores certainly had more cachet with financial sources than most Italian directors of his generation, and *Nirvana* clearly enjoyed a budget larger than the average Italian film; but even his admirably constructed costumes and ingenious and futuristic sets seem out of the league of the Hollywood megapics devoted to the science fiction genre. Nevertheless, working in a film genre not traditionally popular in Italy shows artistic courage, and Salvatores would go on to demonstrate his talent in more substantial genre films treating crime.

Roberto Benigni

Roberto Benigni's career began in the theater, where his authentic Tuscan peasant origins offered him the opportunity to demonstrate his irrepressible comic talents. After gaining popularity on Italian television programs in the 1970s, he turned to the cinema and direction in the early 1980s, and the previously mentioned *Nothing Left to Do but Cry*, shot together with Massimo Troisi, was one of the most successful Italian films of the decade. As an actor for other directors, his work for Jim Jarmusch in *Down by Law* (1986), for Federico Fellini in *The Voice of the Moon* (1990), and for Blake Edwards in *Son of the Pink Panther* (1993) demonstrated his talents to a wide audience beyond Italy. Again, like Moretti, Nichetti, and Troisi, Benigni has frequently directed films in which he played the protagonist. Before his rise to international renown with *Life Is Beautiful*, Benigni shot three very successful comic films, all depending upon his exuberant style of comic acting: *The Little Devil* (*Il piccolo diavolo*, 1988); *Johnny Stecchino*, a.k.a. *Johnny Toothpick* (1991); and *The Monster* (*Il mostro*, 1994). In the first film, Benigni teams up with Walter Matthau, whose dry wit provides the perfect foil to Benigni's hysterical style, in a tale about a Vatican priest (Matthau) who exorcises a devil from a fat woman (Benigni). In *Johnny Stecchino*, Benigni plays two roles: a bumbling school bus driver named Dante and his look-alike, Stecchino, a mobster who testified against some local Mafiosi and whose wife wants Dante killed in her husband's place so the couple can escape to South America. Likewise, in the third film Benigni plays another bumbler, but this time he is mistaken for the famous "monster" that has committed a series of serial murders and sex crimes.[9]

Benigni reached the pinnacle of critical and commercial success with *Life Is Beautiful*, which won numerous awards, including three Oscars (Best Actor, Best Original Dramatic Score, and Best Foreign Language Film) out of seven nominations (the others were Best Picture, Best Director, Best

Screenplay, and Best Editing), recalling the glory days of Bertolucci's *The Last Emperor* and the many nominations and Oscar victories earned by the films of Benigni's idol, Federico Fellini. This bittersweet tragicomedy about the Holocaust created a thunderstorm of critical controversy, producing numerous polemical reviews and articles that bring to mind discussions of another controversial film dealing with the Italian Holocaust, *Seven Beauties*, by Lina Wertmüller. Most Holocaust-related films made in Italy, such as Pontecorvo's *Kapo* (*Kapò*, 1959) or De Sica's *The Garden of the Finzi-Continis* followed traditional patterns of tragic, even hagiographic style in dealing with this unique historical example of human depravity. Both Wertmüller and Benigni, however, followed Chaplin's example in *The Great Dictator* (1940) by selecting a tragicomic approach. In Benigni's case, he even employs an acting style indebted to Chaplin as well. As one hostile reviewer of the film remarked, "Benigni likes to play the slightly bewildered, 'Chaplinesque' little guy caught up in forces beyond his control, who succeeds by his wits and a touch of good fortune."[10] The comparison of Benigni's acting and directing style to Charlie Chaplin is both suggestive and misleading. Benigni's comic gags clearly reflect the example of Chaplin, but Chaplin's comic treatment of Hitler and the Jews appeared early in 1940, before the horrors of the Holocaust had really become common knowledge. Consequently, Chaplin did not encounter an undercurrent of hostility for a tragicomic rather than strictly tragic treatment of the Holocaust and never received harsh critical attacks for an "improper" or "disrespectful" approach. Chaplin's story about a Jewish barber in the mythical state of Tomania ruled by the evil dictator Hynkel, who receives a visit by Napoloni, the dictator of Bacteria, another imaginary state, contains two of the funniest scenes in the history of the cinema: the meeting of Napoloni (Mussolini; played by Jack Oakie) and Hynkel (Hitler/Chaplin) at the train station, and the scene of Hynkel playing with a giant balloon of the world in a mock ballet. Looking backward from what we know now about the conclusion of Hitler's policies—the murder of millions and millions of people, Jews and non-Jews alike—these scenes might be anachronistically construed as disrespectful to these many dead. Nonetheless, one particular sequence in the Italian film, in which Benigni's character, Guido, impersonates a school inspector from Rome and presents himself (an Italian Jew) as the perfect example of the Aryan race, certainly follows Chaplin's example.

Although Benigni may not surpass his model in absolute comic power, he does something else that is remarkable and touching in *Life Is Beautiful*. He turns the often disgusting and shameful events in the camps, where people did anything to survive, into a fabulous world of play inhabited by at least one benign clown, a microcosm of a tiny part of an evil world that affirms life rather than negates it. The film opens in 1939: Guido Orefice (whose last name means "goldsmith") is a slightly crazy bookseller in the

Tuscan city of Arezzo. As a Jew, Guido (Benigni) and his uncle Eliseo (Giustino Durano) suffer the restrictions imposed by Mussolini's racial laws, even though up to this point Italian Jews had seemed completely assimilated into the fabric of Italian society. Indeed, the fact that the regime passed such laws against people who were essentially exactly like everyone else is precisely what explains the profoundly perverse nature of these laws.

Benigni constructs his film around two different subplots. The first part of the film features Guido's comic spoofs of the Italian Fascists, his married life with Dora (Nicoletta Braschi), and the birth of his son, Giosuè, or Joshua (Giorgio Cantarini). The lighter mood of part one changes abruptly when the Germans take the family away to a concentration camp. In this place of horrors, Guido manages to hide his son after being separated from Dora, and in order to survive, he employs all his gifts for fantasy and comic inventiveness, weapons that had been more than sufficient to thwart the Italian Fascists back home in Arezzo but that are challenged to the limits by the far more insidious and savage threat from the Nazis. Guido transforms Giosuè's hidden existence into a game where the child may win points toward the award of a tank. In a variety of tragicomic situations, Guido manages to convince Giosuè that people are not being baked alive in ovens or turned into soap or buttons: imagine, Guido tells his son, losing somebody who is a button from your shirt! Guido's very last act, as he is being taken away for execution, involves a comic imitation of the German goose step, performed to keep the Nazi guards' attention away from his son as they murder the camp's inhabitants before the approaching Allies arrive to liberate the camp. When American soldiers free the prisoners, the surviving Giosuè finally receives the tank ride he anticipates for all those hard earned "points" at the camp. Guido dies but Dora survives, and at the conclusion of the film, Giosuè shouts without fully understanding the depth of the tragedy he has been

In Benigni's *Life Is Beautiful*, Guido's son, Giosué, survives the death camp and finally gets his ride on an American tank which liberates him. *Credit: DVD*

spared, "We won! We won!" Thereafter, an adult Giosuè, a voice-over in the future, remarks: "This is my story. This is the sacrifice my father made. This was his gift to me."[11]

Giosuè's adult voice-over at the end of the film reveals that the voice-over opening the film belonged to the son and not the father: "This is a simple story but not an easy one to tell. Like a fable, there is sorrow, and like a fable, it is full of wonder and happiness."[12] Hostile reviewers of the film stressed its unrealistic tone, but that is precisely the point of the film: Guido turns the life in the camps into a playful game and a children's fable so that his son will continue to believe that goodness can triumph over evil. The film thus commemorates a father's sacrifice by a grateful son. Few critics of the film took time to find out that Benigni's own father spent time in a camp during the war. Using the opening voice-over, Benigni also announces to the attentive viewer that the canons of realism have been suspended and those of the fairy tale have been invoked. This voice-over is accompanied by an image so disturbing that the viewer tends to forget it, because the hilarious picture of Guido and his friend riding a car without brakes through the Tuscan countryside as the credits of the film roll by follows it. This very brief sequence depicts a foggy night in which Guido is walking in what will later be seen as a concentration camp uniform with his son asleep in his arms. Toward the end of the film, this foggy scene repeats itself, but Guido seems to have lost his way and says to his son: "Maybe it's really all a dream. Just a dream, Joshua."[13] Unlike the first sequence, the audience is now forced to relive Guido's experience in the fog from a subjective point-of-view shot that stops Guido dead in his tracks and leaves him, for the first time in his life, speechless. The fog that obscured the first sequence parts a bit to reveal a pile of corpses obscenely and inhumanely stacked up in a mountainous heap. Faced with the real and unspeakable horror of the concentration camps, Guido can only shield his young child from this nightmare by turning it all into a child's fable, and life in the camp into a game. Benigni's film was an audacious treatment of an extremely sensitive topic, but for once the American Academy gave Oscars to the highly original film that deserved them.

Enormous commercial and critical success abroad often leads to a disastrous next film for Italian directors. After *Blow-Up*, the negative reception of Antonioni's *Zabriskie Point* made future English-language films difficult. After *Amarcord*, Fellini failed to score at the box office with *Fellini's Casanova* and never succeeded in obtaining a Hollywood-size budget for his subsequent films. After *Seven Beauties*, Wertmüller's *A Night Full of Rain* ruined her chances of working in Hollywood. Benigni joined their company with *Pinocchio* (2002), an adaptation of Italy's most famous literary work: *The Adventures of Pinocchio: Story of a Puppet* (1883), a classic story for children by Carlo Collodi (1826–90) that has in the past few decades been appropriated by adults. Unlike Benigni, who knew the original Italian tale by heart and had discussed making such a film directed by Federico Fellini with Benigni in the starring role before Fellini's death, most Americans familiar with the Pinocchio story have read bowdlerized versions simplified for children, or believe that the famous animated version Walt Disney produced in 1940 is true to the original literary work. Actually, Collodi's original was a far darker and more foreboding narrative with serious social implications. In the first Italian version Collodi wrote, the book ends with the dramatic hanging of Pinocchio, a grim reminder to the children of the era that if they were not good, honest, hard working, and obedient, they would meet the same kind of fate. Death plays a major role in the book. Not only is Pinocchio hanged, but he also experiences a second, metaphoric death when he is swallowed by the Great Shark and meets his father and creator, Geppetto, inside the fish's belly. The world in which Pinocchio lives is not the saccharine, sentimental universe of Disney where all ultimately ends well, but a harsh, moralistic, Calvinistic, often cruel place where egotism is the rule and kindness extremely rare.

Benigni adapted Collodi's book, not the watered-down version most non-Italian readers have received. Although his production had the largest budget of any Italian film made to that point (around $45 million) and did well in Italy, where readers of Collodi recognized the story as basically true to the original, outside of Italy it was a colossal critical failure and a box-office flop. Still, critics and spectators now consider other films that bombed after the stupendous successes of an important director's previous work (listed above) as far better than they appeared to be when they were first released.[14] So, too, this *Pinocchio* must be reconsidered as a complex work that reflects Benigni's aesthetic. He has been criticized for an "over the top" acting style in other films; but in *Pinocchio* he plays, after all, a wooden puppet that eventually becomes a boy, an undisciplined child, and in this context, his performance may even be deemed rather subdued. Moreover, the creative sets and costumes in the film are wonderfully fanciful and delightful—another testament to the skill in these fields so typical of Italian cinema. In fact, the film is dedicated to Italy's master costume and production designer Danilo Donati, who served as both on *Pinocchio* but died before the film was released. (Donati had previously won two Oscars, for Zeffirelli's *Romeo and Juliet* [1968] and *Fellini's Casanova*, besides working on such important projects as Pasolini's *The Decameron*, Fellini's *Amarcord*, and *Fellini Satyricon*.) Benigni handles Collodi's darker themes beautifully: Pinocchio's hanging against an enormous full moon at night remains one of the most haunting images in the film. And the unhappy death of Pinocchio's best friend, Lucignolo (Kim Rossi Stuart), after being turned into a donkey that is literally worked to death on a farm by a callous peasant, is quite moving. Lucignolo's fate becomes the book's best (or worst) example held up to Pinocchio to illustrate what happens to a boy who does not obey, work hard, and behave properly. Such themes rarely fit well into popular children's literature, and they may well have condemned Benigni's film to commercial failure despite its faithfulness to the original, a fine script, beautiful settings, and good acting.

Benigni's great talent will not be suppressed by a single failure, however, and given his interest in Dante's *Divine Comedy*—he is famous in Italy for declaiming the poet's works and has made two television films dedicated to Canto V of *The Inferno* and Canto XXXIV, the last of *The Paradise*—perhaps a filmed version of *The Divine Comedy* may figure in his future. Like *Pinocchio*, a film of Dante's great poem was one of the unrealized projects of his idol, Fellini, and *The Divine Comedy* has never yet been adequately transferred to the silver screen despite many attempts, particularly in the silent era, to do so.

Giuseppe Tornatore

Giuseppe Tornatore's style has affinities to that of other directors of his generation. Like them, he is interested in reminding the viewer of other, older film traditions, but he generally avoids the kinds of postmodern, metacinematic, and self-reflexive approach, of a Moretti or a Nichetti. Tornatore's treatment in his films of his native Sicily owes a debt to the works of Pietro Germi, and Ettore Scola is no doubt one of his models in treating serious social problems with a comic touch. Little doubt exists, however, that the tone and style of his work owes the most to Federico Fellini. Because of his willingness to manipulate the audience's emotions in what may often be a sentimental and lyrical approach to his subject matter, some negative critics have treated his work with the same kind of suspicion that greeted Fellini's early films.

Two years after the Sicilian-born director debuted in 1986 with a treatment of organized crime in Naples entitled *The Professor*, his second feature film, *Cinema Paradiso*, propelled him into international critical fame, an Oscar for Best Foreign Language Film, and substantial returns at the box office. Its initial release in Italy, however, was a disaster, since it was far too long and somewhat unfocused, but the experienced intervention of the producer Franco Cristaldi encouraged the young director to reedit the work for a second and phenomenally successful release. Its plot provides a nostalgic look back at the place of cinema in Italian society in the postwar period through the eyes of its protagonist, Salvatore Di Vita, nicknamed Totò, who is played at various periods of his life by three actors: Salvatore Cascio as a child, Marco Leonardi as a teenager, and Jacques Perrin as an adult. A young Sicilian boy living in the small town of Giancaldo, Totò befriends Alfredo (Philippe Noiret), the projectionist of the town's only cinema. After Alfredo loses his eyesight due to a fire in his projection room, Salvatore

The projectionist Alfredo kindles Totò's love for the movies, later inspiring him to become a film director in Tornatore's *Cinema Paradiso. Credit: DVD*

replaces him because of his love for the movies Alfredo has screened. For Totò, the projectionist replaces the father he lost in the ill-fated Russian campaign during World War II, and Tornatore follows Totò as he constantly watches films, falls in love for the first time as an adolescent, and eventually becomes a famous Roman film director who leaves Giancaldo, returning thirty years later only for Alfredo's funeral. To highlight Tornatore's nostalgia for the central role films once played in Italian popular culture, as well as his protagonist's nostalgia for his lost innocence as a young apprentice to Alfredo, most of the film unfolds as a series of flashbacks that begin when Salvatore receives a call in Rome from his mother in Sicily to inform him of Alfredo's death. Salvatore Cascio's captivating performance as the young boy both continues and alludes to the long tradition of great child actors in Italian cinema that began with De Sica and the cinema of the 1930s and continued through postwar neorealism. The contrast between the incredibly expressive performance of Cascio as Totò and the robotlike acting style of Perrin as the mature adult Salvatore must surely reflect Tornatore's subtle critique of contemporary Italian cinema's relative emptiness when compared to its glorious past.

Tornatore's nostalgia for the cinema of the immediate postwar period rests upon its role as a social institution. Giancaldo's authentic center, the movie theater is the place where both children and adults retired to experience their fantasies and dream about a better, happier world. Tornatore depicts the crowds inside the theater in the same grotesque, comic style made famous by similar portraits of film audiences in *Fellini's Roma*, *The Clowns*, and *Amarcord*, scenes Wertmüller had previously imitated in *Seven Beauties*. A number of memorable characters in *Cinema Paradiso* constantly remind the viewer of Italian cinematic tradition, such as the parish priest of Giancaldo, who is played by Leopoldo Trieste, the star of Fellini's *The White*

Sheik and *I Vitelloni*, not to mention the wife's comical suitor in Germi's classic portrait of Sicilian culture, *Divorce, Italian Style*, and Totò's mother as an older woman, who is played by Pupella Maggio, the unforgettable mother in Fellini's *Amarcord*. When the building housing the cinema is finally demolished after Alfredo's funeral to make way for a parking lot in Giancaldo, Tornatore dramatically visualizes the loss that Italian culture has suffered by the changes in popular culture that have succeeded in marginalizing Italian cinema (if not that of Hollywood) as the dominant form of mass entertainment.

In Totò's childhood (and in that of Tornatore), the two institutions dominating daily life in Giancaldo were the church and the movie theater, and both were linked not only by similar communal rituals but also by the fact that the parish priest was the local film censor. In Giancaldo, Father Adelfio had the task of screening films during the immediate postwar period, when Catholic censorship laid a heavy hand upon the movies Catholics could watch. The bell the young Totò uses when serving as an altar boy is the same one the priest employs to indicate to Alfredo, the projectionist high up in the projection booth of the cinema, which scenes should be spliced out of the copy of the film that would be screened by the townspeople. Almost inevitably, the censored scenes depict passionate kisses, some of the most famous in film history, including such scenes in Visconti's *The Earth Trembles*, De Santis's *Bitter Rice*, and a host of important Hollywood classics. When the Roman director Salvatore Di Vita attends Alfredo's funeral, he receives Alfredo's legacy to him: a collection of all the scenes the young boy had been prevented from seeing, now spliced together in a final sequence that is *Cinema Paradiso*'s justly celebrated and touching conclusion.

Even though it would be difficult for Tornatore ever to equal the astounding commercial success of *Cinema Paradiso*, his subsequent works—most of which have done well both critically and commercially—offer an authentic auteur's vision of the world: *Everybody's Fine* (*Stanno tutti bene*, 1990); *The Star Maker* (*L'uomo delle stelle*, 1995); *The Legend of 1900*, a.k.a. *The Legend of the Pianist on the Ocean* (*La leggenda del pianista sull'oceano*, 1998); *Malèna* (2000); and *The Unknown Woman* (*La sconosciuta*, 2006). In *Everybody's Fine*, Tornatore employs Fellini's favorite actor, Marcello Mastroianni, who delivers one of his finest late performances as Matteo Scuro, a retired civil servant from Sicily who is accustomed to a yearly birthday visit from his five children, all of whom have moved to what the Sicilians call "the Continent," or the mainland. When they finally inform him that they are unable to come this year for their annual reunion, Matteo decides to pay them a surprise visit. The film unfolds from Matteo's monologue directed to someone whom we discover at the end of the film is his dead wife, with whom he carries on conversations about their children. His trip up the Italian peninsula cannot but recall another famous such filmic journey—from Sicily to Naples, Rome, Florence and the North in Rossellini's *Paisan*, a tragic film that nevertheless held out the hope of a springtime in Italy after the war. In contrast, *Everybody's Fine* offers a pessimistic vision of contemporary Italy: the proud father discovers that all his offspring, who have fabricated lies about their worldly successes, have actually turned out to be quite mediocre people. One son has even committed suicide, yet his siblings concealed this shocking news from his father. When Matteo returns home dejected and his neighbors ask about his children, his vague remark that provides the title of the film delivers a chilling judgment upon the transformations that have taken place within the structure of the Italian family, traditionally the most important institution in Italian culture.

Tornatore's *The Star Maker*, another nostalgic look at the cinematic past of Italy, owes an obvious debt to Tornatore's idol, Federico Fellini. Like *Cinema Paradiso*, it is set in the immediate postwar period in Sicily, when film was the focal point of popular culture and beauty contests and highly publicized star hunts (themes given important treatment in both Fellini's *The Vitelloni* and Visconti's *Bellissima*) testified to the important role cinema played in everyday life. Joe Morelli (Sergio Castellitto), a con artist not unlike Augusto in Fellini's *Il Bidone*, roams around the island looking for would-be actors and charging them for phony screen tests never intended to be shown to a film producer or director in Rome. Morelli even transports his cameras, lights, and microphones in a vehicle that clearly alludes to Zampanò's motorcycle caravan in Fellini's *La Strada*. Joe meets Beata (Tiziana Lodato), a poor girl living on charity in a nunnery, and a Hollywood ending might well have depicted their marriage and hints of a happy life to come. But when Joe, like Fellini's Augusto, lands in jail for his confidence game, it drives Beata mad, and she ends her life in an asylum. Tornatore's indebtedness to Fellini can be discerned in the incredibly interesting array of faces he assembles for Joe's journey. Although Joe's screen tests are a sham, these performances of ordinary people contain deeply affecting scenes. Like Fellini, Tornatore provides us with a kaleidoscope of grotesque, comic, and intensely moving vignettes: police officers declaiming Dante's *Comedy*; three bandit brothers who are persuaded not to rob Joe but to shift to a life in the movies; one of the last members of Garibaldi's Red Shirt Legion, who mutters one of the general's famous slogans; a woman willing to sleep with Joe in order to save her daughter from the life of poverty that she has endured. Perhaps the most hilarious screen tests are sequences devoted to the last lines spoken by Scarlett O'Hara in *Gone with the Wind*: "Tomorrow is another day!" Joe's actors all still have close links to a vibrant oral tradition, and each of them gives a highly personal interpretation of Scarlett's lines, reciting it in Sicilian dialect and applying it to their own lives in a way that underlines how real the cinema's appeal was to the men and women of that postwar generation. Like his mentor Fellini, Tornatore sees drama all around him and in the smallest gestures and expressions of simple human beings.

The *Legend of 1900*, *Malèna*, and *The Unknown Woman* are three films entirely different from one another, even though they are all marked by the same lyrical cinematic style already matured in Tornatore's earlier works. *The Legend of 1900* is an adaptation of a 1994 dramatic monologue by Alessandro Baricco (1958–), one of contemporary Italy's most important writers, perhaps best known abroad for his novels *Silk* (*Seta*, 1996) and *City* (1999). With an enormous budget for an Italian film, it also boasts sets designed by Bruno Cesari (1934–2004), winner of an Oscar for Best Art Direction–Set Direction in Bertolucci's *The Last Emperor*, an award he shared with Ferdinando Scarfiotti (1941–94) and Osvaldo Desideri (1939–), and a stupendous sound track (particularly important in a film about a pianist) by Ennio Morricone, who after five separate and unsuccessful Oscar nominations for Best Original Musical Score (including *Malèna*) finally received an Honorary Oscar for his entire career in 2007. The film, an extended metaphor about artistic creativity, narrates the strange story of a character dubbed 1900 (Tim Roth), a baby abandoned in a box of lemons on the first-class section of the ocean liner *The Virginian* (though the actual ship of that name only launched in 1905). His epithet derives from the fact that he had been born on the first day of the new century, 1900. Growing up on the ship, he never disembarks, and he becomes a piano player so talented that his reputation causes the famous jazz pianist "Jelly Roll" Morton (Clarence Williams III) to board the ship and challenge him to a musical duel. 1900 emerges as the clear victor, leaving "Jelly Roll" a broken man, but 1900 continues to refuse to leave his ship even when it is about to be destroyed for junk. Tornatore's ship reminds us of the ocean liner in Fellini's *And the Ship Sails On*, and like that earlier boat, *The Virginian* serves as a concrete embodiment of an entire epoch.

Another relatively high-budget film, *Malèna*, narrates quite a different kind of Sicilian story, one more in keeping with the tradition of how sexuality is treated in films about that island. Set in the imaginary Sicilian village of Castelcutò during World War II, *Malèna* helped to launch the image of Monica Bellucci (1964–) as an international sexy actress in the tradition of Sophia Loren and Gina Lollobrigida. She plays the title role of a young, sexually liberated woman in a society that does not condone such liberated behavior. Tornatore narrates the story from the perspective of a young boy named Renato Amoroso (Giuseppe Sulfaro), a character who recalls *Cinema Paradiso*'s Totò. Renato is obsessed with Malèna, no matter what kinds of behavior she exhibits after losing her husband and becoming a widow. As he constantly watches her, Renato witnesses her being chased out of her home by her father, sleeping with her lawyer, and then sleeping with a number of Germans during the war. When the Americans liberate the town from the Germans, the jealous townspeople shave Malèna's hair in a frightening scene of the punishment commonly meted out to collaborationists in Italy and France. Later, Renato discovers that Malèna's husband never really died but only pretended to do so, to escape the Fascist police. With her husband, Malèna eventually returns to her native town and finds the courage to face the townspeople who had once humiliated her and driven her away but now greet her as if nothing had ever happened. Tornatore's film represents a strange compromise between different points of view. While the director obviously approves of Malèna's liberated sexuality and her desire to determine how her body is used by the men who constantly ogle her in this male-dominated Sicilian setting, this perspective is conveyed through the eyes of a young boy who objectifies the woman's body in exactly the same manner as the entire village does. The original director's cut of the film contained a number of explicit scenes that were eliminated in the American released print, but they certainly helped to trace Monica Bellucci's trajectory in both Europe and Hollywood as one of the most sensuous contemporary Italian actresses.

The last film completed by Tornatore is *The Unknown Woman*, which may be considered a modern version of a film noir. It treats the problem of prostitution among girls imported into Italy from the former Communist bloc. For an Italian film, it contains numerous scenes of sex and violence that are both shocking and highly effective. Tornatore's recent projects include Baaria (Baaria 2009), a treatment of Sicilian life set between the 1930s and the 1970s in Tornatore's native city of Bagheria (called Baaria in Sicilian dialect), again starring Monica Bellucci, and *Leningrad*, about the famous siege of Leningrad (once again Saint Petersburg since 1991) by the German army during World War II—the grandiose project that Sergio Leone left unrealized after his death, and on which Tornatore has been working for nearly a decade. It remains to be seen if anyone can fill the shoes of Bernardo Bertolucci or Sergio Leone in producing a film epic of such enormous international scope with box-office success. Few, if any, of Tornatore's colleagues would have the courage or the financing to attempt such a film.

Marco Tullio Giordana

Marco Tullio Giordana's earliest works—*To Love the Damned* (*Maledetti vi amerò!* 1980) and *The Fall of the Rebel Angels* (*La caduta degli angeli ribelli*, 1981)—treated student unrest and terrorism. Both attracted critical attention without having much of an effect at the box office. Subsequently, he made *Appointment in Liverpool* (*Appuntamento a Liverpool*, 1988), a fictionalized account of the death of dozens of soccer fans (many of whom were Italian) at Heysel Stadium, Brussels, in 1985. After *Pasolini, an Italian Crime* (*Pasolini, un delitto italiano*, 1995), an attempt to reconstruct Pasolini's last hours before his murder, in which Giordana accepts the standard leftist interpretation of the crime as being the result of a plot, the themes of crime, violence, and terrorism have become part of his narrative signature. We have already examined the fine Mafia biopic he made in 2000, *The Hundred Steps*, one of the films that has moved Italian film toward deeper exploration of genre films involving crime and detection. Giordana's interest in student unrest, violence, and terrorism served him well in the production of the extremely successful six-hour television miniseries *The Best of Youth* (*La meglio gioventù*, 2003) that was released at Cannes and distributed as a true but lengthy feature film with enormous critical and commercial success. In its scope, it recalls such family sagas as Visconti's *Rocco and His Brothers*, Scola's *The Family*, Rosi's *Three Brothers*, Bertolucci's *1900*, or the greatest Italian novel of the twentieth century, Tomasi Giuseppe di Lampedusa's *The Leopard* (also filmed by Visconti). It begins in 1966 and ends in 2003, focusing upon two brothers: Nicola (Luigi Lo Cascio) and Matteo (Alessio Boni) Carati. Preparing for college entrance exams and a trek to Norway's North Cape, the pair splits after Matteo impulsively liberates a young mental patient named Giorgia (Jasmine Trinca) from the asylum where she has been receiving cruel electroshock treatments, leaving Nicola to travel alone at least part of the way to the North Cape. The film ends in 2003 when the son born out of wedlock to Matteo and a Sicilian photographer named Mirella (Maya Sansa) completes his father's interrupted journey with his own girlfriend.

Between 1966 and 2003, Giordana follows with compassion, finesse, and empathy the course of Italian history during this period through the everyday lives of his protagonists. We see the terrible flood in Florence in 1966, the rise of labor violence and Italian terrorism, the attacks upon the state in the Mezzogiorno by the Mafia and their assassinations of important politicians and judges, all through the careers of Nicola, Matteo, and their family. Nicola becomes a psychiatrist fighting against the use of shock treatments, while Matteo, haunted by his own private demons, leaves his university studies and joins the police to subjugate his life to a series of set rules and harsh discipline. Matteo commits suicide out of some unspoken desperation during the holidays, whereas Nicola eventually manages to help Giorgia, the mentally ill young girl who interrupted their trip to Norway, begin a normal life outside the hospital. Nonetheless, Nicola has his own trials: he has a child with Giulia (Sonia Bergamasco), a talented pianist he meets in Florence during the flood; Giulia turns to terrorism, joins the Brigate Rosse, and abandons both Nicola and their daughter, Sara, surfacing only years later after leaving prison shortly before Sara's (Camilla Filippi) marriage in Tuscany.

Matteo joins the police and serves during urban demonstrations that often became violent in Marco Tullio Giordana's epic film about contemporary Italian history, *The Best of Youth. Credit: DVD*

It would be impossible to analyze in detail all the important historical events that Giordana manages to show us fleetingly through the lives of these fascinating but normal characters. That is to say, they are memorable people who lead normal lives—they live, love, grow old, and some even die, but they all persevere and do so through the agency of the nuclear family, that much beleaguered but still crucial institution that dominates Italian culture. What is memorable in a film that might well seem to last forever is that we never notice time passing, so intimately are we allowed to enter into the private lives of this compelling collection of people. Even Giulia, played by an Italian actress with the physical appearance of every terrorist of that era, emerges from the film as a real person, not an ideological stereotype. Giordana's characters engage in little psychological introspection in this made-for-television film; they show what they are thinking by what they are doing. Still, what we see on the surface of their complex personalities remains both appealing and satisfying.

Although *The Best of Youth* contains a great deal of Italian history that non-Italian audiences may not completely comprehend, the film manages to supply most of what an audience needs to know. In Giordana's most recent film, *Wild Blood* (*Sanguepazzo*, 2008), he turns to an earlier period of Italian history to examine the lives of two Fascist-era actors, Luisa Ferida (1914–45) and Osvaldo Valenti (1906–45), who were matinee idols in Italy before the outbreak of the war and until the fall of the Fascist regime in 1943, when part of the Italian film industry moved to the North after the Allied invasion of the peninsula. Ferida and Valenti led what were, by period standards, dissolute lives, marked by addiction to cocaine and their support for the losing side in the civil war that broke out in Italy between 1943 and 1945.[15] Accused of crimes during the last months of the ill-fated Republic of Salò of Benito Mussolini, they were executed by partisans without a trial on the orders of Resistance leaders, including Sandro Pertini (1896–1990), who later became president of Italy. Ferida and Valenti were condemned primarily for their relationship to the infamous Pietro Koch, a sadistic Fascist "dead-ender" who presided over the Villa Triste on Via Paolo Uccello in Milan, where he reputedly entertained his debauched guests (including, according to the accusations of those who executed them, Valenti and Ferida) with drugs, orgies, and torture of the regime's enemies. Koch had had Luchino Visconti arrested in Rome before leaving the city for the North; ironically, it was Visconti who filmed his execution in 1945. *Wild Blood* casts as Ferida Italy's reigning sex goddess, Monica Bellucci, and as Valenti, Luca Zingaretti (1961–), an actor who has earned recognition as the personification of Inspector Montalbano, the detective hero of the novels of Andrea Camilleri, in Italian television films from 1999 to the present.

Gianni Amelio and the Heritage of Neorealism

One of the oldest directors discussed in this chapter, born three months before the liberation of Italy, Gianni Amelio is also the closest to the heritage of neorealism. *The Via Panisperna Boys* (*I ragazzi di Via Panisperna*, 1988) recounts the glory years of Italian physics in the 1930s before Fascist racial laws drove a number of Italian physicists out of the country. During this era, luminaries such as Enrico Fermi, Emilio Segrè, Bruno Pontecorvo, and Ettore Majorana made basic discoveries on slow neutrons and advances on other significant problems in physics that later led to the construction of nuclear reactors and the atomic bomb. A subsequent film, *Open Doors* (*Porte aperte*, 1990), adapted from a 1987 Leonardo Sciascia story about a murderer who demands the death penalty during the Fascist period and a magistrate who tries to prevent that sentence from being passed, is worthy of note. Of particular relevance to Amelio's relationship with Italian neorealism are three subsequent films: *The Stolen Children* (*Il ladro di bambini*, 1992), *Lamerica* (1994), and *The Way We Laughed* (*Così ridevano*, 1998). The first film concerns a young officer in the Carabinieri named Antonio (Enrico Lo Verso, Amelio's favorite actor) from Calabria, who is ordered to return an eleven-year-old girl named Rosetta (Valentina Scalici) and her ten-year-old brother, Luciano (Giuseppe Ieracitano), to the orphanage after her Sicilian mother is arrested for prostituting her in the tenement section of Milan. But the orphanage turns the girl away since she is recognized as the "notorious child prostitute" whose picture has appeared in the tabloids, and the young policeman decides, out of compassion for the children but without the proper authorization, to return them both to their birthplace in Sicily. Thus, the premise of the film reminds one of the opening of Giordana's *The Best of Youth*, where the Carati brothers rescue a mentally ill girl from a cruel asylum; but unlike that high-budget television production, *The Stolen Children* is a low-budget, relatively uncomplicated film with a number of nonprofessional actors, and it continues the neorealist predilection for focusing the camera on the lower classes, especially those from the South. In the film's eloquent but simple conclusion, the two children find a good foster home, while the *carabiniere* suffers no more than a reprimand.

Superior child acting has always been a hallmark of Italian cinema from the Fascist period to the present, although some critics find neorealist children sentimental and melodramatic. Little sentimentality exists, however, in *The Stolen Children*, where Amelio's dispassionate camera style offers scant hope of a better life for the children. Amelio may well intend an ironic reversal of the positive emotional direction we encounter in Rossellini's *Paisan*, like Tornatore's effective reversal in *Everybody's Fine*. Whereas Rossellini moved from South to North and promised moral regeneration and national rebirth after the liberation of Italy, Amelio shows us a tawdry side of Italy's contemporary society: degraded neighborhood bars, endless streets surrounded by dirty yards or enclosed by wire fences, heart-rending expanses of tacky, hastily constructed structures that ruin the magnificent Mediterranean coastline. His skill in obtaining masterful performances from nonprofessional child actors recalls De Sica. Rosetta and Luciano are never "cute"; they are actually unattractive and initially provoke not sympathy but revulsion. The Italian nuclear family, that source of so much energy and emotion in Italian history, seems at an impasse. Little, if anything, could be more destructive of the sacred institution of the family than prostituting a child.

Lamerica examines a theme dear to Italian neorealism—southern Italians traveling from the South to the North or abroad to find work and make a new life, recalling such classics as *The Path of Hope*, by Germi, or Visconti's *Rocco and His Brothers*. Diverging from this tradition, Amelio sets the theme in Albania after the Communist regime collapsed and, in effect, replaces the impoverished peasants of the Mezzogiorno with Albanians. The film opens with documentary footage from the Italian state archives of Mussolini's occupation of Albania and a voice-over that declares: "Finally, thanks to Italy, the mature and robust people of Albania are entering civilization." Amelio's camera then jumps from Mussolini's arrival at the port of Durazzo to the same port (known locally as Durrës) in 1991, where the city teems with poor, starving Albanians desperately trying to leave home for the country they see as the new America—Italy. Once a nation known for dispatching its surplus and impoverished population abroad in North and South America, Italy now has become a rich land that attracts emigrants rather than producing them.

Amelio's narrative focuses upon two Italian entrepreneurs, Gino (Enrico Lo Verso) and Fiore (Michele Placido), who set up a phony shoe factory in Albania in order to defraud the Italian government of subsidies intended to help the Albanians. They need a local front man to set up a bogus Albanian corporation, and, thanks to the good offices of an Albanian official, they find one in an old man who has been in jail for fifty years for political crimes—Spiro Tojaz (Carmelo Di Mazzarelli). Fiore returns to Italy, leaving Gino to handle things on the spot, but their plans begin to unravel. Spiro turns out to be an Italian deserter from the Albanian invasion who hardly remembers his own language. When Gino loses his documents in a robbery, he must return to Italy on an old cargo ship, reduced to the same desperate straits as the Albanians seeking asylum in Italy. Amelio's film thus contains the denunciation of social injustice so important to all neorealist cinema, but *Lamerica* also reminds us of just how much has changed since the postwar period when Rossellini, De Sica, and Visconti portrayed Italy in much the same manner as Amelio has more recently portrayed Albania.

The Way We Laughed, awarded a Golden Lion at the Venice Film Festival, continues Amelio's portrayal of Italian migration, recalling the journey of southerners from Acitrezza to Milan in *Rocco and His Brothers*. Set in Turin between 1958 and 1964, Amelio's film uses a simple camera style and extremely somber lighting to contrast the lives of two brothers, Giovanni (Enrico Lo Verso) and Pietro (Francesco Giuffrida). Devoted to his family, Giovanni is illiterate but clever, and eventually becomes an important labor boss who doles out favors and jobs to poor southerners in return for cash. Pietro has pretensions to becoming a schoolteacher, but his dishonest lazy streak leads him to play hooky from school and to steal to buy expensive clothes. Giovanni sacrifices everything for Pietro and his education, but the younger brother's behavior makes it difficult for Giovanni to assist him. Still, family and blood ties in the South are even more important than religion, just as they were in Visconti's tale. When Pietro finally changes his ways and completes his high-school degree with the assistance of a tutor, he runs in great excitement to tell Giovanni of his good fortune and to show that all his older brother's sacrifices were not in vain. Unfortunately, he appears at the place where Giovanni kills a man, obviously relating to his profession as a labor boss. Following the imperative that family must trump justice, Pietro takes the rap for Giovanni and ends up in a reformatory. *The Way We Laughed* contains little humor or joy, and it presents an extremely dark interpretation of the social customs that southerners brought with them to the North, including their belief in family loyalty.

Ferzan Ozpetek: *Un Turco in Italia* (with Apologies to Rossini)[16]

Unlike Hollywood, which has always constituted a melting pot of cinematic talent, attracting directors, actors, and technicians of genius for decades from all over the world, Cinecittà has not been so clearly identified with such open doors. In most cases, foreigners making films in Italy remained foreigners, most often using the fine facilities of the Italian industry without ever becoming Italian in the process. In an age when the social fabric of Italy itself has been drastically changed by foreign immigration over the past several decades, it is no surprise to find that at least one foreigner of distinction has become virtually naturalized in his work as a film director. Although Turkish by birth, Ferzan Ozpetek has become Italian by inclination, and after working as an assistant on films directed by Massimo Troisi and Ricky Tognazzi, he produced a series of films that have justly attracted a great deal of critical attention and acclaim at film festivals for their originality and high technical competence: *Steam: The Turkish Bath* (*Hamam*, a.k.a. *Il bagno turco*, 1997); *Harem*, a.k.a. *Harem Suaré* (*Harem suaré*, literally, "the last harem"; 1999); *His Secret Life* (*Le fate ignoranti*; literally, "the ignorant fairies"; 2001); *Facing Windows* (*La finestra di fronte*, 2003); and *Saturn in Opposition* (*Saturno contro*, 2007). Although all of his films treat that archetypal Italian cinematic theme of the family, Ozpetek's families are extremely nontraditional and are generally not even heterosexual in nature. His work advances the thesis that one's real family constitutes one's friends and lovers, not just those who represent the traditional Italian nuclear family. Moreover, he injects enough of his Turkish background—including Turkish music on his sound tracks, situating Italians in a Turkish environment abroad, or making Turkish immigrants to Italy part of his fresco of contemporary Italian society—that his films have a genuinely cosmopolitan flavor.

Both the Turkish element of his work and his focus upon homosexuality stand out in *Steam*, *Harem*, and *His Secret Life*. In *Steam*, a young Italian couple's supposedly normal and happy married life is disrupted by the consequences of the husband's inheritance from an aunt who years ago had moved to Turkey and had acquired a popular steam bath. Francesco (Alessandro Gassman, Vittorio's son) goes to Istanbul to sell the bath but becomes caught up in an entirely different kind of world and carries on an affair with a young Turkish man named Mehmet (Mehmet Günsür). When Francesco dies at the hands of a mysterious assassin who stabs him as he opens the front door of Mehmet's home, the film never makes it clear whether "the Italian," as the murderer calls him, dies because of his affair with Mehmet, and thus as the result of a homosexual lover's quarrel, or because Francesco's sudden refusal to sell the Turkish bath property runs afoul of an extremely powerful Turkish businesswoman who needs the land to complete a huge development deal. When his wife, Marta (Francesca d'Aloja), comes to Istanbul after Francesco's death, she develops the same strong attraction to Turkish culture as had her husband's Aunt Anita years earlier, and after she completes the reconstruction of the bath, she remains in Istanbul. Hence, Ozpetek reverses the usual pattern of Italian emigration abroad. Once only the poor and downtrodden of Italy looked to the United States, South America, or Northern Europe and moved for economic reasons, but now successful and wealthy Italians move abroad for many of the same cultural reasons that motivated the members of the so-called Lost Generation of American expatriates who traveled to Europe after World War I.

In contrast, *Harem* recounts the demise of the last harem of the Ottoman sultan in the first decade of the twentieth century and constitutes a historical costume drama, plunging the audience into a beautiful reconstruction of life inside an institution that has always fascinated the West. By presenting the narrative within a series of tales told by the sultan's wives and servants inside the harem, it recalls the structure of *The Arabian Nights*. Impoverished southern Italian parents sell their young daughter, Safiye (Marie Gillain), to the harem. With the assistance of an ambitious but sympathetic black eunuch named Nadir (Alex Descas), she becomes first the sultan's favorite concubine and then his official wife. When the sultan is overthrown, he escapes to exile in Europe, and the harem is dissolved, evicting the women and forcing Safiye to perform for audiences back in Italy at a variety show highlighting the sexual mysteries of the Turkish harem. Ozpetek's interest in this unique institution is predominantly sexual rather than historical, and he suggests that all sorts of unusual liaisons and intrigues took place within the harem. Once again, he mixes Italian and Turkish culture, since Safiye's entry into the harem is facilitated by the sultan's love of Verdi's operas, the libretti of which she translates for him. Her life, parallel to that of Verdi's heroine, Violetta, in *La traviata*, an opera that is performed in the royal palace for the Turkish ruler, seems full of tragic and operatic passion.

His Secret Life and *Facing Windows* confirmed Ozpetek's critical reputation.[17] The first film recalls the supposedly happily married, middle-class Italian couple of *Steam*. After seventeen years of "normal" marriage, Antonia (Margherita Buy) suddenly discovers that her husband, Massimo (Andrea Renzi), has had a homosexual lover named Michele (Stefano Accorsi) for the past seven years when Massimo dies crossing a street while taking a cell phone call (apparently from Michele). The "ignorant fairies" of the original Italian title refer not to Michele and his circle of homosexual friends but, rather, to Michele's inscription on the back of a print that Antonia discovers in her husband's office and that puts her on the trail of his lover. The most intriguing part of the wife's search for the truth of her husband's "secret life" comes from the fact that she is completely incapable of realizing for the longest time that the lover might be a man. As Michele says to Antonia in a comic exchange in his apartment, surrounded by drag queens, unabashedly gay males, transsexuals, and lesbians, "Have you looked around here? Do you need subtitles?"

After recovering from the initial shock, Antonia discovers a strange attraction to the obviously genuine friendship that linked all these strange characters to her husband's life, and she eventually becomes part of it. In short, they become her real family, or at least an important part of her life. Although his representation of homosexuals as just like "normal" people is no original treatment of the issue in the cinema, Ozpetek's film exploits brilliant performances by Buy, Accorsi, and the entire cast (even a Turkish brother and sister belong to this new "family") to produce a moving portrait of gender problems and sexual identification that would have been unthinkable in Italian cinema only a few decades earlier. *Saturn in Opposition* attempts to examine a similar kind of situation, but in spite of its many merits, it seems to be a remake of *His Secret Life*, this time with Accorsi playing the heterosexual husband of Buy, both of whom Ozpetek juxtaposes against a gay couple in the film.

Facing Windows presents a far more complex treatment of "the Other," as it combines Ozpetek's interest in homosexuality with the question of the Holocaust, examining not only the discrimination practiced in Fascist Italy against homosexuals, a theme Scola treated brilliantly in *A Special Day*, but also the roundup of Jews by the Nazis and their Fascist sympathizers in Rome in 1943, an event that takes place in the Roman Ghetto near the ancient ruins of the Teatro di Marcello. Again, we have the traditional heterosexual couple experiencing marital difficulties, Giovanna (Giovanna Mezzogiorno) and Filippo (Filippo Nigro), whose lives are changed by the introduction of a nontraditional hero: an old man wandering around the streets who calls himself Simone but whose real identity eventually emerges. He is Davide Veroli, played by Massimo Girotti, one of Italy's most famous leading men during the Fascist period and the star of such classics as Blasetti's *The Iron Crown*, Visconti's *Obsession*, and Bertolucci's *Last Tango in Paris*. Girotti, who died shortly before the film's release, delivers one of his finest performances in *Facing Windows*. Ozpetek's narrative here has a far more complex structure than in his other works, and a series of flashbacks slowly informs us that the old man is a Holocaust survivor who calls himself Simone because he had been forced to choose between warning the inhabitants of the Ghetto—many of whom despised him for his homosexuality—and his male lover, Simone. Because he chose to warn his neighbors of the threat to their lives, his lover had died, and Davide/Simone has been forever haunted by guilt.

By a quirk of circumstances that are unusual but completely believable by virtue of Ozpetek's outstanding script and masterful narrative technique, Davide and Giovanna meet when she and Filippo offer him hospitality after finding him wandering on the streets during a moment when he has temporarily lost his memory and introduced himself as Simone. Giovanna has always wanted to become a pastry chef, and after the war Davide had become one of Italy's masters in this difficult trade. Teaching Giovanna his skills, Davide is finally able to deal with his guilt and regain his balance. For both, their meeting is a life-changing event, and at the conclusion of the film, she announces that her first attempt at baking an important cake has been praised by the pastry chef with whom she has been apprenticed, thanks to Davide's instructions. She tells Davide, in a moving voice-over of her letter to her mentor, that she has learned the secret of having memories—that everyone who loves you (like Simone in Davide's life) leaves behind something of himself or herself.

Ozpetek's most recent films announce the maturity of a genuinely talented and original film director, and his Turkish origins make him supremely capable of dealing in a creative and perceptive fashion with the problems of religious and sexual identification in an Italian society that has become far more multicultural and tolerant than it was in the past.

Other Names to Remember from the Third Wave Generation of the 1950s

Directors such as Moretti, Salvatores, and Benigni have achieved international, not merely Italian, renown as auteurs with bodies of work that reflect individual cinematic styles, themes, and values. Others from this same generation merit some attention even though they have achieved less renown abroad. For example, the films of Giuseppe Piccioni have done well at the Italian box office ever since his first feature, *Il grande Blek* (literally, "The Great Blek," the name of an old Italian comic book; 1987), and earned a good deal of critical attention within the peninsula, even though Piccioni has not been as prolific as some of his contemporaries. These films include *Not of This World* (*Fuori dal mondo*, 1999), *Light of My Eyes* (*Luce dei miei occhi*, 2001), and *The Life I Want* (*La vita che vorrei*, 2004). The first of these three demonstrates Piccioni's skill in treating one of his basic themes: human loneliness and the difficulty of connecting with others. In a beautifully narrated story, a young nun, Sister Caterina (Margherita Buy), finds an abandoned baby in a park shortly before she is to take her final vows. This event not only causes her to wonder what an alternative life with children might be like but puts her into contact with a lonely man named Ernesto (Silvio Orlando), who owns a laundry in which, it turns out, the abandoned baby's mother once worked. Because Ernesto had had a one-night stand with the mother, the sudden appearance of the nun—who had traced the child back to the laundry through an identifying mark on the baby's blanket—forces Ernesto, like Caterina, to question his own life. A genuine attraction springs up between the two characters, but as the film ends, the changes experienced by both protagonists do not alter the ultimate course of their future lives. Caterina realizes her true vocation is that of a nun serving others, while Ernesto, having discovered he is not the baby's father, at least resolves to be a more humane boss. The entire film reflects masterful performances by Margherita Buy and Silvio Orlando, two of contemporary Italy's best film actors.

In *Light of My Eyes*, Piccioni continues his focus on how complicated relationships may be and how near misses in love are far more frequent than successes. Antonio (Luigi Lo Cascio) is a lonely chauffeur who passes his time imagining that he is a man named Morgan in a science-fiction novel. He meets Maria (Sandra Ceccarelli), who is having a difficult time making a living from a frozen-food shop. Piccioni allows the spark of romance to occur, but it fails to ignite. Silvio Orlando also delivers an expected excellent performance as Saverio, a loan-shark gangster to whom Maria owes money; he befriends Antonio, who begins to work for him in order to help Maria pay her debts. Ultimately, the love that Antonio offers the lonely Maria simply does not suffice to make her love him—a melancholy but certainly not sentimental conclusion to the film. After the film was released, Lo Cascio (the revelation of Giordana's *The Best of Youth*) and Ceccarelli received Best Actor and Best Actress awards at the Venice Film Festival, burnishing Piccioni's reputation as a director whose handling of actors produces stellar performances. Piccioni also employed both Lo Cascio and Ceccarelli in his next film, *The Life I Want*, where they play two actors who fall in and out of love while making a film. The result is another example of metacinema, a film about films, which is a recurrent theme among many of the works produced in the past several decades.

Silvio Soldini's *Bread and Tulips* (*Pane e tulipani*, 2000) represents the best romantic comedy produced by the Italian cinema in recent decades. Unlike the traditional *commedia all'italiana*, this film employs lesser-known faces rather than the traditional comic masks identified with the actors and actresses of the 1960s–80s, and the film swept the 2000 Italian film awards, winning nine David di Donatello prizes in virtually every category. The formula for the film's plot represents no particular innovation: the emotional and passionate rebirth of a middle-aged, neglected housewife named Rosalba (Licia Maglietta), who plays so small a role in her family's life that she is accidentally left behind by them on a vacation trip. After deciding to take her own vacation by herself in Venice, she meets up with a goofy Icelandic waiter named Fernando (played by the veteran Bruno Ganz) who periodically threatens suicide, falls in love with Rosalba, declaims Ariosto's *Orlando furioso*, and encourages Rosalba to fulfill her lifetime dream of playing the accordion. Soldini manages to create a believable cast of lovable and eccentric characters who engage our sympathy without allowing the picturesque quality of the location, Venice, to take over the film. Ultimately Fernando borrows an old delivery van and drives all the way to Rosalba's native Pescara to reclaim her with a bouquet of flowers and a romantic citation from Ariosto in his strange accent, carrying her back to Venice and to a life of playing the accordion at local dancehalls, but most of all, back to a life filled with passion and excitement, even in middle age.

Davide Ferrario's *After Midnight* (*Dopo mezzanotte*, 2004) combines a similar thirst for real romance in an otherwise drab existence in Turin with a metacinematic subplot. Instead of mature, middle-aged protagonists, Ferrario focuses upon young people working in dead-end jobs, or even as car thieves. Martino (Giorgio Pasotti) works during the nights as the caretaker of Turin's stupendous Museo Nazionale del Cinema, which is housed in the Mole Antonelliana, a unique building rising to a height of 113 meters. (The Mole had been designed to be the Jewish Synagogue of Turin shortly after Italy was unified in the nineteenth century and before the capital of the new nation became not Turin, the capital of the Kingdom of Savoy, but Rome.) Martino is the incarnation of the mannerisms and comic behavior of his idol, Buster Keaton, and in fact, clips from Keaton's *One Week* and *The Scarecrow* (both shot in 1920) are employed by Ferrario to highlight Martino's character. Keaton is an appropriate choice, since it is not commonly known that Keaton's last film was an Italian comedy made by Luigi Scattini (1927–2010) entitled *Two Marines* and a *General*, a.k.a. *War Italian Style* (*Due marines e un generale*, 1966), in which Keaton paired up with the zany Italian comic team of Franco Franchi and Ciccio Ingrassia in a send-up of World War II.[18] One of Ferrario's goals in *After Midnight* is to suggest that the rich heritage of silent film, now housed in the Turin museum's substantial archives, may still provide the fertile ground to inspire contemporary filmmaking. Ferrario pairs Keaton's works with an Italian silent classic, Giovanni Pastrone's *The Fire* (*Il fuoco—la favilla, la vampa, la cenere*, 1916), a film about a passionate love affair that stands in contrast to the relationship between Martino and Amanda (Francesca Inaudi), a proletarian employee at a hamburger joint in Turin who meets Martino after she has thrown the hot grease from the french-fry cooker at her arrogant employer and takes refuge from the police in the museum. Her car-thief boyfriend "Angel," a.k.a. Angelo (Fabio Troiano), complicates matters, and Ferrario's narrative turns into a homage to the ménage à trois of Truffaut's *Jules and Jim* (*Jules et Jim*, 1962), the New Wave classic. The role played by the first Fibonacci numbers displayed on one side of the four-sided dome of the Mole Antonelliana gives Ferrario's plot further complexity. These numbers, named after an Italian mathematician (c. 1180–c. 1250), introduce a sequence of numbers beginning with 0 and 1; thereafter each new number in the series is equal to the sum of the previous two: thus 0, 1, 1, 2, 3, 5, 8, and so on. Ferrario suggests that the Fibonacci numbers reflect a kind of universal connection among all sorts of things—natural phenomena, music, economics, and of course human relationships. *After Midnight*'s metacinematic subplot represents yet another use of this theme in the contemporary Italian cinema, while his presentation of the Fibonacci numbers as a mysterious explanation of human relationships represents an amusing (if not developed) definition of romantic love.

In *Don't Move* (*Non ti muovere*, 2004), the actor Sergio Castellitto adapts to the screen a best-selling and prizewinning novel (2001) by his wife, the Irish-born Margaret Mazzantini. Castellitto cast himself as a cowardly surgeon named Timoteo who has a love affair with a poor girl named Italia, played by Penélope Cruz in a completely unpredictable but remarkable performance. Italia dies with her lover by her side in his hospital. As Italy's greatest film historian correctly notes, Castellitto represents perhaps Italy's only contemporary Italian film actor with the versatile skills to adapt himself to very different kinds of film characters that have always been identified with the graduates of the American Actors Studio.[19]

A number of recent Italian films have dealt with the Italian connection to the Holocaust, and an excellent film by the Frazzi brothers, *The Sky Is Falling*, a.k.a. *The Sky Will Fall* (*Il cielo cade*, 2000), merits mention, because it offers an interesting variant on this perennial cinematic theme.[20] In its style, it employs elements from the past history of postwar Italian cinema. Its point of view recalls both the neorealist practice of showing harsh social reality through the eyes of sympathetic children, while its setting—a beautiful Tuscan villa owned by an aristocratic German couple related on the husband's side to the great physicist Albert Einstein—cannot help but remind us of the Edenic world of De Sica's *The Garden of the Finzi-Continis*, where the eruption of German and Fascist anti-Semitism and the subsequent deportation of the Jews that live within the garden destroy an idyllic, even Biblical, paradise. Although a wealthy patrician, the villa's owner, Wilhelm Einstein (Jeroen Krabbé), acts toward his large staff of house servants and peasants as a benevolent and kind father, and his cultured background cannot allow him to believe that the German troops who are battling the Allies in his Tuscan countryside would do him any harm. He and his wife, Katchen (Isabella Rossellini), have two daughters whom they have brought up in the Jewish faith. His generosity extends to a pair of sisters, Penny and Baby, who are distant relatives but Christians whom the Einsteins adopt as their own. One civilized German general, housed at his villa, maintains a level of humanity that reassures Wilhelm, who even dares to beat the general at chess on a regular basis. The general's subsequent transfer and the arrival of the SS leads to Wilhelm's flight with Italian partisans and the barbaric, brutal murder of his wife and his two daughters. Penny and Baby are spared by the cruel Nazi SS officer because he spies a crucifix around their necks, and after Wilhelm returns with the retreat of the German forces, he commits suicide out of guilt and remorse for not dying with his family. A touching postscript concluding this eloquent film invites the viewer to pass by the graves of the Einstein family in Badiuzza sopra Firenze between San Donato in Collina and Rignano sull'Arno and to remember their lives and the horrible events of August 3, 1944, by placing some flowers on their graves.

〜

Since the end of World War II, Italian cinema has fostered numerous popular genres as well as three successful waves of auteurs. The neorealist period produced the first wave of internationally renowned directors, such as Rossellini, De Sica, Antonioni, Visconti, and Fellini, who dominated the scene until the 1970s and continued to produce outstanding works for some time thereafter. The second wave, the postneorealist auteurs—Pasolini, Bertolucci, Bellocchio, Rosi, Petri, Pontecorvo, the Taviani brothers, Scola, and Avati—moved beyond neorealism's heritage to produce a quite different and more socially engaged brand of filmmaking. Some of these figures still continue to create original and significant works. Italy's third wave of auteurs, those discussed in this chapter, who were almost all born in the 1950s, after the initial burst of neorealist creativity, and many of whom came of age during the social and political upheavals around 1968, now form the backbone of Italy's "art" cinema: those films that receive the greatest attention from critics at home and abroad, that have won a very respectable number of international prizes, and that have earned, in many cases, a great deal of money at the box office both nationally and internationally. It has always been a practice in Italy to lament the state of Italian cinema, even during the years when it was unquestionably the most interesting cinema in the world outside of Hollywood, between 1945 and the mid-1970s. Still, even a cursory examination of the many different directors treated in this chapter—along with a new group of talented actors and actresses, not to mention outstanding scriptwriters and technicians—demonstrates that, contrary to this traditional lament of the "crisis" in Italian filmmaking, it is the lack of financial support, not the lack of talent, that has always plagued Italy's contributions to the nation's greatest art form in the modern era.

The concluding chapter of this book presents the notable members of an even younger generation of filmmakers, who look toward the third millennium, and assesses, insofar as this is ever possible in a rapidly changing art form, what the future prospects might be.

CHAPTER SEVENTEEN

Italian Cinema Enters the Third Millennium

The State of the Industry: Promising Signs

IN 2008, ITALIAN BOX-OFFICE FIGURES AND EVENTS at the industry's principal showcases for its products, the international film festivals at Cannes and Venice plus the David di Donatello awards, suggest that Italian cinema may well be healthier than many doom-and-gloom critics realize. According to *Variety*, the share of the local film market in the Italian peninsula has risen from 20 percent in 2004 (where it had remained for almost a decade) to 24 percent in 2005, 29 percent in 2006, and 33 percent in 2008. Hollywood films, such as *Indiana Jones and the Kingdom of the Crystal Skull* and *I Am Legend*, ranked at the top of the box-office charts, but Italian works, such as Matteo Garrone's *Gomorrah* or Carlo Verdone's collection of comic sketches starring himself in what *Variety* has translated as *Big, Bad . . . and Verdone* (*Grande, grosso e . . . Verdone*, 2008), kept neck and neck with American blockbusters for the number of tickets sold. In terms of critical acclaim, the two Italian victories at Cannes—the Grand Prix for Garrone's *Gomorrah* and the Jury Prize for Sorrentino's *Il Divo* (about Giulio Andreotti)—recalled the glory days of 1972, when two Italian films shared the highest award at Cannes, the Palme d'Or: Rosi's *The Mattei Affair*, and Petri's *The Working Class Goes to Heaven*.[1]

The world's first film festival, the Venice Biennale, has for the past decade been making important contributions to raising historical awareness of Italy's contributions to film by sponsoring screenings of important retrospectives of neglected, unknown, or critically overlooked genre films. After wildly successful retrospectives of thrillers, westerns, and crime films (all B genre films), the sixty-fifth Biennale in 2008 sponsored a retrospective entitled "These Phantoms: Italian Cinema Rediscovered (1946–1975)." It featured thirty-three newly restored or rediscovered works from these three decades, including the so-called Golden Age (see Part Three), that have been dusted off from the archives with support from the Biennale, the National Film Archives, and the Italian Ministry of Culture. Works presented include hard-to-locate titles by Luigi Zampa, Duilio Coletti, Mario Bonnard, Dino Risi, Vittorio De Sica, Roberto Rossellini, and numerous other important figures of the period that will now hopefully appear in DVD format for wide distribution. Of particular interest are newly remastered versions of Wertmüller's *The Lizards* and Fellini's *The White Sheik*, as well as a number of difficult-to-find documentaries, including *E il Casanova di Fellini?* (literally, "And *Fellini's Casanova?*"; 1975) by the Fellini collaborators Gianfranco Angelucci and Liliana Betti, originally aired on Italian television.

Only recently have the Italian government and Italy's film industry awakened to the fact that in order to have a flourishing cinema, it is necessary to have a flourishing film *culture*, like the one in France, to encourage a knowledge of a nation's film history and to prepare audiences to seek out the unusual rather than only conventional commercial fare produced in Hollywood or screened on Italian private-television channels. A positive sign is that the newly established Rome Film Festival (held in the fall, after the Venice festival in late August and early September) has been reorganized so as not to compete with Venice. From 2008 to 2012, it was entrusted to the former director at Venice, Gian Luigi Rondi, in an attempt, perhaps futile in Italy, to keep the Rome and Venice venues out of the hands of politicians and bureaucrats in the capital city.

The Italian films presented in competition at the 2008 Venice Festival represented both the old and the new. The veteran Pupi Avati's thriller *Giovanna's Father* (*Il papà di Giovanna*, 2008) joined Ferzan Ozpetek's portrait of twenty-four hours in Rome in *A Perfect Day* (*Un giorno perfetto*, 2008) and a Neapolitan comedy, *Il seme della discordia* (literally, "The Seed of Discord"; 2008), by the newcomer Pappi Corsicato (1960–). At the 2008 David di Donatello Awards, the "favorite" film, with eleven nominations, was *Quiet Chaos* (*Caos calmo*, 2008), by Antonio Luigi Grimaldi (1955–), a film starring Nanni Moretti, veteran director and sometime actor (usually in his own films). Moretti plays a television executive, one who cynically remarks that the health of the Italian cinema is "everybody's priority"—a statement virtually everyone understands to be false—and who has a torrid sex scene onscreen with the actress Isabella Ferrari that prompted an attack by the Vatican. The surprise winner, garnering eight awards out of eleven nominations, one in virtually every possible category, however, was *The Girl by the Lake* (*La ragazza del lago*, 2007), the debut film of Andrea Molaioli (1967–), who had been Moretti's assistant director on *Red Lob, Dear Diary, April*, and *The Son's Room*. This coup is in line with a persistent trend in recent Italian cinema to privilege crime stories and mysteries (like such important recent titles, discussed in chapter 14, as *Crime Novel, La Scorta, The Consequences of Love, The Embalmer, The Family Friend*, and

I'm Not Scared, not to mention *Gomorrah* and *Il Divo*). In Molaioli's film, Toni Servillo (the star of *The Consequences of Love*, *Gomorrah*, and *Il Divo*) plays an aging detective seeking to solve the murder of a young girl found naked by the shore of a lake in the Dolomites. The 2008 David Award for Best Actor went to Servillo, as it had in 2005 for his work in *Consequences*.

In short, the state of the Italian cinema in the first years of the new millennium seems promising. Veterans compete with new faces, and films appear that raise questions, cause scandals, do well at the box office, and earn international recognition, festival prizes, and critical acclaim. The remainder of this chapter discusses the contributions of directors born after 1960—that is, later than those still relatively young figures defined as the "third wave" in chapter 16. They include Paolo Sorrentino (*The Family Friend*, *The Consequences of Love*, *Il Divo*) and Matteo Garrone (*The Embalmer* and *Gomorrah*), both directors discussed in chapter 14 in the context of the evolution of the *poliziesco*; Daniele Lucchetti (1960–), like Molaioli a protégé of Nanni Moretti; Francesca Archibugi (1960–); Emanuele Crialese (1965–); Paolo Virzì (1964–); and Gabriele Muccino (1967–).

Garrone's *First Love*, a.k.a. *Primo Amore* (*Primo amore*, 2004)—his other major feature film besides *The Embalmer* and *Gomorrah*—once again reflects his precocious talent in dealing with dark themes. A goldsmith named Vittorio (Vitaliano Trevisan) seeks an ideal woman, but Sonia (Michela Cescon) has one defect: Vittorio thinks she should lose a few kilos. Because of Sonia's low self-esteem, she allows him to begin to shape her body and control her life as their love affair develops, until they both lose touch with reality and their work, and plunge into a horrifying, masochistic spiral that ends in a severe case of anorexia for Sonia and Vittorio's death at her hands, as she desperately tries to escape his clutches. Garrone's skill at framing his protagonists within all sorts of complex grids, tight spaces, and

In Garrone's *Primo Amore*, sexual passion and anorexia combine. *Credit: DVD*

foreboding sites adds to the building terror in the film, even though very little actually happens in the narrative. The sexual relationship the couple embraces cannot but help recall that in Liliana Cavani's *The Night Porter*, and in fact Sonia's naked body at the film's conclusion suggests the appalling photographs of naked Holocaust survivors from the liberated death camps. Garrone's film poses a troubling question: Just how far are people willing to go for love? The dominating image of the film derives from Vittorio's profession: tragically, he makes a confused attempt to transfer the art of goldsmithing (refining metals down to their purest and lightest essence) to human relationships, a bizarre notion Garrone reveals to be disastrous.

Daniele Lucchetti's career has important links to Nanni Moretti's mentorship (as does Molaioli's, already noted). It was Moretti's production company that released Lucchetti's first film of note, *It's Happening Tomorrow* (*Domani accadrà*, 1988). In *The Yes Man* (*Il portaborse*, 1991), he cast Moretti as a corrupt young government minister who engages a professor (Silvio Orlando) to write his speeches, but the politician's maneuvers and intrigues are so corrupt that the professor returns to his students in disgust and disappointment. *My Brother Is an Only Child* (*Mio fratello è figlio unico*, 2007) resembles the plot of this decade's most important social film, Giordana's *The Best of Youth*. It traces over several decades the tightly intertwined lives of two brothers from a relatively poor family who live in Latina, one of the towns in the Pontine Marshes outside Rome that Mussolini erected as part of a grandiose program of land reclamation there. The film opens in 1962 and concludes in the 1970s during the era of political terrorism; but unlike Giordana in his long television film, Lucchetti focuses upon the developing personalities of the two brothers, rather than the sweep of social events they reflect. Accio Benassi (Elio Germano) first enters a seminary, then leaves and becomes attracted to the right-wing Movimento Sociale Italiano (MSI);

A nostalgic attraction to a neo-fascist movement inspires the young Accio in Luchetti's *My Brother Is an Only Child*. Credit: DVD

meanwhile his brother, Manrico (Riccardo Scamarcio), goes in the opposite direction, eventually moving from labor activity to kneecapping the director of his factory and finally losing his life in a shootout with the antiterrorist police before Accio's very eyes. What complicates the lives of the two brothers is that the Benassi family (with the exception of Accio) are all devout leftists who berate Accio for his tenacious beliefs until, of his own volition, he decides that the politicians who control the MSI are no better than those on the Left he despises and who his family has always worshiped. Manrico has always been the family favorite, but ironically, after Manrico's death, it is the ex-Fascist Accio who breaks into the housing commission of Latina—a completely corrupt coven of bureaucrats who have refused to distribute the completed houses to the Benassi family and hundreds of others who live in Latina—and steals the keys to the empty apartments, provoking a spontaneous occupation of the housing project that the politicians have denied the citizenry for years. What strikes the viewer of this film is that the Benassi brothers never degenerate into abstract symbols: they are always believable, even amusing, and because of Lucchetti's skillful presentation of their very different lives, we are always able to emphathize with their very different personal trajectories. Ultimately, doing the right thing in Lucchetti's film has little to do with political ideology and much more to do with commonly shared humanity (even in an ex-Fascist). Given the leftist tilt of virtually the entire Italian film industry, presenting a complex and nuanced character such as Accio took a good deal of courage on Lucchetti's part and holds future promise.

Francesca Archibugi has amassed a body of work that marks her as Italy's most acclaimed and prolific female director of the group born in the 1960s. With *Mignon Has Come to Stay* (*Mignon è partita*, 1988), *Towards Evening* (*Verso sera*, 1990), *The Great Pumpkin* (*Il grande cocomero*, literally, "the great watermelon"; 1993), *Shooting the Moon* (*L'albero delle pere*, 1998), *Tomorrow* (*Domani*, 2001), and *Flying Lessons* (*Lezioni di volo*, 2007), Archibugi has shown a decided talent for analyzing the world of adolescence within the radically changing nature of the traditional Italian family structure. A recent assessment of her work has defined it as belonging to the so-called bildungsroman tradition, in which Archibugi charts young people's apprenticeship to life as they learn to grow, their ultimate awakening coinciding with a separation of some sort from their parents and their past.[2] While many other directors treat the same theme on a macro level—even such decidedly political films as Giordana's *The Best of Youth* are ultimately as much about the coming of age of young people as they are about grandiose historical and social developments—few have managed to approach this topic with as much sensitivity and originality.

Emanuele Crialese's three feature films were met with moderate commercial success and much critical praise. Crialese, like many of his generation, has studied in the United States, and his first feature, *Once We Were Strangers* (1997), would seem to reflect this experience, as it casts his favorite actor, Vincenzo Amato, as a Sicilian living illegally in New York City and confronting the challenges of a multicultural world. Amato, one of Italy's rising stars, also plays the principal role in Crialese's two next, more successful films, *Respiro: Grazia's Island* (*Respiro*, 2002), and *The Golden Door* (*Nuovomondo*, 2006). In *Respiro*, Crialese treats in an original fashion what one recent critic has defined as the "rural idyll," the dominant theme in such popular recent films as *Cinema Paradiso*, *Mediterraneo*, *Il Postino*, *Malèna*, and *Respiro*, which all take place on an island distant in both time and place from present-day urban Italy.[3] On the remote island of Lampedusa, Grazia (Valeria Golino); her husband, Pietro (Vincenzo Amato); and her three children, Marinella (Veronica D'Agostino), Filippo (Filippo Pucillo), and Pasquale (Francesco Casisa), live the quiet life of a fisherman's family, interrupted only by Grazia's seemingly extravagant behavior which derives from a combination of some form of mental disturbance plus her own exuberant character. Her conduct clashes with the traditional mores of the island's women. She swims naked in the ocean, frees from a kennel dogs that are being held for suppression (leading to a shotgun massacre of the strays by the men of the island), and generally acts in a manner that places her outside the norm. Aided by her son Pasquale, she hides from her husband, causing the townspeople to believe she has died in the ocean. Later, when hunting for rabbits, Pietro sees her swimming below: he and the entire village take her reappearance as a miracle, since it is Saint Bartolo's Day, when they are all at the seashore to light the bonfires traditional of this religious holiday. Of course, this folkloric conclusion begs the question of whether the patriarchal structure of Lampedusa's male-dominated culture will ever change or allow women such as Grazia any personal freedom. Crialese's film combines beautiful photography and music with a neorealist-style emphasis on local dialects, the character of every day life, and many nonprofessional actors, who make up the chorus of the townspeople. The rhythm of his film captures the slow rhythm of the island culture (perhaps a nod to Visconti's famous style in *The Earth Trembles*).

Reflecting Crialese's interest in Sicilian folklore, *The Golden Door* follows a group of highly superstitious Sicilian peasants who immigrate to Ellis Island in 1913. The widower Salvatore Mancuso (Vincenzo Amato) embarks on a boat with his two sons (one a deaf-mute) and his extremely superstitious mother, Fortunata (Aurora Quattrocchi). He meets a strange but attractive British woman named Lucy (Charlotte Gainsbourg), who begs him to marry her to resolve problems with the customs officials when she arrives in America. (Salvatore's fellow citizens report all sorts of rumors about her—that she ran off with an Italian and abandoned her husband, that she became a prostitute.) Some viewers will find the pace of this film too slow, but Crialese manages to alternate authentic period costumes and extremely realistic sets on the boat and at Ellis Island with surrealistic moments of poetic beauty. Unlike most films about immigration to America, we never leave Ellis Island, even though a final dream vision of Italian migrants taking a milk bath in the supposed land of milk and honey suggests that they will succeed in the New World of the film's Italian title. Of particular interest is Crialese's meticulously re-created battery of humiliating tests (mental and physical) that immigrants had to pass in order to come to the United States. It took far more than a stroll across an unguarded border river or highway to leave Ellis Island for the mainland, and many Italians were turned back, like Salvatore's mother, whose strange, superstitious mannerisms are interpreted by the customs officials as mental illness. Fortunata will return to Italy, but even as she decides to do so, Salvatore's deaf-mute son, Pietro (played by the same Filippo Pucillo of *Respiro*), suddenly regains his hearing and powers of speech, as if such miracles occur in the America that Italians had dreamed of as being paved with gold, so that he is allowed to enter this reputed paradise.

Paolo Virzì and Gabriele Muccino both show the kind of talent that may turn them into the comic directors of the future, the successors to Mario Monicelli, Pietro Germi, Ettore Scola, and the other figures who made *commedia all'italiana* one of the industry's main products of quality. Virzì's most recent comedies—*My Name Is Tanino* (2002); *Caterina in the Big City* (*Caterina va in città*, 2003); *Napoleon and Me* (*N / Io e Napoleone*, 2006), and *Your Whole Life Ahead of You*, a.k.a. *Her Whole Life Ahead of Her* (*Tutta la vita davanti*, 2008)—provide proof of his mastery of Italy's most enduring film genre. The first film treats a summer love affair between an Italian and an American girl that takes the action from Sicily to the United States. *Napoleon and Me* represents a change of pace—a costume drama set in the nineteenth century on the island of Elba, where a young teacher (Elio Germano) strongly opposed to the exiled emperor of France (Daniel Auteuil) becomes his secretary and begins to admire Napoleon in spite of himself. *Your Whole Life Ahead of You* attacks the phenomenon of the temporary worker, a policy entirely opposed to traditional Italian labor practices but one that saves employers benefits and salary costs. It stars Isabella Ragonese as a young university graduate in philosophy who, in spite of the usual words of encouragement from those of an older generation—namely, those of the film's title: "Tutta la vita davanti," meaning "You have all your life ahead of you"—must take on the stereotypical dead-end job in a multinational call center where she gets few benefits and even fewer personal satisfactions. As in so many of Italy's great film comedies, *Your Whole Life Ahead of You* reflects a new social reality: millions of Italians working today in "precarious" jobs without a future, rather than landing the traditional *posto* that signified not only a permanent and decent salary but also medical and retirement benefits.

Caterina in the Big City is perhaps the best and most successful of Virzì's films. This brilliant satire of manners focuses upon Caterina (Alice Teghil), a bright, musically talented twelve-year-old who moves with her father, Giancarlo (Sergio Castellitto), and her clueless mother, Agata (Margherita Buy), from the tiny town of Montalto di Castro to the big city of Rome. Caterina's female classmates at her school are divided down the middle into two cliques: one headed by Margherita (Carolina Iaquaniello), a hippie from a leftist family of intellectuals, the other by Daniela (Federica Sbrenna), a preppy from a right-wing family of ex-Fascists whose father is one of Silvio Berlusconi's ministers. First one clique and then the other tries to lure Caterina over to its side, exposing her and us to their shallow values and their ideological blinders. The plot becomes even more complicated because Caterina's parents are so self-absorbed and out of touch with reality. Frustrated by years of teaching completely uninterested pupils in the provinces, Giancarlo dreams of publishing a novel he has secretly written, while Agata is so unhappy at the way she is ignored at home by her husband that she ultimately has an affair with his ex-schoolmate. One of the classic scenes in the film is Giancarlo's farewell to his students in Montalto di Castro. Informing them that they are completely incapable of learning anything, he declares that he has wasted most of his life around them, and on this final occasion, they pay absolutely no attention, in keeping with their past performance!

Virzì obtains an absolutely brilliant performance from the protagonist, who was fourteen when the film was shot. Unlike the characters of other directors (such as Muccino), who seem to make films about young people aimed solely at young people, Caterina stands out against the ridiculous ideological posturings of her classmates (an accurate reflection of the meaningless and outmoded political ideals of their parents) as well as the empty married life she eventually discovers in her own parents, when her father disappears and her mother finds a secret lover. Her resolve to make something of her life succeeds, however, for the final sequence of the film shows her singing with the Santa Cecilia Academy's chorus in Rome. She has been accepted into the famous music school and will no doubt, we are led to believe, make a better life for herself than her parents and her classmates might have led us to expect. Ultimately, Virzì's comic genius in *Caterina in the Big City* derives from his successful attempt to present a realistic, believable teenager who actually reflects greater maturity than the adults and other adolescents who surround her.

Gabriele Muccino has enjoyed a meteoric rise to international success, capped by working in Hollywood on large-budget films headlined by American stars. Like Virzì, Muccino exhibits a mastery of complex camerawork, editing, and narrative rhythm, even though some of the stories he presents involve the kinds of narratives that tend to be identified with Hollywood films aimed at an essentially young audience. *But Forever in My Mind*, a.k.a. *Nobody but You* (*Come te nessuno mai*, 1999) is a good example of Muccino having a very different target audience from that of Virzì. Silvio (Silvio Muccino, the director's brother) is an adolescent obsessed with losing his virginity. The only thing that interests him about the student rebellion sweeping through his high school is the chance it might offer him to have sex with a girl that he likes, but his focus upon her causes him to ignore the fact that another girl named Claudia (Giulia Steigerwalt) actually really likes him. When things are sorted out, Silvio eventually realizes that Claudia should be his real target, and almost without any development in the plot whatsoever, she gives herself to him on the roof of her apartment building. The film concludes with the voice of Silvio telling his best friend that love happens only when you least expect it. Measured against Virzì's much more mature film, Muccino's comedy of errors comes off as extremely shallow, but his mastery of handling scores of nonprofessional actors (the students in the high school) plus his skill at narrating even a slim storyline with energy and aplomb mark him as a highly talented director, one who would eventually do well in Hollywood, with its youth-obsessed film culture.

Muccino's next film, *The Last Kiss* (*L'ultimo bacio*, 2001), constitutes a far more interesting work; it was extremely successful commercially and critically, winning the Sundance Film Festival Audience Award and five David di Donatello awards out of a total of ten nominations. Following *The Last Kiss*, Muccino made *Remember Me, My Love* (*Ricordati di me*, 2003). These two films showed Muccino capable of making more mature comedies about twenty-something men who refuse to grow up and the women who deal with them. It is in this regard that some critics and reviewers have discussed Muccino's *The Last Kiss* by comparing it to Fellini's classic film about Italian males who remain adolescents, *I Vitelloni*.

More important, however, the film's success led to a profitable Hollywood adaptation, also entitled *The Last Kiss* (2006) and filmed by the veteran television director Tony Goldwyn that landed Muccino a Hollywood film contract. Eventually he made a blockbuster film with the superstar Will Smith, *The Pursuit of Happiness* (2006), and a second film starring Smith entitled *Seven Pounds*, released in late 2008. *Seven Pounds* tells the story of an IRS agent who sets out to change his depressing life by helping seven total strangers. *The Pursuit of Happiness* narrates a true story, the struggle of a salesman, Chris Gardner (Will Smith), who hopes to make his fortune selling bone-density scanners. In the process, his wife leaves him, and he and his son go through homelessness, prison, tax problems, and almost crushing despair, before their ultimate triumph. Such a rags-to-riches theme recalls the legendary tales of Italian immigrants being told that America's streets were paved with gold. While Muccino's two Hollywood features are certainly "feel-good" films, it should not be forgotten that Frank Capra, the first Italian American director to succeed in Hollywood, produced a number of equally "feel-good" works that have become American classics. Given the sometimes disastrous results that have occurred when other Italian directors attempted to work in Hollywood, Muccino's success to date represents an almost unique example of transferring one national cinematic culture to another, a feat achieved only by Bernardo Bertolucci in the recent past. Ironically, Muccino's *The Pursuit of Happiness* was even nominated for Best Foreign Film at the David di Donatello Awards in 2007.

~

Italian cinema enters the third millennium with an enviable number of young directors and veterans, talented actors and actresses, and highly competent technicians in all the professions that make moviemaking so demanding (cameramen, film editors, scriptwriters, musicians, set designers). Many of them have been recognized for their abilities and work frequently in Hollywood as well as in Rome. Technological innovations in the film industry will present challenges to the national industry that cannot even be imagined today. Perhaps new electronic means of delivering films directly to homes through the Internet will solve the vexing distribution problems that always hinder the promotion of Italian films abroad. It is always possible that the Italian government will recognize the cinema's unique contribution to Italian culture and will do something serious to promote it commercially.

Italy's cinema has always had a wonderful story to tell us about Italian culture, and in its greatest moments it has managed to provide narratives of universal appeal as well. It has survived many crises over the past century, and has always managed to rise, like the mythical phoenix, from its ashes. Those of us who love the cinema can only hope it will continue to thrive and to serve as a repository of Italy's dreams and aspirations, as it has done so brilliantly for more than a hundred years.

Notes

Chapter One

1. For a catalog of the most important exhibit devoted to the "Mondo nuovo" and its association with the development of the cinema, see Minici, ed., *Il Mondo nuovo: le meraviglie della visione dal '700 alla nascita del cinema*. This essential work contains numerous pictures of perspective views, details on the Remondini establishment, and pictures of the various mechanical devices that led up to the cinema projectors with which we are familiar today.

2. These figures are cited by the silent-cinema scholar Riccardo Redi, "La storia senza le opere," in Redi, ed., *Cinema italiano muto 1905–1916*, p. 7. A very useful synthesis of the many studies done by Italian scholars on film production during the entire history of the national cinema may be found in Barbara Corsi, "Il cinema italiano in cifre," in Brunetta, *Guida alla storia del cinema italiano 1905–2003*, pp. 399–405.

3. Published by Bernardini, *Cinema muto italiano: ambiente, spettacoli e spettatori 1896/1904*, p. 31; English translation cited from John P. Welle, "Early Cinema, *Dante's Inferno* of 1911, and the Origins of Italian Film Culture," in Iannucci, ed., *Dante, Cinema & Television*, p. 25. See also Welle, "Dante in the Cinematic Mode: An Historical Survey of Dante Movies," in Musa, ed., *Dante's Inferno: The Indiana Critical Edition*, pp. 381–95. Bernardini's studies on Italian silent cinema (see Select Bibliography) are fundamental sources for the history of the silent film, and Welle's two essays are fine examples of the renewed critical attention being paid to Italian silent films.

4. Figures cited in Bernardini, *Cinema muto italiano: industria e organizzazione dello spettacolo 1905–1909*, pp. 227–29.

5. I rely upon Welle's studies of this film for my discussion.

6. Note that where the English title for a film is identical to the Italian (including capitalization), the Italian title is *not* duplicated in the text.

7. Figures cited by Brunetta, *Guida alla storia del cinema italiano*, p. 33.

8. For a splendid volume devoted to *Cabiria* that includes more than five hundred stills taken from the individual shots of the film (including samples of those that were tinted with color), the four versions of the film's story, D'Annunzio's intertitles, and a number of letters and contracts associated with the production, see Radicati and Rossi, eds., *"Cabiria": visione storica del III secolo a.C.*

9. For discussions of how the classical era has been depicted in the cinema, see the following: Bondanella, *The Eternal City: Roman Images in the Modern World*; Wyke, *Projecting the Past: Ancient Rome, Cinema and History*; Joshel, Malamud, and McGuire, eds., *Projections: Ancient Rome in Modern Popular Culture*; Malamud, *Ancient Rome and Modern America*; and especially Solomon, *The Ancient World in the Cinema*, rev. and expanded ed.

10. For the list, see Zanelli, *Nel mondo di Federico,* p. 130. For Fellini's relationship to Dante, see essays by Guido Fink and Marguerite R. Waller in Iannucci, ed., *Dante, Cinema & Television;* see also one of Fellini's unrealized story ideas entitled "Inferno" that is reprinted in Tornabuoni, ed., *Federico Fellini,* pp. 75–81. The best treatment of Maciste and the strongman in Italian cinema is Giordano, *Giganti buoni: da Ercole a Piedone (e oltre)—il mito dell'uomo forte nel cinema italiano.*

11. Cited in Brunetta, *Guida alla storia del cinema italiano,* p. 61.

12. A fine study of this phenomenon in the Italian cinema now exists in Angela Dalle Vacche's *Diva: Defiance and Passion in Early Italian Cinema,* and in Marcia Landy's *Stardom, Italian Style.*

13. Leprohoun, *The Italian Cinema,* p. 60.

14. Brunetta, *Guida alla storia del cinema italiano,* p. 252.

15. For a discussion of this unique figure, see Bruno, *Streetwalking on a Ruined Map: Cultural Theory and the City Films of Elvira Notari.*

16. Lizzani, *Il cinema italiano, 1895-1979,* I: 29.

17. See the important screenplay and a discussion of the film's historical significance in Barbina, ed., *Sperduti nel buio.*

18. Unlike so many silent films, *Assunta Spina* has been released in DVD format, accompanied by Mingozzi's previously cited documentary about Francesca Bertini.

19. Cited from Flint, ed. *Marinetti: Selected Writings,* p. 131. The very best discussion of futurist performances, specifically in the theater and the cinema, is Kirby and Kirby, *Futurist Performance.*

20. Pirandello's novel about the cinema—also published subsequently as *The Notebooks of Serafino Gubbio, Cameraman* (*I quaderni di Serafino Gubbio, operatore,* 1916)—has been recently republished in English translation as *Shoot! The Notebooks of Serafino Gubbio, Cinematograph Operator.* I am indebted to Nina Nichols and Jana Bazzoni's extremely thorough outline of Pirandello's links to the cinema in their *Pirandello & Film.*

21. For an important history of this venerable Italian movie studio, see Redi, *La Cines: Storia di una casa di produzione italiana.*

22. Production figures cited in Leprohoun, *The Italian Cinema,* pp. 51, 58.

23. For a discussion of Valentino in America see Bondanella, *Hollywood Italians: Dagos, Palookas, Romeos, Wise Guys, and Sopranos,* pp. 134–45.

Chapter Two

1. For a study of this review, see d'Ardino, *La Revue "Cinema" et le néo-réalisme italien.*

2. Cited by Lino Miccichè, "Il cadavere nell'armadio," in Redi, ed., *Cinema italiano sotto il fascismo,* pp. 9–18, at p. 9 (author's translation). For discussions in English of cinema under Fascism, see: Aprà and Pistagnesi, eds., *The Fabulous Thirties: Italian Cinema 1929-1944;* Hay, *Popular Film Culture in Fascist Italy: The Passing of the Rex;* Landy, *Fascism in Film: The Italian Commercial Cinema, 1931-1943;* and Reich and Garofalo, eds., *Re-viewing Fascism: Italian Cinema, 1922-1943.* The most complete listing of the films produced during the Fascist period may be found in the indispensable catalog by Savio, *Ma l'amore no: realismo, formalismo, propaganda e telefoni bianchi nel cinema italiano di regime 1930-1943.*

3. Miccichè, "Il cadavere nell'armadio," in Redi, ed., *Cinema italiano sotto il fascismo,* pp. 11–13, cites figures relative to the number of extant prints viewable today.

4. For analyses of such newsreels, see: Cardillo, *Il duce in moviola: politica e divismo nei cinegiornali e documentari "Luce"*; Laura, *L'immagine bugiarda: mass-media e spettacolo nella Repubblica di Salò (1943–1945)*; and Hay, *Popular Film Culture in Fascist Italy*, pp. 201–32.

5. For a discussion of the regime's attitudes, see: Mancini, *Struggles of the Italian Film Industry during Fascism, 1930–1935*; Sam Rohdie, "Capital and Realism in the Italian Cinema: An Examination of Film in the Fascist Period," *Screen* 24.4–5 (1983): 37–46; and David Ellwood, "Italy: The Regime, the Nation, and the Film Industry: An Introduction," in Short, ed., *Film & Radio Propaganda in World War II,* pp. 220–29.

6. For Vittorio Mussolini's essay, see "Emancipazione del cinema italiano," *Cinema* 1.6 (September 25, 1936): 213–15.

7. For a brief discussion of the Roach-Mussolini venture, see Rondolino, *Roberto Rossellini,* p. 35.

8. Leo Longanesi, "The Glass Eye," in Aprà and Pistagnesi, eds., *The Fabulous Thirties,* p. 50. Although Longanesi eventually turned away from the regime, as did so many left-wing Fascists who were disappointed with the conservative bent of Mussolini once he attained power, his onetime support had nevertheless been genuine.

9. Zavattini's statement can be read in two versions and two different translations, because the Italian original was a radio broadcast subsequently transcribed and published in various places: "Some Ideas on the Cinema," in MacCann, ed., *Film: A Montage of Theories,* pp. 216–28, and "A Thesis on Neo-Realism," in Overbey, ed., *Springtime in Italy: A Reader on Neo-Realism,* pp. 67–78.

10. For discussions of the Risorgimento in Italian cinema, see: Bouchard, ed., *Risorgimento in Modern Italian Culture,* or Dalle Vacche, *The Body in the Mirror: Shapes of History in Italian Cinema.*

11. For Blasetti's collected writings on the cinema, see Blasetti, *Scritti sul cinema,* ed. Aprà. For the best analysis of *Sole* available, see Aprà and Redi, eds., *"Sole": soggetto, sceneggiatura, note per la realizzazione.* Blasetti's films are discussed in further detail later in this chapter.

12. For a detailed history of this film, see Camerini, ed., *"Acciaio": un film degli anni trenta.*

13. For the best examination of this phenomenon in English, to which this discussion is indebted, see Gianni Rondolino, "Italian Propaganda Films: 1940–1943," in Short, ed., *Film & Radio Propaganda in World War II,* pp. 230–44.

14. For detailed information on the director's career and his films, see Germani and Martinelli, eds., *Il cinema di Augusto Genina*; my own essay, "The Making of *Roma città aperta*: The Legacy of Fascism and the Birth of Neorealism," in Gottlieb, ed., *Roberto Rossellini's "Rome Open City,"* pp. 43–66; or a briefer discussion in Landy, *Fascism in Film,* pp. 218–22.

15. For Antonioni's review and complete credits of the film, see Savio, *Ma l'amore no,* pp. 29–30.

16. Cited from Rondolino, "Italian Propaganda Films," in Short, ed., *Film & Radio Propaganda in World War II,* p. 236; for the complete Italian text of the letter, see Freddi, *Il cinema,* I: 207–11.

17. Cited by Rondolino in ibid., p. 237.

18. In the critical literature, Rossellini's first three feature films made before the end of the war—*The White Ship* (*La nave bianca,* 1942), *A Pilot Returns* (*Un pilota ritorna,* 1942), and *The Man with a Cross* (*L'uomo dalla croce,* 1943)—are generally labeled the "Fascist trilogy." The three films described as his "neorealist trilogy" are *Open City, Paisan,* and *Germany Year Zero* (*Germania anno zero,* 1948). Invented by postwar critics, these terms were never employed by Rossellini himself.

19. Savio, *Ma l'amore no,* p. 379 (author's translation).

20. Ibid., p. 11 (author's translation; italics in the original film titles).

21. Ibid., p. 227 (author's translation). The credits employ the technical term *verismo,* the word Italians use to describe the literary movement of naturalism in Italy championed by Giovanni Verga, the Sicilian novelist whom postwar neorealist critics and directors hoped to emulate in their films and whose masterpiece, *The House by the Medlar Tree* (*I Malavoglia,* 1881), Luchino Visconti rendered into what some critics consider to be the most original of the neorealist classics, *The Earth Trembles* (1948).

22. For the text of the review, see Savio, *Ma l'amore no,* p. 269.

23. During 1943–45, leftist anti-Fascists associated the Redshirts with their own red-kerchief-clad partisan soldiers.

24. Cited by Hay in *Popular Film Culture in Fascist Italy,* p. 55 (Hays's translation); the original review is by Gianni Puccini in *Galleria,* no. 4 (March 10, 1938): p. 172.

25. Marcia Landy makes this point in *Fascism in Film,* p. 265.

26. See Hay, *Popular Film Culture in Fascist Italy,* pp. 103–11, for a detailed analysis of this film.

27. For important discussions of De Sica as actor and director, see Miccichè, ed., *De Sica: Autore, regista, attore,* or Curle and Synder, eds., *Vittorio De Sica: Contemporary Perspectives.*

28. Landy, *Fascism in Film,* p. 55.

29. Cited by Bondanella in *The Eternal City,* p. 187; the original Italian speech may be found in Benito Mussolini, *Opera omnia di Benito Mussolini,* eds. Edoardo and Diulio Susmel (Florence: La Fenice, 1951–62), XXVII: 268–69.

30. For a discussion of these interviews, see Carabba, *Il cinema del ventennio nero,* pp. 52–4; for detailed analyses of this film, see: Hay, *Popular Film Culture in Fascist Italy,* pp. 155–61; Dalle Vacche, *The Body in the Mirror,* pp. 27–52; and Landy, *Fascism in Film,* pp. 194–200.

31. For Nazzari's recollections of the use of prisoners in the fight scene and the two versions of the film, see Savio, *Cinecittà anni trenta: parlano 116 protagonisti del secondo cinema italiano (1930–1943),* III: 826–27.

32. For a history of Titanus, see: Barlozzetti et al., eds., *Modi di produzione del cinema italiano: La Titanus,* and Bernardini and Martinelli, eds., *Titanus: la storia e tutti i film di una grande casa di produzione.*

33. See Farassino and Sanguineti, *Lux Film: Esthétique et système d'un studio italien.*

34. See Barbaro, *Neorealismo e realismo,* ed. Brunetta, especially the essay "Neorealismo" (II: 500–504); and Brunetta, *Umberto Barbaro e l'idea del neorealismo (1930–1943).*

35. Cesare Pavese, *American Literature: Essays and Opinions,* trans. Edwin Fussell, p. 196.

36. For the English text of Visconti's "Anthropomorphic Cinema," see Overbey, ed., *Springtime in Italy,* pp. 83–85. Overbey's anthology also contains English versions of the essays by Antonioni, De Santis, and Alicata discussed here.

Chapter Three

1. Nowell-Smith, *Luchino Visconti*, 3d ed., p. 32. The author rightly reminds the reader that no neorealist film ever followed all these formulae completely.

2. For Bazin's fundamental writings on the Italian cinema, see: Bazin, *Bazin at Work: Major Essays & Reviews from the Forties & Fifties*, ed. Cardullo, trans. Piette and Cardullo; *Qu'est-ce que le cinéma?—IV. Une esthétique de la Réalité: le néo-réalisme*; and *What Is Cinema? Vol. II*, trans. Gray.

3. See Zavattini's "A Thesis on Neo-Realism," in Overbey, ed., *Springtime in Italy: A Reader on Neo-Realism*, pp. 67–78.

4. Rossellini, *My Method: Writings & Interviews*, ed. Aprà, p. 35.

5. Fellini, *Fellini on Fellini*, ed. Keel and Strich, p. 152.

6. De Sica, *Miracle in Milan*, p. 4.

7. When the first edition of Bondanella's *Italian Cinema* appeared in 1983, these ideas seemed debatable; but after over two decades of critical work on Italian neorealism outside of Italy, I believe my original view of neorealism as an aesthetic, not an ideological, revolution has become a critical commonplace, particularly when Italian neorealist fiction is brought into the picture (as this chapter does in some detail).

8. The three-part series "World War II in Color" appeared on The History Channel on February 15–17, 2000. Narrated by John Thaw, it is available on DVD as "World War II—The Lost Color Archives," A&E Home Video, 2000.

9. A number of fine works in English now exist that treat neorealism in all its complexity. Although written over three decades ago, Armes, *Patterns of Realism: A Study of Italian Neo-Realism* still provides a remarkable survey of this body of work. Miccichè's edition of essays, *Il neorealismo cinematografico italiano*, led Italian film historians to question and modify traditional definitions of neorealism. Bondanella, *Italian Cinema*, 1st ed., was one of the first comprehensive discussions of neorealism in English that viewed it primarily as an aesthetic revolution rather than an ideological one, linking its original cinematic features with Italian neorealist fiction, a thesis that the present volume develops at some length. Marcus's *Italian Film in the Light of Neorealism* provides very persuasive formalist criticism of the major neorealist classics. The very titles of six recent works in English show that non-Italian scholars today define Italian neorealism as a far more complex phenomenon than a mere simple-minded "realistic" portrait of postwar Italy: Restivo's *The Cinema of Economic Miracles: Visuality and Modernization in the Italian Art Film (Post-Contemporary Interventions)*; Rocchio's *Cinema of Anxiety: A Psychoanalysis of Italian Neorealism*; P. Adams Sitney's *Vital Crises in Italian Cinema: Iconography, Stylistics, Politics*; Torriglia's *Broken Time, Fragmented Space: A Cultural Map for Postwar Italy*; Shiel's *Italian Neorealism: Rebuilding the Cinematic City*; and Wagstaff's *Italian Neorealist Cinema: An Aesthetic Approach*. In Italian, one original recent work stands out: Giulia Fanara's *Pensare il neorealismo*. For a fine survey of Italian neorealism by Gian Piero Brunetta that, like Fanara's *Pensare*, takes into account not only the traditional views of Bazin but also recent non-Italian scholarly works, see his *Guida alla storia del cinema italiano*, pp. 127–204.

10. For an important discussion of late Fascist culture that argues for continuity in the immediate postwar period in the search for realism in literature and cinema, see Ben-Ghiat's *Fascist Modernities: Italy, 1922–1945*. For excellent discussions of Italian neorealism in English, see Re's *Calvino and the Age of Neorealism: Fables of Estrangement*, or her briefer survey article, "Neorealist Narrative: Experience and Experiment," in Bondanella and Ciccarelli, eds., *The Cambridge Companion to the Italian Novel*, pp. 104–24.

11. Calvino, *The Path to the Nest of Spiders*, trans. Archibald Colquhoun (New York: Ecco Press, 1976), p. vii. The newly added preface was translated by William Weaver.

12. Pavese, *American Literature: Essays and Opinions*, trans. Edwin Fussell (Berkeley: University of California Press, 1970), p. 197.

13. For a listing of films produced and box-office receipts by year of release during the neorealist epoch, see Rondolino, ed., *Catalogo Bolaffi del cinema italiano 1945/1955*, and his *Catalogo Bolaffi del cinema italiano 1956/1965*. For a discussion of the dismal box-office performance of neorealist films in Italy, see Miccichè, ed., *Il neorealismo cinematografico italiano*; or Spinazzola, *Cinema e pubblico: lo spettacolo filmico in Italia 1945–1960*.

14. See Bizzarri and Solaroli, *L'industria cinematografica italiana*, for these statistics as well as the texts of the agreement between ANICA and MPEA.

15. A great deal of criticism of Rossellini and his neorealist masterpieces exists in English. For considerations of his entire career, see Bondanella, *The Films of Roberto Rossellini*; Brunette, *Roberto Rossellini*; and Gallagher, *The Adventures of Roberto Rossellini: His Life and Films*. Specific studies of *Open City* may be found in Foracs, *Rome Open City*, and in Gottlieb, ed., *Roberto Rossellini's "Open City."* English scripts for the war trilogy are available in Rossellini, *The War Trilogy*. Rossellini's writings on the cinema may be consulted in the previously cited Rossellini, *My Method*.

16. Rossellini, *The War Trilogy*, p. 154. All citations from the dialogue of the war trilogy are taken from this edition.

17. Bazin, *What Is Cinema? Vol. II*, p. 137.

18. Brunette, *Roberto Rossellini*, p. 62.

19. Sergio Amidei, one of Rossellini's scriptwriters for *Paisan*, notes this and also states that Rossellini chose the Amalfi Coast location because it was near his then-unnamed mistress's home. See his remarks in the indispensable book on the making of *Paisan* edited by Aprà, *Rosselliniana: bibliografia internazionale, dossier "Paisà,"* p. 108. The most important recent publication on *Paisan* in Italy is Parigi, ed. *"Paisà": Analisi del film*.

20. Massimo Mida, the assistant director on the film, notes this in Aprà, ed., *Rosselliniana*, p. 137.

21. Faldini and Fofi, eds., *L'avventurosa storia del cinema italiano raccontata dai suoi protagonisti 1935–1959*, p. 108.

22. See Massimo Mida's remarks in Aprà, ed., *Rosselliniana*, p. 139.

23. See Fellini's comments in Faldini and Fofi, eds., *L'avventurosa storia del cinema italiano . . . 1935–1959*, p. 108.

24. See Geiger's remarks in Aprà, ed., *Rosselliniana*, pp. 131–32.

25. Massimo Mida, cited in ibid., p. 109.

26. Masi and Lancia, *I film di Roberto Rossellini*, p. 29.

27. Bazin, *What Is Cinema? Vol. II*, p. 37.

28. These seven films (1943–45), produced by the U.S. military, were in the main directed by Frank Capra and Anatole Litvak.

29. Vittorio De Sica, "How I Direct My Films," in *Miracle in Milan*, pp. 1–14, at p. 5. The single indispensable work on this film is Miccichè, ed., *"Sciuscià" di Vittorio De Sica: letture, documenti, testimonianze*. For commentary, see also the previously cited anthologies of essays edited by Miccichè or by Curle and Snyder. One detail of De Sica's casting in *The Bicycle Thief* will be of interest to film buffs: in a scene where father and son stand near German seminary students speaking German, one of them is an almost unrecognizable and beardless Sergio Leone!

30. See Bazin's remarks in *What Is Cinema? Vol. II*, pp. 51, 60.

31. While De Sica himself felt uncomfortable with comparisons to Kafka (see Leprohon, *Vittorio De Sica*, p. 44), claiming that human solitude in his films has social rather than metaphysical causes, the distancing, alienating effects of his cinematic style and the absurd chain of events that leads from one theft of a bicycle to another clearly place *The Bicycle Thief* close to Kafka's narrative technique in its impact upon the viewer.

32. For more on his manifesto, see chapter 2, § "The Search for a New Film Realism."

33. Bazin, *What Is Cinema? Vol. II*, p. 77.

34. A good example of this kind of thinking, an approach to film that would eliminate most of the cinema's best works, may be found in Robert Kolker's attack upon Italian neorealist sentimentality and the frequent use of children in its plots: "None of these filmmakers acknowledged Brecht's principle of sustained, distanced analysis in the work of art, an analysis that disallows emotional identification and passive acceptance of events by the audience. . . . The result was that the neo-realists ultimately failed the people they portrayed by being unable or unwilling to create for them victory over their situation . . . and failed their audience by too often allowing them to sentimentalize rather than analyze character and situation" (*The Altering Eye: Contemporary International Cinema*, p. 68). Poor Rossellini, De Sica, and Visconti, or Shakespeare, for that matter—they did not embrace the aesthetics of Brecht and Godard!

35. Bazin, *What Is Cinema? Vol. II*, p. 78.

36. The essay appears in Overbey, ed., *Springtime in Italy*, pp. 131–38, quote at p. 135.

37. For Visconti's outline of the plots of these three episodes, see "La terra trema—appunti per un film documentario sulla Sicilia (1948)" in Ferrero, ed. *Visconti: il cinema*, pp. 35–42.

38. For an English script, see *Two Screenplays: "La Terra Trema," "Senso,"* trans. Judith Green. The single indispensable work on this film in Italian is *"La terra trema" di Luchino Visconti: analisi di un capolavoro*, ed. Miccichè. The best English-language books on Visconti are Bacon, *Visconti: Explorations of Beauty and Decay*, and Nowell-Smith, *Luchino Visconti*, 3d ed. In Italian, there are numerous works on Visconti, but see in particular Bruni and Pravadelli, eds., *Studi viscontiani*, and Pravadelli, ed., *Il cinema di Luchino Visconti*.

39. See Armes, *Patterns of Realism*, p. 126.

40. Visconti, *Two Screenplays*, p. 96.

Chapter Four

1. For discussion of partisan films, see Armes, *Patterns of Realism*, pp. 93–98; or Faldini and Fofi, eds., *L'avventurosa storia del cinema italiano raccontata dai suoi protagonisti 1935-1959*, pp. 119–23. The most complete discussion of Giuseppe De Santis is Vitti, *Giuseppe De Santis and Postwar Italian Cinema*.

2. For the English text, see Overbey, ed., *Springtime in Italy*, pp. 79–82.

3. For a treatment of this decisive moment in postwar Italy, see Robert A. Ventresca's *From Fascism to Democracy: Culture and Politics in the Italian Election of 1948* (Toronto: University of Toronto Press, 2004).

4. There is a vast bibliography on Antonioni. In English, the best treatments remain Chatman's *Antonioni; or, The Surface of the World* and Brunette's *The Films of Michelangelo Antonioni*.

5. For discussions of Lattuada's early postwar films, see Cosulich, *I film di Alberto Lattuada*; Turroni, *Alberto Lattuada*; and Villa, *Botteghe di scrittura per il cinema italiano: Intorno a "Il bandito" di Alberto Lattuada*. For an analysis of Germi's long career, see Sesti, *Pietro Germi: The Latin Lover*, or his *Tutto il cinema di Pietro Germi*.

6. For a discussion of the Italian "sweater girl," or *maggiorata*, see Masi and Lancia, *Italian Movie Goddesses: Over 80 of the Greatest Women in the Italian Cinema*, pp. 98–121. Other busty women who became famous in the 1950s include Sophia Loren (1934–), Gina Lollobrigida (1927–), and Sylva Koscina (1933–94).

7. Farassino, *Giuseppe De Santis*, pp. 26–27.

8. Verga's story, which he adapted into a play (1884), has also been filmed numerous times, for the big screen and small. In addition to three Italian silent films (1910–24), there have been story-based features directed by Amleto Palermi (1939) and Carmine Gallone (1953) and opera-based films by Franco Zeffirelli (1982), Liliana Cavani (TV, 1996), and others.

9. For a good discussion in English of "rosy neorealism" and of this film in particular, see Marcus, *Italian Film in the Light of Neorealism*, pp. 121–43.

10. De Sica, *Miracle in Milan*, p. 13.

11. See "A Discussion of Neo-Realism: Rossellini Interviewed by Mario Verdone" (Italian original: "Colloquio sul neorealismo," *Bianco e Nero* 2 [1952]: 7–16), trans. Judith White, *Screen* 14 (Winter 1973–74): pp. 69–77, at p. 70; rpt. as "A Discussion of Neorealism, an Interview with Mario Verdone," trans. Annapaola Cancogni, in Rossellini, *My Method: Writings & Interviews*, ed. Aprà, pp. 33–43, at p. 35.

12. Cited by Aristarco in *Antologia di "Cinema nuovo": 1952-1958*, p. 880.

13. Cited in ibid., pp. 881–82 (author's translation). Piero Gobetti (1901–26) and Luigi Salvatorelli (1886–1974) were both anti-Fascist journalists (and Salvatorelli a historian as well).

Chapter Five

1. This film is not to be confused with a foreign-language anthology film, also called *Ways of Love*, assembled by the American distributor Joseph Burstyn and released in 1950. That comprised Jeans Renoir's *A Day in the Country* (*Partie de campagne*, 1936), Marcel Pagnol's *Jofroi* (1933), and Rossellini's *The Miracle* (discussed herein). It was regarding Burstyn's anthology that an attempt was made to ban *The Miracle*.

2. For a discussion of the case and the film's role in it, see Ellen Draper, "'Controversy Has Probably Destroyed Forever the Context': *The Miracle* and Movie Censorship in America in the Fifties," *Velvet Light Trap* 25 (1990): 69–79, and Johnson, *Miracles and Sacrilege: Roberto Rossellini, the Church, and Film Censorship in Hollywood*.

3. Maurice Scherer (pen [and birth] name of Eric Rohmer) and François Truffaut, "Entretien avec Roberto Rossellini," *Cahiers du Cinéma* 37 (154): 1–13, rpt. as "An Interview with *Cahiers du Cinéma*," in Rossellini, *My Method: Writings and Interviews*, ed. Aprà, pp. 47–57, at p. 48.

4. Ibid.

5. Cited by Leprohon in *Michelangelo Antonioni: An Introduction*, pp. 89–90.

6. Antonioni cited by Geduld, ed., *Film Makers on Film Making*, pp. 200–201.

7. Ibid., p. 202.

8. Cameron and Wood, *Antonioni*, p. 66. For the most important discussions of Antonioni's films, see: Arrowsmith, *Antonioni: A Critical Study*; Brunette, *The Films of Michelangelo Antonioni*; Chatman, *Antonioni; or, The Surface of the World*; and Rhodie, *Antonioni*. For a collection of scripts from Antonioni's early films, see *Il primo Antonioni* and *Sei film*, both ed. Di Carlo. For bibliography on Antonioni, see Perry and Prieto, *Michelangelo Antonioni: A Guide to References and Resources*, or Di Carlo, ed., *Michelangelo Antonioni 1942–1965* (in French). A spectacular collection of Antonioni's images is collected in two volumes by Mancini and Perrella, eds., *Architetture della visione / Architecture in Vision*.

9. Richard Roud, "*The Passenger*," *Sight and Sound* 44.3 (Summer 1975): 134–37, at p. 134.

10. Fellini, *Fellini on Fellini*, p. 152. The critical literature on Fellini is voluminous. For an overview in English, see Peter Bondanella and Cristina Degli-Esposti, "Federico Fellini: An Overview of the Critical Literature," in Bondanella and Degli-Esposti, eds., *Perspectives on Federico Fellini*. The most complete bibliography on Fellini in Italian is Bertozzi's three-volume *biblioFellini* published by the Fondazione Federico Fellini in Rimini, which also publishes *Fellini Amarcord*, a fine periodical devoted to Fellini's cinema and influence. In addition, there are three anthologies devoted to Fellini's cinema that offer an overview of this mass of literature: Bondanella, ed., *Federico Fellini: Essays in Criticism*; the previously cited *Perspectives on Federico Fellini*; and Burke and Waller, eds., *Federico Fellini: Contemporary Perspectives*. English biographies of Fellini include Alpert, *Fellini: A Life*; Baxter, *Fellini*; Chandler, *I, Fellini*; and Kezich, *Federico Fellini, His Life and Work*. A recent collection of Fellini's English-language interviews may be examined in Cardullo, ed., *Federico Fellini: Interviews*. For the most complete discussion of Fellini's artistic and intellectual sources, see Bondanella, *The Cinema of Federico Fellini*.

11. Cited by Budgen in *Fellini*, pp. 91–92.

12. Fellini was notoriously unhappy about comparisons of his work to Pirandello, once including in a list of things he did not like both ketchup and this famous Italian playwright! Little doubt exists, however, that he was profoundly influenced by Pirandello's theater in a number of ways, most particularly as a model for his masterpiece of metacinema, 8½. For a consideration of this link, see particularly Bondanella, *The Cinema of Federico Fellini*, and Gieri, *Contemporary Italian Filmmaking*. Pirandello was perhaps the most famous writer in the world during the time Fellini came of

age, and it would have indeed been remarkable if the Sicilian playwright had not been one of his aesthetic sources.

13. No relation to Jean Renoir's film *La règle du jeu* (1939), which has the same English title. Pirandello's play is also known in English as *The Game of Roles*.

14. Pirandello, "Premise," in *Naked Masks*, ed. Eric Bentley (New York: Dutton, 1952), p. 209. In addition to his 1921 *Six Characters in Search of an Author*, this retrospectively designated trilogy included *Each in His Own Way* (*Ciascuno a suo modo*, 1924) and *Tonight We Improvise* (*Questa sera si recita a soggetto*, 1930).

15. Budgen, *Fellini*, p. 92.

16. See Bondanella, *Hollywood Italians: Dagos, Palookas, Romeos, Wise Guys, and Sopranos*, pp. 134–45, for a discussion of Valentino's roles. Fellini clearly means to juxtapose his second-rate Romeo to Valentino's greater example.

17. Fellini, *Early Screenplays: "Variety Lights" and "The White Sheik,"* p. 102. Subsequent citations from this script also come from this edition.

18. Guido Aristarco, "Italian Cinema," in *Film Culture* 1.2 (1955): 30–31; rpt. in Bondanella, ed., *Federico Fellini: Essays*, p. 60; also rpt. in Bondanella and Gieri, eds., *"La Strada": Federico Fellini, Director*, pp. 204–205, at p. 204.

19. For Bazin's polemics with Aristarco, see André Bazin, "La Strada," trans. Joseph E. Cunneen, *Cross-Currents* 6.3 (1956): 200–203, rpt. in Bondanella, ed., *Federico Fellini: Essays*, pp. 54–59, and in Bondanella and Gieri, eds., *"La Strada,"* pp. 199–203; as well as Aristarco, "Italian Cinema," cited in n. 18.

20. Cited in Agel, *Les Chemins de Fellini*, pp. 128–29 (author's translation).

21. Peter Harcourt, "The Secret Life of Federico Fellini," *Film Quarterly* 19.3 (Spring 1966): 4–13, 19, rpt. in Bondanella, ed., *Federico Fellini: Essays*, pp. 239–52, at pp. 241, 247; also rpt. in Bondanella and Gieri, eds., *"La Strada,"* pp. 239–52, at pp. 240, 246.

22. Bazin, "La Strada," in Bondanella, ed., *Federico Fellini: Essays*, p. 58, and in Bondanella and Gieri, eds., *"La Strada,"* p. 203.

23. Murray, *Fellini the Artist*, p. 97.

24. Dante Alighieri, *The Purgatorio*, eds. Peter Bondanella and Julia Conaway Bondanella (New York: Barnes & Noble Classics, 2005), p. 29.

25. André Bazin, "Cabiria: The Voyage to the End of Neorealism," *What Is Cinema? Vol. II*, pp. 83–92; rpt. in Bondanella, ed., *Federico Fellini: Essays*, pp. 94–102, at p. 102.

26. The Criterion Collection DVD of this film (2003) contains two versions of the film: De Sica's full-length version and the edited version screened in the United States—one of the first examples of many that were to follow of studio objections to, and interference with, films shot for Hollywood by Italian directors.

Chapter Six

1. The term "peplum," one popularized by French critics of the era, refers to the kind of short tunic frequently worn by the protagonists of these films.

2. The most complete treatment of this Italian film genre may be found in Lucanio, *With Fire and Sword: Italian Spectacles on American Screens 1958–1968*. Lucanio prefers to call the films "neomythological" rather than peplums, employing a term that the Italian director Vittorio Cottafavi used to define them. The best Italian

treatment of the peplum genre is Giordano, *Giganti buoni: da Ercole a Piedone (e oltre): il mito dell'uomo forte nel cinema italiano*. In English the most comprehensive study of cinema and the classical world is Solomon, *The Ancient World in the Cinema* (rev. and expanded ed.). Although the peplum film has frequently received the worst kind of critical treatment by film reviewers, more recent analyses of this important *filone* (literally, "strand")—the term Italian critics employ to refer to a thematic trend or genre in film history—are more positive. See, for example, Wood, *Italian Cinema*, and Günsberg, *Italian Cinema: Gender and Genre*, for discussion of the sword and sandal epic from the perspective of genre and gender, respectively.

3. Readers with a long memory may recall the parody of bad dubbing in peplum epics on the March 21, 1987, *Saturday Night Live* television broadcast, in particular "Il Returno de Hercules," starring Bill Murray. The television program *Mystery Science Theater 3000*, running 1988–99, featured a man stranded on a space station with two robot sidekicks: all three of them were forced to watch badly made films to pass the time, and some peplums inevitably turned up in this venue and were mercilessly critiqued by the two robots in extremely amusing ways.

4. For a discussion of the traditional epic film on classical times and in particular of Mann's film, see Peter Bondanella, *The Eternal City: Roman Images in the Modern World*.

5. Lucanio, *With Fire and Sword*, p. 2. Lucanio's encyclopedic treatment of the numerous peplum films also contains an exhaustive treatment of the genre's stylistic traits, to which I am indebted.

6. Lucanio's *With Fire and Sword* lists nearly five hundred films, but many are traditional adventure films; other scholars place the figure much lower, at close to two hundred films in the peplum genre.

7. I follow ibid., pp. 12–15, 49–50, for my description of Levine's promotional schemes.

8. Ibid., p. 181.

9. I cite from an interview given to Giordano, *Giganti buoni*, pp. 38–40 (author's translations).

10. These films are discussed in chapter 11.

11. The films, *They Call Me Trinity* (*Lo chiamavano Trinità*, 1970) and *Trinity Is Still My Name* (*Continuavano a chiamarlo Trinità*, 1971), are discussed in chapter 11.

12. Steele would star in other equally important Italian horror films, such as Riccardo Freda's *The Horrible Dr. Hichcock* (*L'orribile segreto del doctor Hichcock*, 1962) and Antonio Margheriti's *Castle of Blood* (*Danza macabre*, 1964); but between these typecast roles, she would also play a small but outstanding part in Federico Fellini's *8½* (*Otto e mezzo*, 1963).

13. This is noted by Lucanio, *With Fire and Sword*, p. 358.

14. See Bruce Headlam, "Revisiting Coen Country for Odd Men," *New York Times*, August 29, 2008, p. 10. The two directors go on to note that their local television affiliate had access to the entire Joseph E. Levine catalog of films, which included at the time not only many Italian peplum epics but also such Fellini masterpieces as *8½*, so "badly dubbed [that] Marcello [Mastroianni] sounded like Hugh Grant. Very stuttery."

15. In this discussion of the Italian film market, I am most indebted to Giordano's *Giganti buoni*; to Spinazzola's *Cinema e pubblico: lo spettacolo filmico in*

Italia 1945–1965; and to Christopher Wagstaff's useful essay, "A Forkful of Westerns: Industry, Audiences, and the Italian Western," in Dyer and Vincendeau, eds., *Popular European Cinema*, pp. 245–61. Wagstaff's treatment focuses upon the spaghetti western, but his description of the Italian film market holds good, in most respects, for all popular genre films, works that might be compared to the so-called B films from Hollywood.
16. Wagstaff, ibid., pp. 249–50.

Chapter Seven

1. For a discussion of comic plots in film comedy, to which I owe this definition, see Mast's *The Comic Mind: Comedy and the Movies*, pp. 5–6, and passim. A number of books on Italian film comedy and the numerous actors associated with this genre are listed in the Bibliography, but almost all of them are written in Italian. Happily, the best and most recent of them is in English: Lanzoni, *Comedy Italian Style: The Golden Age of Italian Film Comedies*.
2. Mast, *The Comic Mind*, p. 7.
3. *The Screenplays of Lina Wertmüller*, p. 194.
4. See John Simon, "Wertmüller's *Seven Beauties*—Call It a Masterpiece," *New York* 9.5 (February 2, 1976): 24–31. The earliest monograph on Wertmüller—Ferlita and May, *The Parables of Lina Wertmüller*—was first published in the United States, not in Italy (as was the previously cited collection of her screenplays); her nomination for an Oscar, though unwon, also reflects her meteoric rise to fame in the United States with this film. Bruno Bettelheim attacked the film for treating the Holocaust in a tragicomic fashion in "Reflections: Surviving," *New Yorker* 52 (August 2, 1976): 31–36, 38–39, 42–52, a position effectively rebutted by Robert Boyers in "Politics & History: Pathways in European Film," *Salmagundi* 38–39 (Summer–Fall 1977): 50–79. More measured analyses of the treatment of sex and politics in Wertmüller or her treatment of the Holocaust may be found in two books by Millicent Marcus: *Italian Film in the Light of Neorealism* and *Italian Film in the Shadow of Auschwitz*. See also an excellent article by William R. Magretta and Joan Magretta, "Lina Wertmüller and the Tradition of Italian Carnivalesque Comedy," *Genre* 12.1 (1979): 25–43. Many of the same criticisms of the image of the Holocaust are directed against Roberto Benigni's *Life Is Beautiful* (*La vita è bella*, 1997).
5. *The Screenplays of Lina Wertmüller*, p. 325.
6. Eco's essay originally appeared in *Diario minimo*, a best-selling collection of his popular essays appearing in 1963; it has been translated in Umberto Eco, *Misreadings*, trans. William Weaver (San Diego and New York: Harcourt Brace, 1993), with the essay on pp. 156–64.
7. Recently Italian film critics have devoted more attention to these types of film comedy. See the following books for more detailed analysis: Bertolino and Ridola, *Franco Franchi e Ciccio Ingrassia*; Buratti, *Fantozzi: una maschera italiana*; and Giordano, *La commedia erotica italiana: vent'anni di cinema sexy "made in Italy."*
8. For discussions of Italian pornography, see Giovannini and Tentori, *Porn'Italia: il cinema erotico italiano*, or Buttasi and D'Agostino, *Dizionario del cinema hard: Attori, attrici, registi e film*. Italian pornography is not discussed in this book, not because I have any moral objections to doing so but, rather, because access to a

sufficiently large number of titles to write a decent historical account of it would be extremely difficult outside Italy. It is worth noting that several Italian porno stars (Ilona Staller or "Cicciolina" [1951—] and Moana Pozzi [1961-94]) have run for election to the Italian Chamber of Deputies, and in 1987 Cicciolina became the first porno actress to win such an election. Pornography in the cinema, even in a country like Italy where the Vatican is located, does not raise the same moral outrage as it does in the United States.

Chapter Eight

1. Leo Braudy, "Rossellini: From *Open City* to *General Della Rovere*," in Braudy and Dickstein, eds., *Great Film Directors*, pp. 655-73, at p. 673.
2. Cited from Gary Crowdus and Dan Georgakas, "'The Audience Should Not Be Just Passive Spectators': An Interview with Francesco Rosi," *Cinéaste* 7.1 (Fall 1975): 2-8, at p. 8.
3. Ibid.
4. Cited by Ghirelli, *Gillo Pontecorvo*, p. 3.
5. David Wilson, "Politics and Pontecorvo," *Sight and Sound* 40 (1971): p. 161.
6. For an interview in English with Volontè, see "Gian Maria Volontè Talks about Cinema and Politics," interview with Guy Braucourt, *Cinéaste* 7.1 (Fall 1975): 10-13.
7. The best introduction to Pasolini's writings in English may be found in *Heretical Empiricism*, ed. Barnett and trans. by Lawton and Barnett.
8. Cited by MacBean, *Film and Revolution*, p. 269.
9. Ibid., p. 272.
10. Pierre Clémenti (1942-99) was extremely popular with young Italian political film directors: Bertolucci's *Partner* (1968)—as big a flop as *The Cannibals*—featured this French actor. Clémenti also stars in Pasolini's *Pigpen*, a.k.a. *Pigsty* (*Porcile*, 1969), and plays a major role in Bertolucci's *The Conformist* (*Il conformista*, 1970).
11. For a sampling of this initial negative criticism, see two reviews: Henry Giroux, "The Challenge of Neo-Fascist Culture," *Cinéaste* 6.4 (1975): 31-32; and Ruth McCormick, "Fascism à la Mode or Radical Chic?," *Cinéaste* 6.4 (1975): 31, 33-34. For an opposing, positive view from the same era, see Teresa de Lauretis, "Cavani's *Night Porter*: A Woman's Film?" *Film Quarterly* 30.2 (Winter 1976-77): 35-38. Less polemical treatments may be found in Marrone, *The Gaze and the Labyrinth*; Marcus, *Italian Film in the Shadow of Auschwitz*; and Ravetto, *The Unmasking of Fascist Aesthetics*.
12. See Cavani's introduction to the script: *Il portiere di notte*, p. viii, and *passim*.

Chapter Nine

1. Unlike both Antonioni and Fellini, who were generally lionized in the United States and were both given Oscars for their entire careers, Visconti was not so fortunate in America. For the history of his American reception, and the frequently vitriolic and negative critiques of his work, see Peter Bondanella, "La (s)fortuna critica del cinema viscontiano in USA" in Bruni and Pravadelli, eds., *Studi viscontiani*, pp. 277-86. The most strident of these attacks, by John Simon, claimed that "there is no more overblown, self-inflated and preposterous reputation in film than that of

Luchino Visconti"; Simon, *Movies into Film: Film Criticism, 1967–1970* (New York: Dial Press, 1971), p. 190.

2. Visconti, "Racconto storie come se raccontassi un Requiem," in Ferrero, ed., *Visconti: il cinema*, pp. 80–81 (author's translation).

3. David Wilson, *Sight and Sound 39.1* (Winter 1969–70): p. 48.

4. See Kriss Ravetto's *The Unmasking of Fascist Aesthetics* for a consideration of this issue. In fact, the "Nazi Bordello" or the "Nazi sexploitation" film is one of the numerous Italian film subgenres that appeared in the wake of such works as Cavani's *The Night Porter*, *The Damned*, or Pasolini's *Salò* (*Salò o le 120 giornate di Sodoma*, 1975). For a discussion of this genre in English, see Mikel J. Koven, "'The Film You Are About to See Is Based on Fact': Italian Nazi Sexploitation Cinema," in Mathijs and Mendik, eds., *Alternative Europe: Eurotrash and Exploitation Cinema since 1945*, pp. 19–31. Basing his work on Visconti's *The Damned* down to recasting both Helmut Berger and Ingrid Thulin in the film, Tinto Brass (1933–) produced a very successful soft-porn Nazi exploitation film on a German Nazi brothel with listening devices employed to eavesdrop upon the secret conversations of Germany's ruling class. Entitled *Salon Kitty* (1976), its success is primarily responsible for setting so many Italian Nazi exploitation films in a brothel. Some sample titles include *SS Experiment Love Camp* (*Lager SSadis Kastrat Kommandantur*, literally, "SS Camp of the Castrated Commandant," 1976) and *SS Camp 5: Women's Hell* (*SS Lager 5: L'inferno delle donne*, 1977), both directed by Sergio Garrone, and *The Gestapo's Last Orgy* (*L'ultima orgia del III Reich*, 1977; dir. Cesare Canevari).

5. Antonioni, *"L'Avventura": A Film by Michelangelo Antonioni*, pp. 213, 215.

6. For the complete translation of the Cannes statement Antonioni read at the film festival, see ibid., pp. 221–23.

7. Alberto Moravia, *The Empty Canvas*, trans. Angus Davidson (New York: Farrar, Giroux and Cudahy, 1961), pp. 3–4.

8. Alberto Moravia, *Man as an End: A Defense of Humanism*, trans. Bernard Wall (New York: Farrar, Straus and Giroux, 1966; rpt. Westport, Conn.: Greenwood Press, 1976), p. 230.

9. Alan Casty, *Development of Film: An Interpretive History* (New York: Harcourt Brace Jovanovich, 1973), p. 277.

10. Antonioni, *"L'Avventura,"* p. 223.

11. "La nuit, l'éclipse, l'aurore: entretien avec Michelangelo Antonioni par Jean-Luc Godard," *Cahiers du Cinéma* 160 (November 1964): 8–17; trans. as "Night, Eclipse, Dawn . . . : an Interview with Michelangelo Antonioni, by Jean-Luc Godard." *Cahiers du Cinéma in English* 1 (January 1966): 19–29. Cited in Andrew Sarris, ed., *Interviews with Film Directors* (New York: Avon, 1969), pp. 28–29.

12. *Ibid.*, p. 23.

13. Cited in Samuels, ed., *Encountering Directors*, p. 72.

14. Leprohon, *Michelangelo Antonioni* (French ed., author's translation), p. 100.

15. Sarris, ed., *Interviews with Film Directors*, p. 29.

16. Antonioni, *Sei film*, p. 497 (author's translation).

17. Antonioni, *Blow-Up*, p. 75.

18. Halprin eventually dropped out of Berkeley and, after living with Frechette in a commune, married the actor Dennis Hopper. Frechette went to jail for bank robbery and murder and died in the prison weight room under suspicious circumstances.

19. For discussions of Fellini's commercials, see Bondanella, *The Cinema of Federico Fellini*; Fabbri, ed., *Lo schermo "manifesto": le misteriose pubblicità di Federico Fellini*; and Angelucci, ed., *Gli ultimi sogni di Fellini*.

20. Cited by Kezich, *Il dolce cinema*, p. 25 (author's translation).

21. Fellini, *Fellini on Fellini*, p. 157.

22. Martelli discusses this issue in Faldini and Fofi, eds., *L'avventurosa storia del cinema italiano raccontata dai suoi protagonisti 1960–1969*, pp. 10–11.

23. See Gherardi's comments in ibid., p. 12.

24. For a discussion of the impact of Fellini's *8½* upon subsequent film directors all over the world, see Peter Bondanella, "La presenza di Federico Fellini nel cinema contemporaneo / Federico Fellini's Presence in the Contemporary Cinema," in *La memoria di Federico Fellini sullo schermo del cinema mondiale*; rpt. as "La presenza di Fellini nel cinema contemporaneo: considerazioni preliminari / Federico Fellini's Presence in the Contemporary Cinema: Some Tentative Observations," in *Federico Amarcord: Rivista di studi felliniani* 7.1–2 (2007): 35–60.

25. *Nine*, the Broadway musical adapted from *8½* in 1982, won the Tony Award for Best Musical in that year and received eleven other Tony nominations (of which it won four). Directed by Tommy Tune, with a musical score by Maury Yeston and texts by Mario Fratti and Arthur Kopit, this enormously successful musical comedy starred Raul Julia and ran for twenty-two months; the successful revival of the musical in 2003 won two Tonys out of eight nominations and starred Antonio Banderas. A film version, directed by Rob Marshall and with Daniel Day-Lewis as Guido, appeared in 2009.

26. Fellini, *"8½": Federico Fellini, Director*, p. 238.

27. Fellini, *Fellini on Fellini*, p. 147.

28. The manuscript of this extraordinary visual work offering great insight into Fellini's creative processes has been published in a facsimile- and normal-format edition in Italy as Fellini, *Il libro dei sogni*, ed. Kezich and Mollica; an English translation is available as *Fellini's Book of Dreams*.

29. Bachmann, "A Guest in My Own Dreams: An Interview with Federico Fellini," p. 7.

30. Sarris, ed., *Interviews with Film Directors*, p. 182.

31. Fellini, *Fellini on Fellini*, p. 151.

32. Fellini's essay *"Amarcord*: The Fascism within Us" may be examined in English in Bondanella, ed., *Federico Fellini: Essays in Criticism*, pp. 20–26; quote at p. 21.

33. Fellini, *Fellini on Fellini*, pp. 157–58.

34. Fellini, *"Amarcord*: The Fascism within Us," in Bondanella, ed., *Federico Fellini: Essays in Criticism*, pp. 21–22.

35. Fellini, *Comments on Film*, ed. Grazzini, trans. Henry, p. 39.

36. Cited in Leo Janos, "The New Fellini: Venice on Ice," *Time* (May 17, 1976), p. 77. For Fellini's most important discussion of the figure of Giacomo Casanova, see Fellini, *"Casanova*: An Interview with Aldo Tassone," in Bondanella, ed., *Federico Fellini: Essays in Criticism*, pp. 27–35.

37. For Fellini's remarks on *The City of Women* and on feminism in general, see Gideon Bachmann, "Federico Fellini: 'The Cinema Seen as a Woman . . .': An Interview on the Day *City of Women* Premiered in Rome," *Film Quarterly* 34.2 (1980): 2–9. The best argument against the facile attacks upon Fellini's film by militant

feminists with no sense of humor may be found in the beautiful essay on Fellini by one of the founders of the feminist movement, Germaine Greer, entitled "Fellinissimo," in Bondanella and Degli Esposti, eds., *Perspectives on Federico Fellini*, pp. 225–39.

38. Fellini, *La voce della luna*, p. 137 (author's translation).

Chapter Ten

1. Günsberg, *Italian Cinema: Gender and Genre*, p. 136.

2. I owe this definition of the Italian horror film to Palmerini and Mistretta's *Spaghetti Nightmares: Italian Fantasy-Horrors as Seen through the Eyes of Their Protagonists*, one of the best English treatments available. See also a number of works listed in the Bibliography devoted to Italian horror films. Of course, calling these works "spaghetti nightmare" films owes its origin to the far more famous definition of Italian films about the American West as "spaghetti westerns."

3. Günsberg, *Italian Cinema: Gender and Genre*, p. 138.

4. See Carol Jenks, "The Other Face of Death: Barbara Steele and *La maschera del demonio*," in Dyer and Vincendeau, eds., *Popular European Cinema*, pp. 149–62, to which I am indebted. The most detailed and authoritative treatment of Bava's cinema is Lucas, *Mario Bava: All the Colors of the Dark*. Lucas has written many of the extremely useful liner notes in the recent DVDs devoted to Bava's work.

5. For a mass of detail on Argento's career, see Jones, *Profondo Argento: The Man, the Myths & the Magic*, which is especially good on the collaborators who create his music, special effects, and photography, and is illustrated with copious photographs from work on his sets. See also McDonagh, *Broken Mirrors/Broken Minds: The Dark Dreams of Dario Argento*.

6. Bennett had already had a long run as the family matriarch, Elizabeth Collins Stoddard, on the vampiric soap opera *Dark Shadows*, a role she repeated on film in Dan Curtis's *House of Dark Shadows* (1970).

7. For a survey of this niche market in Italian cinema to which my discussion is indebted, see Slater, *Eaten Alive! Italian Cannibal and Zombie Movies*.

8. I owe this list of precursors to Slater, ibid. For a specific study of the Italian Nazi sexploitation film, see Mikel J. Koven, "'The Film You Are About to See Is Based On Fact': Italian Nazi Sexploitation Cinema," in Mathijs and Mendik, *Alternative Europe: Eurotrash and Exploitation Cinema since 1945*, pp. 19–31.

9. Other "Mondo" films by these two figures include *Women of the World* (*La donna nel mondo*, 1963); *Mondo Cane Number 2* (*Mondo cane 2*, 1963), *Adios Africa* (*Africa addio*, 1966), and *Goodbye Uncle Tom* (*Addio zio Tom*, 1971).

10. For some academic critics of the later Italian horror film, Radice represents a male image comparable to that of Barbara Steele in an earlier Gothic era. See Patricia MacCormack, "Masochistic Cinesexuality: The Many Deaths of Giovanni Lombardo Radice," and her "Male Masochism, Male Monsters: An Interview with Giovanni Lombardo Radice," in Mathijs and Mendik, *Alternative Europe*, pp. 106–16, 117–23.

11. Better known in the Anglo-Saxon world as Joe D'Amato, Massaccesi had managed to spice up the cannibal theme with soft core even before *Cannibal Holocaust* and *Cannibal Ferox* were released. Directing as Massaccesi, he provides lots of graphic gore and simulated sexual acts in *Emmanuel and the Last Cannibals* (*Emanuelle e gli*

ultimi cannibali, 1977), and his *Erotic Nights of the Living Dead* (*Le notti erotiche dei morti viventi*, 1980) manages to combine simulated sex and zombies.

12. Cited in Slater, *Eaten Alive!* p. 175.

13. Ibid., p. 231.

14. Most American viewers of the film will never have seen an ossuary, or bone-storage site, but they are quite common in Italy and other Catholic countries where, due to a lack of cemetery space, the bones of the buried dead are eventually disinterred after decomposition of the bodies and transferred into an ossuary for safekeeping—there to await the resurrection of the dead, when they will once again become whole.

Chapter Eleven

1. Günsberg, *Italian Cinema: Gender and Genre*, p. 177, notes both of these films.

2. There are a few fundamental books on the Italian western, three by Christopher Frayling: *Once Upon a Time in Italy: The Westerns of Sergio Leone*; *Sergio Leone: Something to Do with Death*; and *Spaghetti Westerns: Cowboys and Europeans from Karl May to Sergio Leone*. For the most complete guide to the entire phenomenon, see Giusti, *Dizionario del western all'italiana*. (Giusti was the organizer of the retrospective on the Italian western at the 2007 Venice Film Festival, where some thirty films were screened.) Finally, for the most detailed analysis of twenty individual Italian westerns, see Howard Hughes, *Once Upon a Time in the Italian West: The Filmgoers' Guide to Spaghetti Westerns*.

3. Cited in Nachbar, ed., *Focus on the Western*, p. 62.

4. Cawelti, "Reflections on the New Western Films," in Nachbar, ed., ibid., pp. 113–17, at p. 113.

5. For Frayling's discussion of spaghetti plots, see his *Spaghetti Westerns*, pp. 51–52. Frayling notes (p. 147) that when Leone was sued by Kurosawa for infringement on his copyright, Kurosawa and his colleagues were awarded exclusive distribution rights for *A Fistful of Dollars* for Japan, Taiwan, and South Korea plus 15 percent of the worldwide box-office receipts. Leone's legal defense rested upon the argument that both authors should have paid Goldoni's estate for the use of Goldoni's original plot. Leone's defense was not as artificial as it might seem to American viewers of his film. In 1947 at the very influential Piccolo Teatro in Milan, Giorgio Strehler (1921–97) put on a celebrated production of Goldoni's play that was repeated numerous times all over Europe. According to some accounts, it was Sergio Corbucci who insisted that Leone see *Yojimbo* (released in Italy as *La sfida del samurai*) when it was first shown in Rome.

6. In Venice, as part of a series of retrospectives called "The Secret History of Italian Cinema," the Prada Foundation (an institution sponsored by the Prada fashion house) presented a program entitled "The Italian Kings of the Bs" in 2004. There, Quentin Tarantino and Joe Dante presented several dozen Italian B pictures. A few years later, Marco Giusti (author of an important reference book on the genre, cited above) organized an exciting retrospective of the spaghetti western at Venice in 2007. Tarantino had been publicizing Italian genre films for some time, not only via citations from *Kill Bill* and other works but also by screening dozens of them at his Quentin Tarantino Film Festival ("QT-Fest") in Austin, Texas, a semiannual event that began in 1997.

7. Cited in Noel Simsolo, "Sergio Leone Talks," *Take One* 3.9 (Jan.–Feb. 1973): 26–32, at p. 30.

8. Frayling, *Spaghetti Westerns*, p. 214.

9. An earlier film had a character named Sartana and played by Garko—*Blood at Sundown*, a.k.a. *One Thousand Dollars on the Black* (*Mille dollari sul nero*, 1966; dir. Alberto Cardone)—and Parolini reused the name and actor but changed the character.

10. Hughes, *Once Upon a Time in the Italian West*, p. 218.

11. For Giusti, the bird's name is Mary Jane (an obvious reference to the marijuana John smokes during the film). It is also possible that the Italian dialogue on the DVD I own gives the name as Marshall, not Marsha. Either Marsha or Mary Jane makes more sense.

12. I owe the amusing details of this film's production and reception to Giusti's inexhaustible *Dizionario del western all'italiana*, pp. 216–21.

13. Cited in ibid., p. 270.

14. The English dialogue dubbed for *They Call Me Trinity* represents a higher quality than was typical of most spaghetti westerns, and it was supervised by Gene Luotto, who also worked for Fellini on *And the Ship Sails On* and other important auteur films.

15. For information on the box-office success of Barboni's two films, see Hughes, *Once Upon a Time in the Italian West*, pp. 238–39; or Giusti, *Dizionario del western all'italiana*, pp. 116, 271. The total box office in Italy came to around 6–7 *billion* lire for each film, in a period when film admissions cost 1,000 lire. In fact, *Trinity Is My Name* came in second behind Bertlolucci's *Last Tango in Paris* only because *Last Tango's* tickets cost an extraordinary 1,800 lire rather than the usual 1,000—and, as Barboni remarked to Bertolucci's producer, Alberto Grimaldi: "And then with all those elements that you inserted in that film—Brando, that girl's ass, the sodomy scene, and all those things—of course you had to win" (Giusti, *Dizionario del western all'italiana*, p. 271; author's translation).

16. Dialogue cited from Hughes, ibid., p. 248.

17. Landis's experiences abroad parallel the often humble origins of many Italian filmmakers, a great many of whom profited from the hundreds of low-budget westerns made during this period, as well as subsequent genre films, to learn their trades. Landis remained grateful for his European experiences and discussed it with an audience of students and film scholars at the international conference "European Cinemas, European Societies, 1895–1995," held at Indiana University from September 28 to October 1, 1995, to celebrate the hundredth anniversary of the *European* invention of the movies. Landis joined Peter Bogdanovich (whose links to the spaghetti western were discussed above) and the Italian director Ettore Scola on the program.

18. Frayling, *Spaghetti Westerns*, p. 254 (where the parable is cited as well).

19. Italian dialogue cited by Giusti, *Dizionario del western all'italiana*, p. 541 (author's translation). Giusti also reports the interesting information on Fellini's "lost" western sequences.

Chapter Twelve

1. The only book in English devoted entirely to the *giallo* is Koven's *La Dolce Morte*, a thought-provoking work to which this chapter is indebted. *Spaghetti Nightmares: Italian Fantasy-Horrors as Seen through the Eyes of Their Protagonists*, by Palmerini and Mistretta, is an excellent treatment in English of Italian genre films but does not really distinguish between the *giallo* and the horror film, as Koven does and as I do in this chapter. The best recent consideration of the literary *giallo* in Italy is Crovi, *Tutti i colori del giallo*. A number of books devoted to the key figures in the history of the *giallo*, Mario Bava and Dario Argento, are listed in the Bibliography. Of special interest are Lucas, *Mario Bava: All the Colors of the Dark*, and Jones, *Profondo Argento: The Man, the Myths & the Magic*.

2. Koven makes two broad sociological claims to explain the *giallo*'s appeal in Italy. He believes that the *giallo* reflects ambivalence about modernity, and this explanation is certainly reasonable, given that the period in which the *giallo* flourished coincided with the end of the Italian "economic miracle." However, his belief that *giallo* protagonists have been traumatized by a particular historical event (what he calls "the defeat and emasculation of Italy in the war and under fascism" [p. 109]) is really too far a leap for me. His criticism of film historians (including me) for ignoring popular film genres in a preference for the so-called Italian art film is well taken, but it must be remembered that most of these films had not been accessible until the advent of DVD remastered prints. I trust that this greatly revised version of my own film history will lay to rest this objection to my own account of the development of Italian cinema, since the present volume includes many new chapters on a number of popular genres and cult figures not included in the three editions of *Italian Cinema*.

3. Koven, ibid., pp. 125–27, advances this reasonable theory, building on the study by Christopher Wagstaff previously cited in chapter 6, "A Forkful of Westerns: Industry, Audiences, and the Italian Western," in Dyer and Vincendeau, eds., *Popular European Cinema*, pp. 245–61. It should be remembered, however, that the hundreds of Italian B films produced may initially have played in the Italian version of grind houses or drive-ins (*seconda* or *terza visione* theaters), but as they become more and more popular, they also moved to first-run theaters. In many instances, during the successive crazes for these B films—that is, between the rise and fall of the peplum to the rise and fall of the *giallo/poliziesco*/horror film craze—some individual B films were box-office hits in first-run theaters. The very nature of the Italian formulaic production of B films requires some huge successes to ensure that the many others produced at much lower cost will nevertheless still make a profit on a very small initial investment.

4. Essay-length analyses of Italian B films in English are rare. For a lengthy discussion of *Bloody Pit of Horror*, see Leon Hunt, "Boiling Oil and Baby Oil: *Bloody Pit of Horror*," in Mathijs and Mendik, *Alternative Europe: Eurotrash and Exploitation Cinema since 1945*, pp. 172–80.

5. It is generally agreed that the key idea of *Alien,* the discovery of a stowaway monster on a space ship in deep space, may have been inspired by another low-budget film by Bava, the science fiction film improbably translated as *Planet of the Vampires*, a.k.a. *Terror in Space* (*Terrore nello spazio*, 1965), on which Rambaldi served as an uncredited model maker before working with Ridley Scott on *Alien*.

6. The best essay on *Deep Red* in English is Giorgio Bertellini's "*Profondo Rosso / Deep Red*" in his own anthology, *The Cinema of Italy*, pp. 213–23. The fact that an Argento *giallo* is included in a book with separate essays on established Italian art film directors or auteurs reflects a growing interest among American Italianists in the Italian B film, for years limited largely to the Italian western. During the 2007–2008 theatrical season in Italy, Argento's most famous film became adapted as a musical: *Profondo rosso: il musical*.

7. Walter's oral biography, *Milking the Moon: A Southerner's Story of Life on This Planet* (New York: Crown, 2001), outlines his multitalented life as a writer, poet, and actor, including friendships with many of the most interesting postwar figures in Italy. Walter lived in Rome during the 1960s and 1970s, where he worked with a number of Italian directors as both actor and translator of scripts. He is best known for his work with Fellini on *8½* (he plays an American journalist) and *Juliet of the Spirits* (where he plays a Mother Superior!); but in the *giallo* genre he has important roles in Pupi Avati's *The House with Laughing Windows* and Paolo Cavara's *The Belly of the Tarantula*, both discussed in this chapter.

8. See Koven, *La Dolce Morte*, pp. 159–71.

9. Since the English subtitles in the currently available DVD incorrectly identify the wife of the owner of a local trattoria as the model, it is impossible to see this early hint about the painter's nature and character without understanding Italian.

Chapter Thirteen

1. For Pasolini's remarks on the meaning of *Medea*, see Duflot, ed., *Entretiens avec Pier Paolo Pasolini*, pp. 112–13.

2. Stack, ed., *Pasolini on Pasolini*, p. 157.

3. Pasolini, "Why That of Oedipus Is a Story: Pier Paolo Pasolini," in Pasolini, *Oedipus Rex*, p. 7.

4. Petraglia, *Pier Paolo Pasolini*, p. 16.

5. For the statistical analysis of Boccaccio's characters, see Thomas G. Bergin, "An Introduction to Boccaccio," in Musa and Bondanella, eds. and trans., *The Decameron: A Norton Critical Edition*, p. 162; or his preface to the 1982 complete translation of *The Decameron* by Musa and Bondanella in New American Library. Auerbach's famous essay on Boccaccio is cited from the *Norton Critical Edition*, p. 284.

6. Pasolini creates a frame of his own making, first and best analyzed in Ben Lawton, "Boccaccio and Pasolini: A Contemporary Reinterpretation of *The Decameron*," in Musa and Bondanella, eds. and trans., *The Decameron: A Norton Critical Edition*, pp. 306–22, to which this discussion is indebted. Other important considerations of Pasolini's literary adaptation may be found in Marcus, *Filmmaking by the Book*, and in Rumble, *Allegories of Contamination*.

7. Cited by Gideon Bachmann, "Pasolini Today: The Interview," *Take One* 4 (1973): 18–21, at p. 21.

8. Vittore Branca, "Boccaccio moderno," *Il Corriere della Sera*, March 20, 1975, p. 3.

9. Snyder, *Pier Paolo Pasolini*, pp. 149–50.

10. Cited from Pasolini, "Abiura della Trilogia della vita," in Pasolini, *Trilogia della vita*, ed. Gattei, pp. 7–11, at p. 11 (author's translation).

11. For an account of Pasolini's death, see the biographies in English by Siciliano and Schwartz.

12. Cited in Marilyn Goldin, "Bertolucci on *The Conformist*," *Sight and Sound* 40.2 (Spring 1971): 64–66, at p. 66; rpt. in Gérard, Kline, and Sklarew, eds. *Bernardo Bertolucci: Interviews*, pp. 63–69, at p. 65. For a detailed discussion of Bertolucci's debt to other directors, see Ungari and Ranvaud, eds., *Scene madri di Bernardo Bertolucci*, and interviews with the director in Gérard et al., ibid.

13. T. Jefferson Klein, "The Unconformist: Bertolucci's *The Conformist* (1971)," in Horton and Magretta, eds., *Modern European Filmmakers and the Art of Adaptation*, pp. 222–37, at p. 231.

14. Cited by Goldin in "Bertolucci on *The Conformist*," p. 66.

15. For an elaboration of this counterintuitive interpretation of Bertolucci's anti-Fascist ideology, see my "Borges, Bertolucci, and the Mythology of Revolution," *Teaching Language through Literature* 27 (1988): 3–14.

16. Cited in Bertolucci, *Bernardo Bertolucci's "Last Tango in Paris*,*" pp. 10, 202.

17. Cited by Joan Mellen in "A Conversation with Bernardo Bertolucci," *Cinéaste* 5.4 (1973): 21–24, at p. 24; rpt. in Gérard, Kline, and Sklarew, eds. *Bernardo Bertolucci: Interviews*, pp. 70–77, at p. 77.

18. Cited by Gideon Bachmann in "Every Sexual Relationship Is Condemned: An Interview with Bernardo Bertolucci apropos *Last Tango in Paris*," *Film Quarterly* 26.3 (Spring 1973): 2–9, at p. 5; rpt. in Gérard et al., eds. *Bernardo Bertolucci: Interviews*, pp. 90–101, at p. 95.

19. Cited by Bachmann, "Every Sexual Relationship Is Condemned," rpt. p. 95.

20. Ibid., p. 7; rpt. p. 97.

21. Bertolucci, *Bernardo Bertolucci's "Last Tango in Paris*,*" pp. 46–47.

22. Julian C. Rice, "Bertolucci's *Last Tango in Paris*," *Journal of Popular Film* 3.2 (1974): 157–72, at p. 161.

23. Marsha Kinder and Beverle Houston, "Bertolucci and the Dance of Danger," *Sight and Sound* 42.4 (Autumn 1973): 186–91, at p. 191.

24. See Tassone, *Parla il cinema italiano*, I: 80.

25. Ibid., I: 82.

26. Bertolucci's film trailed only *Ben-Hur* (1959) with eleven Oscars and *West Side Story* (1961) with ten, but Bertolucci's nine awards ties *Gone with the Wind* (1939) and *Gigi* (1958). (Since then, *Titanic* [1997] and *The Lord of the Rings: The Return of the King* [2003] each won eleven Oscars, and *The English Patient* [1996] nine.) *The Last Emperor* received awards in the following categories: Best Picture, Best Director, Best Adaptation, Best Cinematography, Best Sound, Best Editing, Best Original Music, Best Set Design, and Best Costumes. Antonioni and Fellini received

only Honorary Oscars for their entire careers, never Best Director. Benigni's *Life Is Beautiful* (see chapter 16) received seven Oscar nominations, winning three: Best Actor, Best Original Dramatic Score, and Best Foreign Language Film.

27. Cited by Tony Rayns in "Bertolucci in Beijing," *Sight and Sound* 56.1 (1986–87): p. 39.

28. Cited by Tony Rayns in "Model Citizen: Bernardo Bertolucci on Location in China," *Film Comment* 23.6 (1987): 31–36, at p. 36.

29. Bertolucci himself makes this point in Geoffrey Nowell-Smith and Ilona Halberstadt, "Interview with Bernardo Bertolucci," in Gérard et al., eds., *Bernardo Bertolucci: Interviews*, pp. 241–57, at p. 242. A good example of an "international" film that Bertolucci has not yet realized and has apparently abandoned would be a projected adaptation of Dashiell Hammett's *Red Harvest* (1929) that was originally scheduled for 1984, as well as an update of *1900*, bringing Italian history from 1945 up to the present day. The script for *Red Harvest* now resides in Indiana University's Lilly Library of Rare Books and was written by Bertolucci and the American film critic Marilyn Goldin. For Bertolucci's discussion of this project, see Gian Luigi Rondi, "Bertolucci: The Present Doesn't Interest me," in Gérard et al., eds., ibid., pp. 166–74.

30. Allen Olensky, "Tiptoeing in Tuscany," in Gérard et al., eds., ibid., pp. 235–40, at p. 236.

Chapter Fourteen

1. For a discussion of many of what the eminent mystery writer Carlo Lucarelli calls Italian "mysteries," see the two nonfiction books he published based on his very successful Italian television series: *Misteri d'Italia: I casi di Blu Notte* (Turin: Einaudi, 2002) and *Nuovi misteri d'Italia: I casi di Blu Notte* (Turin: Einaudi, 2004). The books treat such *casi* as the mysterious deaths of Michele Sindona, Roberto Calvi, and Enrico Mattei; the Uno Bianca Gang; the Enimont Scandal; Lucio Gelli and the Masonic Lodge P2; the bombing of the Bologna train station; the death of Pasolini; numerous Mafia murders, including the assassinations of Giovanni Falcone, Paolo Borsellino, and General Carlo Alberto Dalla Chiesa; and the Montesi trial, to name only the most famous postwar scandals. For a chilling discussion of how organized crime in and around Naples, the Camorra, has far outstripped the Sicilian Mafia and morphed into an international corporate conglomerate—in particular, controlling not just narcotics but also the manufacture and distribution of Italian designer fashions all over the world with the usual corruption of civil and governmental officials—see Roberto Saviano's disturbing description in *Gomorra: Viaggio nell'impero economico e nel sogno di dominio della camorra* (Milan: Mondadori, 2006). Translated by Virginia Jewess as *Gomorrah: A Personal Journey into the Violent International Empire of Naples' Organized Crime System* (New York: Farrar, Straus and Giroux, 2007), this book is the source of Matteo Garrone's 2008 film of the same name (discussed later in this chapter). Alexander Stille, *Excellent Cadavers: The Mafia and the Death of the First Italian Republic* (New York: Vintage, 1996), provides a lucid discussion of the interrelationship of politics, finance, and organized crime in Italy until the "Mani pulite" ("Clean Hands") investigations in response to what the Italians called "Tangentopoli" ("Bribeville" or "Graftopolis" might be good translations) brought down by 1992

the major economic and political figures of the postwar regime, the so-called First Republic. Two studies of a decidedly leftist flavor—Philip Willan, *Puppetmasters: The Political Use of Terrorism in Italy* (London: Constable & Company, 1991), and Ganser Daniele, *NATO's Secret Army: Operation Gladio and Terrorism in Western Europe* (London: Routledge, 2005)—discuss the interrelationship of crime, terror, and politics in Italy with particular reference to the involvement of the American CIA and NATO during the Cold War. For the European Left, the CIA remains the bogeyman of international politics and the default explanation for anything sinister that occurs around the world, particularly in Italy.

2. Very little written in English on Italian crime films of this period exists, but a useful survey of the genre may be found in Christopher Barry's "Violent Justice: Italian Cop/Crime Films of the 1970s," in Mathijs and Mendik, eds., *Alternative Europe: Eurotrash and Exploitation Cinema since 1945*, pp. 77–89. In Italian, however, the number of very recent books devoted to the Italian crime film underscores a rebirth of interest in it among a generation of younger critics. See, in particular, Casadio, *Col cuore in gola: assassini, ladri e poliziotti nel cinema italiano dal 1930 ad oggi*; Magni and Giobbio, *Cinici, infami e violenti: guida ai film polizieschi italiani anni '70*; and Curti, *Italia odia: il cinema poliziesco italiano*. For Di Leo, see Davide Pulici's *Fernando di Leo*. Quentin Tarantino's love affair with Italian genre films may also be seen in the title and theme of his latest film, *The Inglourious Basterds* (2009), a reference to his favorite Italian war film (a B film), by Enzo Castellari, *Quel maladetto treno blindato* (1978), released in English as *The Inglorious Bastards*.

3. For a treatment of real Jewish American gangsters, see Richard Cohen, *Tough Jews: Fathers, Sons, and Gangster Dreams* (New York: Vintage, 1999). The numerous histories of the Italian Mafia in America include: Thomas Reppetto, *American Mafia: A History of Its Rise to Power* (New York: Holt, 2004); Selwyn Rabb, *Five Families: The Rise, Decline, and Resurgence of America's Most Powerful Mafia Empires* (New York: St. Martin's Griffin, 2006); and Carl Sifakis, *The Mafia Encyclopedia* (New York: Checkmark Books, 2005). For a consideration of Italian American movie gangsters (always in the back of Leone's mind when he made this film), see Bondanella, *Hollywood Italians: Dagos, Palookas, Romeos, Wise Guys, and Sopranos*. George De Stefano's *An Offer We Can't Refuse: The Mafia in the Mind of America* (New York: Faber and Faber, 2006) analyzes the impact of the Mafia on general American culture.

4. Sergio Leone, "C'era una volta la mia America," *Radio corriere TV* 65.6 (1988): p. 54 (author's translation), an important essay that is reprinted as the introduction to a beautiful collection of photographs from the film in Leone, *"C'era una volta in America": un film di Sergio Leone—Photographic Memories*, ed Garofalo.

5. Cited in De Fornari, *Tutti i film di Sergio Leone*, p. 110 (author's translation); see also his *Sergio Leone: The Great Italian Dream of Legendary America*.

6. The American DVD of this film even provides a cardboard kit to construct a toy white Fiat Uno!

Chapter Fifteen

1. These figures have been compiled from a number of books and articles: Zagarrio, *Cinema italiano anni novanta*, pp. 30–32; Brunetta, *Il cinema italiano contemporaneo da "La dolce vita" a "Centochiodi,"* passim; Maurizio Porro, "Multiplex, tra popcorn

e computer il rischio colonialismo" and Giuseppina Manin, "Cinema, spettatori record nell'anno del Titanic," in *Il Corriere della Sera*, December 29, 1998, p. 34; and Giuseppina Manin, "Crisi del cinema italiano: più ciak, meno incassi," in *Il Corriere della Sera*, February 2, 2000, p. 37.

2. Cited by De Santi and Vittori, *I film di Ettore Scola*, pp. 158–59.

3. For an excellent treatment of the film, see Marcus, *Italian Film in the Shadow of Auschwitz*, which includes on a DVD a copy of one of Scola's short films, entitled *1943–1997* (1997)—yet another investigation of Italy's recent history by this masterful and knowledgeable director.

4. Taviani and Taviani (with Guerra), *Good Morning, Babylon*, p. 80.

5. *Zeffirelli: An Autobiography* is actually one of the most noteworthy Italian autobiographies published in Italy in the postwar period.

6. See Marcus, *Italian Film in the Shadow of Auschwitz*, for a thought-provoking discussion of how Rosi's nostalgia "looks back to a period of Left–Right oppositional thought which allowed no room for the story of Italy's Jews, while simultaneously looking forward to the dissolution of Cold War ideology and the telling of the suppressed history that will emerge full-fledged in the outpouring of films to follow" (p. 81).

Chapter Sixteen

1. Moretti's title *Ecce bombo* comes from a nonsensical cry of a street person in the film, but it certainly recalls the Latin words ("Ecce homo") spoken by Pontius Pilate in the Vulgate Bible (John 19:5 "Behold the man") when he presents Jesus to the crowd. It also, of course, calls to mind the title of one of Nietzsche's most famous works, which, like Moretti's cinema, is autobiographical in nature. (The subtitle of Nietzsche's book is "How One Becomes What One Is," a statement that might well serve to label Moretti's films.)

2. For this distinction between traditional Italian film comedy and Moretti's comedy, see Mazierska and Rascaroli, *The Cinema of Nanni Moretti: Dreams and Diaries*, p. 78.

3. Cited in ibid., p. 115.

4. Cited in Gieri, *Contemporary Italian Filmmaking*, p. 229, from a French article (author's translation).

5. Cited in Mazierska and Rascaroli, *The Cinema of Nanni Moretti*, p. x.

6. Author's translation from the original film sound track.

7. When this tragic event occurred, many of Pasolini's friends on the Left tried to blame the crime on right-wing opponents of Pasolini. Unfortunately, pursuing "rough trade" sex in the suburbs is a dangerous venture under the best of circumstances, and none of these ideological explanations for Pasolini's death has ever really proved convincing. Marco Tullio Giordana made a film about the director's death entitled *Pasolini, an Italian Crime* (*Pasolini, un delitto italiano*, 1995).

8. It has also been published as *El Cartero de Neruda* and *Neruda's Postman*. The original novel was actually preceded by a film version, directed by Antonio Skármeta and screened at Spain's Huelva Latin American Film Festival in December 1983.

9. Since Benigni is a Tuscan, the plot was suggested to him by the actual case of "the Monster of Scandicci," as the Tuscans called him, who had murdered and sexually mutilated a series of couples parked in lovers' lanes over a period of years, from 1968 until the 1980s, near the small town of Scandicci outside of Florence.

10. Stuart Liebman, "If Only Life Were So Beautiful," *Cinéaste* 24.2–3 (1999): 20–22, at p. 20. For two far more positive contributions to this debate, see David Travis, "*La Vita é Bella*: The Political Dimension," *Italian Politics & Society* 49 (Spring 1998): 85–89; and Maurizio Viano, "*Life Is Beautiful*: Reception, Allegory, and Holocaust Laughter," *Annali d'Italianistica* 17 (1999): 155–72. See also Marcus, *After Fellini: National Cinema in the Postmodern Age*, or her *Italian Film in the Shadow of Auschwitz*, the definitive study of the Holocaust in Italian cinema, for its extended discussion of this film on pp. 75–78. Important books that treat Italy and the Holocaust include Renzo Felice, *Storia degli ebrei italiani sotto il fascismo* (Turin: Einaudi, 1961; rev. ed. 1972); Susan Zuccotti, *The Italians and the Holocaust: Persecution, Rescue, Survival* (New York: Basic Books, 1987); and Alexander Stille, *Benevolence and Betrayal: Five Italian Jewish Families under Fascism* (New York: Penguin, 1993).

11. Benigni and Cerami, *Life Is Beautiful (La vita é bella): A Screenplay*, p. 162.

12. Ibid., p. 1.

13. Ibid., p. 147.

14. For instance, *Fellini's Casanova* remains a masterpiece, one of the director's most original and least understood works.

15. For a discussion of this interesting historical episode, see Brancalini, *Celebri e dannati—Osvaldo Valenti e Luisa Ferida: storia e tragedia di due divi del regime.*

16. The reference to Giocchino Rossini (1792–1868), one of Italy's most popular and prolific composers of operas, in regard to Ozpetek's career as a film director is not gratuitous, since several of Rossini's most famous early operas dealt with the interchange between Italy and the Ottoman Empire: *The Italian Girl in Algiers* (*L'italiana in Algeri*, 1813) and *The Turk in Italy* (*Il turco in Italia*, 1814).

17. The best treatment of this film in English may be found in Marcus, *Italian Film in the Shadow of Auschwitz*, pp. 140–52.

18. American stars often ended their careers in Italian pictures, just as many of them (such as Clint Eastwood or Steve Reeves, to name only two of the most notable instances) launched successful careers by first appearing in Italian genre films, such as westerns or peplum epics. Another stalwart of the Hollywood silent cinema and a star of the talkies, Gloria Swanson, made one of her last feature films in *Nero's Mistress*, a.k.a. *Nero's Big Weekend* (*Mio figlio Nerone*, 1956), a comic takeoff on the Roman emperor's life and marriage shot by Steno (a.k.a. Stefano Vanzina) with a cast that included Alberto Sordi, Vittorio De Sica, and Brigitte Bardot.

19. Brunetta, *Il cinema italiano contemporaneo da "La dolce vita" a "Centochiodi,"* p. 635.

20. Again, the most detailed discussion of this film in English may be found in Marcus, *Italian Film in the Shadow of Auschwitz*, pp. 99–110.

Chapter Seventeen

1. For a discussion of these statistics, see Nick Vivarelli, "Will Italy's Cinematic Uprising Continue? Local Films Hit with Critics, Click with Audiences," *Variety* (August 22, 2008).

2. See Flavia Laviosa, "Francesca Archibugi: Families and Life Apprenticeship," in Hope, ed., *Italian Cinema: New Directions*, pp. 201–27.

3. For a discussion of Crialese and this "rural idyll" theme, see Pauline Small, "Representing the Female: Rural Idylls, Urban Nightmares," in Hope, ibid., pp. 151–73.

A Select Bibliography on the History of the Italian Cinema

Note: The following bibliography, organized by topic, includes only the most important items—usually books, anthologies, and scripts, rather than articles.

I. Reference

Bondanella, Peter, ed. *The Italian Cinema Book*. London: Palgrave Macmillan for the British Film Institiute, 2013.

Chiti, Roberto, and Enrico Lancia. *Dizionario del cinema italiano: i film,* vol. 1: *Tutti i film italiani dal 1930 al 1944*. Rome: Gremese, 1993.

Chiti, Roberto, Enrico Lancia, Andrea Orbicciani, and Roberto Poppi. *Dizionario del cinema italiano: le attrici*. Rome: Gremese, 1999.

Di Giammatteo, Fernaldo. *Dizionario del cinema italiano: Dall'inizio del secolo a oggi i film che hanno segnato la storia del nostro cinema*. Rome: Editori Riuniti, 1995.

Filmlexicon degli autori e delle opere. 9 vols. Rome: Edizioni di Bianco e Nero, 1958, 1974.

Finney, Angus. *Developing Feature Films in Europe: A Practical Guide*. London: Routledge, 1996.

Giusti, Marco. *Dizionario dei film italiani stracult*. Milan: Sperling & Kupfer, 1999.

Grant, Barry Keith, ed. *Schirmer Encyclopedia of Film*. 4 vols. Detroit: Thomson Gale, 2007.

Lancia, Enrico. *Dizionario del cinema italiano: i film,* vol. 6: *Dal 1990 al 2000*. Rome: Gremese, 2002.

Lancia, Enrico, and Roberto Poppi, eds. *Dizionario del cinema italiano*: *gli attori,* in two parts: *A–L* and *M–Z*. Rome: Gremese, 2003.

Mereghetti, Paolo. *Dizionario dei Film*. Milan: Baldini & Castoldi, 1995, and subsequent editions.

Nowell-Smith, Geoffrey, with James Hay and Gianni Volpi. *The Companion to Italian Cinema*. London: Cassell, 1996.

Poppi, Roberto. *Dizionario del cinema italiano: i film,* vol. 2: *Tutti i film italiani dal 1945 al 1959*. Rome: Gremese, 2007.

———. *Dizionario del cinema italiano: i film,* vol. 5: *Dal 1980 al 1989,* in two parts: *A–L* and *M–Z*. Rome: Gremese, 2000.

———. *I registi: Dal 1930 ai giorni nostri*. Rome: Gremese, 2002.

Poppi, Roberto, and Mario Pecorari. *Dizionario del cinema italiano: i film,* vol. 3: *Tutti i film italiani dal 1960 al 1969,* in two parts: *A–L* and *M–Z*. Rome: Gremese, 2007.

———. *Dizionario del cinema italiano: i film,* vol. 4: *Dal 1970 al 1979,* in two parts: *A–L* and *M–Z*. Rome: Gremese, 2000.

Rondolino, Gianni, ed. *Catalogo Bolaffi del cinema italiano 1945/1955*. Turin: Bolaffi, 1967.

——. ed. *Catalogo Bolaffi del cinema italiano 1956/1965.* Turin: Bolaffi, 1967.

——. ed. *Catalogo Bolaffi del cinema italiano 1966/1975.* Turin: Bolaffi, 1975.

——. ed. *Catalogo Bolaffi del cinema italiano 1975/1976.* Turin: Bolaffi, 1976, and subsequent annuals: *1976/1977,* 1977; *1977/1978,* 1978; *1978/1979,* 1979; *1979/1980,* 1980.

——. ed. *Dizionario del cinema italiano 1945-1969.* Turin: Einaudi, 1969.

Schedario cinematografico. 8 vols. Rome: Centro dello spettacolo e della communicazione sociale, 1972.

Stewart, John. *Italian Film: A Who's Who.* Jefferson, N.C.: McFarland, 1994.

Un secolo di cinema italiano. Atti del Convegno "Cent'Anni di Cinema Italiano," Accademia delle scienze, Torino, 3–5 giugno 1999. Milan: Il Castoro, 2000.

II. Backgrounds to Italian Cinematic Culture: Modern Italian History, Culture, and Literature

Asor Rosa, Alberto. *Dizionario della letteratura italiana del Novecento.* Turin: Einaudi, 1992.

Baranski, Zygmunt G., and Rebecca West, eds. *The Cambridge Companion to Modern Italian Culture.* Cambridge: Cambridge University Press, 2001.

Barzini, Luigi. *The Italians.* New York: Atheneum, 1964.

Bethemont, Jacques, and Jean Pelletier. *Italy: A Geographical Introduction.* London: Longman, 1983.

Bondanella, Peter, and Andrea Ciccarelli, eds. *The Cambridge Companion to the Modern Italian Novel.* Cambridge: Cambridge University Press, 2003.

Bondanella, Peter, and Julia Conaway Bondanella, eds.-in-chief. *Dictionary of Italian Literature,* 2d rev. ed. Westport, Conn.: Greenwood Press, 1996.

Bonsaver, Guido, and Robert S. C. Gordon, eds. *Culture, Censorship, and the State in Twentieth-Century Italy.* Oxford: European Humanities Research Centre, 2004.

Brand, Peter, and Lino Pertile, ed. *The Cambridge History of Italian Literature.* Cambridge: Cambridge University Press, 1996.

Cannistraro, Philip V., ed. *Historical Dictionary of Fascist Italy.* Westport, Conn.: Greenwood Press, 1982.

Coppa, Frank J., ed. *Dictionary of Modern Italian History.* Westport, Conn.: Greenwood Press, 1985.

Di Scala, Spencer M. *Italy from Revolution to Republic: 1700 to the Present.* Boulder, Colo.: Westview, 1995.

Dombroski, Robert S, and Dino S. Cervigni, eds. *Italian Cultural Studies.* Special issue of *Annali d'Italianistica* 16 (1998).

Foracs, David, and Robert Lumley, eds. *Italian Cultural Studies: An Introduction.* Oxford: Oxford University Press, 1996.

Ginsborg, Paul. *A History of Contemporary Italy: Society and Politics 1943-1988.* London: Penguin, 1990.

——. *Italy and Its Discontents: Family, Civil Society, State 1980-2001.* New York: Palgrave Macmillan, 2003.

Gundle, Stephen, and Simon Parker, ed. *The New Italian Republic: From the Fall of the Berlin Wall to Berlusconi.* London: Routledge, 1996.

Heiney, Donald. *America in Modern Italian Literature.* New Brunswick: Rutgers University Press, 1964.

Jeannet, Angela, and Louise Barnett, eds. and trans. *New World Journeys: Contemporary Italian Writers and the Experience of America.* Westport, Conn.: Greenwood Press, 1977.

Jones, Tobias. *The Dark Heart of Italy.* New York: Farrar, Straus and Giroux, 2005.

Kogan, Norman. *A Political History of Italy: The Postwar Years.* New York: Praeger, 1983.

Mack Smith, Denis. *Italy: A Modern History.* Ann Arbor: University of Michigan Press, 1969; rev. ed. 1998.

———. *Mussolini.* New York: Knopf, 1982.

Marrone, Gaetana, and Paolo Puppa, eds. *Encyclopedia of Italian Literary Studies.* 2 vols. New York: Routledge, 2007.

Moliterno, Gino, ed. *Encyclopedia of Contemporary Italian Culture.* London: Routledge, 2000.

Ruland, Richard. *America in Modern European Fiction: From Image to Metaphor.* New Brunswick: Rutgers University Press, 1976.

Russell, Rinaldina, ed. *The Feminist Encyclopedia of Italian Literature.* Westport, Conn.: Greenwood Press, 1997.

Spagnoletti, Giacinto. *La letteratura italiana del nostro secolo.* 3 vols. Milan: Mondadori, 1985.

Spignesi, Stephen J. *From Michelangelo to Mozzarella: The Complete Italian IQ Quiz.* New York: Citadel Press, 2007.

Spotts, Frederic, and Theodore Wieser. *Italy: A Difficult Democracy—A Survey of Italian Politics.* Cambridge: Cambridge University Press, 1986.

Ward, William. *Getting It Right in Italy: A Manual for the 1990s.* London: Bloomsbury, 1990.

White, Jonathan. *Italy: The Enduring Culture.* New York: Ungar, 2001.

Wood, Sharon. *Italian Women's Writing 1869–1994.* London: Athlone Press, 1995.

III. General Histories of Italian Cinema

A. Comprehensive Studies

Argentieri, Mino. *Storia del cinema italiano.* Milan: Newton & Compton, 2006.

Bernardini, Aldo, and Jean A. Gili, eds. *Le cinéma italien: de "La prise de Rome" (1905) à "Rome, ville ouverte" (1945).* Paris: Éditions du Centre Pompidou, 1986.

Bertellini, Giorgio, ed. *The Cinema of Italy.* London: Wallflower Press, 2004.

Bertetto, Paolo. *Il più brutto del mondo: il cinema italiano oggi.* Milan: Bompiani, 1982.

———. ed. *Storia del cinema italiano*: vol. 1, *Dal 1985 a oggi—uno sguardo d'insieme.* Venice: Marsilio, 2011.

Bizio, Silvia. *Cinema Italian Style: Italians at the Academy Awards.* Trans. Carl Haber. New York: Gremese International, 2002.

Bondanella, Peter. "America and the Post-War Italian Cinema," *Rivista di studi italiani* 2.1 (June 1984): 106–25.

———. *Italian Cinema: From Neorealism to the Present.* 1st ed. New York: Frederick Ungar, 1983. 3d rev. ed. New York: Continuum, 2001.

———. "Italy." In William Luhr, ed. *World Cinema since 1945.* New York: Ungar, 1987.

———. "Recent Work on Italian Cinema." *Journal of Modern Italian History* 1.1 (1995): 101–23.

Brunetta, Gian Piero. *Buio in sala: cent'anni di passioni dello spettatore cinematografico.* Venice: Marsilio Editori, 1989.

———. *Cent'anni di cinema italiano.* Rome: Laterza, 1991.

———. *Cent'anni di cinema italiano.* 2 vols.: 1, *Dalle origini alla seconda guerra mondiale.* 2, *Dal 1945 ai giorni nostri.* Rome: Laterza, 2003.

———. *Guida alla storia del cinema italiano 1905–2003.* Turin: Einaudi, 2003. English edition: *The History of Italian Cinema 1905–2003.* Trans. Jeremy Parzen. Princeton: Princeton University Press, 2009.

———. *Storia del cinema italiano 1895–1945.* Rome: Editori Riuniti, 1979.

———. *Storia del cinema italiano dal 1945 agli anni ottanta.* Rome: Editori Riuniti, 1982.

———. *Storia del cinema italiano.* 4 vols.: 1, *Il cinema muto 1895–1929.* 2, *Il cinema del regime 1929–1945.* 3, *Dal neorealismo al miracolo economico 1945–1959.* 4, *Dal miracolo economico agli anni novanta 1960–1993.* Rome: Editori Riuniti, 1993.

———. *Storia del cinema mondiale.* 4 vols. Turin: Einaudi, 1999– .

Buache, Freddy. *Le cinéma italien 1945–1979.* Lausanne: Éditions L'Age d'Homme, 1979.

Buss, Robin. *Italian Films.* New York: Holmes & Meier, 1989.

Caprara, Valerio. *Il buono, il brutto, il caltivo: storie della storia del cinema italiano.* Naples: Guida Editori, 2006.

Carpi, Fabio. *Cinema italiano del dopoguerra.* Milan: Schwarz, 1966.

Celli, Carlo, and Margo Cottino-Jones. *A New Guide to Italian Cinema.* New York: Palgrave Macmillan, 2007.

Dalle Vacche, Angela. *The Body in the Mirror: Shapes of History in Italian Cinema.* Princeton: Princeton University Press, 1992.

Di Giammatteo, Fernaldo. *Storia del cinema.* Venice: Marsilio, 2005.

Forshaw, Barry. *Italian Cinema: Art House to Exploitation.* London: Pocket Essentials, 2006.

Garofalo, Piero, and Daniela Selisca. *Ciak . . . si parla italiano: Cinema for Italian Conversation.* Newburyport, Ma.: Focus Publishing, 2005.

Giacovelli, Enrico. *Un secolo di cinema italiano 1900–1999.* 2 vols. Turin: Lindau, 2002.

Jaratt, Vernon. *The Italian Cinema.* New York: Arno Press, 1972 (1st ed., 1951).

Landy, Marcia. *Italian Film.* New York: Cambridge University Press, 2000.

Leprohon, Pierre. *The Italian Cinema.* Trans. Roger Greaves and Oliver Stallybrass. London: Secker & Warburg, 1972. [rev. ed. of orig. French ed., Paris: Éditions Seghers, 1966]

Liehm, Mira. *Passion and Defiance: Film in Italy from 1942 to the Present.* Berkeley: University of California Pres, 1984.

Lizzani, Carlo. *Il cinema italiano, 1895–1979.* 2 vols. Rome: Editori Riuniti, 1979. 2d ed. published as *Il cinema italiano dalle origini agli anni ottanta.* Rome: Editori Riuniti, 1982.

Moliterno, Gino, ed. *Historical Dictionary of Italian Cinema.* Lanham, Md.: Scarecrow Press, 2008.

Sorlin, Pierre. *Italian National Cinema 1896–1996.* London: Routledge, 1996.

Spinazzola, Vittorio. *Cinema e pubblico: lo spettacolo filmico in Italia 1945–1960.* Milan: Bompiani, 1974.

Torri, Bruno. *Cinema italiano: dalla realtà alle metafore.* Palermo: Palumbo, 1973.

Turconi, Davide, and Antonio Sacchi, eds. *Bianconero rosso e verde: immagini del cinema italiano 1910–1980.* Florence: La Casa Usher, 1983.

Wood, Mary P. *Italian Cinema.* Oxford: Berg, 2005.

B. The Silent Era

Alovisio, Silvio. *Voci del silenzio: La sceneggiatura nel cinema muto italiano.* Milan: Il Castoro, 2005.

Barbina, Alfredo, ed. *Sperduti nel buio.* Turin: Nuova ERI, 1987.

Bernardini, Aldo. *Cinema italiano delle origini: gli ambulanti.* Gemona: La Cineteca del Friuli, 2001.

———. *Cinema muto italiano: ambiente, spettacoli e spettatori 1896–1904.* Rome and Bari: Laterza, 1980.

———. *Cinema muto italiano: arte, divismo e mercato 1910–1914.* Rome and Bari: Laterza, 1982.

———. *Cinema muto italiano: i film "dal vero" 1895–1914.* Gemona: La Cineteca del Friuli, 2002.

———. *Cinema muto italiano: industria e organizzazione dello spettacolo 1905–1909.* Rome and Bari: Laterza, 1981.

———. ed. *Storia del cinema italiano*: vol. 2, *1895–1911.* Venice: Marsilio, forthcoming.

Bernardini, Aldo, and Flavia De Lucis, eds. *C'era il cinema: l'Italia al cinema tra Otto e Novecento (Reggio Emilio 1986–1915).* Modena: Edizioni Panini, 1983.

Brunetta, Gian Piero. *Il cinema muto italiano.* Rome: Laterza, 2008.

Bruno, Giuliana. *Streetwalking on a Ruined Map: Cultural Theory and the City Films of Elvira Notari.* Princeton: Princeton University Press, 1993.

Campagnoni, Donata Pesente, and Carla Ceresa, eds. *Tracce: Documenti del cinema muto torinese del Museo nazionale del cinema.* Milan: Il Castoro, 2007.

Canosa, Michele, and Giulia Carluccio, eds. *Storia del cinema italiano*: vol. 3, *1912–1923.* Venice: Marsilio, forthcoming.

Carillo, Massimo. *Tra le quinte del cinematografo: cinema, cultura e società in Italia 1900–1937.* Bari: Edizioni Dedalo, 1987.

Dalle Vacche, Angela. *Diva: Defiance and Passion in Early Italian Cinema.* Austin: University of Texas Press, 2008.

Degrada, Elena, Elena Mosconi, and Silvio Paoli, eds. *Moltiplicare l'istante: Beltrami, Comerio e Pacchioni tra fotografia e cinema.* Milan: Il Castoro, 2007.

Flint, R. W., ed. and trans. *Marinetti: Selected Writings.* New York: Noonday Press, 1972.

Kirby, Michael, and Victoria Nes Kirby. *Futurist Performances.* New York: Dutton, 1971; rpt. New York: PAJ Publications, 1986.

Martinelli, Vittorio, ed. *Il cinema muto italiano: i film degli anni venti,* in two parts: *1921–1922, Bianco e nero* 42.1–3; *1923–1931, Bianco e nero* 42.4–6 (1981).

———. ed. *Il cinema muto italiano: i film del dopoguerra,* in two parts: *1919, Bianco e nero* 41.1–3; *1920, Bianco e nero* 41.4–6 (1980).

———. ed. *Le dive del silenzio.* Bologna: Le Mani, 2001.

Minici, Carlo Alberto Zotti, ed. *Il Mondo nuovo: Le meraviglie della visione dal '700 alla nascita del cinema*. Bassano del Grappa: Mazzotto, 1988.

Paolella, Roberto. *Storia del cinema muto*. Naples: Giannini, 1956.

Raffaelli, Sergio. *L'Italiano nel cinema muto*. Florence: Cesati, 2003.

Redi, Riccardo. *Ti parlerò . . . d'amor: cinema italiano fra muto e sonoro*. Turin: Edizioni ERI, 1986.

———. ed. *Cinema italiano muto 1905-1916*. Rome: CNC Edizioni, 1991.

Scaglione, Massimo. *Le dive del ventennio*. Turin: Lindau, 2003.

Tosi, Virgilio. *Il cinema prima del cinema*. Milan: Il Castoro, 2007; trans. *Cinema before Cinema: The Origins of Scientific Cinematography*. London: British Universities Film & Video, 2005.

Troianelli, Enza. *Elvira Notari: pioniera del cinema napoletano (1875-1946)*. Rome/Naples: Euroma–La Goliardica, 1989.

Verdone, Mario. *Cinema e letteratura del futurismo*. Rome: Edizioni di Bianco e Nero, 1968.

———. ed. *Poemi e scenari cinematografici d'avanguardia*. Rome: Officina Edizioni, 1975.

C. Sound and the Fascist Era

Aprà, Adriano, and Patrizia Pistagnesi, eds. *The Fabulous Thirties: Italian Cinema 1929-1944*. Milan: Electa International, 1979.

Argentieri, Mino. *L'occhio del regime*. Rome: Bulzoni, 2003.

Ben-Ghiat, Ruth. *La cultura fascista*. Bologna: Il Mulino, 2000. English edition: *Fascist Modernities: Italy, 1922-1945*. Berkeley: University of California Press, 2001.

Bernagozzi, Giampaolo. *Il mito dell'immagine*. Bologna: Editrice CLUEB, 1983.

Brancalini, Romano. *Celebri e dannati: Osvaldo Valenti e Luisa Ferida—storia e tragedia di due divi del regime*. Milan: Longanesi, 1985.

Brunetta, Gian Piero. *Cinema italiano tra le due guerre: fascismo e politica cinematografica*. Milan: Mursia, 1975.

Caldiron, Orio, ed. *Storia del cinema italiano*: vol. 5, *1934-1939*. Venice: Marsilio, 2006.

Carabba, Claudio. *Il cinema del ventennio nero*. Florence: Vallecchi, 1974.

Cardillo, Massimo. *Il duce in moviola: politica e divismo nei cinegiornali e documentari "Luce."* Bari: Edizioni Dedalo, 1983.

Casadio, Gianfranco. *Il grigio e il nero: spettacolo e propaganda nel cinema italiano degli anni Trenta (1931-1943)*. Ravenna: Longo, 1991.

Casadio, Gianfranco, Ernesto G. Laura, and Filippo Cristiano. *Telefoni bianchi: realtà e finzione nella società e nel cinema italiano degli anni Quaranta*. Ravenna: Longo, 1991.

Falasca-Zamponi, Simonetta. *Fascist Spectacles: The Aesthetics of Power in Mussolini's Italy*. Berkeley: University of California Press, 1997.

Fogu, Claudio. *The Historic Imaginary: Politics of History in Fascist Italy*. Toronto: University of Toronto Press, 2003.

Gili, Jean A. *L'Italie de Mussolini et son cinéma*. Paris: Henri Veyrier, 1985.

———. *Stato fascista e cinematografia: repressione e promozione*. Rome: Bulzoni, 1981.

Hay, James. *Popular Film Culture in Fascist Italy: The Passing of the Rex*. Bloomington: Indiana University Press, 1987.

Landy, Marcia. *Fascism in Film: The Italian Commercial Cinema, 1931–1943*. Princeton: Princeton University Press, 1986.

———. *The Folklore of Consensus: Theatricality in the Italian Cinema, 1930–1943*. Albany: State University of New York Press, 1998.

Laura, Ernesto G. *L'immagine bugiarda: mass-media e spettacolo nella Repubblica di Salò (1943–1945)*. Rome: ANCCI, 1987.

———. ed. *Storia del cinema italiano*: vol. 6, *1940–1944*. Venice: Marsilio, 2010.

Mancini, Elaine. *Struggles of the Italian Film Industry during Fascism, 1930–1935*. Ann Arbor: UMI Research Press, 1985.

Mida, Massimo, and Lorenzo Quaglietti, eds. *Dai telefoni bianchi al neorealismo*. Rome: Laterza, 1980.

Nuovi materiali sul cinema italiano 1929–1943. 2 vols. Ancona: Mostra internazionale del nuovo cinema, 1976.

Quaresima, Leonardo, ed. *Storia del cinema italiano*: vol. 4, *1924–1933*. Venice: Marsilio, forthcoming.

Redi, Riccardo, ed. *Cinema italiano sotto il fascismo*. Venice: Marsilio Editori, 1979.

———. ed. *Cinema scritto: il catalogo delle riviste italiane di cinema: 1907–1944*. Rome: Associazione italiana per le ricerche di storia del cinema, 1992.

Redi, Riccardo, and Claudio Camerini, eds. *Cinecittà 1: industria e mercato nel cinema italiano tra le due guerre*. Venice: Marsilio Editori, 1985.

Reich, Jacqueline, and Piero Garofalo, eds. *Re-viewing Fascism: Italian Cinema, 1922–1943*. Bloomington: Indiana University Press, 2002.

Ricci, Steven. *Cinema and Fascism: Italian Film and Society, 1922–1943*. Berkeley: University of California Press, 2008.

Savio, Francesco. *Ma l'amore no: realismo, formalismo, propaganda e telefoni bianchi nel cinema italiano di regime 1930–1943*. Milan: Sonzogno, 1975.

Short, R.K.M., ed. *Film & Radio Propaganda in World War II*. Knoxville: University of Tennessee Press, 1983.

Stone, Marla. *The Patron State: Culture & Politics in Fascist Italy*. Princeton: Princeton University Press, 1998.

Zagarrio, Vito. *Cinema e fascismo: film, modelli, immaginari*. Venice: Marsilio Editori, 2004.

D. Neorealism and Its Heritage: 1945–1968

Aprà, Adriano, and Claudio Carabba, eds. *Neorealismo d'appendice: per un dibattito sul cinema popolare—il caso Matarazzo*. Florence: Guaraldi, 1976.

Aristarco, Guido. *Antologia di "Cinema nuovo" 1952–1958: dalla critica cinematografica alla dialettica culturale*. Florence: Guaraldi, 1975.

———. *Sciolti dal giuramento: il dibattito critico-ideologico sul cinema negli anni Cinquanta*. Bari: Edizioni Dedalo, 1981.

Armes, Roy. *Patterns of Realism: A Study of Italian Neo-Realism*. Cranbury, N.J.: A. S. Barnes, 1971.

Bernagozzi, Giampaolo. *Il cinema corto: il documentario nella vita italiana 1945–1980*. Florence: La Casa Usher, 1980.

Bernardi, Sandro, ed. *Storia del cinema italiano*: vol. 9, *1954–1959*. Venice: Marsilio, 2004.

Bondanella, Peter. "From Italian Neorealism to the Golden Age of Cinecittà." In Elizabeth Ezra, ed. *European Cinema*. Oxford: Oxford University Press, 2004, pp. 119–38.

———. "Italian Neorealism." In Linda Badley, R. Barton Palmer, and Steven Jay Schneider, eds. *Traditions in World Cinema*. Edinburgh: University of Edinburgh Press, 2006, pp. 29–40.

Brunetta, Gian Piero. *Il cinema neorealista italiano: storia economica, politica, e culturale*. Rome Laterza, 2009.

Caldiron, Orio. *C'era una volta il '48: La grande stagione del cinema italiano*. Rome: Minimum Fax, 2008.

Canova, Gianni, ed. *Storia del cinema italiano*: vol. 11: *1965–1969*. Venice: Marsilio, 2002.

Canziani, Alfonso, and Cristina Bragaglia. *La stagione neorealista*. Bologna: Cooperativa Libraria Universitaria Editrice, 1976.

Capussotti, Enrica. *Gioventù perduta: Gli anni Cinquanta dei giovani e del cinema in Italia*. Florence: Giunti, 2004.

Casadio, Gianfranco. *Adultere, fedifranghe, innocenti: la donna del neorealismo popolare nel cinema italiano degli anni Cinquanta*. Ravenna: Longo, 1991.

Celant, Germano, ed. *The Italian Metamorphosis, 1943–1968*. New York: Guggenheim Museum, 1994 (also available as a CD-ROM of the same title).

Cosulich, Callisto, ed. *Storia del cinema italiano*: vol. 7, *1945–1948*. Venice: Marsilio, 2003.

d'Ardino, Laurent Scotto. *La Revue "Cinema" et le néo-realisme italien: autonomisation d'un champ esthétique*. Vincennes: Presses Universitaires de Vincennes, 1999.

Debreczeni, François, and Heinz Steinberg, eds. *Le néo-réalisme italien: bilan de la critique*. Études Cinématographiques, nos. 32–35. Paris: Lettres modernes Minard, 1964.

De Giusti, Luciano, ed. *Storia del cinema italiano*: vol. 8, *1949–1953*. Venice: Marsilio, 2003.

De Vincenti, Giorgio. *Storia del cinema italiano*: vol. 10, *1960–1964*. Venice: Marsilio, 2002.

Falaschi, Giovanni, ed. *Realtà e retorica: la letteratura del neorealismo italiano*. Florence: G. D'Anna, 1977.

Faldini, Franca, and Goffredo Fofi, eds. *L'avventurosa storia del cinema italiano raccontata dai suoi protagonisti 1935–1959*. Milan: Feltrinelli, 1979.

———. eds. *L'avventurosa storia del cinema italiano raccontata dai suoi protagonisti 1960–1969*. Milan: Feltrinelli, 1981.

Fanara, Giulia. *Pensare il neorealismo: Percorsi attraverso il neorealismo cinematografico italiano*. Rome: Lithos, 2000.

Farassino, Alberto, ed. *Neorealismo: cinema italiano 1945–1949*. Turin: EDT, 1989.

Ferrero, Adelio, Giovanna Grignaffini, and Leonardo Quaresima. *Il cinema italiano degli anni '60*. Florence: Guaraldi, 1977.

Ferretti, Gian Carlo, ed. *Introduzione al neorealismo*. Rome: Editori Riuniti, 1977.

Gaiardoni, Laura, ed. *Mario Serandrei, gli scritti: un film, "Giorni di Gloria."* Rome: Il Castoro, 1998.

Günsberg, Maggie. *Italian Cinema: Gender and Genre*. New York: Palgrave Macmillan, 2005.

Haaland, Torunn. *Italian Neorealist Cinema*, Edinburgh: Edinburgh University Press, 2013.

Kolker, Robert Phillip. *The Altering Eye: Contemporary International Cinema*. New York: Oxford University Press, 1983.

Marcus, Millicent. *Italian Film in the Light of Neorealism*. Princeton: Princeton University Press, 1986.

Materiali sul cinema italiano degli anni '50. Pesaro: Mostra internazionale del nuovo cinema, 1978.

Miccichè, Lino, ed. *Il neorealismo cinematografico italiano*. Venice: Marsilio Editori, 1975.

Morreale, Emiliano, ed. *Lo schermo di carta: Storia e storie dei cineromanzi*. Milan: Il Castoro, 2007 (includes DVD of 1950s cartoon versions of films that were extremely popular in the period).

Olivieri, Angelo. *L'imperatore in platea: i grandi del cinema italiano dal "Marc'Aurelio" allo schermo*. Bari: Edizioni Dedalo, 1986.

Overbey, David, ed. and trans. *Springtime in Italy: A Reader on Neo-Realism*. Hamden, Conn.: Archon Books, 1979.

Pellizzari, Lorenzo, ed. *Cineromanzo: il cinema italiano 1945–1953*. Milan: Longanesi, 1978.

Pintus, Pietro. *Storia e film: trent'anni di cinema italiano (1945–1975)*. Rome: Bulzoni, 1980.

Prédal, René, ed. *Le néoréalisme italien*. Special issue of *CinémAction* no. 70 (January 1994).

Re, Lucia. *Calvino and the Age of Neorealism: Fables of Estrangement*. Stanford: Stanford University Press, 1990.

———. "Neorealist Narrative: Experience and Experiment." In Peter Bondanella and Andrea Ciccarelli, eds. *The Cambridge Companion to the Italian Novel*. Cambridge: Cambridge University Press, 2003, pp. 104–24.

Restivo, Angelo. *The Cinema of Economic Miracles: Visuality and Modernization in the Italian Art Film (Post-Contemporary Interventions)*. Durham, N.C.: Duke University Press, 2002.

Rocchio, Vincent F. *Cinema of Anxiety: A Psychoanalysis of Italian Neorealism*. Austin: University of Texas Press, 1999.

Rossitti, Marco. *Il film a episodi in Italia tra gli anni cinquanta e settanta*. Bologna: Hybris, 2005.

Ruberto, Laura, and Kristi Wilson, eds. *Italian Neorealism and Global Realism*. Detroit: Wayne State University Press, 2007.

Shiel, Mark. *Italian Neorealism: Rebuilding the Cinematic City*. London: Wallflower Press, 2006.

Sitney, P. Adams. *Vital Crises in Italian Cinema: Iconography, Stylistics, Politics*. Austin: University of Texas Press, 1995; rpt. New York: Oxford University Press, 2013.

Steinmatsky, Noa. *Italian Locations: Reinhabiting the Past in Postwar Cinema*. Minneapolis: University of Minnesota Press, 2008.

Taylor, John Russell. *Cinema Eye, Cinema Ear*. New York: Hill and Wang, 1964.

Tinazzi, Giorgio, ed. *Il cinema italiano degli anni '50*. Venice: Marsilio Editori, 1979.

Tinazzi, Giorgio, and Marina Zancan, eds. *Cinema e letteratura del neorealismo.* Venice: Marsilio Editori, 1983.

Torriglia, Anna Maria. *Broken Time, Fragmented Space: A Cultural Map for Postwar Italy.* Toronto: University of Toronto Press, 2002.

Venti anni di cinema italiano nei saggi di ventotto autori. Rome: Sindicato nazionale giornalisti cinematografici italiani, 1965.

Villa, Federica. *Storia del cinema italiano:* vol. 11, *1965–1969.* Venice: Marsilio, 2002.

Vitzizzai, Elisabetta Chicco, ed. *Il neorealismo: antifascismo e popolo nella letteratura dagli anni trenta agli anni cinquanta.* Turin: Paravia, 1977.

Wagstaff, Chris. *Italian Neorealist Cinema: An Aesthetic Approach.* Toronto: University of Toronto Press, 2008.

Williams, Christopher, ed. *Realism and the Cinema: A Reader.* London: Routledge & Kegan Paul, 1980.

E. Italian Cinema from 1968 to the End of the Twentieth Century

Attolini, Vito. *Sotto il segno del film (cinema italiano 1968/1976).* Bari: Mario Adda, 1983.

Borra, Antonello, and Cristina Pausini. *Italian through Film: A Text for Italian Courses.* New Haven: Yale University Press, 2004.

Brunetta, Gian Piero. *Il cinema italiano contemporaneo da "La dolce vita" a "Centochiodi."* Rome: Laterza, 2007.

D'Arcangelo, Maresa, and Giovanni M. Rossi, eds. *1975/1985: gli anni maledetti del cinema italiano.* Florence: Mediateca Regionale Toscana, 1986.

De Bernardinis, Flavio. *Storia del cinema italiano:* vol. 12, *1970–1976.* Venice: Marsilio, 2009.

Dyer, Richard, and Ginette Vincendeau. *Popular European Cinema.* London: Routledge, 1992.

Eleftheriotis, Dimitris. *Popular Cinemas of Europe: Studies of Texts, Contexts and Frameworks.* New York: Continuum, 2001.

Faldini, Franca, and Goffredo Fofi, eds. *Il cinema italiano d'oggi 1970–1984 raccontato dai suoi protagonisti.* Milan: Mondadori, 1984.

Gieri, Manuela. *Contemporary Italian Filmmaking: Strategies of Subversion—Pirandello, Fellini, Scola, and the Directors of the New Generation.* Toronto: University of Toronto Press, 1995.

Kovács, András Bálint. *Screening Modernism: European Art Cinema, 1950–1980.* Chicago: University of Chicago Press, 2008.

Miccichè, Lino, ed. *Cinema italiano degli anni '70: cronache 1969–78.* Venice: Marsilio, 1980.

———. ed. *Il cinema italiano degli anni '60.* Venice: Marsilio, 1975.

Montini, Franco, ed. *Una generazione in cinema: esordi ed esordienti italiani 1975–1988.* Venice: Marsilio, 1988.

Morabito, Mimmo, ed. *Nostri autori prossimi venturi.* Florence: Mediateca Regionale Toscana, 1987.

Nowell-Smith, Geoffrey. *Making Waves: New Cinemas of the 1960s.* New York: Continuum, 2007.

Pirro, Ugo. *Soltanto un nome nei titoli di testa: i felici anni Sessanta del cinema italiano.* Turin: Einaudi, 1998.

Vannini, Andrea, ed. *1975/1985: le strane occasioni del cinema italiano—i registi e i film*. Florence: Mediateca Regionale Toscana, 1987.

Vighi, Fabio. *Traumatic Encounters in Italian Film: Locating the Cinematic Unconscious*. Bristol: Intellect, 2006.

Witcombe, Roger T. *The New Italian Cinema*. New York: Oxford University Press, 1982.

Zagarrio, Vito. *Cinema italiano anni novanta*. Venice: Marsilio, 1998; 2d ed. 2001.

———. ed. *Storia del cinema italiano*: vol. 13, *1977–1985*. Venice: Marsilio, 2005.

F. The New Italian Cinema: Beyond the Millennium

Cristiano, Anthony. *Contemporary Italian Cinema: Images of Italy at the Turn of the Century*. Polypus Press, 2008.

Eugeni, Ruggero, and Sandra Lischi, eds. *Storia del cinema italiano*: vol. 14, *1986–2000*. Venice: Marsilio, forthcoming.

Guerrini, Riccardo, Giacomo Tagliani, and Francesco Zucconi, eds. *Lo spazio del reale nel cinema italiano contemporaneo*. Bologna: Le Mani, 2009.

Hope, William, ed. *Italian Cinema: New Directions*. Oxford: Peter Lang, 2005.

Macchitella, Carlo. *Nuovo cinema italia: autori, industria, mercato—conversazione con Marianna Rizzini*. Venice: Marsilio, 2003.

Marcus, Millicent. *After Fellini: National Cinema in the Postmodern Age*. Baltimore: Johns Hopkins University Press, 2002.

Marrone, Gaetana. "The New Italian Cinema." In Elizabeth Ezra, ed. *European Cinema*. Oxford: Oxford University Press, 2004, pp. 233–49.

———. ed. *Annali d'Italianistica* 17 (1999). Special issue dedicated to "New Landscapes in Contemporary Italian Cinema."

Martini, Giulio, and Guglielmina Morelli, eds. *Patchwork due: geografia del nuovo cinema italiano*. Milan: Il Castoro, 1997.

Montini, Franco, ed. *Il cinema italiano del Terzo Millennio: I protagonisti della rinascita*. Turin: Lindau, 2002.

Sesti, Mario. *Nuovo cinema italiano: gli autori, i film, le idee*. Rome: Edizioni Theoria, 1994.

Zagarrio, Vito, ed. *La meglio gioventù: Nuovo cinema italiano 2005–2006*. Venice: Marsilio, 2006.

IV. Thematic or Generic Studies

A. Literature or the Sister Arts and Italian Cinema

Attolini, Vito. *Dal romanzo al set: cinema italiano dalle origini ad oggi*. Bari: Edizioni Dedalo, 1988.

Beccastrini, Stefano. *Il messaggio incompiuto: Masaccio e il cinema*. Florence: Aska, 2006.

Bonsaver, Guido, Martin McLaughlin, and Franca Pellegrini, eds. *Senergie narrative: Cinema e letteratura nell' Italia contemporanea*. Florence: Franco Cesati, 2008.

Bragaglia, Cristina. *Il piacere del racconto: narrativa italiana e cinema (1895–1990)*. Florence: La Nuova Italia, 1993.

Brunetta, Gian Piero, ed. *Letteratura e cinema*. Bologna: Zanichelli, 1976.

Càllari, Francesco. *Pirandello e il cinema*. Venice: Editori Marsilio, 1991.

Campari, Roberto. *Il fantasma del bello: iconologia del cinema italiano*. Venice: Marsilio, 1994.

Caputo, Roland. "Literary Cineastes: The Italian Novel and the Cinema." In Peter Bondanella and Andrea Ciccarelli, eds. *The Cambridge Companion to the Italian Novel*. Cambridge: Cambridge University Press, 2003, pp. 182–96.

Casadio, Gianfranco. *Opera e cinema*. Ravenna: Longo, 1995.

Costa, Antonio. *Cinema e pittura*. Turin: Loescher, 1991.

———. *Immagine di un'immagine: cinema e letteratura*. Turin: UTET, 1993.

———. *Il cinema e le arti visive*. Turin: Einaudi, 2002.

Dalle Vacche, Angela. *Cinema and Painting: How Art Is Used in Film*. Austin: University of Texas Press, 1996.

D'Avack, Massimo. *Cinema e letteratura*. Rome: Canesi, 1964.

Fumagalli, Armando. *I vestiti nuovi del narratore: l'adattamento da letteratura a cinema*. Milan: Il Castoro, 2004.

Galluzzi, Francesco. *Il cinema del pittore: Le arti e il cinema italiano 1940–1980*. Milan: Skira, 2007.

Geduld, Harry, ed. *Authors on Film*. Bloomington: Indiana University Press, 1972.

Gambacorti, Irene. *Storie di cinema e letteratura: Verga, Gozzano, D'Annunzio*. Florence: Società Editrice Fiorentina, 2003.

Guidorizzi, Ernesto. *La narrativa italiana e il cinema*. Florence: Sansoni, 1973.

Horton, Andrew S, and Joan Magretta, eds. *Modern European Filmmakers and the Art of Adaptation*. New York: Frederick Ungar, 1981.

Iannucci, Amilcare A., ed. *Dante, Cinema & Television*. Toronto: University of Toronto Press, 2004.

Lauretta, Enzo, ed. *Pirandello e il cinema*. Agrigento: Atti del Centro Nazionale di Studi Pirandelliani, 1978.

Marcus, Millicent. *Filmmaking by the Book: Italian Cinema and Literary Adaptation*. Baltimore: Johns Hopkins University Press, 1993.

McDougal, Stuart Y., ed. *Made into Movies: From Literature to Film*. New York: Holt, Rinehart & Winston, 1985.

Nichols, Nina Davinci, and Jana O'Keefe Bazzoni. *Pirandello & Film*. Lincoln: University of Nebraska Press, 1995.

Pellizzari, Lorenzo, ed. *L'avventura di uno spettatore: Italo Calvino e il cinema*. Bergamo: Pierluigi Lubrina, 1990.

Pirandello, Luigi. *Shoot! The Notebooks of Serafino Gubbio, Cinematograph Operator*. Trans. C. K. Scott Moncrieff. Chicago: University of Chicago Press, 2006.

Testa, Carlo. *Italian Cinema and Modern European Literatures: 1945–2000*. Westport, Conn.: Praeger, 2002.

———. *Masters of Two Arts: Re-creation of European Literatures in Italian Cinema*. Toronto: University of Toronto Press, 2002.

Vannini, Andrea, ed. *Vasco Pratolini e il cinema*. Florence: Edizioni La Bottega del Cinema, 1987.

Welle, John. "The Cinema of History: Film in Italian Poetry of the 1960s and 1970s." In John Butcher and Mario Moroni, eds. *From Eugenio Montale to Amelia Rosselli: Italian Poetry in the Sixties and Seventies*. Leicester: Troubadour, 2004, pp. 50–62.

———. "Dante in the Cinematic Mode: An Historical Survey of Dante Movies." In Mark Musa, ed. *Dante's Inferno: The Indiana Critical Edition*. Bloomington: Indiana University Press, 1995, pp. 381–95.

———. "Early Cinema, *Dante's Inferno* of 1911, and the Origins of Italian Film Culture." In Amilcare A. Iannucci, ed. *Dante, Cinema & Television*. Toronto: University of Toronto Press, 2004, pp. 21–50.

B. Women, Feminism, Sex, and Censorship in Italian Cinema

Argentieri, Mino. *La censura nel cinema italiano*. Rome: Editori Riuniti, 1974.

Baldi, Alfredo. *Schermi proibiti: La censura in Italia 1947–1988*. Venice: Marsilio Editori, 2003.

———. *Lo sguardo punito: Film censurati 1947–1962*. Rome: Bulzoni, 1994.

Baragli, Enrico, S.J. *Cinema cattolico: documenti della S. Sede sul cinema*. Rome: Città Nuova Editrice, 1965.

Boarini, Vittorio, ed. *Erotismo, eversione, merce*. Bologna: Cappelli, 1974.

Bruno, Giuliana, and Maria Nadotti, eds. *Offscreen: Women & Film in Italy*. London: Routledge, 1988.

Bruscolini, Elisabetta, ed. *Diveantidive del cinema italiano*. Venice: Marsilio, 2002.

Buttasi, Vanni, and Patrizia D'Agostino. *Dizionario del cinema hard: attori, attrici, registi e film*. Rome: Gremese, 2000.

Carrano, Patrizia. *Malafemmina: la donna nel cinema italiano*. Florence: Guaraldi, 1977.

Curti, Roberto, and Tommaso La Selva. *Sex and Violence: percorsi nel cinema estremo*. Turin: Lindau, 2003.

Fantuzzi, Virgilio. *Cinema sacro e profano*. Rome: Edizioni "La civiltà cattolica," 1983.

Gaudino, Luigi. *Cinema alla sbarra: Trent'anni di avventure e sventure giudiziarie del cinema italiano*. Udine: Forum Edizioni, 2007.

Giovannini, Fabio, and Antonio Tentori. *Porn'Italia: il cinema erotico italiano*. Viterno: Nuovi Equilibri, 2004.

Grazzini, Giovanni. *Eva dopo Eva: la donna nel cinema italiano dagli anni Sessanta a oggi*. Rome: Laterza, 1980.

Grossini, Giancarlo. *120 film di Sodoma: analisi del cinema pornografico*. Bari: Edizioni Dedalo, 1982.

Gundle, Stephen. *Bellissima: Feminine Beauty and the Idea of Italy*. New Haven: Yale University Press, 2007.

Jeffries, Giovanna Miceli. *Feminine Feminists: Cultural Practices in Italy*. Minneapolis: University of Minnesota Press, 1994.

Masi, Stefano, and Enrico Lancia. *Italian Movie Goddesses: Over 80 of the Greatest Women in Italian Cinema*. Trans. Lucia Alma Braconi, Charles Nopar, and Lenore Rosenburg. Rome: Gremese International, 1997.

Massaro, Gianni. *L'occhio impuro: cinema, censura e moralizzatori nell'Italia degli Anni Settanta*. Milan: SugarCo, 1976.

Mellen, Joan. *Women and their Sexuality in the New Film*. New York: Horizon Press, 1973.

Pastore, Sergio. *Proibitissimo: la censura nel tempo*. Naples: Adriano Gallina, 1980.

Turroni, Giuseppe. *Viaggio nel corpo: la commedia erotica nel cinema italiano*. Milan: Moizzi, 1979.

Tyler, Parker. *Screening the Sexes: Homosexuality in the Movies*. New York: Doubleday, 1973.

C. Italian Film Comedy

Aprà, Adriano, and Patrizia Pistagnesi, eds. *Comedy, Italian Style 1950–1980*. Turin: Edizioni RAI, 1986.

Argentieri, Mino, ed. *Risate di regime: la commedia italiana 1930–1944*. Venice: Marsilio, 1991.

Commedia sexy all'italiana. Milan: Mediane, 2007 (sound track collection on CD with accompanying book).

d'Amico, Masolino. *La commedia all'italiana: il cinema comico in Italia dal 1945 al 1975*. Milan: Mondadori, 1985.

Gili, Jean A. *Arrivano i mostri: i volti della commedia italiana*. Bologna: Cappelli, 1980.

———. *La comédie italienne*. Paris: Henri Veyrier, 1983.

Giacovelli, Enrico. *La commedia all'italiana: La storia, i luoghi, gli autori, gli attori, i film*. Rome: Gremese, 1995. 2d rev. ed.

Giordano, Michele. *La commedia erotica italiana: vent'anni di cinema sexy "made in Italy."* Rome: Gremese, 2002.

Lanzoni, Rémi. *Comedy Italian Style: The Golden Age of Italian Film Comedies*. New York: Continuum, 2008.

Laura, Ernesto G. *Comedy Italian Style*. Rome: ANICA, n.d.

———. *Italian History, Comedy Style*. Rome: ANICA, n.d.

Mast, Gerald. *The Comic Mind: Comedy and the Movies*. Indianapolis: Bobbs-Merrill, 1973.

Salizzato, Claver, and Vito Zagarrio, eds. *Effetto commedia: teoria, generi, paesaggi della commedia cinematografica*. Rome: Di Giacomo, 1985.

Serceau, Michel, ed. *La comédie italienne de Don Camillo à Berlusconi. CinémAction* 42 (March 1987).

Trionfera, Claudio, ed. *Age & Scarpelli in commedia*. Rome: Di Giacomo, 1990.

D. Political or Historical Themes and Film Genres

Argentieri, Mino, and Angelo Turchini. *Cinema e vita contadina: "Il mondo degli ultimi" di Gian Butturini*. Bari: Edizioni Dedalo, 1984.

Bertelli, Sergio, with Ileana Florescu. *Corsari del tempo: quando il cinema inventa la storia (guida pratica per registi distratti)*. Florence: Edizioni Ponte alle Grazie, 1994.

Bondanella, Peter. *Hollywood Italians: Dagos, Palookas, Romeos, Wise Guys, and Sopranos*. New York: Continuum, 2004.

Bouchard, Norma. *Risorgimento in Modern Italian Culture: Revisiting the Nineteenth-Century Past in History, Narrative, and Cinema*. Madison, N.J.: Fairleigh Dickinson University Press, 2005.

Brunetta, Gian Piero, Roberto Campari, Marcello Flores, Peppino Ortoleva, Pierre Sorlin, and Nicola Tranfaglia, eds. *La cinepresa e la storia: fascismo, antifascismo, guerra e resistenza nel cinema italiano*. Milan: Edizioni scolastiche Bruno Mondadori, 1985.

Carotti, Carlo. *Alla ricerca del paradiso: l'operaio nel cinema italiano, 1945–1990*. Genoa: Graphos, 1992.

Casadio, Gianfranco. *La guerra al cinema: i film di guerra nel cinema italiano*. 2 vols. 1, *Dal Risorgimento alla seconda guerra mondiale*. 2, *Dalla seconda guerra mondiale alla Resistenza*. Ravenna: Longo, 1997–78.

Casella, Paola. *Hollywood Italian: Gli italiani nell'America di celluloide*. Milan: Baldini & Castoldi, 1998.

Clarke, David B., ed. *The Cinematic City*. London: Routledge, 1997.

Fink, Guido. "Ferrara e il cinema," in two parts: I, "Dai primordi fino alla seconda guerra mondiale" and II, "Ferrara e il cinema dal dopoguerra." In Francesca Bocchi, ed. *Storia illustrata di Ferrara*, vol. 4. Milan: Nuova Editoriale AIEP, 1989, pp. 1009–24 and 1025–40.

Fontanelli, Mario, ed. *Emilia–Romagna, terra di cineasti: antologia di testi, interviste e saggi critici*. Parma: Grafiche STEP, 1990.

Freda, Riccardo. *Divoratori di celluloide: 50 anni di memorie cinematografiche e non*. Ed. Goffredo Fofi and Patrizia Pistagnesi. Rome: Il Formichiere, 1981.

Gili, Jean A., ed. *Fascisme et résistance dans le cinéma italien (1922–1968)*. Études Cinématographiques, nos. 82–83. Paris: Lettres modernes Minard, 1970.

Gori, Gianfranco, ed. *Passato ridotto: gli anni del dibattito su cinema e storia*. Florence: La Casa Usher, 1982.

———. ed. *La storia al cinema: ricostruzione del passato, interpretazione del presente*. Rome: Bulzoni, 1994.

Landy, Marcia. *Cinematic Uses of the Past*. Minneapolis: University of Minnesota Press, 1996.

———. *Film, Politics, and Gramsci*. Minneapolis: University of Minnesota Press, 1994.

Marcus, Millicent. *Italian Film in the Shadow of Auschwitz*. Toronto: University of Toronto Press, 2007.

Michalczyk, John J. *The Italian Political Filmmakers*. Rutherford, N.J.: Fairleigh Dickinson University Press, 1986.

Muscio, Giovanna, and Giovanni Spagnoletti, eds. *Quei bravi ragazzi: il cinema italoamericano contemporaneo*. Venice: Marsilio, 2007.

Pesce, Sara. *Memoria e immaginario: La seconda guerra mondiale nel cinema italiano*. Bologna: Le Mani-Microart's, 2008.

Ravetto, Kriss. *The Unmasking of Fascist Aesthetics*. Minneapolis: University of Minnesota Press, 2001.

Rosenstone, Robert A., ed. *Revisioning History: Film and the Construction of a New Past*. Princeton: Princeton University Press, 1995.

Sorlin, Pierre. *European Cinemas, European Societies 1939–1990*. New York: Routledge, 1991.

———. *The Film in History: Restaging the Past*. Oxford: Basil Blackwell, 1980.

Zanotto, Piero, and Fiorello Zangrando. *L'Italia di cartone*. Padua: Livia Editrice, 1973.

E. The B-Film Genres of the Golden Age

1. The "Peplum," or "Sword and Sandal," Epic

Bondanella, Peter. *The Eternal City: Roman Images in the Modern World*. Chapel Hill: University of North Carolina Press, 1987.

Brunetta, Gian Piero, and Jean A. Gili, eds. *L'ora d'Africa del cinema italiano 1911–1989*. Mori, Trent: La Grafica, 1990.

Cammarota, Domenico. *Il cinema peplum: La prima guida critica ai film di Conan, Ercole, Goliath, Maciste, Sansone, Spartaco, Thaur, Ursus.* Rome: Fanucci, 1987.

Casadio, Gianfranco. *I mitici eroi: il cinema "peplum" nel cinema italiano dall'avvento del sonoro ad oggi (1930–1993).* Ravenna: Longo, 2007.

Elley, Derek. *The Epic Film: Myth and History.* London: Routledge & Kegan Paul, 1984.

Farassino, Alberto, and Tatti Sanguineti, eds. *Gli uomini forti.* Milan: Mazzotta, 1983.

Giordano, Michele. *Giganti buoni: da Ercole a Piedone (e oltre): il mito dell'uomo forte nel cinema italiano.* Rome: Gremese, 1998.

Joshel, Sandra R., Margaret Malamud, and Donald T. McGuire Jr., eds. *Projections: Ancient Rome in Modern Popular Culture.* Baltimore: Johns Hopkins University Press, 2001.

Lucanio, Patrick. *With Fire and Sword: Italian Spectacles on American Screens 1958–1968.* Metuchen, N.J.: Scarecrow Press, 1994.

Malamud, Margaret. *Ancient Rome and Modern America.* West Sussex: John Wiley, 2009.

Solomon, Jon. *The Ancient World in the Cinema.* Cranbury, N.J.: A. S. Barnes, 1978; rev. and expanded ed., New Haven: Yale University Press, 2001.

Winkler, Martin M., ed. *Classical Myth & Culture in the Cinema.* Oxford and New York: Oxford University Press, 2001.

———. ed. *Gladiator: Film and History.* Oxford: Blackwell, 2004.

Wyke, Maria. "Italian Cinema and History." In Valentina Vitali and Paul Willemen, eds. *Theorising National Cinema.* London: British Film Institute, 2006, pp. 61–71.

———. *Projecting the Past: Ancient Rome, Cinema and History.* New York: Routledge, 1997.

2. The Spaghetti Western

Beatrice, Luca. *Al cuore, Ramon, al cuore: la leggenda del western all'italiana.* Florence: Tarab, 1996.

Casadio, Gianfranco. *Se sei vivo, spara! Storie di pistoleri, banditi e bounty killers nel western all'italiana (1942–1998).* Ravenna: Longo, 2004.

Cawelti, John G. *The Six-Gun Mystique.* Bowling Green, Ohio: Bowling Green State University Popular Press, 1970.

Ferrini, Franco, ed. *L'antiwestern e il caso Leone.* Special issue of *Bianco e Nero* (nos. 9–10). Rome: Società Gestioni Editoriali, 1971.

Frayling, Christopher. *Spaghetti Westerns: Cowboys and Europeans from Karl May to Sergio Leone.* London: Routledge & Kegan Paul, 1981; rev. ed. London: I. B. Tauris, 2006.

Giusti, Marco. *Dizionario del western all'italiana.* Milan: Mondadori, 2007.

Hughes, Howard. *Once Upon a Time in the Italian West: The Filmgoers' Guide to Spaghetti Westerns.* London: I. B. Tauris, 2004.

Morricone western. Milan: Mediane, 2006 (sound track collection on CD with accompanying book).

Moscati, Massimo. *Western all'italiana: guida ai 407 film, ai registi, agli attori.* Milan: Pan Editrice, 1978.

Nachbar, Jack, ed. *Focus on the Western.* Englewood Cliffs, N.J.: Prentice-Hall, 1974.

Roth, Lane. *Film Semiotics, Metz, and Leone's Trilogy.* New York: Garland, 1983.

Staig, Laurence, and Tony Williams. *Italian Western: The Opera of Violence.* London: Lorrimer, 1975.

Weisser, Thomas. *Spaghetti Westerns: The Good, the Bad and the Violent—A Comprehensive, Illustrated Filmography of 558 Eurowesterns and Their Personnel, 1961–1977.* Jefferson, N.C.: McFarland, 1992.

3. *The Spaghetti Horror, Cannibal, Zombie, and Exploitation Films*

Balun, Chas. *Beyond Horror Holocaust: A Deeper Shade of Red.* Key West, Fla.: Fantasma Books, 2003.

Fenton, Harvey, Julian Grainger, and Gian Luca Castoldi, eds. *Cannibal Holocaust and the Savage Cinema of Ruggero Deodato.* London: Fab Press, 1999.

Harper, Jim. *Italian Horror.* Baltimore: Luminary Press, 2005.

———. *Legacy of Blood: A Comprehensive Guide to Slasher Movies.* Manchester: Headpress/Critical Vision, 2004.

Lupi, Gordiano. *Cannibal: Il cinema selvaggio di Ruggero Deodato.* Rome: Mondo Ignoto, 2003.

Manti, Davide. *Ca(u)se perturbanti: Architetture horror dentro e fuori lo schermo—Fonti, figure, temi.* Turin: Lindau, 2003.

Martin, John. *Cannibal: The Most Disgusting Consumer Guide Ever!* Liskeard: Straycat, 2007.

Mathijs, Ernest, and Xavier Mendik, eds. *Alternative Europe: Eurotrash and Exploitation Cinema since 1945.* London: Wallflower Press, 2004.

Morsiani, Alberto, ed. *Rosso italiano (1977/1987): dieci anni di horror con Argenti, Bava, Fulci e . . . gli altri.* Modena: Avofilm, 1988.

Palmerini, Luca M., and Gaetano Mistretta. *Spaghetti Nightmares: Italian Fantasy—Horrors as Seen through the Eyes of Their Protagonists.* Key West, Fla.: Fantasma Books, 1996.

Paul, Louis. *Italian Horror Film Directors.* Jefferson, N.C.: McFarland, 2005.

McCallum, Lawrence. *Italian Horror Films of the 1960s: A Critical Catalog of 62 Chillers.* Jefferson, N.C.: McFarland, 2002.

Rhodes, Gary D., ed. *Horror at the Drive-In: Essays in Popular Americana.* Jefferson, N.C.: McFarland, 2003.

Schneider, Stephen Jay, and Tony Williams, eds. *Horror International.* Detroit: Wayne State University Press, 2005.

Slater, Jay, ed. *Eaten Alive! Italian Cannibal and Zombie Movies.* London: Plexus, 2002.

Stine, Scott Aaron. *The Gorehound's Guide to Splatter Films of the 1980s.* Jefferson, N.C.: McFarland, 2003.

Tohill, Cathal, and Pete Tombs. *Immoral Tales: European Sex and Horror Movies 1956–1984.* New York: St. Martin's Griffin, 1995.

4. *The Italian* Giallo, *or Mystery Thriller*

Boyd, David, and B. Barton Palmer, eds. *After Hitchcock: Influence, Imitation, and Intertextuality.* Austin: University of Texas Press, 2006.

Crovi, Luca. *Tutti i colori del giallo: il giallo italiano da De Marchi a Scerbanenco a Camilleri.* Venice: Marsilio, 2002.

Forlai, Luigi, and Augusto Bruni. *Detective thriller e noir: Teoria e tecnica della narrazione.* Rome: Dino Audino, 2003.

Giuffrida, Sergio, and Riccardo Mazzoni, eds. *Giallo: poliziesco, thriller e detective story.* Milan: Leonardo Arte, 1999.

Koven, Mikel J. *La Dolce Morte: Vernacular Cinema and the Italian "Giallo" Film.* Lanham, Md.: Scarecrow Press, 2006.

Navarro, Antonio José, ed. *El giallo italiano: La oscuridad y la sangre.* Madrid: Nuer Ediciones, 2001.

Rea, Luca. *I colori del buio: Il cinema thrilling italiano dal 1930 al 1979.* Florence: Igor Molino, 1999.

Smith, Adrian Luther. *Blood & Black Lace: The Definitive Guide to Italian Sex and Horror Movies.* Liskeard: Straycat, 2000.

——. *The Delirium Guide to Italian Exploitation Cinema 1975–1979.* London: Media Publications, 1997.

5. The Italian Poliziesco *Film*

Attori a mano armata: The Main Actors of the Most Violent Season of the Italian Cinema. Milan: Mediane, 2007 (sound track collection on CD with accompanying book).

Casadio, Gianfranco. *Col cuore in gola: assassini, ladri e poliziotti nel cinema italiano dal 1930 ad oggi.* Ravenna: Longo, 2002.

Curti, Roberto. *Italia odia: il cinema poliziesco italiano.* Turin: Lindau, 2006.

Magni, Daniele, and Silvio Giobbio. *Cinici, infami e violenti: guida ai film polizieschi italiani anni '70.* Milan: Bloodbuster, 2005.

Padovani, Gisella, and Rita Verdirame, eds. *L'almanacco del delitto: I racconti polizieschi del "Cerchio Verde."* Palermo: Sellerio, 1996.

Tomas Milian: The Tough Bandit, The Rough Cop, and the Filthy Rat in Italian Cinema / Il bandito, lo sbirro e Er Monnezza. Milan: Mediane, 2007 (sound track collection on CD with accompanying book).

Torlasco, Domietta. *The Time of the Crime: Phenomenology, Psychoanalysis, Italian Film.* Palo Alto: Stanford University Press, 2008.

F. Miscellaneous Topics

Albano, Lucilla. *Lo schermo dei sogni: Chiavi psicoanalitiche del cinema.* Venice: Marsilio, 2004.

Arosio, Mario, Giuseppe Cereda, and Franca Iseppi. *Cinema e cattolici in Italia.* Milan: Editrice Massimo, 1974.

Bandy, Mary Lea, and Antonio Monda, eds. *The Hidden God: Film and Faith.* New York: Museum of Modern Art, 2003.

Basili, Giancarlo. *Spazio e architettura nel cinema italiano.* Ed. Gianni Canova. Ancona: Alexa Edizioni, 2000.

Beccastrini, Stefano. *Un tessuto d'armonie profonde: l'Umbria e il cinema.* Florence: Aska, 2003.

——.*Vista nova: Il cinema in Toscana, la Toscana nel cinema.* Florence: Aska, 2002.

Bellocchio, Lella Ravasi. *Gli occhi d'oro: il cinema nella stanza dell'analisi*. Bergamo: Moretti & Vitali, 2004.

Bernardi, Sandro. *Il paesaggio nel cinema italiano*. Venice: Marsilio, 2004.

Bertozzi, Marc. *L'idea documentaria: Altri sguardi dal cinema italiano*. Turin: Lindau, 2003.

——. *L'occhio e la pietra: Il cinema, una cultura urbana*. Turin: Lindau, 2003.

——. *Storia del documentario italiano: Immagini e culture dell'altro cinema*. Venice: Marsilio, 2008.

Brunetta, Gian Piero. *Il colore dei sogni: Iconografia e memoria nel manifesto cinematografico italiano*. Chieri: Testo & Immagine, 2002.

Bruscolini, Elisabetta. *Rome in Cinema between Fiction and Reality*. Rome: Fondazione Scuola Nazionale di Cinema, 2001.

Cattini, Alberto. *Strutture e poetiche nel cinema italiano*. Rome: Bulzoni, 2002.

Curi, Umberto. *Lo schermo del pensiero: Cinema e filosofia*. Milan: Raffaello Cortini, 2000.

Delli Colli, Laura. *Il gusto del cinema italiano in 100 recette*. Milan: Elle U Multimedia, 2002.

Di Biagi, Flaminio. *Il cinema a Roma: Guida alla storia e ai luoghi del cinema nella capitale*. Rome: Palombi, 2003.

Della Casa, Steve. *Italiana: Il cinema attraversa l'Italia*. Milan: Electa Mondadori, 2005.

Di Marino, Bruno. *L'ultimo fotogramma: I finali nel cinema*. Rome: Editori Riuniti, 2001.

Giuliani, Gianna. *Le strisce interiori: cinema italiano e psicoanalisi*. Rome: Bulzoni, 1980.

Kehr, Dave. *Italian Film Posters*. New York: Museum of Modern Art, 2003.

Lapertosa, Viviana. *Dalla fame all'abbondanza: Gli italiani e il cibo nel cinema italiano dal dopoguerra a oggi*. Turin: Lindau, 2002.

Lev, Peter. *The Euro-American Cinema*. Austin: University of Texas Press, 1993.

Menarini, Roy. *La parodia nel cinema italiano*. Bologna: Alberto Perdisa, 2001.

Ruggeri, Giovanni, and Mario Guarino. *Berlusconi: inchiesta sul signor TV*. Rome: Editori Riuniti, 1987.

Scrocco, Francesco J., Paolo Taggi, and Adriano Zanacchi. *Spot in Italy: 30 anni di pubblicità televisiva italiana*. Turin: Edizioni ERI, 1987.

Vitti, Antonio, ed. *Incontri con il cinema italiano*. Caltanissetta-Roma: Salvatore Sciascia, 2003.

West, Rebecca, ed. *Pagina Pellicola Pratica: Studi sul cinema italiano*. Ravenna: Longo, 2000.

Wrigley, Richard, ed. *Cinematic Rome*. Leicester: Troubador Press, 2008.

V. Studies of Individual Actors

Alberico, Giulia. *Il corpo gentile: Conversazione con Massimo Girotti*. Rome: Luca Sossella, 2003.

Bernardini, Aldo. *Nino Manfredi*. Rome: Gremese, 1999.

Bernardini, Aldo, and Claudio G. Fava. *Ugo Tognazzi*. Rome: Gremese, 1978; 2d ed., 1985.

Bertolino, Marco, and Ettore Ridola. *Franco Franchi e Ciccio Ingrassia*. Rome: Gremese, 2003.

———. *Bud Spencer & Terence Hill*. Rome: Gremese, 2002.

Buratto, Fabrizio. *Fantozzi: una maschera italiana*. Turin: Lindau, 2003.

Caldiron, Orio. *Totò*. Rome: Gremese, 1980.

———. ed. *"Totò a colori" di Steno: Il film, il personaggio, il mito*. Rome: Edizioni Interculturali, Federazione Italiana Circoli del Cinema, 2003.

Cammarota, Domenico. *Il cinema di Totò*. Rome: Fanucci, 1986.

Caputo, Marcello Gagliani, ed. *. . . . Altrimenti ci arrabbiamo: Il cinema di Bud Spencer e Terence Hill*. Rome: Un Mondo a Parte, 2008.

Carrano, Patrizia. *La Magnani*. Milan: Rizzoli, 1986 (preface by Federico Fellini); rpt. Turin: Lindau, 2004.

Causo, Massimo, ed. *Tognazzi: l'alterUgo del cinema italiano*. Nardò: BESA, 2001.

Degioanni, Bernard. *Vittorio Gassman*. Paris: Éditions PAC, 1980.

De Berti, Raffaele. *Un secolo di cinema a Milano*. Milan: Il Castoro, 1996.

Della Casa, Stefano, and Franco Prono, eds. *Torino città del cinema*. Milan: Il Castoro, 2001.

Delli Colli, Laura. *Monica Vitti*. Rome: Gremese, 1987.

Deriu, Fabrizio. *Gian Maria Volontè: il lavoro d'attore*. Rome: Bulzoni, 1997.

Detassis, Piera, and Mario Sesti, eds. *Bellissimi: generazioni di attori a confronto—L'ultima onda" del cinema italiano e la grande tradizione del dopoguerra*. Ancona: Il Lavoro Editoriale, 1987.

Diva italiana: An Exclusive Collection of Rare Photos. Milan: Mediane, 2005 (sound track collection on CD with accompanying book).

Divo italiano: An Exclusive Collection of Rare Photos of the Italian Movie Stars. Milan: Mediane, 2006 (sound track collection on CD with accompanying book).

Faldini, Franca, and Goffredo Fofi. *Totò: l'uomo e la maschera*. Milan: Felltrinelli, 1977; *Totò*. 2d rev. ed. Naples: Tullio Pironti, 1987.

———. *Totò: Storia di un buffone serissimo*. Milan: Mondadori, 2004.

Fava, Claudio G. *Alberto Sordi*. Rome: Gremese, 1979.

Fava, Claudio G., and Matilde Hochkofler. *Marcello Mastroianni*. Rome: Gremese, 1980.

Fabrizi, Aldo. *Ciavéte fatto caso?* Ed. Marco Giusto. Milan: Mondadori, 2004 (book and videocassette).

Fofi, Goffredo. *Alberto Sordi: l'Italia in bianco e nero*. Milan: Mondadori, 2004.

Francione, Fabio, and Lorenzo Pellizzari, eds. *Ugo Tognazzi regista*. Alessandria: Edizioni Falsopiano, 2002.

Gambetti, Giacomo. *Vittorio Gassman*. Rome: Gremese, 1982.

Gassman, Vittorio. *Un grande avvenire dietro le spalle: vita, amori e miracoli di un mattatore narrati da lui stesso*. Milan: Longanesi, 1981.

Guback, Thomas A. *The International Film Industry: Western Europe and America since 1945*. Bloomington: Indiana University Press, 1994.

Gubitosi, Giuseppe. *Amedeo Nazzari*. Bologna: Il Mulino, 1998.

Harris, Warren G. *Sophia Loren: A Biography*. New York: Simon & Schuster, 1998.

Hochkofler, Matilde. *Anna Magnani*. Rome: Gremese, 1984.

———. *Anna Magnani: Lo spettacolo della vita*. Rome: Bulzoni, 2005.

Kezich, Tullio. *Giulietta Masina*. Bologna: Cappelli, 1991.

———. *Giulietta Masina (La Chaplin Mujer): Entrevista realizada por Tullio Kezich.* València: Fernando Torres, 1985.

Landy, Marcia. *Stardom, Italian Style: Screen Performance and Personality in Italian Cinema.* Bloomington: Indiana University Press, 2008.

Laura, Ernesto G. *Alida Valli.* Rome: Gremese, 1979.

Lupi, Gordiano. *Le dive nude: Edwige Fenech e Gloria Guida.* Rome: Mondo Ignoto, 2006.

———. *Tomas Milian, il trucido e lo sbirro.* Rome: Mondo Ignoto, 2004.

Masi, Stefano. *Roberto Benigni Superstar.* Trans. Sandra E. Tokunaga. Rome: Gremese International, 1999.

Masi, Stefano, and Enrico Lancia. *Italian Movie Goddesses.* Rome: Gremese, 1997.

———. *Sophia Loren.* Rome: Gremese, 1985.

Mingozzi, Gianfranco, ed. *Francesca Bertini.* Bologna: Le Mani, 2003.

Montini, Franco, and Piero Spila, eds. *Gian Maria Volontè: Un attore contro.* Milan: Rizzoli, 2004 (book with DVD by Ferruccio Marotti).

Moscati, Italo. *Anna Magnani: Vita, amori e carriera di un'attrice che guarda dritto negli occhi.* Rome: Ediesse, 2003.

———. *Gioco perverso: La vera storia di Osvaldo Valenti e Luisa Ferida, tra Cinecittà e guerra civile.* Turin: Lindau, 2007.

———. *Sophia Loren: La storia dell'ultima diva.* Turin: Lindau, 2005.

Navarro, Giorgio, and Fabio Zanello. *Tomas Milian: Er cubbano de Roma.* Florence: Igor Molino, 1999.

Pistagnesi, Patrizia, ed. *Anna Magnani.* Milan: Fabbri, 1988.

Ponzi, Maurizio. *Gina Lollobrigida.* Rome: Gremese, 1982.

Pruzzo, Pierro, and Enrico Lancia. *Amedeo Nazzari.* Rome: Gremese, 1983.

Reich, Jacqueline. *Beyond the Latin Lover: Marcello Mastroianni, Masculinity, and Italian Cinema.* Bloomington: Indiana University Press, 2004.

Tatò, Francesco, ed. *The Stuff That Dreams Are Made Of: The Films of Marcello Mastroianni.* Rome: Cinecittà International, 1998.

Small, Pauline. *Sophia Loren: Moulding the Star.* Bristol: Intellect, 2009.

Tognazzi, Ugo. *L'abbuffone: Storie da ridere e ricette da morire.* Cava de' Tirreni: Avagliano, 2004.

VI. Economic or Sociological Analyses of Italian Cinema (Including Film Studios, Producers, and Related Governmental Institutions)

Alloway, Lawrence. *The Venice Biennale 1895–1968: From Salon to Goldfish Bowl.* Greenwich, Conn.: New York Graphic Society, 1968.

Aprà, Adriano, Giuseppe Ghigi, and Patrizia Pistagnesi, eds. *Cinquant'anni di cinema a Venezia.* Venice: Edizioni RAI, 1982.

Barlozzetti, Guido, Stefania Parigi, Angela Prudenzi, and Claver Salizzato, eds. *Modi di produzione del cinema italiano: La Titanus.* Rome: Di Giacomo, 1985.

Bernardini, Aldo, and Vittorio Martinelli, eds. *Titanus: la storia e tutti i film di una grande casa di produzione.* Milan: Coliseum, 1986.

Bizzarri, Libero. *Il cinema italiano: industria, mercato, pubblico.* Rome: Edizioni Gulliver, 1987.

Bizzarri, Libero, and Libero Solaroli. *L'industria cinematografica italiana.* Florence: Parenti, 1958.

Brunetta, Gian Piero, ed. *Identità italiana e identità europea nel cinema italiano dal 1945 al miracolo economico.* Turin: Edizioni della Fondazione Giovanni Agnelli, 1996.

Campari, Roberto. *Hollywood–Cinecittà: il racconto che cambia.* Milan: Feltrinelli, 1980.

Casetti, Francesco, ed. *La cineteca italiana: una storia milanese.* Milan: Il Castoro, 2005.

Chiarini, Luigi. *Un leone e altri animali: cinema e contestazione alla Mostra di Venezia 1968.* Milan: Sugar, 1969.

Contaldo, Francesco, and Franco Fanelli. *L'affare cinema: multinazionali, produttori, e politici nella crisi del cinema italiano.* Milan: Feltrinelli, 1979.

Corsi, Barbara. *Con qualche dollaro in meno: storia economica del cinema italiano.* Rome: Editori Riuniti, 2001.

Del Buono, Oreste, and Lietta Tornabuoni, eds. *Era Cinecittà: vita, morte e miracoli di una fabbrica di film.* Milan: Bompiani, 1979.

Della Fornace, Luciana. *Il film in Italia dalla ideazione alla proiezione: strutture e processi dell'industria cinematografica.* Rome: Bulzoni, 1978.

Di Monte, Ezio, Amedeo Fago, and Roberto Farina, eds. *La città del cinema (produzione e lavoro nel cinema italiano 1930/1970).* Rome: Editrice Roberto Napoleone, 1979.

Farassino, Alberto, and Tatti Sanguineti. *Lux Film: Esthétique et système d'un studio italien.* Locarno: Éditions du Festival international du Film de Locarno, 1984; Italian ed., Alberto Farassino. *Lux Film.* Milan: Il Castoro, 2000.

Franchi, Mariagrazia, and Elena Mosconi. *Spettatori: forme di consumo e pubblici del cinema in Italia 1930–1960.* Venice: Marsilio, 2002.

Freddi, Luigi. *Il cinema.* 2 vols. Rome: L'Arnia, 1949; rpt. as *Il cinema: il governo dell'immagine.* Rome: Gremese, 1994.

Grassi, Giovanna, ed. *L'altro schermo: libro bianco sui cineclub, le sale d'essai e i punti di diffusione cinematografica alternativa.* Venice: Marsilio, 1978.

Huaco, George A. *The Sociology of Film Art.* New York: Basic Books, 1965.

Ivaldi, Nedo. *La prima volta a Venezia: mezzo secolo di Mostra del cinema nei ricordi della critica.* Padua: Edizioni Studio Tesi, 1982.

Kaufman, Hank, and Gene Lerner. *Hollywood sul Tevere.* Milan: Sperling & Kupfer Editori, 1982.

Kezich, Tullio, and Alessandra Levantesi. *Dino: De Laurentiis, la vita e i film.* Turin: Feltrinelli, 2001. Eng. ed. *Dino: The Life and the Films of Dino De Laurentiis.* Trans. James Marcus. New York: Miramax Books/Hyperion, 2004.

Laura, Ernesto G., ed. *Tutti i film di Venezia 1932–1984.* 2 vols. Venice: La Biennale, 1985.

Macchitella, Carlo, and Alberto Abruzzese, eds. *Cinemitalia 2005: Sogni, industria, tecnologia, mercato.* Venice: Marsilio, 2005.

Magrelli, Enrico, ed. *Sull'industria cinematografica italiana.* Venice: Marsilio Editori, 1986.

Mariotti, Franco, ed. *Cinecittà tra cronaca e storia 1937–1989.* 2 vols. Rome: Presidenza del Consiglio dei Ministri, 1989.

Monicelli, Mino, ed. *Cinema italiano: ma cos'è questa crisi?* Bari: Laterza, 1979.

Nowell-Smith, Geoffrey, and Steven Ricci, eds. *Hollywood & Europe: Economics, Culture, National Identity 1945–95.* London: British Film Institute, 1998.

Quaglietti, Lorenzo. *Storia economico-politica del cinema italiano 1945–1980.* Rome: Editori Riuniti, 1980.

Redi, Riccardo. *La Cines: Storia di una casa di produzione italiana.* Rome: CNC Edizioni, 1991.

Redi, Riccardo, and Claudio Camerini, eds. *Cinecittà 1: industria e mercato nel cinema italiano tra le due guerre.* Venice: Marsilio Editori, 1985.

Repetto, Monica, and Carlo Tagliabue, eds. *La vita è bella? Il cinema italiano alla fine degli anni Novanta e il suo pubblico.* Milan: Il Castoro, 2000.

Rocca, Carmelo. *Le leggi del cinema: Il contesto italiano nelle politiche comunitarie.* Franco Angeli, 2003.

Savio, Francesco. *Cinecittà anni trenta: parlano 116 protagonisti del secondo cinema italiano (1930-1943).* Ed. Tullio Kezich. 3 vols. Rome: Bulzoni, 1979.

Sorlin, Pierre. *Sociologia del cinema.* Trans. Luca S. Budini. Milan: Garzanti, 1979; trans. of original French ed. of 1977.

Viganò. Dario. *Un cinema ogni campanile: chiesa e cinema nella diocesi di Milano.* Milan: Il Castoro, 1997.

Vivere il cinema: cinquant'anni del Centro Sperimentale di Cinematografia. Rome: Presidenza del Consiglio dei Ministri, 1987.

Zagarrio, Vito, ed. *Dietro lo schermo: ragionamenti sui modi di produzione cinematografici in Italia.* Venice: Marsilio, 1988.

VII. Film Theory and Film Criticism

A. Film Theory

Andrew, J. Dudley. *Concepts in Film Theory.* New York: Oxford University Press, 1984.

———. *The Major Film Theories: An Introduction.* New York: Oxford University Press, 1976.

Aristarco, Guido. *Il dissolvimento della ragione: discorso sul cinema.* Milan: Feltrinelli, 1965.

———. *Marx, le cinéma, et la critique de film.* Études Cinématographiques, nos. 88–92. Paris: Lettres modernes Minard, 1972.

———. *Il mito dell'attore: come l'industria della star produce il sex symbol.* Bari: Edizioni Dedalo, 1983.

———. *Storia delle teoriche del film.* Turin: Einaudi, 1951.

Barbaro, Umberto. *Film: soggetto e sceneggiatura.* Rome: Edizioni Bianco e Nero, 1939.

———. *Il film e il risarcimento marxista dell'arte.* Rome: Editori Riuniti, 1974.

———. *Neorealismo e realismo.* Ed. Gian Piero Brunetta. 2 vols. Rome: Editori Riuniti, 1976.

Bazin, André. *Bazin at Work: Major Essays & Reviews from the Forties & Fifties.* Ed. Bert Cardullo. Trans. Alain Piette and Bert Cardullo. New York: Routledge, 1977.

———. *Qu'est-ce que le cinéma?—IV. Une esthétique de la Réalité: le néo-réalisme.* Paris: Éditions du Cerf, 1962.

———. *What Is Cinema? Vol. II.* Trans. Hugh Gray. Berkeley and Los Angeles: University of California Press, 1971.

Bettetini, Gianfranco. *L'indice del realismo.* Milan: Bompiani, 1971.

——. *The Language and Technique of the Film.* The Hague: Mouton de Gruyter, 1973.

Bordwell, David. *Narration in the Fiction Film.* Madison: University of Wisconsin Press, 1985.

Branigan, Edward. *Point of View in the Cinema: A Theory of Narration and Subjectivity in Classical Film.* Berlin: Mouton, 1984.

Braudy, Leo, and Marshall Cohen, eds. *Film Theory and Criticism: Introductory Readings.* 6th rev. ed. New York: Oxford University Press, 2004.

Bruno, Edoardo, ed. *Teorie del realismo.* Rome: Bulzoni, 1977.

——. ed. *Teorie e prassi del cinema in Italia 1950-1970.* Milan: Mazzotta, 1972.

Casetti, Francesco. *Dentro lo sguardo: il film e il suo spettatore.* Milan: Bompiani, 1986.

——. *Teorie del cinema 1945-1990.* Milan: Bompiani, 1993. *Theories of Cinema, 1945-1995.* Trans. Francesca Chiostri and Elizabeth Gard Bartolini-Salimbeni with Thomas Kelso. Rev. English ed. Austin: University of Texas Press, 1999.

Chiarini, Luigi. *Cinema e film: storia e problemi.* Rome: Bulzoni, 1972.

——. *Cinema quinto potere.* Bari: Laterza, 1954.

——. *Il film nella battaglia delle idee.* Rome: Fratelli Bocca, 1954.

Chiarini, Luigi, and Umberto Barbaro, eds. *L'arte dell'attore.* Rome: Bianco e Nero, 1950.

De Lauretis, Teresa. "Semiotics, Theory and Social Practice: A Critical History of Italian Semiotics." *Cine-Tracts* 5 (2.1) (1978): 1–14.

Eco, Umberto. "On the Contribution of Film to Semiotics." *Quarterly Review of Film Studies* 2.1 (1977): 1–14.

——. "Towards a Semiotic Inquiry into the Television Message." Trans. Paola Splendore. *Working Papers in Cultural Studies* 3 (1972): 103–22.

Gambetti, Giacomo. *Zavattini mago e tecnico.* Rome: Ente dello spettacolo, 1986.

MacCann, Richard, ed. *Film: A Montage of Theories.* New York: Dutton, 1966.

Miccichè, Lino. *Filmologia e filologia: Studi sul cinema.* Venice: Marsilio, 2002.

Nichols, Bill, ed. *Movies and Methods.* 2 vols. Berkeley: University of California Press, 1976, 1985.

Pasinetti, Francesco. *L'arte del cinematografo: articoli e saggi teorici.* Ed. Ilario Ierace and Giovanna Grignaffini. Venice: Marsilio Editori, 1980.

Pasolini, Pier Paolo. "The Catholic Irrationalism of Fellini." *Film Criticism* 9.1 (1984): 63–73.

——. "The Cinema of Poetry." Trans. Marianne de Vettimo and Jacques Bontemps. *Cahiers du Cinéma in English* 6 (1966), 34–43. Rpt. in Nichols, *Movies and Methods*, vol. 1, pp. 524–58.

——. "Cinematic and Literary Stylistic Figures." *Film Culture* 24 (Spring 1962): 42–43.

——. *Empirismo eretico.* Milan: Garzanti, 1972; *Heretical Empiricism.* Ed. Louise K. Barnett and trans. Ben Lawton and Louise K. Barnett. Bloomington: Indiana University Press, 1988; new ed. New Accademia Publishing, 2005.

——. "The Pesaro Papers." *Cinim* 3 (1969): 6–11.

——. "Pier Paolo Pasolini: An Epical-Religious View of the World." *Film Quarterly* 18 (1965): 31–45.

——. "The Scenario as a Structure Designed to Become Another Structure." *Wide Angle* 2.1 (1978): 40–47.

Rosen, Philip, ed. *Narrative, Apparatus, Ideology: A Film Theory Reader*. New York: Columbia University Press, 1986.

Stam, Robert. *Reflexivity in Film and Literature: From Don Quixote to Jean-Luc Godard*. Ann Arbor: UMI Research Press, 1985.

B. Film Criticism in Italy (Excluding Theory)

Aristarco, Guido. *Neorealismo e nuova critica cinematografica: cinematografia e vita nazionale negli anni quaranta e cinquanta: tra rotture e tradizioni*. Florence: Nuova Guaraldi Editrice, 1980.

Bianca, Pividori, ed. *Critica italiana primo tempo: 1926–1934*. Rome: Studi monografici di Bianco e Nero, 1973.

Bolzoni, Francesco, ed. *Critici e autori: complici e/o avversari? Atti del convegno di Ferrara 9–10 novembre 1974*. Venice: Marsilio Editori, 1976.

Brunetta, Gian Piero. *Gli intellettuali italiani e il cinema*. Milan: Bruno Mondadori, 2004.

———. *Umberto Barbaro e l'idea di neorealismo (1930–1943)*. Padua: Liviana Editrice, 1969.

d'Amico, Masolino. *Persone speciali*. Turin: Nino Aragno, 2003.

De Marchi, Bruno, ed. *La critica cinematografica in Italia: rilievi sul campo*. Venice: Marsilio Editori, 1977.

De Santis, Giuseppe. *Verso il neorealismo: un critico cinematografico degli anni quaranta*. Ed. Callisto Cosulich. Rome: Bulzoni Editori, 1982.

Farassino, Alberto. *Scritti strabici: Cinema, 1975–1988*. Ed. Tatti Sanguineti. Milan: Baldini Castoldi Dalai, 2004.

Flaiano, Ennio. *Un film alla settimana: 55 critiche da "Cine Illustrato" (1939–1940)*. Ed. Tullio Kezich. Rome: Bulzoni, 1988.

———. *Lettere d'amore al cinema*. Ed. Cristina Bragaglia. Milan: Rizzoli, 1978.

Fofi, Goffredo. *Capire con il cinema*. Milan: Feltrinelli, 1977.

———. *Il cinema italiano: servi e padroni*. Milan: Feltrinelli, 1971.

Furno, Mariella, and Renzo Renzi, eds. *Il neorealismo nel fascismo: Giuseppe De Santis e la critica cinematografica 1941–1943*. Bologna: Edizioni della Tipografia Compositori, 1984.

Grazzini, Giovanni. *Il cinemondo: dieci anni di film, 1976–1986*. 11 vols. Rome: Laterza, 1987.

Hiller, Jim, ed. *Cahiers du Cinéma: The 1950s—Neo-Realism, Hollywood, New Wave*. Cambridge, Mass.: Harvard University Press, 1985.

Kezich, Tullio. *Il centofilm [1]: un anno al cinema 1977–1978*. Milan: Edizioni Il Formichiere, 1978.

———. *Il dolce cinema: Fellini & altri*. Milan: Bompiani, 1978.

———. *Il filmottanta: cinque anni al cinema 1982–1986*. Milan: Mondadori, 1986.

———. *Il millefilm: dieci anni al cinema 1967–1977*. 2 vols. Milan: Edizioni Il Formichiere, 1978.

———. *Il nuovissimo millefilm: cinque anni al cinema 1977–1982*. Milan: Mondadori, 1983.

Moravia, Alberto. *Al cinema: centoquarantotto film d'autore*. Milan: Bompiani, 1975.

Renzi, Renzo. *Il fascismo involontario e altri scritti*. Bologna: Cappelli, 1975.

———. *La sala buia: diario di un disamore*. Bologna: Cappelli, 1978.

———. *Da Starace ad Antonioni: diario critico di un ex balilla*. Padua: Marsilio Editori, 1964.

Torri, Bruno, eds. *Nuovo cinema (1965–2005): Scritti in onore di Lino Miccichè*. Venice: Marsilio, 2005.

VIII. Collections of Interviews with Directors

Garibaldi, Andrea, Roberto Giannarelli, and Guido Giusti, eds. *Qui comincia l'avventura del signor . . . : Dall'anonimato al successo ventitre protagonisti del cinema italiano raccontano*. Florence: La Casa Usher, 1984.

Geduld, Harry, ed. *Film Makers on Film Making*. Bloomington: Indiana University Press, 1967.

Georgakas, Dan, and Lenny Rubenstein, eds. *The Cinéaste Interviews on the Art and Politics of the Cinema*. Chicago: Lake View Press, 1983.

Gili, Jean, ed. *Le cinéma italien*. Paris: Union Générale d'Éditions, 1978.

———. ed. *Italian Filmmakers: Self Portraits—A Selection of Interviews*. Trans. Sandra E. Tokunaga. New York: Gremese, 1998.

Samuels, Charles Thomas, ed. *Encountering Directors*. New York: Putnam's, 1972.

Tassone, Aldo, ed. *Parla il cinema italiano*. 2 vols. Milan: Edizioni il Formichiere, 1979–80.

IX. Italian Directors: Critical Works and Scripts

Gianni Amelio

Amelio, Gianni. *"Lamerica": film e storia del film*. Ed. Piera Detassis. Turin: Einaudi, 1994.

———. *Il vizio del cinema: vedere, amare, fare un film*. Milan: Einaudi, 2004.

Amelio, Gianni, Sandro Petraglia, and Stefano Rulli. *Le chiavi di casa*. Venice: Marsilio, 2004.

Crowdus, Gary, and Richard Porton. "Beyond Neorealism: Preserving a Cinema of Social Conscience—An Interview with Gianni Amelio." *Cinéaste* 21.4 (1995): 6–13.

Domenico, Scalzo, ed. *Gianni Amelio: un posto al cinema*. Torino: Lindau, 2001.

Martini, Emanuela. *Gianni Amelio*. Milan: Il Castoro, 2006.

———. ed. *Gianni Amelio: le regole e il gioco*. Turin: Lindau, 1999.

Michelangelo Antonioni

Achilli, Alberto, Alberto Boschi, and Gianfranco Casadio, eds. *Le sonorità del visibile: immagini, suoni e musica nel cinema di Michelangelo Antonioni*. Ravenna: Longo, 2000.

Antonioni, Michelangelo. *"L'Avventura": A Film by Michelangelo Antonioni*. Ed. George Amberg. New York: Grove Press, 1969.

———. *Blow-Up*. New York: Frederick Ungar, 1971.

———. *Chung Kuo Cina*. Ed. Lorenzo Cucco. Turin: Einaudi, 1974.

———. *Comincio a capire*. Catania: Girasole Edizioni, 1999.

———. *Il deserto rosso*. Ed. Carlo Di Carlo. Bologna: Cappelli, 1978.

———. *"L'eclisse" di Michelangelo Antonioni*. Ed. John Francis Lane. Bologna: Cappelli, 1962.

———. *Identificazione di una donna*. Ed. Aldo Tassone. Turin: Einaudi, 1983.

——. *I film nel cassetto.* Ed. Carlo di Carlo and Giorgio Tinazzi. Venice: Marsilio, 1995. English edition: *Unfinished Business: Screenplays, Scenarios, and Ideas.* Ed. Carlo di Carlo and Giorgio Tinazzi. Trans. Andrew Taylor. New York: Marsilio, 1998.

——. *Il mistero di Oberwald.* Ed. Gianni Massironi. Turin: Edizioni RAI, 1981.

——. *The Passenger.* Ed. Mark Peploe, Peter Wollen, and Michelangelo Antonioni. New York: Grove Press, 1975.

——. *Il primo Antonioni.* Ed. Carlo Di Carlo. Bologna: Cappelli, 1973.

——. *Professione: reporter.* Ed. Carlo Di Carlo. Bologna: Cappelli, 1975.

——. *Screenplays of Michelangelo Antonioni.* Trans. Louis Brigante. New York: Orion Press, 1963.

——. *Sei film.* Turin: Einaudi, 1964.

——. *Tecnicamente dolce.* Ed. Aldo Tassone. Turin: Einaudi, 1976.

——. *That Bowling Alley on the Tiber: Tales of a Director.* Trans. William Arrowsmith. New York: Oxford University Press, 1986.

——. *"Zabriskie Point" di Michelangelo Antonioni.* Bologna: Cappelli, 1970.

Arrowsmith, William. *Antonioni: A Critical Study.* New York: Oxford University Press, 1995.

Biarese, Cesare, and Aldo Tassone. *I film di Michelangelo Antonioni.* Rome: Gremese, 1985.

Brunette, Peter. *The Films of Michelangelo Antonioni.* New York: Cambridge University Press, 1998.

Cameron, Ian, and Robin Wood. *Antonioni.* London: Studio Vista, 1968.

Chatman, Seymour. *Antonioni; or, The Surface of the World.* Berkeley: University of California Press, 1985.

Di Carlo, Carlo. *Il cinema di Michelangelo Antonioni.* Milan: Il Castoro, 2002.

——. *Les images d'Antonioni.* Rome: Cinecittà International, 1988.

——. *Michelangelo Antonioni.* Rome: Edizioni di Bianco e Nero, 1964.

——. ed. *Cher Antonioni. . . .* Rome: Ente Autonomo di Gestione per il Cinema, 1988.

——. ed. *Michelangelo Antonioni 1942–1965.* Rome: Ente Autonomo di Gestione per il Cinema, 1988.

Estève, Michel, ed. *Michelangelo Antonioni: L'homme et l'objet.* Paris: Études Cinématographiques, nos. 36–7. Paris: Lettres modernes Minard, 1964.

Huss, Roy, ed. *Focus on "Blow-Up."* Englewood Cliffs, N.J.: Prentice–Hall, 1971.

Leprohon, Pierre. *Michelangelo Antonioni.* 4th ed. Paris: Éditions Seghers, 1969.

——. *Michelangelo Antonioni: An Introduction.* Trans. Scott Sullivan. New York: Simon & Schuster, 1963.

Lyons, Robert J. *Michelangelo Antonioni's Neo-Realism: A World View.* New York: Arno Press, 1976.

Mancini, Michele, and Giuseppe Perrella, eds. *Architetture della visione / Architecture in Vision.* 2 vols. Rome: Coneditor, 1985.

Moore, Kevin Z. "Eclipsing the Commonplace: The Logic of Alienation in Antonioni." *Film Quarterly* 48.4 (1995): 22–34.

Nowell-Smith, Geoffrey. "*L'avventura.*" Bloomington: Indiana University Press, 1998.

Perry, Ted, and Rene Prieto. *Michelangelo Antonioni: A Guide to References and Resources.* Boston: G. K. Hall, 1986.

Orsini, Maria, ed. *Michelangelo Antonioni: i film e la critica 1943–1995: un'antologia.* Rome: Bulzoni, 2002.

Ranieri, Nicola. *Amor vacui: il cinema di Michelangelo Antonioni.* Chieti: Métis, 1990.

Renzi, Renzo. *Album Antonioni: Une biographie impossible.* (Vol. 3 of *L'Oeuvre de Michelangelo Antonioni.* Ed. Carlo Di Carlo.) Rome: Cinecittà International, 1990.

Rhodie, Sam. *Antonioni.* London: British Film Institute, 1990.

Tinazzi, Giorgio. *Michelangelo Antonioni.* Milan: Il Castoro, 2002.

———. ed. *Michelangelo Antonioni: Écrits 1936/1985.* (Vol. 4 of *L'Oeuvre de Michelangelo Antonioni.* Ed. Carlo Di Carlo.) Rome: Cinecittà International, 1988.

———. ed. *Michelangelo Antonioni: identificazione di un autore.* 2 vols. Parma: Pratiche, 1983, 1985.

Trebbi, Fernando. *Il testo e lo sguardo: antitesi, circolarità, incrociamento in "Professione: reporter": saggio su M. Antonioni.* Bologna: Pàtron, 1976.

Wenders, Wim. *My Time with Antonioni: The Diary of an Extraordinary Experience.* Trans. Michael Hofmann. London: Faber and Faber, 2000.

Zumbo, Saverio. *Al di là delle immagini: Michelangelo Antonioni.* Alessandria: Edizioni Falsopiano, 2002.

Dario Argento

Carluccio, Giulia, Giacomo Manzoli, and Roy Menarini, eds. *L'eccesso della visione: il cinema di Dario Argento.* Turin: Lindau, 2003.

Cozzi, Luigi, ed. *Giallo Argento: Tutto il cinema di Dario Argento.* Rome: Mondo Ignoto, 2003. Rev. ed. of *Dario Argento: il suo cinema, i suoi personaggi, i suoi miti.* Rome: Fanucci Editori, 1991.

Dario Argento. Milan: Mediane, 2007 (sound track collection on CD with accompanying book).

Della Casa, Stefano, ed. *Dario Argento, il brivido della critica: scritti sul cinema.* Turin: Testo & Immagine, 1996.

Gallant, Chris, ed. *Art of Darkness: The Cinema of Dario Argento.* London: Fab Press, 2001.

Giovanni, Fabio. *Dario Argento: il brivido, il sangue, il thrilling.* Bari: Edizioni Dedalo, 1986.

Jones, Alan. *Profondo Argento: The Man, the Myths & the Magic.* Surrey: Fab Press, 2004.

McDonagh, Maitland. *Broken Mirrors/Broken Minds: The Dark Dreams of Dario Argento.* London: Sun Tavern Fields, 1991.

Pugliese, Roberto. *Dario Argento,* 2d ed. Milan: Il Castoro, 1996.

Pupi Avati

Avati, Pupi. *Il cuore altrove e altre storie.* Rome: Gremese, 2002.

Maraldi, Antonio, ed. *Pupi Avati: cinema e televisione.* Gambettola: Centro Cinema Città di Cesena, 1980.

Romano, Paolo, and Roberto Tirapelle, eds. Sequenze 6. *Il cinema di Pupi Avati.* Verona: Nuova Grafica Cierre, 1987.

Sarno, Antonello. *Pupi Avati.* Milan: Il Castoro, 1993.

Mario Bava

Cozzo, Luigi. *Mario Bava: i mille volti della paura*. Rome: Mondo Ignoto, 2001.

Howarth, Troy. *The Haunted World of Mario Bava*. London: Fab Press, 2002.

Lucas, Tim. *Mario Bava: All the Colors of the Dark*. Introduction by Martin Scorsese. Foreward by Riccardo Freda. Cincinnati: Video Watchdog, 2007.

Pezzotta, Alberto. *Mario Bava*, 2d ed. Milan: Il Castoro, 1997.

Marco Bellocchio

Aprà, Adriano, ed. *Marco Bellocchio: il cinema e i film*. Venice: Marsilio, 2005.

Bellocchio, Marco. *China Is Near*. Ed. Tommaso Chiaretti. New York: Orion Press, 1969.

——. *Marcia trionfale*. Ed. Anna Maria Tatò. Turin: Einaudi, 1976.

——. *"Nel nome del padre" di Marco Bellocchio*. Ed. Goffredo Fofi. Bologna: Cappelli, 1971.

——. *"I pugni in tasca": un film di Marco Bellocchio*. Ed. Giacomo Gambetti. Milan: Garzanti, 1967.

——. *Salto nel vuoto*. Ed. Alberto Barbera and Gianni Volpi, with an essay by Massimo Fagioli. Milan: Feltrinelli, 1981.

Bernardi, Sandro. *Marco Bellocchio*. Milan: Il Castoro, 1998.

Ceretto, Luisa, and Giancarlo Zappoli. *Le forme della ribellione: il cinema di Marco Bellocchio*. Turin: Lindau, 2004.

Lodato, Nuccio. *Marco Bellocchio*. Milan: Moizzi, 1977.

Ventura, Francesco. *Il cinema e il caso Moro*. Recco: Le Mani–Microart'S, 2008.

Carmelo Bene

Saba, Cosetta B. *Carmelo Bene*, 2d ed. Milan: Il Castoro, 2005.

Roberto Benigni

Benigni, Roberto. *Io un po' Pinocchio: Roberto Benigni racconta il suo film tra le pagine del romanzo di Collodi*. Florence: Giunti, 2002.

Benigni, Roberto, and Vincenzo Cerami. *Life Is Beautiful (La vita é bella): A Screenplay*. Trans. Lisa Taruschio. New York: Hyperion, 1998.

Borsatti, Cristina. *Roberto Benigni*. Milan: Il Castoro, 2002.

Bullaro, Grace Russo, ed. *Beyond "Life is Beautiful": Comedy and Tragedy in the Cinema of Roberto Benigni*. Leicester: Troubadour, 2005.

Celli, Carlo. *The Divine Comic: The Cinema of Roberto Benigni*. Blue Summit, Pa.: Scarecrow Press, 2001.

Denby, David. "In the Eye of the Beholder: Another Look at Roberto Benigni's Holocaust Fantasy." *New Yorker* (March 15, 1999), 96–99.

Masi, Stefano. *Roberto Benigni Superstar*. Trans. Sandra E. Tokunaga. Rome: Gremese International, 1999.

Bernardo Bertolucci

Alley, Robert. *Last Tango in Paris*. New York: Dell, 1972.

Behr, Edward. *The Last Emperor*. London: Futura, 1987.

Bernardo Bertolucci. Milan: Mediane, 2007 (sound track collection on CD with accompanying book).

Bertolucci, Bernardo. *Bernardo Bertolucci's "Last Tango in Paris."* New York: Delta, 1973.

——. *Ultimo tango a Parigi*. Turin: Einaudi, 1973.

Bertolucci, Bernardo, Franco Arcalli, and Giuseppe Bertolucci. *Novecento: atto primo* and *Novecento: atto secondo*. 2 vols. Turin: Einaudi, 1973.

Burgoyne, Robert. *Bertolucci's "1900."* Detroit: Wayne State University Press, 1991.

Carroll, Kent E., ed. *Closeup: "Last Tango in Paris."* New York: Grove Press, 1973.

Casetti, Francesco. *Bernardo Bertolucci.* Florence: La Nuova Italia, 1978.

Costa, Francesco, ed. *Bernardo Bertolucci.* Rome: Dino Audino, 1993.

Di Giovanni, Norman Thomas. *1900.* New York: Dell, 1976.

Estève, Michel, ed. *Bernardo Bertolucci.* Études Cinématographiques, nos. 122–26. Paris: Lettres modernes Minard, 1979.

Gérard, Fabien S. *Ombres jaunes: journal de tournage "Le dernier empereur" de Bernardo Bertolucci.* Paris: Cahiers du Cinéma, 1987.

Gérard, Fabien S., T. Jefferson Kline, and Bruce Sklarew, eds. *Bernardo Bertolucci: Interviews.* Oxford: University Press of Mississippi, 2000.

Halligan, Benjamin. *La Luna.* Trowbridge, England: Flicks Books, 2001.

Kline, T. Jefferson. *Bertolucci's Dream Loom: A Psychoanalytic Study of Cinema.* Amherst: University of Massachusetts Press, 1987.

Kolker, Robert Phillip. *Bernardo Bertolucci.* New York: Oxford University Press, 1985.

Loshitzky, Yosefa. *The Radical Faces of Godard and Bertolucci.* Detroit: Wayne State University Press, 1994.

Prono, Franco. *Bernardo Bertolucci: "Il conformista."* Turin: Edizioni Lindau, 1998.

Sklarew, Bruce H., Bonnie S. Kaufman, Ellen Handler Spitz, and Diane Borden, eds. *Bertolucci's "The Last Emperor": Multiple Takes.* Detroit: Wayne State University Press, 1998.

Thompson, David. *Last Tango in Paris.* London: British Film Institute, 1998.

Tonetti, Claretta Micheletti. *Bernardo Bertolucci: The Cinema of Ambiguity.* New York: Twayne, 1995.

Ungari, Enzo, and Donald Ranvaud, eds. *Scene madri di Bernardo Bertolucci*, 2d rev. ed. Milan: Ubulibri, 1987.

Wagstaff, Christopher. *Il Conformista (The Conformist).* London: British Film Institute, 2012.

Giuseppe Bertolucci

Giraldi, Massimo. *Giuseppe Bertolucci.* Milan: Il Castoro, 2000.

Alessandro Blasetti

Aprà, Adriano, and Riccardo Redi, eds. *"Sole": soggetto, sceneggiatura, note per la realizzazione.* Rome: Di Giacomo, 1985.

Blasetti, Alessandro. *Il cinema che ho vissuto.* Ed. Franco Prono. Bari: Edizioni Dedalo, 1982.

———. *Scritti sul cinema.* Ed. Adriano Aprà. Venice: Marsilio Editori, 1982.

Gori, Gianfranco. *Alessandro Blasetti.* Florence: La Nuova Italia, 1984.

Salizzato, Claver, and Vito Zagarrio, eds. *"La corono di ferro": un modo di produzione italiano.* Rome: Di Giacomo, 1985.

Verdone, Luca. *I film di Alessandro Blasetti.* Rome: Gremese, 1989.

Mauro Bolognini

Brancati, Vitaliano. *Bell'Antonio.* Trans. Stanley Hochman. New York: Frederick Ungar, 1978.

Di Montezemolo, Vittorio Cordero, ed. *Bolognini*. Rome: Istituto Poligrafico dello Stato, 1977.

Franco Brusati

Occhipinti, Andrea, ed. *Un castello disincantato: film e scritti di Franco Brusati*. Milan: Il Castoro, 2003.

Mimmo Calopresti

Sesti, Mario. *Mimmo Calopresti*. Alessandria: Edizioni Falsopiano, 2003.

Mario Camerini

Germani, Sergio Grmek. *Mario Camerini*. Florence: La Nuova Italia, 1980.

Renato Castellani

Castellani, Renato. *"Giulietta e Romeo" di Renato Castellani*. Ed. Stelio Martini. Bologna: Cappelli, 1956.
———. *Quattro soggetti*. Rome: Centro Cattolico Cinematografico, 1983.
Trasatti, Sergio. *Renato Castellani*. Florence: La Nuova Italia, 1984.

Enzo G. Castellari

Lupi, Gordiano, and Fabio Zanello, eds. *Il cittadino si ribella: il cinema di Enzo G. Castellari*. Rome: Mondo Ignoto, 2006.

Liliana Cavani

Buscemi, Francesco. *Invito al cinema di Liliana Cavani*. Milan: Mursia, 1996.
Cavani, Liliana. *"Milarepa" di Liliana Cavani*. Ed. Italo Moscati. Bologna: Cappelli, 1974.
———. *Il portiere di notte*. Turin: Einaudi, 1975.
Cavani, Liliana, and Enrico Medioli. *Oltre la porta*. Turin: Einaudi, 1982.
Cavani, Liliana, and Italo Moscati. *Lettere dall'interno: racconto per un film su Simone Weil*. Turin: Einaudi, 1974.
Marone, Gaetana. *The Gaze and the Labyrinth: The Cinema of Liliana Cavani*. Princeton: Princeton University Press, 2000.
Tallarigo, Paola, and Luca Gasparini, eds. *Lo sguardo libero: il cinema di Liliana Cavani*. Florence: La Casa Usher, 1990.
Tiso, Ciriaco. *Liliana Cavani*. Florence: La Nuova Italia, 1975.

Daniele Ciprì and Franco Maresco

Morreale, Emiliano. *Ciprì e Maresco*. Alessandria: Edizioni Falsopiano, 2003.

Luigi Comencini

Comencini, Luigi. *Al cinema con cuore 1938–1974*. Ed. Adriano Aprà. Milan: Il Castoro, 2007.
———. *Infanzia, vocazione, esperienze di un regista*. Milan: Baldini & Castoldi, 1999.
———. *"Tutti a Casa": Un film di Dino De Laurentiis*. Caltanissetta: Salvatore Sciascia, 1960.
Gili, Jean A. *Luigi Comencini*. Paris: Edilig, 1981. Enlarged and updated in Italian as *Luigi Comencini*. Trans. Cristiana Latini. Rome: Gremese, 2005.
Gosetti, Giorgio. *Luigi Comencini*. Florence: La Nuova Italia, 1988.
Pirro, Ugo, and Luigi Comencini. *Delitto d'amore*. Milan: Vangelista, 1974.
Trionfera, Claudio. *Luigi Comencini*. Rome: ANICA, n.d.

Vittorio Cottafavi

Rondolino, Gianni. *Vittorio Cottafavi: cinema e televisione*. Bologna: Cappelli, 1980.

Ruggero Deodato

Fenton, Harvey, Julian Grainger, and Gian Luca Castoldi, eds. *Cannibal Holocaust and the Savage Cinema of Ruggero Deodato*. London: Fab Press, 1999.

Giuseppe De Santis

Camerino, Vincenzo, ed. *Il cinema di Giuseppe De Santis*. Lecce: Elle Edizioni, 1982.

De Santis: l'avventura neorealista. Special issue of *Cinema & Cinema* 9.30 (January–March 1982).

De Santis, Giuseppe. *"Riso amaro": un film diretto da Giuseppe De Santis*. Ed. Carlo Lizzani. Rome: Officina Edizioni, 1978.

———. *Verso il neorealismo: un critico cinematografico degli anni quaranta*. Ed. Callisto Cosulich. Rome: Bulzoni, 1982.

Farassino, Alberto. *Giuseppe De Santis*. Milan: Moizzi, 1978.

Gili, Jean, ed. *Alle origini del neorealismo: Giuseppe De Santis a colloquio con Jean Gili*. Rome: Bulzoni, 2008.

Masi, Stefano. *Giuseppe De Santis*. Florence: La Nuova Italia, 1982.

Parisi, Antonio. *Il cinema di Giuseppe De Santis tra passione e ideologia*. Rome: Cadmo, 1983.

Vitti, Antonio. *Giuseppe De Santis and Postwar Italian Cinema*. Toronto: University of Toronto Press, 1996.

Vittorio De Seta

De Seta, Vittorio. *"Un uomo a metà" di Vittorio De Seta: analisi di un film in costruzione*. Ed. Filippo De Sanctis. Bologna: Cappelli, 1966.

Vittorio De Sica

Agel, Henri. *Vittorio De Sica*, 2d ed. Paris: Éditions Universitaires, 1964.

Alonge, Andrea Giaime. *Vittorio De Sica: "Ladri di biciclette."* Turin: Edizioni Lindau, 1998.

Bartolini, Luigi. *Bicycle Thieves*. Trans. C.J. Richards. New York: Macmillan, 1950.

Bolzoni, Francesco. *Quando De Sica era Mister Brown*. Turin: Edizioni ERI, 1985.

Bruni, Davide. *Vittorio De Sica: "Sciuscià."* Turin: Lindau, 2007.

Caldiron, Orio, ed. *Vittorio De Sica*. Special issue of *Bianco e Nero* 36.9–12 (September–December 1975).

Cassarini, Maria Carla. *"Miracolo a Milano" di Vittorio De Sica: Storia e preistoria di un film*. Genoa: Le Mani–Microart'S, 2000.

Curle, Howard, and Stephen Snyder, eds. *Vittorio De Sica: Contemporary Perspectives*. Toronto: University of Toronto Press, 2000.

Darretta, John. *Vittorio De Sica: A Guide to References and Resources*. Boston: G. K. Hall, 1983.

De Santi, Gualtiero. *Vittorio De Sica*. Milan: Il Castoro, 2003.

De Sica, Vittorio. *The Bicycle Thief*. New York: Simon & Schuster, 1968.

———. *Lettere dal set*. Ed. Emi De Sica and Giancarlo Governi. Milan: SugarCo, 1987.

———. *Miracle in Milan*. Baltimore: Penguin, 1969.

Gordon, Robert S. C. *Bicycle Thieves*. London: British Film Institute, 2008.

Mercader, Maria. *La mia vita con Vittorio De Sica.* Milan: Mondadori, 1978.

Miccichè, Lino, ed. *De Sica: autore, regista, attore.* Venice: Editori Marsilio, 1993.

———. ed. *"Sciuscià" di Vittorio De Sica: letture, documenti, testimonianze.* Rome: Centro Sperimentale di Cinematagrafia, 1994.

Mollica, Vincenzo, ed. *Le canzoni di Vittorio De Sica: antologia storica.* Montepulciano: Editori del Grifo, 1990.

Moscati, Italo. *Vittorio De Sica: Vitalità, passione e talento in un'Italia dolceamara.* Rome: Ediesse, 2004.

Pecori, Franco. *Vittorio De Sica.* Florence: La Nuova Italia, 1980.

Fernando Di Leo

Pulici, Davide. *Fernando di Leo.* Milan: Nocturno Libri, 2001.

Luciano Emmer

Moneti, Guglielmo. *Luciano Emmer.* Florence: La Nuova Italia, 1992.

Roberto Faenza

Faenza, Roberto, Sergio Vecchio, with Antonio Tabucchi and Marcello Mastroianni, and photography by Ottavio Ferrario. *"Sostiene Pereira": film book.* Milan: Il Castoro, 1995.

Federico Fellini

Agel, Geneviève. *Les Chemins de Fellini.* Paris: Éditions du Cerf, 1956.

Angelucci, Gianfranco, ed. *Federico Fellini da Rimini a Roma 1937–1947: Atti del convegno di studi e testimonianze Rimini, 31 ottobre 1997.* Rimini: Pietroneno Capitani, 1998.

———. ed. *"La dolce vita": un film di Federico Fellini.* Rome: Editalia, 1989.

———. ed. *Gli ultimi sogni di Fellini.* Rimini: Pietroneno Capitani, 1997.

Alpert, Hollis. *Fellini: A Life.* New York: Atheneum, 1986.

Antonelli, Lamberto, and Gabriele Paolini, eds. *Attalo e Fellini al "Marc'Aurelio": Scritti e disegni.* Rome: Roberto Napoleone, 1995.

Arpa, Angelo, S.J. *"La Dolce vita": Cronaca di una Passione.* Naples: Parresìa, 1996.

———. *Fellini: persona e personaggio.* Naples: Parresìa, 1996.

Bachmann, Gideon. "A Guest in My Own Dreams: An Interview with Federico Fellini." *Film Quarterly* 47.3 (1994): 2–15.

Baxter, John. *Fellini.* New York: St. Martin's Press, 1993.

Benderson, Albert E. *Critical Approaches to Federico Fellini's "8½."* New York: Arno Press, 1974.

Benzi, Luigi "Titta." *Patachédi: Gli amarcord di una vita all'insegna della grande amicizia con Federico Fellini.* Rimini: Guaraldi, 1995.

Betti, Liliana. *Fellini: An Intimate Portrait.* Trans. Joachim Neugroschel. Boston: Little, Brown, 1979.

———. *Io e Fellini (Ma sei sicuro che non ci siano gli indiani?).* Milan: Archinto, 2000.

———. ed. *Federico A.C.: disegni per il "Satyricon" di Federico Fellini.* Milan: Milano Libri Edizioni, 1970.

Betti, Liliana, and Gianfranco Angelucci, eds. *Casanova rendez-vous con Federico Fellini.* Milan: Bompiani, 1975.

Betti, Liliana, and Oreste Del Buono, eds. *Federcord: disegni per "Amarcord" di Federico Fellini.* Milan: Milano Libri Edizioni, 1974.

Benevelli, Elio. *Analisi di una messa in scena: Freud e Lacan nel "Casanova" di Fellini.* Bari: Dedalo Libri, 1979.

Bertozzi, Marco, with Giuseppe Ricci and Simone Casavecchia, eds. *biblioFellini.* 3 vols. 1, *Monografie, soggetti e sceneggiature, saggi in volume.* 2, *Saggi, recensioni e articoli nella stampa periodica.* 3, *Recensioni sui quotidiani; vignette e scritti umoristici; programmi radiofonici; regie e collaborazioni cinematografiche; pubblicità; film, documentari, programmi televisivi su Fellini; scritti di Fellini.* Rimini: Fondazione Federico Fellini, 2002–2004.

Bìspuri, Ennio. *Federico Fellini: il sentimento latino della vita.* Rome: Editrice Il Ventaglio, 1981.

———. *Interpretare Fellini.* Rimini: Guaraldi, 2003.

Boledi, Luigi, and Raffaele De Berti, eds. *"Luci del Varietà": pagine scelte.* Milan: Il Castoro, 1999.

Bondanella, Peter. "Fellini." In *Action!: How Great Filmmakers Direct Actors.* Ed. Paolo Bertetto. Rome: Fondazione Cinema per Roma, 2007, pp. 225–31.

———. "*Amarcord*: Fellini and Politics." *Cinéaste* 19.1 (1992): 36–43.

———. "Beyond Neorealism: Calvino, Fellini and Fantasy." *Michigan Romance Studies* 16 (1996): 103–20.

———. *The Cinema of Federico Fellini.* Foreword by Federico Fellini. Princeton: Princeton University Press, 1992. Italian edition with a new preface by the author: *Il cinema di Federico Fellini.* Rimini: Guaraldi, 1994.

———. *The Films of Federico Fellini.* New York: Cambridge University Press, 2002.

———. "Introduzione a *La famiglia* e *Happy Country* / An Introduction to *La famiglia* and *Happy Country*." *Federico Amarcord: Rivista di studi felliniani* 6.1–2 (2006): 9–14.

———. "La presenza di Federico Fellini nel cinema contemporaneo / Federico Fellini's Presence in the Contemporary Cinema." In *La memoria di Federico Fellini sullo schermo del cinema mondiale.* Ed. Giuseppe Ricci and Alessandra Fontemaggi. Rimini: Fondazione Federico Fellini, 2004. Rpt. as "La presenza di Fellini nel cinema contemporaneo: considerazioni preliminari / "Federico Fellini's Presence in the Contemporary Cinema: Some Tentative Observations." *Fellini Amarcord: Rivista di studi felliniani* 7.1–2 (2007): 35–60.

———. "*La strada* e il cinema della poesia: dal soggetto al film" / "*La Strada* and the Cinema of Poetry: From Soggetto to Film," *Fellini Amarcord: Rivista di studi felliniani* 4.2–3 (2004): 7–18.

———. ed. *Federico Fellini: Essays in Criticism.* New York: Oxford University Press, 1978.

Bondanella, Peter, and Cristina Degli-Esposti, eds. *Perspectives on Federico Fellini.* New York: G. K. Hall/MacMillan, 1993.

Borin, Fabrizio. *Federico Fellini.* Rome: Gremese, 1999; English version *Federico Fellini: A Sentimental Journey into the Illusion and Reality of a Genius.* Trans. Charles Nopar with Sue Jones. Rome: Gremese International, 1999.

Boyer, Deena. *The Two Hundred Days of "8½."* New York: Garland, 1978.

Budgen, Suzanne. *Fellini.* London: British Film Institute, 1966.

Burke, Frank. "Fellini's Commercials: Biting the hand that feeds." *The Italianist* 31.2 (2011): 205–42.

———. *Fellini's Films: From Postwar to Postmodern.* New York: Twayne, 1996.

Burke, Frank, and Marguerite R. Waller, eds. *Federico Fellini: Contemporary Perspectives*. Toronto: University of Toronto Press, 2002.

Cardullo, Bert, ed. *Federico Fellini: Interviews*. Oxford: University Press of Mississippi, 2006.

Caruso, Rossella, and Giuseppe Casetti, eds. *Il mio amico Pasqualino: Federico Fellini 1937–1947*. Rome: Il museo del Louvre and Associazione Federico Fellini, 1997.

Casanova, Alessandro. *Scritti e immaginati. I film mai realizzati di Federico Fellini*. Rimini: Guaraldi, 2005.

Chandler, Charlotte. *I, Fellini*. New York: Random House, 1995. Italian edition: *Io, Federico Fellini*. Trans. Marzio Tosello. Milan: Mondadori, 1995. French edition: *Moi, Fellini: Treize ans de confidences*. Trans. Annick Granger de Scriba, Sabine Boulogne, and Philippe Bonnet. Paris: Editions Robert Laffont, 1994.

Cianfarani, Carmine, ed. *Federico Fellini: Leone d'Oro, Venezia 1985*. Rome: ANICA, 1985.

Ciment, Gilles, ed. *Federico Fellini: Dossier Positif–Rivages*. Paris: Éditions Rivages, 1988.

Cini, Roberta. *Nella città delle donne: femminile e sogno nel cinema di Fellini*. Tirrenia, Pisa: Edizioni del Cerro, 2008.

Cirio, Rita. *Il mestiere di regista: intervista con Federico Fellini*. Milan: Garzanti, 1994.

Collet, Jean. *La création selon Fellini*. Paris: José Corti, 1990.

Costantini, Costanzo. *L'inferno di Fellini*. Rome: Sovera, 2003.

Costello, Donald. *Fellini's Road*. Notre Dame, Ind.: University of Notre Dame Press, 1983.

De Benedictis, Maurizio. *Linguaggi dell'aldilà: Fellini e Pasolini*. Rome: Lithos, 2000.

De Miro, Ester, and Mario Guaraldi, eds. *Fellini della memoria*. Florence: La Casa Usher, 1983.

De Santi, Pier Marco. *I disegni di Fellini*. Rome: Laterza, 1982; rpt. 2004.

De Santi, Pier Marco, and Raffaele Monti, eds. *Saggi e documenti sopra "Il Casanova" di Federico Fellini*. Pisa: Quaderni dell'Istituto di storia dell'arte dell'Università di Pisa, 1978.

Di Biagi, Flaminio. *La Roma di Fellini*. Recco: Le Mani-Microart'S, 2008.

Estève, Michel, ed. *Federico Fellini: aux sources de l'imaginaire*. Études Cinématographiques, nos. 127–30. Paris: Lettres modernes Minard, 1981.

———. ed. *Federico Fellini: "8½."* Études Cinématographiques, nos. 28–29. Paris: Lettres modernes Minard, 1963.

Fabbri, Paolo, ed. *Lo schermo "manifesto": le misteriose pubblicità di Federico Fellini*. Rimini: Guaraldi, 2002.

Fantuzzi, Virgilio. *Il vero Fellini*. Rome: Ave Editrice, 1994.

Fava, Claudio G., and Aldo Viganò. *I film di Federico Fellini*. 2d ed. Rome: Gremese, 1987. English edition: *The Films of Federico Fellini*. Trans. Shula Curto. Secaucus, N.J.: Citadel Press, 1985.

Federico Fellini & Dario Fo: disegni geniali. Milan: Mazzotta, 1999.

Fellini, Federico. *Block-notes di un regista*. Milan: Longanesi, 1988.

———. *Ciò che abbiamo inventato è tutto autentico: Lettere a Tullio Pinelli*. Venice: Marsilio, 2008.

———. *La città delle donne*. Milan: Garzanti, 1980.

———. *I clowns.* Ed. Renzo Renzi. Bologna: Cappelli, 1970; 2d ed., 1988.

———. *La Dolce Vita.* Trans. Oscar De Liso and Bernard Shir-Cliff. New York: Ballantine, 1961.

———. *La dolce vita.* Milan: Garzanti, 1981.

———. *Early Screenplays: "Variety Lights" and "The White Sheik."* New York: Grossman, 1971.

———. *"8½": Federico Fellini, Director.* Ed. and trans. Charles Affron. New Brunswick, N.J.: Rutgers University Press, 1987.

———. *E la nave va.* Ed. Federico Fellini and Tonino Guerra. Milan: Longanesi, 1983.

———. *"La famiglia / The Family."* Ed. and trans. Peter Bondanella and Federico Pacchioni. *Fellini Amarcord: Rivista di studi felliniani* 6.1–2 (October 2006): 31–48.

———. *Fare un film.* Turin: Einaudi, 1980.

———. *Fellini on Fellini.* Ed. Anna Keel and Christian Strich. New York: Da Capo Press, 1996. Original English edition: Trans. Isabel Quigly. London: Eyre Methuen, 1976.

———. *Fellini Satyricon.* Ed. Dario Zanelli. Bologna: Cappelli, 1969. English edition: *Fellini's Satyricon.* Trans. Eugene Walter and John Matthews. New York: Ballantine, 1970.

———. *Fellini TV: "Blocknotes di un regista" / "I clowns."* Ed. Renzo Renzi. Bologna: Cappelli, 1972.

———. *Il film "Amarcord."* Ed. Gianfranco Angelucci and Liliana Betti. Bologna: Cappelli, 1974.

———. *Ginger e Fred: rendiconto di un film.* Ed. Mino Guerrini. Milan: Longanesi, 1986.

———. *Giulietta.* Genoa: Il melangolo, 1994.

———. *Giulietta degli Spiriti.* Ed. Tullio Kezich. Bologna: Cappelli, 1965. English edition: *Juliet of the Spirits.* Trans. Howard Greenfeld. New York: Orion Press, 1965.

———. *"Happy Country (Paese Felice) / Happy Country."* Ed. and trans. Peter Bondanella and Federico Pacchioni. *Fellini Amarcord: Rivista di studi felliniani* 6.1–2 (October 2006): 49–150.

———. *Intervista sul cinema.* Ed. Giovanni Grazzini. Rome: Laterza, 1983; rpt. 2004. English edition: *Comments on Film.* Trans. Joseph Henry. Fresno: Press of California State College at Fresno, 1988.

———. *Il libro dei sogni.* Ed. Tulio Kezich and Vittorio Boarini, with a contribution by Vincenzo Mollica. Milan: Rizzoli, 2007. English edition: *The Book of Dreams.* Trans. Aaron Maines, David Stanton. New York: Rizzoli International, 2008.

———. *La mia Rimini.* Bologna: Cappelli, 1987. 2d rev. ed. Rimini: Guaraldi, 2003.

———. *Il mio amico Pasqualino.* Rimini: Edizione della Fondazione Federico Fellini, 1997.

———. *"Moraldo in the City" & "A Journey with Anita."* Ed. and trans. John C. Stubbs. Urbana: University of Illinois Press, 1983.

———. *Le notti di Cabiria.* Milan: Garzanti, 1981.

———. *"8½" di Federico Fellini.* Ed. Camilla Cederna. Bologna: Cappelli, 1965.

———. *Il primo Fellini: "Lo sciecco bianco," "I vitelloni," "La strada," "Il bidone."* Ed. Renzo Renzi. Bologna: Cappelli, 1969.

———. *Prova d'orchestra.* Milan: Garzanti, 1980.

———. *Quattro film*. Introduction ("Autobiografia di uno spettatore") by Italo Calvino. Turin: Einaudi, 1974.

———. *Raccontando di me: Conversazioni con Costanzo Costantini*. Rome: Editori Riuniti, 1996. English version: *Fellini on Fellini*. Ed. Costanzo Costantini. Trans. Sohrab Sorooshian. London: Faber & Faber, 1995.

———. *Racconti umoristici*. Ed. Claudio Carabba. Turin: Einaudi, 2004.

———. *"Roma" di Federico Fellini*. Ed. Bernardino Zapponi. Bologna: Cappelli, 1972.

———. *Satyricon Politikon: le vignette tra "guerra" e "partiti."* Ed. Angelo Olivieri. Rome: Un mondo a parte, 2005.

———. *Lo sceicco bianco*. Milan: Garzanti, 1980.

———. *La Strada*. Special issue of *L'Avant-Scène du Cinéma* 102 (April 1970): 7–51.

———. *"La strada" di Federico Fellini: transcrizione del film*. Ed. Giuseppe Ricci. *Fellini Amarcord: Rivista di studi felliniani* 4.2–3 (2004): 47–159.

———. *"La Strada": Federico Fellini, Director*. Ed. Peter Bondanella and Manuela Gieri. New Brunswick: Rutgers University Press, 1987.

———. *La Strada, un film di Federico Fellini*. Ed. François-Regis Bastide, Juliette Caputo, and Chris Marker. Paris: Éditions du Seuil, 1955.

———. *"La strada": sceneggiatura originale di Federico Fellini e Tullio Pinelli*. Rome: Edizioni Bianco e Nero, 1955.

———. *"La strada*: soggetto di Tullio Pinelli e Federico Fellini." Ed. Peter Bondanella and Giuseppe Ricci. *Fellini Amarcord: Rivista di studi felliniani* 4.2–3 (2004): 21–48.

———. *Three Screenplays: "I Vitelloni," "Il Bidone," "The Temptations of Dr. Antonio."* New York: Grossman, 1970.

———. *Il viaggio di G. Mastorna*. Introduction by Tullio Kezich; afterword by Enrico Ghezzi. Milan: Bompiani, 1995. Rpt.: Ed. Ermanno Cavazzoni. Preface by Vincenzo Mollica. Macerata: Quodlibet, 2008.

———. *"I vitelloni" e "La strada": soggetto e sceneggiatura*. Milan: Longanesi, 1989.

———. *La voce della luna*. Turin: Einaudi, 1990.

———. *La voce della luna*. Ed. Lietta Tornabuoni. Florence: La Nuova Italia, 1990.

Fellini, Federico, and Georges Simenon. *Carissimo Simenon–Mon cher Fellini: carteggio di Federico Fellini e Georges Simenon*. Ed. Claude Gauteur and Silvia Sager. Milan: Adelphi, 1998.

Fellini, Federico, and Bernardino Zapponi. *Casanova: sceneggiatura originale*. Turin: Einaudi, 1976.

———. *Fellini's Casanova*. Ed. Bernardino Zapponi. Trans. Norman Thomas di Giovanni and Susan Ashe. New York: Dell, 1977.

Fellini! Milan: Skira, 2003.

Fellini Amarcord: Rivista di studi felliniani / Fellinian Studies Magazine. Rimini: Petroneno Capitani Editori, 2001–2009.

Filippini, Massimiliano, and Vittorio Ferorelli, eds. *Federico Fellini autore di testi: Dal "Marc'Aurelio" a "Luci del Varietà" (1939–1950)*. Bologna: Quaderni IBC, 1999.

Fofi, Goffredo, and Gianni Volpi, eds. *Federico Fellini: l'arte della visione*. Grugliasco: Tipografia Torinese, 1993.

Fontemaggi, Alessandra, and Giuseppe Ricci, eds. *Gli attori di Fellini: Giulietta 50 anni dopo "La strada."* Rimini: Fondazione Federico Fellini, 2005.

——. eds. *Il cinema di carta: L'eredità di Fellini in mostra*. Milan: Edizioni Nuages, 2004.

——. eds. *Il mio Fellini: Atti del Convegno—Rimini, 25–26 novembre 2005*. Rimini: Fondazione Federico Fellini, 2006.

Giacci, Vittorio, and Gianfranco Angelucci, eds. *La voce della luce: Federico Fellini*. Rome: Progetti Museali Editori/ENEL, 1995.

Giacovelli, Enrico. *Tutti i film di Federico Fellini*. Turin: Lindau, 2002.

Gieri, Manuela. *Contemporary Italian Filmmaking: Strategies of Subversion—Pirandello, Fellini, Scola, and the Directors of the New Generation*. Toronto: University of Toronto Press, 1995.

Gori, Gianfranco Miro, ed. *Rimini e le cinema: images, cinéastes, histoires*. Paris: Éditions du Centre Pompidou / Rimini: Ville de Rimini, 1989.

Gundle, Stephen. *Death and the Dolce Vita: The Dark Side of Rome in the 1950s*. Edinburgh: Canongate Books, 2011.

Hughes, Eileen Lanouette. *On the Set of "Fellini Satyricon": A Behind-the-Scenes Diary*. New York: Morrow, 1971.

Kauffmann, Stanley. "Fellini, Farewell." *New Republic* 210.5 (January 31, 1994): 28–30.

Ketcham, Charles B. *Federico Fellini: The Search for a New Mythology*. New York: Paulist Press, 1976.

Kezich, Tullio. *Il dolce cinema*. Milan: Bompiani, 1978.

——. *Federico Fellini, la vita e i film*. Milan: Feltrinelli, 2002. English edition: *Federico Fellini: His Life and Work*. Trans. Minna Proctor. New York: Faber and Faber, 2006.

——. *Fellini*. Milan: Camunia Editrice, 1987.

——. *Fellini del giorno dopo: con un alfabetiere felliniano*. Rimini: Guaraldi, 1996.

Lupo, Gordiano. *Federico Fellini: A Cinema Greatmaster*. Milan: Mediane, 2009 [English and Italian text]

Manara, Milo. *Due viaggi con Federico Fellini: Viaggio a Tulum—Il viaggio di G. Mastorna detto Fernet*. Ed. Vincenzo Mollica. Milan: Mondadori, 2001.

Maraldi, Antonio, ed. *"8½" di/de/by Federico Fellini: fotografie di / photographies de / photographs by Paul Ronald*. Cesena: Il ponte vecchio, 2007. Rimini: Fondazione Federico Fellini, 2007.

Miller, D. A. *8½*. Houndsmill, U.K.: Palgrave Macmillan, for British Film Institute, 2008.

Mollica, Vincenzo. *Fellini: parole e disegni*. Turin: Einaudi, 2000. Eng. Trans. *Fellini: Words and Drawings*. Trans. Nina Marino, with an introduction by Peter Bondanella. Welland, Ont.: Éditions Soleil, 2001.

——. ed. *Fellini sognatore: omaggio all'arte di Federico Fellini*. Firenze [Montepulciano]: Editori del Grifo, 1992.

——. ed. *Il grifo: speciale Oscar Fellini*, 3.22 (March 1993).

——. ed. *Scenari: il fumetto e il cinema di Fellini*. Montepulciano: Editori del Grifo, 1984.

——. ed. *Viaggio a Tulum: disegni di Milo Manara da un soggetto di Federico Fellini per un film da fare*. Montepulciano: Editori del Grifo, 1991.

Mollica, Vincenzo, and Alessandro Nicosia, eds. *Romarcord Fellini 1993–2003*. Milan: Skira, 2003.

Monetti, Domenico, and Giuseppe Ricci, eds. *Giulietta degli spiriti raccontato dagli Archivi Rizzoli*. Rome: Centro Sperimentale di Cinematografia / Rimini: Fondazione Federico Fellini, 2005.

Monti, Fiorella, and Elisabetta Zanzi, eds. *Fellini e dintorni: Cinema e psicoanalisi.* Cesena: Il Ponte Vecchio, 1996.

Monti, Raffaele, ed. *Bottega Fellini: "La città della donne": progetto, lavorazione, film.* Rome: De Luca, 1981.

Monti, Raffaele, and Pier Marco De Santi, ed. *L'invenzione consapevole: disegni e materiali di Federico Fellini per il film "E la nave va."* Florence: Artificio, 1984.

Murray, Edward. *Fellini the Artist.* 2d ed. New York: Frederick Ungar, 1985.

Pacchioni, Federico M. *Inspiring Fellini: Literary Collaboration Behind the Scenes.* Toronto: University of Toronto Press, 2013.

Pecori, Franco. *Federico Fellini.* Florence: La Nuova Italia, 1974.

Perry, Ted. *Filmguide to "8½."* Bloomington: Indiana University Press, 1975.

Pettigrew, Damian. *Federico Fellini: Sono un gran bugiardo: l'ultima confessione del Maestro raccolta da Damien Pettigrew.* Rome: Eleu, 2003.

———. *Fellini: I'm a Born Liar (Fellini: Je suis un grand menteur).* Documentary film (2002) on DVD. Los Angeles: First Look Pictures, 2003.

———. *I'm a Born Liar: A Fellini Lexicon.* New York: Abrams, 2003.

Piccini, Carmen. *The Magic of Fellini.* Documentary film (2002) on DVD. Distributor—Chatsworth, Calif.: Image Entertainment, 2004.

Pieri, Françoise. *Federico Fellini conteur et humoriste 1939–1942: avec des textes de Federico Fellini et un entretien inédits.* Perpignan: Collection Institut Jean Vigo, 2000.

Pinelli, Tullio. *"Le notti di Cabiria" con un'intervista di Maricla Boggio.* Nardò: BESA, n.d.

Pinkus, Karen. *The Montesi Scandal: The Death of Wilma Montesi and the Birth of the Paparazzi in Fellini's Rome.* Chicago: University of Chicago Press, 2003.

Prats, A. J. *The Autonomous Image: Cinematic Narration & Humanism.* Lexington: University Press of Kentucky, 1981.

Price, Barbara Anne, and Theodore Price. *Federico Fellini: An Annotated International Bibliography.* Metuchen, N.J.: Scarecrow Press, 1978.

Provenzano, Roberto C. *Invito al cinema di Fellini.* Milan: Mursia, 1995.

Real Dreams: Into the Dark with Federico Fellini. BBC documentary film, aired on *Omnibus*, May 15, 1987.

Ricci, Giuseppe, ed. *Federico in costume.* Rimini: Fondazione Federico Fellini, 2003.

———. *Fellini e i suoi film nei disegni della collezione Renzi.* Ed. Giuseppe Ricci. Rimini: Fondazione Federico Fellini, 2004.

———. *Il mio Fellini—seconda parte: Atti del Convegno—Rimini, 15–16 dicembre 2006.* Rimini: Fondazione Federico Fellini, 2007.

Ricci, Giuseppe, and Marco Bertozzi, eds. *Il corpo, gli interni, la città nell'opera grafica di Federico Fellini.* Rimini: Fondazione Federico Fellini, 2002.

Rohdie, Sam. *Fellini Lexicon.* London: British Film Institute, 2002.

Rondi, Brunello. *Il cinema di Fellini.* Rome: Edizioni di Bianco e Nero, 1965.

Rosenthal, Stuart. *The Cinema of Federico Fellini.* New York: A. S. Barnes, 1976.

Rossi, Moraldo, and Tatti Sanguineti. *Fellini & Rossi: il sesto vitellone.* Bologna: Le Mani, 2001.

Salachas, Gilbert. *Federico Fellini: An Investigation into His Films and Philosophy.* Trans. Rosalie Siegel. New York: Crown, 1969.

Sanguineti, Tatti, eds. *Voci del varietà / Federico delle voci: I direttori di doppiaggio di Fellini.* Rimini: Fondazione Federico Fellini, 2005.

Scolari, Giovanni. *L'Italia di Fellini.* Cantalupo in Sabina: Edizioni Sabinae, 2008.

Secchiaroli, Tazio. *Federico Fellini*. Ed. Giovanni Bertelli. Milan: Rizzoli, 2003.

Sesti, Mario, and Andrea Crozzoli, eds. *8½: Il viaggio di Fellini—fotografie di Gideon Bachmann*. Pordenone: Cinemazero, 2003.

Solmi, Angelo. *Fellini*. London: Merlin Press, 1967.

Strich, Christian, ed. *Fellini's Faces*. New York: Holt, Rinehart & Winston, 1982.

———. ed. *Fellini's Films: The Four Hundred Most Memorable Stills from Federico Fellini's Fifteen and a Half Films*. New York: Putnam's, 1977.

Stubbs, John C. *Federico Fellini: A Guide to References and Resources*. Boston: G. K. Hall, 1978.

———. *Federico Fellini as Auteur: Seven Aspects of His Films*. Carbondale: Southern Illinois University Press, 2006.

Tornabuoni, Lietta, ed. *Federico Fellini*. Milan: Rizzoli, 1994.

Trasatti, Sergio, Andrea Piersanti, and Francesco Bolzoni, eds. *Tutto Fellini su CD-ROM*. Rome: Editoria Elettronica Editel/Ente dello spettacolo, 1994.

Van Order, M. Thomas. *Listening to Fellini: Music and Meaning in Black and White*. Madison. N.J.: Fairleigh Dickinson University Press, 2009.

Verdone, Mario. *Federico Fellini*. Milan: Il Castoro, 2006 (1st ed., 1994).

Zanelli, Dario. *L'inferno immaginario di Federico Fellini: cose dette da F. F. a proposito de "Il Viaggio di G. Mastorna."* Ravenna: Guaraldi, 1995.

———. *Nel mondo di Federico: Fellini di fronte al suo cinema (e a quello degli altri)*. Preface by Federico Fellini. Turin: Nuova ERI Edizioni RAI, 1987.

Zanzotto, Andrea. *Filò: per il "Casanova" di Fellini*. Milan: Mondadori, 1988. English edition: *Peasants Wake for Fellini's "Casanova" and Other Poems*. Ed. and trans. John P. Welle and Ruth Feldman. Urbana: University of Illinois Press, 1997.

Zapponi, Bernardino. *Il mio Fellini*. Venice: Marsilio Editori, 1995.

Davide Ferrario

Maraldi, Antonio. *Il cinema di Davide Ferrario*. Cesena: Il Ponte Vecchio, 2007.

Marco Ferreri

Accialini, Fulvio, and Lucia Coluccelli. *Marco Ferreri*. Milan: Edizioni il Formichiere, 1979.

Ferreri, Marco. *Chiedo asilo*. Ed. Maurizio Grande. Milan: Feltrinelli, 1980.

———. *L'ultima donna*. Ed. Anna Maria Tatò. Turin: Einaudi, 1976.

Grande, Maurizio. *Marco Ferreri*. Florence: La Nuova Italia, 1974.

Standola, Alberto. *Marco Ferreri*. Milan: Il Castoro, 2004.

Lucio Fulci

Albiero, Paolo, and Giacomo Cacciatore. *Il terrorista dei generi: tutto il cinema di Lucio Fulci*. Rome: Un mondo a parte, 2004.

Bruschini, Antonio, and Antonio Tentori. *Lucio Fulci: il poeta della crudeltà*. Rome: Mondo Ignoto, 2004.

Chianese, As, and Gordiano Lupi. *Filmare la morte: il cinema horror e thriller di Lucio Fulci*. Piombino, Livorno: Edizioni Il Foglio Letterario, 2006.

Gomarasca, Manlio. *L'opera al nero: il cinema di Lucio Fulci*. Milan: Nocturno, 2003.

Romagnoli, Michele. *L'occhio del testimone: il cinema di Lucio Fulci*. Rome: Granata Press, 1992.

Thrower, Stephen. *Beyond Terror: The Films of Lucio Fulci*. New York: Fab Press, 1999.

Matteo Garrone

De Sanctis, Pierpaolo, Domenico Monetti, and Luca Pallanch. *Non solo Gomorra: tutto il cinema di Matteo Garrone*. Cantalupo in Sabina: Edizioni Sabinae, 2008.

Augusto Genina

Costa, Antonio. *I leoni di Schneider: percorsi intertestuali nel cinema ritrovato*. Rome: Bulzoni, 2002.

Germani, Sergio G., and Vittorio Martinelli, eds. *Il cinema di Augusto Genina*. Pasian di Prato, Udine: Edizioni Biblioteca dell'Immagine, 1989.

Pietro Germi

Aprà, Adriano, Massimo Armenzoni, and Patrizia Pistagnesi, eds. *Pietro Germi, ritratto di un regista all'antica*. Parma: Pratiche Editrice, 1989.

Caldiron, Orio. *Pietro Germi, la frontiera e la legge*. Rome: Bulzoni, 2004.

Germi, Pietro. *"L'uomo di paglia" di Pietro Germi*. Ed. Fausto Montesanti. Bologna: Cappelli, 1958.

Giacovelli, Enrico. *Pietro Germi*, 2d ed. Milan: Il Castoro, 1997 (1st ed., Florence: La Nuova Italia, 1991).

Sesti, Mario. *Tutto il cinema di Pietro Germi*. Milan: Baldini & Castoldi, 1997.

———. ed. *Pietro Germi: The Latin Loner*. Milan: Olivares, 1999.

Marco Tullio Giordana

Errico-Reiter, Rosa. *"I cento passi": Marco Tullio Giordana*. Perugia: Guerra Edizioni, 2007.

Maraldi, Antonio, ed. *"I cento passi": un film di Marco Tullio Giordana*. Florence: Edizioni Il Ponte Vecchio, 2005.

Petraglia, Sandro, and Stefano Rulli. *"La meglio gioventù": un film di Marco Tullio Giordana*. Rome: RAI ERI, 2004.

Alberto Lattuada

Boledi, Luigi, and Raffaele De Berti, eds. *"Luci del Varietà": pagine scelte*. Milan: Il Castoro, 1999.

Bruno, Edoardo. *Alberto Lattuada*. Rome: ANICA, n.d.

Camerini, Claudio. *Alberto Lattuada*. Florence: La Nuova Italia, 1982.

Cosulich, Callisto. *I film di Alberto Lattuada*. Rome: Gremese, 1985.

Lattuada, Alberto. *"La steppa" di Alberto Lattuada*. Ed. Franco Calderoni. Bologna: Cappelli, 1962.

Oldoini, Enrico. *A proposito di "Così come sei": dall'idea al film— fatti personaggi e indiscrete avventure rubate dietro lo schermo*. Bologna: Cappelli, 1978.

Turroni, Giuseppe. *Alberto Lattuada*. Milan: Moizzi, 1977.

Villa, Federica. *Botteghe di scrittura per il cinema italiano: Intorno a "Il bandito" di Alberto Lattuada*. Venice: Marsilio, 2002.

Umberto Lenzi

Gomarasca, Manlio. *Umberto Lenzi*. Milan: Nocturno Libri, 2001.

Sergio Leone

Cèbe, Gilles. *Sergio Leone*. Paris: Henri Veyrier, 1984.

Cumbow, Robert C. *Once Upon a Time: The Films of Sergio Leone*. Metuchen, N.J.: Scarecrow Press, 1987.

De Fornari, Oreste. *Sergio Leone*. Milan: Moizzi, 1977.

——. *Sergio Leone: The Great Italian Dream of Legendary America*. New York: Gremese International, 1997.

——. *Tutti i film di Sergio Leone*. Milan: Ubulibri, 1984.

Di Claudio, Gianni. *Directed by Sergio Leone*. Chieti: Libreria Universitaria Editrice, 1990.

Donati, Roberto. *Sergio Leone: America e nostalgia*. Alessandria: Edizioni Falsopiano, 2004.

Fawell, John. *The Art of Sergio Leone's "Once Upon a Time in the West": A Critical Appreciation*. Jefferson, NC: McFarland, 2005.

Frayling, Christopher. *Once Upon a Time in Italy: The Westerns of Sergio Leone*. New York: Abrams, 2005.

——. *Sergio Leone: Something to Do with Death*. London: Faber and Faber, 2000.

Gabutti, Diego. *C'era una volta in America*. Milan: Rizzoli, 1984.

Garofalo, Marcello. *Tutto il cinema di Sergio Leone*. Milan: Baldini Castoldi Dalai, 1999.

Leone, Sergio. *"C'era una volta in America": un film di Sergio Leone—Photographic Memories*. Ed. Marcello Garofalo. Rome: Editalia, 1988.

——. *Per un pugno di dollari*. Ed. Luca Verdone. Bologna: Cappelli, 1979.

Martin, Adrian. *Once Upon a Time in America*. London: British Film Institute, 1998.

Meyer, David N. "Once Upon a Time, an Epic Was Shorn of Grandeur." *New York Times*, February 14, 1999, Arts Section, p. 26.

Mininni, Francesco. *Sergio Leone*. Milan: Il Castoro, 2007 (1st ed., Firenze: La Nuova Italia, 1989).

Moscati, Italo. *Sergio Leone: Quando il cinema era grande*. Turin: Lindau, 2007.

Roth, Lane. *Film Semiotics, Metz, and Leone's Trilogy*. New York: Garland, 1983.

Saccutelli, Gianluca. *C'era una volta Sergio Leone*. Porto Sant'Elpidio, Ascoli Piceno: Ottava Musa Edizioni, 1999.

Smith, Paul. *Clint Eastwood: A Cultural Production*. Minneapolis: University of Minnesota Press, 1993.

Carlo Lizzani

De Santi, Gualtiero. *Carlo Lizzani*. Roma: Gremese, 2001.

Lizzani, Carlo. *Il cinema italiano, 1895–1979*. 2 vols. Rome: Editori Riuniti, 1979. 2d ed. published as *Il cinema italiano dalle origini agli anni ottanta*. Rome: Editori Riuniti, 1982.

——. *"Fontamara" dal romanzo di Ignazio Silone*. Turin: Edizioni ERI, 1980.

——. *"L'oro di Roma" di Carlo Lizzani*. Ed. Giovanni Vento. Bologna: Cappelli, 1961.

——. *"Il processo di Verona" di Carlo Lizzani*. Ed. Antonio Savignano. Bologna: Cappelli, 1963.

Luigi Magni

Montini, Franco, and Piero Spila, eds. *Il mondo di Luigi Magni*. Rome: RAI ERI, 2000.

Mario Martone

Ranucci, Georgette, and Stefanella Ughi, eds. *Mario Martone*. Rome: Dino Audino, 1995.

Francesco Maselli

Parigi, Stefania. *Francesco Maselli.* Florence: La Nuova Italia, 1992.

Raffaele Matarazzo

Prudenzi, Angela. *Raffaele Matarazzo.* Florence: La Nuova Italia, 1990.

Mario Mattoli

Della Casa, Stefano. *Mario Mattoli.* Florence: La Nuova Italia, 1990.

Mario Monicelli

Borghini, Fabrizio, ed. *Mario Monicelli: cinquant'anni di cinema.* Pisa: Edizioni Master, 1985.

Della Casa, Stefano. *Mario Monicelli.* Florence: La Nuova Italia, 1986.

Mario Monicelli. Milan: Mediane, 2007.

Mondadori, Sebastiano. *La commedia umana: Conversazioni con Mario Monicelli.* Milan: Il Saggiatore, 2005.

Monicelli, Mario. *L'arte della commedia.* Ed. Lorenzo Codelli. Bari: Edizioni Dedalo, 1986.

———. *"I compagni" di Mario Monicelli.* Ed. Pio Baldelli. Bologna: Cappelli, 1963.

Giuliano Montaldo

Miles, Keith, and David Butler. *Marco Polo.* New York: Dell, 1982.

Montaldo, Giuliano, and Vincenzo Labella. *"Marco Polo": come nasce un film.* Ed. Giacomo Gambetti. Turin: Edizioni RAI, 1980.

Nanni Moretti

Coco, Giuseppe. *Nanni Moretti: cinema come diario.* Milan: Bruno Mondadori, 2006.

De Bernardinis, Flavio. *Nanni Moretti.* Milan: Il Castoro, 2006.

Gili, Jean. *Nanni Moretti.* Rome: Gremese, 2006.

Giovannini, Memmo, Enrico Magrelli, and Mario Sesti. *Nanni Moretti.* Naples: Edizioni scientifiche italiane, 1986.

Mascia, Gianfranco. *Qualcosa di sinistra: intervista a Nanni Moretti.* Genoa: Frilli, 2002.

Mazierska, Ewa, and Laura Rascaroli. *The Cinema of Nanni Moretti: Dreams and Diaries.* New York: Columbia University Press and Wallflower Press, 2004; rpt. *Il cinema di Nanni Moretti: Sogni & diari.* Rome: Gremese, 2006.

Menarini, Roy. *Nanni Moretti: "Bianca."* Turin: Lindau, 2007.

Ranucci, Georgette, and Stefanella Ughi, eds. *Nanni Moretti.* Rome: Dino Audino, 2001.

Villa, Federica. *Nanni Moretti: "Caro diario."* Turin: Lindau, 2007.

Mauruzio Nichetti

Orto, Nuccio. *Maurizio Nichetti: un comico, un autore.* Chieti: Métis, 1990.

Pistoia, Marco. *Maurizio Nichetti.* Milan: Il Castoro, 1997.

Ermanno Olmi

Allegretti, Elisa, and Giancarlo Giraud, eds. *Ermanno Olmi: L'esperienza di Ipotesi Cinema.* Genoa: Le Mani–Microart'S, 2001.

Aprà, Adriano, ed. *Il cinema di Ermanno Olmi.* Parma: Incontri Cinematografici Monticelli Terme, 1979.

Dillon, Jeanne. *Ermanno Olmi*. Florence: La Nuova Italia, 1986.

Olmi, Ermanno. *L'albero degli zoccoli*. Ed. Giacomo Gambetti. Turin: Edizioni RAI, 1980.

———. *"E venne un uomo": un film di Ermanno Olmi*. Ed. Giacomo Gambetti and Claudio Sorgi. Milan: Garzanti, 1965.

Tabanelli, Giorgio. *Ermanno Olmi: nascita del documentario poetico*. Rome: Bulzoni, 1987.

Ferzan Ozpetek

Gabriele, Marcello. *Ferzan Ozpetek: La leggerezza e la profondità*. Bologna: Le Mani, 2009.

Pier Paolo Pasolini

Bandeau, Agnès. *Pasolini, Chaucer and Boccaccio: Two Medieval Texts and Their Translation to Film*. Jefferson, N.C.: McFarland, 2006.

Bertini, Antonio. *Teoria e tecnica del film in Pasolini*. Rome: Bulzoni, 1979.

Boccaccio, Giovanni. *The Decameron: A Norton Critical Edition*. Ed. and trans. Mark Musa and Peter Bondanella. New York: Norton, 1977.

De Benedictis, Maurizio. *Linguaggi dell'aldilà: Fellini e Pasolini*. Rome: Lithos, 2000.

De Giusti, Luciano. *I film di Pier Paolo Pasolini*. Rome: Gremese, 1983.

Duflot, Jean, ed. *Entretiens avec Pier Paolo Pasolini*. Paris: Éditions Pierre Belfond, 1970.

Estève, Michel, ed. *Pier Paolo Pasolini*, 2 vols. 1, *Le Mythe et le sacré*. Études Cinématographiques, nos. 109–11. 2, *Un "Cinéma de poésie."* Études Cinématographiques, nos. 112–14. Paris: Lettres modernes Minard, 1976–77.

Ferrero, Adelio. *Il cinema di Pier Paolo Pasolini*, 2d ed. Venice: Marsilio, 2005.

Fusillo, Massimo. *La Grecia secondo Pasolini: mito e cinema*. Florence: La Nuova Italia, 1996.

Gervais, Marc. *Pier Paolo Pasolini*. Paris: Éditions Seghers, 1973.

Gordon, Robert S. C. *Pasolini: Forms of Subjectivity*. New York: Oxford University Press, 1996.

Green, Naomi. *Pier Paolo Pasolini: Cinema as Heresy*. Princeton: Princeton University Press, 1991.

Luzi, Alfredo, and Luigi Martellini, eds. *Pier Paolo Pasolini*. Urbino: Argalia, 1973.

Maggi, Armando. *The Resurrection of the Body: Pier Paolo Pasolini from Saint Paul to Sade*. Chicago: University of Chicago Press, 2008.

Manzoli, Giacomo. *La voce e il silenzio nel cinema di Pier Paolo Pasolini*. Bologna: Pendragon, 2001.

Moscati, Italo. *Pasolini passione: vita senza fine di un artista trasparente*. Rome: Ediesse, 2005.

Murri, Serafino. *Pier Paolo Pasolini*. Milan: Il Castoro, 2000.

Pasolini, Pier Paolo. *"Edipo re": un film di Pier Paolo Pasolini*. Ed. Giacomo Gambetti. Milan: Garzanti, 1967.

———. *Heretical Empiricism*. Ed. Louise K. Barnett and trans. by Ben Lawton and Louise K. Barnett. Bloomington: Indiana University Press, 1988; rpt. Washington: New Academia Publishing, 2005.

———. *"Medea": un film di Pier Paolo Pasolini*. Milan: Garzanti, 1970.

———. *Oedipus Rex*. Trans. John Matthews. New York: Frederick Ungar, 1971.

———. *Poems*. Trans. Norman MacAfee. New York: Vintage, 1982.

———. *The Ragazzi.* Trans. Emile Capouya. New York: Grove Press, 1968.

———. *Teorema.* Milan: Garzanti, 1968.

———. *Trilogia della vita.* Ed. Giorgio Gattei. Milan: Mondadori, 1987.

———. *Uccellacci e uccellini,* 2d ed. Milan: Garzanti, 1975.

———. *Il vangelo secondo Matteo.* Ed. Giacomo Gambetti. Milan: Garzanti, 1964.

———. *A Violent Life.* Trans. William Weaver. London: Johathan Cape, 1968.

Passannanti, Erminia. *Il Corpo & il Potere: "Salò o le 120 Giornate di Sodoma" di Pier Paolo Pasolini.* Leichester: Troubadour, 2004.

Petraglia, Sandro. *Pier Paolo Pasolini.* Florence: La Nuova Italia, 1974.

Pier Paolo Pasolini. Milan: Mediane, 2007.

Pier Paolo Pasolini: A Future Life. Rome: Fondazione Pier Paolo Pasolini, 1989.

Quintavalle, Uberto Paolo. *Giornate di Sodoma: ritratto di Pasolini e del suo ultimo film.* Milan: SugarCo, 1976.

Rhodes, John David. *Stupendous, Miserable City: Pasolini's Rome.* Minneapolis: University of Minnesota Press, 2007.

Rohdie, Sam. *The Passion of Pier Paolo Pasolini.* Bloomington: Indiana University Press, 1995.

Rumble, Patrick. *Allegories of Contamination: Pier Paolo Pasolini's "Trilogy of Life."* Toronto: University of Toronto Press, 1995.

Rumble, Patrick, and Bart Testa, eds. *Pier Paolo Pasolini: Contemporary Perspectives.* Toronto: University of Toronto Press, 1994.

Ryan-Scheutz, Colleen. *Sex, the Self, and the Sacred: Women in the Cinema of Pier Paolo Pasolini.* Toronto: University of Toronto Press, 2007.

Salvini, Laura. *I frantumi del tutto: ipotesi e letture dell'ultimo progetto cinematografico di Pier Paolo Pasolini—"Porno-teo-kolossal."* Bologna: Editrice CLUEB, 2004.

Schwartz, Barth David. *Pasolini Requiem.* New York: Pantheon, 1992.

Siciliano, Enzo. *Vita di Pasolini.* Milan: Mondadori, 2005. English edition (of 1978 1st ed.): *Pasolini: A Biography.* Trans. John Shepley. New York: Random House, 1982.

Snyder, Stephen. *Pier Paolo Pasolini.* Boston: Twayne, 1980.

Stack, Oswald, ed. *Pasolini on Pasolini.* Bloomington: Indiana University Press, 1970.

Viano, Maurizio. *A Certain Realism: Making Use of Pasolini's Film Theory and Practice.* Berkeley: University of California Press, 1993.

Villani, Simone. *Il Decameron allo specchio: Il film di Pasolini come saggio sull'opera di Boccaccio.* Rome: Donzelli, 2004.

Willemen, Paul, ed. *Pier Paolo Pasolini.* London: British Film Institute, 1977.

Giovanni Pastrone

Alovisio, Silvio, and Alberto Barbera, eds. *Cabiria & Cabiria.* Introduction by Martin Scorsese. Milan: Il Castoro, 2006.

Berretto, Paolo, and Gianni Rondolino, eds. *"Cabiria" e il suo tempo.* Milan: Il Castoro, 1998.

Radicati, Roberto, and Ruggero Rossi, eds. *"Cabiria": visione storica del III secolo a.C.* Turin: Museo Nazionale del Cinema, 1977.

Usai, Paolo Cherchi. *Giovanni Pastrone.* Florence: La Nuova Italia, 1986.

Elio Petri

Bacci, Federico, Nicola Guarneri, and Stefano Leone, eds. *Elio Petri, appunti su un autore.* Milan: Feltrinelli, 2005.

Gili, Jean A., ed. *Elio Petri*. Nice: Université de Nice, Faculté des Lettres et Sciences Humaines, Section d'histoire, 1974.

Petri, Elio. *Scritti di cinema e di vita*. Rome: Bulzoni, 2007.

Rossi, Alfredo. *Elio Petri*. Florence: La Nuova Italia, 1979.

Antonio Pietrangeli

Maraldi, Antonio. *Antonio Pietrangeli*. Florence: La Nuova Italia, 1991.

Morelli, Guglielmina, Giulio Martini, and Giancarlo Zappoli. *Un'invisibile presenza: Il cinema di Antonio Pietrangeli*. Milan: Il Castoro, 1998.

Marco Ponte

Ponte, Marco. *A/A Andata & Ritorno*. Ed. Sara Beltrame. Venice: Marsilio Editori, 2004.

Gillo Pontecorvo

Bignardi, Irene. *Memorie estorte a uno smemorato: vita di Gillo Pontecorvo*. Milan: Feltrinelli, 1999.

Celli, Carlo. *Gillo Pontecorvo: From Resistance to Terrorism*. Lanham, Md.: Scarecrow Press, 2005.

Ghirelli, Massino. *Gillo Pontecorvo*. Florence: La Nuova Italia, 1979.

Mellen, Joan. *Filmguide to "The Battle of Algiers."* Bloomington: Indiana University Press, 1973.

Pontecorvo, Gillo. *Gillo Pontecorvo's "The Battle of Algiers."* Ed. Piernico Solinas. New York: Scribner's, 1973.

Dino Risi

Bellumori, Cinzia. *Dino Risi*. Rome: ANICA, n.d.

D'Agostini, Paolo. *Dino Risi*. Milan: Il Castoro, 1995.

Miccichè, Lino, ed. *"Una vita difficile" di Dino Risi: risate amare nel lungo dopoguerra*. Venice: Marsilio, 2000.

Risi, Dino. *I miei mostri*. Milan: Mondadori, 2004.

Viganò, Aldo. *Dino Risi*. Milan: Moizzi, 1977.

Francesco Rosi

Bolzoni, Francesco. *I film di Francesco Rosi*. Rome: Gremese, 1986.

Gili, Jean A. *Francesco Rosi: Cinéma et pouvoir*. Paris: Éditions du Cerf, 1976.

Mancino, Anton Giulio, and Zambetti, Sandro. *Francesco Rosi*, 2d ed. Milan: Il Castoro, 1998.

Rosi, Francesco. *Salvatore Giuliano*. Ed. Tullio Kezich. Rome: Edizioni FM, 1961.

———. *"Uomini contro" di Francesco Rosi*. Ed. Callisto Cosulich. Bologna: Cappelli, 1970.

Rosi, Francesco, and Eugenio Scalfari. *"Il caso Mattei": un corsaro al servizio della repubblica*. Bologna: Cappelli, 1972.

Testa, Carlo, ed. *Poet of Civic Courage: The Films of Francesco Rosi*. Westport, Conn.: Praeger, 1996.

Roberto Rossellini

Aprà, Adriano, ed. *"Roma città aperta" di Roberto Rossellini*. Rome: Comune di Roma Assessorato alla cultura, 1994.

———. ed. *Rosselliniana: bibliografia internazionale, dossier "Paisà."* Rome: Di Giacomo, 1987.

———. ed. *Rossellini India 1957*. Rome: Cinecittà International, 1991.

Baldelli, Pio. *Roberto Rossellini: i suoi film (1936–1972) e la filmografia completa*. Rome: Edizioni Samonà e Savelli, 1972.

Bondanella, Peter. *The Films of Roberto Rossellini*. New York: Cambridge University Press, 1993.

Braudy, Leo, and Morris Dickstein, eds. *Great Film Directors: A Critical Anthology*. New York: Oxford University Press, 1978.

Brunette, Peter. *Roberto Rossellini*. New York: Oxford University Press, 1987.

Bruni, David. *Roberto Rossellini "Roma città aperta."* Turin: Lindau, 2006.

Bruno, Edoardo. *Rossellini Bergman: Europe Six*. Rome: Cinecittà Estero, 1990.

———, ed. *R. R. Roberto Rossellini*. Rome: Bulzoni, 1979.

De Marchis Rossellini, Marcella. *Un matrimonio riuscito*. Milan: Il Castoro, 1996.

Di Giammatteo, Fernaldo. *Roberto Rossellini*. Florence: La Nuova Italia, 1990.

Foracs, David. *Rome Open City*. London: British Film Institute, 2000.

Foracs, David, Sarah Lutton, and Geoffrey Nowell-Smith, eds. *Roberto Rossellini: Magician of the Real*. Bloomington: Indiana University Press, 2001.

Gallagher, Tag. *The Adventures of Roberto Rossellini: His Life and Films*. New York: Da Capo Press, 1998.

Gottlieb, Sidney, ed. *Roberto Rossellini's "Rome Open City."* New York: Cambridge University Press, 2004.

Guarner, José Luis. *Roberto Rossellini*. Trans. Elisabeth Cameron. New York: Praeger, 1970.

Johnson, William Bruce. *Miracles and Sacrilege: Roberto Rossellini, the Church, and Film Censorship in Hollywood*. Toronto: University of Toronto Press, 2008.

MacBean, James Roy. *Film and Revolution*. Bloomington: Indiana University Press, 1975.

Masi, Stefano, and Enrico Lancia. *I film di Roberto Rossellini*. Rome: Gremese, 1987.

Michelone, Guido. *Invito al cinema di Rossellini*. Milan: Mursia, 1996.

Parigi, Stefano, ed. *"Paisà": Analisi del film*. Venice: Marsilio, 2005.

Ranvaud, Dan, ed. *Roberto Rossellini*. BFI Dossier no. 8. London: British Film Institute, 1981.

Roberto Rossellini. Rome: Ente autonomo di gestione per il cinema, 1987.

Roncoroni, Stefano. *La storia di "Roma città aperta."* Bologna: Le Mani–Microart'S, 2006.

Rondolino, Gianni. *Roberto Rossellini*, 2d ed. Florence: La Nuova Italia, 1977.

———. *Roberto Rossellini*. Turin: UTET, 1989.

Rossellini, Isabella. *In the Name of the Father, the Daughter, and the Holy Spirits: Remembering Roberto Rossellini*. Munich: Schirmer–Mosel, 2006.

Rossellini, Roberto. *"Era notte a Roma" di Roberto Rossellini*. Ed. Renzo Renzi. Bologna: Cappelli, 1960.

———. *Il mio metodo: scritti e intervisti*. Ed. Adriano Aprà. Venice: Marsilio Editori, 1987. English edition: *My Method: Writings & Interviews*. Trans. Annapaola Cancogni. New York: Marsilio, 1992.

———. *Quasi un'autobiografia*. Ed. Stefano Roncoroni. Milan: Mondadori, 1987. French edition: *Fragments d'une autobiographie*. Trans. Stefano Roncoroni. Paris: Éditions Ramsay, 1987.

———. *La trilogia della guerra*. Ed. Stefano Roncoroni. Bologna: Cappelli, 1972. English edition: *The War Trilogy*. Trans. Judith Green. New York: Grossman, 1973.

Serceau, Michel. *Roberto Rossellini*. Paris: Éditions du Cerf, 1986.

Trasatti, Sergio. *Rossellini e la televisione*. Rome: La Rassegna Editrice, 1978.

———. ed. CD-ROM: *Roberto Rossellini su CD-ROM*. Rome: Editoria Elettronica Editel, 1994.

Verdone, Mario. *Roberto Rossellini*. Paris: Éditions Seghers, 1963.

Walter Ruttman

Camerini, Claudio, ed. *"Acciaio": un film degli anni trenta*. Turin: Nuova ERI Edizioni RAI, 1990.

Gabriele Salvatores

Ammaniti, Niccolò. *I'm Not Scared*. Trans. Jonathan Hunt. Edinburgh: Canongate Books, 2003.

Grassi, Raffaella. *Territori di fuga: il cinema di Gabriele Salvatores*. Alessandria: Edizioni Falsopiano, 1997.

Malavasi, Luca. *Gabriele Salvatores*. Milan: Il Castoro, 2005.

Merkel, Flavio, ed. *Gabriele Salvatores*. Rome: Dino Audino, 1992.

Ettore Scola

Bertini, Antonio. *Ettore Scola: Il cinema e io—Conversazione con Antonio Bertini*. Rome: Officina Edizioni Cinecittà Internazional, 1996.

Bíspuri, Ennio. *Ettore Scola, un umanista nel cinema italiano*. Rome: Bulzoni, 2006.

Bondanella, Peter. "La comédie 'métacinématographique' d'Ettore Scola." In Michel Serceau, ed., *La comédie italienne de Don Camillo à Berlusconi*. *CinémAction* 42 (March 1987): 91–99.

De Santi, Pier Marco, and Rossano Vittori. *I film di Ettore Scola*. Rome: Gremese, 1987.

Ellero, Roberto. *Ettore Scola*, 2d ed. Milan: Il Castoro, 1996.

Gieri, Manuela. *Contemporary Italian Filmmaking: Strategies of Subversion—Pirandello, Fellini, Scola, and the Directors of the New Generation*. Toronto: University of Toronto Press, 1995.

Kezich, Tullio, and Alessandra Levantesi, eds. *"Una giornata particolare": un film di Ettore Scola—incontrarsi e dirsi addio nella Roma del '38*. Rome: Edizioni Lindau, 2003.

Marinucci, Vincio. *Ettore Scola*. Rome: ANICA, n.d.

Masi, Stefano. *Ettore Scola*. Rome: Gremese, 2006.

Scola, Ettore. *Una giornata particolare*. Milan: Longanesi, 1977.

Zagarrio, Vito, ed. *Trevico-Cinecittà: L'avventuroso viaggio di Ettore Scola*. Venice: Marsilio Editori, 2002.

Mario Soldati

Malavasi, Luca. *Mario Soldati*. Milan: Il Castoro, 2006.

Silvio Soldini

Colombo, Silvia. *Il cinema di Silvio Soldini*. Alessandria: Edizioni Falsopiano, 2002.

Luciano, Bernadette. *The Cinema of Silvio Soldini: Dream—Image—Voyage*. Leichester: Troubadour, 2008.

Gianluca Tavarelli

Volpi, Gianni. *Gianluca Tavarelli*. Alessandria: Edizioni Falsopiano, 2003.

Paolo and Vittorio Taviani

Accialini, Fulvio, and Lucia Coluccelli. *Paolo e Vittorio Taviani*. Florence: La Nuova Italia, 1979.

Aristarco, Guido. *Sotto il segno dello scorpione: il cinema dei fratelli Taviani*. Florence: Casa Editrice G. D'Anna, 1977.

Cooperativa Nuovi Quaderni, eds. *Cinema e utopia: i fratelli Taviani, ovvero il significato dell'esagerazione*. Parma: Nuovi Quaderni, 1974.

De Poli, Marco. *Paolo e Vittorio Taviani*. Milan: Moizzi, 1977.

De Santi, Pier Marco. *I film di Paolo e Vittorio Taviani*. Rome: Gremese, 1988.

Ferrucci, Riccardo, ed. *La bottega Taviani: un viaggio nel cinema da San Miniato a Hollywood*. Florence: La Casa Usher, 1987.

———. *Paolo and Vittorio Taviani: Poetry of the Italian Landscape*. Trans. Patricia Fogarty. New York: Gremese International, 1996.

Ledda, Gavino. *Padre Padrone: The Education of a Shepherd*. Trans. George Salmanazar. New York: Urizen Books, 1979.

Orto, Nuccio. *La notte dei desideri: il cinema dei fratelli Taviani*. Palermo: Sellerio, 1987.

Paolo & Vittorio Taviani: Leone d'Oro, Venezia 1986. Rome: ANICA, 1986.

Taviani, Paolo, and Vittorio Taviani. *Padre padrone*. Bologna: Cappelli, 1977.

———. *San Michele aveva un gallo—Allonsanfan*. Bologna: Cappelli, 1974.

———. *Sotto il segno dello scorpione—Il prato*. Turin: ERI, 1981.

———. with Tonino Guerra. *Good Morning, Babylon*. London: Faber and Faber, 1987.

Giuseppe Tornatore

Hope, William. *The Films of Giuseppe Tornatore*. Market Harborough: Troubador, 2001.

Tornatore, Giuseppe. *Nuovo cinema Paradiso*. Palermo: Sellerio, 1990.

Roberta Torre

Marcus, Millicent. "Postmodern Pastiche, the *Sceneggiata*, and the View of the Mafia from Below in Roberta Torre's *To Die for Tano*." In *After Fellini: National Cinema in the Postmodern Age*. Baltimore: Johns Hopkins University Press, 2002, pp. 234–50.

Massimo Troisi

Giusti, Marco, ed. *Massimo Troisi: Il mondo intero proprio—pensieri e battute*. Milan: Mondadori, 2004.

Skármeta, Antonio. *The Postman*. Trans. Katherine Silver. New York: Hyperion, 1993.

Troisi, Massimo, and Anna Pavignano. *"Ricomincio da tre": sceneggiatura dal film*. Milan: Feltrinelli, 1981.

Tonino Valerii

Curti, Roberto, ed. *Il mio nome è Nessuno: lo spaghetti western secondo Tonino Valerii*. Rome: Un mondo a parte, 2008.

La Selva, Tommaso. *Tonino Valerii*. Milan: Nocturno Libri, 2000.

Florestano Vancini

Gambetti, Giacomo. *Florestano Vancini*. Rome: Gremese, 2000.

Daniele Vicari

Detassis, Piera. *Daniele Vicari*. Alessandria: Edizioni Falsopiano, 2003.

Paolo Virzì

Virzì, Paolo, and Francesco Bruni. *Caterina va in città*. Venice: Marsilio Editori, 2003.

Virzì, Paolo, Francesco Gruni, and Francesco Piccolo. *My Name Is Tanino*. Rome: Arcana Fiction, 2002.

Luchino Visconti

Bacon, Henry. *Visconti: Explorations of Beauty and Decay*. Cambridge: Cambridge University Press, 1998.

Baldelli, Pio. *Luchino Visconti*. Milan: Mazzotta, 1973; rev. ed. 1982.

Bencivenni, Alessandro. *Luchino Visconti*, 2d ed. Milan: Il Castoro, 1999.

Bruni, David, and Veronica Pravadelli, eds. *Studi viscontiani*. Venice: Marsilio Editori, 1997.

De Carvalho, Caterina d'Amico, ed. *Viscontiana: Luchino Visconti e il melodramma verdiano*. Milan: Mazzotta, 2001.

de Carvalho, Caterina d'Amico, and Renzo Renzi. *Luchino Visconti: il mio teatro*. 2 vols. 1, *1936–1953*; 2, *1954-1976*. Bologna: Cappelli, 1979.

De Giusti, Luciano. *I film di Luchino Visconti*. Rome: Gremese, 1985.

Di Giammatteo, Fernaldo, and Aldo Bernardini, eds. *La controversia Visconti*. Rome: Edizioni dell'Ateneo e Bizzarri, 1976.

Estève, Michel, ed. *Luchino Visconti: L'histoire et l'esthétique*. Études Cinématographiques, nos. 26–7. Paris: Lettres modernes Minard, 1963.

Ferrara, Giuseppe. *Luchino Visconti*, 2d ed. Trans. Jean-Pierre Pinaud. Paris: Éditions Seghers, 1970.

Ferrero, Adelio, ed. *Visconti: il cinema*. Modena: Stampa Cooptip, 1977.

Mancini, Elaine. *Luchino Visconti: A Guide to References and Resources*. Boston: G. K. Hall, 1986.

Miccichè, Lino. *Luchino Visconti: un profilo critico*. Venice: Marsilio Editori, 1996.

———. ed. *"Il gattopardo."* Naples: Electa, 1996.

———. ed. *"La terra trema" di Luchino Visconti: analisi di un capolavoro*. Turin: Centro Sperimentale di Cinematografia, 1994.

Nowell-Smith, Geoffrey. *Luchino Visconti*. 3d ed. London: British Film Institute, 2003.

Partridge, Colin. *"Senso": Visconti's Film and Boito's Novel*. Lewiston, N.Y.: Edwin Mellen Press, 1991.

Pravadelli, Veronica, ed. *Il cinema di Luchino Visconti*. Rome: Marsilio, 2000.

———. ed. *Visconti a Volterra: La genesi di "Vaghe stelle dell'Orsa. . . ."* Turin: Lindau, 2000.

Rohdie, Sam. *Rocco and His Brothers*. London: British Film Institute, 1993.

Rondolino, Gianni. *Luchino Visconti*. Turin: UTET, 1981.

Schifano, Laurence. *Luchino Visconti: Les feux de la passion*. Paris: Perrin, 1987. Italian edition: *I fuochi della passione: la vita di Luchino Visconti*. Trans. Sergio

Ferrero; Milano: Longanesi, 1988. *Luchino Visconti: The Flames of Passion*, trans. William S. Byron. London: Collins, 1990.

Servadio, Gaia. *Luchino Visconti: A Biography*. New York: Franklin Watts, 1983.

Stirling, Monica. *A Screen of Time: A Study of Luchino Visconti*. New York: Harcourt Brace Jovanovich, 1979.

Tonetti, Claretta. *Luchino Visconti*. Boston: Twayne, 1983.

Tramontana, Gaetano. *Invito al cinema di Luchino Visconti*. Milan: Mursia, 2003.

Villien, Bruno. *Visconti*. Barcelona: Calmann-Lévy, 1986.

Visconti, Luchino. *Bellissima*. Ed. Enzo Ungari. Bologna: Cappelli, 1977.

——. *"La caduta degli dei (Götterdämmerung)" di Luchino Visconti*. Ed. Stefano Roncoroni. Bologna: Cappelli, 1969.

——. *Il film "Il gattopardo" e la regia di Luchino Visconti*. Ed. Suso Cecchi D'Amico. Bologna: Cappelli, 1963.

——. *Gruppo di famiglia in un interno*. Ed. Giorgio Treves. Bologna: Cappelli, 1975.

——. *"Il lavoro."* In *Boccaccio '70 di De Sica, Fellini, Monicelli, Visconti*. Ed. Carlo Di Carlo and Gaio Fratini. Bologna: Cappelli, 1962, pp. 183–203.

——. *"Ludwig" di Luchino Visconti*. Ed. Giorgio Ferrara. Bologna: Cappelli, 1973.

——. *"Morte a Venezia" di Luchino Visconti*. Ed. Lino Miccichè. Bologna: Cappelli, 1971.

——. *"Le notti bianche" di Luchino Visconti*. Ed. Renzo Renzi. Bologna: Cappelli, 1957.

——. *Ossessione*. Ed. Enzo Ungari (with G. B. Cavallaro). Bologna: Cappelli, 1977.

——. *"Rocco e i suoi fratelli" di Luchino Visconti*. Ed. Guido Aristarco and Gaetano Carancini. Bologna: Cappelli, 1960.

——. *"Senso" di Luchino Visconti*. Ed. G. B. Cavallaro. Bologna: Cappelli, 1955.

——. *La terra trema*. Ed. Enzo Ungari (with Claudio Battistini and G. B. Cavallaro). Bologna: Cappelli, 1977.

——. *Three Screenplays: "White Nights," "Rocco and His Brothers," "The Job."* Trans. Judith Green. New York: Orion Press, 1970.

——. *Two Screenplays: "La Terra Trema," "Senso."* Trans. Judith Green. New York: Orion Press, 1970.

——. *Vaghe stelle dell'Orsa*. Ed. Pietro Bianchi. Bologna: Cappelli, 1965.

——, Michelangelo Antonioni, and Antonio Pietrangeli. *Il processo di Maria Tarnowska: la sceneggiatura di un film mai realizzato*. Ed. Gianno Rondolino. Milan: Il Castoro, 2006.

—— and Suso Cecchi d'Amico. *Alla ricerca del tempo perduto*. Milan: Mondadori, 1986.

Lina Wertmüller

Bullaro, Grace Russo. *Man in Disorder: The Cinema of Lina Wertmüller in the 1970s*. Leichester: Troubadour, 2007.

Cerulo, Maria Pia, Luigi Cipriani, Mauro Conciatori, Massimo Giraldi, and Lilia Ricci, eds. *Lina Wertmüller: il grottesco e il barocco in cinema*. Assisi: ANCCI, 1993.

Ferlita, Ernest, and John R. May. *The Parables of Lina Wertmüller*. New York: Paulist Press, 1977.

Masucci, Tiziana. *I chiari di Lina.* Catalpo in Sabina: Edizioni Sabinae, 2009.

Prats, A. J. *The Autonomous Image: Cinematic Narration & Humanism.* Lexington: University Press of Kentucky, 1981.

Wertmüller, Lina. *The Head of Alvise.* New York: Morrow, 1982.

———. *The Screenplays of Lina Wertmüller.* Trans. Steven Wagner. New York: Quadrangle, 1977.

Luigi Zampa

Zampa, Luigi. *Il prima giro di manovella: il romanzo sull'ambiente del cinema.* Rome: Trevi, 1980.

Franco Zeffirelli

Zeffirelli, Franco. *Il mio Gesù.* Milan: Sperling & Kupfer, 1977.

———. *Zeffirelli: An Autobiography.* New York: Weidenfeld & Nicolson, 1986.

Valerio Zurlini

Martini, Giacomo, ed. *Valerio Zurlini: una regione piena di cinema.* Regione Emilia-Romagna / Cinecittà Holding, n.d.

Minotti, Gianluca. *Valerio Zurlini.* Milan: Il Castoro, 2001.

X. Italian Cameramen, Scriptwriters, Musicians, and Special Effects Technicians

Amidei, Sergio. *Soggetti cinematografici.* Ed. Lorenzo Codelli. Gorizia: Comune di Gorizia, 1985.

Bernardini, Aldo, and Jean A. Gili, eds. *Cesare Zavattini.* Paris: Éditions du Centre Pompidou / Bologna: Regione Emilia–Romagna, 1990.

Bertelli, Gian Carlo, and Pier Marco De Santi, eds. *Omaggio a Flaiano.* Pisa: Giardini, 1987.

Borin, Fabrizio, ed. *La filmografia di Nino Rota.* Florence: Olschki, 1999.

Cecchi d'Amico, Suso. *Storie di cinema (e d'altro).* Ed. Margherita d'Amico. Milan: Bompiani, 2002.

De Leonardis, Giancarlo. *Le mani nei capelli: il mestiere del parrucchiere nel cinema.* Pomezia, Rome: Peliti Associati, 2004.

De Santi, Pier Marco. *La musica di Nino Rota.* Rome: Laterza, 1983.

———. ed. *Omaggio a Nino Rota.* Pistoia: Assessorato per gli Istituti Culturali del Comune di Pistoia, 1981.

Flaiano, Ennio. *Un film alla settimana: 55 critiche da Cine Illustrato (1939–1940).* Ed. Tullio Kezich (with Cinzia Romani). Rome: Bulzoni, 1988.

Giacomini, Stefania. *Alla scoperta del set: con venti personaggi che il cinema lo fanno.* Rome: RAI ERI, 2004.

Lombardi, Francesco, ed. *Fra cinema e musica del Novecento: il caso Nino Rota.* Florence: Olschki, 2000.

Masi, Stefano. *Costumisti e scenografi del cinema italiano.* 2 vols. L'Aquila: La Lanterna Magica, 1989–90.

———. *Nel buio della moviola: introduzione alla storia del montaggio.* L'Aquila: La Lanterna Magica, 1985.

———. *Storie della luce.* L'Aquila: La Lanterna Magica, 1983.

Monda, Antonio, and Maria-Christina Villaseñor, eds. *Conversations between Shadows and Light: Italian Cinematography*. Milan: Edizioni Olivares, 2001.

Parigi, Stefania. *Fisiologia dell'immagine: Il pensiero di Cesare Zavattini*. Turin: Lindau, 2006.

Pellizzari, Lorenzo, ed. *Carlo Rambaldi e gli effetti speciali*. San Marino: AIEP, 1987.

Perugini, Simone. *Nino Rota e le musiche per il Casanova di Federico Fellini*. Catalpo in Sabina: Edizioni: Sabinae, 2009.

Pirro, Ugo. *Celluloide*. Milan: Rizzoli, 1983. Rpt. Turin: Einaudi, 1995.

Praturlon, Pierluigi. *Pierluigi on Cinema*. Milan: Photology, 2006.

Prédal, René. *La photo de cinéma; suivi d'un dictionnaire de cent chefs opérateurs*. Paris: Éditions du Cerf, 1985.

Storaro, Vittorio. *Scrivere con la luce*. 3 vols. 1, *La luce / The Light*; 2, *I colori / Colors*; 3, *Gli elementi / The Elements*. Rome: Electa/Accademia dell'Immagine, 2001–2003.

Tonino Guerra. Ed. Dicastero Cultura, Rep. di San Marino. Rimini: Maggioli, 1985.

Tonti, Aldo. *Odore di cinema*. Florence: Vallecchi, 1964.

Zavattini, Cesare. *Basta coi soggetti!* Ed. Roberta Mazzoni. Milan: Bompiani, 1979.

———. *Diario cinematografico*. Ed. Valentina Fortichiari. Milan: Bompiani, 1979. Rev. ed. Milan: Mursia, 1991.

———. *"I misteri di Roma" di Cesare Zavattini*. Ed. Francesco Bolzoni. Bologna: Cappelli, 1963.

———. *Neorealismo ecc*. Ed. Mino Argentieri. Milan: Bompiani, 1979.

———. *Opere: romanzi, diari, poesie*. Ed. Renato Barilli. Milan: Bompiani, 1974.

———. *Zavattini: Sequences from a Cinematic Life*. Trans. William Weaver. Englewood Cliffs, N.J.: Prentice-Hall, 1970.

Photo Credits

Photographs and stills are courtesy the following sources, also noted in the captions:

AB (Archivio Brunetta, Padua)

Cinecittà Archives

CSC (Centro Sperimentale di Cinematografia Fototeca, Rome)

Donald Krim Jr. and United Artists (New York)

DVD (screen captures)

Ettore Scola and Mass Films (Rome)

MoMA (Museum of Modern Art, Film Stills Archive, New York)

Museo Nazionale del Cinema (Turin)

Nanni Moretti and SACIS (Rome)

Paolo and Vittorio Taviani

Sergio Leone

Index

Note: This index concentrates on names, titles, film genres, and movements. Each film is listed here by its director and English release title, if there is one; its original Italian title is also provided in the text proper. Whenever possible and available, biographical dates and film-release dates are also included here. In some cases (especially with minor actors and actresses), no reliable dates are available.